Public Finance and Public Policy in the New Century

The CESifo Seminar Series
Hans-Werner Sinn, editor

Inequality and Growth: Theory and Policy Implications, ed. Theo S. Eicher and Stephen J. Turnovsky (2003)

Public Finance and Public Policy in the New Century, ed. Sijbren Cnossen and Hans-Werner Sinn (2003)

Public Finance and Public Policy in the New Century

Sijbren Cnossen and
Hans-Werner Sinn, editors

CESifo Seminar Series

The MIT Press
Cambridge, Massachusetts
London, England

336
P9764

This book was set in Palatino on 3B2 by Asco Typesetters, Hong Kong, and was printed and bound in the United States of America.

Library of Congress Cataloging-in-Publication Data

Public finance and public policy in the new century / Sijbren Cnossen and Hans-Werner Sinn, editors.
  p.   cm. — (The CESifo seminar series)
  Includes bibliographical references and index.
  ISBN 0-262-03304-6 (hc. : alk. paper)
  1. Finance, Public. 2. Fiscal policy. 3. Public welfare—Finance. I. Cnossen, Sijbren.
II. Sinn, Hans-Werner. III. Series.
HJ141 .P795   2003
336—dc21   2002043182

10 9 8 7 6 5 4 3 2 1

Contents

Henry J. Aaron

II   **Taxation and Tax Reform**   125

4   **Perfect Taxation with Imperfect Competition**   127
    Alan J. Auerbach and James R. Hines Jr.

    Comments   155
    Harvey S. Rosen

5   **Bridging the Tax-Expenditure Gap: Green Taxes and the
    Marginal Cost of Funds**   159
    Agnar Sandmo

    Comments   179
    Jeremy Edwards

6   **Taxes and Privatization**   185
    Roger H. Gordon

    Comments   213
    Ray Rees

7   **The Property Tax: Competing Views and a Hybrid
    Theory**   217
    John Douglas Wilson

    Comments   237
    Panu Poutvaara

8   **The Dutch Presumptive Capital Income Tax: Find or
    Failure?**   241
    Sijbren Cnossen and Lans Bovenberg

    Comments   263
    Alfons J. Weichenrieder

Series Foreword

This book is part of the CESifo Seminar Series in Economic Policy, which aims to cover topical policy issues in economics from a largely European perspective. The books in this series are the products of the papers presented and discussed at seminars hosted by CESifo, an international research network of renowned economists supported jointly by the Center for Economic Studies at Ludwig-Maximilians-Universität, Munich, and the Ifo Institute for Economic Research. All publications in this series have been carefully selected and refereed by members of the CESifo research network.

Introduction and Summary

Sijbren Cnossen and
Hans-Werner Sinn

1 Purpose and Dedication

This book of essays and commentaries has been especially written to celebrate Richard Musgrave's ninetieth birthday and to commemorate the tenth anniversary of CES, the Center for Economic Studies at the University of Munich.

In an eloquent tribute, Henry Aaron characterizes Richard Musgrave as the midwife of modern public economics. He reviews Musgrave's celebrated branches of government—allocation, distribution, and stabilization—as well as his analytically useful distinction of three kinds of incidence: balanced budget, differential, and specific. However, he reserves his most laudatory remarks for the intellectual tradition, going back to Adam Smith, in which Musgrave has chosen to place his contributions to economics. That tradition treats economics as derived from moral philosophy and views government as an instrument that can be used to help establish the good society. This stands in contrast to the individualistic framework within which much of modern economic analysis, stripped of all institutional context or relevance, is being undertaken. Aaron believes that Musgrave's successors will be impoverished if they do not recapture the intellectual breadth and seriousness of purpose to which Richard Musgrave's life and work stand as eloquent testimony.

David Bradford pays tribute to CES, the tenth anniversary of which fell within a month of Richard Musgrave's ninetieth birthday and which therefore organized the event. Richard Musgrave is not only a former student of the University of Munich but also one of the founding fathers of CES. He has participated in the scientific advisory Council of CES from the very first moment and has helped shape the structure of CES throughout the years, including

the foundation of the CESifo network. It made sense to celebrate the
two "birthdays" together, summing the ages of the laureates to one
hundred.

The essays in this volume take stock of and extend the theory and
practice of public finance and public policy. They try to come to
grips with the evolving role of government and the Welfare State,
the interaction between taxation and markets, the future of pension
and healthcare systems, and the problems posed by open borders.

2   The Welfare State and Trust in Government

The role of government in establishing the good society is evident
in the social Welfare State, the evolution of which since the end
of World War II is surveyed by Assar Lindbeck (chapter 1). The
underlying thesis, which is frequently associated with him, is that
changes in the labor market and the structure and preferences of
the family represent the same type of systematic changes in social
arrangements in modern economies as those that came about as the
result of the Industrial Revolution and Tayloristic production at the
onset of the twentieth century. Some of these changes are exogenous
from the point of view of the Welfare State; other changes may be
regarded as endogenous behavior adjustments of individuals in
response to the Welfare State itself. Lindbeck describes and hypo-
thesizes about the underlying causes as well as shifts in the policy
paradigms. He considers a number of Welfare State reforms, including changes in the pension system and the adjustment of income
insurance and personal ("social") services to a new family structure
characterized by a high incidence of two-earner households and
single-parent families. In addition, Lindbeck discusses the pros and
cons of more competition and greater freedom of choice in the field
of personal services.

In his comments, Richard Musgrave wonders whether Lindbeck's
view on the continuing role of the Welfare State may not be too
optimistic. The capacity to finance the Welfare State is weakened by
fiscal competition brought about by the current shift to an open and
global world. A shift to a global budget, the logical counterpart of
global markets, would require a global view of equity in distribution
that is unlikely to materialize.

The financing of the modern Welfare State is critically dependent
on people's attitude toward, or trust in, government. This attitude

can influence their tax compliance behavior and in turn alter the cost of raising revenue. The results of Joel Slemrod's study (chapter 2) reveal that tax cheating is lower in countries that exhibit more (not-government-related) trustworthiness. However, holding that constant, tax cheating becomes more acceptable as government grows, to a significant and large degree. Holding income constant, though, a more accepting attitude toward tax cheating does limit the size of government. All in all, there is some weak evidence that the strong positive correlation between the size of government and tax cheating masks the fact that big government induces tax cheating while, at the same time, tax cheating constrains big government. Slemrod also produces clear evidence of a Wagner's Law relationship such that prosperity increases government size.

In his comments, Michael Burda wonders whether trust is the appropriate framework for thinking about citizen-government interactions. Taxpayers' honesty could just as well result from social norms as from trust relationships. He finds it hard to believe that Europeans trust their governments any less than Americans do. Widespread tax evasion and avoidance observed in Europe is as consistent with a deterioration of social norms as with a breakdown in trust. Burda thinks that Slemrod shares some of this ambivalence.

Not only can government be mistrusted, but language can be too. David Bradford (chapter 3) examines the ambiguity of budgetary language, which can hide as much as it reveals. Bradford revisits Musgrave's conceptual division of the government's functions into Allocation, Distribution, and Stabilization Branch subbudgets in the context of several examples of problems associated with present budgetary conventions. He suggests that progress towards Musgrave's ideal of a more informative budgetary "language"—one less dependent on arbitrary institutional labeling—must be based on the nonarbitrary description of the individual's economic environment, as it is affected by government. As a first approximation, this environment can be summed up in terms of the individual's budget constraint and levels of public goods provided. Simple models suggest that an unambiguous budgetary language may be feasible, but there remains much to clarify about both the objectives of the exercise and the specifics of methods to deal with particular problems.

Henry Aaron, who shares Bradford's frustrations, suggests in his comments, however, that conceptually correct solutions to the problems raised by Bradford are vastly beyond our capacity to implement—so far beyond it, in fact, that trying to implement them would make matters worse. He does not pretend to have a full list of "fixes" for actual and potential budget abuses, but suggests serious consideration of some modest changes launched earlier by Robert Reischauer, former director of the U.S. Congressional Budget Office.

3   Taxation, Markets, Incidence, and Tax Reform

Musgrave has always had a keen interest in the interaction among taxation and markets, incidence issues, and the design of an equitable income tax. Accordingly, the five essays in part II examine various aspects of, respectively, optimal taxation in imperfect markets, the use of Pigouvian taxes in imperfect markets, the role of the corporation tax with state ownership of firms, the incidence of the property tax, and the problems encountered in trying to tax capital income.

Alan Auerbach and Jim Hines (chapter 4) analyze features of perfect taxation—also known as optimal taxation—when one or more private markets are imperfectly competitive. When governments cannot use lump-sum taxes to provide corrective subsidies that render outcomes efficient, perfect tax policies represent compromises between the benefits of subsidizing output in the imperfectly competitive sectors of the economy and the costs of imposing higher taxes elsewhere. The authors' analysis draws together and extends the results of the previous literature. Among its new contributions are a demonstration of the close relationship between the policy rules for correcting externalities and competitive imperfections, and an investigation of how governments should behave in an environment in which the degree of market imperfection is uncertain. When governments have uncertain knowledge of the degree of competition in product markets, perfect corrective tax policy is generally of smaller magnitude than that when the degree of competition is known with certainty.

In his comments, Harvey Rosen points out that once one opens the door to differential tax rates, politicians may take advantage of it to tax some goods heavily and subsidize others based on political rather than efficiency or equity considerations. Hence, a rule that all rates be equal may ultimately be more efficient than the *actual* result if differentiation is permitted.

Imperfect markets are also the subject of Agnar Sandmo's contribution (chapter 5). Green or Pigouvian taxes have the potential to *increase* the efficiency of the market system. This appears to imply that the marginal cost of public funds (MCF)—usually greater than one in the presence of distortionary taxes—could be less than one. Sandmo shows, however, that in a number of cases and studies, this simple intuition fails to meet the conditions that must be satisfied for the intuition to hold. In a setting of two taxes—one on labor income and one on a "dirty" consumption good—with optimal rates, there is a common MCF for both sources of tax finance, but little can be said about its value. Furthermore, when the green tax is the only source of finance, its MCF is not necessarily less than one; this depends on whether its level is greater or less than the marginal social damage from the environmental externality. Sandmo also considers a fixed distortion in the labor market, as well as the case where the income tax is the marginal source of finance and where the green tax is fixed. Here, the approach taken is not that of optimal tax analysis but rather the reform perspective, where one considers a balanced budget change in public expenditure and taxes, and looks at the condition for such a change to be welfare improving.

Jeremy Edwards concurs with Sandmo's conclusion that simple intuition about the MCF has to be handled with great care, and limits his comments to an application of its analysis to versions of the double dividend hypothesis.

Roger Gordon's essay (chapter 6) focuses on the interaction between the corporate income tax and state ownership of firms. Some recent work has argued that if the tax rate is high enough, state-owned firms can avoid the distortions to managerial incentives. If this argument were right, then the capital intensity of state-owned firms should fall with privatization. However, as Gordon points out, the data show instead that firms lay off part of their workforce when they are privatized, suggesting that state firms are unusually labor-intensive. He proposes an explanation for these observations. To begin with, the government can use cheap loans from state-owned banks rather than state ownership of firms more generally to maintain the capital stock. In the event, there is no reason to expect that state-owned firms will be more capital-intensive than privately owned firms. Furthermore, the author argues that state-owned firms can hire relatively more low-skilled workers than would an equivalent privately owned firm, because they are less subject to labor market distortions such as the minimum wage and unemployment insurance programs.

In his comments, Ray Rees questions Gordon's positive explanations of the evidence. In his view, the explanation for the excessive
labor intensity of state-owned firms, for instance, is to be found in
the nature of the control and decision structure of these firms, and
the role played by unions within this, rather than in an attempt
to correct for general labor market distortions. Indeed, the drive
towards privatization is to be understood as an attempt to achieve
transformation of this control and decision structure.

In the next essay, Jay Wilson (chapter 7) develops a hybrid model
of the property tax that combines features of two competing views
on the incidence of the property tax: the "new view," which postulates that residential property taxes lower the after-tax return on
capital by approximately the average tax rate, and the "benefit
view," which argues that a property tax represents a user fee for
local public goods. He compares his property tax with two other
taxes: a head tax and a tax on land. Taken as a whole, the results
partially support the benefit view by demonstrating that a move
from the land tax to the property tax induces jurisdictions to raise
their public good supplies above the inefficiently low levels that
prevail under the land tax. But these supplies remain inefficiently
low. Moving from the property tax to a system of head taxes restores
efficiency, while also raising the after-tax return on capital, as predicted by the new view. Thus, the incidence results from the new
view receive some support.

In his comments, Panu Poutvaara indicates that Wilson's model
could be extended by changing the assumptions on political process,
costless mobility, and the single use of capital.

Musgrave's interest in equitable tax design is reflected in Sijbren
Cnossen and Lans Bovenberg's essay (chapter 8) on various ways of
taxing capital income, as exemplified by the Dutch experience.
Recently, the Netherlands has abolished the tax on actual personal
capital income and has replaced it by a presumptive capital income
tax, which is in fact a net wealth tax. Cnossen and Bovenberg contrast this wealth tax with a conventional realization-based capital
gains tax, a retrospective capital gains tax with interest on the
deferred tax, and a mark-to-market tax, which taxes capital gains as
they accrue. They conclude that the effective and neutral taxation
of capital income can best be ensured through a combination of (a) a
mark-to-market tax to capture the returns on easy-to-value financial

products and (b) a capital gains tax with interest to tax the returns on hard-to-value real estate and small businesses.

Alfons Weichenrieder points out that if, as indicated by the Dutch experience, the valuation problems under a wealth tax can be handled, a mark-to-market tax should be feasible.

4   The Future of Pension and Healthcare Systems

Aging populations put pressure on pension systems and social insurance and medical programs in Welfare States. In the first essay in part III, Hans-Werner Sinn (chapter 9) points out that the population of Germany is aging faster than those of most other countries. Consequently, without reform, the German pay-as-you-go pension system will face a severe crisis in the near future. Sinn discusses the options using a model developed by him and his coworkers at CES for the Council of Advisers to the Federal Ministry of Economics and Technology. He argues that the German pay-as-you-go (PAYGO) pension system is efficient in a present-value sense but will nevertheless need the support of a funded system, based on individual accounts, to avoid a financial crisis. Sinn recommends obligatory private saving at a variable rate where the time path of the saving rate is chosen so as to stabilize the sum of this rate and the PAYGO contribution rate, given the time path of pensions as defined in the present system. He contrasts this recommendation with the proposal that the German government made in 2000.

In a careful analysis of Sinn's essay, Georges de Menil believes that in addition to introducing individual accounts, the German government should begin now to scale back existing PAYGO entitlements. This is the only way to protect the credibility of the PAYGO system in the future.

Individual savings accounts are also the subject of Peter Sørensen's contribution (chapter 10). He notes that in the modern European Welfare State, a substantial part of the tax bill is transferred back to taxpayers themselves in the form of social transfers. To avoid the accompanying "excessive" distortions, the author proposes the introduction of individual mandatory savings accounts to finance part of social insurance for people of working age. Workers drawing higher Social Security benefits would receive a lower supplementary retirement income from their savings accounts. Using a simple overlapping generations model, Sørensen finds that his proposal would generate a Pareto improvement, even if the preexisting tax-transfer system had been optimized. He illustrates his contribution by describing a specific Danish proposal for an individual savings accounts system and by reviewing an estimate of the effects of this system on the distribution of income.

Sørensen's savings account could be used to finance healthcare for people of working age. However, government cannot withdraw completely from the health insurance market, as argued by Robin Boadway, Manuel Leite-Monteiro, Maurice Marchand, and Pierre Pestieau (chapter 11). They show that government intervention in health insurance markets is welfare improving and that social insurance is generally desirable particularly when there is a negative correlation between labor productivity and loss probability. Boadway and his colleagues draw this conclusion in a study of linear income taxation and redistributive social insurance when the former has the traditional labor distortion and the latter generates both ex ante and ex post moral hazard. Private insurance is available and individuals differ in labor productivity and loss probability.

In his comments, Dominique Demougin observes that the contribution by Boadway, Leite-Monteiro, Marchand, and Pestieau provides an interesting efficiency-based justification for the use of a dual healthcare system, partly publicly funded and partly privately financed. He believes that the assumption of a linear income tax unnecessarily restricts the analysis.

Health insurance coverage is low among the self-employed in the United States, relative to the coverage among wage earners. This is causing substantial public policy concern. Using data from the Medical Expenditure Panel Survey conducted in 1996, Craig Perry and Harvey Rosen (chapter 12) suggest that the link between insurance and utilization of healthcare services is not as strong as assumed in the policy debate. For a number of medical care services, the self-employed have the same rates of utilization as wage earners, despite the fact that they are substantially less likely to be insured. In addition, when the self-employed are less likely than wage earners to utilize a particular medical service, the differences generally do not seem very large. The self-employed thus appear to be able to finance access to healthcare from sources other than insurance. Further, analysis of out-of-pocket expenditures on healthcare suggests that doing so does not lead to substantial reductions in their ability to consume other goods and services. Finally, there is no evidence that the children of the self-employed have less access to healthcare than the children of wage earners. Hence, the public policy concerns that the relative lack of health insurance among the self-employed substantially reduces utilization of healthcare services or creates economic hardship appear to be misplaced.

In his comments, Gebhard Flaig reviews various extensions and amendments to the empirical specification of the Perry/Rosen study in order to get a feeling of whether the results are robust with respect to the underlying assumptions. He believes that analyzing cross-section data with reduced form models may not be the most efficient way to extract as much useful information as possible from the data. A more structural approach combined with the use of panel data would probably deliver more insights.

5   International Tax Issues and Fiscal Federalism

International tax issues have always been contentious, but never more so than over the last few years, when expanded trade and investment relations have combined with new financial and electronic technology to cast doubt on how well the existing "OECD consensus" on international taxation can cope. The essay by Richard Bird and Jack Mintz (chapter 13) first explores the (limited) usefulness of cooperative game theory in understanding how international tax issues are resolved in practice and then considers in some detail some of the rules of the tax coordination game that seem critical in developing agreement in this area. In particular, the authors stress the importance of such concepts as "inter-nation equity" and "fair shares" in understanding both the evolution of the present system of international taxation and its likely future development. Finally, since the critical question is the institutional setting within which countries play the game of sharing the international tax base in this changing world, Bird and Mintz offer some thoughts on how the ongoing process of developing a new international tax system for the new world economy might best proceed.

In his comments, Thomas Moutos shares Bird and Mintz's preference for a pragmatic approach that focuses on the general principles that should guide the procedure leading to an agreement considered "fair" by the interested parties. These principles do not necessarily include worldwide efficiency, the yardstick most economists would apply. Yet, in Moutos's view, the authors' guidelines can also fall short of general applicability.

Moving from the international to the federal scene, Henry Tulkens (chapter 14) draws attention to "Musgravian" externalities, formulated and illustrated by Musgrave in a 1966 paper on "social goods." The author sees these externalities as one form of the interactions that occur between the components of a federation. In the context of the original formal apparatus, Tulkens considers whether and how alternative forms of federal structures are likely to achieve efficiency. Following suggestions from the literature, three such forms are dealt with: "planned," "cooperative," and "majority-rule" federalism. Next, the relevance of noncooperative equilibria is examined in the light of an interpretation of them as "fallback positions" when disagreement occurs among members of a federation. Finally, the question is evoked of what economics and public finance may have to say on the limits to institutional decentralization, that is, on the choice between federal, confederal, and secessional structures. The chapter concludes with a reminder of Musgrave's view on this issue.

In reviewing Tulkens's essay, Clemens Fuest examines the arguments in favor of decentralized policymaking that are found in the literature: information advantages, commitment to maintain previous capital tax rates, and, perhaps most importantly, improvements in the efficiency of the political process. Fuest notes that Musgrave is often associated with the issue of externalities, which call for government intervention. However, quoting from his work, he shows that Musgrave is also aware of the workings of political processes.

Next, Kai Konrad and Helmut Seitz (chapter 15) revisit the fundamental trade-off between risk sharing and incentives for local governments under a system of unconditional transfers between states in the German federation. The central aspect that they address is asymmetry in regions' population size, a prominent feature of most existing federations. If two states differ in size, the best mutual insurance outcome would be obtained if both states were to collect their risky tax revenue, sum these revenues, and divide the total between them (not necessarily evenly). However, moral hazard incentives would typically make this maximum mutual insurance suboptimal. With revenue sharing, each state's incentive to enforce the (uniform federal) tax laws and to spend money on tax auditing is diminished. Under linear mutual insurance schemes, the authors show that the per capita share of a region's tax revenue that should enter the insurance scheme is higher the larger the relative size of this region. Furthermore, even though the optimal insurance scheme features larger contributions by larger regions, which increases their moral hazard incentives, it holds that, for optimal contribution shares, the moral hazard incentives in the smaller region are larger than those in the larger region even in the optimum.

In his comments, Marko Köthenbürger calls for more information and analysis about how the German transfer system actually meets the demand for interregional insurance, about the impact of population size, and about the interaction between revenue sharing and fiscal equalization. He considers that it would be useful to extend the analysis by introducing some explicit modeling of the political economy.

Finally, Wolfram Richter (chapter 16) takes on the issue of "Delayed Integration"—namely, the rule under which mobile individuals are assigned to jurisdictions to which they have moved only after a coordinated period of transition. Delayed Integration, which is a compromise between the Home Country Principle and the Employment Principle, contrasts with current policy in the European Union, which relies heavily on the Employment Principle. This principle is known to impede production efficiency and to work against the interest of immobile factors. Precisely the opposite can be said about the Home Country Principle. However, the Home Country Principle is nonintegrational and weakens competition among jurisdictions even when this competition is efficiency enhancing. Richter argues that Delayed Integration may be a principle that policymakers should seriously consider as an option for coordinating the policies of autonomous jurisdictions committed to the free movement of all their citizens.

Søren Bo Nielsen notes in his comments that the taxation of mobile labor is of particular relevance in Germany, which has experienced pronounced internal labor mobility since its unification and also has the second-largest share in the European Union of immigrants from Eastern Europe. For the principle of Delayed Integration to work, however, it should be able to handle rather complicated patterns of mobility.

Inevitably, the summary and synthesis of the essays and commentaries in this volume have had to be selective. No doubt, we have not done justice to their richness, and therefore we invite readers to study the contributions for themselves.

Acknowledgments

The essays and commentaries in this volume were originally presented at a conference at the Center for Economic Studies (CES) of Ludwig-Maximilians-Universität, Munich, in January 2001. Subsequently, the essays were revised, subjected to a thorough refereeing process, and, again, revised. We gratefully acknowledge the cooperation of all authors and commentators. In the course of editing the volume, most helpful comments were received from Henry Aaron, Reuven Avi-Yonah, Tim Besley, Paul Besseling, Robin Boadway, Alex Boersch-Supan, Massimo Bordignon, Donald Brean, Sam Bucovetsky, Michael Burda, Len Burman, Bev Dahlby, Richard Doernberg, Jeremy Edwards, Lars Feld, Clemens Fuest, Don Fullerton, Peter Heller, Bernd Huber, Harry Huizinga, Robert Inman, Theo van de Klundert, Maurice Marchand, Ken Messere, Peter Mieszkowski, Ruud de Mooij, Peggy Musgrave, Richard Musgrave, Gareth Myles, Michael Orszag, Pierre Pestieau, Panu Poutvaara, Assar Razin, Ray Rees, Manfred Rose, Agnar Sandmo, Deborah Schenk, Jon Skinner, Vito Tanzi, Hans-Jürgen Vosgerau, and Aart de Zeeuw. As this long list indicates, the work on this volume has truly been a joint effort. Thanks are due to Judith Payne, who did an impeccable job in processing the essays and commentaries.

We also wish to thank Martina Grass, Ulrich Hange, and the staff of CES who did a marvelous job in organizing the celebrations and the conference. A booklet with all the speeches and tributes by Henry Aaron, David Bradford, Georges de Menil, Andreas Heldrich, Bernd Huber, Assar Lindbeck, Peggy Musgrave, Richard Musgrave, Agnar Sandmo, Paul Samuelson, Hans-Werner Sinn, Peter Sørensen, and Henry Tulkens can be ordered from office@CESifo.de. The booklet and videos of the festivities are also available on the CESifo homepage: ⟨www.CESifo.de⟩.

Tribute to Richard Abel Musgrave

Henry J. Aaron

No invitation I can recall has caused me as much pleasure as Hans-Werner's letter inviting me to participate in this celebration of Richard Musgrave's ninetieth birthday. I am confident that all who are participating in this event share a similar feeling. We all recognize in Richard Musgrave a combination of quite extraordinary personal and intellectual integrity and creativity, leavened with broad cultural sophistication, and seasoned with charm at once gruff and warm. He is one of those rare people who elicit both respect and affection and who display both dignity and warmth. We have all been touched personally, intellectually, or emotionally by a life that spans and has surmounted the catastrophic, yet miraculous, century just ended. Although I never took a course from him, Richard Musgrave was my teacher through his writings, as he was to every public finance economist who passed through graduate school for the two decades from 1960 to 1980. We are all honored by the privilege of celebrating his life with him. Let me amend that—we are all honored by being privileged to celebrate the lives of Richard and Peggy with *them*, for much of Musgrave's work is the work of the Musgraves.

This invitation caused me, as it did many others, to try to take stock of Richard Musgrave's intellectual contributions and to assess, at a more personal level, what they mean to me. Doing so is not easy for two reasons. The contributions are numerous, but the greater challenge lies elsewhere. The intellectual constructs that he pioneered are now so much a part of our thinking that it is hard now to recover our pre-Musgrave mindsets, a necessary step in measuring his contributions.

I reopened the covers of my copy of *The Theory of Public Finance* to find a book with more underlining, more marginal notes, and more inserted sheets of note paper with derivations, elaborations, and comments than in any other book I own. Doing so underscored the fact that, as others have noted, Richard Musgrave was the midwife of modern public economics. Various sections of that book provoked different thoughts.

First, some of the most liberating contributions of the book involved categorizations that helped people organize their thinking in ways that encouraged further analysis. The most celebrated is the division of the operations of the public sector into three branches responsible for allocation, distribution, and stabilization. It not only defined the outline of *The Theory of Public Finance* but also became a way of thinking about the activities of the public sector. With the passage of time, however, it has become clear that these functions, which are separable in logic, are intertwined in practice.

Furthermore, the evolution of economics has reduced the relative importance of the Stabilization Branch. Much of the responsibility for stabilization has migrated from public finance to monetary analysis. Tax and expenditure policy are now regarded as relatively unimportant or clumsy *short-run* stabilization tools, but they remain preeminent long-term influences on national saving and hence long-term economic growth, as well as on resource allocation and income distribution.

As one of the three functions of public finance has slowly faded from view, the other two—distribution and allocation—have merged. By answering the nineteenth-century question about how to collect taxes with least overall sacrifice, the optimal tax literature has shown that questions of distribution and allocation are inextricably linked.

Of perhaps even greater analytic use was the distinction among three kinds of incidence—balanced budget, differential, and specific. Most incidence analysis—and debates—dwell on the implicit or explicit evaluation of the distributional impact of taxes the revenue from which is returned to taxpayers through lump-sum transfers distributed in a distributionally and allocatively neutral manner. There is only one problem with this convention. Distributionally and allocatively neutral ways of distributing tax revenue in practice are never used. The analytical convention is a fiction. It complies in a formal way with Musgrave's strictures regarding the need to pair a tax with what it buys if one is to get meaningful results. But it would be far more constructive, I think, to evaluate the distributional consequences of actual taxes in combination with the actual expenditures or tax cuts they finance. This approach to incidence analysis forces the analyst to interpret political events and intentions as well as to do standard economic analysis, because one has to try to understand how elected officials use tax legislation to advance objectives that often transcend tax policy.

Two examples illustrate the point. Under standard tax analysis, the U.S. payroll tax is regressive, except in the very bottom brackets, when households are classified by income, and roughly proportional when classified by consumption. Analyzing the payroll tax as a means of financing social insurance converts it into a progressive policy under either method of classification. As a second example, standard comparisons of the U.S. and, say, the French and German tax systems would conclude that the former is more progressive than are the latter, because the U.S. system relies more than do continental European systems on progressive personal income and capital income taxes while European systems rely more on regressive commodity taxes. But the relatively regressive European taxes are also very large. They pay for generous social services that are distributed in a highly progressive fashion. The difference between the U.S. and Franco/German finance systems is best understood, I think, by linking the taxes to the public spending they finance. Analyzing the distribution of public sectors as a whole is difficult, but that is what counts, more than the isolated incidence of individual taxes offset by wholly imaginary lump-sum transfers.

Musgrave's work reflects an intellectual tradition that is no longer dominant within economics but that still survives and, I believe, will endure. That tradition, which goes back to Adam Smith, treats economics as derived from moral philosophy. All of Richard Musgrave's work is in that tradition. The people who form the government in Musgrave's analytical universe may worry a lot about staff size or power or income—their own or their class's—but government officials in the Musgravian world are not maximizing staffs or budgets. At least, that is not the focus of his analysis. Rather, government is an instrument that can be used to help establish the good society. The Musgravian government is an entity that is receptive to what should be done based on popular preferences expressed through a democratic voting rule and his analysis is intended to help elected officials know what they *should* do to maximize public welfare.

No person who has left his homeland in protest against Naziism could harbor any illusion regarding the capacity of governments to run amok. So it is not naivete that Musgrave expresses in this approach to the role of government. It is, I believe, a deep moral commitment that governments must be shown how they *should* behave, how they *must* behave, and how in a democracy, if shown, they *will* behave.

Of course, they do not always behave as they should. As a whole subdiscipline in public economics has shown, government officials often act from self-interest, not in the public interest. And even if they always intended to stick to the public's interest, people who are charged with the three distinct functions of the public sector would be bound to see the world differently and to conflict with one another. But we know from other research that not everyone behaves selfishly and that most people behave altruistically at least some of the time. The tradition in economics that Musgrave's work exemplifies reminds officials how they should behave if they have the public interest in mind.

A striking and appealing, if currently unfashionable, feature of Musgrave's work is a willingness to incorporate and wrestle with unabashedly moral principles. Take merit goods, for example. Wrestle is the right metaphor. In *The Theory of Public Finance*, Musgrave explicitly disavowed so-called organic national preferences. Having lived through the results of philosophies that incorporated organic theories of the state, he opted instead for models based on individual preferences. But he then also rejected "extreme individualism" which would leave no room for democratic leadership to amend and modify individual preferences, particularly when those preferences rest on incomplete information or are distorted, for example, by advertising that "screams" (his word) at people through the mass media.

Contrast this treatment of merit wants with that of Anthony Atkinson and Joseph Stiglitz, whose superlative 1980 text, *Lectures in Public Economics*, succeeded Musgrave's treatise as the bible of public economics courses. Atkinson and Stiglitz mention merit wants in one short paragraph in the introduction and then say no more. There is simply no place for merit wants within the individualistic framework they explore with relentless consistency. There is no place, that is, unless one declares as legitimate individual preferences regarding the consumption of others. But that assumption would hopelessly complicate much of microeconomics.

Richard Musgrave represents a generation of scholars for whom responsible scholarship was coterminous with confronting large, if messy, problems, rather than limiting oneself to questions drained of their historical and philosophical meaning. They could do no less because, as they saw it, the preservation of culture and civilization depended on it. Liberals such as Musgrave or conservatives such as Friedrich von Hayek or James Buchanan were engaged in a similar enterprise. However much they may have disagreed about policy, they saw—and see—problems in historical and philosophical context. They began to apply the language of mathematics to these problems. But they and their students discovered that, while mathematics was liberating, it was also constraining—liberating because it provided harder conclusions than verbal reasoning permitted, but constraining because restrictive assumptions were necessary to realize that potential. Willy-nilly, the restrictive assumptions accumulated. The energy and time necessary to master the new skills mounted. The nuanced ambiguities of the political and historical context of economic problems that suffuses the work of Musgrave and his contemporaries faded away until, as David Colander and Arjo Klamer reported in the late 1980s, more than two-thirds of U.S. economics graduate students thought it was unimportant to have a thorough knowledge of the economy. If mid-twentieth-century scholars could be faulted for tackling problems so large and important they were insoluble, some of their successors can be faulted for being willing to apply technically virtuosic methods to problems so stripped of institutional context or relevance that no serious person could care about the answers.

Countertrends are evident, however. A small group of economists persist in paying careful attention to philosophical questions. Amartya Sen is only the best known. In a different vein, behavioral economics holds out the promise of moving beyond the mechanical simplicities of the standard utility function and incorporating valid empirical findings about how people in fact make decisions, why behavioral violations of the postulates of revealed preference are not aberrations to be explained away but the only possible response of sane human beings trying to cope with the complexity of real-world decisions, and how social interaction shapes individual decisions.

Our successors will be richer for the flowering of theoretical and
econometric tools that has marked the last third of the twentieth
century and continues now. But they will be impoverished if we do
not also recapture the intellectual breadth and seriousness of purpose to which Richard Musgrave's life and work stand as eloquent
testimony.

Ten Years of CES

David F. Bradford

Richard Musgrave's ninetieth birthday coincided with the tenth anniversary of CES, the Center for Economic Studies at the University of Munich. Richard Musgrave is not only a former student of the University of Munich but also one of the founding fathers of CES and has been a CES Council Member ever since. So this volume offers a felicitous opportunity to celebrate two significant landmarks.

CES emerged as a formal university institute in January 1991, funded by the Bavarian Ministry of Culture and chaired by Hans-Werner Sinn. Its original focus was not on research positions but on a visitors' program for the benefit of economic research in Munich. Later, CES expanded into a true university research institute with several full-time research positions.

CES has hosted about three hundred scholars from the world's best universities for extended research visits. These visitors were carefully selected by the CES Council, whose international members include Martin Beckmann, Mervyn King, Richard Musgrave, Agnar Sandmo, Karlhans Sauernheimer, Robert Solow, Joseph Stiglitz, Charles Wyplosz, and me. Out of the growing number of visitors, an informal research network emerged. When Hans-Werner Sinn became president of the Ifo Institute, one of Germany's top economics think tanks, the network was given a formal status within a new CESifo organization.

CES has gradually evolved over its ten-year existence. Then, Hans-Werner Sinn managed alone. Now, it has four directors for the visiting program: Bernd Huber, Gerhard Illing, Ray Rees, and Klaus Schmidt. Then, it was housed in a suite of offices on Ludwigstrasse in lovely old Munich. Now, it occupies two large floors in Schackstrasse 4, a lovely old building, still, I'm glad to report, in lovely old Munich.

Now, as then, you arrive as a visitor to find a comfortable office, equipped with everything you need to get right to work, including assistance in all mundane needs and the attentiveness of the young CES researchers. You find yourself in the company of three or four other visitors, from all over the world, with a great diversity of interests, all relaxed and willing to talk.

The genius of CES is its combination of a sense of community and a subtle force that I call leverage. A visitor typically gives a research seminar in the Munich Economics Department and will attend a selection of the four or five weekly seminars that CES helps organize in the faculty and at the Ifo Institute. Rather more special, a visitor is normally invited to give a series of lectures, usually one a week for three weeks, covering an area of his or her expertise. The other guest scholars typically attend, as do interested Munich faculty, the young scholars affiliated with CES, and Munich doctoral students. For the doctoral students, especially, the result is an exposure to the current work of leading thinkers, with plenty of chances to interact very directly, that is unique in Germany and, really, in the world.

A highlight of the CES year is the Distinguished CES Fellow award, given to an outstanding economist who is also asked to present the Munich Lectures in Economics. Award winners include Anthony Atkinson, Peter Diamond, Avinash Dixit, Rudiger Dornbusch, Oliver Hart, Paul Krugman, Guido Tabellini, and Jean Tirole. Their lectures appear in a book series published by The MIT Press.

In March 1998, James Buchanan and Richard Musgrave were invited to CES for a week-long debate on the role of the state in the modern economy, which was attended by a large number of economists from Asia, Europe, and the United States. This was an important event in the history of economic thought, clarifying the roots of our thinking. The papers and comments presented at the symposium have been published as *Public Finance and Public Choice: Two Contrasting Visions of the State* by The MIT Press.

CES and its creators should take enormous pride in what has been accomplished. Much has been ventured and much has been gained. All who have an interest in the welfare of economics in Munich, in Germany, in Europe, and in the world should be grateful for what is happening at CES.

I   Modernizing Public Policy

1 Changing Tides for the Welfare State: An Essay

Assar Lindbeck

1.1 Introduction

The Welfare State is an inheritance from political responses to changes in socioeconomic conditions and values in the past. But the situation today is very different from that which prevailed when the Welfare State was constructed. Still, it has turned out to be difficult to adjust Welfare State arrangements to new circumstances. The ensuing misalignment between the Welfare State and contemporary conditions does not mean that today's Welfare State arrangements have become obsolete or that voters have turned their backs on the Welfare State. According to opinion polls, the Welfare State is still quite popular, even though there are specific complaints and popular support for some narrowly targeted Welfare State programs is often rather weak (Taylor-Gooby 1996; Boeri, Börsch-Supan, and Tabellini 2001). But as we shall see, new socioeconomic developments and changes in values help explain why proposals for Welfare State reform abound and why some such reforms have already been initiated in a number of countries. These are the issues focused on in this chapter.

The socioeconomic background of the Welfare State is well known. Industrialization meant that periods of work and nonwork became more discrete and more random events than before (Piore 1987; Atkinson 1991). The resulting temporal desynchronization of an individual's consumption requirements and actual income flows created a need (justification) for new arrangements to reallocate income over his life cycle and to protect him against income risks. At the same time, urbanization reduced the family's ability to satisfy these needs, partly because family members of different generations often became separated geographically. It is also well known that voluntary market solutions could not live up to these new needs because of myopic behavior and free riding of some individuals, and because of familiar limitations in private insurance markets as a result of adverse selection, cream skimming, and moral hazard. Nor could the family alone satisfy the increased need for education and healthcare in industrial and urban societies. All this, of course, is the background for the (reasonable) assertion that the Welfare State can be justified not only on distributional (social) grounds but also with reference to efficiency aspects (Barr 1992). Moreover, we may speculate that destitution among minorities became less socially acceptable during the course of the twentieth century. In this sense, social (political) preferences gradually changed, perhaps to some extent as a result of higher income and more widespread education. Meanwhile, we may quarrel about whether social preferences of this type reflect altruism or "enlightened self-interest."

Macroeconomic instability in an industrial society, not least the depression in the 1930s, highlighted the need for income protection. Moreover, rapid economic growth during the first decades after World War II created the economic resources necessary to satisfy these needs to a considerable degree. Indeed, during these decades, Welfare State arrangements in many developed countries were gradually transformed from poverty relief and basic ("minimum") income support into broad income maintenance programs and further expansion of tax-financed services in education and health. A number of socioeconomic features during the early postwar decades also contributed to making the Welfare State both financially viable and reasonably well adjusted to the new needs. These features include a rather homogeneous labor force, full employment (mainly for men), quite stable families, and favorable demography (a large fraction of the population of working age).

General franchise provided political channels through which the new needs could gradually be translated into concrete action, even though embryos of Welfare State arrangements already existed. By the time the modern Welfare State was basically completed in the 1970s, it was mainly adapted to the needs of "standard" families with a male breadwinner and a housewife, though it also provided special arrangements to mitigate poverty for individuals and families without a regularly employed income earner. In several countries in Western Europe, job protection legislation was added, in particular in the 1970s, as a complement to or a substitute for unemployment benefits and social assistance.

It is well known, however, that socioeconomic changes in recent decades have created new needs (justifications) for intertemporal reallocation of income and protection against new types of income risk. These changes have also generated new service needs that are not well met by traditional Welfare State arrangements. Some socio-economic changes have also undermined the financial viability of a number of traditional Welfare State arrangements. As in the case of industrialization and urbanization a century ago, the most important changes have taken place in the labor market and the family.

Several driving forces behind these developments may be regarded as exogenous from the point of view of the Welfare State. Obvious examples are new technologies, advances in medicine, and increased international economic integration. Other driving forces—including changes in demography, work, cohabitation patterns, the life cycle of individuals, and macroeconomic developments—are most realistically regarded as combined results of exogenous events and endogenous behavioral adjustments of individuals in response to the Welfare State itself, including tax- and benefit-induced distortions of economic incentives. I will also argue that the views ("philosophies") among voters and politicians regarding the relation between the individual and the state have changed in recent decades. Important examples are new ways of viewing an individual's responsibility for his own destiny and his right and ability to exert free choice among alternative types of income protection and social services.

In some countries, the dynamics of the political process may also have generated an "overshooting" of the Welfare State, in the sense that voters would have chosen smaller aggregate Welfare State spending if incentives for political action had been more symmetric between beneficiaries and taxpayers. As argued by many observers (e.g., Olson 1965 and Tullock 1959), since benefits are often selective while taxes are usually general, the incentives of individuals belonging to special-interest groups to exert political pressure for new favors are often stronger than the incentives of the general taxpayer to resist such favors. The recursive and incremental nature of the political decision-making process may accentuate this tendency, since different spending programs are seldom weighted against each other simultaneously (Lindbeck 1985, 1994). Additions to Welfare State arrangements also create new interest groups for Welfare State spending. Indeed, in societies where a large part of the electorate get the bulk of their income from the government—via benefits or public-sector employment—the interest in large Welfare State spending becomes solidly anchored among voters; Sweden is an extreme example (Lindbeck 1997b, 1279, 1315).

When discussing these issues, it is important to keep in mind that economic behavior is influenced not only by economic incentives but also by values including social norms and individual ethics (internalized norms). In particular, norms inherited from the past may constrain the (dis)incentive effects in the short run. In a long-term perspective, however, these norms themselves may adjust in response to changes in economic incentives (Lindbeck 1995). If this hypothesis is correct, the (dis)incentive effects of Welfare State arrangements, and their financing, would in some cases be stronger in the long run than in a short- and medium-term perspective. Such behavioral inertia may accentuate the earlier mentioned tendency to "overshoot" aggregate Welfare State spending, since it is difficult for policymakers and voters to predict induced long-term changes in social norms when new Welfare State programs are launched.

These new developments constitute the background for this essay on "changing tides" for the Welfare State. It is then important to note that the "welfare regimes" differ considerably among developed countries, with different relative roles of the state, the family, and the market for economic security and personal services. I begin by discussing changes in the labor market (section 1.2). Next, I deal with changes in the structure and stability of the family (section 1.3). I then turn to contemporary changes in the macroeconomy with important consequences for the functioning of the Welfare State (section 1.4). Here, I deal with three macroeconomic features—short-term macroeconomic instability, economic growth, and the internationalization of national economies. Some concluding remarks are offered in section 1.5.

1.2   Structural Changes in the Labor Market

1.2.1   Labor Supply

What, then, are the most important examples of "changing tides" in the labor market from the point of view of the Welfare State? With respect to labor supply, it is a commonplace that the aging of the population—a combined result of the baby boom in the 1940s, low birth rates since the 1970s, and increasing longevity after retirement—threatens the financial viability of the Welfare State, in particular the pension system. Indeed, birth rates in most European countries today are considerably below the reproduction level. The average birth rate in Western Europe (the number of children born divided by the average number of women in fertile cohorts) was only 1.47 in 1998 (U.S. Bureau of the Census 1998). Life expectancy at age 65 in Western Europe has increased by slightly more than 1 year per decade after World War II, the increase ranging from somewhat less than 1 year per decade in the Netherlands to more than 1.5 years per decade in France (United Nations 1949, 1960, 1997). Instead of 45–50 years of work and 5–10 years of retirement half a century ago, a typical young individual today can expect to work for 30–35 years and be retired for about 17 years (OECD 1998).[1]

Most likely, the fall in birth rates is related to higher costs of raising children (reflecting higher real wages) and the increased labor-force participation of females (Becker 1981). Some Welfare State arrangements have also contributed to the fall in birth rates, since it is no longer essential to have children in order to be supported in old age; PAYGO pension systems, for instance, imply that the children of other families support me when I grow old. Government subsidies to education have also delayed the entry of individuals into the labor force. This has reduced the number of taxpayers, though the related accumulation of human capital per individual, and hence increased labor productivity, have counteracted (or even reversed) the negative effects on the tax base in the long run.

Since the demographic problems are about the same in most countries in Western Europe, attempts to mitigate these problems via immigration of young and low-middle-age workers would have to rely on immigrants from Eastern Europe and non-European countries. Although such immigration certainly makes sense from an economic point of view, we know from experience that ethnic conflicts may be triggered if the size or speed of immigration exceeds certain (hitherto unknown) limits. This is particularly likely to occur if immigration is thought to result in downward pressure on the wages of low-skilled workers or upward pressure on social assistance spending. Such developments would also complicate the ambitions of Welfare States to mitigate segregation and promote social accord. A likely future strategy of governments to deal with this issue would be to favor the immigration of skilled rather than unskilled workers.

Welfare State arrangements have also contributed a growing number of pensioners, not only via a lower statutory retirement age and more generous subsidies to early retirement but also through subsidized healthcare, which is likely to have contributed to the rise in longevity. Moreover, government spending on pensions has been boosted by a tendency among politicians to add new types of benefits gradually to existing pension systems—for instance, by successively allotting pension rights for compulsory military service, unemployment periods, the care of children, and so forth. These new commitments have given rise to unavoidable cost increases associated with the gradual "maturing" of PAYGO pension systems.

Since better health among elderly citizens usually enhances their ability to work, it may not be too far-fetched to alleviate the financial difficulties of the pension system by raising the age of mandatory retirement (the "statutory" retirement age) and reducing subsidies to early retirement. As an illustration of the potential importance of such reforms, in the late 1990s, average labor-force participation in the European Union (EU) in the 55–65 age group was only about 40 percent, ranging from 24 percent in Belgium to 88 percent in Iceland (OECD 1999).

References to the political power of retirees and cohorts close to retirement probably do not suffice to explain why it seems so difficult to restrain mandatory pension spending by cuts in pension benefits, increases in the statutory retirement age, and reduction in subsidies to early retirement. For instance, some young and middle-age individuals may be pleased with the idea of not having to support their parents individually in the future. Moreover, with today's incentive structure in favor of early retirement, it is not surprising that rather young cohorts look forward to early retirement themselves, often at no later than 60—at least, this is what opinion polls tell us. Moreover, in all Western European countries, unions and firms use early retirement, at the taxpayers' expense, as a way of cutting the workforce in individual firms (when this is regarded as necessary) at the lowest possible cost to firms. A common argument is that this reduces aggregate unemployment, which might be true in a short-term perspective.

Considering the wide variability in the capacity and willingness to work among the elderly, there is a strong case for combining the removal of subsidies to early retirement with a more flexible retirement age (possibly with actuarial adjustments of yearly pensions).

Elderly workers in poor health could then be referred to the sick or disability insurance system rather than to the pension system. Another, possibly complementary, reform could be to allow the elderly to continue to work after receiving a pension (without it being reduced), hence partly separating retirement and pension. Indeed, this is rather common in Japan, where employees are often able to continue working at reduced wages after receiving pensions—either by performing new tasks in the same firm or by shifting to other firms.

We know that many countries also contemplate more far-reaching reforms of their pension systems, either within the context of existing PAYGO systems or by partial or total shifts to fully funded, actuarially fair pension systems. These reforms have usually been designed not only to improve the financial stability of the pension system but also to induce individuals to take greater responsibility for their future pensions. Indeed, some countries have already implemented such reforms. (I return to this issue in section 1.3.2.)

Besides these demographic developments, the most important change on the labor-supply side is presumably the rise in labor-force participation of women. The EU average of labor-force participation among adult females (aged 15–64) has increased from 42 percent in 1960 to 58 percent today, ranging from 44 percent in Italy to 75 percent in Denmark (OECD 1998; Eurostat 1998a). The background is well known: rationalization of household work, improved education of women relative to men, fewer children per family, and probably also increased preferences among females for economic and social independence.[2]

By boosting the tax base, increased labor-force participation of females obviously helps finance the Welfare State. But it also increases the political pressure for Welfare State spending aimed at helping individuals, mostly women, to combine family life and working life. Indeed, there is an obvious possibility of "mutual causation" between female labor-force participation and voting behavior regarding the size and composition of government spending. There is strong empirical evidence that working women tend to vote for parties that favor high government spending in the social sphere, including childcare, healthcare, and old-age care (Edlund and Pande 2001). Females are also employed proportionally more than males in the production of government-subsidized services, which means that they also have an interest as employees in voting for parties that support government subsidies of this type.

So far, however, only a few countries have adjusted their Welfare State arrangements to the new situation with rising labor-force participation of women (OECD 1998). The Nordic countries are an exception, where such labor-force participation has, in fact, been systematically stimulated by Welfare State arrangements, including elaborate systems of income transfers to families during parental leave and generous subsidies to childcare and old-age care outside the family.

The rise in female labor-force participation is, of course, an important explanation for the increase in part-time work, which is a rather natural arrangement among adults with small children. Indeed, part-time work averages about 17 percent of total employment in Western Europe, ranging from 6 percent in Greece to 39 percent in the Netherlands (Eurostat 1998b; OECD 1998). But existing benefit rules are often not well adjusted to part-time work. An illustration is that Welfare State benefits are often reduced if one of the adults in a family decides to work longer hours outside the household.

1.2.2 Labor Demand

Some recent and expected changes on the labor-demand side also have important consequences for the functioning of the Welfare State. For instance, is there any guarantee that future pension reforms, designed to boost the labor supply of elderly workers (in the age group 55–70), will actually raise employment rather than boosting unemployment for such workers? Economists typically react to this question by suggesting policies that encourage lower relative wage rates or reduced payroll taxes for this group of workers. The first alternative is not easy to implement in the context of collective bargaining because incumbent workers ("insiders"), who often dominate union policies, may regard such wage adjustments as underbidding of prevailing wages. As an alternative, the government may encourage elderly workers to sign individual wage contracts—for instance, by no longer favoring collective-bargaining contracts. But insiders may be able to resist this as well. First, they may have sufficient political clout to prevent such legislation from the outset. Second, they often have market powers to prevent individuals from underbidding wages and firms from encouraging such underbidding. This may be achieved by threatening to harass potential underbidders or by refusing to cooperate with them in the production process (Lindbeck and Snower 1988). Lower payroll taxes for elderly workers are perhaps a more realistic alternative than lower relative wages as a way of boosting labor demand for this group. But insiders might use their political powers to resist such policies as well.

In a similar vein, how can we prevent increased labor supply of women from resulting in higher unemployment either for this specific group or for men who feel the pinch of increased competition from more able females? In the United States, this problem has been solved by the invisible hand, mainly in the market for private services, whereby the demand for female labor has expanded and relative wages of unskilled males have fallen. In the Nordic countries, a corresponding increase in labor demand for women has been brought about via the visible hand of increased government service production. Both "hands" have thus far been tied in the rest of Europe.

Moreover, it is rather generally agreed that the widening of the dispersion of earnings, particularly in the United States and the United Kingdom in the 1980s and early 1990s, and the widening of the distribution of unemployment (in percentage points) in many countries in Western Europe are largely due to changes in the composition of labor demand in favor of high-skilled workers. Although some observers have referred to increased international competition for labor-intensive products, the most generally accepted explanation is certainly that during this period, Tinbergen's (1975) celebrated "race between technology and education" was won by the former. Lindbeck and Snower (1996) emphasize a third explanation—namely, that the well-documented, ongoing reorganization of firms, including the decentralization of authority and initiatives, has favored the demand for *versatile* workers, that is, individuals who are able to face up to increased responsibility (often due to idiosyncratic characteristics). This explanation is consistent with the observation that wage dispersion has recently increased also *within* narrowly defined educational groups, professions, and job categories.[3]

This development tends to make centralized wage bargaining relatively less attractive to firms, since the reorganization of work increases job heterogeneity and, as a result, also the heterogeneity of the labor force. It thus becomes more difficult than before to acquire appropriate information about job characteristics on the central level and hence to set appropriate wages from an efficiency point of view. Since centralized wage bargaining often results in a squeeze of wage differentials, shifts to more decentralized bargaining—a likely outcome of the reorganization of work—are likely to accentuate the tendencies toward wider wage dispersion (Lindbeck and Snower 2001a). However, since relative wages would then be better adjusted to the composition of demand and supply of various types of labor (more "market-conforming" wages), tendencies toward a wider dispersion of job opportunities and unemployment are likely to be mitigated.

Recent changes in *types* of labor-market contracts have also contributed to more heterogeneity in the labor market. Nowadays, there is a bewildering mixture of permanent ("indefinite") work contracts, fixed-period (temporary) work, project work, bonus systems, stock options, and so forth. For instance, whereas few workers were on fixed-term contracts in Western Europe during the first decades after World War II, the current EU average is 13 percent, with the highest figure being 33 percent for Spain (Eurostat 1998a). By allowing fixed-term contracts, the hiring of outsiders is likely to be boosted in business upswings. However, as pointed out by Bentolila and Bertola (1990), temporarily employed workers also function as an "employment buffer" for insiders, which further strengthens their job security and market power.

There is no doubt that these developments in the labor market complicate the egalitarian ambitions of the Welfare State. So far, however, in countries with elaborate Welfare State arrangements, the dispersion of the distribution of *disposable* income has increased considerably less than that of the distribution of earnings (Gottschalk and Smeeding 2000; Atkinson 1999b, 2000). On this count, the Welfare States in Western Europe have had some success in counteracting tendencies toward a wider dispersion of income.

The standard policy prescription to counteract tendencies toward a wider dispersion of wages has been to stimulate education and training. It is not obvious, however, that *general* educational subsidies (to all income groups) will have this effect. For instance, it has been argued by Hassler, Rodriguez More, and Zeira (2001) that such subsidies tend to stimulate education among the well-to-do more than among other groups, since the former devote more resources than others to education. By contrast, Nickell and Bell (1997) have hypothesized that a rise in the general level of education enhances individuals' ability to adjust to changes in the composition of labor demand in favor of high skills, and that this will mitigate tendencies toward higher relative wages for high-skilled workers. The notion that better education also makes workers more versatile would further mitigate tendencies toward a wider dispersion of wages as a result of the reorganization of work. However, to the extent that versatility depends on an innate idiosyncratic ability to accept responsibility, take initiative, and cooperate with others, education and training will not be sufficient to prevent a widening of the dispersion of earnings and job opportunities inherent in the contemporary reorganization of work within firms.

Selective education subsidies to low-skilled workers, or potentially low-skilled workers, are more likely to reduce wage differentials. Such subsidies would also stimulate social mobility, thereby enhancing equality of opportunity, in the sense that some previously low-skilled workers would become high-skilled. The long-term effect of selective education subsidies on social mobility is a more complex matter. While mobility is stimulated by greater economic resources for investment in education among families with low factor income, this effect is counteracted by a negative disincentive effect on education due to smaller wage differences (Hassler, Rodriguez More, and Zeira 2001).[4]

1.2.3 The Unemployment Experience

It is well known that during the last quarter of the twentieth century, Western Europe has been less successful in promoting full employment than in mitigating tendencies toward a wider dispersion of disposable income—presumably in part because of its highly institutionalized, centralized, and regulated system of wage formation, which could be expected to constrain relative wage flexibility. Lower employment rates have then not only contributed to undermining the Welfare State financially; the insider-outsider divide in society has also sharpened—contrary to the idea that the Welfare State should enhance social integration.

Moreover, while traditional Welfare State arrangements provide pensioners with adequate protection against income risks, such risks have instead begun to increase for young and elderly workers and their families—reflected in high unemployment among the former and dropout from the labor force among the latter (partly via early retirement). During the last two decades of the twentieth century, the youth unemployment rate (individuals in the age group 15–24) has typically been about 15–20 percent in most of Western Europe. Exceptions are countries with well-developed apprentice systems, such as Austria, Germany, and Switzerland, where the rate has oscillated between 5 and 10 percent. Spain and Italy are extreme cases in the opposite direction; their rates have recently hovered in the interval of 20–30 percent. As mentioned earlier, *employment* rates for older workers (aged 55–64) have become as low as 40 percent in the European Union as a whole (OECD 1999).

The reverse causation, from the Welfare State to unemployment, is a more controversial issue. It is unavoidable that both equilibrium unemployment (the natural rate or NAIRU) and unemployment persistence (prolonged deviations from the equilibrium rate) may be accentuated by certain types of Welfare State arrangements. Obvious examples are high subsidies of nonwork, such as generous and long-lasting unemployment benefits, social assistance ("welfare" in U.S. terminology) for unemployed workers without work requirements, and poverty traps created by means-tested benefits. There are certainly strong ethical (distributional) justifications for such benefits. But the more generous the benefits and the longer they may be kept, the greater the risk that they reduce active job search and job acceptance, in particular when administration is lax—a well-known example of moral hazard. Sufficiently generous subsidies of nonwork may also raise the wage costs for low-skilled workers by boosting the reservation wage, with similar unemployment consequences as in the case of (sufficiently high) minimum wages. These general comments are not very controversial. What *is* controversial is the quantitative importance of these employment effects, and hence the intensity of the conflict between ambitions to provide income support in connection with nonwork and a desire to fight long-term unemployment.

The consequences of job-security legislation are an even more complex issue, since such legislation increases the costs of both hiring and firing workers, with ambiguous *direct* effects on the average unemployment rate over the business cycle. But this is not the end of the story. Since the market power of insiders in the labor market is augmented by such legislation, wages are boosted and the demand for workers reduced. If these negative indirect effects on labor demand are sufficiently strong, the *average* unemployment rate over the business cycle would increase even if the direct effects are not negative, or are even positive (Lindbeck and Snower 2001b). Other types of legislation that enhance the bargaining power of unions will accentuate these effects—for instance, laws and regulations that extend collective agreements to nonunion workers and nonunion firms and that facilitate sympathy strikes, blockades, and picketing. I then assume that unions are more concerned about the welfare of insiders than of outsiders.

Moreover, regardless of whether or not job-security legislation increases equilibrium unemployment, there is no doubt that it increases unemployment persistence, that is, movements either away from or toward the equilibrium unemployment rate will decelerate. More specifically, this type of legislation tends to stabilize (un)employment at the level that happens to exist. If the economy is initially close to full employment, unemployment tends to be stabilized at a low level; this was the situation in most Western European countries in the period 1955–1975. The welfare implications are grimmer if unemployment is high initially—for instance, as a result of a recent negative macroeconomic shock, such as in the period 1975–1995. In this case, unemployment is stabilized at a high level. Indeed, I have argued elsewhere that the prolonged period of high unemployment in Western Europe during the 1980s and 1990s had more to do with high unemployment persistence than with an asserted increase in the equilibrium unemployment rate (Lindbeck 2002).

Such unemployment persistence may be the result of behavioral adjustments of either insiders or outsiders or both. One example is that after a recession, insiders may use their market powers to push up wages in a subsequent business upswing without much concern for the employment prospects of outsiders, thereby reducing the willingness of firms to hire workers. It is also well known that outsiders' possibilities of returning to work tend to fall by the length of their unemployment spells. Losses in skills and self-confidence also reduce the reemployment of outsiders. These are some reasons why both job-security legislation and long-lasting unemployment benefits tend to increase unemployment persistence. It is often hypothesized that low investment in real capital during prolonged periods of recession results in sluggish demand for labor in the aftermath, which may also reduce the demand for labor and contribute to unemployment persistence.

Unemployment persistence may be further accentuated by endogenous changes in the work ethic and social norms in conjunction with long periods of mass unemployment. In a short- and medium-term perspective, ethics and social norms in favor of work, and against living on benefits, are likely to constrain the disincentive effects on work of labor income taxes and subsidies of nonwork. But this inertia is likely to recede if a large fraction of the population are unemployed for long periods of time, assuming that social norms are upheld by the approval or disapproval of employed workers. Thus, the greater the number of individuals who live on benefits, the more socially accepted we would expect this way of life to become (Lindbeck 1995; Lindbeck, Nyberg, and Weibull 1999). Here, then, is another potentially important mechanism behind unemployment persistence. It is reflected in common talk about "unemployment cultures," although we know little about the quantitative importance of this asserted phenomenon.[5]

Needless to say, some Welfare State arrangements may instead *reduce* structural unemployment. The most obvious example is the school system. An upgrading of general skills among low-skilled workers presumably helps them to get jobs—at least when there are effective wage floors due to high minimum wages or when there are high reservation wages due to generous transfers to individuals out of work. Thus, the existence of wage floors, which in themselves may contribute to unemployment among unskilled workers (if the floor is high enough), strengthens the case for policy actions to improve the education and training of low-skilled workers.

Reduced payroll taxes for low-skilled workers, or outright "in-work benefits," comprise another strategy to boost their employment prospects in the case of rigid money wages. But since such subsidies are reduced when an individual acquires more skill, they necessarily imply increased implicit marginal taxes on investment in human capital. This, of course, may be counteracted by higher education subsidies. In this sense, employment subsidies and education subsidies are complements rather than substitutes.

So-called "active" labor-market policy might also be expected to mitigate structural unemployment through better matching between jobs and workers, which is likely to reduce both the equilibrium unemployment rate and unemployment persistence. A large number of studies, however, indicate that the quantitative effects of such policies are quite limited (e.g., Calmfors, Manning, and Saint-Paul 1998; Katz, Stanley, and Krueger 1998).[6]

One specific problem with active labor-market policy is that it facilitates the manipulation of unemployment statistics. By simply putting a book in the hands of all unemployed workers and calling them students or trainees, "open" unemployment could, in principle, be reduced to zero without any increase in regular employment. Moreover, not only workers with early retirement but frequently also "discouraged" workers are often removed from labor-force statistics. This means that the employment situation in a country is often better described by the fraction of individuals of working age who are employed—"employment rates" for short—than by the unemployment rate. While these rates were about the same (approximately 65 percent) in most OECD countries in the early 1960s, the figures have recently diverged considerably. In the United States and the Nordic countries, the rates had reached the interval 70–77 percent by the end of the 1990s (after having been above 80 percent in Finland and Sweden in the late 1980s), while the EU average had fallen to about 60 percent (OECD 1998, 1999).

The division of workers into insiders, with good and stable jobs, and outsiders, with recurrent periods of (often prolonged) unemployment or work in the informal sector, also has wide repercussions beyond the labor market. Since outsiders have smaller economic resources than insiders, they are often forced to abstain from social activities enjoyed by others, which weakens their social networks. Moreover, many important Welfare State entitlements and subsidized services are tied to current or previous work, which contributes to excluding outsiders from such Welfare State arrangements. In particular, youngsters without a foothold in the labor market often have to rely on quite ungenerous, often means-tested social assistance—when they do not live on handouts from their parents. Here, then, is a clear example of a conflict between incentives and distributional aspects. On the other hand, when expected future benefits are (positively) tied to work, such benefits have positive incentive effects on work, which counteract various work disincentives of taxes and means-tested benefits.

Social exclusion may also be intensified by conditions in the housing market. There is always a general tendency toward segregation in the housing market based on income and profession. A specific type of segregation may arise in urban housing markets with rent control and a related housing shortage (excess demand for housing). There will be a division between housing-market insiders, with direct rental contracts, and housing-market outsiders, without such contracts. In this situation, apartments will mainly be acquired via personal networks and black-market transactions. Low-income groups, including many young people and immigrants, are particularly hard hit in this respect. A positive correlation would also be expected between being an outsider in the labor market and being an outsider in the housing market.

The punchline of this discussion is that the Welfare State has a long way to go in order to adjust to changing tides in the structure of the labor market.

1.3   Changes in the Family

1.3.1   *Household Types and Life Cycle*

The ambitions of the traditional Welfare State to protect male-breadwinner families against income losses explain its emphasis on full employment, unemployment insurance, sick-leave insurance, and pensions for the breadwinner and his survivors in case of death. Recent changes in household structure, life cycle, and values make this type of Welfare State less relevant than it used to be. In particular, male-breadwinner households now constitute less than a third of families in most developed countries (Mclanahan, Casper, and Sorensen 1995, table 11.3). Two-earner households constitute (on average) about 40 percent of households in the Nordic countries and about 25 percent in Southern Europe (Italy and Spain), with other countries in Western Europe in between—usually about 30 percent (Luxembourg Income Study 2001). Single-parent households now average 14 percent of households in EU countries, ranging from 8 percent in Greece and Spain to 23 percent in the United Kingdom (Eurostat 1998b).

Growing numbers of two-earner and single-parent households have heightened the political pressure for subsidized childcare outside the household. Up to a point, subsidies to childcare and old-age care outside the household can also be justified on efficiency grounds, since they counteract tax distortion in favor of household work. In the case of small families, for example, this tax distortion discourages the exploitation of returns to scale in childcare and old-age care. The issue becomes more complex, however, if we add political complications. For instance, it has been observed in many countries that politicians often tend to combine such subsidies with highly arbitrary rules and costly regulations regarding the conduct of such care—namely, in terms of the physical premises, including space, construction, and administration, and, in the case of childcare, types of toys, curriculum, and so forth. Moreover, in some Nordic countries—for instance, Sweden—childcare subsidies outside the family are now higher than required to compensate for the tax distortion, at least for families with more than one child. This, of course, means that the government-imposed distortion changes sign in the case of such families.

For families with little education or severe problems (including criminality and alcohol or drug abuse), subsidized childcare outside the household may also promote investment in human capital. Indeed, there is empirical support for this view (Leibowitz 1996; Heckman 1999). There may also be an externality argument for subsidies to childcare outside the family in such cases, for the purpose of mitigating social misbehavior later on in life.

Whereas two-earner households rarely exhibit poverty, it is well documented that households with a single adult, in particular with children, are highly exposed to economic distress and even poverty. For instance, child poverty in one-earner households is often three or four times as frequent as the corresponding rates in two-earner households (Mclanahan, Casper, and Sorensen 1995; Bradbury and Jäntti 2001). A basic reason is that labor-force participation among single adults with children is low in most countries. Another reason is that returns to scale in household service production cannot be exploited in such households. Moreover, there are no adult household members with whom income risk can be pooled. Indeed, besides long-term unemployment, single parenthood seems to be the most important socioeconomic factor behind poverty, including child poverty (Esping-Andersen 1999, 161–163).

Although explanations of the rise in single parenthood are manifold, including increased labor-force participation of females, it is obvious that various Welfare State arrangements also have an impact. There is a strong ethical case for government support to single parents, usually mothers[7]—not least to mitigate child poverty.

But it is unavoidable that women then find it financially easier to become single mothers, through childbearing as well as divorce—another example of moral hazard in Welfare State policies. It is also likely that social norms against being a single mother have diminished in recent decades. There is probably mutual causation in this case: While weaker norms against being a single mother result in more of them, more single mothers are likely to weaken the norms.

The generosity of Welfare State support to single motherhood differs considerably among countries. In the United Kingdom, the United States, and some countries on the European continent, such support is usually modest, and mainly confined to transfer payments. In the Nordic countries, not only are transfers more generous but also they are combined with priority for single mothers to receive strongly subsidized childcare outside the household. The latter, of course, helps explain the high labor-force participation of single mothers in these countries. For instance, more than 80 percent of single mothers in Sweden worked in the early 1990s, while the EU average was 68 percent and the figure for the United Kingdom only about 50 percent. The situation in the United States is not much different—about 45 percent (Gornick 1994). The question of how problems related to single motherhood should be dealt with politically is a complex and controversial issue. The policy trend, however, is to require single mothers to work or acquire education and training, which often presupposes subsidized childcare.

Another aspect of the increased heterogeneity of households is based on tendencies to choose a less "linear" *life cycle* among education, work, and nonwork than earlier. Specifically, individuals tend increasingly to shift back and forth between periods of work, studies, sabbatical, work abroad, and so forth. One explanation may be that higher incomes in society result in increased diversity of individual "life projects," similar to the way rising income diversifies product demand. But it is also likely that preferences and attitudes are gradually undergoing change in the sense that individuals with given income want to realize idiosyncratic life projects; for evidence of such changes in values, see Inglehart and Baker (2000). This "individualization" of preferences may be a result of higher education and/or of demonstration effects from other countries. It is clear that traditional Welfare State arrangements, based on the assumption of a linear life cycle, are too inflexible to satisfy the needs and desires of individuals today to finance periods of nonwork for reasons other than bad health, unemployment, or old age.

Moreover, pensions are often tied to income earned late in working life, such as in the last ten or fifteen years of work. In a society with idiosyncratic fluctuations in income over the life cycle, sometimes with particularly high income early in life, such arrangements are not appropriate. From this point of view, there is now a stronger case for tying pensions to lifetime income, or lifetime contributions, rather than to income late in working life.

Increased family instability in many countries after World War II has also created intrafamily distributional problems for social insurance entitlements. The traditional system was largely designed to protect widows and their children. But since females increasingly have their own income from work, the need for special social insurance benefits for widows has declined. Here, a delicate normative issue is how fast pension rights for widows should be phased out. (In Sweden, phasing-out has been so rapid that many widows—a group with little political clout—have become severely disadvantaged.) In addition to problems for widows and their children, there is a growing social problem for divorcees when one partner (usually the woman) has lost momentum in her labor-market career because of childbirth and has not yet accumulated enough pension claims. In some cases, this is bound to create economic hardship in old age for at least one partner. An obvious solution in the event of separation is to split pension claims between spouses—and perhaps also between other types of long-term cohabitants. Here, then, is another example where contemporary Welfare State arrangements are not well adjusted to today's social conditions.

Recent socioeconomic changes also have important implications for housing policy. Greater instability of family structure—due to divorce, remarriage, changes in cohabitation patterns, and ambitions among the young to set up housekeeping on their own—has made rent control, with a resulting "housing shortage" (excess demand for housing), a more severe social problem than in the past. Unstable families require a flexible housing market, which presupposes equilibrating rents ("market rents") with a reserve (a few percent) of empty apartments at every point in time.

1.3.2 Individual Responsibility

In addition to new socioeconomic developments and changing values among voters, new views and values among politicians also explain current approaches to Welfare State reforms. One important example involves encouraging greater individual and family responsibility—a parallel to the increased responsibility recently given to individual workers in reorganized firms. This tendency may be seen as a reaction against the paternalistic notion that the government, in popular jargon, should take care of an individual from "cradle to grave."

The new emphasis on "workfare" rather than "welfare," not just for single mothers, is one such attempt to boost individual responsibility. More generally, politicians and policy advisers seem to be increasingly sympathetic toward shifting away from policies that subsidize nonwork. There is a tendency either to take a neutral stance regarding the choice between work and nonwork or, more frequently, to adopt policies that actively promote work (as in the case of employment subsidies or tax credits for low-wage groups).

Even leaders of traditional left-wing parties, such as the U.K. Labour party, have recently emphasized the individual's responsibility for his own economic situation. Some leaders of the Democratic party in the United States, including the Clinton administration, have expressed the same view; indeed, this vision is behind the 1997 social assistance reform in the United States—designed to abolish "welfare as we know it" in President Clinton's words. Although macroeconomic efficiency would clearly be improved by such a shift, the consequences for the financial position of the government are less clear.[8]

Another important example of reforms designed to enhance individual responsibility concerns proposals for shifting to pension systems with individual accounts. This may be achieved either by establishing a tight link between contributions and benefits in the context of PAYGO systems with "notional" accounts—a so-called "notional defined contribution" system—or by shifting to fully funded, actuarially fair systems. If only weak links (or no links at all) exist between contributions and benefits in an existing PAYGO pension system, such shifts also imply less distortion of work and hence higher economic efficiency.

The emergence of broad and highly liquid international capital markets, and the development of new types of capital market instruments that provide more options regarding the degree of risk exposure, have strengthened the case for fully funded pension systems with individual accounts. However, a shift to a fully funded system also has intergenerational and intragenerational redistributional consequences. For instance, if one or a few early ("transition") generations are forced to honor the pension claims of existing

PAYGO pensioners, subsequent generations will be favored at the expense of earlier generations. Subsequent generations will enjoy a return on their mandatory saving equal to the market interest rate, which is usually higher than the returns in PAYGO systems (which tend to equal the growth rate of aggregate labor income). Under this scheme for honoring the claims of existing PAYGO pensioners, a shift to a fully funded system would tend to increase aggregate national saving for a while, which is also to the advantage of future generations. Indeed, this is often regarded as a main rationale for such a shift (Feldstein 1995; Kotlikoff 1998). This rationale, of course, is basically an issue of redistribution of income—from current to future generations.

It is also unavoidable that shifts to fully funded systems, with individual choice of fund managers, widen the dispersion of pensions *within* generations, since some managers will be more successful than others. This merely illustrates the general principle that greater individual freedom of choice tends to create increased differences in outcome.

The case is stronger for a partial rather than a total shift to a fully funded pension system, since better diversification of the "portfolio" of pension claims is achieved in the former situation. Not only does the market risk differ between PAYGO and funded pension systems—risk regarding the development of the tax base in the first system and capital market risk in the second; the political risks also differ, and are probably, as a rule, greater in the case of PAYGO systems, since property rights are likely to be stronger in fully funded systems with individual accounts. Anyway, by combining the two systems, it would be possible to pool various types of market risks and political risks, and hence achieve a reduction in total risk.

One serious problem with mandatory fully funded pension systems is that it may be difficult to prevent future politicians from intervening in the portfolio management of pension funds created by the government, and from exercising voting powers in firms in which the funds hold shares. It would be tempting for future politicians to argue "Why should taxpayers in our country finance investments in other countries, when many of our own industries and regions need more investment?" and "Why is it that politicians, representatives of the people, should not appoint board members of firms in which the voters' pension contributions have been invested?" In other words, capital cannot be nationalized—whether in government-run pension funds or otherwise—without risking politicization of the national economy. It is not necessarily helpful to instill a regulation according to which mandatory pension funds should invest in mutual funds or foreign stocks. Future politicians with ambitions of power can always change such regulations. The most promising way of minimizing the risk of politicization is probably to let each citizen choose among a number of competing private funds from the very beginning. This is likely to impede future politicization since outright nationalization of private pension funds would then be necessary.

Of course, the administrative costs for competing pension funds are likely to be higher than for a unitary government-operated fund, at least in countries with a reasonably well-functioning government administration. But adherents of a pluralistic society may be willing to pay a price, not only in terms of greater dispersion of the distribution of pensions but also in the form of higher administrative costs, in order to enhance the survival of a pluralistic society. Administrative arrangements could also be implemented to curtail these costs—for instance, by lids on the fees in mandatory pension funds, which would prompt many fund managers to choose index-type funds.

A more radical proposal, also designed to confer on the individual more responsibility for his own income security, would be to replace the many different types of Welfare State arrangements currently in effect with a unified system of compulsory saving with individual accounts and "drawing rights" (Fölster 1999; Orszag and Snower 1999). The characteristic feature of such a system is that an individual would be allowed to draw on his account before retirement for certain specified purposes, such as education, sabbatical, sick leave, and unemployment. What remains in the account at the time of retirement would determine the size of his pension. Thus, an individual would have greater freedom than today to reallocate Welfare State entitlements over his life cycle according to idiosyncratic preferences. This reform also fits nicely with individuals' desire to choose a less linear life cycle than in the past. For the time being, the most obvious real-world example of such a system is the central provident fund in Singapore.

1.3.3 Production and Provision of Welfare State Services

While contemporary changes in family structure increase the demand for childcare and old-age care, higher real income and increased longevity tend to raise the demand for education and healthcare, probably also as a share of gross domestic product (GDP). The mechanism of Baumol's (1967) law, based on a relatively slow increase in productivity for many personal ("human") services, also tends to raise aggregate spending on personal services as a share of GDP. In addition, medical advances will most likely contribute to higher aggregate healthcare spending as a share of GDP— for instance, due to new surgical procedures for "repairing" the human body. In all of these cases, Welfare State policies, of course, boost these demands via subsidies or mandatory insurance.

These developments accentuate the problem of deciding who should provide and produce the services. In several countries in Western Europe, again notably the Nordic nations, the public sector is in charge of both the provision and the production of these services. This has been brought about by a combination of regulations and subsidies mainly confined to the public sector. In fact, personal (human) services—education, healthcare, childcare, and old-age care—have largely been socialized in these countries. This is reflected in employment statistics. While the public service sector accounts for about 25 percent of total employment in the Nordic countries, the average for Western Europe is about 18 percent (OECD 1998). In the United States, where taxes are relatively low and the dispersion of wages relatively wide, market purchases of such services (including arrangements provided by employers) are instead relatively large. As a result, while the number of individuals (officially) engaged in personal services in the private sector is only 5–6 percent of the labor force in Western Europe, it is about twice as large in the United States (Elfring 1988, table V.3).

At the same time as several personal (human) services have shifted to the government sector, the production of a number of "material services" has shifted from the market to the household (Lindbeck 1988). The reason is that the tax system favors home production of services *in general*—including repairs, cleaning, and gardening. I suppose Karl Marx would have been surprised by this combination of socialized household production of personal services and a shift of various material services from the market to the household— while manufacturing production has remained in the private sector.

It is not obvious why governments in some countries have thus created near–public sector monopolies for both provision and production of important personal services. One conceivable explanation is that such policies tend to change the distribution of income to the

disadvantage of high-income families that choose to buy nonsub-
sidized private services at the same time as they have to pay taxes to
finance services for others. They then have to "pay twice" (Besley
and Coate 1991; Blomquist and Christiansen 1995). Another explanation may be that public sector service monopolies make it easier
for politicians and public sector administrators to control the type,
quality, and distribution of such services. But why would a majority
of voters support such arrangements, which largely do away with
individual freedom of choice in these areas? Today, it may well be
that only a small minority of voters are concerned about freedom of
choice for services such as childcare and old-age care, in particular if
most families are basically content with the quality of government-
produced services. The absence of freedom of choice may be a serious concern only for those who adhere strongly to the *principle* that
individuals should be free to choose.

However, as time goes by, higher income and better education
are likely to increase households' interest in obtaining more individually adjusted services and hence more individual freedom of choice
in the future. Again, this would be a parallel to the observed high
income elasticity of demand for product variability in the case of
private goods and services. As a result, Welfare States that favor
public sector service monopolies are likely to be less and less in
touch with the values of a large number of their citizens.

One increasingly popular way of creating competition in the production of such services is different forms of outsourcing, sometimes
after competitive bidding among private service producers. While
this procedure may increase efficiency and innovation in production,
it hardly increases the freedom of choice among consumers. As we
know by now, it is not administratively difficult to combine freedom
of choice with subsidies to "social services." Service checks (vouchers) allow households to buy services wherever they like, or to cash
the checks and produce the services themselves. It is not obvious
why the case for freedom of choice, competition, and innovation
(experimentation) should be weaker in these areas than for ordinary
consumer goods. Administratively, voucher systems are much easier
in the case of childcare and education than in the case of old-age
care, since the service needs of the elderly vary greatly depending on
the individual's health situation.

The most common argument against vouchers seems to be that
they might increase institutional segregation along the lines of in-

come, education, and profession. But this argument is far from obvious. There is considerable housing segregation in most countries,
which means that service vouchers give low-income families living in
geographical areas with poor service institutions a chance to acquire
services from better institutions in other geographical areas—today
a privilege mainly confined to the rich. Vouchers may then, in fact,
contribute to institutional *desegregation* of childcare, education, and
old-age care services.

In the case of education, a specific argument against vouchers is
that public sector schools may lose some of their best students and
most-able teachers, and that this will lower the quality of education
for the remaining pupils in such schools (Hirschman 1960; Epple and
Romano 1998). But there is also an opposite hypothesis—namely,
that increased competition stimulates the performance of *all* schools,
including those in the public sector, and that, as a result, education
becomes better adjusted to children's different needs and parents'
different wishes also in public sector schools (Hoxby 1994). The
empirical studies carried out so far do not lend support to the negative hypothesis; there is, rather, some support for the positive one.[9]
However, a difficult political question in this context is whether
parents should be allowed to add cash payments to vouchers to
obtain more expensive education for their children. Individuals sub-
scribing to the view that certain types of personal services should be
more equally distributed than purchasing power in general are likely
to argue in favor of restrictions on allowing parents to add private
cash to vouchers.

Contemporary changes in information and communication technology (ICT) are likely to have important consequences for public
service production. Trivially, ICT reduces the individual's costs of
acquiring information about public sector activities, including rules
concerning social insurance and Welfare State services. ICT also
makes it cheaper to administrate individually adjusted, and hence
more differentiated, social insurance systems, including both pension
systems with individual accounts and compulsory saving with individual drawing rights.

The World Wide Web also enables individuals to learn from the
experiences of others regarding specific public sector services, evaluated from the consumer's point of view. Moreover, as new forums
gradually emerge on the Internet, individual citizens can express
their opinions not only about goods in the private sector but also

about specific public sector services, such as childcare, education, healthcare, and old-age care at specific institutions. An individual will then be able to air his views not only on the Web site of politicians and public sector institutions but also on nongovernment sites: virtual communities, news groups, and chat groups managed by independent agents. When many individuals openly express their views in cyberspace, politicians and public sector administrators will find it difficult to neglect complaints and suggestions (Lindbeck and Wikström 2000).

In other words, the Internet is likely to enhance the individual's "voice" option, in Hirschman's (1960) terminology, regarding public sector services. This is important in the sense that voting is a very inefficient way of voicing opinions about specific public sector services, such as a particular school or childcare institution. After all, general elections only enable an individual to comment on broad "packages" of policy measures proposed by political parties or individual candidates.

A voice option via the Internet would be even more powerful if it were accompanied by an expanded "exit" option, which is exactly what vouchers would bring about. Correspondingly, exit options are more valuable if the individual is well informed—for instance, via the Web. Thus, voice options by way of the Web and exit opportunities by way of voucher systems are highly complementary mechanisms.

1.3.4 Family Orientation versus Individual Orientation

The developments discussed above—concerning family structure, life cycle, and values—challenge both the family-oriented, transfer-heavy Welfare States on the European continent and the more individually oriented, public-service-heavy Welfare States in the Nordic countries. The former type of Welfare State emphasizes family stability and family-provided services to family members, while female labor-market participation is discouraged.[10] The fact that birth rates today are not higher in these countries than in countries where more women work outside the home suggests that low labor-force participation among females is no guarantee for high fertility.

Generally speaking, the Nordic Welfare States are more individual oriented in the sense that taxes and benefits are tied to individuals rather than to families and that Welfare State arrangements are adapted to women's ambitions to participate in the labor market. In particular, the availability of subsidized childcare and old-age care outside the family is likely to mitigate the conflict between female labor-market participation and personal services for household members. One obvious "cost" is high tax rates and, in reality (though not by necessity), strongly restricted freedom of households to choose a service provider since public sector provision and production of personal services is emphasized. In practice, these countries also exhibit strong gender segregation in the labor market—a concentration of women in the public sector and men in the private sector. For instance, in Sweden, 51 percent of the female labor force work in the public sector, and 73 percent of the employees in this sector are females (Statistics Sweden 2001).

Some advocates of Nordic-type Welfare States regard generous transfers to households as instruments for making individuals less dependent on the labor market—a "de-commodation" of individuals in Marxian jargon (a concept elaborated by Polanyi 1944). But, somewhat paradoxically, it is precisely in this type of Welfare State that married (and cohabiting) women are actually "commodized," since their high labor-force participation makes them *directly* dependent on the labor market (Esping-Andersen 1999). Moreover, a common assessment is that families with two adult labor-market participants often find that time is extremely scarce, a point made forcefully long ago by Burenstam Linder (1970). Married females have adjusted to this dilemma not only by working part time but also by cutting the number of hours of work in the home as compared with housewives (Esping-Andersen 1999, 629).

The answer to the question of what would be an appropriate strategy for Welfare State reforms from a normative point of view depends, of course, on what type of society we strive to realize. Moreover, women's ambitions to participate in the labor market can be satisfied in different ways. One way is through a U.S.-type strategy of high flexibility (and wide dispersion) of relative wages, possibly combined with negative income taxes associated with work (such as "in-work benefits" or tax credits to individuals with small earnings). Another way is the Nordic strategy of generous subsidies to childcare and old-age care outside the household. It turns out that total social spending (public sector plus private)[11] does not differ dramatically between these two types of countries, even though the proportions of government and private financing and provision differ considerably (Forsell, Medelberg, and Ståhlberg 2000; Esping-Andersen 1999, 175–178).

1.4 Macroeconomic Developments: Instability, Growth, and Internationalization

1.4.1 Short-Term Macroeconomic Instability

Recent experiences of short-term macroeconomic fluctuations in developed countries provide interesting lessons for the Welfare State. The traditional Keynesian view, of course, was that generous Welfare State arrangements help reduce cyclical fluctuations in aggregate output and employment since disposable income is held stable by the "automatic fiscal stabilizer." This theory is still relevant in the case of modest business cycles. But, as we know, this view has recently been challenged. Then I do not refer to the "Ricardian equivalence" hypothesis, according to which the effects on aggregate demand (abstracting from disincentive effects via tax distortions) are independent of the way in which government spending is financed (by taxes or borrowing). Nor do I refer to views developed by a number of German economists in the 1980s to the effect that higher government spending may create expectations about permanently higher taxes in the future, which are assumed to reduce private spending and hence have negative macroeconomic effects (see the discussion in Giavazzi and Pagano 1990).[12]

Instead, I consider recent experience in Finland and Sweden, which suggests that the automatic fiscal stabilizer may turn into an automatic destabilizer in the case of *huge* negative macroeconomic shocks if these undermine confidence in the ability of the government to live up to its financial commitments. There are at least two reasons for such a destabilizing effect due to increased uncertainty about government behavior. If the budget deficit and, as a consequence, public sector debt explode, lenders may lose confidence in the government's ability to service the galloping debt. They then require higher—possibly much higher—interest rates, with restrictive macroeconomic effects as a result. The crowding-out of private spending may then be much larger than that predicted by traditional static Keynesian (IS-LM) models (where the crowding-out effect can never be larger than the initial stimulation of aggregate demand via a higher budget deficit).[13]

Another reason why galloping government debt during a recession may have restrictive rather than expansionary macroeconomic effects on the national economy is that households may lose confidence in the government's ability to grant promised Welfare State entitlements. A predicted effect of such an increase in uncertainty is a rise in the financial saving rate of households, in particular via reduced purchases of durable consumer goods. This also tends to deepen a recession.[14]

All this means that the harmony that used to be assumed between the Welfare State and macroeconomic stability, in the Keynes-Beveridge tradition, has been shattered to some extent (Lindbeck 1997a). In particular, this may happen in countries where the budget balance is very sensitive to changes in macroeconomic activity, which is the case in countries with highly ambitious Welfare State arrangements.

1.4.2 Economic Growth

While rapid economic growth during the first decades after World War II facilitated the financing of Welfare State spending, it is a commonplace that the growth slowdown from the mid-1970s contributed to the emerging financial problems of the Welfare State. At the same time as the tax base became more sluggish, various Welfare State entitlements, often based on earlier macroeconomic developments, continued to expand. This helps explain the emergence of budget deficits in several countries.

But what about the possibility of reverse causation—from the Welfare State to long-term economic growth? The most obvious example of *positive* growth effects, at least during a period of transition, is probably government subsidies to investment in human capital—education, training programs, and, to some extent, also healthcare (though perhaps not in the case of retired individuals). It is also generally believed that income protection contributes to social tranquility, and that this in turn promotes economic efficiency and growth by preventing disruptive social conflicts. Indeed, there is some empirical support for this hypothesis (Alesina et al. 1996).[15]

One widely quoted Welfare State arrangement with *negative* effects on GDP growth, at least during a period of transition, is the introduction of PAYGO social insurance systems. The reason is that the "gift" to the first generations of PAYGO pensioners increased their consumption and hence reduced aggregate saving. Moreover, as pointed out, in particular by Feldstein (1995), existing capital income taxes are likely to have depressed physical capital formation over a number of years. Various asymmetries in such taxes also distort the allocation of investment among sectors and firms, with negative effects on economic growth. Similarly, progressive taxes on earnings are likely to have reduced the incentives to invest in human capital, hence counteracting the positive effects of various educational subsidies on such investment. Most likely, gradually larger marginal tax wedges on labor earnings during the 1960s, 1970s, and early 1980s in many countries reduced not only economic efficiency but also economic growth during a period of transition.

I would hypothesize that the negative growth effects will be particularly pronounced if Welfare State egalitarianism spreads to the business sector. An example is attempts by the government to squeeze profits and to tax wealth of small entrepreneurs as part of redistribution policy, since real investment then tends to fall. If the government, as in Sweden during the 1960s and 1970s, responds to such a fall by selective subsidies to ailing firms, the allocation of resources is bound to be distorted, and economic efficiency and (at least during a period of transition) the growth rate bound to decline. A combination of double taxation of profits, high wealth taxes, and high inheritance taxes is also likely to harm the entry and expansion of small firms.[16]

The basic issue, however, is not whether the Welfare State *as a whole* boosts or retards economic growth, but rather at what level of Welfare State arrangements, and related financing, the negative effects of additional spending start to dominate the positive effects. This way of looking at the issue is evidently based on the observation that the marginal disincentive effects of explicit and implicit taxes increase with the rates, and the assumption that governments, to begin with, choose growth-enhancing rather than growth-retarding programs. This is the background for the usual hypothesis of a nonlinear (concave) relation between Welfare State spending and economic growth, with an internal maximum point for the growth rate. This view of the world, however, is complicated by the fact that the consequences of Welfare State arrangements (and their financing) for economic growth depend crucially on the exact design of these arrangements, including the structure of taxes—a point pursued, for instance, by Atkinson (1999a). Indeed, there is not even any guarantee that a government will initially choose taxes with modest rather than huge distortions and that it will begin the Welfare State buildup by implementing systems with positive rather than negative effects on economic efficiency and growth.

All this means that we cannot hope to find a robust empirical relation between the aggregate level of Welfare State spending, on one hand, and economic efficiency and aggregate economic growth, on the other hand. Thus, it is very difficult to ascertain the level of Welfare State spending at which unfavorable effects on efficiency and growth start to dominate the favorable ones.[17]

1.4.3 Internationalization

It is a commonly held view today that the gradual internationalization of the economic system ("globalization") will force countries to scale down their Welfare State ambitions. It is true that the possibilities of taxing capital much more highly in one country than in others have receded considerably, and that this may generate "downward tax competition" in the case of capital taxation. Government revenues from capital taxes, however, usually comprise only a few percent of total government tax revenues. Thus, the main problem with receding national autonomy in capital taxation is not really that it becomes more difficult to finance the Welfare State. Nevertheless, there will certainly be an increased conflict between attempts to reduce disposable income of the very rich (for whom income from capital is important) and ambitions to keep up domestic capital formation. Presumably, this conflict is particularly strong in the case of owners of small and medium-sized firms, because they require family capital and other types of domestic equity capital.

Moreover, to the extent that the internationalization of product and labor markets is responsible for the recent widening of the distribution of earnings in some countries, it becomes more difficult to squeeze the distribution of earnings. A long time ago, Myrdal (1968) pointed out that countries with generous Welfare State arrangements and strongly egalitarian ambitions will undergo strong pressure for immigration of low-skilled workers. He predicted that this will induce such countries to pursue quite restrictive immigration policies for low-skilled workers. Moreover, to mitigate tendencies toward downward benefit competition, some authors, such as Sinn (2000), have suggested that benefits for immigrants should be tied to the benefit levels in their home countries rather than in their host country.

So much for capital and (low-skilled) labor. It is more difficult to judge whether national autonomy has dwindled much, or is likely to do so in the future, in the case of taxation of human capital. Several factors have certainly increased the mobility of human capital: internationalization of firms (including increased role of multinational firms), improved knowledge of foreign languages among younger generations, and better information about conditions in other countries. Thus, the risk that countries with high and strongly progressive taxes will face a brain drain has certainly increased, though from quite low levels. While countries have some control of immigration of low-skilled workers through quantitative regulations, attempts to counteract emigration of high-skilled individuals have to rely on other methods, including economic incentives. An individual's choice of country of residence, however, does not depend mainly on *marginal* tax rates, but rather on his *total* tax burden relative to *total* benefits received. It is mainly this relation governments should consider when worrying about brain drain in connection with Welfare State policies. So far, however, the quantitative importance of this type of brain-drain problem has not been overwhelming for rich countries, except possibly for some English-speaking countries. The situation may well change in the future. But it is still too early to say whether much coordination and centralization of Welfare State and tax arrangements will be necessary later on in order to limit brain drain and downward tax competition in the case of human capital.

There is, no doubt, a case for making social insurance entitlements internationally transferable—a parallel to attempts to make occupational pensions transferable among production sectors in the domestic economy. One way of bringing this about is to base entitlements on individual accounts that the individual can take with him when shifting his domicile from one country to another—a method reminiscent of Sinn's (2000) suggestion to tie benefits for migrants to the benefit level in their home countries. While such accounts are typical for fully funded benefit systems, as well as for forced saving with "drawing rights" of individuals, *notional* accounts in the context of PAYGO systems may also be made internationally transferable.

One reason to be somewhat skeptical about assertions that the internationalization process will force countries to make drastic reductions in Welfare State spending is that the most internationalized countries in the Organization for Economic Cooperation and Development (OECD) area—a number of "small open" Western European countries—have traditionally had particularly generous Welfare State arrangements without pronounced brain-drain problems.[18] As mentioned before, the problem for these countries is rather to limit immigration of low-skilled workers.

There is, however, another way of looking at the increased obstacles to national governments keeping domestic taxes high on human and financial capital in an ever more internationalized economy. Rather than looking at this as a problem for governments, increased international mobility of human and financial capital may be seen as protection of minorities against threats of being "robbed" by the government or by a majority of voters. The ability of the individual to "vote with his feet" may be regarded as a complement to his right to vote at the ballet box. The exit option is strengthened.

1.5 Concluding Remarks

How, then, have different countries responded to "changing tides" for the Welfare State? In most countries, not much has yet been done to adjust the Welfare State to new income risks and new service needs. Although attempts have been made in several countries to raise the average pension age, this has turned out to be a politically difficult task. Only a few OECD countries—including Italy, Sweden, and Germany—have started major reforms of their pension systems through shifts to "notional defined contribution" pension systems or partial shifts to fully funded systems.

Adjustment to changes in family structure has also been quite modest in most OECD countries. The most far-reaching change has taken place in the Nordic countries, reflected in legislated paid leave for the care of small children and subsidies to childcare outside the family. This is an important explanation as to why labor-force participation in these countries is as high as it is in the United States, where it is kept up by wide wage dispersion and relatively low taxes. In one important respect, however, the Nordic countries have moved closer to the Welfare State regimes on the European continent: Benefits have recently been tied more closely to contributions paid earlier (the "Bismarck tradition"), rather than constituting "citizens' rights" independent of contributions. In the United Kingdom, there has instead been a pronounced shift from universal to means-tested benefits (Atkinson 1999a).

Reforms of the labor market in response to shifts in supply and demand for labor have also been modest. For instance, not much has been done to improve wage flexibility to accommodate shifts in the composition of the labor force and to mitigate tendencies toward unemployment persistence. The insider-outsider divide in the labor market and society at large also prevails; the Netherlands is perhaps an exception.

There are only modest tendencies to encourage greater freedom of choice concerning types of personal services—for instance, via service vouchers, which could potentially strengthen individuals' "exit options." The ICT revolution, which could provide individuals with new tools for a stronger "voice" in the sector of public services, has at most only started to emerge.

The most important adjustment of Welfare State policies during the last two decades is probably that aggregate Welfare State spending—defined as transfers (excluding interest payments) plus public consumption (excluding defense)—has stagnated as a percentage of GDP since the mid-1980s in most OECD countries (OECD 1999). I then abstract from cyclical fluctuations. One interpretation is that governments have become more aware of the difficulties of financing ever higher Welfare State expenditures without severe disincentive effects (tax distortions and moral hazard). In only a very few countries, however, can we observe a clear trend toward lower Welfare State spending during the last two decades—in particular, in the Netherlands and Belgium—though several countries (such as Denmark, Finland, and Sweden) have cut aggregate Welfare State spending substantially from the cyclical peak levels in the early 1990s.

The overall impression is that it is politically difficult to adjust Welfare State arrangements to new socioeconomic conditions and changing values. One explanation for the difficulties, of course, is that new arrangements have to compete with established programs for which there already exist interest groups, often with strong political influence. In line with Khaneman-Tversky-type theories, it is also natural to assume that voters who lose benefits that they already have will be more perturbed than voters who do not secure new benefits. Hence, the risk of losing votes among the former is probably greater than the possibilities of gaining votes among the latter. The outcome is either that new arrangements will not develop in response to new demands (the situation in the United Kingdom and in most countries in continental Europe) or that new arrangements are piled on top of the old ones, which, during the 1970s and 1980s, resulted in very high tax rates in the Nordic countries.

Notes

I am grateful to Jon Dutrieux Anderson, Alessandra Bonfiglioli, and Christina Håkansson for help in collecting data. Anders Björklund, Peter Heller, Richard Musgrave, and Solveig Wikström provided useful comments on a draft of the chapter. I am also grateful for comments from two anonymous referees.

1. According to projections by the EU Secretariat, the pension rules in effect in the early 1990s imply that the average age dependency ratio (the number of retirees relative to the number of individuals of working age) will increase by 50 percent between the mid-1990s and 2020 in the EU area (Commission of the European Communities 1994).

2. It is true that some factors have operated in the opposite direction, hence discouraging female labor-force participation. In particular, do-it-yourself tasks have been stimulated by a gradual increase in the relative price of purchased household services. Moreover, in the same way as tariffs favor autarky rather than international trade for a nation, income and consumption taxes favor autarky for the household (do-it-yourself work) rather than purchases of services in the open market (Lindbeck 1988). Evidently, in the case of females, these two negative effects on labor-force participation have been overridden by the above-mentioned positive effects (in contrast to the case of males).

3. There are now systematic empirical studies showing that this type of reorganization of firms is a widespread phenomenon; for a survey of the empirical literature, see Lindbeck and Snower (2001a). A hardline believer in the technological explanation might be tempted to argue that the reorganization of firms is simply a subset of technological change. Even with that terminology, an explanation in terms of reorganization of work would still be of interest in clarifying what *type* of technological change is behind the recent widening of the dispersion of earnings and job opportunities. This explanation then emphasizes the role of versatility rather than just technical skills.

4. Long ago, Myrdal and Myrdal (1934) argued that a broadening of educational opportunities would ultimately result in genetic sorting on income classes and that this would subsequently harm the genetic pool among low-income classes and, as a result, slow down social mobility.

5. It is true that unemployment has tapered off cyclically during boom periods in Western Europe in the mid-1990s and early 2000s, but only to about 8 percent (open unemployment). This figure, of course, is vastly higher than those typical of boom periods during the 1960s and 1970s. It is difficult to know exactly how institutional conditions should be altered so as to contribute to reduced unemployment. While

some unemployment-reducing reforms were brought about via confrontation with labor unions during the Thatcher era in the United Kingdom, reforms and adjustments with favorable employment effects turned out to be feasible in the Netherlands via agreements among unions, employers, and the government.

6. It could be that these studies underestimate the long-term positive employment effects of such policies. More specifically, it is conceivable that unemployed workers involved in active labor-market programs, such as training and public works, do not lose their skills and work habits as fast as openly unemployed workers. If so, active labor-market policy may make the supply of skilled labor more elastic in *subsequent* booms, thereby contributing to lower structural unemployment in later upswings. So far, there is not much systematic empirical information about such conceivable long-term effects.

7. Women account for 84 percent of single parents in Western Europe (Eurostat 1998b).

8. The effects depend partly on the elasticity of labor demand with respect to real wage costs. While some authors, such as Sinn (2000), have argued that the financial position of the government will improve, others, such as Burtless (1994), assert that the opposite is likely to be the case.

9. For a survey of the literature, see Bergström and Sandström (2001), who also present a study for Sweden.

10. Childcare by grandparents and other relatives is important in all countries. Esping-Andersen (1999, 64) reports that such childcare accounts for about 30 percent of total childcare in Denmark, 50 percent in the United States, and 83 percent in the United Kingdom—and probably the lion's share also in Germany, Italy, and Spain.

11. I include in this concept childcare, education, healthcare, and old-age care outside the family.

12. These studies have looked mainly at the possibility that *lower* government spending has expansionary macroeconomic effects.

13. In the early 1990s, real interest rates on private loans in Finland and Sweden increased to 10–15 percent.

14. For instance, in the early 1990s, the household saving rate in Sweden increased from *minus* 3 to *plus* 9 percent, which corresponded to a fall in domestic aggregate demand by about 7 percent. The difficulties in stimulating household consumption via budget deficits in Japan in the 1990s may be a similar phenomenon.

15. It has also been argued by Sinn (1996) that increased income security provided by various Welfare State arrangements promotes economic growth, since entrepreneurs are then willing to accept greater risk. This cannot possibly be a decisive point. The big risk for entrepreneurs involves losing their equity capital, and Welfare State arrangements and/or taxes do not compensate for such risks. As a rule, the probable alternatives for an entrepreneur are to start a new firm or to accept becoming an employee—rather than living on Welfare State benefits, such as unemployment benefits or social assistance.

16. Indeed, in Sweden during the 1960s and 1980s, tax rates on capital investment by owners of small firms were often close to, or even higher than, 100 percent in real terms. I have hypothesized that this "extension" of redistribution policies to the busi-

ness sector was an important explanation for the slow growth in Sweden relative to other countries during the last quarter of the twentieth century (Lindbeck 1997b). This policy was gradually abandoned in the late 1980s and early 1990s.

17. Overall, in the case of rich countries, ambitious econometric studies tend to find a negative relation between the share of aggregate government spending (or taxes) and economic growth; see, for instance, Fölster and Henrekson (2001). Even if this result makes sense to many observers, including myself, we cannot feel confident about the quantitative aspects.

18. A celebrated explanation as to why these countries have built up quite ambitious programs of income protection is that highly open economies are particularly exposed to the risk of income disturbances emanating from worldwide developments; see Cameron (1978) and Rodrik (1998).

References

Alesina, A., S. Ozler, N. Roubini, and P. Swagel. 1996. "Political Instability and Economic Growth." *Journal of Economic Growth* 2: 189–213.

Atkinson, A. B. 1991. "Social Insurance." *Geneva Papers on Risk and Insurance Theory* 16: 113–131.

Atkinson, A. B. 1999a. "The Economics of the Welfare State: An Incomplete Debate." In *The Welfare State in Europe*, ed. M. Buti, D. Franco, and L. Pench. Cheltenham, UK: Edward Elgar.

Atkinson, A. B. 1999b. "Is Rising Inequality Inevitable? A Critique of the Transatlantic Consensus." Wider Annual Lecture 3, University of Oslo, Norway, November 1.

Atkinson, A. B. 2000. "Income and Earnings Inequality in OECD Countries. Seeking to Explain Recent Developments." Paper presented at Center for Business and Policy Studies (SNS) and Swedish Trade Union Conference, Stockholm, Sweden.

Barr, N. 1992. "Economic Theory and the Welfare State: A Survey and Interpretation." *Journal of Economic Literature* 30: 741–803.

Baumol, W. 1967. "The Macroeconomics of Unbalanced Growth." *American Economic Review* 57: 415–426.

Becker, G. 1981. *A Treatise on the Family*. Cambridge: Harvard University Press.

Bentolila, S., and G. Bertola. 1990. "Firing Costs and Labour Demand: How Bad Is Eurosclerosis?" *Review of Economic Studies* 57: 381–402.

Bergström, F., and M. Sandström. 2001. *Konkurrens Bildar Skola: En ESO-Rapport om Friskolornas Betydelse för de Kommunala Skolorna*. (Competition Founds a School: An ESO Report on the Effects of Private Schools on Local Public Schools.) ESO Report, Stockholm, Sweden.

Besley, T., and S. Coate. 1991. "Public Provision of Private Goods and the Redistribution of Income." *American Economic Review* 81: 979–984.

Blomquist, S., and V. Christiansen. 1995. "Public Provision of Private Goods as a Redistributive Device in an Optimum Income Tax Model." *Scandinavian Journal of Economics* 97: 547–567.

Boeri, T., A. Börsch-Supan, and G. Tabellini. 2001. "Would You Like to Shrink the Welfare State? A Survey of European Citizens." *Economic Policy* 32(April): 7–50.

Bradbury, B., and M. Jäntti. 2001. "Child Poverty across the Industrialised World: Evidence from the Luxembourg Income Study." In *Child Well-Being, Child Poverty and Child Policy in Modern Nations*, ed. K. Vleminckx and T. M. Smeeding. Bristol, UK: Policy Press.

Burenstam Linder, S. 1970. *The Harried Leisure Class*. New York: Columbia University Press.

Burtless, G. 1994. "Paychecks or Welfare Checks: Can AFDC Recipients Support Themselves?" *Brookings Review* 12(4): 34–37.

Calmfors, L., A. Manning, and G. Saint-Paul. 1998. "A Balanced Approach to Employment Policy in Europe." HM Treasury Working Paper No. 70, London.

Cameron, D. 1978. "The Expansion of the Public Economy: A Comparative Analysis." *American Political Science Review* 72: 1243–1261.

Commission of the European Communities. 1994. *Social Protection in Europe 1993*. Directorate-General for Employment, Industrial Relations, and Social Affairs. Luxembourg: Office for Official Publications of the European Communities.

Edlund, L., and R. Pande. 2001. "Gender Politics: The Political Science of Marriage." Mimeo., Columbia University, New York.

Elfring, T. 1988. "Service Employment in Advanced Economies." Ph.D. diss., University of Groningen, Netherlands.

Epple, D., and R. E. Romano. 1998. "Competition between Private and Public Schools, Vouchers and Peer-Group Effects." *American Economic Review* 88: 33–67.

Esping-Andersen, G. 1999. *Social Foundations of Postindustrial Economies*. Oxford: Oxford University Press.

Eurostat. 1998a. *Statistics in Focus* Volumes 3–11. Labour Force Survey, Principal Results 1998. Luxembourg: Luxembourg Statistical Office of the European Communities.

Eurostat. 1998b. *Statistics in Focus, Population and Social Conditions*. Vol. 12, *Lone Parent Families: A Growing Phenomenon*. Luxembourg: Luxembourg Statistical Office of the European Communities.

Feldstein, M. 1995. "The Missing Piece in Policy Analysis: Social Security Reform." *American Economic Review* 85: 1–14.

Fölster, S. 1999. "Social Insurance Based on Personal Savings Accounts: A Possible Reform Strategy for Overburdened Welfare States?" In *The Welfare State in Europe*, ed. M. Buti, D. Franco, and L. Pench. Cheltenham, UK: Edward Elgar.

Fölster, S., and M. Henrekson. 2001. "Growth Effects of Government Expenditure and Taxation in Rich Countries." *European Economic Review* 45: 1501–1520.

Forsell, Å., M. Medelberg, and A.-C. Ståhlberg. 2000. "Olika Transfereringssystem men Olika Inkomster." (Different Transfer Systems but Different Incomes.) *Ekonomisk Debatt* 28: 143–158.

Giavazzi, F., and M. Pagano. 1990. "Can Severe Fiscal Contractions Be Expansionary? Tales of Two Small European Countries." In *NBER Macroeconomics Annual 1990*, ed. O. J. Blanchard and S. Fisher. Cambridge: MIT Press.

Gornick, J. 1994. "Economic Gender Gaps in Industrialized Countries." *Luxembourg Income Study*. Mimeo., Data and Program Library Service, University of Wisconsin-Madison.

Gottschalk, P., and T. Smeeding. 2000. "Empirical Evidence on Income Inequality in Industrialized Countries." In *Handbook of Income Distribution*, Vol. 1, ed. A. B. Atkinson and F. Bourguignon. Amsterdam: Elsevier Science.

Hassler, J., J. Rodriguez More, and J. Zeira. 2001. "Inequality, Mobility and Distribution." Mimeo., Institute for International Economic Studies, Stockholm, Sweden.

Heckman, J. J. 1999. "Policies to Foster Human Capital." Paper presented at the Aaron Wildavsky Forum, University of California, Berkeley.

Hirschman, A. 1960. *Exit, Voice, and Loyalty*. Cambridge: Harvard University Press.

Hoxby, C. M. 1994. "Do Private Schools Provide Competition for Public Schools?" National Bureau of Economic Research Working Paper No. 4975, Cambridge, MA.

Inglehart, R., and W. Baker. 2000. "Modernization, Cultural Change, and the Persistence of Traditional Values." *American Sociological Review* 65: 19–51.

Katz, L., M. Stanley, and A. Krueger. 1998. "Impact of Employment and Training Programs: The American Experience." HM Treasury Working Paper No. 70, London.

Kotlikoff, L. 1998. "Simulating the Privatization of Social Security in General Equilibrium." In *Privatizing Social Security*, ed. M. Feldstein. Chicago: University of Chicago Press.

Leibowitz, A. 1996. "Child Care: Private Costs or Public Responsibility." In *Individual and Social Responsibility*, ed. U. Fuchs. Chicago: University of Chicago Press.

Lindbeck, A. 1985. "Redistribution Policy and the Expansion of the Public Sector." *Journal of Public Economics* 28: 309–328.

Lindbeck, A. 1988. "Consequences of the Advanced Welfare State." *The World Economy* 11: 19–38.

Lindbeck, A. 1994. "Overshooting, Reform and Retreat of the Welfare State." Tinbergen Lecture. *De Economist* 142: 1–19.

Lindbeck, A. 1995. "Hazardous Welfare-State Dynamics." *American Economic Review, Papers and Proceedings* 85: 9–15.

Lindbeck, A. 1997a. "Full Employment and the Welfare State." Seidman Lecture. *The American Economist* 42: 3–14.

Lindbeck, A. 1997b. "The Swedish Experiment." *Journal of Economic Literature* 35: 1273–1319.

Lindbeck, A. 2002. "Unemployment—Structural." In *International Encyclopedia of the Social and Behavioral Sciences*, ed. N. J. Smelser and P. B. Baltes. Oxford: Pergamon, Elsevier Science.

Lindbeck, A., and D. Snower. 1988. "Cooperation, Harassment and Involuntary Unemployment." *American Economic Review* 78: 167–188.

Lindbeck, A., and D. Snower. 1996. "Reorganization of Firms and Labor Market Inequality." *American Economic Review* 86: 315–321.

Lindbeck, A., and D. Snower. 2001a. "Centralized Bargaining and Reorganized Work: Are They Compatible?" *European Economic Review* 45: 1851–1875.

Lindbeck, A., and D. Snower. 2001b. "Insiders versus Outsiders." *Journal of Economic Perspectives* 15(1): 165–188.

Lindbeck, A., and S. Wikström. 2000. "The ICT Revolution in Consumer Product Markets." *Consumption, Markets and Culture* 4: 1–20.

Lindbeck, A., S. Nyberg, and J. W. Weibull. 1999. "Social Norms and Economic Incentives in the Welfare State." *Quarterly Journal of Economics* 114: 1–35.

Luxembourg Income Study. 2001. www.lis.ceps.lu. Data and Program Library Service, University of Wisconsin-Madison.

Mclanahan, S., L. Casper, and A. Sorensen. 1995. *Growing Up with a Single Parent.* Cambridge: Harvard University Press.

Myrdal, A., and G. Myrdal. 1934. *Kris i Befolkningsfrågan.* (The Population Crisis.) Stockholm: Bonniers.

Myrdal, G. 1968. *Beyond the Welfare State: Economic Planning and its International Implications.* New Haven: Yale University Press.

Nickell, S., and B. Bell. 1997. "Changes in the Distribution of Wages and Unemployment in OECD Countries." *American Economic Review* 87: 302–308.

OECD. 1998. *Historical Statistics, 1960–1995.* Paris: Organization for Economic Cooperation and Development.

OECD. 1999. *Employment Outlook.* Paris: Organization for Economic Cooperation and Development.

Olson, M. 1965. *The Logic of Collective Action: Public Goods and the Theory of Groups.* Cambridge: Harvard University Press.

Orszag, M., and D. Snower. 1999. "Expanding the Welfare System: A Proposal for Reform." In *The Welfare State in Europe*, ed. M. Buti, D. Franco, and L. Pench. Cheltenham, UK: Edward Elgar.

Piore, M. J. 1987. "Historical Perspectives and the Interpretation of Unemployment." *Journal of Economic Literature* 25: 1834–1850.

Polanyi, K. 1944. *The Great Transformation.* New York: Rhinehart.

Rodrik, D. 1998. "Why Do More Open Economies Have Bigger Governments?" *Journal of Political Economy* 106: 997–1032.

Sinn, H.-W. 1996. "Social Insurance, Incentives and Risk Taking." *International Tax and Public Finance* 3: 259–280.

Sinn, H.-W. 2000. "The Threat to the German Welfare State." CESifo Working Paper No. 320, Munich, Germany.

Statistics Sweden. 2001. Central Bureau of Statistics. Available online at ⟨www.scb.se⟩.

Taylor-Gooby, P. 1996. "The United Kingdom: Radical Departures and Political Consensus." In *Squaring the Welfare Circle*, ed. V. George and P. Taylor-Gooby. London: Macmillan.

Tinbergen, J. 1975. *Income Distribution*. Amsterdam: North-Holland.

Tullock, G. 1959. "Some Problems of Majority Voting." *Journal of Political Economy* 67: 571–579.

United Nations. 1949. *Demographic Yearbook, 1949*. New York: United Nations.

United Nations. 1960. *Demographic Yearbook, 1960*. New York: United Nations.

United Nations. 1997. *Demographic Yearbook, 1997*. New York: United Nations.

U.S. Bureau of the Census. 1998. International Data Base, Washington, DC.

Comments

Richard A. Musgrave

The chapter by Assar Lindbeck is an informative and timely one. Current problems of the Welfare State are traced to changes in the economic, demographic, and social environment in which welfare policies operate, and possible solutions are explored in a constructive spirit. Demographic change, changes in the structure of the labor market, changes in the role of the family, and changes in the setting of macro policy have posed new problems, and new solutions are required. These factors are considered with a rich mix of attention to institutional detail, economic analysis, and allowance for political and ethical considerations—a fine example of how political economy should be done. Having debated such matters with the author half a century ago, when Assar visited us at the University of Michigan, I especially enjoyed this revisit.

Space limitation does not permit me to review these many aspects in detail, and only a few general comments will have to suffice. To begin with, I applaud the positive spirit in which the role of the Welfare State is viewed. The problem is seen as one of adapting outdated instruments to changing circumstances, with manageable solutions in sight, and with continuing support for its basic objectives. This, however, may be too optimistic a view. Some of the structural changes that have occurred, especially the demographic factor, have greatly complicated the task of welfare policy and we cannot assume that acceptance of the Welfare State—that is, public responsibility for providing a reasonably secure and equitable society—will remain unchanged.

Such may be the case for the Nordic countries and perhaps also for a substantial part of continental Europe, but I wonder. I especially wonder whether that premise holds for the United States. Views regarding the role of the State and distributive equity, inevitably

involved in the design of Welfare State policy, are subject to change
and we may well move toward a period where the Welfare State will
have harder going. The chapter, in various connections, suggests
that shifts toward privatizing may offer an acceptable solution, but
it also recognizes that public regulation and control will then be
needed, measures that may well meet the same resistance. Moreover,
welfare policy inevitably involves some degree of redistribution, an
essential feature that could not be met in a fully privatized system.
Support of the needy, after all, cannot be financed by the needy—a
fact that perhaps needs more attention than given in the chapter.

There is also the ominous impact that the current shift to an open
and global world may bring. Increased trade may be all the good,
but the fiscal implications of globalization are a different matter.
Given the high mobility of capital and of skilled labor, the capacity
to finance the Welfare State is weakened by fiscal competition. To
this is added the tendency for beneficiaries to move to the place of
highest support, which will increase program costs. Lest globalization should permit reduction in military outlays, which does not
seem evident, the fiscal crisis that globalization will impose on the
budgets of nation states may well leave Welfare State policies its
primary victim. The threat of downward equalization which fiscal
competition imposes may thus need more attention than given it in
the chapter. In theory at least, there are two possible solutions. One
is to seek measures that coordinate the revenue and outlay sides of
welfare policies across countries, so as to permit each to conduct its
own policy. The other is to abolish national budgets and shift to a
global fisc. A global budget (the very opposite of the EU's subsidiarity rule!) would indeed be the logical counter to the globalization
of markets. But its logic would also require a global view of equity
in distribution—the residents of high-income regions would have to
extend their distributive concerns to the less well-off locations—and
this would hardly be accepted by the former.

In conclusion, I offer a brief comment on Lindbeck's final section, which addresses the macroeconomics of the Welfare State. The
Welfare State will, of course, be better off in a prosperous and full-
employment economy. To secure this, the chapter calls for reliance
on monetary policy and low interest rates, and against the use of
fiscal policy. The latter is viewed as ineffective, with deficits inducing increased saving in the private sector. As I see it, the assumption
of perfect "rational foresight" that underlies the so-called Ricardian

equivalence does not in fact prevail. Moreover, foresight effects also enter with monetary policy, where rate reduction may generate expectations of subsequent return to a "normal" level and with it discourage long-term lending. Such will especially be the case as a recession deepens. To be sure, the political process renders tax changes less flexible than monetary adjustments, but I would not write them off as part of the stabilization arsenal. Economics aside, the use of fiscal policy for stabilization also has important bearing on the size of the budget. In the Great Depression and up to the 1960s, expansionary policy was thought of in terms of expenditure increase while restrictive policy was thought of in terms of tax increase. Over time, this practice came to be reversed, with expansionary measures by way of tax reduction and restriction by way of expenditure cuts. Thus while fiscal stabilization used to be biased toward raising the size of the public sector, it now tends to work the other way.[1]

No less important to the Welfare State, especially in view of an aging population, is the premise of economic growth, based on saving, capital formation, and technical progress. Here, the chapter calls for care in the taxation of capital, lest investment and, with it, economic growth be retarded. This may be the case, but the chapter also holds that exclusion of capital from the tax base will not damage the finance of the Welfare State since capital taxation anyhow contributes only a small share of total revenue. I wonder. If the taxation of capital income, as well as capital taxes proper, is included, the share in revenue thus collected is by no means small. Moreover, capital income comprises a large share of income received by high-income groups, that is, of income that can hardly be bypassed in financing the Welfare State. An answer might be found in taxing high-income consumption, but that also has its problems.

The closest link between financing the Welfare State and macro policy, however, arises via the way in which old-age retirement and medical care are financed. Provision for retirement in an aging population requires saving and the accumulation of assets in which these savings can be held. Use of surplus finance to retire publicly held debt and its transfer into a reserve fund offers a solution, but it requires heavy reliance on responsible fiscal management in the future. Investment in the market in turn is resisted, based on a fear of governmental interference with capital allocation, and so forth. The chapter discusses these difficult choices in an intelligent fashion, anticipating in some respects their current debate in the United States.

While I find some aspects of the section on macro policy less satisfactory, that section is only attached at the end and is not the chapter's main focus. What matters is the penetrating, balanced, and instructive discussion of the preceding sections of how structural changes in various parts of the economy have developed and now call for reconsideration of the instruments by which the goals of the Welfare State can best be met. That review, as I noted at the outset, offers a most valuable and constructive contribution.

Note

1. I am pleased to credit my wife for this point.

2   Trust in Public Finance

Joel Slemrod

Although good economic analysis calls for joint consideration of both (the expenditure and revenue sides), the practice is to deal with them as more or less separate issues.

—Richard and Peggy Musgrave, *Public Finance in Theory and Practice*

Some people are happy that there are externalities everywhere, and others would prefer that there be none at all.

—Richard Musgrave, on the occasion of receiving the honorary degree of Doctor of Laws from the University of Michigan, December 15, 1991 [paraphrased]

2.1 Introduction

With a few exceptions, the positive and normative analysis of taxation has proceeded as if the purposes for which the funds are being raised and the efficiency with which they are utilized are irrelevant. As the first statement above makes clear, Richard (and, in this case, Peggy) Musgrave lamented this dichotomy.[1] He argued that analytical blinders blurred important questions such as the net distributional impact of government and prevented fruitful discussion of policies such as the earmarking of revenues. Throughout his career, Professor Musgrave also took seriously the vital role government can play in an economy and a society, including but not limited to achieving an appropriate allocation of resources in the presence of externalities. In the second statement quoted above, he recognizes that not all people enjoy the interaction among people—the sense of community—that the presence of externalities compels. But clearly he himself does. He writes: "I think of the state as an association of individuals, engaged in a cooperative venture, formed to resolve problems of social coexistence and do so in a democratic and fair manner." And also: "Overrepresented in my German and underrepresented in my U.S. years, I am well aware that the concept of community is subject to abuse ... At the same time, the concept of community should not be exorcised for that reason" (Buchanan and Musgrave 1999, 31, 33).

In this chapter, I argue that the idea of community, fostered by trust among citizens and perhaps also by trust in government, ties together these two lifelong concerns of Professor Musgrave. Moreover, consideration of these issues may shed light on some important public finance issues, including whether taxpayers' evaluations of government expenditures or the fairness of the tax system affect their willingness to comply with the tax law, and whether variations in trust are an important factor in explaining the cross-country patterns in levels of taxation and the type of taxes used.[2]

In what follows, I first critically review some of the literature on trust among private parties and between citizens and government, and its implications for tax compliance behavior. Then, I discuss some empirical explorations into untangling the complex causal interactions between trust, government, and prosperity. I focus on whether trust in public finance can shed light on such longstanding questions as Wagner's Law, the effect of government on prosperity, and under what circumstances taxpayers act as free riders.

2.2   Trust and Trustworthiness among Private Parties

The notions of trust and the more recently coined term social capital have received much recent attention in social science, stimulated in part by the work of Putnam (1993) and Fukuyama (1995), but with antecedents in, for example, Coleman (1990). Economists have recognized the critical role played by trust in economic performance. Arrow (1972) has remarked that "virtually every commercial transaction has within itself an element of trust, certainly any transaction conducted over a period of time. It can plausibly be argued that much of the economic backwardness in the world can be explained by the lack of mutual confidence." In high-trust societies, individuals need to spend less resources to protect themselves from being exploited in economic transactions. Knack and Keefer (1997) argue that trusting societies tend to have stronger incentives to innovate and to accumulate both physical and human capital. Lack of trust in government may also have costs. Clague (1993, 412) argues that "a society with very low levels of rule obedience cannot ... have a net of institutions that is conducive to economic progress."

The idea of reputation—the level of trust one is perceived to merit—has also been examined. As Axelrod (1986) puts it, an individual's reputation derives from adherence to or violation of a norm that others view as a signal about the individual's future behavior in a wide variety of situations. In Cripps and Thomas (1995), one establishes a reputation as others learn, in games with incomplete information, about one's propensity to use a particular strategy. Such reputation effects are common in multiple-player games modeling contributions to public good provision. For example, Marks and Schansberg (1997) find that providing the group with individual-specific information about past contributions partially offsets free riding.

Reputation also matters in interactions between individuals and firms. As explained by Campbell (1995), in a market economy, a firm has two sets of rivals: other firms and consumers. Competition with other firms keeps the return to capital low, so a firm must do years of business in order to pay off its initial expenditures on capital. This means that its strategy against consumers takes on a time dimension, as the firm relies on repeated interactions. The consumer's choice to "cooperate with," or buy from, the firm will then depend on whether the firm has "defected," or been misleading about its product, in the past. A firm's reputation, then, is simply the record of its past performance. The return to a firm's reputation comes in the willingness of others to enter into future incomplete contracts with the firm.

The flip side of trust is trustworthiness. Just as reputation is the ability to elicit trust from others, social capital—according to Glaeser et al. (1999)—is the ability to elicit trustworthiness from others. They distinguish between trusting behavior, which they define as "the commitment of resources to an activity where the outcome depends upon the cooperative behavior of others," and trustworthy behavior, which "increases the returns to people who trust you." Glaeser et al. report the results of two experiments. The first operationalizes trust and trustworthiness as behavior in the two roles of a trust game in which the first player (the "sender," who is in a position to exhibit trusting behavior) is given $15 and can choose how much of that to send to the second player (the "recipient," who is in a position to exhibit trustworthy behavior). The recipient receives, through the experimenters, twice whatever the sender sends, and then can choose how much to send back. In their second experiment, subjects report their willingness to pay for an envelope containing $10 that is addressed to them and dropped in different public places; this experiment measures only trusting behavior.

One of their findings has important implications for evaluating much of the empirical research I discuss below. It turns out that the answer that their subjects gave to the survey question often used to measure trust in others in empirical studies—"Generally speaking, would you say that most people can be trusted or that you can't be too careful in dealing with people?"—correlates with *trustworthy, but not with trusting*, behavior. Moreover, high-status individuals tend to be trusting because their status induces people to act in a trust-worthy manner toward them, ensuring a high return to trust. They suggest that much of the past research on individual behavior based on this and similar "trust" questions should therefore be re-interpreted, and conjecture that such questions are best used to predict "the overall level of trustworthiness in society." The distinc-tion and relationship between trust and trustworthiness are impor-tant in the empirical analysis reported later.

2.3   Trust and Government

2.3.1   Trust in Government

What affects the relationship between citizens and the government has a quite different flavor from what affects relationships among private parties. The crucial difference is not the relative size of the two parties. After all, a consumer dealing with a large corporation is in the same relative size position as a citizen is in with respect to most federal governments.

What is unique to government is its role as the sole provider of public and other goods and services, its coercive power to collect taxes to pay for these goods and services, and, critically, the absence of a link between what the citizen receives from government and what he or she pays to government. Firestone Tire Company wants to establish a reputation for a high-quality product because con-sumers need not buy its tires. Citizens, however, do not purchase public goods from government the way consumers purchase tires; the amount they pay in taxes does not determine the amount or quality of government services they receive. If, as the standard model of taxpayer behavior maintains, the perceived quality of government goods does not influence the level of taxes remitted, a government does not have a *financial* incentive to invest in its reputation for public goods production, since it will be unable to capture the return to such an investment. (It might, of course, have a political motive to do so.)

A more apt analogy is with a large charitable organization. As with government, any one person's contribution is a drop in the bucket and will not materially affect the organization's activities. Of course, unlike government, a charity cannot coerce (other than via peer pressure) donations. However, if one values what use the money is put to, then the donor or taxpayer might consider the donation to be a purchase rather than an exaction.

Note that there is at least anecdotal evidence that donors do respond to information about the trustworthiness of large charitable organizations. For example, after its national president was charged, and later convicted, of diverting charitable funds to his own use, the United Way, the premier fundraising organization in the United States, experienced a drop in donors and donations of about 20 percent (Johnston 1997). Moreover, there is considerable evidence that consumers' purchasing decisions may depend on aspects of their perceptions of the producing company that are unrelated to the value-for-price trade-off. The consumer boycotts of goods produced by Nike is a recent example. Kahneman, Knetsch, and Thaler (1986) discuss evidence that the response to a consumer good price increase will be more favorable if people judge the price increase to be necessitated by input cost increases rather than by the desire for increased profits. Thus, even in the realm of purely private goods, some consumers may override their opportunistic impulses and be influenced by their approval of or trust in the producer.

The distinctive element of the relationship between taxpayer and government is the free-rider problem, also known as the zero contribution thesis. Because one's own outcome is unaffected by one's own "contribution," no one should voluntarily contribute to a public good—pay taxes—unless the threat of punishment makes it sensible.[3] Thus, governments have a political, but not a financial, incentive to invest in their trustworthiness, and taxpayers have no incentive to be trustworthy toward the government, unless the enforcement regime makes it in their financial interest.[4]

It is undeniable that free-riding behavior is ubiquitous. The story does not, though, end there. For example, a vast amount of experimental work (not to say anecdotal evidence) suggests that free-riding behavior is context-specific. Ostrom (2000, 140) remarks that the finding that "the rate of contribution to a public good is affected by various contextual factors" is one of seven phenomena that "have been replicated so frequently that these can be considered the core facts that theory needs to explain." The challenge, then, is to identify aspects of government expenditure and tax policies that mediate the free-rider impulse in an empirically important way.

Although trust in other people and trust in government are not the same thing, they may be related. Brehm and Rahn (1997) argue that confidence in government may be partly a reflection of the more general relationship of trust in people—if people are untrustworthy in general, then people in government are untrustworthy as well. Of course, as Brehm (1998) points out, taxpayers may not see people in government as being ordinary people, perhaps because they believe that being in government creates opportunities for people to exploit others that are not available to ordinary people.

Furthermore, confidence in government can be a positive force in trusting others, in part because government can act as a safeguard for our willingness to extend trust to others. Establishing a fair and efficient legal system is the best example of this, but there are others. Fukuyama (1995) stresses the role of government in lowering the personal investments and providing the assurances that make possible the trust that lubricates cooperation. On the other hand, some argue that the centralized state undermines cooperation and destroys trust among individuals. Taylor (1982) argues that the centralized state drives out spontaneous coordination that depends on small groups and "thick" networks of interaction.

2.3.2 Trustworthiness and Reputation of Government

In a competitive political system such as a democracy, governments face incentives to establish good reputations in order to encourage the electorate to select them rather than their rivals in the future.

Moreover, to the extent that capital is mobile, governments with good reputations for cooperating with business will find that more businesses choose their country in the future.

The role of government reputation and credibility has been extensively examined, most often in the context of monetary policy (e.g., Barro and Gordon 1983), but reputation has also been used to interpret actors' responses to other sorts of government policies. For example, Epple (1998) discusses local government reputation with respect to whether a town will continue a no-rent-control policy if it is not bound to do so, and the choices that property owners make that are dependent on that reputation.

In these situations, it is in individuals' interest to evaluate whether commitments made by the government are credible. The question on the table is, though, quite different—whether trust in government can cause citizens to abandon their short-term financial interest of free riding. In this context, Levi (1998) argues that citizens are likely to trust government only to the extent that they believe that it will act in their interests, that its procedures are fair, and that their trust of the state and others is reciprocated. She argues that government trustworthiness, plus the perception that others are doing their share, can induce people to become "contingent consenters" who cooperate even when their short-term material self-interest would make free riding the individual's best option. She writes that "the willingness to pay taxes quasi-voluntarily or to give one's contingent consent to conscription often rests on the existence of the state's capacity and demonstrated readiness to secure the compliance of the otherwise noncompliant" (Levi 1998, 91).

The operating definitions of trustworthiness of government and trust in government that I will adopt are in the spirit of Levi. Government trustworthiness is all those actions that may induce people to forgo their opportunistic behavior and become contingent compliers. Trust in government is a belief that the government is carrying out those actions. The first two aspects of this trust do not depend on the reciprocal actions of other citizens, and in these cases trust is close to "approval." The third aspect—the perception that others are doing their share—is more closely related to the notions of trust in others that I have already touched on, because it is about whether people act as if others will follow through on what they have promised to do. Clearly, the survey questions on which the empirical investigations that follow rely do not precisely correspond to these definitions; they are, though, close enough to be worth examining.

2.4   Trustworthiness of Taxpayers: Tax Compliance

With regard to free-rider behavior toward the government, tax compliance poses the foremost temptation. Although officially the U.S. income tax system is based on voluntary compliance,[5] in one sense that characterization is purely Orwellian. An elaborate system of employer withholding, matching of information reports, and audits with penalties for detected evasion "encourages" compliance. The fact that, line item by line item, there is a clear positive correlation between the so-called voluntary compliance rate with the U.S. income tax and the presence of these enforcement mechanisms confirms their importance.[6]

Some have argued, however, that the idea of voluntary compliance is not just Orwellian Newspeak. The argument is sometimes loosely based on the observation that, given the probability of audit and the penalties typically assessed, evasion seems to be a winning proposition for many more people than actually do evade. For example, Feld and Frey (2002) assert that it is "impossible to account for tax compliance in terms of expected punishment." From this perspective, the puzzle is not to explain why people evade, but rather to explain why people pay (so much) taxes. Solutions to this puzzle generally require pushing beyond the standard economic model, in the context of which people who voluntarily comply are exhibiting nothing short of "pathological honesty."

I discuss below these attempts to solve the puzzle of apparently voluntary, or pathological, compliance. Before doing so, I must record my objection to the proposition that the standard economic model of tax evasion, due to Allingham and Sandmo (1972), has been discredited. The dismissive argument runs along the following lines. The average audit rate in the United States is less than 2 percent. With that probability of evasion being detected, and with the penalty rates in effect, what we know about the degree of risk aversion from other contexts suggests that compliance should be much, much lower than it apparently is. The flaw in this argument is that the 2 percent probability of detection is certainly a vast understatement for the bulk of income subject to tax. A wage or salary earner whose employer submits this information electronically to the Internal Revenue Service (IRS), but who does not report that income on his or her own personal return, will be flagged for further scrutiny with a probability much closer to 100 percent than to 2 percent.[7]

Thus, this simple argument for the failure of the utility-maximization approach itself fails. There is, though, some experimental evidence for this proposition, such as Spicer and Becker (1980) and Alm, Jackson, and McKee (1992), in which subjects respond not only to the probabilities and stakes of a tax evasion game, but also to context provided to them. In contrast, Mason and Calvin (1984), in an analysis of survey data in Oregon, find that dissatisfaction with the tax system is not directly related to reported noncompliance, although it changes other attitudes and beliefs. Cowell (1990, 219) reports on other experimental evidence that fails to find links between perceived inequities in the tax system and noncompliance. Kaplan and Reckers (1985) find that beliefs about tax morality are more important than beliefs about the tax fairness of the tax system.

Also worthy of note is the ambitious recent attempt of Scholz and Lubell (1998a, b) to examine whether trust in government affects tax compliance, using data from a one-hour in-person survey supplemented by tax return data. They have no direct measure of noncompliance, but use instead a measure based on answers to twelve questions about compliance over a three-year period with specific sources of income, general income, deductions, and overall tax reporting. Their measure of trust in government is the summed response to two statements: "You can generally trust the government to do what is right" and "Dishonesty in government is pretty rare." To measure trust in citizens, they use the survey answers to "What percentage of taxpayers at your income level ... pay less taxes than they legally owe?"[8] Scholz and Lubell argue that the amount of benefits from public activities depends on the amount of taxes collected, which in turn depends on the fraction of honest taxpayers, so that greater trust measured in this way should correspond to a belief in greater benefits from the collective. This reasoning requires a set of tenuous assumptions, and may be related to noncompliance as a rationalization.

Scholz and Lubell also control for attitudes about tax fairness and equity, civic duty, political efficacy, tax duty, opportunity for evasion, and being in a high noncompliance occupation. With these controls, they find that high scores on both trust measures significantly decrease the likelihood of noncompliance. Surprisingly and apparently contradictorily, political efficacy (whether the respondent has a "say" in what the government does and whether it is run "mainly for the benefit of special interests") increases noncompliance. The authors rationalize this finding by suggesting that political efficacy may lead to a perceived ability to manipulate the system without risk.

Because of several methodological weaknesses, the Scholz-Lubell study is far short of being definitive. Overall, there is no compelling evidence to discard the Allingham-Sandmo model of tax compliance, but there are also compelling reasons to believe that free riding in other areas is suppressed, and that tax evasion free riding is suppressed in experimental situations—to take seriously that tax compliance does respond to taxpayers' attitudes toward government.[9]

In their review of tax compliance research, Andreoni, Erard, and Feinstein (1998) identify three classes of explanation for why observed evasion is apparently lower than conventional economic models of tax evasion predict: moral rules or sentiments that determine the psychic costs of evasion, evaluations of the fairness of the tax code and its enforcement, and evaluation of government expenditures and corruption. Frey (1997) links the first two classes of explanation by differentiating between intrinsic and extrinsic motivation. With intrinsic motivation, taxpayers pay because of "civic virtue;" with extrinsic motivation, they do so because of threat of punishment. Frey argues that increasing extrinsic motivation—say, with more punitive enforcement policies—"crowds out" intrinsic motivation by making people feel that they pay taxes because they have to, rather than because they want to.[10] Similarly, in Cullis and Lewis (1997), individuals not only care about their own consumption but also value their own compliance with the social convention of tax compliance and separately the extent of others' compliance with the norm, either directly or indirectly via pecuniary consequences. Falkinger (1995) argues that if tax equity strengthens the social norm against evasion, then evasion becomes more costly in terms of bad conscience (if not caught) or bad reputation (if caught) in a society with a more equitable system. Moreover, as Andreoni, Erard, and Feinstein (1998) point out, perceived unfairness can be used to rationalize evasion in one's self-interest, thereby decreasing psychic costs.

In Bordignon (1993), a relationship exists between the individual and the government that involves exchange rather than mere coercion. The taxpayer computes the terms of trade between his private consumption and the government provision of public goods, and evades (up to his level of risk aversion or up to the level he feels reestablishes fairness) if he finds these terms unfair. Unfairness in this model reflects either an inadequate level of goods provision with respect to the required tax payment, an unfair tax structure, or evasion by other taxpayers. Andreoni, Erard, and Feinstein add that an individual can also find unfairness in goods provision due to the provision of the *wrong* goods, that is, someone such as Thoreau may avoid taxes because he thinks government policy wrong. But, as Daunton (1998) points out, this is not a simple matter. Expenditures on warfare might be tolerated in a patriotic period but rejected during another period characterized by antimilitarism. Expenditure on welfare might at times be seen as a socially desirable pooling of risk and at other times be seen as a source of national decay.

Feld and Frey (2002) link all three ideas with what they call a psychological contract between the tax authority and citizens, which they believe is the model that describes taxation in areas with high levels of direct, rather than merely representative, democracy. They argue that where the relationship between the individual and the tax authority is seen as involving an implicit contract sustained by trust, individuals will comply due to high "tax morale." To sustain citizens' commitment to the contract and therefore their morale, the tax authority must act respectfully toward citizens while at the same time protecting the honest from the free rider. It does this by giving taxpayers the benefit of the doubt when it finds a mistake, by sanctioning small violations more mildly, and by sanctioning large and basic violations (for example, the failure to file a return) more heavily. In a study of local governments in Switzerland, Feld and Frey find that these policies are in fact used more in more direct democracies.

They claim that such contracts are stronger—and therefore the authority relies on the above techniques more heavily—in direct democracies for several reasons. First, citizens in these areas have selected (or at least, Feld and Frey assume, felt comfortable with the selection process of) the programs that their taxes support, and therefore should feel more willing to pay for them (this assumption falls in line with Andreoni, Erard, and Feinstein's third idea). After all, they can express discontent with either tax or spending policy by changing the laws, so they do not need to rely on a violation of the psychological contract. Since the authority knows this, it feels justified in treating citizens as trustworthy.

Of course, an alternative theory could be that in a direct democracy, citizens simply choose tax policies that involve respect because they prefer them, rather than that there is a psychological contract in place that makes such policies the most efficient way of collecting taxes. However, Feld and Frey's finding that blatant violations of the tax code are punished more heavily in direct democracies does provide some evidence that citizens in more direct democracies are not simply pushing for leniency but rather evaluating behavior as upholding or violating a basic contract.

Whether one calls this behavior pathological honesty, or alternatively good citizenship, the fact is that the cost of raising taxes, and of running the government, is lower to the extent that taxpayers "volunteer" to comply. It is as if there is a stock of goodwill, or social capital, the return to which is the more efficient operation of government. This social capital stock may be reduced by a policy change that decreases the incentive to be a law-abiding citizen.

It is interesting to note that all of the literature about whether attitudes affect compliance applies to individual taxpayers, although in most countries the bulk of taxes are remitted (as opposed to borne, in the sense of ultimate incidence) by businesses, either because the taxes are levied on business entities or because labor income taxes are withheld by the employer. Whether a company's policy would react as an individual is a fascinating and completely open question, one that is related to the motivations behind corporate charitable contributions.[11]

Paying taxes in excess of the remittance that is in one's utility-maximizing interest can be considered a voluntary contribution to government.[12] There is a more direct way to make such contributions—just send money.[13] In the United States, people have always been able to do this, but since 1961, Congress has allowed people to earmark contributions for reducing the national debt and has kept records on the amount of contributions. Moreover, since 1982, the Internal Revenue Service has included instructions in its tax packet on how to make such a contribution. In fiscal year 2000, these contributions totaled $1.855 million, which amounts to about

0.00001 percent of federal tax collections in that year and about 0.0008 percent of financial contributions to charities. Less than 10 percent of these gifts are included with federal tax returns. In fiscal year 1996, 366 Americans slipped checks totaling just $85,378 to reduce the federal debt inside their tax returns.[14]

Slemrod and Oltmans (2001) investigate the aggregate annual amount of such gifts since 1961, to see if their magnitude is systematically related to attitudes toward government or objective measures of government expenditure patterns, tax structure, and the deficit. They do discover such relationships. For example, gifts to government are higher in years when the national debt is higher, suggesting a need-driven motive for gifts. Perhaps surprisingly, gifts are higher when the proportion of the population who endorse the belief that government wastes taxes is higher. This is consistent with donors embracing the earmarked nature of the gift—to a good use, reducing the debt, rather than a bad use, wasteful government spending. More generally, the systematic nature of these gifts is consistent with the notion that the gifts implicit in extraordinary tax compliance levels may also be related to attitudes and objective measures of government expenditure, taxation, and deficit policies.

2.5 Previous Literature on the Relationship among Trust, Government, and Prosperity

It is one thing to hypothesize about the role of trust in government in taxpaying behavior and the efficient operation of an economy. It is quite another, and more demanding, task to identify its role empirically. This section briefly reviews some of the existing literature related to that task, while the next section presents research that extends our empirical knowledge of the interrelationship within and, mostly, across countries.

2.5.1 *Evidence on the Determinants of Taxation and Government Spending*

Trust and social capital may provide a clue to explaining one of the most striking empirical regularities in public finance—the positive association between a country's tax-to-GDP ratio and its level of affluence, as measured for example by its per capita GDP. Two classes of explanation have been offered to explain this association.[15] The first, called Wagner's Law, is a demand explanation. It posits that rising incomes and associated structural changes (such as urbanization) engender a demand for more government involvement. Another explanation is that affluence is associated with demographic characteristics (such as literacy and less reliance on agriculture) that facilitate raising tax revenue, which in turn leads to expanded government activity. Of course, these explanations are not mutually exclusive, and the research challenge, as in many settings, is to disentangle the supply and demand explanations for government expenditure and taxation.[16]

Professor Musgrave, in his 1969 book *Fiscal Systems*, notes the high positive correlation, both across countries and over time, between GDP per capita and the total tax ratio, as does Goode (1968). Goode suggests that rather than income being the driving factor, this correlation may result from the positive correlation between per capita income and other social and economic conditions that make direct taxes acceptable and effective, such as a high level of literacy, wide use of standard accounting methods, effective public administration, and political stability. Musgrave himself notes that the relationship between income and the tax ratio is solely a result of comparing low- and high-income groups of countries, and does not hold within each group of countries. More recently, Tanzi (1992) investigates the determinants of the share of tax in GDP in eighty-three developing countries during the period 1978–1988. He finds that, by itself, the log of per capita income is positively associated with the tax ratio, but the share of agricultural output in GDP (highly negatively correlated with per capita GDP) explains more of the variation in tax shares than does per capita income and it has a negative sign. When both variables are included, per capita income no longer has a significant positive effect, although the negative effect of the agricultural share survives.

2.5.2 Evidence on the Effect of Trust (and Government) on Prosperity

2.5.2.1 Trust

There is some empirical evidence that trust and civic duty among a country's citizens contribute to growth.[17] Knack and Keefer (1997) test the impact of these attitudes on both growth and investment rates in a cross section of twenty-nine countries, using measures of trust and civic norms from the World Values Surveys (WVSs) of 1981 and 1990. To assess the level of trust in others in a society, they use the WVS question discussed in section 2.6.1. The strength of norms of civic cooperation was assessed from attitudes toward five particular actions, including the tax evasion question used here already.

Knack and Keefer find that social capital variables exhibit a strong and significant positive relationship to economic growth. As they note, the causality of this relationship could go in either direction: Trust could be a product of optimism generated by high or growing incomes, or it could be that trust facilitates prosperity. However, they find that trust is more correlated with per capita income in later years than with income in earlier years, suggesting that the causation runs from trust to growth more so than vice versa.

One possible channel through which trust might affect economic outcomes is its impact on the performance of government. To investigate this, Knack and Keefer construct an index of how much confidence people profess in various governmental and societal institutions and find that, controlling for per capita income and education enrollments, the only significant determinant of government performance is the trust variable: A trusting citizenry facilitates a successful government. It is, though, conceivable that the causation is reversed—that it is the behavior of governments that influences levels of trust.

Zak and Knack (2001) extend the Knack and Keefer framework by separately testing for the effect on growth of proxies for the presence of formal institutions, social distance, and discrimination and for whether their effect remains significantly correlated with growth controlling for measures of trust. They find that trust is positively and significantly related to growth even in the presence of measures of formal institutions or of social distance, but that most of the influence of the latter on growth occurs through their impact on trust. The one exception is a measure of property rights, which retains its independent positive association with growth even in the presence of a trust variable. They justify this finding by noting that this index includes government actions against private agents. In contrast, the trust measure is "likely to be little affected by perceptions of the trustworthiness of government" (316).

La Porta et al. (1999) find that, across countries, a one-standard-deviation increase in the measure of trust increases judicial efficiency by 0.7 of a standard deviation and reduces government corruption by 0.3 of a standard deviation. Putnam (1993) examines cross-regional Italian data and concludes that local governments are more efficient where there is greater civic engagement.

2.5.2.2 Government
In recent years, there has been an explosion of cross-country studies of the impact of government taxation and expenditure on prosperity. In contrast to the literature on the determinants of the size of government discussed earlier, and to the new analyses presented later, the prosperity indicator in all these studies is a measure not of the level of prosperity, but rather of its rate of growth.

In the most influential of these studies, Barro (1991) examines a cross section of ninety-eight countries for the period 1960–1985 and, among other concerns, investigates the impacts on economic growth of government expenditures, measured as the ratio to real GDP of real government consumption purchases less spending on education and defense. He finds a significantly negative association of this government expenditure variable, averaged over the period 1970–1985, with real growth from 1960 to 1985. Barro suggests that one interpretation of these findings is that government consumption introduces distortions, such as high tax rates, but does not provide an offsetting stimulus to investment and growth.

Several subsequent studies—most notably, Levine and Renelt (1992) and Easterly and Rebelo (1994)—have, however, demonstrated that this negative association is by no means robust to reasonable alternative formulations. Easterly and Rebelo, using several different measures of fiscal policy, find that measures of the level of taxes tend to be insignificant in Barro-style growth rate regressions. They ascribe this finding to the strong positive correlation between their fiscal variables and the initial (1960) level of per capita income, making it difficult to disentangle the effects of fiscal variables from those of the initial level of income—the "convergence" effect discussed in Barro and Sala-i-Martin (1992) and elsewhere. Slemrod (1995) reviews this literature and concludes that it has not resolved many of the problems with interpreting the estimated coefficient of a measure of the level of government activity in a growth equation.

2.6   New Evidence on the Structural Relationship among Trust, Government, and Prosperity

Although there is a growing and, in some cases, large empirical literature on the determinants of growth, size of government, and aspects of trust and trustworthiness, it is fair to say that no empirical analysis has attempted to untangle the structural relationships among them. This section begins that task. As is inevitable for a first step, it leaves many open questions. Nevertheless, it is promising in that the data analysis is supportive of several of the hypotheses raised earlier in this chapter.

2.6.1   Data

The data on trust and trustworthiness come from the 1990 wave of the World Values Survey, the purpose of which is to facilitate cross-national comparisons of values, norms, and attitudes. The survey was conducted, with limited national modifications, in forty-five countries. It asked about attitudes concerning work, family, religion, politics, and contemporary social issues and gathered a limited amount of demographic data as well. The twenty-five capitalist countries in the survey for which sufficient other data are available make up my sample.[18] Although the data are subject to the usual reservations about attitude surveys, and in particular cross-country attitude surveys, the data have been widely and fruitfully used by political scientists and sociologists, not to mention Knack and Keefer (1997) and Zak and Knack (2001); for an extensive, albeit incomplete, list of its use in research, see Inglehart, Basanez, and Moreno (1998).

Along with other variables that are used in the analysis (for a description, see appendix 2A), I will use three WVS variables as indicators of trust and trustworthiness. These come from the following questions:

Generally speaking, would you say that most people can be trusted or that you can't be too careful in dealing with people?

Please tell me whether you think that lying in your own interest can always be justified, never be justified, or something in between. (scale from 1 = never justified to 10 = always justified)

Please tell me whether you think that cheating on tax if you have the chance can always be justified, never be justified, or something in between. (scale from $1 =$ never justified to $10 =$ always justified)

The weighted mean values are used as country-level measures of trust in others, (lack of) trustworthiness, and acceptability of tax evasion, respectively.[19] The responses are rescaled to lie in a 0–100 range.

2.6.2 Correlations without Causation

As background for the empirical exercises, tables 2.1 and 2.2 present correlation matrices. (Summary statistics are presented in appendix 2B.) Table 2.1 refers to within-country responses for the United States and West Germany. Among respondents from each country, trust in others is positively associated with both financial satisfaction and income. The story is slightly different for tax evasion as a measure of trustworthiness. The acceptability of tax evasion falls with financial satisfaction in both countries, but increases with income in Germany and, although not with statistical significance, in the United States. Trustworthiness as measured by refraining from lying is also positively correlated with financial satisfaction, but negatively associated with income. This suggests that the attractiveness of opportunistic behavior follows a "satisficing" pattern: People of any income who are satisfied with their lot are more likely to abstain from this kind of behavior.

There is also generally a clear positive association between trust in others and the two measures of trustworthiness. By far the highest correlation is between the two measures of trustworthiness ("Is lying okay?" and "Is tax evasion okay?"), suggesting that whatever mechanism inculcates these norms affects both one's behavior towards people for whom establishing a reputation may have a payoff and one's behavior toward the government, for which it is unlikely to have a payoff in the private sector. However, in both countries, those who trust or have confidence in government are less likely to find tax evasion acceptable.[20]

In both countries, more educated people are more likely to trust others, but are also more likely to find lying and, in Germany only, tax evasion to be acceptable. They exhibit less confidence in government. Religious people are on average both more trusting and, particularly, more trustworthy. Those on the right of the political

Table 2.1
Within-country correlations for the United States (in bold) and West Germany

	(1) Age	(2) Acceptability of tax evasion	(3) Confidence in government institutions	(4) Education	(5) Financial satisfaction	(6) Income scale	(7) Male	(8) Nonreligious	(9) Right political orientation	(10) Trust in others	(11) Trust in government	(12) Trustworthiness
(1) Age	**1.000** / 1.000											
(2) Acceptability of tax evasion	**−0.192*** / −0.221***	**1.000** / 1.000										
(3) Confidence in government institutions	**0.053** / 0.190***	**−0.051** / −0.249***	**1.000** / 1.000									
(4) Education	**−0.222*** / −0.341***	**0.002** / 0.138***	**−0.059** / −0.118***	**1.000** / 1.000								
(5) Financial satisfaction	**0.204*** / 0.166***	**−0.085*** / −0.146***	**0.087*** / 0.238***	**0.031** / 0.002	**1.000** / 1.000							
(6) Income scale	**−0.170*** / −0.249***	**0.019** / 0.071***	**−0.038** / 0.022	**0.340*** / 0.278***	**0.246*** / 0.250***	**1.000** / 1.000						
(7) Male	**0.029** / −0.118***	**0.024** / 0.118***	**−0.034** / −0.046**	**0.071*** / 0.082***	**0.067*** / 0.003	**0.086*** / 0.095***	**1.000** / 1.000					
(8) Nonreligious	**−0.121*** / −0.259***	**0.137*** / 0.266***	**−0.051** / −0.174***	**0.049* / 0.142***	**−0.067*** / −0.176***	**0.044** / 0.029	**0.084*** / 0.159***	**1.000** / 1.000				
(9) Right political orientation	**0.058* / 0.236***	**−0.031** / −0.142***	**0.082*** / 0.240***	**−0.032** / −0.110***	**0.116*** / 0.182***	**0.025** / 0.049**	**0.062** / 0.017	**−0.173*** / −0.245***	**1.000** / 1.000			
(10) Trust in others	**0.105*** / −0.047*	**−0.115*** / −0.033	**−0.017** / 0.098***	**0.148*** / 0.143***	**0.104*** / 0.123***	**0.099*** / 0.098***	**−0.019** / 0.001	**−0.053** / −0.024	**−0.076*** / −0.018	**1.000** / 1.000		
(11) Trust in government	**0.001**	**−0.099***	**0.106***	**0.040**	**0.129***	**0.032**	**−0.060**	**−0.092***	**0.066***	**0.093***	**1.000**	
(12) Trustworthiness	**0.149*** / 0.249***	**−0.383*** / −0.505***	**0.066*** / 0.172***	**−0.065*** / −0.084***	**0.063*** / 0.123***	**−0.054** / −0.083***	**−0.021** / −0.085***	**−0.122*** / −0.274***	**0.027** / 0.121***	**0.097*** / 0.063**	**0.041* /	**1.000**

*significant at 10 percent level; **significant at 5 percent level; ***significant at 1 percent level.

spectrum have less trust in others in the United States but not significantly in Germany and, perhaps surprisingly, have more trust in
government in the United States. In the United States, those with a
right-wing political orientation are neither more nor less trustworthy
on average to a significant degree; they are clearly more trustworthy
in Germany.

The positive correlation in the United States between trust in
others and trust in government is consistent with the finding of
Brehm (1998), who argues, based on the 1996 National Election
Survey data from the United States, that there is a strong positive
relationship between social trust and government trust. However,
Newton (1999) shows that the positive correlation between trust in
others and trust in government is not a general result. He finds that
among twelve countries in the 1990 World Values Survey that have
both questions, the correlation between trust in government and
trust in others is small and a *negative* 0.03. Newton concludes that
political trust is not caused so much by social or economic factors
as by political ones, including the record and orientation of the party
in power; for example, right-leaning people will be more likely to
express distrust when the left is in power. Newton (1999) does,
though, find that the positive correlation of social trust with satisfaction with life, age, religiosity, income, and education level is quite
robust across seven developed countries.

Table 2.2 is a weighted correlation matrix of the country means
of the measures of trust, the measures of trustworthiness, and other
country-specific indicators. Because the number of observations is so
much lower, the significance levels are on average much lower than
for the within-country correlations of table 2.1, although the correlations themselves are often much higher in absolute value.

Across countries, trust in others is still strongly a phenomenon of
affluence. However, the relationship between financial satisfaction
and evasion flips sign in the cross-country context. While within the
United States and Germany those who profess to be more financially
satisfied are less likely to condone evasion, across countries more
financial satisfaction is positively correlated with condoning evasion. Across countries, the correlation between trust in others and
the acceptability of evasion reverses sign and becomes positive,
although the statistical significance is not strong. It is also true that
across countries the relationship between either religion or political
orientation changes notably. Although within the United States reli-

Table 2.2
Cross-country correlations

	(1) Agriculture	(2) Cheating on taxes	(3) Education	(4) Financial satisfaction	(5) GDP per capita (log)	(6) Government expenditure ratio	(7) Illiteracy	(8) Legal origin EGS	(9) Nonreligious	(10) Openness	(11) Right political orientation	(12) Trust in others	(13) Trustworthiness
(1) Agriculture	1.000												
(2) Cheating on taxes	-0.434**	1.000											
(3) Education	-0.516**	0.119	1.000										
(4) Financial satisfaction	-0.512***	0.386*	0.474**	1.000									
(5) GDP per capita (log)	-0.877***	0.388*	0.654***	0.658***	1.000								
(6) Government expenditure ratio	-0.465**	0.515***	0.296	0.720***	0.618***	1.000							
(7) Illiteracy	0.914***	-0.316	-0.646***	-0.452**	-0.884***	-0.418**	1.000						
(8) Legal origin EGS	-0.026	-0.266	0.460**	0.311	0.298	0.124	-0.120	1.000					
(9) Nonreligious	-0.390*	0.128	0.415**	0.025	0.383*	0.090	-0.349*	0.138	1.000				
(10) Openness	-0.278	0.525***	0.208	0.475**	0.310	0.446**	-0.346*	-0.034	0.008	1.000			
(11) Right political orientation	0.044	-0.126	0.420**	0.002	0.052	-0.240	-0.060	0.619***	0.049	0.184	1.000		
(12) Trust in others	-0.348*	0.201	0.692***	0.651***	0.553***	0.564***	-0.393*	0.618***	0.326	0.180	0.284	1.000	
(13) Trustworthiness	0.292	-0.697***	0.231	-0.124	-0.121	-0.123	0.073	0.496***	-0.012	-0.244	0.202	0.261	1.000

Note: All correlation coefficients are computed from twenty-five data points.
*significant at 10 percent level; **significant at 5 percent level; ***significant at 1 percent level.

gious people are both more trusting and more trustworthy, across countries the opposite is true for trust in others, and no clear relationship exists for the other measures.

For later purposes, one further set of correlations is worth noting. In countries with a high level of government involvement, people are more likely to find tax evasion to be acceptable, even though their residents are not notably less trustworthy generally (as measured by their response to the question about the acceptability of lying in one's own interest) and are *significantly more trusting of others*. In fact, the highest absolute correlants with evasion attitudes, other than the other measure of trustworthiness, are measures of the country's level of government.

2.6.3 A Structural Model

2.6.3.1 Tax Cheating and Size of Government

I begin by investigating a model of the extent of tax cheating and the size of government that recognizes the interdependence of the two. In what follows, I use G to denote the extent of government involvement in the economy, TC to denote attitudes toward tax cheating, TW to denote trustworthiness, and TO to stand for trust in others. Finally, Y will denote a measure of prosperity, measured by the log of GDP per capita.

The two structural relationships are summarized as follows:

$$TC = TC(G, TW, \mathbf{ZTC}), \tag{1}$$

$$G = G(Y, TC, \mathbf{ZG}). \tag{2}$$

Equation (1) refers to the determination of attitudes toward tax cheating. It is presumed to depend on the degree of overall trustworthiness in the society, assumed to be exogenous in this analysis, and on the extent of government involvement. The only other exogenous variable (and the only element of the vector $\mathbf{ZTC}$) is the average age of the survey respondents.[21] In other studies, age has been found to be negatively associated with the propensity to evade taxes.

Equation (2) represents the determination of the extent of government involvement in a country. This may depend, via Wagner's Law, on the level of prosperity. I hypothesize that it also depends on the extent to which people are willing to suspend their free-rider impulses and forgo tax cheating opportunities; the more people do so, the lower is the cost of raising resources for government and the larger government will be. Included in the vector of explanatory variables, ZG, are standard indicators of either the demand for or cost of providing government services. In particular, ZG includes the age dependency ratio, the percentage of the economy that is agricultural, the extent of illiteracy, and the extent of openness. Some of these variables may affect the size of government both via the cost of raising revenue and via the demand for government services, so that the interpretation of these variables' coefficients is problematic. Finally, in ZG there is a dummy variable for whether the country's legal system is of English, Scandinavian, or German (but not French) origin. Following La Porta et al. (1999), this variable may represent a historical tradition of limiting government power.

The results of estimating this system using three-stage least squares[22] are shown as model 1 of table 2.3. The equation explaining attitudes toward tax cheating is crisp and reasonable. It says that tax cheating is lower in countries that exhibit more (not-government-related) trustworthiness. However, holding that constant, tax cheating becomes more acceptable as government grows, to a significant and large degree. An older population reduces the average acceptability of tax evasion.

The second column of model 1 shows the results of estimating a structural equation explaining the level of government. There is clear evidence of a Wagner's Law relationship, as evidenced by the significant and large coefficient on the log level of income. Holding income (and the ZG variables) constant, though, a more accepting attitude toward tax cheating does limit the size of government. True, the estimated relationship does not reach standard levels of statistical significance. Nevertheless, there is some weak evidence that the strong positive correlation between the size of government and tax cheating masks the fact that big government induces tax cheating while, at the same time, tax cheating constrains big government. Certainly, more research is needed to clarify this structure.

Among the exogenous variables, the openness measure is significantly positive, corroborating the findings of Rodrik (1998) and Cameron (1978) before him. The illiteracy variable is also positive, suggesting that it serves more as a measure of the demand for social services than as a measure of the difficulty of raising revenue. Neither the age dependency variable nor the agriculture variable is

Table 2.3
Results of three-stage least squares estimation of structural models

Independent variables	Dependent variables							
	Model 1		Model 2			Model 3		
	Cheating on taxes	G/GDP	Cheating on taxes	G/GDP	GDP per capita (log)	Cheating on taxes	G/GDP	GDP per capita (log)
Cheating on taxes		−1.10 (0.832)		−0.046 (0.593)			−1.18 (0.864)	
G/GDP	0.405 (0.116)***		0.396 (0.101)***		0.0255 (0.0211)	0.387 (0.130)***		0.0255 (0.0250)
(G/GDP) squared					−0.000336 (0.000295)			−0.000405 (0.000357)
GDP per capita (log)		43.5 (15.4)***		35.2 (16.1)**			51.7 (20.8)**	
Age	−0.686 (0.426)		−0.584 (0.392)			−0.640 (0.447)		
Age dependency ratio		0.607 (0.575)		0.233 (0.468)			0.713 (0.631)	
Agriculture/GDP		−0.898 (1.30)		0.0472 (1.03)			−0.582 (1.39)	
Capital per worker (log)					0.557 (0.113)***			0.721 (0.158)***
Illiteracy		1.83 (0.865)**		1.21 (0.712)*	−0.0149 (0.00634)**		2.00 (0.947)**	−0.00977 (0.00768)
Legal origin EGS		−10.2 (7.33)		−5.15 (6.50)			−13.0 (8.43)	

Openness		0.302 (0.139)**					0.303 (0.143)**	
Trust				0.162 (0.102)	0.00379 (0.00329)			0.00142 (0.00507)
Trustworthiness	-0.665 (0.140)***		-0.654 (0.135)***			-0.671 (0.140)***		
Constant	82.7 (16.3)***	-396 (160)**	78.0 (15.7)***	-314 (167)*	3.29 (1.16)***	82.0 (16.2)***	-479 (215)**	1.88 (1.69)
Number of observations	25	25	25	25	25	25	25	25
Chi-squared test	50.9***	23.7***	54.4***	29.8***	371.7***	48.1***	19.8***	296.2***

Note: Numbers in parentheses are standard errors of the estimates above them.
* significant at 10 percent level; ** significant at 5 percent level; *** significant at 1 percent level.

significant. The legal system dummy variable does enter as hypothesized, in that an English, German, or Scandinavian system of law is associated, although not significantly at conventional levels, with smaller governments than otherwise.

2.6.3.2 Tax Cheating, Size of Government, and Prosperity

I next expand the ambitiousness of this exercise by adding to the structural model an equation determining the level of prosperity, equation (3) below. In its structural equation, I allow prosperity to depend on the level of government (and the level squared, to allow that the marginal impact can change sign at a certain level), on trust in others (as emphasized by Knack and Keefer [1997] and others), and on a short vector of exogenous variables. The two exogenous variables measure the physical capital stock (specifically the capital-labor ratio) and the human capital stock (measured by the level of illiteracy). Together with the trust-in-others variable, a measure of social capital, equation (3) posits that prosperity depends on four kinds of capital—physical, human, social, and public.[23]

The system now becomes:

$$TC = TC(G, TW, \mathbf{ZTC}), \tag{1}$$

$$G = G(Y, TC, \mathbf{ZG}), \tag{2}$$

$$Y = Y(G, G^2, TO, \mathbf{ZY}). \tag{3}$$

Model 2 of table 2.3 describes the results of the three-stage least squares estimation of this system of three equations. The estimated equation for income is quite reasonable. More physical capital and more human capital significantly increase real income per capita. So does more trust in others, although the coefficient only barely exceeds its estimated standard error. To put the magnitudes in perspective, a one-standard-deviation increase in trust in others is associated with a 5.5 percent higher level of per capita income. The pattern of influence of government on prosperity takes the form suggested by Barro (1991): Its marginal effect is positive until a turning point is reached. The turning point is estimated to be at a government that represents 37.9 percent of GDP. Note, though, that the t-statistics are only slightly above one.[24]

One consequence of expanding the system to three equations is that, compared with model 1, the coefficient on tax cheating in the size of government equation essentially goes to zero, and the absolute size and significance of the other variables decline, although the qualitative results are unchanged.

Finally, in model 3, I show the results of replicating model 2, but replacing the survey measure of trust with the survey measure of trustworthiness as a determinant of prosperity. According to this specification, variations in trustworthiness cannot explain variations in prosperity as well as variations in trust can. However, this change sharpens the evidence for most of the other hypotheses I am concerned with. In particular, the negative coefficient of tax cheating on the size of government is restored, and the first positive, then negative effect of government on prosperity becomes more statistically significant (with a turning point at 31.5 percent). This illustrates the fragility of at least some of the conclusions that can be drawn from these exercises.

2.6.4 Is It All Just Well-Tossed Spaghetti?

Even without considering trust in government, Putnam (2000, 137) despairs that "the causal arrows among civic involvement, reciprocity, honesty, and social trust are as tangled as well-tossed spaghetti."[25] Clearly there are plausible stories that, of trust, trustworthiness, attitudes toward tax evasion, size of government, and prosperity, almost any variable has a direct effect on almost any other variable. Of course, to an econometrician, a bowl of spaghetti-like causal arrows raises issues of simultaneity bias, which requires defensible "exclusion restrictions" to assert that the estimated coefficients reflect true causal, structural effects. The specifications I have investigated in this chapter are based on a careful reading of the existing literature and introspection about, to put it directly, what affects what. In the process of this research, I have learned that many of the findings are not robust to alternative, reasonable, specifications. Some are apparently more robust than others, as I suggest below. Nor have I even waded into the issues of data reliability, which are serious issues not only with respect to the survey-based measures of trust and trustworthiness, but also with respect to the measure of government size and other variables. Nevertheless, I believe that empirical analysis that simply ignores the interrelationships may be seriously misleading, and an important research challenge is to try to untangle the well-tossed spaghetti. I summarize the insights from this exercise in what follows.

I find some evidence that both prosperity and government involvement are higher in more trusting societies. Moreover, holding these measures of trust constant, the association of government size with prosperity is positive until a level of government spending somewhere between 31.5 and 37.9 percent of GDP, after which its marginal effect is negative.

There is a caveat to this neat story, however. In countries with bigger governments, there is a breakdown in the trustworthiness its citizens exhibit toward government, as measured by the acceptability of tax evasion. Thus, although a trusting citizenry allows larger government, the tax burden this entails erodes the rule obedience taxpayers exhibit toward government. Whether this is the reason that at some high level, further government is associated with less prosperity is an intriguing, but still open, question.

2.7 Conclusion: Trust in Public Finance

Not surprisingly, these empirical exercises have uncovered neither the elixir of prosperity nor the key to establishing trust among all mankind. Nor have they established that considering trust, social capital, and community constructs the conceptual bridge between government expenditure and taxation that Professor Musgrave despaired that the profession was overlooking.

Even if it were clear that taxpaying behavior depended on attitudes toward government, the policy implications are not clear. To be sure, these attitudes cannot be easily changed. Blumenthal, Christian, and Slemrod (2001) report on the results of a field experiment in which Minnesota taxpayers were sent one of two letters, one that detailed the good things that taxes supported (without invoking the free-rider problem) and the other reporting the high rate of aggregate taxpayer compliance (playing down the "sucker" syndrome). Taxpayers who received either letter exhibited no significant increase in income tax compliance compared with a control group of taxpayers who did not receive either letter. Apparently, one-shot exhortations are not successful, a result that would not surprise many who are familiar with the marketing literature on this subject.[26]

One fascinating area for future research is whether our models of the behavioral response to the tax system fail when the free-rider assumption fails. To put the question starkly, can social capital explain why people continue to work, save, and invest in the face of the high marginal tax rates in many countries? When Social Security benefits are tied to payroll tax payments via a formula, economists (e.g., Feldstein and Samwick 1992) have questioned whether the incentive effects need to be adjusted for the marginal benefits that accrue. More generally, if for most taxpayers their tax payments are the optimal Allingham-Sandmo payment plus a "gift" to government, will they respond to taxes as our standard model suggests?

I do not know the answer to this question, but I do know that is one aspect of a fundamental methodological question: "Is the positive theory of taxation a straightforward application of price theory, or is it something quite different?" Consider the tax-augmented relative price term that applies to a commodity in an individual's budget set, $p(1 + t)$, where t is the tax wedge inserted by a consumption tax or an income tax (in the latter case, the relative price is usually written as $w(1 - t)$, where w is the wage rate). Using this notation, the methodological question is whether individuals respond to the relative price $p(1 + t)$, or whether the response to the p part and the $(1 + t)$ part are systematically different. In the standard model, they are not.

I have argued elsewhere (Slemrod 2001) that because of avoidance and evasion, the response to p and the response to $(1 + t)$ will be different. The idea is that a change in t changes the return–risk trade-off of avoidance and evasion in ways that a change in p does not, and the former involves the tax avoidance technology and not only taxpayer preferences. The ideas explored in this chapter suggest another reason why the two responses may be systematically different.[27] Taxpayers' attitudes toward government affect how they react to $(1 + t)$ but not how they react to p.

I am sure that Professor Musgrave would agree that public finance is much, much more than applied price theory. Indeed, he has written that his fascination with the field is "rooted in its broad scope, a joining of economics, politics, and social ethics" and that "the existence of externalities and the need to confront the issues of distribution enrich social life, the challenge of freedom and with it the human status of its members" (Buchanan and Musgrave 1999, 29, 49). No one has more eloquently stated the task before scholars of the public sector.

Appendix 2A: Data Appendix

Variable description	Source and notes
Population (in thousands, 1990)	PWT 5.6
GDP per capita (in 1990 PPP $)	PWT 5.6
Capital per worker (in 1990 PPP $)	PWT 5.6
Openness = sum of imports and exports as a proportion of GDP for 1990	PWT 5.6
Age dependency ratio = ratio of population under age 15 and above age 65 to the working-age population aged 15–64 (in %) in 1990	WDI CD-ROM
Illiteracy rate = number of people aged 15 and above who cannot, with understanding, read and write a short, simple statement of their everyday life, as a proportion of total population (in %) in 1990	WDI CD-ROM; based on information from WDR; the missing values were filled in by zeros for all countries with missing values except for Iceland and Ireland, for which 0 was substituted based on background information from CIA World Factbook
Share of agriculture in GDP = sum of value added from forestry, hunting, fishing, cultivation of crops, and livestock production as a proportion of GDP (in %) in 1990	WDI CD-ROM; datum for West Germany taken from WDR; datum for Switzerland taken from NAS
Share of consolidated government tax expenditure in GDP = sum of consolidated central (C.II), state/regional (St.C.II), and local (L.C.II) government expenditures, less transfers from all the three levels of government (T.I), as a proportion of GDP (in %) in 1990	GFSY for fiscal data; WDI CD-ROM for GDP; GDP datum for Germany taken from NAS; shares calculated in 1988 for Chile, 1989 for Italy and Japan, and 1991 for Switzerland; missing data substituted for by zeros
Legal origin EGS = legal origin of the Company Law or Commercial Code; there are four possible origins: (1) English Common Law, (2) French Commercial Code, (3) German Commercial Code, and (4) Scandinavian Commercial Code; "legal origin EGS" is 1 if English, German, or Scandinavian, and 0 otherwise	La Porta et al. (1999)
Trust in others = weighted average (or individual-level data for West Germany and United States), normalized to scale 0 to 100, of survey responses to question: "Generally speaking, would you say that most people can be trusted or that you can't be too careful in dealing with people?" (0 = can't be too careful; 1 = most people can be trusted)	WVS

Variable description	Source and notes
Trust in government = weighted average (or individual-level data for West Germany and United States), normalized to scale 0 to 100, of survey responses to question: "How much do you trust the government in [national capital] to do what is right? Do you trust it almost always, most of the time, only some of the time, or almost never?" (1 = almost never, . . . , 4 = almost always)	WVS
Acceptability of tax evasion = weighted average (or individual-level data for West Germany and United States), normalized to scale 0 to 100, of survey responses to question: "Please tell me whether you think cheating on tax if you have the chance can always be justified, never be justified, or something in between." (using scale from 1 = never justified to 10 = always justified)	WVS
Trustworthiness = weighted average (or individual-level data for West Germany and United States), normalized to scale 0 to 100, of survey responses to question: "Please tell me whether you think lying in your own interest can always be justified, never be justified, or something in between." (using scale from 1 = always justified to 10 = never justified)	WVS
Confidence in government institutions = weighted average (or individual-level data for West Germany and United States) of sum of total, divided by 4, normalized to scale 0 to 100, of number of survey responses of "a great deal" or "quite a lot" to question: "Please look at this card and tell me, for each item listed, how much confidence you have in them. Is it a great deal, quite a lot, not very much or none at all? (a) The education system (b) The legal system (c) The police (d) The civil service"	WVS
Age = weighted average (or individual-level data for West Germany and United States) of survey respondent age in years	WVS
Education = individual-level data for West Germany and United States of survey responses to question: "At what age did you or will you complete your full-time education, either at school or at an institution of higher education? Please exclude apprenticeships." (responses truncated at 12 years from below and at 21 years from above)	WVS

Variable description	Source and notes
Financial satisfaction = individual-level data for West Germany and United States, normalized to scale 0 to 100, of survey responses to question: "How satisfied are you with the financial situation of your household?" (using scale from 1 = dissatisfied to 10 = satisfied)	WVS
Income scale = individual-level data for West Germany and United States, normalized to scale 0 to 100, of survey responses to question: "Here is a scale of incomes and we would like to know in what group your household is, counting all wages, salaries, pensions and other incomes that come in. Just give the letter of the group your household falls into, before taxes and other deductions." (using nation-specific codes, 1 = lowest, 10 = highest)	WVS
Male = individual-level data indicator, for West Germany and United States, for a survey respondent being male	WVS
Nonreligious = individual-level data for West Germany and United States, normalized to scale 0 to 100, of survey responses to question: "Independently of whether you go to church or not, would you say that you are: 1 = a religious person; 2 = not a religious person; 3 = a convinced atheist."	WVS
Right political orientation = individual-level data, normalized to scale 0 to 100, of survey responses to question: "In political matters, people talk of 'the left' and 'the right.' How would you place your views on this scale, generally speaking?" (using scale from 1 = left to 10 = right)	WVS

Key:

PWT 5.6 is from ⟨http://pwt.econ.upenn/edu⟩, described in Summers and Heston (1991).

WDI CD-ROM is *World Development Indicators* 2001 CD-ROM, World Bank, Washington, DC, 2001.

WDR is *World Development Report*, World Bank, Washington, DC, 1992.

CIA World Factbook is *The World Factbook*, Central Intelligence Agency, Washington, DC, 2000, ⟨http://www.cia.gov/cia/publications/factbook⟩.

NAS is *National Accounts Statistics*, United Nations, New York, 1994.

GFSY is *Government Finance Statistics Yearbook*, International Monetary Fund, Washington, DC, 1995 and 1997.

WVS is World Values Survey, R. Inglehart et al., *World Values Surveys and European Values Surveys, 1990–1993*, Institute for Social Research, Ann Arbor, 2000.

Appendix 2B

Table 2B.1
Within-country summary statistics for the United States and West Germany

Variable	Number of observations	Mean	Standard deviation	Minimum	Maximum
United States					
Age	1,787	44.171	17.944	17	85
Cheating on taxes	1,818	11.217	20.880	0	100
Confidence in government institutions	1,796	61.864	24.954	0	100
Education	1,624	18.807	2.168	12	21
Financial satisfaction	1,830	64.594	26.970	0	100
Income scale	1,696	38.270	21.783	0	100
Male	1,799	0.498	0.500	0	1
Nonreligious	1,785	9.152	20.875	0	100
Right	1,587	52.653	19.932	0	100
Trust	1,782	50.000	50.014	0	100
Trust in government	1,829	46.633	25.059	0	100
Trustworthiness	1,821	84.372	22.395	0	100
West Germany					
Age	2,093	45.778	18.020	18	85
Cheating on taxes	2,053	21.798	26.508	0	100
Confidence in government institutions	2,091	56.890	33.478	0	100
Education	2,068	16.441	2.354	14	21
Financial satisfaction	2,075	63.904	24.497	0	100
Income scale	1,932	34.158	28.674	0	100
Male	2,101	0.467	0.499	0	1
Nonreligious	1,740	18.777	27.021	0	100
Right	1,846	47.770	18.819	0	100
Trust	1,725	37.831	48.511	0	100
Trust in government	0	—	—	—	—
Trustworthiness	2,013	71.765	26.076	0	100

Note: All means and standard deviations are calculated using survey weights.

Table 2B.2
Cross-country summary statistics

Variable	Number of obser- vations	Mean	Standard deviation	Mini- mum	Maxi- mum
Age	25	42.316	3.094	34.074	47.048
Age dependency	25	53.060	8.275	43.639	73.956
Agriculture	25	6.340	6.332	1.825	30.766
Capital per worker (log)	25	10.076	0.767	7.576	11.204
Cheating on taxes	25	16.680	8.458	2.720	34.381
GDP per capita (log)	25	9.394	0.629	7.317	9.990
Government expen- diture	25	40.846	14.169	16.222	61.280
Government expen- diture squared	25	1,861.161	1,052.557	263.146	3,755.248
Illiteracy	25	4.712	10.985	0.000	50.700
Legal origin EGS	25	0.600	0.500	0	1
Openness	25	59.089	30.695	15.180	144.960
Trust	25	40.206	14.617	9.980	66.102
Trustworthiness	25	80.621	7.3517	64.008	91.507

Notes

I am grateful to Peter Katuscak and Elizabeth Oltmans for expert research assistance and extended conversations on the themes of this chapter. I also thank two referees, David Bradford, Michael Burda, Christopher Clague, Bruno Frey, John T. Scholz, Daniel Shaviro, and the participants at the New York University Tax Symposium, February 1, 2001, and the CESifo conference, "Public Finances and Public Policy in the New Millennium," University of Munich, January 12–13, 2001, for helpful comments on an earlier draft.

1. Note that I am speaking here of why public finance theorists treat expenditures and taxation separately, and not about why in *practice* expenditure programs are not tied to particular tax instruments, the practice known as earmarking. Opponents of earmarking argue that it leads to a fragmented and inefficient tax system, and that tying expenditure amounts to specified tax revenues causes inefficient resource allocation decisions.

2. The idea that the structure of the public finances can be instrumental in developing a sense of national community has a long history in the United States. Discussing Alexander Hamilton's plans to have the U.S. federal government assume the revolutionary debts of the states and combine them into existing federal debts, Sandel (1998, 134) says, "Fearful that local sentiments would erode national authority and doubtful that disinterested virtue could inspire allegiance to the nation, Hamilton saw in public finance an instrument of nation-building."

3. The same argument, of course, applies to other decisions, such as whether anyone should expend the time and effort to vote.

4. Note that citizens cannot invest in reputation by being trustworthy towards government. Tax compliance lacks the characteristic—vital to building reputation by signaling trustworthiness—of being observable. In only the rarest cases, after all, is one's tax evasion made publicly known.

5. The IRS Mission Statement, as cited in Steuerle (1986, 1), lists as its first task to "encourage and achieve the highest degree of voluntary compliance in accordance with the tax laws and regulations." IRS measures of the level of tax compliance are all couched in this language, featuring concepts such as the "voluntary" reporting percentage and "voluntary" compliance level.

Some tax protesters in the United States have used references in court cases to the voluntary nature of taxes as a justification for nonpayment. A quotation frequently cited is the following by the U.S. Supreme Court: "Our tax system is based upon voluntary assessment and payment and not upon distraint" (*Flora v. United States*, 362 U.S. 145, 175). This quotation is taken out of context, and other courts' statements make clear that the opposite is true, such as: "Any assertion that the payment of income taxes is voluntary is without merit. It is without question that the payment of taxes is not voluntary" (*United States v. Gerads*, 999 F.2d 1255, 1256 (8th Cir., 1993), *per curiam*). These quotations are collected in "The Tax Protestor FAQ," created by Daniel Evans; see ⟨http://evans-legal.com/dan/tpfaq.html⟩.

6. See Klepper and Nagin (1989).

7. In addition, to the extent that past years' returns may be audited, the relevant probability is the probability of audit over a number of years rather than in a single year.

8. This latter question is obviously much different from the trust question used in most of the other studies discussed in what follows.

9. Victor Hugo, in *Les Misérables* (1862, vol. 1, bk. 5, sec. 7, 209), observed the following relationship between tax compliance and prosperity in eighteenth-century Paris:

When the population suffers, when work is lacking, when there is no commerce, the tax-payer resists imposts through penury, he exhausts and oversteps his respite, and the state expends a great deal of money in the charges for compelling and collection. When work is abundant, when the country is rich and happy, the taxes are paid easily and cost the state nothing. It may be said, that there is one infallible thermometer of the public misery and riches; the cost of collecting the taxes.

Note that this behavior would produce a Wagner's Law phenomenon in which tax collections as a fraction of income are higher when income is higher. I am grateful to Jonathan Skinner for bringing this quotation to my attention.

10. Scholz and Lubell (2001), in an experimental setting, find that the level of cooperation in certain settings declines significantly when penalties are introduced, suggesting that the increased deterrence motivation does not compensate for the change in decision frame brought about by the penalties.

11. See, for example, Clotfelter (1985).

12. The tax payments, or lack thereof, of some taxpayers may reflect "pathological dishonesty," if they underpay compared with their rational utility-maximizing calculus because of their aversion to government.

13. Some fraction of purchases of U.S. Savings Bonds might be considered to be a contribution to the government, to the extent that the return-for-risk is lower than a nongovernment alternative, and this is known to the purchaser.

14. There are also fascinating localized examples of gifts to government. For example, in 2000, the state of Pennsylvania mailed out 2.5 million income tax rebates to its tax-payers; the rebate was prompted by a large budget surplus and was described as an offset to local property taxes. The Associated Press (2000) reports that hundreds of these checks have been signed over to local school districts. One donor was quoted as saying that "It's important that schools have more money to meet their needs."

15. By the way, the same relationship holds for most countries over time: The tax-GDP ratio has grown as the country has become richer.

16. See Slemrod (1995) for the problems involved in this enterprise.

17. There is also an older literature of cross-country research on national development that argues that nations whose people generally support government policies progress more rapidly than nations in which obedience must be coerced. See Almond and Verba (1963).

18. The countries are Argentina, Austria, Belgium, Canada, Chile, Denmark, Finland, France, (West) Germany, Iceland, India, Ireland, Italy, Japan, (Republic of) Korea, Mexico, the Netherlands, Norway, Portugal, Spain, Sweden, Switzerland, Turkey, the United Kingdom, and the United States.

19. I also ran the same set of models using *unweighted* country means from the WVS data. The results are very similar both qualitatively and quantitatively to those reported here.

20. The trust in government question ("How much do you trust the government in [national capital] to do what is right?") was asked in only seven of the twenty-five sample countries, so it is unfortunately not used in the analysis that follows.

21. Holding trustworthiness constant, elderly people may have different attitudes toward evasion because they may have less direct involvement with the income tax system.

22. Joint significance tests on the slope coefficients in each of the first-stage instru-menting regressions were carried out in each of the three models considered. After adjusting the estimated variance matrices by the White heteroskedasticity correction, each of the tests displays significance at a 1 percent level, except for the equations for G and G^2 in model 3, which are significant at a 5 percent level.

23. Lack of data does not allow also including a measure of natural resources, or nat-ural capital.

24. Joint tests were performed on G and G^2 in models 2 and 3 to test the hypothesis that government spending affects prosperity. In both tests, the chi-squared statistic with two degrees of freedom failed to reach standard levels of significance.

25. In a similar vein, Messere (1993) characterizes as "fishing expeditions" efforts to relate tax levels and structure to measures of economic performance.

26. There is, though, a school of marketing science experts who argue that one-shot advertising is nearly as effective as multiple communications.

27. Rosen (1976) and Konig et al. (1995) explore yet another reason, that taxpayers are unaware of their tax rate.

References

Allingham, M. G., and A. Sandmo. 1972. "Income Tax Evasion: A Theoretical Analysis." *Journal of Public Economics* 1: 323–338.

Alm, J., B. Jackson, and M. McKee. 1992. "Estimating the Determinants of Taxpayer Compliance with Experimental Data." *National Tax Journal* 45: 107–114.

Almond, G., and S. Verba. 1963. *The Civic Culture*. Princeton: Princeton University Press.

Andreoni, J., B. Erard, and J. Feinstein. 1998. "Tax Compliance." *Journal of Economic Literature* 36: 818–860.

Arrow, K. 1972. "Gifts and Exchanges." *Philosophy and Public Affairs* 1: 343–367.

Associated Press. 2000. "Taxpayers Return Their Rebates to Help Pennsylvania's Schools." November 25.

Axelrod, R. 1986. "An Evolutionary Approach to Norms." *American Political Science Review* 80: 1095–1111.

Barro, R. J. 1991. "A Cross-Country Study of Growth, Saving, and Government." In *National Saving and Economic Performance*, ed. B. D. Bernheim and J. B. Shoven. Chicago: University of Chicago Press.

Barro, R. J., and D. B. Gordon. 1983. "Rules, Discretion, and Reputation in a Model of Monetary Policy." *Journal of Monetary Economics* 12: 101–121.

Barro, R. J., and X. Sala-i-Martin. 1992. "Public Finance in Models of Economic Growth." *Review of Economic Studies* 59: 645–661.

Blumenthal, M., C. Christian, and J. Slemrod. 2001. "Do Normative Appeals Affect Tax Compliance? Evidence from a Controlled Experiment in Minnesota." *National Tax Journal* 54: 125–138.

Bordignon, M. 1993. "A Fairness Approach to Income Tax Evasion." *Journal of Public Economics* 52: 345–362.

Brehm, J. 1998. "Who Do You Trust? People, Government, or Neither?" Mimeo., Duke University, Durham, NC.

Brehm, J., and W. Rahn. 1997. "Individual Level Evidence for the Causes and Consequences of Social Capital." *American Journal of Political Science* 41: 999–1023.

Buchanan, J. M., and R. A. Musgrave. 1999. *Public Finance and Public Choice: Two Contrasting Visions of the State*. Cambridge: MIT Press.

Cameron, D. R. 1978. "The Expansion of the Public Economy: A Comparative Analysis." *American Political Science Review* 72: 1243–1261.

Campbell, D. E. 1995. *Incentives: Motivation and the Economics of Information*. New York: Cambridge University Press.

Clague, C. 1993. "Rule Obedience, Organizational Loyalty, and Economic Development." *Journal of Institutional and Theoretical Economics* 149: 393–414.

Clotfelter, C. 1985. *Federal Tax Policy and Charitable Giving*. Chicago: University of Chicago Press.

Coleman, J. 1990. *Foundations of Social Theory*. Cambridge: Harvard University Press.

Cowell, F. 1990. *Cheating the Government*. Cambridge: MIT Press.

Cripps, M. W., and J. P. Thomas. 1995. "Reputation and Commitment in Two-Person Repeated Games without Discounting." *Econometrica* 63: 1401–1419.

Cullis, J. G., and A. Lewis. 1997. "Why People Pay Taxes: From a Conventional Economic Model to a Model of Social Convention." *Journal of Economic Psychology* 18: 305–321.

Daunton, M. 1998. "Trusting Leviathan: British Fiscal Administration from the Napoleonic Wars to the Second World War." In *Trust and Governance*, ed. M. Levi and V. Braithwaite. New York: Russell Sage Foundation.

Easterly, W., and S. Rebelo. 1994. "Fiscal Policy and Economic Growth: An Empirical Investigation." *Journal of Monetary Economics* 32: 417–458.

Epple, D. 1998. "Rent Control with Reputation: Theory and Evidence." *Regional Science and Urban Economics* 28: 679–710.

Falkinger, J. 1995. "Tax Evasion, Consumption of Public Goods, and Fairness." *Journal of Economic Psychology* 16: 63–72.

Feld, L., and B. Frey. 2002. "Trust Breeds Trust: How Taxpayers Are Treated." *Economics of Governance* 3(2): 87–99.

Feldstein, M., and A. Samwick. 1992. "Social Security Rules and Marginal Tax Rates." *National Tax Journal* 45: 1–22.

Frey, B. 1997. "A Constitution for Knaves Crowds Out Civic Virtues." *Economic Journal* 107: 1043–1053.

Fukuyama, F. 1995. *Trust*. New York: Basic Books.

Glaeser, E. L., D. Laibson, J. A. Scheinkman, and C. L. Soutter. 1999. "Measuring Trust." *Quarterly Journal of Economics* 65: 811–846.

Goode, R. 1968. "The Tax Burden in the United States and Other Countries." *Annals of the American Academy of Political and Social Science* 379: 83–89.

Hugo, V. 1862. *Les Misérables*. University of Virginia Electronic Text Center. Available online at ⟨http://etext.lib.virginia.edu/etcbin/toccer-new2?id=Hug1Mis.sgm&images=images/modeng&data=/texts/english/modeng/parsed&tag=public&part=all⟩.

Inglehart, R., M. Basanez, and A. Moreno. 1998. *Human Values and Beliefs: A Cross-Cultural Sourcebook*. Ann Arbor: University of Michigan Press.

Johnston, D. C. 1997. "United Way, Faced with Fewer Donors, Is Giving Away Less." *New York Times*, November 9.

Kahneman, D., J. L. Knetsch, and R. Thaler. 1986. "Fairness and the Assumptions of Economics." *Journal of Business* 59: S285–S300.

Kaplan, S. E., and P. M. J. Reckers. 1985. "A Study of Tax Evasion Judgments." *National Tax Journal* 38: 97–102.

Klepper, S., and D. Nagin. 1989. "The Anatomy of Tax Evasion." *Journal of Law, Economics, and Organization* 5: 1–24.

Knack, S., and P. Keefer. 1997. "Does Social Capital Have an Economic Payoff? A Cross-Country Investigation." *Quarterly Journal of Economics* 112: 1251–1288.

Konig, H., F. Laisney, M. Lechner, and W. Pohlmeier. 1995. "Tax Illusion and the Labor Supply of Married Women: Evidence from German Data." *Kyklos* 48: 347–368.

La Porta, R., F. Lopez-de-Silanes, A. Shleifer, and R. Vishny. 1999. "The Quality of Government." *Journal of Law, Economics, and Organization* 15: 222–279.

Levi, M. 1998. "A State of Trust." In *Trust and Governance*, ed. M. Levi and V. Braithwaite. New York: Russell Sage Foundation.

Levine, R., and D. Renelt. 1992. "A Sensitivity Analysis of Cross-Country Growth Regressions." *American Economic Review* 82: 942–963.

Marks, M. B., and E. D. Schansberg. 1997. "Fairness and Reputation Effects in a Provision Point Contributions Process." *Nonprofit Management and Leadership* 7: 235–251.

Mason, R., and L. D. Calvin. 1984. "Public Confidence and Admitted Tax Evasion." *National Tax Journal* 37: 489–496.

Messere, K. C. 1993. *Tax Policy in OECD Countries: Choices and Conflicts*. Amsterdam: IBFD Publications BV.

Musgrave, R. A. 1969. *Fiscal Systems*. New Haven: Yale University Press.

Musgrave, R. A., and P. B. Musgrave. 1989. *Public Finance in Theory and Practice*. 5th ed. New York: McGraw-Hill.

Newton, K. 1999. "Social and Political Trust in Established Democracies." In *Critical Citizens: Global Support for Democratic Government*, ed. P. Norris. Oxford: Oxford University Press.

Ostrom, E. 2000. "Collective Action and the Evolution of Social Norms." *Journal of Economic Perspectives* 14(3): 137–158.

Putnam, R. 2000. *Bowling Alone*. New York: Simon & Schuster.

Putnam, R. (with R. Leonardi and R. Y. Nanetti). 1993. *Making Democracy Work*. Princeton: Princeton University Press.

Rodrik, D. 1998. "Why Do More Open Economies Have Bigger Governments?" *Journal of Political Economy* 106: 997–1032.

Rosen, H. S. 1976. "Tax Illusion and the Labor Supply of Married Women." *Review of Economics and Statistics* 58: 167–172.

Sandel, M. J. 1998. *Democracy's Discontent: America in Search of a Public Philosophy*. Cambridge, MA, and London, UK: Belknap Press of Harvard University Press.

Scholz, J. T., and M. Lubell. 1998a. "Trust and Taxpayers: Testing the Heuristic Approach to Collective Action." *American Journal of Political Science* 42: 398–417.

Scholz, J. T., and M. Lubell. 1998b. "Adaptive Political Attitudes: Duty, Trust, and Fear as Monitors of Tax Policy." *American Journal of Political Science* 42: 903–920.

Scholz, J. T., and M. Lubell. 2001. "Cooperation, Reciprocity, and the Collective Action Heuristic." *American Journal of Political Science* 45: 160–178.

Slemrod, J. 1995. "What Do Cross-Country Studies Teach about Taxes, Prosperity, and Economic Growth?" *Brookings Papers on Economic Activity* 2: 373–415.

Slemrod, J. 2001. "A General Model of the Behavioral Response to Taxation." *International Tax and Public Finance* 8: 119–128.

Slemrod, J., and E. Oltmans. 2001. "Gifts to Government." Mimeo., University of Michigan, Ann Arbor.

Spicer, M. W., and L. A. Becker. 1980. "Fiscal Inequity and Tax Evasion: An Experimental Approach." *National Tax Journal* 33: 171–175.

Steuerle, C. E. 1986. *Who Should Pay for Collecting Taxes? Financing the IRS.* Washington, DC: American Enterprise Institute.

Summers, R., and A. Heston. 1991. "The Penn World Table (Mark 5): An Expanded Set of International Comparisons, 1950–1988." *Quarterly Journal of Economics* 106: 327–368.

Tanzi, V. 1992. "Structural Factors and Tax Revenue in Developing Countries: A Decade of Evidence." In *Open Economies: Structural Adjustment and Agriculture*, ed. I. Goldin and L. A. Winters. Cambridge, UK: Cambridge University Press.

Taylor, M. 1982. *Community, Anarchy, and Liberty.* Cambridge, UK: Cambridge University Press.

Zak, P., and S. Knack. 2001. "Trust and Growth." *Economic Journal* 111: 295–321.

Comments

Michael Burda

While not a scholar of the public sector, I must add my name to the many grateful thousands who have thanked Professor Musgrave for the pleasure of studying the subject using *Public Finance in Theory and Practice*. Musgrave's never ending quest for a unified understanding of taxation and expenditures is honored by Joel Slemrod's challenging chapter, which surveys the role of trust in public economics. As I see it, Slemrod's most important conclusions are that: (1) Trust has a theoretical role to play in public finance; (2) Lack of exclusion restrictions makes testing this role difficult if not impossible; and (3) The evidence on trust and taxpaying behavior in both macro and micro data sets, while not overwhelming, suggests that high-taxation jurisdictions exhibit lower trust and lower trustworthiness. Citizens in high-tax countries seem to consider tax evasion more acceptable and in all likelihood engage in the activity, indirect evidence for the still poorly substantiated Laffer curve.

The discussion of trust is new in economics and still lacks a clear, agreed-upon definition. Slemrod's chapter reflects this ambiguity. Trust must be distinguished from credibility, which characterizes how economic agents anticipate and solve for the optimal policies chosen by policymakers. I also believe trust is different from "social capital," which I will discuss below. For Slemrod, trust is equivalent to "letting down your guard," or forgoing costly measures that defend against opportunistic behavior of others. Trust arises when a cooperative strategy played by individuals vis-à-vis the government has a higher expected payoff, and when government in equilibrium plays a strategy of trustworthiness. Trustworthiness means forsaking opportunistic behavior, which can in turn induce trust. Both trust and trustworthiness appear necessary for any equilibrium involving trust to get off the ground.

1   Trust or Social Norms?

But is trust the appropriate framework for thinking about citizen-government interactions, or are other mechanisms at work? Taxpayers' honesty could just as well result from social norms as from trust relationships, and the two alternatives may be far from semantic. The trust paradigm described by Slemrod typically involves repeated bilateral interactions, possibly with changing partners. While a repeated "revolving door" ultimatum game with many agents could rationalize some of what we understand as trust, it seems artificial applied in the public finance context, since the same government is always at the other end. Moreover, externalities, ever present in the work of Musgrave, are not of immediate relevance in a world of trust. In a model of social norms, the average behavior of others affects my own utility as well as the disutility of my own actions. This suggests another model—a model of enforceable social norms such as that used to study free-riding behavior in unions (Cripps and Naylor 1993), cheating on the Welfare State (Lindbeck 1997), or taxpaying (Falkinger 1995). The norm originates in the aggregate behavior of the economy and offers a benchmark against which benefits and costs of various choices can be defined. Arguably, social norms may be more appropriate for explaining multiple equilibria and path dependence than models of trusting citizenry. Social norms are related to the notion of "social capital," which can be thought of as a pure public good generated by the sum of individuals' behavior.

It is natural to ask whether trust or norms are the central characteristic explaining behavioral variation between Europe and the United States. Despite enormous differences in attitudes, I find it hard to believe that Europeans trust their governments any less than Americans do—and in some countries, may trust them more! Widespread tax evasion and avoidance observed in Europe is as consistent with a deterioration of social norms as with a breakdown in trust. The U.S. institution of tax withholding—implemented during World War II—is the most egregious sign of mistrust by a government one can imagine, effectively ignoring any trustworthy behavior on the part of the taxpayer. In Europe, tax withholding is far from universal—not only as regards capital income (e.g., in Germany), but also as regards wages and salaries (e.g., in France).

2   Trust and Econometrics

The U.S.-European comparison suggests that models with norms and multiple equilibria are a necessary component for understanding citizen-government interactions. But can a social-norm-based economy be distinguished from a trust economy? Clearly one needs to ask questions such as "Are externalities really involved in individuals' behavior?" and "Are there sharper, more differentiated measures of trust across time and countries?" Evidence on trust *within* countries (across states or counties of the United States, for example) could help us in this respect by "controlling" for national preferences. Correlations, while a good start, hardly demonstrate causation, nor do they discriminate between competing theories.

Any critical reader of Slemrod's chapter must be concerned about the use of econometrics to estimate links between trust, government activity, and economic well-being. The red flag, of course, is identification. Because trust can potentially depend on everything, exogenous variation in trust must be identified to detect effects on government spending, taxation, income, or growth. Time variation or exclusion restrictions might work, but Slemrod admits being far from finding acceptable instruments. Exploiting local and regional variation of attitudes with a better-designed survey in large countries such as the United States, Canada, or Russia might help, as could looking for "events" or natural experiments such as the breakup of the Czech and Slovak republics and Yugoslavia, or the unification of Germany. It might be informative to repeat some of the regressions for subgroupings (continental European, Anglo-Saxon, Asian). More and better theory will be needed to guide us in the search for instruments.

3   Concluding Remarks

Do people pay taxes because they trust or because they feel that they must? Apparent violations of utility-maximization behavior challenge us to modify existing theories or to reject them and develop new paradigms. While many efforts to incorporate sociological aspects have been successful, any inductive form of theorizing based on observation alone will ultimately disappoint us as economists. I think Slemrod shares some of this ambivalence: He describes some of the newer theories of trust and government, but seems unconvinced about the evidence. For me at least, the evidence does not yet warrant giving up on positive theorizing based on normative analysis—most important, optimization. Social norm theory, while admitting powerful interdependent effects among agents, remains susceptible to those methods. I am not sure the same holds for trust and trustworthiness.

References

Cripps, M., and R. Naylor. 1993. "An Economic Theory of the Open Shop." *European Economic Review* 37: 1599–1620.

Falkinger, J. 1995. "Tax Evasion, Consumption of Public Goods, and Fairness." *Journal of Economic Psychology* 16: 63–72.

Lindbeck, A. 1997. "Incentives and Social Norms in Household Behavior." *American Economic Review* 87: 370–377.

3 Reforming Budgetary Language

David F. Bradford

The administrative case for budget consolidation is self-evident ... But this consolidation is a matter of administrative expediency only; we must not lose sight of the basic principle that the consolidated budget has no rationale on its own ...

Consolidation, to be sure, presents no dangers in our imaginary model of efficient budgeting.... But in the real world the matter is regarded differently; there the tendency is to view the budget in consolidated terms from the outset, and thus to confuse the underlying issues in the planning stage.

—Richard A. Musgrave, *The Theory of Public Finance* [emphasis in the original]

3.1 Introduction

I was introduced to Richard Musgrave's magisterial treatise as a student in Kenneth Arrow's public finance course at Stanford in the early 1960s. Musgrave's application of relatively simple but rigorous economic theory to a wide range of important problems was terribly exciting for a young graduate student. His book was thus a major reason that I chose the field of public finance—or, as Musgrave himself called it in the subtitle of his book, public economy—for the principal preoccupation of my career. It is a pleasure to contribute to this volume to express our appreciation to him on the occasion of his ninetieth birthday.

Among the most important of the ideas that we students encountered in *The Theory of Public Finance* was the conceptual division of the government's budget into Allocation, Distribution, and Stabilization Branches. It is to the consolidation of the subbudgets of these three branches, each informative about the function served, that Musgrave refers in the quotation at the start of this chapter. In his preface (p. v), Musgrave begs the reader "not to discard this some-what utopian scheme (of three informative subbudgets) with the sterile objection of 'utterly impracticable.' Let its practicability be tested not by the prospects for speedy enactment but by the contri-bution it has to make to orderly thinking about the basic issues of budget policy." In this chapter, I revisit, in the light of develop-ments in economics since Musgrave wrote, the question of whether budgetary practices could be made more directly informative about two of Musgrave's conceptual functions of government. Reflecting my inadequacies as a macroeconomist, I restrict my attention to the allocative and distributional branches.

My subject is the budget as a way of describing what the govern-ment does, monitoring its performance, and planning for its future. My easy thesis is that there is a serious problem of meaning in the terms we use—such as taxes, spending, deficits—what I call the "budgetary language." My harder thesis is that it is within our reach to improve the situation significantly. The general ideas that I pre-sent may seem obvious to professional readers. But not very many people outside the profession seem to understand them, or, perhaps better said, a great many people clearly do not understand them. And even trained economists oft go astray.

Given the stakes involved and the complexity of the material, it is not surprising that we find in budgetary debates a great deal of "smoke and mirrors." Our present budgetary concepts invite such manipulation because they are not economically well defined. It is always difficult to tell whether people are able to see through accounting data to underlying realities. A good example from the private sphere would be the treatment of retirement pensions. Under early standards, companies with very different obligations could have identical balance sheets. Changes in the rules to make infor-mation about pension obligations explicit in financial accounts were the subject of bitter controversy. On the other hand, it is possible that the valuation placed on a company by financial experts was already independent of these accounting data. Such experts could ferret out the company's real situation, using information supplemental to standard financial accounts (see Beaver and Landsman 1983).

Experience suggests to me, however, that misunderstanding of the economic reality behind government budgetary information seriously influences policy. While I would not advocate or expect immediate replacement of present rules with economically meaningful alternative conventions, I do believe there is a case for fairly radical overhaul of our budgetary language. At a minimum, supplementary accounting information, based on economically meaningful conventions, could go a long way toward achieving improved transparency about what is going on and more effective planning for the future.

In this chapter, I propose as the building blocks of such a language the elements of the standard description of the household's economic circumstances: the level of its budget constraint, the prices it faces, and the economic environment (read levels of public goods) in which it finds itself. Before getting to this image of the road to reform, I illustrate the need for it with four examples of problems with existing budgetary language in the United States. If some of these examples seem a bit dated, it is because I used them some time ago in teaching public finance. No doubt, I could bring them up to date but, unlike undergraduates, today's readership does not need the excitement provided by connection with today's *New York Times*. I am sure the problems I describe persist today, at least in the United States. In that regard, I must apologize for the parochial attachment to the U.S. budgetary institutions that I know reasonably well. A referee has suggested that substantial transparency has been achieved in Australia, New Zealand, and the United Kingdom. Regrettably, I have not been able to determine the extent to which these countries have solved the puzzles posed here. Reliance in Europe on criteria such as the Maastricht standards for budgetary discipline, which are subject to the criticisms raised in what follows, suggests to me that there is plenty of room for improvement in the practices of other countries.

3.2 Four Examples

3.2.1 *Example 1: Are They Spending Cuts or Tax Increases?*

The first parable is drawn from debate I observed as an interested participant in discussion of fiscal plans that emerged as William Clinton moved from U.S. president elect to president. Conservative voters had deserted President George Bush after he violated his pledge for "no new taxes." Reflecting the same political mood, candidate Clinton campaigned as a New Democrat on a theme of cutting deficits by controlling spending rather than by raising taxes.

At Senate hearings for his confirmation, Clinton's nominee for Director of the Office of Management and Budget, Leon Panetta, asserted his aim to achieve deficit reduction by cutting spending and raising taxes, with three dollars of spending cuts for each dollar of tax increases. Later, as December turned to January, Panetta suggested it might be possible to achieve two dollars of spending cuts for each dollar of tax increases. Shortly before the President's economic message late in the month, his spokesman hinted on a Sunday talk show that the President was aiming for "balance" in his budgetary proposals. In the event, President Clinton announced in his speech his intention to implement $247 billion in spending cuts over a five-year period, together with, surprise, $246 billion in tax increases.

In the subsequent debate, critics redid the numbers in many ways. In a typical example, the Senate Budget Committee minority (Republican) staff concluded that the version of the Clinton program that passed the House incorporated $6.35 in taxes for each $1 in spending cuts. The argument involved, in part, matters of defining baselines and of netting. My interest here, however, concerns the debate over what is a tax increase and what is a spending cut. An excellent example was the Clinton administration's proposal to increase the portion of Social Security retirement benefits that is subject to income taxation (a proposal that was subsequently enacted). The administration described this proposal as a reduction in spending of $21.4 billion over five years. It did not count the change in its table of "revenue provisions," where tax changes are customarily summarized. Critics cried foul and they found support in the analysis by the even-handed Congressional Budget Office that placed the provision in the category of "revenue proposals."

What is the nonpartisan truth here? Was the Social Security proposal a spending cut or a tax increase? Economics tells us that the label is *uninformative*. It is a commonplace of public finance that transfer payments (such as Social Security retirement benefits, commonly classified as expenditures) and taxes (such as income taxes) are entirely symmetric. Thus, Musgrave (1959, 272) notes that "In a formal sense, transfers may again be looked upon as negative taxes." But to do so is not normal practice in budgetary debate. Interestingly, it is also still not the standard approach taken in courses in public finance. On the same page of *The Theory of Public Finance*, Musgrave observes in connection with transfer payments that "consumer behavior may be affected from the expenditure as well as from the tax side of the budget," thereby implicitly accepting a useful distinction, as do his textbook successors.

We have here a problem due to aggregation along the lines Musgrave pointed out in the quotation at the head of this chapter. Sometimes there is a real difference to be concerned about. But in the circumstances that spending and taxes are really the same thing, the classification shouldn't matter, should it?

3.2.2 Example 2: A Balanced Budget Policy Change May Be Hard on Future Generations

The present distinction between taxes and spending is based on institutional convention, not economics. One might say "so much the worse for economics," were it not for the evident problems occasioned by mistaken reliance on the tax/spending distinction. Nowhere is this clearer than in present budgetary politics in the United States. The first example worked mainly off the equivalence of taxes and transfers. The second example is closely related, in that it involves, in effect, taxes and transfers as they affect different generations of citizens. At the time of writing (August 2001), politicians in the United States are debating the best use of large budget surpluses; not long ago, they were struggling to overcome budget deficits. Arguably, in the recent past, they were understating the fundamental intergenerational distributional problem. By the same token, today they are probably overly optimistic about the future, in the sense that they would behave differently if they had better budgetary language.

We can easily illustrate the problem with present conventions with the case of an extension of some benefit flowing to older residents—for example, an improvement in the prescription drug provisions under Medicare (the health insurance provided to the elderly). If such an improvement were financed by an increase in the payroll tax, there would be a net transfer to existing elderly residents at the expense of younger residents, including the as yet unborn. Alternatively, finance through, say, an increase in the premiums paid by the current elderly would leave unchanged the anticipated net tax on currently young and future cohorts. Both of these programs would, however, have the same impact on the budget deficit, current and projected. Does the budget deficit matter?

3.2.3 Example 3: Tax Expenditures and Their Opposites (Taxes?)

The third example involves real expenditures. It may seem a bit quaint, as it comes from those days when we worried about how to cut the deficit, not how to spend the surplus, but the generic point is no less apt today. The example features the secret Bradford plan to balance the budget without raising taxes and without reducing defense capability (or any other real spending program).

Step 1 of the Bradford plan is to cut the weapons procurement request in the defense budget to zero. Taken by itself, this would harm defense capacity. Step 2, designed to offset this unfortunate effect, calls for enactment of a new "weapons supply tax credit" (WSTC). To qualify for the WSTC, manufacturers will sign appropriate documents prescribed by the secretary of defense (looking much like today's procurement contracts) and deliver to appropriate depots weapons systems of prescribed characteristics. The WSTC, which may be transferred to other taxpayers without limit, may only be used in payment of income tax. Step 2 is, apparently obviously, a tax cut.

A time of concern about budget deficits is patently not a time for a tax cut, so step 3 is a revenue-neutral tax *reform*, under which the new tax credits are offset by including all Social Security benefits in taxable income and eliminating the mortgage interest deduction.

Steps 1 and 2 would have a large effect on the budgetary totals, resulting in a large cut in spending and an equal cut in taxes. But the economic reality would be unaffected until step 3, which would more or less radically change the distributive impact of the fiscal system under the cover of revenue-neutral reform.

It is true that the chances are pretty good that some astute politician or journalist would notice what is going on in this case. Maybe the policy process would see through to the economic substance. But maybe not; permit me to doubt. In any case, I believe the implied description of present budgetary language is completely accurate.

3.2.4 Example 4: How to Spend (and Tax) without Spending (or Taxing): Mandates

The fourth situation calling for better economic description is the use of regulation to influence the allocation of resources and distribution of income. Consider a mandate that employers provide health insurance for their workers as an approach to healthcare reform. Such a scheme would have rather complex incidence but, except for the unlikely case that the mandate matches what people would do on their own, we know there will be gainers and losers and there would be allocative effects from its introduction, just as there would be for a program of taxes and subsidies or for a program of public provision of health insurance that would generate the same result. Yet (neglecting such features as the deductibility of the employers' outlays under the income tax) the mandated system would have no direct budgetary consequences. (Bradford and Max [1997] quantify the taxes and transfers implicit in an illustrative mandate for the United States.)

Or consider, for example, the requirement under U.S. law that makes potentially responsible parties (PRPs), defined very broadly, jointly and severally liable for cleaning up abandoned hazardous wastes. Here, a large program of expenditure is being financed by an implicit tax on the PRPs.

Environmental regulation is increasingly important in most advanced economies and, while it may well be worth it, it is often expensive. For example, the U.S. government estimated that just one law—the Clean Air Act Amendment (an amendment to the already existing rules), passed in 1990—would, when fully phased in, impose roughly $25 billion per year in compliance costs. Other examples of regulations include requirements that local governments assure that waste water released into waterways be up to national drinking standards and requirements that governments and businesses provide handicapped access to all public facilities.

With a little imagination, we can generally construct a program of taxes and expenditures, as the terms are conventionally understood, that will exactly duplicate the effect of regulatory programs such as these. The duplicating provisions would be reflected in conventional budgets. Yet the regulatory programs do not show up there. What should our objective be in approaching the measurement of such regulatory programs?

3.3   Toward Improvement in Budgetary Language

Budget information concerns how the world looks (or would look, in the case of proposed budget plans) compared with some hypothetical *status quo ante*. In general, the implicit status quo ante is the absence of government. To be sure, the actual numerical figures are probably best thought of as some sort of approximation to such a description. For example, when we say that the United States is spending $300 billion on national defense, we must mean something like that if we eliminated all those programs, there would be $300 billion of other goods and services available in the economy. We know we cannot take such a figure literally. Matters such as the speed with which such a huge hypothetical policy change might be effected would radically influence the actual impact. But the figure still is presumably to be interpreted as a measure of difference from the counterfactual baseline "null" policy of no expenditures on national defense.

As Musgrave (1959, 184–185) points out in his discussion of budget items in the social accounts, most of the use of aggregates such as the level of defense expenditures is to assess year-to-year changes. To interpret the effect of an increase in defense outlays from $300 billion to $320 billion as the value of alternative goods and services forgone is likely to make reasonable sense.

The strategy that I suggest is to base accounting conventions on the building blocks of budget constraints and prices. We know, in principle, how to describe people's economic situations in ways that are quite independent of fiscal institutions. With due regard for the level of abstraction involved, we may say that the economic situation of an individual is described by budget constraints, intratemporal and intertemporal, together with environmental variables, including government-provided services. Putting it loosely, we can describe the economic reality by the amount of money people have to spend, the prices they face, and the amounts of public goods available to them. This can be done in ways that are independent of the many possible institutional arrangements that could give rise to the same set of economic circumstances of individuals.

The same tools should permit us to describe alternative policies unambiguously. The real content of defense "spending" is a measure of the quantity of troops and tanks, whether paid for by check or by tax credit. The real effect of an investment subsidy is to change a certain price facing producers, whether the subsidy is implemented by a Commerce Department program or by accelerated depreciation in an income tax. The real effects of an income tax and an income-related phaseout of welfare benefits are the same, and would be identically described in a system of real fiscal accounts.

The ideal set of budget accounts should show how much we are spending and what we are spending it on, and it should be more refined about who the "we" is than a single aggregate "we." It should show the amounts subsets of us are gaining and other subsets are losing, including importantly an identification of gains and losses by generational cohorts.

Finally, the budget should show impacts of programs implemented through mandates or regulation.

3.4   Budgetary Language in Some Simple Model Economies

In the Musgrave tradition, we might ask how the problem would look in a simple model economy, consisting of two people; let us call them A and B.

3.4.1   Taxes and Transfers: Intratemporal

To capture the basic distributive problem, consider a world with just one private good—call it X—in addition to labor. Each person i acquires a quantity x_i of X by working l_i units of time subject to a budget constraint determined by his (pardon the gender convention) productivity (assumed equal to his wage), w_i, less a lump-sum tax paid to the government, Ta_i, plus a lump-sum transfer received from the government, Tr_i:

$$x_A = w_A l_A - Ta_A + Tr_A, \tag{1}$$

$$x_B = w_B l_B - Ta_B + Tr_B, \tag{2}$$

$$Ta_A + Ta_B = Tr_A + Tr_B, \tag{3}$$

where (3) expresses the government's budget constraint.

Note that the aggregates of taxes and transfers are uninformative about the distributive properties of the budget. They could both be large but each person's tax could exactly equal his transfer. To describe the government's program in this economy, it suffices to record the net tax paid or net transfer received by each of the two citizens; let us call the net tax Tan_i. Then all we need to know about the government's policy is captured unambiguously by the pair (Tan_A, Tan_B). (A detail: Because of the government's budget constraint, we only need to specify $n - 1$ of these, where n is the number of people. When, as in the example, there are just two

people, this makes a big difference. In the more general case, with
large n, the government's budget constraint will provide very little
information.)

3.4.2   Taxes and Transfers: Intertemporal

Bringing in time poses serious challenges to meaningful budgetary
language. To isolate the key issues, consider a two-period world.
Now we need to add period superscripts, 1 or 2, to everything in
sight. The following system describes the budget constraints as of
period 1 in terms of the basic economic system plus net taxes:

$$x_i^1 + \delta x_i^2 = w_i(l_i^1 + \delta l_i^2) - (Tan_i^1 + \delta Tan_i^2) \text{ for } i = A, B, \tag{4}$$

$$Tan_A^1 + Tan_B^1 + \delta(Tan_A^2 + Tan_B^2) = 0, \tag{5}$$

where the wage rates are presumed the same in both periods and
where δ is the discount factor in the model economy.

In this depiction, I have taken for granted that the budgetary
information will have dealt with the netting of taxes and transfers.
Specification of the net transfers in period 1 is, however, uninformative about the impact of the fiscal plan on the two people in the
economy. Thus, we could give everyone a "tax cut" in period 1, so
that both Tan_A^1 and Tan_B^1 are negative. This would accord with usage
in policy debates in the United States today. The government's budget constraint tells us, however, that this is, at best, an incomplete
description of policy.

In the intertemporal framework, one needs to specify the full set
of net taxes through time, or, sufficiently, their discounted value,
to capture the distributive impact of the budget. Here, that would
mean specifying the discounted net transfers to each taxpayer (or
class of taxpayers), $Tan_A^1 + \delta Tan_A^2$ and $Tan_B^1 + \delta Tan_B^2$. (In this case, the
government's budget constraint makes one of the two redundant
but, as before, this is an artifact of the two-person example.)

In a real-world setting, with an indefinite horizon, policy is never
projected through time in a way consistent with the government's
intertemporal budget constraint. More practically, one could hope to
specify some sort of current projection of the future net taxes, say in
the form $Tan_A^1 + \delta Tan_A^{2, projected}$ and $Tan_B^1 + \delta Tan_B^{2, projected}$. Some summary of the unresolved intertemporal budget requirement would be
needed to complete the budgetary description. In our simple econ-

omy, it could be a statement of the net tax in the aggregate that remains to be assigned to the two people in the next period, $Tan^{2,residual}_{aggregate}$. Using the intertemporal budget constraint, we relate this quantity to the known and projected net taxes by

$$Tan^{2,residual}_{aggregate} = -\frac{Tan^1_A + Tan^1_B + \delta(Tan^{2,projected}_A + Tan^{2,projected}_B)}{\delta}. \tag{6}$$

The idea generalizes to the setting of an indefinite horizon, except that some way is needed to normalize, in order to express the net tax residual on an annual basis. For example, one could ask what uniform annual aggregate net tax, starting next period, $Tan^{starting\ in\ 2,residual}_{aggregate}$, would be sufficient to satisfy the intertemporal budget constraint. This quantity would be related to the projected net taxes by

$$Tan^{starting\ in\ 2,residual}_{aggregate} = -r \sum_{j=0}^{\infty} \delta^j (Tan^{j+1,\ projected}_A + Tan^{j+1,\ projected}_B), \tag{7}$$

where r is the discount rate implicit in the discount factor, δ. Alternatively, and perhaps more helpfully, one could express the undetermined residual as the constant per capita amount, or as the constant fraction of some measure of per capita income, that would do the job.

3.4.3 Public Goods

Returning to the single-period context, let us add a public good, G. Assume it is measured in units of its cost in the private good forgone to produce it; in these units, the production possibility frontier of G and X, given labor inputs, is linear with slope -1. The budget constraints of the two citizens would be the same as in the previous case, but the outcome that they would value would now be expressed in terms of a quantity of the private good and the level of provision, g, of the public good. The government's budget constraint would become

$$Ta_A + Ta_B = Tr_A + Tr_B + g. \tag{8}$$

Now, to describe the impact of the government on the two citizens, we need the three items (Tan_A, Tan_B, g). In other words, we

need to add to the net (private good) distributive impacts of the
budget the amount of the public good provided.

One might, in addition, be interested in the *valuation* placed on the
public good. Public good provision would be the province of the
Allocation Branch in Musgrave's scheme. He conceived of the Allocation Branch as assessing the amount citizens would be willing to
pay for the public good. In his illustrative analysis, in my notation, the Allocation Branch sets a tax on citizen i of Ta_i^a, where it is
assumed that the benefit provided to i (measured by willingness to
pay in terms of the private good) is at least as great as Ta_i^a. These
taxes would be set to balance the Allocation Branch budget:

$$Ta_A^a + Ta_B^a = g. \tag{9}$$

A perhaps minor matter: The surplus generated by optimizing the
choice of g drops out of this account. (Also omitted are the shortfalls
that might be generated for one or another citizen if the level of the
public good is inefficient or if the willingness to pay is incorrectly
estimated in setting the Allocation Branch taxes.)

We would then need to put a Distribution Branch superscript on
the net taxes charged by that branch, and they would always satisfy

$$Tan_A^d + Tan_B^d = 0. \tag{10}$$

By construction, the Distribution Branch net taxes would capture
the idea of "true" redistribution of the consumption equivalent generated by the economy.

Musgrave's ideal Allocation Branch taxes raise an interesting
philosophical issue about the purpose of budgetary data. One might
argue that the objective of the budgetary figures is to give us "the
facts" about the policies of the government, leaving it to further, and
more controversial, analyses to decide on the valuation of what
government does or proposes. By contrast, Musgrave's Allocation
Branch's further step of estimating the value placed on public goods
requires a higher order of analysis that is, indeed, "utopian," relative
to today's practice which, at best, stops at accounting for the level g
of the public good provided.

3.4.4 Distorting Commodity Taxes and Subsidies

A further set of issues arises when we have more than one private
good, with the possibility of taxes and subsidies applied to them. Let

the second good be Y. To simplify, let us maintain the linearity of the production possibility frontier and choose the units of Y so that the marginal rate of transformation between X and Y is always one. Let the rate of tax on purchases of commodity j be t_j and the rate of subsidy be s_j. With these new policy instruments (and abandoning the separate Allocation and Distribution Branch distinctions), the three budget constraints of our little one-period economy become

$$(1 + t_x - s_x)x_A + (1 + t_y - s_y)y_A = w_A l_A - Tan_A, \tag{11}$$

$$(1 + t_x - s_x)x_B + (1 + t_y - s_y)y_B = w_B l_B - Tan_B, \tag{12}$$

$$Tan_A + Tan_B + t_x(x_A + x_B) + t_y(y_A + y_B) = s_x(x_A + x_B) + s_y(y_A + y_B) + g, \tag{13}$$

where the previously defined tax and transfer terms refer now just to the lump-sum components of the government's program.

An obvious point to make about this system is that it is redundant in policy instruments. Present budgetary language would, however, attach significance to the separate pieces. The bits labeled "subsidies" would be identified as expenditures, characterized not by the rates but rather by the product of rates and quantities. So the expenditure on the subsidy to good X would be recorded as $s_x(x_A + x_B)$ and the subsidy to Y as $s_y(y_A + y_B)$.

It seems that the distinction between a subsidy and a tax in the conventional sense is a matter of intent. A subsidy in the conventional sense is "on purpose" and a tax in the conventional sense (apart from a Pigouvian offset to an externality) is an unfortunate necessity. It is unclear, however, whether one can construct a satisfactory accounting distinction based on intent. If consumers and producers are looking only at real trade-offs, rather than labels, the economically significant quantities are the net tax (or subsidy) rates. If we normalize on earnings and denote the net tax on good X by tn_x, and so forth, the system of budget constraints becomes

$$(1 + tn_x)x_A + (1 + tn_y)y_A = w_A l_A - Tan_A, \tag{14}$$

$$(1 + tn_x)x_B + (1 + tn_y)y_B = w_B l_B - Tan_B, \tag{15}$$

$$Tan_A + Tan_B + tn_x(x_A + x_B) + tn_y(y_A + y_B) = g. \tag{16}$$

The key budgetary information, expressed in revenue terms, would be the net tax revenue totals, $tn_x(x_A + x_B)$ and $tn_y(y_A + y_B)$. Typically, such net tax revenue quantities would include both positive and negative (i.e., net subsidy) values. Note that this accounting would neglect the deadweight loss that might be due to the distorting taxes. Including estimates of these distortionary effects raises the same philosophical and analytical issues as does including estimates of the valuation of public goods.

Even with normalization on earnings along the lines described (so there is no tax or subsidy on working), there remains a question of how to summarize the impact of the government budget when there are many commodities. How do we summarize the set of effective taxes that come between the producer prices (unity, by choice of units) and the prices facing the consumer or worker? I have not tried to identify an answer, but perhaps one could choose some reasonable aggregates of goods and services (say, food, housing, transportation, all others) and use an aggregation of their before- and after-tax/subsidy prices derived from the index number literature.

Some thought needs to be given to how best to characterize the distributive impact of net commodity taxes on individuals. In the illustrative case, if there were no lump-sum taxes, we would have no obvious distributive information. The budget situation of the individual would nonetheless be changed by the policy compared with the situation of no net taxes and no public good provision. The impact of the policy on each individual would be captured, from a formal perspective, by the statement that the net price of X is increased by tn_x, the net price of Y by tn_y, and the level of the public good by g. All three of the measures have, in this case, the quality of public goods. But this is too much information. A useful budgetary convention would be based on a measure of the incidence of the policy package, a measure I have not tried to derive here.

3.4.5   Taxes on Earnings

The big enchilada of distorting taxes is the tax on labor supply. Suppose only a labor income tax and lump-sum taxes are used, and that the labor income tax rate applied to person i is τ_i. Then, for the single-commodity case, our budget constraints become

$$x_i = (1 - \tau_i)w_i l_i - Tan_i \text{ for } i = A, B, \tag{17}$$

$$Tan_A + \tau_A w_A l_A + Tan_B + \tau_B w_B l_B = g. \tag{18}$$

Present practice in this case would be to define the net tax on citizen i as $\tau w_i l_i + Ta_i$. This gets the story wrong, in the first place by failing to net taxes and transfers, to make it $\tau w_i l_i + Tan_i$. Further, the "proper" sign convention would call for treating the tax on labor as a negative net tax (subsidy) on nonmarket time that we conventionally call leisure. Consistency with the suggested description of commodity taxes and subsidies would suggest describing the budget in terms of the net lump-sum tax elements plus the leisure subsidies. (Also, although not strictly speaking an element of budgetary aggregates, the common characterization assigns an incidence to one transaction tax instrument—the tax on labor—that neglects proper treatment of leisure forgone as well as general equilibrium effects.)

An approach that I find intriguing is a normalizing convention such that all distorting taxes are expressed as what we conventionally call commodity taxes. This would capture the idea of a fundamental trade-off between work and various desired goods. So, a 10 percent tax on earnings would be expressed, instead, as a uniform 11 percent (i.e., $1/(1 - 0.1)$) tax on goods. Where the earnings tax rate varies from worker to worker, such net taxes on goods would be person-specific, an awkward but accurate description of economic substance. Note, however, that the approach would require identifying not simply earnings in general, but earnings at a specific time (e.g., the present), if this idea were extended to an income tax context. In that setting, there would typically be a different rate of tax on the same good at different distances into the future. Thus the rate of tax on a standard consumption good at successive dates in the future, expressed in terms of current earnings, would be higher and higher, reflecting the penalty on saving imposed by an income tax. Such a way of describing the budget's impact might affect people's attitudes toward an income tax.

Alternatively, one could normalize on some standard private good. To illustrate, consider A's budget constraint with an earnings tax and a pair of net commodity taxes, as discussed earlier:

$$(1 + tn_x)x_A + (1 + tn_y)y_A = (1 - \tau_A)w_A l_A - Tan_A. \tag{19}$$

Suppose we were to take good X as numeraire. Then the normalized budget constraint would be

$$x_A + \frac{1 + tn_y}{1 + tn_x}y_A = \frac{1 - \tau_A}{1 + tn_x}w_A l_A - \frac{Tan_A}{1 + tn_x}. \tag{20}$$

The normalization would need to be carried through all of the budget constraints, including the government's. Let me describe the resulting net tax rates, and so forth, by putting a superscript on them, so the new budget constraint looks like

$$x_A + (1 + tn_y^x)y_A = (1 - \tau_A^x)w_A l_A - Tan_A^x, \tag{21}$$

where

$$tn_y^x \equiv \frac{1 + tn_y}{1 + tn_x} - 1, \tag{22}$$

$$\tau_A^x \equiv 1 - \frac{1 - \tau_A}{1 + tn_x}, \tag{23}$$

$$Tan_A^x \equiv \frac{Tan_A}{1 + tn_x}. \tag{24}$$

A normalization of this kind can reveal some surprises. To put some illustrative numbers on the story, suppose taxpayer A is paying a 25 percent tax on earnings and getting a $1,000 net transfer; there is a 20 percent tax on commodity X and a 10 percent tax on commodity Y. Such magnitudes might well be encountered in a system with a VAT and an income or a payroll tax. With the suggested normalization, we would say that taxpayer A faces an earnings tax of 37.5 percent (reflecting the impact of the system on his ability to trade working for the numeraire good, X) and gets a net transfer of 833 units of X, with a subsidy of his purchases of Y at a rate of 8.33 percent.

Of course, the choice of numeraire good is arbitrary. More plausible than a single commodity, a standard bundle of consumer goods—purchasing power—would be a more natural choice in a real application. Thus if, in this example, we had chosen to normalize the net-of-commodity-tax prices of the goods based on some bundle of X and Y, instead of on X alone, the story would imply some small (less than the 20 percent nominal rate) net tax on X and a smaller than 8.33 percent net subsidy of purchases of Y.

Before leaving this set of issues, I might add yet one more complicating factor: If the linearity assumption about the production system is invalid, specifying for each person the applicable rate of earnings tax, the appropriate net commodity taxes, and the lump-sum tax (together with the level of public goods provided) is, in principle, no longer sufficient to determine the impact of the government's program on that person. That is because the program overall will generally affect wage rates, quite possibly the most important way a program affects a person. Allen (1982) provides a striking example in which "standard" views about the progressivity of a tax are overturned by general equilibrium effects on skill-related wages.

3.4.6 Tax Expenditures

Finally, this setup of the problem may yield some insight into the problem of tax expenditures. Returning to the two-commodity example, take the case in which the taxes and subsidies on X are zero (or where we have normalized on commodity X), but a deduction is allowed from the earnings tax base for the purchase of Y. Then the budget constraints become

$$x_A + (1 + t_y - s_y)y_A = (1 - \tau_A)[w_A l_A - (1 + t_y - s_y)y_A] - Ta_A + Tr_A, \quad (25)$$

$$x_B + (1 + t_y - s_y)y_B = (1 - \tau_B)[w_B l_B - (1 + t_y - s_y)y_B] - Ta_B + Tr_B, \quad (26)$$

where I have neglected the government's budget constraint in the interest of reducing the clutter. These budget constraints can be reduced to a "canonical" form (prices times quantities of goods on the left, and after-tax wage times labor supply plus lump-sum transfer on the right) by some algebra. I reproduce here A's budget constraint:

$$x_A + [1 + t_y - s_y + (1 - \tau_A)(1 + t_y - s_y)]y_A = (1 - \tau_A)w_A l_A - Tan_A. \quad (27)$$

One way to describe this constraint is to say it involves a net tax, $tn_{y,i}$, on Y, specific to person i, which is defined (for the case of person A) by

$$tn_{y,A} \equiv t_y - s_y + (1 - \tau_A)(1 + t_y - s_y). \quad (28)$$

If we wanted to describe the resulting government program as "spending" on Y (e.g., as a subsidy program for housing), we could multiply the implicit subsidy rates and quantities, to obtain a total:

$$tn_{y,A}y_A + tn_{y,B}y_B. \quad (29)$$

I would not claim it is beautiful, but it is unambiguous.

3.5 Application to the Four Examples

Having in mind the ideas developed somewhat formally for our little model economy, we may consider whether there is any practical progress to be made on the four illustrative problem cases.

3.5.1 Tax and Expenditure Sides of the Budget

With respect to the example of the alternative views of including more Social Security benefits in the base of the income tax, the basic point is that it should not make the slightest difference whether something is called a tax increase or an expenditure cut, and therefore it should not affect our view of the policy, whether we like it or not. We should be looking for a language that describes the underlying reality. Note that it is not just that present conventions are arbitrary, the way a foot or a meter is an arbitrary unit of length. As these cases clearly indicate, an arbitrary standard could have plenty of meaning. It is that present conventions are not grounded in economic reality, and therefore cannot suffice to describe it.

It seems to me an approach worth exploring would be to reserve the term "spending" or "expenditures" for something like government purchases of goods and services as inputs to the production of public goods. Assuming for the moment that we can make such a distinction among outlays (for purposes of national income accounting, we already identify purchases of goods and services), it would seem to provide a useful normalization of the amount of public goods provided in the budget.

The term "taxes" might be used to refer to the net transfer of funds to the government in a year. Under this convention, the president would be obliged to say, "In my plan, I propose to change the income tax rules to increase the taxes on retirees by $21.4 billion, to increase the taxes on higher-income individuals by $120 billion (or whatever it is), etc." If there is too much emotional freight attached to the term "taxes," one could, alternatively, use language of net transfers from the government. Under this convention, the president would say, "In my plan, I propose to change the income tax rules to reduce the net transfers from the government to retirees by $21.4 billion, to reduce the net transfer to higher-income individuals by $120 billion (or whatever it is), etc." It is true that this would take some getting used to. But, even if we did not insist on the president changing his rhetorical stripes, we could insist on the government keeping its books on such a basis.

Once we have expressed the government's accounts on a meaningful basis, it should be easier to focus the policy debate on the substance. The substance, in this case, is essentially distributive, and so it is most unlikely that aggregates (e.g., the statement that the net transfers increase by $60 billion this year) are going to answer the questions that ought to interest people. We can see this clearly if we conceive of a government that engages only in redistribution. In that case, for every dollar paid in to the government in "taxes," there would be a dollar paid out in "transfers." The aggregate is algebraically zero. Further, even if we distinguish the payments in from the payments out (as we probably should not, unless incentives are involved), the aggregate of either is of little consequence. In particular, it tells us little of interest about the size of government. What matters is the net gain or loss of one or another group in the society, and it is this that ought to be available to us, at various levels of detail, in the information on the budget.

As in the example of the president's speech, the interesting questions to be addressed with information about net transfers concern who gives and who receives, on net. We presume it does not matter to the retiree whether his Social Security benefit is cut by $200 or his income tax is increased by $200 (although maybe people do care about this). It seems to me that there are likely to be many ways of disaggregating net transfers according to the characteristics of the people involved. Ability to pay or "income" of the payer or recipient is an obvious category of interest. This is the information addressed in a standard "distribution table," commonly used to describe income taxes. The perspective suggested here would involve relating a measure of net transfers to some measure of a person's pre-fiscal-system opportunities or abilities, in contrast to the typical procedure followed today, in the United States at least, that counts explicit transfers, if at all, as part of the income "classifier." An ideal presentation would take a comprehensive approach, encompassing, for example, corporation income taxes, in-kind transfer programs, excise taxes, and state and local income and sales taxes. (Bradford 1995 provides an overview of these procedures and a discussion of alternatives in the U.S. context.)

Age or generation is likely to be of interest as well as perhaps health status. A well-constructed set of budget accounts should make it easy for policymakers and citizens to explore the impact of programs, and especially changes in programs, on various groups of concern.

This general approach would cry out for elaboration. For example, should one attempt to keep track of net transfers from government on the basis of an extended time, perhaps a person's lifetime? (Such issues would naturally arise in connection with the incidence of sharp transitions in policy, as, e.g., in some versions of a transition from the present income tax to some versions of consumption tax.) In thinking about categories of affected individuals, what is the place for "special-interest" groups, such as farmers or auto workers or tort lawyers?

I leave these questions for future speculation. But one assumption I have blithely made above deserves to be revisited—namely, the assumption that we can distinguish outlays that provide public goods, with the presumption that other outlays belong in the transfer category. For one thing, many outlays for goods and services are pretty clear substitutes for cash transfers to people: Clinics providing healthcare to people of limited economic means would be an example. But government statisticians should be able to make reasonable calls about these. For another thing, some outlays have as their purpose advancing the economic interests of some constituency. A subsidy to domestic construction of merchant ships would be an example. It would add too much to the length of this chapter to pursue these issues here.

3.5.2 Budget Deficits

As it affects the budget sets of individuals, the problem of the government budget "deficit" is essentially one of distribution across generations. "Controlling the deficit" or "protecting the surplus" generally means, economically, shifting net fiscal burdens toward presently living (and perhaps especially the older among them) and away from future (and perhaps the younger among the presently living) generations. This viewpoint has been translated into practical accounting procedures in considerable detail in the "generational accounting" framework originated by Alan Auerbach, Laurence Kotlikoff, and colleagues. (For an early exposition of the approach, see Auerbach, Gokhale, and Kotlikoff 1991. Kotlikoff [1992] provides an extended and entertaining treatment that documents the widespread confusion about the issues in the profession. Auerbach, Kotlikoff, and Leibfritz [1999] present an application of generational accounting to the budgetary pictures of many countries around the world. Unfortunately, official generational account estimates for the United States were discontinued in 1994.)

The interests of different subgroups of the population would be expressed by a variety of "cuts" at the distribution of net transfers. The essential idea of generational accounts is to present the distribution according to birth cohorts. Auerbach and his colleagues have suggested various ways to characterize what I have called the "residual" net tax needed to comply with the intertemporal budget constraint. For example, one way is to calculate the hypothetical average uniform tax on earnings levied on all people with birth dates after the accounting year that would be required. Both generational accounting and this particular way of quantifying what Shaviro (1997) calls the "budget lag" are controversial and require a great many more or less speculative steps. On the other hand, they seem to me essential tools for fiscal planning.

3.5.3 Tax Expenditures

How should we deal with the problem exemplified by my WSTC? Here, we have the government acquiring some goods and services for purposes of providing a public good, national defense. The aggregate of such goods and services is, arguably, reasonably measured by the expenditure, and the expenditure is the same, whether it is the result of appropriating money and paying contractors in the usual way or of providing a credit against income tax for people who supply the desired goods and services. It is therefore compelling that these two approaches to the problem of dealing with national defense should show up comparably in the budget.

The term "tax expenditures" was coined by then Assistant Secretary of the U.S. Treasury Stanley Surrey. (His viewpoint can be found in Surrey and McDaniel 1985; see also the discussion in Bradford 1986.) In his attempt to capture the equivalence between spending programs and features of the income tax law, Surrey conceived of tax expenditures as deviations from some sort of ideal or normal version of the tax. Application of the idea therefore requires identification of the normal or reference tax. Insofar as the reference tax has tended to be interpreted normatively, as what the system "should" be, it has naturally attracted controversy and reduced the appreciation of the analytically unassailable point of the exercise.

My particular policy preference for consumption rather than Haig-Simons income taxation provides a case in point. The consumption-type treatment of retirement saving under the existing income tax is regarded by tax expenditure analysis as a subsidy to such saving. By contrast, if a consumption-type tax is taken as the reference standard, the retirement saving provisions are "correct" and capital income taxes would be regarded as a negative subsidy (i.e., a tax!) on saving.

The missing element in this structure is the neutral status quo ante, corresponding to the zero expenditure on defense against which the defense outlay is measured. Unlike the conventional income tax baseline used in current tax expenditure accounting, there is no controversy about the baseline in the case of conventional expenditures. As our simple two-person economy suggests, it is conceptually possible to construct a measure of the expenditure programs implicit in our "tax" provisions that has the same normative neutrality as other budgetary information. The example also suggests that a great deal of work is required to make that translation in a manner that can be understood in a policy context. In the meantime, we can take two messages from this discussion. First, it is essential to provide tax expenditure estimates. Second, the reference baseline used should be treated as analytically convenient, and not normative.

3.5.4 Regulatory Taxing and Spending

A first principle ought to be that whatever measures we adopt recognize as equivalent policies that accomplish the same thing through "conventional" budgetary programs and through regulatory programs. In each of these cases, we could, with some ingenuity perhaps, construct a program of lump-sum grants and price subsidies that accomplishes the same thing as the regulatory program. Programs that translate into the same lump-sum grant plus price subsidies effects should be recognizable as equivalent.

As an aside, the examples I cite differ in one interesting respect: The environmental regulation is producing a public good; the healthcare insurance regulation is producing a more complicated result, more like a requirement that people eat three times a day up to a certain standard.

It ought to be emphasized that regulatory programs can accomplish significant redistributive effects. Indeed, while there are some market failure arguments, it seems to me that the distributive issues are often the dominant ones in the case of regulation. The nominal objective of obligatory health insurance, for example, is to redistribute from those with good health characteristics toward those with poor health characteristics, and typically even more important, from the relatively better-off toward the relatively poor. In addition, transition effects may imply intergenerational impacts. (The implied redistribution from younger toward older cohorts in the population that would be effected by compulsory health insurance using age-independent "community rating" premiums is examined in Bradford and Max 1997.)

The practical approach to recognizing the implicit taxing and spending in regulations is to push, to the extent possible, the careful translation of these programs into conventional taxing and spending programs and the adding of them to the budgetary information. This would be a substantial departure from current practices.

3.6 Conclusion

Musgrave's conceptual division of the government's program into Allocation and Distribution Branch subbudgets retains its analytical power, even if the Stabilization Branch now may require a rather different treatment. The present chapter has argued that progress towards Musgrave's ideal of a more informative budgetary language—one less or, ideally, not at all dependent on arbitrary institutional labeling—must be based on the nonarbitrary description of the individual's economic environment, as it is affected by government. As a first approximation, that environment can be summed up in terms of the individual's budget constraint and levels of public goods provided. Simple models suggest that an unambiguous budgetary language may be feasible but there remains much to clarify about both the objectives of the exercise and the specifics of methods to deal with particular problems. I conclude that significant improvement is possible, although both practical and conceptual problems present an interesting agenda for future research.

Notes

I would like to thank William Gale, Sherry Glied, Deborah Lucas, Daniel Shaviro, and Joel Slemrod, as well as participants at the CESifo conference, "Public Finances and Public Policy in the New Millennium," University of Munich, January 12–13, 2001, especially Henry Aaron, for helpful comments and conversations.

References

Allen, F. 1982. "Optimal Linear Income Taxation with General Equilibrium Effects on Wages." *Journal of Public Economics* 17: 135–143.

Auerbach, A. J., J. Gokhale, and L. J. Kotlikoff. 1991. "Generational Accounts: Meaningful Alternative to Deficit Accounting." In *Tax Policy and the Economy*, vol. 5, ed. D. F. Bradford, 55–110.

Auerbach, A. J., L. J. Kotlikoff, and W. Leibfritz. 1999. *Generational Accounting Around the World*. Chicago: University of Chicago Press.

Beaver, W. H., and W. Landsman. 1983. *Incremental Information Content of Statement Thirty-Three Disclosures*. Financial Accounting Standards Board.

Bradford, D. F. 1986. *Untangling the Income Tax*. Cambridge: Harvard University Press.

Bradford, D. F., ed. 1995. *Distributional Analysis of Tax Policy*. Washington, DC: AEI Press.

Bradford, D. F., and D. A. Max. 1997. "Implicit Budget Deficits: The Case of a Mandated Shift to Community-Rated Health Insurance." In *Tax Policy and the Economy*, vol. 11, ed. J. M. Poterba, 129–167. (Revised version issued as *Intergenerational Transfers Under Community Rating*. 1996. Washington, DC: AEI Press.)

Kotlikoff, L. J. 1992. *Generational Accounting: Knowing Who Pays, and When, for What We Spend*. New York: Free Press.

Musgrave, R. A. 1959. *The Theory of Public Finance: A Study in Public Economy*. New York: McGraw-Hill.

Shaviro, D. 1997. *Do Deficits Matter?* Chicago: University of Chicago Press.

Surrey, S. S., and P. R. McDaniel. 1985. *Tax Expenditures*. Cambridge: Harvard University Press.

Comments

Henry J. Aaron

David Bradford points out that budget categories, in the United States and elsewhere, contain conventions that make no economic sense. He proposes modifications to correct those flaws. The modifications would end certain arbitrary distinctions expressed in current budget categories. They would also create a new system of hyperlinked accounts. The scars and frustrations of a Princeton don who has jousted with the political barbarians are apparent in his examples. As a full-time resident in the land of the philistines—that is, Washington, DC—I share his frustrations and more. But I believe that the solutions he proposes are both impracticable and subject to as much abuse as the current system he correctly deplores. Simpler, less elegant, and less intellectually defensible changes, in my view, would do more practical good. My comments stem from the view that "'Good in theory, but bad in practice' really means 'Bad in theory.'"

The topic Bradford addresses is particularly timely in the United States, Europe, and elsewhere. Under current budget conventions, the United States is experiencing sizable budget surpluses that are projected to grow for many years. Eventually, however, current projections indicate that deficits will emerge. Deficits return because outlays on health and pension benefits for the elderly will rise sharply under current law. The difference between the short- and long-run situations raises the question of whether the United States should regard its budget as being in surplus or in deficit. Over the next year, the answer is clear. But the reliability of the estimates diminishes sharply as one looks further into the future.[1] There is no reason to think that current long-run projections are biased, but there is ample reason to believe that one can place little or no confidence in point estimates of distant future budgets.

To drive home this point, I cite revisions of the budget for the year 2005 produced by the U.S. Congressional Budget Office (CBO) over the period from 1995 to 2000. In 1995, the CBO forecast a deficit of approximately $400 billion for the year 2005. In 2000, it forecast a surplus of nearly $500 billion for the year 2005—a swing of nearly $1 trillion in the balance for a single year—based entirely on changes in the real economy and in healthcare spending and *apart from all changes in public policy*. I return to this matter of uncertainty later in my comments.

But even if one ignores uncertainty, are current budget measures or future projections meaningful? I begin with the problem that I think Bradford is addressing and restate why the current accounts are arbitrary, misleading, and subject to abuse. But I suggest that conceptually correct solutions to these problems are vastly beyond our capacity to implement—so far, in fact, that trying to implement them would make matters much, much worse. Along the way, I explain why I think Bradford's proposed "fixes," as well as others that he praises such as generational accounts, are unsatisfactory and as subject to manipulation as the current system.

Budget accounts are a collection of date-stamped, financial flows classified more or less arbitrarily as taxes, transfers, and exhaustive expenditures. These flows may affect factor incomes as well. As a result, they have both direct and indirect effects on resource allocation and the distribution of real incomes among individuals and over time. The generic problem can be stated simply. Voters reward elected officials for achieving budget balance and for providing various tax breaks and expenditures. These goals conflict. For that reason, elected officials try to do good things for their constituents without jeopardizing budget balance. Furthermore, at least in the United States, voters regard keeping the government small as a political virtue. For this reason, elected officials structure their actions to make it appear that they have kept budgets small and government employment low.

Bradford's examples illustrate such efforts. Example 1 shows that changes in transfers and taxes are not logically distinct. He might also have cited the convention in the United States of labeling that portion of the tax-based earnings subsidy that reduces payments by the taxpayer as a negative tax and the portion that results in positive payments to the taxpayer as a transfer. This practice attaches a sig-

nificance to the zero point on the number line that should shame
anyone who has taken first-year algebra.

The author points out with his example 2 that the effects of budgets measured over a year or even a few years into the future may be
altogether different from the effects of that budget policy over the
very long run. In addition, he might have cited the example of the
extension by Congress of a deduction for saving structured to encourage short-term realizations of capital income. This bit of legerdemain
permitted legislators to brag that a tax change that cut revenues in
present-value terms was actually a revenue raiser measured over the
ten-year budget window now in use in the United States.

Example 3 illustrates the well-known preference of U.S. elected
officials for tax incentives over direct government spending to
achieve the same purpose. The former make taxes smaller, while the
latter makes expenditures bigger. Functional similarity be damned!
Cutting taxes makes the government smaller, you see, even if it
extends government influence, while expenditure increases that are
functionally similar make the government larger.

Example 4 extends the same principle to central government regulations, which can mandate spending by individuals, businesses,
or subsidiary governments without significantly modifying central
government spending or taxes.

I am not sure that Bradford's list exhausts the ways in which
budget accounts can present misleading or flatly false pictures of
what the government is really doing, but it is a very good start.

How could one correct these problems? The answer, I think, is
that the only way to escape them entirely would be to have a fully
articulated and completely reliable general equilibrium model, all of
whose parameters are generally accepted, that shows the effects on
the discounted, present value of each individual's (or family's) and
each business's real, infinite-horizon net worth. Without such a tool,
some important potential effects of government policy are omitted
from one's calculation. And if something is omitted, elected officials
will be tempted to frame proposals so that costs are excluded and
benefits are included or so that government appears smaller than it
really is. Forestalling such misleading practices is what Bradford
hopes to achieve with his reforms.

Well, we do not have that fully articulated, completely reliable,
universally accepted general equilibrium model. And we never will.

So, the problem of finding the correct set of budget concepts is unsolvable as a practical matter. Budget reformers will be updating Bradford's chapter forever. The good news is that abuses of any given set of rules are likely eventually to elicit budget reforms that correct them. The bad news is that the new rules will call forth new abuses.

Furthermore, I think that Bradford's observation that government statisticians are capable of making the judgments necessary to produce the hyperlinked budget accounts he proposes is incorrect. In support of this charge, I cite generational accounts, whose departure from official U.S. accounts he mourns and I celebrate. Generational accounts are based on projections stretching more than a century into the future of the tax rates that will have to be paid by particular cohorts based on extrapolations of various assumptions regarding program structure, economic growth, and real interest rates. In addition, generational accounts entirely exclude the value to particular cohorts of various publicly financed expenditures, such as those on education. A reform of the U.S. Medicare health program for the elderly and disabled enacted in 1997 that modestly changed the structure of the Medicare program lowered the projected tax rate applicable to the unborn by an estimated 30 percentage points. Assumed changes in compound growth rates of healthcare spending stretching into the indefinite future were responsible for the shift.

In fact, public healthcare spending is impossible to forecast accurately even a few years into the future because it is driven principally by technological changes and by constantly evolving private and public policies for which no analyst has satisfactory models. Such revision played a major part in that $1 trillion shift in the projected annual U.S. budget balance for the year 2005 that I cited earlier.

If analysts could be so wrong about compound growth rates over just a five- to ten-year period, what hope is there for agreement on growth rates stretching into the distant future? The speed with which such large errors can emerge raises very large questions regarding the weight that should be attached to projected out-year expenditures and revenues in current budget debates. This whole area has received scant attention from public finance economists and cries out for serious analysis.

Generational accounts are splendid tools for instruction and for seminar papers. They teach useful lessons to graduate students in economics. But they are terrible instruments if made central to the political process, for two reasons. First, they fail to attach probability weights or uncertainty ranges to far-distant projections. Let me emphasize that it is not at all clear how this matter of uncertainty should be handled. But generational accounts simply ignore uncertainty. Second, they sublimate profoundly significant political questions as technical matters that few citizens or elected officials can be expected to understand and about which consensus is unlikely even if they do understand them. To assume that laws that have been revised frequently in response to actual conditions will remain unchanged for a century or more is indefensible. To expect budget accounts, economists, or statisticians, to say nothing of elected officials for whom projections are matters of political life and death, to reach consensus on the likely course of distant events is ivory-tower nonsense.

So, where does that leave us? Let me suggest as a metaphor the story of the little Dutch boy who finds a hole in the dike and puts his finger in it until the grown-ups come along to plug it. In this case, public finance economists and budget analysts are a team of little boys tending a budgetary dike that has lots of holes. Only, these holes are different—they leak water only when someone is looking at them. Unfortunately, there are bad people—let us call them politicians—who tirelessly try to spot holes so that they can make them leak. When nasty politicians spot a hole and make it leak, alert economists must scurry over to stick their fingers in the holes until eventually the hole is plugged. Some people—let us call them Bradfords—think that when the current set of holes are plugged, the problem is solved. But the dastardly politicians never sleep, and there is an infinite stock of holes. The game will never end. But it takes time to find new holes. So, with sufficient vigilance by the Bradfords, the dikes will hold and the land will be safe.

In considering what sorts of budget accounting rules we should adopt, I think it is important to remember not only that unabusable rules do not, and never will, exist but also that the requirements for serviceable official accounts differ from the standards of academic analysis. Nonetheless, I urge certain principles.

First, official accounts should be reasonably simple, reasonably stable, and not readily subject to manipulation in ways that cannot readily be detected or corrected by laypersons. They should be simple because elected officials communicate in simple terms. Elected officials do not, cannot, and will not communicate in confidence intervals, probability distributions, or multiple alternatives. Budget categories must be simple so that manipulations of data can be easily understood. By simple, I mean that most of the policy elite—lawyers, business executives, and journalists, for example, few of whom are mathematically sophisticated and many of whom are nearly innumerate—can understand what is going on.

Second, stability of concepts is important because *changes* in budgets, rather than *levels*, are most important for political purposes. If revisions of assumptions or methods cause large year-to-year changes in reported expenditures or taxes, few people will be able to distinguish such changes from those caused by policy shifts. If official series are subject to large changes originating in assumptions or methods or from events that are palpably minor, most people will assume that the statistics are worthless and will disregard them. That means that official budget data should not, in general, depend on discounted present values which are acutely sensitive to variations in assumed growth or discount rates.

On these standards, many of the budgetary innovations that economists celebrate are harmful. Generational accounts are notoriously unstable, with the long-term tax rates jumping 30 or 40 percentage points in a single year because of legislation that has small effects today but is estimated to affect compound growth rates of variables fifty to one hundred or more years into the future. More generally, generational accounts also depend sensitively on judgments about which honest analysts can honestly disagree.

Similar criticisms can be leveled against the inclusion of tax expenditures in official budgets. As Bradford notes, what constitutes a tax expenditure depends on one's principles of taxation, a matter on which reputable economists and others disagree. Capital budgets are also potentially mischievous. What is capital or consumption is easily manipulated and the rewards to successful manipulation are high, since prudent finance dictates that we pay for consumption with current taxes, but it is responsible to borrow to pay for capital.

Bradford's proposed budget devices would entail a proliferation of accounts that depend with exquisite sensitivity on a myriad of elasticities and projections. Each of the accounts may well be useful to someone, just as each of the myriad of current national income accounts now is of value to someone. But, in the end, what counts for political debate is less the *level* of each of the aggregates than the *changes* from year to year. For that reason, conceptual errors that distort the *levels* of taxes or expenditures may offend our senses of intellectual purity, but they do less harm to public debate than do distortions of *changes* from year to year. For similar reasons, budget accounts that depend on estimates of behavioral elasticities, such as those for labor supply or saving, should be avoided. The reason is not that these elasticities are unimportant or that we do not ache to know them. Quite the reverse. They are so important but consensus is so elusive that we lack the standards for fiscal honesty necessary to minimize and police political manipulation. Those are the holes in the dike. By increasing their salience in political debate, Bradford's reforms would exacerbate the very problems he seeks to solve.

My own view is that in the U.S. context, the most serious threats to good budgetary accounting come from time-based manipulations. U.S. budget debates focus on flows estimated over a ten-year period. Placing increased expenditures or reduced taxes outside the ten-year budget window reduces the apparent cost of the proposal and increases its chance of enactment. It also places budget effects in a future we are unable to foresee accurately. And so, we get tax cuts that are phased in slowly over our ten-year budget horizon and are fully effective only in the ninth or tenth year. We also get expenditure proposals that start small but explode in cost in the "out years." Given our incapacity to forecast accurately for more than a few months into the future, we are making commitments that we cannot know our capacity to honor.

I do not pretend to have a full list of "fixes" for actual and potential budget abuses. But I would suggest serious consideration of some modest changes suggested by Robert Reischauer, former director of the U.S. Congressional Budget Office. These modifications include the following:

1. Accounts of government pensions should be excluded from the annual budget debate. These and possibly other programs constitute long-term commitments. This exclusion does not excuse such programs from periodic scrutiny, but it should signal that legislative modifications will not be negotiated as frequently as are changes in outlays for current services.

2. Legislatures should adopt limits on the proportion of projected future surpluses that can be currently committed. The proportion should diminish with time in recognition of our limited capacity to foresee the future.

3. Legislatures should adopt explicit procedures for estimating the current cost of credit programs and future expenditures and revenues of programs financed by earmarked taxes. It is more important that these rules be stable and transparent so that abuses can be readily detected than that they be precisely correct.

4. To the extent that legislative rules or constitutions permit, changes in budget rules should be inhibited. The requirement of the U.S. Senate that its own rules can only be changed by a 60 percent majority is illustrative.

These reforms will not solve the problem that Bradford has addressed. But neither will the measures he has proposed. The difference is that the ones I have suggested have some chance of being implemented and understood. And it will be easier to detect when they have been violated.

Note

1. These projections, based on the situation in early 2001 when the CESifo conference was held, have turned out to be remarkably short-lived. Tax cuts, a recession, and increased homeland defense and military spending in the wake of the September 11, 2001, terrorist attacks converted projected surpluses into projected deficits. The longer-run prospects are correspondingly worse, as well.

II

Taxation and Tax Reform

4

Perfect Taxation with Imperfect Competition

Alan J. Auerbach and
James R. Hines Jr.

4.1 Introduction

Perfect taxation—or, as it is more commonly known, optimal taxation—typically entails distorting the economy in order to redistribute resources, provide public goods, or advance other government objectives. Tax policy is defined to be "perfect" if it minimizes distortions and thereby maximizes economic efficiency subject to meeting other government requirements. In the case of economies already distorted by imperfect competition in private markets, corrective taxation has the potential to enhance the efficiency of private resource allocation. In order to realize this potential, governments must be able and willing to use their available tax instruments in an informed and sensible fashion.

Richard Musgrave's ninetieth birthday is an appropriate occasion to reexamine the features of perfect taxation, since much of Musgrave's work is devoted to characterizing optimal government policies. His influential classic *The Theory of Public Finance* categorizes these settings, providing nuggets of detailed insight while embedding its analysis in a general equilibrium consideration of the many ramifications of government policy. On the subject of imperfect competition, Musgrave (1959, 149–150) describes the corrective subsidy, following it with the observation: "Since the assumption of pure competition is unrealistic, our earlier conclusions must be qualified accordingly. At the same time, allocation in the market is not altogether chaotic. Therefore, we are still well advised to prefer the general tax unless there is a clear case for correcting a specific imperfection."

The purpose of this chapter is to consider in some detail the nature of perfect tax policies in imperfectly competitive markets. Section

4.2 uses a partial equilibrium setting to characterize tax policies that induce imperfectly competitive firms to select efficient output levels. These policies generally take the form of subsidies that encourage firms to expand output. Section 4.3 then reviews several of the general second-best welfare issues that arise whenever governments are forced to rely on distortionary tax instruments in order to raise revenue.

Section 4.4 analyzes the impact of distortionary taxation on the design of specific taxation in the presence of imperfect competition. The need to raise tax revenue with distortionary instruments naturally dampens the enthusiasm of the government to provide subsidies to output by firms in imperfectly competitive industries. Section 4.5 considers the same issues with ad valorem rather than specific taxation. While ad valorem taxes are generally welfare-superior to specific taxes in environments with imperfect competition, perfect government policy with either type of tax entails the same trade-offs between optimal correction of market imperfection and the cost of raising revenue with distorting taxes.

Section 4.6 offers a numerical analysis of perfect corrective taxation (of both the specific and ad valorem varieties) in a simple economy. Section 4.7 investigates the impact on government policy of uncertainty over the degree of market competition. The perfect response to uncertainty is generally to reduce the magnitude of the corrective tax policy, since states of the world in which little or no correction is necessary are also those in which corrective policies have the greatest market impact. Section 4.8 is the conclusion.

4.2 Perfect Commodity Taxation with Cournot Competition

It is helpful to start by considering the behavior of a firm acting as a Cournot competitor in an industry with a fixed number n of firms.[1] Firms in this industry produce homogeneous products. The government imposes a specific tax on output at rate t, so firm i's profit is given by

$$Px_i - tx_i - C(x_i), \tag{1}$$

in which P is the market price of the firm's output, x_i the quantity it produces, and $C(x_i)$ the cost of producing output level x_i. In this partial equilibrium setting, it is appropriate to take P to be a univariate function of industry output, denoted X.

The firm's first-order condition for profit maximization is

$$P + x_i \frac{dP}{dX}(1 + \theta) - t = C'(x_i), \tag{2}$$

in which θ is firm i's conjectural variation, corresponding to $dX/dx_i - 1$. Differing market structures correspond to differing values of θ. In a Cournot-Nash setting, in which firm i believes that its quantity decisions do not affect the quantities produced by its competitors, $\theta = 0$. In a perfectly competitive setting, $\theta = -1$. Various Stackelberg possibilities correspond to values of θ that can differ from these, and, indeed, need not lie in the $[-1, 0]$ interval.

It is useful to consider the pricing implications of (2).[2] Differentiating both sides of (2) with respect to t, taking θ to be unaffected by t, and limiting consideration to symmetric equilibria (so that $x_i = X/n$, $C(x_i) = C(X/n)$, and, since $dX/dt = (dP/dt)/(dP/dX)$, it follows that $dx_i/dt = (dP/dt)/(n\,dP/dX)$), then

$$\frac{dP}{dt} = \left\{ 1 + \frac{1+\theta}{n}(1+\eta) - \frac{C''(X/n)}{n\,dP/dX} \right\}^{-1}, \tag{3}$$

in which $\eta \equiv (d^2P/dX^2)X/(dP/dX)$ is the elasticity of the inverse demand function for X. From (3), it is clear that dP/dt can exceed unity, a possibility that is consistent with the firm's second-order condition for profit maximization and with other conditions (discussed by Seade 1980a, b) that correspond to industry stability. The possibility that dP/dt exceeds unity corresponds to situations in which the specific tax is overshifted. Overshifting has intrigued public finance economists at least since the time of Edgeworth.

Equations (2) and (3) identify the potential welfare impact of taxation in the presence of imperfect competition. From (2), the combination of imperfect competition ($\theta > -1$) and a downward-sloping inverse demand function ($dP/dX < 0$) implies that firms choose output levels at which price exceeds marginal cost. Hence, there is deadweight loss in the absence of taxation, and, in this simple partial equilibrium setting, tax policies that stimulate additional output reduce deadweight loss, while those that reduce output increase it. In some circumstances, the imposition of a tax may reduce industry output sufficiently that after-tax profits actually rise.

Tax policy can be used to reduce or eliminate the allocative inefficiency due to imperfect competition, though other policy instruments (such as antitrust enforcement) are also typically available and may be more cost-effective at correcting the problem.[3] Taking alternative remedies to be unavailable, the perfect policy, if the government has access to lump-sum taxation, is to guarantee marginal cost pricing by setting $t = (X/n)(dP/dX)(1 + \theta)$.[4] Since $dP/dX < 0$, this corrective method entails subsidizing the output of the imperfectly competitive industry.

Quite apart from what one might think about the normative desirability of offering subsidies to oligopolists,[5] any such corrective scheme encounters three immediate difficulties. The first is that government funds used to subsidize the output of oligopolists must be obtained with taxes that typically distort the rest of the economy. The second is that the degree of competition in an oligopoly is typically not known with certainty. And the third is that subsidies encourage industry entry, which can reduce the oligopolistic cohesion of competitors but may do so at the cost of wasted resources, since a firm's average cost typically exceeds its marginal cost in these settings. Sections 4.4 and 4.5 consider the implications of distortionary taxation for perfect corrective taxation and section 4.7 introduces uncertainty.[6]

4.3   Optimal Taxation

In order to evaluate the effect of costly tax revenue on the design of perfect corrective policies, it is necessary to impose an exogenous revenue requirement on a setting in which the government has access to distortionary tax instruments. Ramsey (1927) introduced this problem and analyzed its main features. This section first reviews the properties of the basic Ramsey result and then considers important extensions to cases in which producer prices change and in which there are consumption externalities.

4.3.1   Distortionary Tax Revenue

The simplest version of the Ramsey tax problem abstracts from population heterogeneity and posits that the government must raise a fixed sum of tax revenue with proportional commodity taxes, leaving to the side how such revenue is to be spent. With a population of identical individuals, typically analyzed as a single representative individual, the goal of perfect tax design is to minimize the excess burden associated with raising the needed revenue. We typically rationalize government's inability to use lump-sum taxes by saying that such taxes are inequitable, although this may seem a bit forced in a setting with identical individuals. It may help to think of this simple problem as a necessary building block, rather than as one that adequately models a realistic situation.

The representative consumer maximizes utility, $U(\mathbf{x})$, over a vector of commodities x_i ($i = 0, 1, \ldots, N$), subject to the budget constraint $\mathbf{p}'\mathbf{x} \leq y$, where $\mathbf{p}$ is the corresponding vector of consumer prices and y is lump-sum income. To raise the required level of revenue, R, the government imposes a vector of specific taxes on the commodities, $\mathbf{t}$, driving a wedge between consumer prices and producer prices, $\mathbf{q}$. It is useful to assume initially that this vector of producer prices is fixed. With given producer prices, the government in setting tax rates is effectively choosing the consumer price vector, since $\mathbf{p} = \mathbf{q} + \mathbf{t}$. Thus, the government's optimal tax problem can be modeled as

$$\max_{\mathbf{p}} \; V(\mathbf{p}, y), \text{ subject to } (\mathbf{p} - \mathbf{q})'\mathbf{x} \geq R, \tag{4}$$

where $V(\cdot)$ is the household's indirect utility function.

With no lump-sum income, two tax systems are equivalent if they differ by proportional taxes on all commodities. Without lump-sum income, one is therefore free to normalize one of the taxes, say on good 0, to zero, and for convenience choose the same good as numeraire, that is, $q_0 = p_0 = 1$. The maximization problem in (4), with the multiplier μ associated with the budget constraint, yields N first-order conditions:

$$-\lambda x_i + \mu \left[x_i + \sum_j t_j \frac{dx_j}{dp_i} \right] = 0 \qquad \text{for } i = 1, \ldots, N, \tag{5}$$

in which $\lambda \equiv \partial V(\mathbf{p}, y)/\partial y$ is the marginal utility of income. Making use of the Slutsky decomposition, (5) implies

$$\sum_j t_j S_{ji} = -\frac{\mu - \alpha}{\mu} x_i \qquad \text{for } i = 1, \ldots, N, \tag{6}$$

where S_{ji} is the jith element of the Slutsky matrix $S \equiv d\mathbf{x}^c/d\mathbf{p}$ and $\alpha = \lambda + \mu \sum_j t_j (dx_j/dy)$ is the "social" marginal utility of income that includes the value of the additional tax revenue raised when the household receives another unit of income.[7] Before interpreting (6), it is useful to consider the more general case of variable producer prices.

4.3.2 Changing Producer Prices

Since the excess burden of a tax is a function of the extent to which the tax changes producer prices, it follows intuitively that allowing producer prices to vary alters the first-order conditions for the optimal tax schedule. Let the general production function be characterized by

$$f(\mathbf{z}) \leq 0, \tag{7}$$

where $\mathbf{z}$ is the production vector and perfect competition ensures that $q_i/q_j = f_i/f_j$ for all i and j. Without loss of generality, the units of the production function can be chosen such that $q_i = f_i$ for all i. If there are constant returns to scale, then $f(\cdot)$ is homogeneous of degree zero in $\mathbf{z}$. Otherwise, there may be pure profits, $\pi = \mathbf{q}'\mathbf{z} > 0$.

With changing producer prices, it is not appropriate to specify the constraint in the optimal tax problem as a scalar value of tax revenue to be collected, so it is necessary to posit that the government absorbs a vector $\mathbf{R}$ of commodities. This implies that the consumption vector $\mathbf{x}$ satisfies $f(\mathbf{x} + \mathbf{R}) \leq 0$, thereby incorporating both revenue and production constraints. The optimal tax problem, then, is to maximize the indirect utility function $V(\mathbf{p}, \pi)$ subject to this constraint, and not that given in (4). The associated Lagrangean expression is

$$V(\mathbf{p}, \pi) - \mu f(\mathbf{x} + \mathbf{R}), \tag{8}$$

and the government's problem is still that of choosing the consumer price vector $\mathbf{p}$, rather than the tax vector $\mathbf{t}$, even though the relationship between changes in the two vectors is more complicated than when producer prices are fixed.[8] The resulting first-order conditions are (recalling the normalization that $q_i = f_i$)[9]

$$-\lambda x_i + \lambda \frac{d\pi}{dp_i} + \mu \left[-\sum_j q_j \frac{dx_j}{dp_i} \right] = 0 \quad \text{for } i = 1, \dots, N. \tag{9}$$

Differentiating the household's budget constraint $\mathbf{p}'\mathbf{x} = \pi$ with respect to p_i yields

$$x_i + \sum_j p_j \frac{dx_j}{dp_i} - \frac{d\pi}{dp_i} = 0 \qquad \text{for } i = 1, \ldots, N, \tag{10}$$

and adding the left-hand side of this equation to the expression inside the brackets in (9) yields

$$-\lambda x_i + \lambda \frac{d\pi}{dp_i} + \mu \left[x_i + \sum_j t_j \frac{dx_j}{dp_i} - \frac{d\pi}{dp_i} \right] = 0 \qquad \text{for } i = 1, \ldots, N. \tag{11}$$

Since producer prices, and hence profits, change with $\mathbf{p}$, the derivative dx_j/dp_i in (11) includes the indirect effect of p_i on profits through changes in production:

$$\frac{dx_j}{dp_i} = \frac{\partial x_j}{\partial p_i} + \frac{dx_j}{dy} \frac{d\pi}{dp_i}. \tag{12}$$

Using this and the preceding definition of the marginal social utility of income, α, (11) can be rewritten as

$$-\lambda x_i + \mu \left[x_i + \sum_j t_j \frac{\partial x_j}{\partial p_i} - \frac{\mu - \alpha}{\mu} \frac{d\pi}{dp_i} \right] = 0 \qquad \text{for } i = 1, \ldots, N, \tag{13}$$

or, using the Slutsky decomposition, as

$$-\sum_j t_j S_{ji} = \frac{\mu - \alpha}{\mu} \left(x_i - \frac{d\pi}{dp_i} \right) \qquad \text{for } i = 1, \ldots, N, \tag{14}$$

which differs from (6)—the first-order condition in the case of fixed producer prices—by the term $d\pi/dp_i$ on the right-hand side. Thus, if there are constant returns to scale ($\pi \equiv 0$), the first-order conditions are identical (Diamond and Mirrlees 1971). The same is true if the government imposes a pure profits tax, so that the after-tax value of y accruing to households is uniformly zero (Stiglitz and Dasgupta 1971).

4.3.3 Externalities

A similarly intuitive set of results appears when the simple Ramsey problem is extended to incorporate externalities, as in Sandmo (1975). Suppose that an externality, E, enters into each person's utility function and cannot be avoided, so that the representative individual's indirect utility function may be written $V(\mathbf{p}, y, E)$. Suppose also, for simplicity, that the externality is the product of aggregate consumption of a single good, say the good with the highest index, N, and that there are H identical individuals. In order to focus on externalities, consider the case in which production exhibits constant returns to scale, so that there are no pure profits. Then, the Lagrangean,

$$HV(\mathbf{p}, 0, X_N) - \mu f(\mathbf{X}), \qquad (15)$$

implies the following N first-order conditions with respect to the prices of goods $1, \ldots, N$ (compare with (5)):

$$-\lambda x_i + \mu \left[x_i + \sum_j t_j^* \frac{dx_j}{dp_i} \right] = 0 \qquad \text{for } i = 1, \ldots, N, \qquad (16)$$

where $t_j^* = t_j$ for $j \neq N$ and $t_N^* = t_N + HV_E/\mu = t_N + (HV_E/\lambda)/(\mu/\lambda)$. Expression (16) is the standard perfect tax solution, except that it calls for the tax on the externality-producing good, t_N, to equal the sum of the "perfect" tax that ignores the externality, t_N^*, plus a term that reflects the cost of the externality. This second term equals the corrective Pigouvian tax—the social cost per unit of consumption of the good, measured in terms of the numeraire commodity—divided by the marginal cost of public funds, μ/λ.

4.4   Perfect Specific Taxation with Distortionary Tax Instruments

In order to explore the impact of distortionary taxation on perfect corrective taxation, consider the setup of section 4.3.1, in which all commodities are produced at constant cost. There are $N+1$ commodities, of which the first N, indexed $0, \ldots, N-1$, are produced by competitive firms, and commodity N is produced in an imperfectly competitive market whose pricing satisfies (2).[10] Denoting the (constant) per-unit production cost of commodity i by q_i, it follows that $p_i = q_i + t_i$ for $i = 0, \ldots, N-1$. As in section 4.3.1, we assume that the tax on the numeraire commodity, good 0, equals zero. Firms in the imperfectly competitive industry generate profits, and someone in the economy receives these profits as income.[11] Taking consumers in the economy to be identical, it follows that the utility of the representative consumer can be represented by

$$V(\mathbf{p}, \pi), \qquad (17)$$

in which $\mathbf{p}$ is the vector of $N+1$ commodity prices and π represents profits earned by the imperfectly competitive firms. Commodity demands are then functions of $\mathbf{p}$ and π, but to simplify the calculations that follow, we consider the case in which firms ignore the indirect impact of their pricing decisions on demand through induced changes in profits.[12] The representative firm's first-order condition for profit maximization becomes $p_N + [X_N(1+\theta)]/[n(\partial X_N/\partial p_N)] - t_N = q_N$. Thus, the price-cost margin imposed by imperfect competition is $m = -X_N(1+\theta)/[n(\partial X_N/\partial p_N)]$.

The optimal taxation problem can be conveniently analyzed by maximizing (17) over the choice of $\mathbf{p}$, t_N, and π, subject to the constraints that

$$\sum_{j=1}^{N} t_j X_j = R, \tag{18}$$

$$(p_N - t_N - q_N)X_N = \pi, \tag{19}$$

$$-\frac{X_N}{n}\frac{1+\theta}{\partial X_N/\partial p_N} = p_N - t_N - q_N. \tag{20}$$

This approach to the optimal tax problem defines tax rates on the first $N-1$ commodities implicitly by the relationship $t_i = p_i - q_i$. Equation (18) corresponds to the government's budget constraint, (19) to the definition of profits, and (20) to the first-order condition for profit maximization in the imperfectly competitive industry.[13]

The first-order condition corresponding to maximizing (17) over the choice of p_i ($i < N$), subject to (18), (19), and (20), may be written[14]

$$-\lambda X_i + \mu \left[X_i + \sum_{j=1}^{N} t_j \frac{\partial X_j}{\partial p_i} \right] + \varphi_1 \left[(p_N - t_N - q_N)\frac{\partial X_N}{\partial p_i} \right]$$

$$+ \varphi_2 \left[\frac{(p_N - t_N - q_N)}{X_N}\frac{\partial X_N}{\partial p_i} - \frac{(p_N - t_N - q_N)}{\partial X_N/\partial p_N}\frac{\partial^2 X_N}{\partial p_N \partial p_i} \right] = 0, \tag{21}$$

in which, as before, the Lagrange multiplier μ is associated with the revenue constraint, while the new Lagrange multipliers φ_1 and φ_2 correspond to the additional constraints (19) and (20). The first-order condition corresponding to the choice of p_N is

$$-\lambda X_N + \mu \sum_{j=1}^{N} t_j \frac{\partial X_j}{\partial p_N} + \varphi_1 \left[(p_N - t_N - q_N) \frac{\partial X_N}{\partial p_N} + X_N \right]$$

$$+ \varphi_2 \left[-1 + \frac{(p_N - t_N - q_N)}{X_N} \frac{\partial X_N}{\partial p_N} - \frac{(p_N - t_N - q_N)}{\partial X_N / \partial p_N} \frac{\partial^2 X_N}{\partial p_N^2} \right] = 0.$$

$$(22)$$

The first-order conditions corresponding to choices of t_N and π are given by

$$\mu X_N - \varphi_1 X_N + \varphi_2 = 0, \tag{23}$$

$$\lambda + \mu \sum_{j=1}^{N} t_j \frac{\partial X_j}{\partial \pi} - \varphi_1 \left(1 - m \frac{\partial X_N}{\partial \pi} \right) + \varphi_2 \frac{\partial m}{\partial \pi} = 0. \tag{24}$$

To simplify and interpret these first-order conditions, we note first that by substituting (23) into (22), we obtain (21) for $i = N$. Thus, this expression holds for $i = 1, \ldots, N$. Next, it is possible to combine (23) and (24) to solve for the multipliers φ_1 and φ_2 in terms of other parameters. Doing so, we find that $\varphi_1 = \{\lambda + \mu \sum_{j=1}^{N} t_j (\partial X_j / \partial \pi) - \mu X_N (\partial m / \partial \pi)\} / \{1 - X_N (\partial m / \partial \pi) - m(\partial X_N / \partial \pi)\}$ and that $\varphi_2 = -(\mu - \varphi_1) X_N$. Substituting these expressions into (21), we obtain the following expression, for $i = 1, \ldots, N$:

$$-\lambda X_i + \mu \left[X_i + \sum_{j=1}^{N} t_j \frac{\partial X_j}{\partial p_i} \right] + \varphi_1 m \frac{\partial X_N}{\partial p_i} + (\mu - \varphi_1) X_N$$

$$\times \left[-\frac{(p_N - t_N - q_N)}{X_N} \frac{\partial X_N}{\partial p_i} + \frac{(p_N - t_N - q_N)}{\partial X_N / \partial p_N} \frac{\partial^2 X_N}{\partial p_N \partial p_i} \right] = 0. \tag{25}$$

The second term in brackets in (25) equals minus the change in the price-cost margin in industry N with respect to p_i, $\partial m / \partial p_i$. From (19) and (20), the effect of price changes on industry N profits, holding income constant, is $\partial \pi / \partial p_i = m(\partial X_N / \partial p_i) + X_N(\partial m / \partial p_i)$. The total change in industry N profits is given by $d\pi / dp_i = (\partial \pi / \partial p_i)/(1 - \partial \pi / \partial y)$, in which $\partial \pi / \partial y = m\partial X_N / \partial \pi + X_N \partial m / \partial \pi$. Making these substitutions, it is possible to rewrite (25) as

$$-\lambda X_i + \mu \left[X_i + \sum_{j=1}^{N} t_j^* \frac{\partial X_j}{\partial p_i} - \frac{\mu - \alpha^*}{\mu} \frac{d\pi}{dp_i} \right] = 0, \tag{26}$$

in which $t_j^* = t_j$ for $j \neq N$, $t_N^* = p_N - q_N$ is the total wedge in market j, equal to $t_N + m$ in industry N, and $\alpha^* = \lambda + \mu \sum_{j=1}^{N} t_j^* \partial X_j / \partial \pi$ is the "social" marginal utility of income, inclusive of its effect on profits.

Equation (26) has features that are analogous to (16), carrying the interpretation offered by Sandmo (1975) for the perfect tax conditions in the presence of externalities, with the added aspect that pure profit levels are affected by price changes. Intuitively, the "externality" in the case of imperfect competition is the outcome of the oligopolistic output selection, resulting in the extra markup m. The definition of t_N^* takes into account the need to correct this preexisting distortion. Without the last term in the brackets in (26), it would be optimal to correct fully for the extra distortion in industry N and then impose the standard perfect taxes. Presumably, the net result in industry N would be an incomplete offset of the oligopolistic markup, the optimal tax component normally being positive. The last term in brackets in (26) accounts for the existence of profits, taking the form laid out in (13) above and explained in that context. In this instance, tax-induced price changes affect the profitability of the imperfectly competitive industry, the difference $\mu - \alpha^*$ capturing the welfare effect of increasing industry profits by one unit. To the extent that a higher price of a commodity directly or indirectly augments oligopoly profits, this must be included in computing the price change's overall welfare effect. Doing so has the effect of making the price increase less attractive as a policy tool.

Although the preceding derivation of (26) elucidates the role played by taxes in influencing the noncompetitive industry's markup, one may arrive at the same result more directly by incorporating the constraints of the problem in a different manner. Doing so also facilitates an extension to the case in which more than one industry is noncompetitive. Assume that the revenue constraint still obeys (18), but that profits are now

$$\sum_{j=M+1}^{N} (p_j - t_j - q_j)X_j = \pi, \tag{19'}$$

where the characterization of producer behavior in noncompetitive industries $j > M$ is

$$p_j - t_j - q_j = -\frac{X_j}{n_j} \frac{1 + \theta_j}{\partial X_j / \partial p_j}, \tag{20'}$$

where n_j and θ_j are defined for industry j in the usual way. Combining (19′) with the revenue constraint, (18), we may recast the problem as one of maximizing (17) with respect to $\mathbf{p}$, subject to the constraint

$$\sum_{j=1}^{N}(p_j - q_j)X_j \geq R + \pi,\tag{27}$$

where profits are given by

$$\pi = - \sum_{j=M+1}^{N} \frac{X_j}{n_j}\frac{1+\theta_j}{\partial X_j/\partial p_j}X_j.\tag{28}$$

With μ defined as the multiplier of the constraint given in (27), the first-order conditions for this problem are

$$-\lambda X_i + \lambda\frac{d\pi}{dp_i} + \mu\left[X_i + \sum_{j=1}^{N}(p_j - q_j)\frac{\partial X_j}{\partial p_i} + \sum_{j=1}^{N}(p_j - q_j)\frac{\partial X_j}{\partial y}\frac{d\pi}{dp_i} - \frac{d\pi}{dp_i}\right] = 0$$

for $i = 1, \ldots, N$,$\qquad\qquad$(29)

where, as before, λ is the marginal utility of income. This may be rewritten to produce (26), with t_j^*, for $j > M$, equal to the total wedge in industry j.[15]

The preceding discussion presumes that the government is unable to use a complete set of tax instruments, being restricted instead to linear taxes on output. If the government has access to a tax on pure profits, then it can improve efficiency by using it. A 100 percent pure profit tax would effectively remove the $d\pi/dp_i$ term from (26), thereby modifying the perfect output tax configuration to consist of Ramsey-like revenue-raising taxes plus a corrective subsidy to output in the imperfectly competitive industry. The use of pure profit taxes together with other tax instruments relies, however, on the ability of the government to identify pure profits with precision in all situations. Consequently, in the analysis that follows, the government is assumed not to have the option of imposing pure profit taxes.

4.5 Specific and Ad Valorem Taxation

In competitive markets, the distinction between specific and ad valorem taxation arises only from minor tax enforcement considerations. In imperfectly competitive markets, these two tax instruments are no longer equivalent, since the imposition of an ad valorem tax makes the tax rate per unit of sales a function of a good's price, which is partly under the control of individual firms. As a result, ad valorem and specific taxes that raise equal tax revenue will typically differ in their implications for economic efficiency, ad valorem taxation being associated with much less deadweight loss.[16] Intuitively, ad valorem taxation removes a fraction (equal to the ad valorem tax rate) of a firm's incentive to restrict its output level in order to raise prices.

4.5.1 Welfare Effects

Now, the government is assumed to have access both to an ad valorem tax and to a specific tax. In this setting, the firm's profits equal

$$(1 - \tau)Px_i - tx_i - C(x_i), \tag{30}$$

in which τ is the ad valorem tax rate. Assuming the n-firm outcome to be symmetric, the first-order condition for profit maximization becomes

$$(1 - \tau)\left[P + \frac{X}{n}\frac{dP}{dX}(1 + \theta)\right] - t = C'\left(\frac{X}{n}\right), \tag{31}$$

and its pricing implications are

$$\frac{dP}{dt} = \left\{(1 - \tau)\left[1 + \frac{1 + \theta}{n}(1 + \eta)\right] - \frac{C''(X/n)}{n\,dP/dX}\right\}^{-1}, \tag{32}$$

$$\frac{dP}{d\tau} = \left[P + \frac{X}{n}\frac{dP}{dX}(1 + \theta)\right]\frac{dP}{dt}. \tag{33}$$

Since a unit change in τ raises more tax revenue than does a unit change in t, it is unsurprising that $dP/d\tau > dP/dt$. Much more revealing is the effect of these tax instruments normalized by dollar of marginal tax revenue. Since total tax revenue is given by $Rev = \tau PX + tX$, it follows that

$$\frac{d(Rev)}{dt} = X\left(1 + \tau\frac{dP}{dt}\right) + (t + \tau P)\frac{\partial X}{\partial P}\frac{dP}{dt}, \tag{34}$$

$$\frac{d(Rev)}{d\tau} = PX\left(1 + \frac{\tau}{P}\frac{dP}{d\tau}\right) + (t + \tau P)\frac{\partial X}{\partial P}\frac{dP}{d\tau}. \tag{35}$$

In this simple partial equilibrium model, the change in dead-weight loss, DWL, associated with one of these tax changes is equal to the product of the induced change in X and the difference between marginal cost and price. Consequently,

$$\frac{d(DWL)/dt}{d(DWL)/d\tau} = \frac{-(\partial X/\partial P)\,(dP/dt)}{-(\partial X/\partial P)\,(dP/d\tau)}\,\frac{P - C'\left(\dfrac{X}{n}\right)}{P - C'\left(\dfrac{X}{n}\right)} = \frac{dP/dt}{dP/d\tau}, \tag{36}$$

which, together with (34) and (35), implies that

$$\frac{\dfrac{d(DWL)/dt}{d(DWL)/d\tau}}{\dfrac{d(Rev)/dt}{d(Rev)/d\tau}} = \frac{X\left(\dfrac{P}{dP/d\tau} + \tau\right) + (t + \tau P)\dfrac{\partial X}{\partial P}}{X\left(\dfrac{1}{dP/dt} + \tau\right) + (t + \tau P)\dfrac{\partial X}{\partial P}}. \tag{37}$$

From (33), $dP/d\tau < P(dP/dt)$, so if tax revenue is an increasing function of tax rates, then the right-hand side of (37) is greater than unity. Hence, revenue-equal substitution of ad valorem for specific taxation reduces deadweight loss at any (t, τ) combination.[17] Of course, such substitution works at the expense of firm profitability, and would, if used excessively, drive profits negative and supply presumably to zero. But assuming the firm profitability constraint not to bind, the optimal tax configuration entails ad valorem rather than specific taxation.

4.5.2 Optimal Taxation with Distortionary Ad Valorem Tax Instruments

The preceding comparison of ad valorem and specific taxation compares their effectiveness per dollar of forgone revenue, but it does not address the question of the optimal rate of ad valorem taxation when the government is unable or unwilling to provide specific subsidies. While this problem might be thought to entail a very different solution from that for specific taxation, properly framed it becomes clear that the solution has the same character regardless of the type of available tax instrument.

Following the analysis of specific taxes, we seek to maximize the indirect utility function in (17) subject to the revenue constraint,

$$\sum_{j=1}^{N} \tau_j p_j X_j \geq R, \tag{38}$$

the definition of profits,

$$[p_N(1 - \tau_N) - q_N]X_N = \pi, \tag{39}$$

and the characterization of producer behavior,

$$p_j(1 - \tau_j) - q_j = 0 \text{ for } j = 1, \ldots, M;$$

$$-(1 - \tau_j)\frac{X_j}{n_j}\frac{1 + \theta_j}{\partial X_j / \partial p_j} \text{ for } j = M+1, \ldots, N. \tag{40}$$

As before, we express this as a problem of choosing the consumer prices, **p**, by using (40) to eliminate τ from the problem and using (39) to substitute for the explicit expression for the markup, m. The result is that we may rewrite the problem as one of maximizing (17) with respect to **p**, subject to the constraint

$$\sum_{j=1}^{N}(p_j - q_j)X_j \geq R + \pi, \tag{41}$$

where profits are given by

$$\pi = \sum_{j=M+1}^{N}\frac{q_j}{p_j - \phi_j}\phi_j X_j, \tag{42}$$

where $\phi_j = -[X_j / n_j][(1 + \theta_j) / (\partial X_j / \partial p_j)]$.

Note that (42) differs from (28) by the term multiplying $\phi_j X_j$ on the right-hand side of (42), which equals $1 - \tau_j$. Otherwise, the problem is identical to that for specific taxes, and the first-order conditions given in (26) still hold, for τ_i inserted in place of t_i / p_i. The resulting equilibrium will generally be different, of course, because profits, and hence the terms $d\pi / dp_i$, will be different.

4.6   An Example

In order to illustrate the trade-offs implicit in corrective tax policies with imperfect competition, it is useful to consider a concrete example. Suppose that the economy consists of identical consumers with utility functions over two goods, 1 and 2, and leisure of the form

$$U(x_1, x_2, l) = (x_1 - a)^{\beta_1} x_2^{\beta_2} l^{\beta_3}, \tag{43}$$

where the exponents β_i sum to one. This is the Stone-Geary or displaced Cobb-Douglas specification, where the quantity a of good 1 may be interpreted as a basic need. If $a > (<) 0$, then good 1 is a relative necessity (luxury).

We assume that the labor market and the market for good 1 are competitive, but that the market for good 2 is noncompetitive in the manner discussed above. The market demands for goods 1 and 2 are

$$X_1 = a + \beta_1 \frac{y - p_1 a}{p_1}, \tag{44}$$

$$X_2 = \beta_2 \frac{y - p_1 a}{p_2}, \tag{45}$$

where y is the household's full income, equal to its labor endowment plus profits.

From (26), we obtain the following expressions for perfect taxes on goods 1 and 2, assuming that labor is untaxed:

$$-\lambda X_i + \mu \left[X_i + t_1 \frac{\partial X_1}{\partial p_i} + t_2^* \frac{\partial X_2}{\partial p_i} \right] - (\mu - \alpha^*) \frac{d\pi}{dp_i} = 0 \text{ for } i = 1, 2, \tag{46}$$

which, rewritten using the demand expressions in (44) and (45), are

$$(\mu - \lambda) X_1 - \mu \left[\frac{t_1}{p_1} \frac{\beta_1 y}{p_1} + \frac{t_2^*}{p_2} \beta_2 a \right] - (\mu - \alpha^*) \frac{d\pi}{dp_1} = 0, \tag{47}$$

$$(\mu - \lambda) X_2 - \mu \left[\frac{t_2^*}{p_2} X_2 \right] - (\mu - \alpha^*) \frac{d\pi}{dp_2} = 0. \tag{48}$$

The implications of these conditions depend on the manner in which taxes are imposed. For specific taxes, because the elasticity of demand for good 2 is unity, the markup in industry 2 is, from equation (20),

$$p_2 - t_2 - q_2 = p_2 \frac{1 + \theta}{n}. \tag{49}$$

Thus, profits are $\pi = p_2(1 + \theta)X_2 / n$, which, using (45), equals $\beta_2(y - p_1 a)(1 + \theta)/n$. Because the household's full income, y, equals its labor endowment, say L, plus π, one may express profits in terms of underlying parameters as

$$\pi = \gamma \frac{L - p_1 a}{1 - \gamma}, \tag{50}$$

where $\gamma = \beta_2(1 + \theta)/n$. Using (50), it is possible to rewrite the first-order conditions in (47) and (48) as

$$(\mu - \lambda)X_1 - \mu \left[\frac{t_1}{p_1} \frac{\beta_1 y}{p_1} + \frac{t_2^*}{p_2} \beta_2 a \right] - (\mu - \alpha^*) \left[-a \frac{\gamma}{1 - \gamma} \right] = 0, \tag{51}$$

$$(\mu - \lambda)X_2 - \mu \left[\frac{t_2^*}{p_2} X_2 \right] = 0. \tag{52}$$

In (51), the impact on profits of an increase in the price of the competitive good depends on the sign of a. (The corresponding term in (52) is zero, in this case.) If a is positive (negative), this impact on profits is negative (positive), which will contribute, ceteris paribus, to a higher (lower) tax on that good. As will be seen shortly, this effect works in the same direction as the tax differential prevailing in the absence of imperfect competition. Rearranging (52) in terms of the proportional wedge, t_2^*/p_2, and substituting this expression and the expression for X_1 in (44) into (51), we obtain the following expressions:

$$\frac{t_1}{p_1} = \frac{\mu - \lambda}{\mu} \left(1 + \frac{p_1 \beta_3 a}{\beta_1 y} \right) + \frac{p_1 a}{\beta_1 y} \frac{\mu - \alpha^*}{\mu} \frac{\gamma}{1 - \gamma}, \tag{53}$$

$$\frac{t_2^*}{p_2} = \frac{\mu - \lambda}{\mu}. \tag{54}$$

These expressions are informative about the ways in which different parameters affect the relative tax rates on goods 1 and 2. Consider first what happens in the absence of imperfect competition ($n = \infty$ or $\theta = -1$). In this case, taxes on the two goods will be equal only if $\beta_3 = 0$ (in which case labor is supplied inelastically and a uniform tax on the two goods is nondistortionary) or $a = 0$ (in which case neither good is a relative necessity). Introducing imperfect competition works to enlarge the differential wedge between the two industries, based on the full wedge in industry 2, t_2^*. However, there are limits to the conclusions one can draw based on these expressions, because they are not complete solutions for the tax rates but depend on multipliers that are themselves endogenous. Also, the conditions for the ad valorem tax case, using the markup condition based on (40) instead of (49), yields somewhat messier conditions

Table 4.1
Perfect commodity taxes with Stone-Geary utility functions

Basic need (a)	$\dfrac{1+\theta}{n}$	Specific taxation			Ad valorem taxation		
		t_1	t_2	t_2^*	t_1	t_2	t_2^*
0.0	0.0	0.176	0.176	0.176	0.176	0.176	0.176
0.0	0.1	0.242	0.118	0.242	0.231	0.129	0.240
0.0	0.2	0.316	0.053	0.316	0.296	0.070	0.320
−0.1	0.0	0.104	0.257	0.257	0.104	0.257	0.257
−0.1	0.1	0.169	0.214	0.349	0.154	0.225	0.336
−0.1	0.2	0.244	0.166	0.457	0.210	0.189	0.439
0.1	0.0	0.238	0.074	0.074	0.238	0.074	0.074
0.1	0.1	0.300	0.003	0.115	0.296	0.007	0.118
0.1	0.2	0.365	−0.072	0.160	0.367	−0.075	0.175

Note: The table presents distortion minimizing tax rates for an economy in which identical consumers have utility functions given by $U = [(x_1 - a)x_2 l]^{1/3}$, in which x_1 is consumption of commodity 1, x_2 is consumption of commodity 2, l is leisure, and a denotes the consumer's basic need for commodity 1. Commodity 1 is produced by a competitive industry, while commodity 2 is produced by an imperfectly competitive industry consisting of n firms, each of which selects its output level with a conjectural variation of θ. Thus, lower values of $(1 + \theta)/n$ correspond to greater industry competition. Consumers have unit wages and unit labor endowments, and constant producer costs of both commodities are fixed at unity as well. The government's revenue requirement equals 10 percent of the economy's labor endowment. The variables t_1 and t_2 are tax rates on commodities 1 and 2 respectively, while t_2^* is the total wedge between consumer price and producer cost for commodity 2, inclusive both of the effect of taxes and of the markup due to imperfect competition.

than (53) and (54). Thus, for further insight, we turn to numerical simulations.

Table 4.1 presents simulations for this Stone-Geary case, for a range of values of the basic need, a, and the markup term, $(1 + \theta)/n$. In all simulations, the intensity parameters β_i each equal $\frac{1}{3}$, the value of the labor endowment and all producer prices equal 1, and required revenue equals 0.1. For ease of comparison, the taxes presented are in specific units, rather than as a fraction of the price, even in the case of ad valorem taxation.

There are a number of interesting results one can observe from inspection of the table. First, for all variations in the preference parameter a, the total wedge on the noncompetitive good increases with the degree of noncompetitiveness, as tax reductions occur but do not completely offset the extra wedge induced by increases in $(1 + \theta)/n$. For all values of a, the tax on the competitive good rises with the markup in industry 2, as needed to reduce the tax rate on the noncompetitive good. Following the intuition provided based on (53) and (54), the wedge under specific taxation between t_2^* and t_1 grows with $(1+\theta)/n$, becoming more negative when $a > 0$, more positive when $a < 0$, and remaining constant when $a = 0$.

When $(1+\theta)/n > 0$, the tax on good 2 is generally higher in the case of ad valorem taxation, because the ad valorem tax acts to moderate noncompetitive behavior. Because of this moderation, the total wedge facing purchases of good 2 is sometimes lower under ad valorem taxation, despite the higher tax. The one exception to the rule of higher taxation of good 2 under ad valorem taxation is in the last row of the table. Here, the tax on good 2 is initially low, even without noncompetitive behavior, because good 1 is a relative necessity $(a > 0)$. As $(1+\theta)/n$ rises, this contributes to a further lowering of t_2, to the point that it becomes negative when $(1+\theta)/n = 0.2$—corresponding to a five-firm industry under Cournot conjectures. However, once the tax rate on good 2 is negative, applying it as an ad valorem tax *exacerbates* noncompetitive behavior. This can be seen by the fact that the markup (the difference between t_2 and t_2^*) is higher for the ad valorem tax case in this row, in contrast to the rest of the table.

4.7 Uncertainty

One of the difficulties facing tax authorities attempting to implement perfect corrective policies is that the extent of imperfect competition in an industry is generally not known with certainty. This section explores the impact of uncertainty on the design of corrective policy. We consider the case in which the extent of competition, as captured by θ, is unknown. As in section 4.4, the government has access to specific tax instruments with which to tax industries producing output at constant costs. As a result, the government directly controls the prices of commodities other than that produced by imperfectly competitive firms. In order to focus the analysis on uncertainty, the government is assumed to have no revenue needs and access to lump-sum taxation. In the absence of lump-sum taxation, the optimal tax configuration would presumably exhibit at least some of the features analyzed in section 4.4.

Taking the measure of welfare to be expected utility, the government maximizes

$$E[V(\mathbf{p_0}, p_N, \pi - T)], \tag{55}$$

in which $\mathbf{p_0}$ is the vector of N commodity prices for goods produced by firms in competitive industries, p_N is the price of the output sold in the imperfectly competitive industry, π represents profits earned by the imperfectly competitive firms, and T equals lump-sum taxes. $E[\cdot]$ is the expectations operator.

The government selects a vector of commodity taxes $\mathbf{t}$ and lump-sum taxes T to maximize (55) subject to

$$\sum_{j=1}^{N} t_j X_j + T = 0, \tag{56}$$

$$(p_N - t_N - q_N)X_N = \pi, \tag{57}$$

$$-\frac{X_N}{n} \frac{1+\theta}{\partial X_N / \partial p_N} = p_N - t_N - q_N. \tag{58}$$

Denoting the imperfectly competitive markup, $p_N - t_N - q_N$, by m, it follows that expected utility can be written as

$$E\left[V\left(p_0, \{q_N + t_N + m(\mathbf{t}, \theta)\}, \left\{X_N(\mathbf{t}, \theta)m(\mathbf{t}, \theta) + \sum_{j=1}^{N} t_j X_j(\mathbf{t}, \theta)\right\}\right)\right], \tag{59}$$

in which use is made of reduced-form functions to denote the dependency of m and X_j on prices and income that in turn are functions of $\mathbf{t}$ and θ. The first-order conditions corresponding to the maximum of (59) over the choice of the elements of the vector $\mathbf{t}$ are

$$E\left[\lambda(\mathbf{t}, \theta)\left\{m(\mathbf{t}, \theta)\frac{\partial X_N(\mathbf{t}, \theta)}{\partial t_i} + \sum_{j=1}^{N} t_j \frac{\partial X_j(\mathbf{t}, \theta)}{\partial t_i}\right\}\right] = 0 \qquad \text{for } i = 1, \ldots, N. \tag{60}$$

In the absence of uncertainty over the value of θ, it is clear that (60) is satisfied by a tax vector in which $t_j = 0$ for all $j < N$ and $t_N = -m$. Equation (60) illustrates the channels through which uncertainty over the extent of competition influences the optimal tax rule. One such channel concerns risk aversion as reflected by the $\lambda(\mathbf{t}, \theta)$ function. The marginal utility of income, λ, is generally a decreasing function of θ, since a greater degree of monopoly leads to higher prices (recall that nominal income is fixed) and therefore lower utility associated with marginal nominal income. The extent to which θ affects λ is, however, attenuated by the reduced utility due to monopoly and the associated higher marginal utility of income.

It is useful to put risk considerations aside, in order to focus on issues that are specific to the imperfectly competitive setting of the problem. To do so, we take λ in (60) to be unaffected by θ, and consider the simplifying case in which $t_j = 0$ for all $j < N$. Then (60) implies

$$E\left[(m(\mathbf{t}, \theta) + t_N)\frac{\partial X_N(\mathbf{t}, \theta)}{\partial t_N}\right] = 0. \tag{61}$$

Denoting the expectation of m, $E[m(\mathbf{t}, \theta)]$, by $\bar{m}(\mathbf{t})$, (61) indicates that the dependency of $\partial X_N / \partial t_N$ on θ implies that the perfect corrective tax is not simply $t_N = -\bar{m}(\mathbf{t})$. If we express this partial derivative as

$$\frac{\partial X_N(\mathbf{t}, \theta)}{\partial t_N} = \frac{\partial X_N(\mathbf{t}, \theta)}{\partial p_N} \frac{\partial p_N(\mathbf{t}, \theta)}{\partial t_N}, \tag{62}$$

then the first-order condition (61) becomes

$$E\left[\frac{\partial X_N(\mathbf{t}, \theta)}{\partial p_N} \{m(\mathbf{t}, \theta) + t_N\} \frac{\partial p_N(\mathbf{t}, \theta)}{\partial t_N}\right] = 0. \tag{63}$$

This condition is satisfied when

$$\{\bar{m}(\mathbf{t}) + t_N\}E\left[\frac{\partial X_N(\mathbf{t}, \theta)}{\partial p_N} \frac{\partial p_N(\mathbf{t}, \theta)}{\partial t_N}\right] + \operatorname{cov}\left\{m(\mathbf{t}, \theta), \frac{\partial X_N(\mathbf{t}, \theta)}{\partial p_N} \frac{\partial p_N(\mathbf{t}, \theta)}{\partial t_N}\right\}$$

$$= 0, \tag{64}$$

so that the optimal tax rule is

$$t_N = -\bar{m}(\mathbf{t})\left[1 + \frac{\operatorname{cov}\left\{m(\mathbf{t}, \theta), \dfrac{\partial X_N(\mathbf{t}, \theta)}{\partial p_N} \dfrac{\partial p_N(\mathbf{t}, \theta)}{\partial t_N}\right\}}{\bar{m}(\mathbf{t})E\left[\dfrac{\partial X_N(\mathbf{t}, \theta)}{\partial p_N} \dfrac{\partial p_N(\mathbf{t}, \theta)}{\partial t_N}\right]}\right]. \tag{65}$$

Equation (65) reflects the impact of uncertainty over the value of θ. High values of θ tend to depress $\partial p_N / \partial t_N$, since oligopolistic output determination is based on marginal revenue curves that are steeper than demand curves. Unless $\partial X_N / \partial p_N$ is strongly affected by θ—which is unlikely—then the covariance in the numerator of the term on the right-hand side of (65) is negative. States of the world in which θ takes a high value are also states of the world in which higher tax subsidies are relatively less effective at stimulating demand. It follows that states of the world in which θ is small are also those in which tax subsidies have a significant impact on resource allocation. The relative ineffectiveness of tax subsidies when needed (i.e., when θ is large) makes the perfect corrective tax policy smaller in magnitude than it would be if the degree of competition were known with certainty.

In order to see this relationship more clearly, consider the case of a linear demand curve, for which $\partial X_N(\mathbf{t}, \theta)/\partial p_N$ is constant. In this case, (63) becomes

$$E\left[\{m(\mathbf{t}, \theta) + t_N\} \frac{\partial p_N(\mathbf{t}, \theta)}{\partial t_N}\right] = 0. \tag{66}$$

In order to interpret (66), it is useful to refer to (3), which describes the effect of t_N on p_N in a partial equilibrium setting. Note that in the assumed case of a linear demand curve, the elasticity of inverse demand for good N, $\eta \equiv (d^2 p_N/dX_N^2)[X_N/(dp_N/dX_N)]$, equals zero. With constant marginal cost as well, (3) reduces to

$$\frac{\partial p_N}{\partial t_N} = \left(1 + \frac{1+\theta}{n}\right)^{-1} = \frac{n}{1+n+\theta}, \tag{67}$$

which lies between zero and one (for the realistic cases in which $\theta \geq -1$) and is a decreasing function of θ. Denoting the (linear) demand function $X_N = a - b p_N$, it follows that $\partial X_N/\partial p_N = -b$, and the pricing equation (58) implies

$$X_N = \frac{n[a + b(q_N + t_N)]}{1 + n + \theta}. \tag{68}$$

Combining (58) and (66)–(68) produces the first-order condition

$$t_N E\left[\frac{n}{1+n+\theta}\right] = E\left[\frac{X_N(1+\theta)}{1+n+\theta}\right] \frac{1}{\partial X_N/\partial p_N}. \tag{69}$$

Since $m = -X_N(1+\theta)/[n(\partial X_N/\partial p_N)]$, (68) implies that $\bar{m} = -\{a - b(q_N + t_N)\}\{E[(1+\theta)/(1+n+\theta)]\}/\{\partial X_N/\partial p_N\}$. Then (68) and (69) together imply

$$t_N = -\bar{m}\left\{\frac{E\left[\dfrac{1+\theta}{(1+n+\theta)^2}\right]}{E\left[\dfrac{1}{1+n+\theta}\right] E\left[\dfrac{1+\theta}{1+n+\theta}\right]}\right\}. \tag{70}$$

In order to interpret (70), it is helpful to define $\gamma \equiv 1/(1+n+\theta)$, from which it follows that $1 + \theta = (1/\gamma) - n$. Then (70) becomes

$$t_N = -\bar{m} \frac{E\left[\gamma^2\left(\frac{1}{\gamma} - n\right)\right]}{E[\gamma]E[1 - n\gamma]} = -\bar{m} \frac{E[\gamma] - nE[\gamma^2]}{E[\gamma] - n\{E[\gamma]\}^2}. \tag{71}$$

Defining $\bar{\gamma} \equiv E[\gamma]$ and using the definition of the variance to substitute $\sigma^2(\gamma) \equiv E[\gamma^2] - \{E[\gamma]\}^2$, it follows from (71) that

$$t_N = -\bar{m}\left\{1 - \frac{\sigma^2(\gamma)}{\bar{\gamma}\left(\frac{1}{n} - \bar{\gamma}\right)}\right\}. \tag{72}$$

Since the variance $\sigma^2(\gamma) \geq 0$, and the restriction that $\theta \geq -1$ implies that $1/n \geq \bar{\gamma} > 0$, it follows that (72) implies that t_N is less than or equal to $\bar{m}$ in absolute value.

Equation (71) characterizes corrective taxation in a way that permits a simple evaluation of the potential importance of the correction due to uncertainty over the appropriate value of θ. Consider, for example, the case in which $n = 10$ and γ is uniformly distributed over the interval $\left(\frac{1}{40}, \frac{1}{10}\right)$. Then $E[\gamma] = 0.0625$, $E[\gamma^2] = 0.004375$, and (71) implies that $t_N = -\bar{m}(0.8)$. If, instead, $n = 2$ and θ is uniformly distributed over the interval $(-1, 5)$, then $E[\gamma] = 0.231$, $E[\gamma^2] = 0.0625$, and (71) implies that $t_N = -\bar{m}(0.86)$. Alternatively, if $n = 10$ and θ is uniformly distributed over the interval $(-1, 5)$, then $E[\gamma] = 0.0783$, $E[\gamma^2] = 0.00625$, and (71) implies that $t_N = -\bar{m}(0.93)$. These examples, which need not be representative, share the feature that perfect corrective policy is approximately 10 to 20 percent smaller in magnitude in the presence of modest uncertainty over the degree of market competition.

4.8 Conclusion

The ability of the government to alter private incentives through the tax system affords policymakers a range of options that are often more attractive than regulatory alternatives. When it is possible to identify imperfectly competitive market structures, an appropriate set of taxes and subsidies can be used to correct misallocations due to oligopolistic price setting. These taxes and subsidies reflect a tension between the efficiency gains from subsidizing output in the imperfectly competitive sector of the economy and the cost of taxing the rest of the economy to pay for the subsidies. In those cases in which the extent of competition is not known with certainty, a more moderate set of corrective taxes and subsidies is typically indicated.

The focus of this analysis is the efficiency of resource allocation, which, while perfectly appropriate for economic research, represents only a part of the information necessary in order to implement sound policy. Musgrave (1959, 157) reminds the reader that "the avoidance of excess burden is only one consideration among others in choosing between different taxes." He continues (159): "Society must ask itself what price, in terms of excess burden, it wishes to pay to secure certain policy objectives. In this sense, the narrow criterion of efficiency as avoidance of excess burden must be subordinated to a broader concept of efficiency under which conflicting objectives are reconciled." The reconciliation of these diverse objectives is the task of political and social organizations, whose job is made easier by its thoughtful conceptualization in the work of Richard Musgrave and others.

Notes

We thank Gareth Myles, Harvey Rosen, Agnar Sandmo, two anonymous referees, and participants in the CESifo conference, "Public Finances and Public Policy in the New Millennium," University of Munich, January 12–13, 2001, for helpful comments on earlier drafts.

1. The analysis in this section, and in several of the sections that follow, draws heavily on that provided in Auerbach and Hines (2002). For an early analysis of the impact of taxation in the presence of monopoly, see Cournot (1838) and Edgeworth (1925).

2. See Stern (1987) for a more general analysis of price responses to tax changes in a variety of settings.

3. One possibility, explored by Katz and Rosen (1985), is that tax authorities design corrective policies on the basis of imperfect understanding of the extent of competition in oligopolistic industries.

4. Such a corrective subsidy was proposed by Robinson (1933, 163–165), who attributes it to her husband and presents it as an "ingenious but impractical scheme." For an elaboration, see Higgins (1943).

5. See Musgrave (1976).

6. The issue of entry is considered in Auerbach and Hines (2002), based on earlier work by Seade (1980a, b), Besley (1989), Myles (1989), Delipalla and Keen (1992), and de Meza, Maloney, and Myles (1995). In order to focus on the first two of these three issues, the models in this chapter take the number of industry competitors to be fixed.

7. Samuelson (1951) uses the symmetry of the Slutsky matrix ($S_{ij} = S_{ji}$) to interpret equation (6) as implying that optimal taxes entail equiproportionate compensated reductions in demands for all commodities. While valid locally, this interpretation relies on constancy of the elements of the Slutsky matrix as tax rates change, a feature they do not generally exhibit.

8. As discussed in Auerbach (1985), $d\mathbf{p}/d\mathbf{t} = [I - HS]^{-1}$, where H is the Hessian of $f(\cdot)$, so there is a one-to-one relationship between changes in $\mathbf{t}$ and changes in $\mathbf{p}$ as long as $[I - HS]$ is of full rank.

9. Note that we still assume a zero tax rate on the numeraire commodity, good 0. In the presence of pure profits, the ability to impose a tax on this good would facilitate a revenue-raising nondistortionary uniform tax on all commodities, equivalent to a lump-sum profits tax.

10. We follow much of the literature in assuming that preferences and technology support a unique stable market equilibrium, which, as Roberts and Sonnenschein (1977) note, need not exist in the presence of imperfect competition. Guesnerie and Laffont (1978) analyze cases in which preferences and production technologies make it impossible for any tax policies to support first-best outcomes. They note that, in other cases, corrective government policies produce outcomes that are highly unstable.

11. In the competitive context, assuming a zero tax rate on one commodity restricts the government effectively from imposing a tax on pure profits through a uniform tax on all commodities. Here, though, before-tax profits would respond to such uniform taxation, leaving the government's problem unchanged. See Auerbach and Hines (2002) for a more formal demonstration of this point.

12. Assuming that firms ignore the indirect impact of profits on demand for their own products is reasonable and serves to simplify greatly the calculations that follow in equations (21)–(25). Although it will affect the underlying equilibrium, this simplification has no impact on the results as presented in (26), since the impact is concentrated in the term $d\pi/dp_i$ appearing in that expression. This point is made evident by the fact that the alternative derivation (presented in (29)) does not rely on any particular pricing rule.

13. See Myles (1989; 1995, 363–369) for an alternative approach to characterizing the solution to the optimal tax problem in the presence of imperfect competition. This approach produces first-order conditions for the optimal tax configuration expressed in terms of price and profit reactions to tax changes at the optimum. These conditions do not then permit the simple interpretation offered for equation (26). The appendix to Myles (1989) analyzes a more general version of this problem in which consumers are heterogeneous. The advantage of sidestepping the complication of consumer heterogeneity is that doing so clarifies the interpretation of the resulting efficiency conditions, though it does not address some broader welfare issues.

14. The last term in brackets in equation (21) results from substituting (20) into the actual first-order condition.

15. As noted in note 12, the derivation of equation (29) does not depend on the particular specification of profits given in (28).

16. Suits and Musgrave (1953) provide a classic analysis of this comparison; their treatment is greatly expanded and elaborated by Delipalla and Keen (1992), and extended by Skeath and Trandel (1994) and Denicolo and Matteuzzi (2000).

17. Consequently, if the government is able to impose negative specific taxes (specific subsidies), then it can completely eliminate the distortion due to imperfect competition through a judicious combination of ad valorem tax and specific subsidy, as noted by Myles (1996). The effectiveness of this corrective method is limited by any constraints on specific tax rates, such as a restriction that they be nonnegative—in which case the optimal specific tax rate is zero.

References

Auerbach, A. J. 1985. "The Theory of Excess Burden and Optimal Taxation." In *Handbook of Public Economics*, Vol. 1, ed. A. J. Auerbach and M. Feldstein. Amsterdam: North-Holland.

Auerbach, A. J., and J. R. Hines Jr. 2002. "Taxation and Economic Efficiency." In *Handbook of Public Economics*, Vol. 3, ed. A. J. Auerbach and M. Feldstein. Amsterdam: North-Holland.

Besley, T. 1989. "Commodity Taxation and Imperfect Competition: A Note on the Effects of Entry." *Journal of Public Economics* 40: 359–366.

Cournot, A. 1838. *Researches into the Mathematical Principles of the Theory of Wealth.* Translated by N. T. Bacon. New York: Macmillan, 1929. Reprinted as "Of Monopoly and of the Influence of Taxation on Commodities Produced under a Monopoly." In *Readings in the Economics of Taxation*, ed. R. A. Musgrave and C. S. Shoup. Homewood, IL: Richard D. Irwin, 1959.

Delipalla, S., and M. Keen. 1992. "The Comparison between *Ad Valorem* and Specific Taxation under Imperfect Competition." *Journal of Public Economics* 49: 351–366.

De Meza, D., J. Maloney, and G. D. Myles. 1995. "Price-Reducing Taxation." *Economics Letters* 47: 77–81.

Denicolo, V., and M. Matteuzzi. 2000. "Specific and *Ad Valorem* Taxation in Asymmetric Cournot Oligopolies." *International Tax and Public Finance* 7: 335–342.

Diamond, P. A., and J. A. Mirrlees. 1971. "Optimal Taxation and Public Production I: Production Efficiency and II: Tax Rules." *American Economic Review* 61: 8–27 and 261–278.

Edgeworth, F. Y. 1925. "The Pure Theory of Taxation." In *Papers Relating to Political Economy*, Vol. 2, ed. F. Y. Edgeworth. London: Macmillan. Reprinted as "The Pure Theory of Taxation." In *Readings in the Economics of Taxation*, ed. R. A. Musgrave and C. S. Shoup. Homewood, IL: Richard D. Irwin, 1959.

Guesnerie, R., and J.-J. Laffont. 1978. "Taxing Price Makers." *Journal of Economic Theory* 19: 423–455.

Higgins, B. 1943. "Post-War Tax Policy (Part I)." *Canadian Journal of Economics and Political Science* 9. Reprinted as "Fiscal Control of Monopoly." In *Readings in the Economics of Taxation*, ed. R. A. Musgrave and C. S. Shoup. Homewood, IL: Richard D. Irwin, 1959.

Katz, M. L., and H. S. Rosen. 1985. "Tax Analysis in an Oligopoly Model." *Public Finance Quarterly* 13: 3–20.

Musgrave, R. A. 1959. *The Theory of Public Finance*. New York: McGraw-Hill.

Musgrave, R. A. 1976. "ET, OT, and SBT." *Journal of Public Economics* 6: 3–16.

Myles, G. D. 1989. "Ramsey Tax Rules for Economies with Imperfect Competition." *Journal of Public Economics* 38: 95–115.

Myles, G. D. 1995. *Public Economics*. Cambridge, UK: Cambridge University Press.

Myles, G. D. 1996. "Imperfect Competition and the Optimal Combination of *Ad Valorem* and Specific Taxation." *International Tax and Public Finance* 3: 29–44.

Ramsey, F. P. 1927. "A Contribution to the Theory of Taxation." *Economic Journal* 37: 47–61.

Roberts, J., and H. Sonnenschein. 1977. "On the Foundations of the Theory of Monopolistic Competition." *Econometrica* 45: 101–113.

Robinson, J. 1933. *The Economics of Imperfect Competition*. London: Macmillan.

Samuelson, P. A. 1951. "Theory of Optimal Taxation." Unpublished memorandum for the U.S. Treasury. Published in *Journal of Public Economics* 30 (1986): 137–143.

Sandmo, A. 1975. "Optimal Taxation in the Presence of Externalities." *Swedish Journal of Economics* 77: 86–98.

Seade, J. 1980a. "On the Effects of Entry." *Econometrica* 48: 479–489.

Seade, J. 1980b. "The Stability of Cournot Revisited." *Journal of Economic Theory* 23: 15–26.

Skeath, S. E., and G. A. Trandel. 1994. "A Pareto Comparison of *Ad Valorem* and Unit Taxes in Noncompetitive Environments." *Journal of Public Economics* 53: 53–71.

Stern, N. 1987. "The Effects of Taxation, Price Control and Government Contracts in Oligopoly and Monopolistic Competition." *Journal of Public Economics* 32: 133–158.

Stiglitz, J. E., and P. S. Dasgupta. 1971. "Differential Taxation, Public Goods and Economic Efficiency." *Review of Economic Studies* 38: 151–174.

Suits, D. B., and R. A. Musgrave. 1953. "*Ad Valorem* and Unit Taxes Compared." *Quarterly Journal of Economics* 67: 598–604.

Comments

Harvey S. Rosen

The chapter by Alan Auerbach and James Hines is sure to find a place on the reading lists of graduate courses in public finance. It nicely presents some results that are well-known but have not always been exposited with the greatest clarity. A good example is the proposition that, in the presence of imperfect competition, a tax can be overshifted. I especially liked the elegant demonstration that optimal taxation in an imperfectly competitive environment is formally similar to optimal taxation in the presence of an externality.

The chapter also has some important new results. One of the most interesting concerns optimal taxation when there is uncertainty about market structure. In their model, Auerbach and Hines characterize market structure with a single parameter, which essentially measures the extent of market power. They show that, under certain conditions, one goes less far in the direction of levying the corrective tax when one is uncertain about the magnitude of this parameter.

Several links exist between this chapter and the work of Richard Musgrave. To begin, it is useful to note that Musgrave was quite sensitive to the fact that understanding oligopoly pricing was potentially an important issue in tax analysis. With respect to how such pricing is done, Musgrave noted in *The Theory of Public Finance* that "In a market characterized by a small number of sellers supplying a standardized product, price will be set somewhere between the competitive price and the monopoly price, but there is no way of telling just where it will come to rest. *The solution depends on the strategy pursued by the participating firms*" (280, italics added). The italicized statement is essentially equivalent to the proposition that the equilibrium depends on the variable that Auerbach and Hines call θ. Thus, many years before the formalization of oligopoly theory upon which Auerbach and Hines build, Musgrave was able to discern intuitively some of its key insights.

This Auerbach-Hines chapter is theoretical, and it is therefore entirely appropriate that they stress Musgrave's "thoughtful conceptualization" of tax analysis in oligopolistic markets. But it is important to remember that in addition to conceptualizing on this topic, Musgrave also did some famous empirical work on overshifting and imperfect competition—his book with Marian Krzyzaniak, *The Shifting of the Corporation Income Tax*. This bold and courageous effort to go beyond theory and actually see what the data had to say about overshifting was roundly attacked. Much of the attack, in my mind, was generated by its conclusion that the corporation tax is overshifted, implying that markets are imperfectly competitive. Many economists, particularly in the United States, simply were not willing to contemplate this possibility.

As Auerbach and Hines correctly note, "overshifting has intrigued public finance economists at least since the time of Edgeworth," and there has been more empirical work on this topic since the Krzyzaniak-Musgrave volume. Much of that work has come to the same general conclusion that they did—many taxes are in fact overshifted. Unfortunately, such results have been received with much the same skepticism as Krzyzaniak and Musgrave's and for much the same reason—an a priori belief that market imperfections cannot be a serious empirical phenomenon.

I would now like to turn to the policy implications of this line of research. In particular, would it be wise to give decision makers advice based on the analysis of taxation in oligopoly models? As Auerbach and Hines note, in *The Theory of Public Finance* Musgrave is rather cautious on this matter: "... allocation in the market is not altogether chaotic. Therefore, we are still well advised to prefer the general tax unless there is a clear case for correcting a specific imperfection." Thus, Musgrave provides an *informational* motivation for ignoring market imperfections when giving advice on optimal tax rates. This is in the same spirit as Auerbach and Hines's interesting result, noted above, that uncertainty with respect to market structure reduces the size of the optimal corrective tax.

I believe that other strains of Musgrave's thought reinforce the view that caution is in order here. The key insight is that policymakers need not follow economists' advice, a phenomenon that Musgrave observed directly: "like most economists of my generation, I had the benefit of direct association with policy making and policy makers, thus observing the link—or the gap, as it may be— between pure theory and affairs of state" (1959, v). Given the existence of such a gap, one has to think about how the advice will be used by politicians, which is part of what Musgrave called the "sociology of fiscal politics" and what we call "political economy" today. It may be the case that once one opens the door to differential tax rates, politicians will take advantage of it to tax some goods heavily and subsidize others based on political rather than efficiency or equity considerations. Hence, a rule that all rates be equal may ultimately be more efficient than the *actual* result if differentiation is permitted. This is similar to the "rules versus discretion" controversy in the literature on monetary economics. In short, both the informational issue raised by Musgrave and political economy considerations may suggest that giving policy advice as if the economy were competitive may be the most sensible strategy. None of this takes away, of course, from the importance of understanding both the positive and normative aspects of taxation under imperfect competition, as so nicely exposited in this chapter.

References

Musgrave, R. A. 1959. *The Theory of Public Finance*. New York: McGraw-Hill.

Musgrave, R. A., and M. Krzyzaniak. 1963. *The Shifting of the Corporation Income Tax*. Baltimore: Johns Hopkins University Press.

5 Bridging the Tax-Expenditure Gap: Green Taxes and the Marginal Cost of Funds

Agnar Sandmo

5.1 Introduction

On several occasions, Richard Musgrave has lamented the tendency in the theory of public finance to analyze questions of taxation and of the supply of public goods[1] in separate compartments. Although this practice can often be justified in terms of analytical tractability, it is true that a joint perspective on taxes and public expenditure is sometimes very important. In the recent literature, this point has been emphasized in numerous studies of the concept of the marginal cost of (public) funds (MCF). The basic idea in this literature is that when public goods are financed by distortionary taxes, the efficiency costs that this entails should, in a cost-benefit analysis of public projects, be reflected in a multiplicative adjustment of the marginal social cost of increased supply. If public goods supply could have been financed by lump-sum taxes, an increased supply involving a cost of 1 million euro and benefits of 1.2 million euro should definitely be carried out. But if each euro of tax revenue involves 0.3 euro of tax efficiency cost, then the MCF is 1.3 and the social cost should be computed as 1.3 times the direct resource cost. With a social cost of 1.3 million euro, the proposed increase in public goods supply no longer passes the cost-benefit test, which can be written more generally as

Marginal social benefit $\geq$ MCF $\times$ Marginal social cost.

Thus, the concept of the marginal cost of public funds is the modern theory's response to Musgrave's critique. Its origin lies in the tax side of the public budget, and its application is to the determination of the expenditure side.

Like a number of other fundamental ideas in public finance, this one can be traced back to Pigou (1928). It reentered the literature through the theory of optimal taxation, notably in a famous article by Atkinson and Stern (1974), although the MCF terminology was apparently introduced by Browning (1976). More recent contributions include Wildasin (1984), Mayshar (1991), Ballard and Fullerton (1992), and Håkonsen (1998). While most analyses of the MCF interpret it as a pure measure of inefficiency, some authors, such as Wilson (1991), Dahlby (1998), and Sandmo (1998), have argued that the MCF should also incorporate a measure of the possible distributional gains from distortionary taxes. The basic argument for this is that taxes are distortionary precisely because one wants to achieve some distributional objective; hence, the MCF should reflect the redistributional gain as well as the efficiency loss.

Underlying most of this literature is the crucial assumption that when lump-sum taxes are not available, taxes used to finance the supply of public goods must be distortionary. But this is not necessarily the case. In the case of commodities or factors of production generating negative external effects, we know that the imposition of a tax reflecting the difference between marginal social and private cost (or between marginal private and social benefit) does not create any inefficiency; on the contrary, it leads to an efficiency gain. This insight has recently given rise to a large number of analyses of the so-called double dividend from a green tax reform, in which one studies the substitution of green or Pigouvian taxes[2] for standard distortionary taxes, assuming that government revenue is to be held constant. That the existence of a double dividend turns out not to be so obvious as might be suggested by partial equilibrium analysis comes essentially from the theoretical ambiguity of the direction of the cross-price effects between markets, an aspect not captured in the partial equilibrium approach.[3]

The definition of the double dividend with constant tax revenue as the point of reference is, however, not the only one possible. If one believes that a distortionary tax system keeps the supply of public goods at an inefficiently low level, one way in which to reap the benefits of a less distortionary system would be to expand public expenditure, seeing that the MCF is now lower than it used to be. This idea also has a considerable appeal to economic intuition. In fact, partial equilibrium analysis would suggest that if increased public expenditure could be financed by Pigouvian or green taxes, the MCF should be *less than one*, since there is now an efficiency *gain* from tax finance which should be subtracted from the direct resource cost. But experience from following the double dividend debate should warn us that there may be complications ahead and that a more general analysis is called for.

Among the contributions that already address this or related questions from a theoretical angle, van der Ploeg and Bovenberg (1994) and Kaplow (1996) are particularly noteworthy. Van der Ploeg and Bovenberg study the effects of varying environmental preferences on the optimal supply of public goods, but they do not discuss the role of environmental taxes in determining the MCF. Kaplow's main concern is to study the role of optimal nonlinear income taxation; under special assumptions about preferences, he shows that we should think of the MCF in first-best terms.[4] The articles by Ballard and Medema (1993) and Brendemoen and Vennemo (1996) use computable general equilibrium models to study alternative sources of finance for public projects and find that the MCF for environmental taxes is much lower than that for traditional taxes, sometimes indeed considerably below unity.

5.2 Individual Behavior and the First-Best Allocation

A desire for redistribution is essential for understanding why existing tax systems are distortionary. The efficiency loss from distortionary taxes therefore has to be balanced against redistributional gains, and to focus solely on the loss side, as is done in most of the literature on the marginal cost of funds, may therefore be misleading. However, in the interests of analytical simplicity, this is nevertheless what we shall do in the following, keeping in mind that distributional concerns can be relatively easily added to the model—for example, in the way it is done in Sandmo (1998). Hence, it is assumed that all n consumers are alike and that the representative consumer's utility function can be written as

$$U = U(y, x, l, z, e), \tag{1}$$

where y and x are the quantities of two consumer goods, l is leisure, z is the supply of a public good, and e is environmental pollution. U is increasing in the first four arguments and decreasing in the fifth.

Environmental pollution is generated by the aggregate consumption of the x good, so that $e = nx$. Labor supply is denoted by h, with $h + l = T$, which is the time endowment.

Each consumer maximizes his utility, taking the supply of public goods and the amount of environmental pollution as given, subject to the budget constraint

$$y + Px = w(1 - t)h + a. \tag{2}$$

The y good is the numeraire, while the consumer price of the x good is $P = p + \tau$, where p is the producer price and τ is the tax rate. Labor income is subject to tax at the rate t, so that the after-tax wage rate is $w(1 - t)$. The variable a is any exogenous income that the consumer might have; if $a < 0$, it is a lump-sum tax.

Utility maximization leads to the first-order conditions

$$\frac{U_l}{U_y} = w(1 - t), \tag{3}$$

$$\frac{U_x}{U_y} = P. \tag{4}$$

This gives rise to a supply function for labor,

$$h = h[w(1 - t), P, a, z, e], \tag{5}$$

and demand functions for the two consumer goods. In particular, the demand function for the x good or "dirty good" is

$$x = x[w(1 - t), P, a, z, e]. \tag{6}$$

We assume that the dirty good is normal ($\partial x/\partial a > 0$), implying that demand is a decreasing function of price ($\partial x/\partial P < 0$).

Note the dependence of these functions on the state of the environment, e. While this is an exogenous variable from the point of view of each single individual,[5] changes in prices, taxes, and public goods supply will in the aggregate affect individual behavior through their effects on e and the feedback effects on labor supply and commodity demands. Many writers have chosen to neglect these feedback effects; the case in which there is a rigorous justification for it is, of course, where the utility function is weakly separable between the state of the environment and other goods, so that

$$U = U[\varphi(y, x, l, z), e]. \tag{1'}$$

Separability is hardly a realistic assumption, and for a number of environmental problems, such as traffic congestion, nonseparability and feedback effects are obviously very important. Nevertheless, it will be adopted in what follows, basically because it simplifies the analysis without distorting the qualitative conclusions that can be drawn from it.

Optimizing behavior also implies the indirect utility function

$$V = V[w(1 - t), P, a, z, e],$$ (7)

with the Roy conditions

$$V_t = -\lambda wh; V_P = -\lambda x; V_a = \lambda,$$ (8)

where the Lagrange multiplier λ is the marginal utility of income.

We now turn from individual behavior to social welfare maximization. With all individuals being alike, a natural choice for a social welfare function is the utilitarian sum of utilities, which is simply $W = nU$. The production possibility schedule is assumed to be of the linear Ricardian form, so that it can be written as

$$-wnh + ny + pnx + qz = 0.$$ (9)

Here, w, p, and q are the technical production coefficients. The symbols have been chosen to reflect the fact that under competitive conditions, the coefficients will be equal to equilibrium producer prices, again with the y good as the numeraire.

Social welfare maximization is now characterized by the first-order optimality conditions

$$\frac{U_l}{U_y} = w,$$ (10)

$$\frac{U_x}{U_y} + n\frac{U_e}{U_y} = p,$$ (11)

$$n\frac{U_z}{U_y} = q.$$ (12)

Comparing (10) and (11) with the conditions for individual utility maximization, (3) and (4), we can characterize the first-best optimal tax structure. This is simply $t = 0$ and $\tau = -nU_e/U_y$. There should be no distortionary tax in the labor market, and the tax on the dirty good should reflect the marginal social damage, that is, the sum of the marginal damages imposed on all individuals. Finally, the public good should be supplied according to the Samuelson (1954) optimality rule: The sum of the marginal willingness to pay across all individuals should equal the marginal cost or the marginal rate of transformation. In this case, the MCF is unity, since the marginal social benefit is simply equated to the marginal social cost. If this combination of taxes and public goods supply leads to a deficit or surplus in the government's budget constraint, the gap should be filled by a lump-sum transfer from or to the consumers, that is, by an adjustment of the lump-sum income term, a.

5.3   Public Goods Supply with Distortionary Taxes

We now abandon the assumption that lump-sum taxes are feasible. In the real world of heterogeneous consumers, individualized lump-sum taxes would be the ideal way of raising revenue while simultaneously redistributing income, but, for well-known reasons, such taxes are not practically feasible. In a model economy of identical individuals, however, there is no real reason why it should be impossible to collect the same amount in taxes from all individuals. In this context, the assumption must therefore be seen simply as an ad hoc device to concentrate on the efficiency properties of a second-best optimum situation. The government has to finance the cost of supplying the public good partly by means of the distortionary income tax and partly through the Pigouvian tax on the dirty good. As a natural point of reference, we begin by deriving the conditions for a second-best optimum. What is the optimal supply of the public good, and what is the best combination of the labor income tax and the Pigouvian tax?

The government's budget constraint says that taxes collected must equal expenditure, so that

$$ntwh + n\tau x = qz, \tag{13}$$

while the social welfare function can be written in dual form as

$$W = nV[w(1-t), P, a, z, e], \tag{14}$$

where a must now be understood as constrained to zero.

We are now in a position to study how the cost of public goods supply depends on the costs of tax finance. There are, in principle, two ways in which this can be done. We could, as Atkinson and

Stern (1974) did, adopt the framework of optimal taxation and public goods, or we could, as is more or less implicit in cost-benefit analysis, consider a balanced budget change in public expenditure and taxes without assuming anything about optimality. The first approach gives the most straightforward definition of the MCF as a shadow price emerging from the optimality conditions. The second, however, is much less restrictive and more relevant for the view of the MCF as a practical tool for the evaluation of public projects. In the following, we shall pursue both approaches and see how they are related.

Starting within the optimality framework, the problem is to maximize (14) with respect to the tax rates t and τ, subject to the budget constraint (13). The Lagrangean can be written as

$$\Lambda = nV[w(1-t), P, z, e] + \mu(ntwh + nt\tau x - qz). \tag{15}$$

Keeping in mind that $e = nx$ and that producer prices are constant, the first-order conditions for this optimization problem[6] are

$$\frac{\partial \Lambda}{\partial t} = -n\lambda wh + nV_e n \frac{\partial x}{\partial t} + \mu \left(nwh + ntw \frac{\partial h}{\partial t} + n\tau \frac{\partial x}{\partial t} \right) = 0, \tag{16}$$

$$\frac{\partial \Lambda}{\partial \tau} = -n\lambda x + nV_e n \frac{\partial x}{\partial P} + \mu \left(nx + ntw \frac{\partial h}{\partial P} + n\tau \frac{\partial x}{\partial P} \right) = 0, \tag{17}$$

$$\frac{\partial \Lambda}{\partial z} = nV_z + nV_e n \frac{\partial x}{\partial z} + \mu \left(ntw \frac{\partial h}{\partial z} + n\tau \frac{\partial x}{\partial z} - q \right) = 0. \tag{18}$$

Although the three conditions provide a joint characterization of the optimal tax-expenditure policy, it is natural to see (18) as the optimality condition for public goods supply. Dividing through this equation by λ and rearranging terms, we obtain

$$n\frac{V_z}{\lambda} + n\frac{V_e}{\lambda} n \frac{\partial x}{\partial z} = \gamma \left(q - ntw \frac{\partial h}{\partial z} - n\tau \frac{\partial x}{\partial z} \right), \tag{19}$$

where $\gamma = \mu/\lambda$. The interpretation of condition (19) is straightforward. The first term on the left is the Samuelson sum of the marginal rates of substitution—that is, the direct benefit of the increase in public goods supply. The second term is the indirect benefit that arises because the public good may cause a change in the amount of environmental damage. This benefit is positive if the dirty good and the public good are substitutes ($\partial x/\partial z < 0$) and negative if they are complements $(\partial x / \partial z > 0)$. On the right-hand side, q is the direct resource cost of the public good, as before. The direct resource cost is modified by the remaining two terms in parentheses. These terms represent the change in tax revenue that is generated by an increased public goods supply; to the extent that the public good increases the tax bases, it counteracts the adverse distortionary effects of the taxes, so that real resource costs are lowered. Finally, the parameter γ represents the ratio of the marginal utilities of income in the private and public sectors and is a measure of the inefficiency of the tax system. It is this parameter that will be identified with the marginal cost of public funds, so that MCF $= \gamma$.

However, a question may be raised as to whether γ alone is too restrictive as a measure of the MCF. In particular, one might argue that the tax revenue effects should also somehow be included, since they too characterize the second-best optimality condition in contrast to the first-best Samuelson rule. Something may be said for this, but the issue depends on how one sees the practical role of the concept of the MCF. The point of view taken here is that the potential usefulness of the MCF lies in cost-benefit analyses of public goods projects funded by general tax finance, and that it should be defined in a way that will make it the same for all projects. But the bracketed expression in (19) is project-specific, since the only realistic assumption is that each public good is characterized by a different degree of substitutability or complementarity with private taxed goods. On the other hand, γ is a characteristic of the system of tax finance and does not vary with the nature of the project. Thus, the modification of the direct resource cost via the effect of the public good on the tax base should be seen as a separate operation, to be performed before the MCF is applied to the net resource cost of the project.[7]

5.4 An Optimal Tax Structure

When both tax rates have been chosen in accordance with the second-best optimal tax criterion,[8] it follows that the MCF at the optimum must be the same, *whatever the source of tax finance*. This follows by noting that when (16) and (17) both hold, we must have

$$\frac{wh - n \dfrac{V_e}{\lambda} \dfrac{\partial x}{\partial t}}{wh + tw \dfrac{\partial h}{\partial t} + \tau \dfrac{\partial x}{\partial t}} = \gamma = \frac{x - n \dfrac{V_e}{\lambda} \dfrac{\partial x}{\partial P}}{x + tw \dfrac{\partial h}{\partial P} + \tau \dfrac{\partial x}{\partial P}}. \tag{20}$$

Can anything be said about the common value of the two expressions for the MCF? Simple conditions in terms of these demand and supply derivatives seem difficult to derive. Still, there are two important messages to take away from (20). The first is the equality of the two measures of the MCF, and that it is only in the case where the whole tax system has been optimized that the concept of *one* MCF is a valid one. The second message has the form of a caution. It might be tempting to conclude that the common value of the MCF must be lower in this case than it would have been, had the green tax for some reason not been available—the reason being presumably that the value of the objective function must increase with the number of policy instruments that can be used. The fallacy in this line of reasoning is that it is not the MCF but social welfare that is the policy objective, and that there is no one-to-one correspondence between social welfare and the value of the MCF. We might still think that this would be a reasonably realistic conclusion, but it does not follow directly from the simple logic of optimization theory.

5.5 Beyond Optimization: The Reform Perspective

In the previous section, we considered the marginal cost of public funds as a shadow price related to the solution of an optimization problem. But if the MCF is to be used in an evaluation of particular proposals for increased supply of a public good, the optimality setting is very restrictive. A more natural framework is that of the theory of tax reform, although extended to take account of a possible increase in public expenditure. The question is then whether increased expenditure increases welfare, given the nature of the taxes that are used to finance it.

We begin by studying the condition for welfare improvement following a simultaneous change in tax rates and public goods supply. If we take the differential of the social welfare function (14), the condition can be written as

$$
dW = \left(-n\lambda wh + nV_e n \frac{\partial x}{\partial t} \right) dt + \left(-n\lambda x + nV_e n \frac{\partial x}{\partial P} \right) d\tau
$$

$$
+ \left(nV_z + nV_e n \frac{\partial x}{\partial z} \right) dz > 0. \tag{21}
$$

The increased expenditure must be balanced by a corresponding increase in tax revenue, so that from the government's budget constraint, we must have

$$\left(nwh + ntw\frac{\partial h}{\partial t} + n\tau\frac{\partial x}{\partial t}\right)dt + \left(nx + ntw\frac{\partial h}{\partial P} + n\tau\frac{\partial x}{\partial P}\right)d\tau$$

$$+ \left(ntw\frac{\partial h}{\partial z} + n\tau\frac{\partial x}{\partial z} - q\right)dz = 0. \tag{22}$$

We can now use (21) and (22) to analyze the conditions for increased public goods supply to be welfare-improving under alternative assumptions about the source of tax finance.

An interesting issue is, of course, the extent to which the analysis of optimal taxation provides any insights that are useful for the reform perspective. It is useful to explore the connection between the two approaches via the simple case where the green tax is the only source of finance. One might perhaps think that this implies a reversion to the first-best. This is not true, however, since there is no guarantee that the revenue generated by the first-best level of the green tax would finance an optimal amount of the public good. The optimal resource cost of the public good might be either higher or lower than this, and budget balance must be achieved through a simultaneous adjustment of the tax and the public goods supply. The next section therefore considers the MCF for pure green finance and contrasts the optimum tax approach with that of the reform perspective.

5.6   The Case of Pure Green Finance

We start by considering the analysis in an optimal tax framework. With $t = 0$, (19) becomes

$$n\frac{V_z}{\lambda} + n\frac{V_e}{\lambda}n\frac{\partial x}{\partial z} = \gamma\left(q - n\tau\frac{\partial x}{\partial z}\right). \tag{23}$$

The MCF, which will now be written as γ_τ to indicate the source of finance, can now be obtained from the last part of (20), after setting $t = 0$, as

$$\gamma_\tau = \frac{x - n\dfrac{V_e}{\lambda}\dfrac{\partial x}{\partial P}}{x + \tau\dfrac{\partial x}{\partial P}}. \tag{24}$$

As pointed out earlier, intuition might suggest that with purely green taxation, the MCF could well be below one. However, the form of (24) does not immediately indicate that this is the case. A more careful analysis of this equation is accordingly called for.

Note first that the expression in the denominator represents the derivative of tax revenue with respect to the green tax. In standard optimal tax theory, the tax revenue effect is positive at the optimum; an increase in the tax rate inflicts a loss on consumers, and to offset this loss, the tax revenue effect must be positive. In other words, each tax rate must be on the rising part of its "Laffer curve." In the case of a green tax, however, this is not necessarily the case. An increase in the price $P = p + \tau$ involves a loss to the consumer through the negative effect on purchasing power, but at the same time it improves the environment, which is a gain. A higher tax at the margin might therefore represent a net gain for the consumer, and in this case it could happen that the marginal tax revenue effect could be negative at the optimum.[9] But the conventional assumption of a positive revenue effect seems to be the more interesting and relevant one, and I shall concentrate on this. Given that assumption (in addition to the assumption that the dirty good is normal, so that $\partial x/\partial P$ is negative), it is easy to see that (24) implies the following:

$$\gamma_\tau > 1 \text{ if and only if } \tau > -n\frac{V_e}{\lambda}. \tag{25}$$

In words, the marginal cost of public funds exceeds one in the case where the optimum green tax rate exceeds its Pigouvian level; conversely, it is less than one if the tax is below this level. The intuition behind the result is easy to understand. When the tax exceeds its Pigouvian level, its role *on the margin* becomes that of an ordinary distortionary tax; it is higher than required to equalize marginal social benefits and costs. In that case, the MCF must necessarily be greater than one. When, on the other hand, it is below that level, an additional increase goes further in the direction of internalizing the externality, so that there is a social benefit involved in a higher tax rate. The higher tax leads to a lower degree of distortion, so that the MCF becomes less than one.

It is worth noting that the borderline case $\tau = -n(V_e/\lambda)$, where the second-best tax rate coincides with the first-best, also has the implication that the condition for optimal public goods supply (23)

becomes simply $n(V_z/\lambda) = q$. When the green tax—by coincidence—
internalizes the externality perfectly, there is no need to take account
of the effect of public goods supply on the environmental externality,
and the Samuelson optimality condition holds without modification.

Having studied the case of pure green finance from an optimum
taxation viewpoint, we now revert to the reform perspective. Here,
no assumption is being made about the optimality of taxes and
expenditure. With pure green finance, we have that $dt = t = 0$ in (21)
and (22). Eliminating $d\tau$ from the last expression, we can rewrite (21)
as

$$\frac{dW}{dz} > 0 \text{ if and only if } n\frac{V_z}{\lambda} + n\frac{V_e}{\lambda}n\frac{\partial x}{\partial z} > \gamma_\tau\left(q - n\tau\frac{\partial x}{\partial z}\right), \qquad (26)$$

where, as before,

$$\gamma_\tau = \frac{x - n\dfrac{V_e}{\lambda}\dfrac{\partial x}{\partial P}}{x + \tau\dfrac{\partial x}{\partial P}}. \qquad (27)$$

The expression for the MCF is the same as (24), while the condition
for welfare improvement has the same form as (23); the difference
is simply that the equality sign in (23) has been replaced by an
inequality. Whether the MCF is greater or less than one depends on
whether the green tax is above or below its first-best level. Thus, the
basic logic of the analysis and the usefulness of the MCF concept are
valid outside of the optimal tax-expenditure framework.

In considering the identical expressions (24) and (27), it should, of
course, be kept in mind that although the expressions have the
same form, the actual *value* of the MCF is unlikely to be the same.
In the case represented by (24), the value has been derived as a
shadow price in a second-best optimization problem, while in (27)
there are no such restrictions on taxes and quantities. The important
message—which is easily seen to be valid beyond this particular
example—is that the correct way to think about the components of
the MCF is independent of any optimality assumptions. This is consistent with the more general analysis of the principles of cost-benefit
analysis by Drèze and Stern (1987), who also point out that the definition of shadow prices does not depend on the assumption that the
government has carried out an optimal plan.

5.7 A Fixed Distortion in the Labor Market

A natural extension of the previous analysis is to the case where the green tax is still the marginal source of finance, but where there is a fixed tax distortion in the labor market. This case can be seen as representing the more general case where the income tax system has been designed to a large extent with distributional objectives in mind and where the marginal tax rate accordingly is not adjusted to finance the marginal expenditure on public goods.

With the insights established in the previous section, it is now natural to focus on the reform framework. Thus, in (21) and (22) we have $t > 0$ but $dt = 0$. Proceeding as we did earlier, we derive the expression for the MCF as

$$\gamma_\tau = \frac{x - n\dfrac{V_e}{\lambda}\dfrac{\partial x}{\partial P}}{x + tw\dfrac{\partial h}{\partial P} + \tau\dfrac{\partial x}{\partial P}}. \tag{28}$$

To study the condition for $\gamma_\tau > 1$, we continue to assume that the effect on tax revenue of raising τ is positive. The condition then becomes

$$\left(\tau + n\dfrac{V_e}{\lambda}\right)\dfrac{\partial x}{\partial P} < -tw\dfrac{\partial h}{\partial P}. \tag{29}$$

Dividing through by $\partial x/\partial P$, which is negative, we may conclude that

$$\gamma_\tau > 1 \text{ if and only if } \tau + n\dfrac{V_e}{\lambda} > -tw\dfrac{\partial h}{\partial P}\bigg/\dfrac{\partial x}{\partial P}. \tag{30}$$

The left-hand side of the inequality is the deviation of the green tax from its first-best level.[10] The right-hand side has the sign of $\partial h/\partial P$. In the absence of quantitative information about the relationships involved, one firm conclusion that can be drawn is the following:

$$\gamma_\tau > 1 \text{ if } \tau > -n\dfrac{V_e}{\lambda} \text{ and } \dfrac{\partial h}{\partial P} < 0. \tag{31}$$

It also follows that

$$\gamma_\tau < 1 \text{ if } \tau < -n\dfrac{V_e}{\lambda} \text{ and } \dfrac{\partial h}{\partial P} > 0. \tag{32}$$

Both (31) and (32) state *sufficient* conditions for the MCF to be greater than or less than one, respectively, but each of them also alerts us to the difficulties involved in providing necessary conditions in this type of setting. From our previous discussion of the benchmark case of pure green finance, we would indeed expect the MCF to exceed one in the case where the green tax is above its Pigouvian level. If $\partial h/\partial P = 0$, so that labor supply had been independent of the level of green taxation, that result would have carried over to the present case. But when the cross-price effect differs from zero, the increase in the price of the dirty good affects the magnitude of the labor market distortion. Suppose that the conditions in (31) hold, so that labor and the dirty good are complements. Then, a further increase in τ would exacerbate the distortion in the market for the dirty good, while simultaneously making the distortion in the labor market more severe by lowering the supply of labor. This makes the MCF unequivocally greater than one. If, on the other hand, labor and the dirty good had been substitutes, an increase in τ would involve an increase in one distortion and a decrease in the other. Depending on the relative strengths of the two effects, the MCF could be either less than or equal to one.

Condition (32) has a similar interpretation. A value of τ below its Pigouvian level would seem to indicate an MCF less than one. But because of the effect on labor supply of an increase in the price of the dirty good, it is only in the case of substitutability $(\partial h/\partial P > 0)$ that this conclusion can be firmly extended to the case of a distorted labor market.

In connection with (32), there is a special case that deserves particular attention—namely, that where the initial value of τ is zero. In discussions of the double dividend from a green tax reform, the thought experiment that some people seem to have in mind is where green taxes are introduced into an overall tax system where they were previously not present. In general, (28) indicates that such a reform will imply an MCF below unity provided that the green tax does not sufficiently strongly magnify the effects of previous tax distortions in the economy.

5.8   The Income Tax as the Marginal Source of Funds

As a further thought experiment, we may briefly consider the case where the increase in public expenditure is financed by means of increased income taxation and where the level of green taxes is held constant. Going back to the inequalities (21) and (22), this involves setting $d\tau = 0$, and the marginal cost of funds can then be derived as

$$\gamma_t = \frac{wh - n\dfrac{V_e}{\lambda}\dfrac{\partial x}{\partial t}}{wh + tw\dfrac{\partial h}{\partial t} + \tau\dfrac{\partial x}{\partial t}}. \tag{33}$$

Again assuming the denominator of the right-hand side to be positive, it follows that

$$\gamma_t > 1 \text{ if and only if } \left(\tau + n\frac{V_e}{\lambda}\right)\frac{\partial x}{\partial t} < -tw\frac{\partial h}{\partial t}. \tag{34}$$

This condition does not give us a clear answer as to the numerical magnitude of γ_t. It does, however, give rise to the same type of classification as (30), which, it will be recalled, concerns the "reverse" case, where t is fixed and the green tax is the marginal source of funds. Let us assume that labor supply is a decreasing function of the marginal tax rate. Sufficient conditions for the condition in (34) to hold are then either

• that the green tax is below its Pigouvian level and that the demand for the dirty good is an increasing function of the income tax rate, or

• that the green tax is above its Pigouvian level and that the demand for the dirty good is a decreasing function of the income tax rate.

In both cases, the economic intuition behind the conclusion that $\gamma_t > 1$ is that the increase in the rate of income tax, in addition to worsening labor market efficiency, also magnifies the existing distortion in the market for the dirty good. It is also worth pointing out that while in the standard analysis of the income tax, the MCF equals one if the labor supply elasticity is zero, this is not the case here. This is easily seen from (33). The two cases of sufficient conditions mentioned above would in that case continue to yield an MCF in excess of one, since the income tax affects the demand for the dirty good.

These are not the only sets of sufficient conditions that lead to firm qualitative conclusions about the magnitude of the marginal cost of funds for income tax finance. A number of other combinations of assumptions could be listed (one could, for example, repeat the above exercise for the case of $\partial h/\partial t > 0$), but they do not yield much additional insight into the nature of the problem. The general message is, as before, that under second-best conditions, it is essential to consider the interaction between distortions in different markets.

5.9   A Simplified Rule for Green Taxes

A weak point of optimal tax theory is its neglect of the administrative costs of the tax system. Including the administrative costs of taxes explicitly in the optimization framework raises a number of difficulties, particularly with regard to the nonconvexities involved, and to tackle these is far beyond the scope of this chapter. However, one topic that deserves discussion in the present context is the question of decentralization of tax decisions. If green taxes and environmental charges come to be more widely used in the coming decades, there will be a heavy burden on the ministry of finance, in terms of information collection and decision-making capacity, if all decisions about taxes are to be its responsibility. A more realistic scenario is one where decisions about a large number of environmental taxes and charges become decentralized to the ministry of the environment or perhaps regional authorities with responsibility for local pollution control. In that case, it would be unreasonable and impractical to ask all these units to take account of all possible secondary effects of the tax system—for example, the green tax effects on labor market performance. Instead, the central government should provide more simple guidelines for lower-level units, and one such guideline might be to set environmental taxes according to the first-best Pigouvian formula $\tau = -n(V_e/\lambda)$. Calculations of the MCF for the central government would then be based on the assumption that revenue is to be generated through variations in the income tax rate t, assuming that those responsible for environmental taxes keep these linked to the expression for marginal social damage.

The MCF can now be derived as a special case of (33)—namely, where $\tau = -n(V_e/\lambda)$. We then get

$$\gamma_t = \frac{wh + \tau \dfrac{\partial x}{\partial t}}{wh + tw \dfrac{\partial h}{\partial t} + \tau \dfrac{\partial x}{\partial t}}. \tag{35}$$

It follows immediately, assuming again that the tax revenue effect is positive, that

$\gamma_t > 1$ if and only if $tw\dfrac{\partial h}{\partial t} < 0.$ $\hspace{3cm}$ (36)

With a positive tax rate, the MCF exceeds one if the labor supply elasticity with respect to the tax rate is negative, and is below one if it is positive. This is a very simple condition, providing a clear focus on what determines the magnitude of the efficiency costs of financing public goods through central government finance. The decentralization scheme on which this condition is based is suboptimal in the sense that one can always do better by coordinating decisions—in principle. But the decentralization rule is likely to be better in terms of administrative resource use, representing a practically feasible division of responsibilities within the public sector.

5.10   Concluding Remarks

Simple economic intuition suggests that when the supply of public goods can be financed by means of environmental taxes, the method of finance yields an efficiency gain to the economy; hence, the marginal cost of public funds should be less than one. This chapter has shown that this intuition should be handled with care. Even in the case with no traditional income or commodity taxes, the intuition fails to be valid if the initial level of the Pigouvian tax is above its first-best level. In the more general case where there exist both traditional and environmental taxes, the implications for the MCF depend crucially on the nature of interaction between markets. The existence of environmental taxes also has important implications for the magnitude of the MCF from traditional taxes such as the income tax. However, in all the thought experiments that we have considered, there emerges a formula for the MCF which has a strong appeal to the not-so-simple intuition that one develops from the study of optimal second-best tax systems. Moreover, these formulae can be shown to be valid not only when the tax system is assumed to satisfy the conditions for second-best optimality, but also in the much less restrictive framework of a balanced-budget expansion of public goods supply.

Notes

I am grateful to the discussant, Jeremy Edwards, for his perceptive comments on the original version of the chapter, and to the referees for useful suggestions. I am also grateful to Don Fullerton for a very careful reading of the chapter and for a number of extremely helpful remarks on both its form and its substance.

1. Or, more generally, publicly provided goods. These might—and indeed do—also comprise private goods in areas such as healthcare and education.

2. Thus, the present chapter can be seen as utilizing and combining two of Pigou's important contributions to the public economics literature—the possibility of efficiency-improving environmental taxes and the link between tax distortions and public goods supply. The idea of what we now refer to as Pigouvian taxes was first introduced in Pigou (1920); see in particular page 99 of the fourth edition (1932).

3. For a more detailed analysis, see Sandmo (2000, chap. 6) and the review of the literature by Bovenberg (1999).

4. This is closely related to an earlier result in an important paper by Christiansen (1981).

5. This may require a comment in view of the assumption that all individuals are identical. The essential part of the assumption is that each consumer's use of the dirty good is small relative to aggregate consumption and pollution. Under that assumption, even when individuals are not identical, each one of them may know that others respond to prices and income in the same way as he does himself, but it is still not rational for him to take this into account in his own consumption decisions. This is simply the assumption of perfectly competitive behavior.

6. The form of the optimality conditions reflects the assumption of separability of e. In the general case, the partial derivatives such as $\partial h/\partial t$ would have to be replaced by derivatives dh/dt, and so forth, which would take account of the environmental feedback on demands and supplies. See Sandmo (2000, chap. 6) for details.

7. Atkinson and Stern (1974), in their comparison of the optimality rules for public goods under first-best and second-best conditions, do not make this conceptual distinction between the two types of effects, but it should be kept in mind that their paper was written long before the modern focus on the MCF as a tool for decentralized decision making in the public sector.

8. The reader may check that conditions (16) and (17) together imply the property of additivity, as it was called in Sandmo (1975), or the principle of targeting. Solving the two equations for t and τ, it can be shown that the characterization formula for the income tax rate is a generalized version of the Ramsey inverse elasticity and is independent of the marginal social damage, while the formula for the green tax is the weighted sum of a Ramsey term and one reflecting the marginal social damage. Of the available taxes, it is only the tax on the dirty good that, in the optimal design of the tax system, is targeted on improving the environment.

9. It is easy to understand why an optimal green tax might be on the downward-sloping part of its Laffer curve. If the marginal social damage is high enough, as in the case of toxic waste, it might indeed be optimal to set the tax at a level where a reduction of the tax would increase revenues. One of the reasons why, in this particular context, this case is of less interest is that when the optimal tax is close to being prohibitive, regulations—for example, in the form of outright prohibition—would do just as well as taxes.

10. Or, more correctly, the deviation of the tax from its first-best *characterization*. In a distorted equilibrium, the value of an environmental improvement will, in general,

differ from what it would have been under first-best conditions, although its analytical representation has the same form.

References

Atkinson, A. B., and N. H. Stern. 1974. "Pigou, Taxation and Public Goods." *Review of Economic Studies* 41: 119–128.

Ballard, C. L., and D. Fullerton. 1992. "Distortionary Taxes and the Provision of Public Goods." *Journal of Economic Perspectives* 6 (Summer): 117–131.

Ballard, C. L., and S. G. Medema. 1993. "The Marginal Efficiency Effects of Taxes and Subsidies in the Presence of Externalities: A Computational General Equilibrium Approach." *Journal of Public Economics* 52: 199–216.

Bovenberg, A. L. 1999. "Green Tax Reforms and the Double Dividend: An Updated Reader's Guide." *International Tax and Public Finance* 6: 421–443.

Brendemoen, A., and H. Vennemo. 1996. "The Marginal Cost of Funds in the Presence of Environmental Externalities." *Scandinavian Journal of Economics* 98: 405–422.

Browning, E. K. 1976. "The Marginal Cost of Public Funds." *Journal of Political Economy* 84: 283–298.

Christiansen, V. 1981. "Evaluation of Public Projects under Optimal Taxation." *Review of Economic Studies* 48: 447–457.

Dahlby, B. 1998. "Progressive Taxation and the Social Marginal Cost of Public Funds." *Journal of Public Economics* 67: 105–122.

Drèze, J., and N. Stern. 1987. "The Theory of Cost-Benefit Analysis." In *Handbook of Public Economics*, vol. 2, ed. A. J. Auerbach and M. Feldstein. Amsterdam: North-Holland.

Håkonsen, L. 1998. "An Investigation into Alternative Representations of the Marginal Cost of Public Funds." *International Tax and Public Finance* 5: 329–343.

Kaplow, L. 1996. "The Optimal Supply of Public Goods and the Distortionary Cost of Taxation." *National Tax Journal* 49: 513–533.

Mayshar, J. 1991. "On Measuring the Marginal Cost of Funds Analytically." *American Economic Review* 81: 1329–1335.

Pigou, A. C. 1920. *The Economics of Welfare*. London: Macmillan. (4th ed., 1932.)

Pigou, A. C. 1928. *A Study in Public Finance*. London: Macmillan. (3rd ed., 1947.)

Samuelson, P. A. 1954. "The Pure Theory of Public Expenditure." *Review of Economics and Statistics* 36: 387–389.

Sandmo, A. 1975. "Optimal Taxation in the Presence of Externalities." *Swedish Journal of Economics* 77: 86–98.

Sandmo, A. 1998. "Redistribution and the Marginal Cost of Public Funds." *Journal of Public Economics* 70: 365–382.

Sandmo, A. 2000. *The Public Economics of the Environment*. Oxford, UK: Oxford University Press.

Van der Ploeg, F., and A. L. Bovenberg. 1994. "Environmental Policy, Public Goods and the Marginal Cost of Public Funds." *Economic Journal* 104: 444–454.

Wildasin, D. A. 1984. "On Public Good Provision with Distortionary Taxation." *Economic Inquiry* 22: 227–243.

Wilson, J. 1991. "Optimal Public Good Provision with Limited Lump Sum Taxation." *American Economic Review* 81: 153–166.

Comments

Jeremy Edwards

The question that Agnar Sandmo addresses in this chapter is how the cost-benefit rule for public good provision is affected if the tax revenue used to finance such provision is raised not by imposing distortionary taxes, but by imposing green taxes which correct negative externalities. Simple intuition might suggest that if distortionary taxes are used to finance public goods, the efficiency costs of such taxes should be included in the cost-benefit calculation, and result in a marginal cost of public funds (MCF) that is greater than one. Correspondingly, if green taxes are used to finance public good provision, simple intuition might suggest that the efficiency gains from imposing such externality-correcting taxes should also be included in the cost-benefit analysis of public good provision, in this case by means of an MCF that is less than one. The chapter shows very clearly that the simple intuition that suggests that the MCF is less than one when green taxes are used to finance public goods is not generally correct. This conclusion complements the result that the MCF is not necessarily greater than one in the case where distortionary taxes are used to finance public goods (Atkinson and Stern 1974). I concur entirely with the chapter's conclusion that simple intuition about the MCF has to be handled with great care, and my comments are limited to an application of its analysis to versions of the double dividend hypothesis.

A standard version of the double dividend hypothesis is based on a reform in which green taxes are substituted for distortionary taxes while holding total tax revenue constant. Such a reform is claimed to yield two dividends: the environmental gain from imposing taxes on externality-generating activities and the tax efficiency gain from substituting green for distortionary taxes. In the introduction to this chapter, Sandmo points out that there is an alternative version of the double dividend hypothesis, in which green taxes yield an environmental gain and the revenue they generate is used to finance additional public good provision while holding revenue from distortionary taxes constant. The chapter analyzes the relationship between green tax revenue and public good provision in detail, but does not subsequently consider the two different versions of the double dividend hypothesis mentioned in its introduction. It is worthwhile indicating how the framework set out in this chapter can be used to analyze these two versions of the double dividend hypothesis.

I assume in most of what follows that there is no optimization of policy, and focus on reforms from an arbitrary starting point. The policymaker has three policy instruments available—the distortionary income tax t, the green tax τ, and the supply of the public good z. A change in the green tax must result in a change in either the distortionary tax or the level of public good provision in order to preserve equilibrium. The Lagrangean for the policymaker's problem (equation (15) of the chapter) is

$$\Lambda = nV[w(1-t), p+\tau, z, nx] + \mu[ntwh + n\tau x - qz]. \tag{1}$$

Consider the case in which τ and z are fixed at some values, so that they are parameters of the policymaker's problem. The value of t will then be determined by the requirement that the government budget balances: In other words, t is the variable that adjusts to ensure equilibrium.[1] In this case, t is nevertheless the control variable with which the problem represented by the Lagrangean (1) is solved, and hence two first-order conditions can be obtained by partially differentiating (1) with respect to t and μ. Although the policymaker is doing no genuine policy optimization and has to choose t simply to satisfy the government budget constraint, the analysis can still make use of some first-order conditions. In their survey of the theory of cost-benefit analysis, Drèze and Stern (1987) describe this as the "fully-determined" case.

The two first-order conditions obtained by differentiating (1) with respect to t and μ are, respectively,[2]

$$-n\lambda wh + nV_e n\frac{\partial x}{\partial t} + \mu\left(nwh + ntw\frac{\partial h}{\partial t} + n\tau\frac{\partial x}{\partial t}\right) = 0, \tag{2}$$

$$ntwh + n\tau x - qz = 0. \tag{3}$$

Equation (3) determines the value of t at which the government budget balances; given this value, and the associated values of x and h, (2) determines the value of μ implied by the requirement that the government budget is balanced. These equations imply that, in this case of no genuine policy optimization and budget balance ensured by t, the MCF is

$$\gamma_t \left(\equiv \frac{\mu}{\lambda} \right) = \left(wh - \frac{V_e}{\lambda} n \frac{\partial x}{\partial t} \right) \Big/ \left(wh + tw \frac{\partial h}{\partial t} + \tau \frac{\partial x}{\partial t} \right). \tag{4}$$

The variable γ_t is the marginal social welfare gain (measured in terms of private income) that can be achieved by cutting t if the public sector receives a gift of one unit of tax revenue.

Now suppose that there is a small increase in the green tax τ from its parametric value. The welfare effect of this small increase, with t adjusting to ensure government budget balance, can be found (using the Envelope Theorem) by differentiating (1) with respect to τ. Doing so gives, after some manipulation, the following condition for such a green tax reform to raise social welfare:

$$\frac{V_e}{\lambda} n \frac{\partial x}{\partial P} + \gamma_t \left(tw \frac{\partial h}{\partial P} + x + \tau \frac{\partial x}{\partial P} \right) > x. \tag{5}$$

This condition expresses the effects of a green tax reform on social welfare along the lines of the standard version of the double dividend hypothesis, in which the net revenue effect leads to an offsetting change in distortionary tax revenue. The term on the right-hand side of (5) represents the cost to consumers of the dirty good of increasing the green tax. The benefits of this increase are given by the left-hand side of (5). The first term here is the value of the environmental change due to the increase in the green tax, while the second is the consequent net effect on tax revenue, adjusted by γ_t, the value of which reflects the efficiency cost of distortionary taxation. These two terms constitute the potential double dividend in this case. The first term is positive, given the assumptions of the chapter. However, the net effect on revenue can be positive or negative, while, as the discussion in section 5.8 of the chapter shows, γ_t can be greater or less than one.

The alternative version of the double dividend hypothesis is to suppose that the revenue from the green tax reform is used not to reduce the distortionary tax, but to increase public good provision.

Formally, this is the case in which τ and t are fixed at some values, so that they are parameters of the policymaker's problem, while the value of z is determined by the requirement that the government budget balances. The control variable that solves the problem represented by the Lagrangean (1) is now z instead of t, and hence two first-order conditions can be obtained by partially differentiating (1) with respect to z and μ. Consequently, (2) is replaced by

$$nV_z + nV_e n \frac{\partial x}{\partial z} + \mu \left(ntw \frac{\partial h}{\partial z} + n\tau \frac{\partial x}{\partial z} - q \right) = 0, \tag{6}$$

and in this case of no genuine policy optimization and budget balance ensured by adjustments in z, the MCF is

$$\gamma_z = \left(\frac{V_z}{\lambda} + \frac{V_e}{\lambda} n \frac{\partial x}{\partial z} \right) \Big/ \left(\frac{q}{n} - tw \frac{\partial h}{\partial z} - \tau \frac{\partial x}{\partial z} \right). \tag{7}$$

The variable γ_z is the marginal social welfare gain (measured in terms of private income) that can be achieved by increasing z if the public sector receives a gift of one unit of tax revenue.

The welfare effect of a small increase in the green tax τ, with z adjusting to ensure government budget balance, is, as before, found (using the Envelope Theorem) by differentiating (1) with respect to τ. The condition for this green tax reform to raise social welfare is

$$\frac{V_e}{\lambda} n \frac{\partial x}{\partial P} + \gamma_z \left(tw \frac{\partial h}{\partial P} + x + \tau \frac{\partial x}{\partial P} \right) > x. \tag{8}$$

The form of condition (8) differs from (5) only in that the net effect of the green tax increase on tax revenue is now adjusted by γ_z. The reason for this is that the net revenue effect now leads to a change in public good provision, and the value of γ_z reflects the benefits of such provision. It is clear from (7) that γ_z can also be greater or less than one. Since there is no assumption of any genuine policy optimization, there is no reason at all to suppose that $\gamma_z = \gamma_t$. It is, for example, perfectly possible that $\gamma_z > 1$ while $\gamma_t < 1$.

If, however, the policymaker can use both t and z as control variables, so that some genuine policy optimization occurs, (2) and (6) will both apply (together with (3)), and hence $\gamma_t = \gamma_z$. In this case, the effect of a green tax reform on social welfare is independent of whether the change in net revenue leads to a reduction in distortionary taxation or an increase in public good provision.

Notes

1. I assume that, for arbitrary values of any two of the policy instruments, a value of the third satisfying the government budget constraint always exists.

2. These first-order conditions reflect the chapter's assumption of weak separability of the representative consumer's utility function between the state of the environment and other goods.

References

Atkinson, A. B., and N. H. Stern. 1974. "Pigou, Taxation and Public Goods." *Review of Economic Studies* 41: 119–128.

Drèze, J. P., and N. H. Stern. 1987. "The Theory of Cost-Benefit Analysis." In *Handbook of Public Economics*, vol. 2, ed. A. J. Auerbach and M. S. Feldstein. Amsterdam: North-Holland.

6   Taxes and Privatization

Roger H. Gordon

6.1   Introduction

Public ownership of firms and banks was a common phenomenon during the first few decades following World War II, not just under Communist governments but even in many developed market economies. Such ownership was rationalized in the academic literature by Lange (1938) and Lerner (1944), who argued that in *theory* a state-owned firm can replicate the allocation decisions of a privately owned firm, and yet can avoid misallocations resulting from externalities or market failures. The strong economic performance of the most market-based economies, and of private relative to state-owned firms, during this period likely explains the shift in both political and academic views toward one favoring complete and immediate privatization of state-owned firms. The expectation now appears to be that privatization is always appropriate, and that productivity of firms should jump following privatization, once market forces more freely come into play, inducing firms to exploit rapidly any efficiency-enhancing reallocations.[1]

Since the 1970s, Latin American and Western European countries, as well as Japan, have privatized many firms that had long been state-owned. More recently, one of the first priorities in many transition countries has been to privatize their existing state-owned firms quickly and fully. This occurred not just in what had been the GDR, where available market institutions in the rest of Germany provided an appropriate legal, tax, and regulatory environment for a market economy. It occurred as well in countries such as Russia and the Czech Republic, where these other institutional changes often occurred gradually following the initial privatizations. Again, the initial expectation seemed to be that productivity would jump quickly in these firms.

Outcomes, however, have been surprisingly mixed, raising questions about whether this immediate privatization in fact was well advised. For example, the most successful transition countries— China and Poland—have been very slow in privatizing at least their larger state-owned firms. While privatized firms in Russia may have been successful at reducing their tax obligations and transferring wealth from outside investors to insiders in the firm, productivity gains within these firms have been limited, and investment in these firms has been stagnant.

One possible explanation for the poor initial performance among the newly privatized firms is that institutions that ensure effective corporate governance were initially weak, yet are an essential prerequisite for efficient operation of at least larger privately owned firms.[2] Without these institutions, managers can easily gain at the expense of outside shareholders as well as the government, by hiding profits—for example, by transferring funds to a private firm fully owned by the manager. In contrast, managers may have only weak incentives to undertake real investments in the firm in the hopes of future profits. The personal cost to them of forgoing current payouts in order to finance new investment is clear. Given that these individuals may no longer be in control in the future, they may not be able to reap directly the future profits from the new investment. In addition, given the poor information flows to the financial market, they may see little current capital gains in the price of their shares in the firm.

These arguments, however, would not be relevant for Western European, and presumably Latin American, countries, where the appropriate institutions ensuring effective corporate governance are long-standing. Even in well-developed market economies, however, recent papers have raised questions about whether private ownership always dominates state ownership.[3] These papers accepted the premise that state-owned firms operate less efficiently than private firms *if* the private firms face efficient incentives. However, due to corporate tax distortions, private firms have an incentive to reduce their capital stock (and their *reported* taxable profits) whenever the resulting efficiency costs are more than offset by the implied tax savings. The overall excess burden of the resulting misallocations should roughly be proportional to the square of the tax rate the firm faces. In contrast, they argued, the efficiency costs from state owner-ship should not directly depend on the tax structure.[4] If tax rates are high enough, then state ownership can be less inefficient than private ownership, and conversely.

Based on this argument, we should expect to see state ownership primarily in countries where tax rates are high. Privatization should then occur in response to a fall in tax rates, around the date when the relative efficiencies of state-owned and privately owned firms are equal, in which case there may be no immediate efficiency conse-quence when a firm is privatized. In contrast, if privatizations occur following a sharp drop in tax rates, the resulting efficiency gain could be large. Conversely, if a firm is privatized when tax rates are still too high (as perhaps was the case in Russia), then efficiency can fall in response to a privatization. Since the excess burden from cor-porate tax distortions should be higher the more capital-intensive the firm, whereas the inefficiencies from government ownership would not clearly be linked to the firm's capital intensity, the past papers forecast that more labor-intensive firms should be privatized first, with the most capital-intensive firms privatized only when corporate tax rates have fallen yet further. In any case, a firm's capital-labor ratio should drop, output should fall, and after-tax profits should rise following privatization, since the firm then maximizes after-tax rather than before-tax profits. Section 6.2 provides a summary of these past arguments.

Unfortunately, some of these forecasts seem to be counterfactual. For example, during the 1980s and 1990s, as Chinese state-owned firms have faced increasingly strong market incentives, managers commonly complained about having excess workers (and particu-larly excess low-skilled workers), rather than excess capital.[5] Simi-larly, when privatizations occur, the key policy concern is commonly not a resulting drop in investment but rather a fear of large-scale layoffs.[6] For example, the Treuhand often imposed constraints on those acquiring privatized firms to maintain employment for at least some time period.

The objective of this chapter is to provide a possible explanation for why state-owned firms seem to be unusually labor-intensive, contrary to the forecasts in earlier papers. The argument has two parts. First, we will argue that cheap credit from state-owned banks is sufficient in itself to avoid the underinvestment otherwise caused by high corporate tax rates, even if nonbank firms remain privately owned.[7] With bank subsidies for *marginal* investments, the corporate tax becomes a tax on *inframarginal* profits. If a state-owned bank were as effective at allocating funds across firms as privately owned banks, then ownership of a state bank alone accomplishes the desired reallocation of resources while avoiding the costs incurred from state ownership of firms more broadly. Capital-labor ratios should then be comparable in private and any nonbank state-owned firms, contrary to the previous forecasts. This argument is developed in detail in section 6.3.

While the role of state banks can explain why state-owned firms are not *more* capital-intensive than privately owned firms, it cannot explain why they are *less* capital-intensive. The second part of the argument is that the corporate tax is by no means the only distortion resulting in inefficient (or inequitable) allocation decisions by private firms. As discussed in section 6.4, many of the other distortions result in too few workers, and particularly too few low-skilled workers, being hired. Examples are income taxes on labor income, the minimum wage, unemployment insurance programs, and unions. Cheap loans from a state-owned bank do nothing to offset these tax or regulatory distortions affecting the labor market. We examine below conditions under which state ownership of some firms can be used to address these labor market distortions. The resulting state-owned firms will be more labor-intensive (and more low-skilled-intensive) than equivalent private firms, consistent with the available evidence.

6.2   Overview of the Role of State Ownership

Why are state-owned firms less efficient than privately owned firms? The reasons can be many. As Kornai (1979) has emphasized, state-owned firms appear to face a soft-budget constraint, so that funds are not normally cut off if the firm pursues inefficient investments.[8] Alternatively, the government-owned sector may simply be too large to be efficient—as argued by Coase (1988), there is an optimal size for the firm, which in practice seems to be dramatically smaller than the size of the state-owned sector. In addition, state firms normally do not have publicly traded shares, making it much more difficult to tie the compensation of managers of state-owned firms to the value of the firm.

The most obvious explanation, however, for the inefficiency of state-owned firms is that they are vulnerable to political interference with respect to almost any dimension of their operations. Private owners, in contrast, should care only about firm value, that is, the discounted present value of firm profits. As argued by Boycko, Shleifer, and Vishny (1996), one key role of privatization is to make such political interference more difficult.

But using political interference to explain why state-owned firms are less efficient simply shifts the question to explaining why political interference will end up being used in ways that reduce efficiency. Possible explanations here are easy. As emphasized, for example, by Buchanan and Tullock (1962), political decisions at best respond to the preferences of the median voter. Except under unusually restrictive assumptions, the implied political preferences will not maximize efficiency or any other reasonable objective function.[9] Once government bureaucrats have independent powers, opportunities for inefficient outcomes expand—campaign contributions and other forms of side payments can induce government officials to aid special interests at the expense of overall efficiency. Government officials would then favor state ownership as a way to gain access to such bribes. Even ignoring these political economy problems, governments appropriately have many objectives in addition to efficiency,[10] implying willingness to accept some inefficiency if the resulting gains in other objectives are large enough.

In spite of these efficiency losses from state ownership, recent papers by Gordon, Bai, and Li (1999) and by Huizinga and Nielsen (2001) explore conditions under which state ownership of firms can increase the sum of the utilities of residents, and even efficiency, if tax distortions are high enough. Rather than modeling these various sources of inefficiency from state ownership explicitly, they simply assume that state-owned firms operate less efficiently.[11] In particular, assume that a private firm chooses to produce output worth $f(K_p, L_p)$, using inputs of K_p units of capital and L_p workers. In contrast, a state-owned firm would produce output worth only $g(K_g, L_g)$,[12] choosing inputs of K_g and L_g, where $f(K,L) > g(K,L)$ for all K and L.

The social surplus from production can be measured by the value to consumers of the output minus the loss to suppliers of the factor inputs. Therefore, the social surplus from a private firm equals $S_p \equiv f(K_p, L_p) - wL_p - rK_p$, whereas that of the public firm equals $S_g \equiv g(K_g, L_g) - wL_g - rK_g$. Here, w is the opportunity cost for workers while r is the opportunity cost of capital on the world market. Let K^* and L^* denote the inputs that maximize the surplus from a private firm—that is, the inputs that would be chosen by a private firm operating in a competitive environment free of any distortions. For any choice of inputs for the public firm, we know that $S_g(K_g, L_g) < S_p(K_g, L_g) \leq S_p(K^*, L^*)$. Let α measure the efficiency loss from public ownership, as a fraction of surplus under private ownership, so that $\alpha = 1 - S_g(K_g, L_g)/S_p(K^*, L^*)$.

Due to tax distortions, however, a private firm would not choose K^* and L^*. Instead, the firm would choose input levels to maximize after-tax profits. If the firm faces a corporate income tax at rate τ, then it will choose inputs to maximize[13]

$$[f(K_p, L_p) - wL_p](1 - \tau) - rK_p. \tag{1}$$

If the firm takes all prices as given and $\tau = 0$, then the outcome should be efficient. If $\tau \neq 0$, then the equilibrium value of K_p is smaller than the efficient level. In particular, starting from the market equilibrium, the marginal efficiency gain from a dollar increase in K_p equals $\tau r/(1 - \tau)$. The average gain per dollar increase in K_p when moving from the market equilibrium to the efficient allocation is approximately $0.5\tau r/(1 - \tau)$. The efficiency loss from the corporate tax is therefore $0.5\tau r \Delta K_p/(1 - \tau)$, where ΔK_p measures the difference between the efficient K_p and the market-chosen value of K_p. Note that

$$\Delta K_p \approx \frac{\partial K_p}{\partial p_K}\left(\frac{\tau r}{1 - \tau}\right), \tag{2}$$

where p_K is the cost of capital.[14] Therefore, the efficiency loss from the corporate tax can be expressed as $0.5\tau^2 r\varepsilon K_p/(1 - \tau)$, where ε is the price elasticity of the demand for capital.

One key simplifying assumption made in the past papers, which we will continue to make, is that the behavior of state-owned firms is not affected by tax distortions. In particular, since the government controls the compensation package of the manager and workers in the firm, it can link compensation to before-tax rather than after-tax profits. In any case, taxes and dividends are functionally equivalent for a state-owned firm, so that all that matters is the sum, not the composition, of these payments, and dividends can adjust to offset any changes in tax rates.

Under these assumptions, the efficiency loss from state ownership is simply $\alpha S_p(K^*, L^*)$, regardless of the tax rate. State ownership then dominates on efficiency grounds if $\alpha S_p < 0.5\tau^2 r\varepsilon K_p/(1 - \tau)$, or if $\tau > \sqrt{2\alpha(1 - \tau)S_p/(\varepsilon r K_p)}$. Therefore, a government can rationally favor state ownership on efficiency grounds, if for whatever reason it chooses a high enough corporate tax rate.[15]

Similarly, if the firm is not a price taker in some market, then again the chosen allocation under private ownership will be inefficient. Regulatory policies may reduce this inefficiency—for example, by imposing government controls over the output price but not over other choices of the firm. As emphasized in the regulatory literature, inefficiencies inevitably will remain—for example, gold-plating if the rate of return allowed exceeds that available elsewhere. Whether private ownership, perhaps subject to regulatory control, is more or less efficient than state ownership, ignoring taxes, depends on the size of the relevant parameters. Taxes, however, further lower the efficiency under private ownership, thereby tending to favor state ownership.

The starting point for this chapter is the apparently counterfactual implications of the earlier stylized model. According to this model, state ownership should be more common when tax rates are high, which does seem consistent with the stylized facts. State ownership should also be more common in industries where monopoly power is an unavoidable problem, again very much consistent with the data. However, the theory forecasts that state-owned firms should be more capital-intensive than equivalent privately owned firms in the same industries. Their capital intensity should then drop following privatization.

These latter forecasts all seem inconsistent with the available evidence. To begin with, managers of state-owned firms complain about having "too many" workers, rather than too much capital. In addition, the commonly cited form of political interference in the operations of state-owned firms is pressure to hire more workers, rather than pressure to invest more. Furthermore, when a state-owned firm is privatized, the fear is layoffs of workers more than disinvestment.

In the next section, we explore how state ownership of the banking system alone may be sufficient to avoid tax distortions to the amount of capital investment, even when other firms are privately owned. This seems a plausible explanation for why state ownership and control of banks has been so common.

6.3   Role of State Ownership of Banks

Before we can sensibly explore the role of state ownership of banks, we need to begin by providing a rationale for the existing tax distortions. In particular, if the assumed tax system does not maximize the government's objective, then any of a variety of policies might provide a third-best means of pushing the incentives faced by private agents towards those consistent with the optimal tax system, including policies affecting bank lending. We therefore begin by constructing a base case in which the tax system is second-best optimal, and then explore whether other nontax policies may improve the resulting allocation.

In the previous models, the corporate tax played a key role. There are various reasons for use of a corporate income tax in the overall tax system. One role, emphasized in Musgrave (1959) and explored empirically recently by Gordon and Slemrod (2000), is to prevent income shifting from the personal to the corporate tax base, undertaken to avoid personal taxes on labor income. Whenever the corporate tax rate is below an individual's personal tax rate, the individual can save on taxes by receiving compensation in a form that is taxed as corporate rather than personal income. For employees in large firms in the United States, the main approach that is available to reclassify personal as corporate income for tax purposes is qualified stock options, use of which is tightly limited by law. For a closely held firm, however, where owners are also workers in the firm, simply retaining income rather than paying wages is sufficient, and here there are no legal restrictions. The best way to prevent this income shifting is to impose a corporate tax rate equal to the maximum personal tax rate. This is exactly the policy, and rationale, seen in Bradford (1989) in his proposed X-tax and in McLure (1991) in his proposed SAT (simplified alternative tax). If conversions between corporate and noncorporate status involve no real costs, then this tax policy ensures that firm owners pay tax at the same rate as they owe on their other personal income.

A second rationale for the corporate tax, also emphasized in Musgrave (1959), is as a needed supplement to existing personal income taxes on income from equity. While interest income is taxed in full under the personal income tax, income from equity largely takes the form of capital gains, which face a lower effective tax rate due to deferral of the tax until realization, due to a lower statutory tax rate if the stock is held until the gains are "long-term," and due to the possible write-up of basis at death. One possible aim of the corporate tax is to provide enough of a supplementary tax on income from equity that the effective tax rates on income from equity and debt are equalized.

Unless the tax rates on income from equity and debt are equalized, the tax system will distort a firm's financial policy.[16] In particular, if the net-of-corporate-tax interest rate paid on corporate debt is below the net-of-tax interest rate that shareholders can earn if they buy these corporate bonds, then there are arbitrage gains when the firm borrows from these investors. Firms will then use debt finance until the offsetting real costs, at the margin, arising plausibly from the resulting higher risks of bankruptcy, are large enough to offset the tax savings from further debt finance.

The key complication is that the corporate tax rate that avoids distorting corporate debt decisions is very different from the rate that avoids any shifting of labor income. As shown, for example, in Gordon and Bradford (1980), the effective personal tax rate on interest income that is embodied in equity prices in theory should equal a weighted average of the personal tax rates faced by all investors, with the weight on each individual's tax rate equal to the value of that person's financial assets divided by a measure of his risk aversion.[17] This weighted average tax rate is necessarily below the maximum personal tax rate. Yet, if the corporate rate is below the maximum personal tax rate, then all individuals in higher personal tax brackets will gain from income shifting. In short, because of the progressive nature of the personal tax, the corporate tax rate cannot be chosen to accomplish both objectives simultaneously. For simplicity of notation, assume that the pressures from income shifting dominate.[18] The chosen corporate tax rate, τ, should then equal the maximum personal tax rate, t_M.[19] In contrast, the weighted average personal tax rate on interest income is denoted by t.

Given these assumptions, firms choose the size of K and L and the amount of debt finance,[20] D, to maximize the net income of equity holders:

$$[f(K,L) - wL - rD - c(D/K)K](1 - t_M) - r(K - D)(1 - t). \qquad (3)$$

Here, $c(D/K)$ measures expected bankruptcy and other agency costs per dollar of capital, as a function of the debt-to-capital ratio.[21] For simplicity, assume that $c(0) = c'(0) = 0$, $c' > 0$, and $c'' > 0$.[22] We assume in addition that $c'(1)$ is sufficiently large that a firm would never be 100 percent debt financed.

The implied first-order condition for K equals[23]

$$f_K = r + c - \gamma c' + r \frac{t_M - t}{1 - t_M}, \tag{4}$$

where $\gamma \equiv D/K$, while the first-order condition for D is

$$c' = r \frac{t_M - t}{1 - t_M}. \tag{5}$$

Note, conditional on the firm's choice for γ, that the efficiency-maximizing level of K would be such that $f_K = r + c$. Equation (4) therefore implies underinvestment in the competitive equilibrium due to the tax distortions. The more progressive is the personal tax structure, and the higher are tax rates more generally, the larger are the efficiency costs from these combined tax distortions, arising both from the underinvestment in capital and from the agency costs c.

To begin with, how could state ownership of firms be used to lessen these combined efficiency costs (though at the expense perhaps of generating other efficiency losses)? If the government owns the firm and induces the manager to maximize pre-tax profits, providing government funds for new investment at an accounting price of r, then the manager should invest until $f_K = r$ and choose D so that $c' = 0$. With privately owned banks but state ownership of firms, this outcome arises only with no use of debt finance, and with all investment financed instead either by retained earnings or by budgetary transfers from the government. The question is then whether the resulting efficiency gains are enough to offset the lower assumed rate of return earned by these firms, due to other implications of state ownership.

What if the banks are state-owned but the firms are privately owned? To what degree can state banks induce firms to choose the efficient level of capital and to avoid the bankruptcy costs c? If the bank simply considers fully financing an extra dollar of capital, there is no net gain for either the firm or the government: The firm faces no tax distortion at the margin when it uses debt to finance extra capital, since all resulting costs are tax deductible.[24] In particular, the resulting change in pre-tax firm profits would equal $f_K - r - c - (1 - \gamma)c'$. Using (4) and (5), it immediately follows that this expression equals zero, implying no change either in after-tax profits for the firm or in tax revenues.

To provide any efficiency gain through lending from a state-owned bank, the bank would need to reduce the bankruptcy costs, $c + (1 - \gamma)c'$, incurred on extra debt-financed investment. What if the state-owned bank entirely ignores enforcement efforts on its own loans to the firm, so that (to take the extreme case) loan repayments are zero and any associated bankruptcy costs are also zero?[25] What happens to overall bankruptcy costs, including those arising from loans from private banks? Can the state bank successfully push K to the efficient level? In short, will a state-owned bank choose to make loans to a private firm, knowing that the loans will not be repaid?

Assume that the government is indifferent between firms having an extra dollar in profits and the government receiving an extra μ dollars in tax revenue. Presumably, government revenue is valued more highly than firm profits (i.e., $\mu < 1$), both due to the marginal costs to the government of raising revenue through other taxes and due to the equity gains from transferring revenue from shareholders through the government to the population more broadly.

Starting from the competitive allocation described by (4) and (5), what happens if a state bank lends a dollar to the firm? If the government gains from this change, then there is a potential role for a state bank.

If the firm can continue to choose the amount of equity finance and debt finance freely, so that (4) and (5) continue to be satisfied, then the real allocation decisions of the firm cannot change. The only consequence of the loan from the state bank is that the funds will be transferred directly to shareholders. For the loan to have any real effect on the level of investment, the government must impose some constraint preventing the transfer of the funds to shareholders. In particular, assume that the total payouts to equity holders, whether through dividend payments or equity repurchases, can at most equal the after-tax profits of the firm. Such constraints are in fact common covenants in private loan contracts, so that this assumption should be a reasonable one.

With this restriction, (4) will no longer be satisfied. Instead, the amount of capital contributed by equity holders will be held fixed at its initial level, due to the binding constraint limiting payouts.[26] Since the extra funds cannot be paid out to equity holders, they must either be invested or used to retire private loans.[27] Assume that private bank loans, denoted by D, remain unrestricted.

The question is then how much of any funds from the state bank will be used to add to the capital stock. The net profits of the firm now equal $[f - wL - rD - (D + E)c\{D/(D + E)\}](1 - t_M)$, where E is the market value of the equity in the firm. Note that the previous identity that $K = D + E$ no longer holds: Due to the binding constraint limiting payouts, the market value of equity understates the replacement cost of the capital whose return goes to equity holders. I assume that the agency costs from debt finance then depend on the debt-to-value ratio as perceived by the firm's private owners, multiplied by the value of assets they jointly have at stake.

To judge whether there is *any* role for a state bank, consider the net welfare change when the state bank lends an extra dollar to the firm for new investment starting from the competitive equilibrium. Given that the government values a dollar of firm profits and μ dollars of tax revenue equally, the objective of the government is to maximize

$$W = [t_M + \mu(1 - t_M)][f - wL - rD - (D + E)c] - rK. \tag{6}$$

Due to the new loan, net profits of the firm go up by[28] $[f_K - (c - c'\gamma)(\partial E/\partial K)](1 - t_M)$. In contrast, the resulting change in tax revenue, minus the lost income of the state bank, equals $t_M[f_K - (c - c'\gamma)(\partial E/\partial K)] - r$. As a result, the weighted sum of the net gains to both the firm and the government equals

$$\frac{\partial W}{\partial K} = [\mu(1 - t_M) + t_M]\left[f_K - (c - c'\gamma)\frac{\partial E}{\partial K}\right] - r. \tag{6'}$$

At the competitive equilibrium, equity holders would invest until the market value of the returns to extra investment just equals the cost of the investment, so that $\partial E/\partial K = 1$. With only a marginal change from this competitive equilibrium, we still have $\partial E/\partial K = 1$. Therefore, given (4) and (5), (6') also equals

$$\frac{\partial W}{\partial K} = \mu r(1 - t) - r\left[\frac{1 - t_M(2 - t)}{1 - t_M}\right]. \tag{7}$$

Under what conditions is this expression positive? If the term in brackets is negative, then the expression is certainly positive, since government revenue goes up even though the loan is never repaid.

This occurs if $t_M > 1/(2-t)$. For example, if $t = 0.25$, then tax revenue goes up if $t_M > 0.57$. In general, the expression is positive as long as

$$\mu > 1 - \frac{t_M - t}{(1-t_M)(1-t)}. \tag{8}$$

For example, if $t_M = 0.5$ and $t = 0.25$, then the expression is positive if $\mu > 0.33$, so that the government values a dollar of profits at least at a third the value of a dollar in tax revenue.

If some lending is worthwhile, then lending should continue until the expression in (6′) equals zero, or until

$$f_K = \frac{r}{A} + (c - \gamma c') \frac{\partial E}{\partial K}, \tag{9}$$

where $A \equiv \mu + (1-\mu)t_M$ measures the social value of a dollar of extra profits to the firm.

To calculate $\partial E/\partial K$, we know that

$$E = \frac{[f - wL - rD - (D+E)c](1-t_M)}{r(1-t)}. \tag{10}$$

Differentiating with respect to K and making use of (9), we find that

$$\frac{\partial E}{\partial K} = \frac{1 - t_M}{A(1-t)}. \tag{11}$$

By (8), we infer that $\partial E/\partial K < 1$ as long as any state loans are worthwhile. Intuitively, the government induces the firm to expand its capital stock, pushing the return per unit of capital below the point sufficient to compensate equity holders for additional new equity-financed investments.

Given (11), we find that the capital stock implied by (9) is larger than it would be without a state bank. In particular, given (4), (9), and (11), we find that $f_K^s/f_K = \partial E/\partial K < 1$, where f_K^s is the value implied by (9) with state loans and where f_K is the value in (4) without state loans. The optimal capital stock can even be larger than the efficient level, where $f_K = r$,[29] since extra government-financed capital reduces bankruptcy costs.

In addition, (11) implies that $\partial E/\partial K$ is a declining function of t_M, so that f_K^s/f_K is also a declining function of t_M. Therefore, if the effective corporate tax rate varies by firm, then state banks should focus their lending on firms that face higher effective corporate tax rates, so presumably on larger firms.

Note that in this equilibrium, the state bank necessarily loses money. In fact, under our admittedly extreme assumptions, there are no loan repayments at all. In addition, there will be no new equity finance for any firm receiving loans from the state bank—the marginal return on new investment will be below the shareholders' opportunity cost of funds, that is, $\partial E/\partial K < 1$.

What happens to private lending in the process? Private lending to the firm continues until $\partial E/\partial D = -1$, implying that (5) is still satisfied. With unchanging tax rates, γ remains unchanged as well. Therefore, $\partial D/\partial K = [\gamma/(1 - \gamma)]\partial E/\partial K > 0$. Rather than extra loans from the state bank being used to retire private loans, we find instead that the resulting capital investment provides more collateral for private loans, leading to increased private lending as well.[30]

Unless state ownership per se reduces the efficiency of operation of a bank, therefore, there are strong reasons to expect to see lending from state-owned banks in equilibrium. Inevitably, however, state banks will not be able to allocate funds as effectively as was assumed in this model. When firms can receive loans without any need for repayment, all firms will want as many loans as they can get. The bank no longer receives any credible information from firms, based on their willingness to take on extra debt. The bank, therefore, rather than the firms, must decide what level of capital stock is appropriate for each firm. The bank, of course, has poorer information than the firm has, resulting in a worse allocation of available funds across firms. The cost of these misallocations can potentially be very high.

If private investors *must* contribute a large enough fraction of the costs of new investment, however, then the government can potentially rely on their willingness to invest to guide and constrain the lending undertaken by the state bank. Assume, for example, that a firm is required to finance some fraction γ^* of any new investments I, in order to qualify for a state loan for the remaining fraction of the investment cost, $(1 - \gamma^*)I$. If the firm is allowed to choose I freely, then the state bank no longer needs to be relied on to make these allocation decisions. What value of γ^* maximizes the government's objective, and how does this equilibrium compare with the previous one?

With this requirement, the firm will choose I to maximize $[f - wL - rD - (D + E_0 + \gamma^*I)c](1 - t_M) - r(E_0 + \gamma^*I)(1 - t)$, where E_0

is the market value of shares in the initial capital stock, K_0. In equilibrium, the firm will continue to request further funds until $\partial E_0/\partial D = \partial E_0/\partial I = 0$. The optimal value for D still satisfies (5), so that γ is unaffected by the choice of γ^*. In contrast, the optimal value for I satisfies

$$f_K = \gamma^* \left[r + c + (1 - \gamma)r\frac{t_M - t}{1 - t_M} \right]. \tag{12}$$

Comparing (4) and (12), given (5), we immediately conclude that the capital stock will be larger than in the competitive equilibrium when the firm receives loans from the state bank for any $\gamma^* < 1$.

The government in contrast hopes to maximize

$$W^a \equiv [t_M + \mu(1 - t_M)][f - wL - rD - (D + E_0 + \gamma^*I)c]$$

$$- \mu r(E_0 + \gamma^*I) - (1 - \gamma^*)rI. \tag{13}$$

Its desired level of γ^* then satisfies[31]

$$\frac{\partial W^a}{\partial I} = \frac{AIc - rI(1 - \mu)}{\partial I/\partial \gamma^*}. \tag{14}$$

In order to make sense of this equation, note that the optimum would require $\partial W^a/\partial I = 0$ if there were no tax distortions and the government cared only about economic efficiency. Equation (14) captures two reasons why the government would want to deviate from this allocation. First, on distributional grounds, it would want to increase γ^* further, to the extent that $\mu < 1$, since it gains from shifting more of the cost of new investment onto private investors. In addition, however, the government would gain from reducing γ^* to the extent that $c > 0$, since more government financing means lower bankruptcy costs.

If we compare government welfare here with the level of welfare that arose without the financing constraints, we find that welfare is necessarily higher. In particular, if γ^* is set equal to the level of γ chosen under the policies that optimize (6), then firms would demand unlimited amounts of credit—credit is effectively free to the firm, since the constraint on γ is nonbinding, yet equity holders get to keep some of the return from the resulting investment. The desired value of new investment, I, is clearly a declining function of the fraction γ^* that the firm must self-finance. Therefore, to induce firms to choose the same level of K as the government would choose without financing constraints, the resulting value of γ^* is necessarily greater than the equilibrium γ in the previous allocation. Therefore, with the financing constraint, the same capital stock is feasible, but the government no longer needs to finance as much of it. Since $\mu < 1$, welfare is necessarily higher. In general, the optimal capital stock will change, so that the government can do yet better.

In theory, a subsidy through cheap state loans is equivalent to a subsidy allowing the expensing of new investment under the corporate tax. With expensing, there is no distortion to marginal investment decisions even though the tax continues to collect revenue from existing capital.[32] With a state bank, rather than saving the firm t_M in taxes through making each dollar of new investment immediately deductible, the government instead can provide a loan of t_M (that need not be repaid) to help finance the investment.[33]

If t_M were the same for all firms, allowing expensing should be a far easier way to correct marginal investment incentives than setting up a state bank. However, the *effective* tax rate on new investment inevitably varies substantially across firms, depending on varying statutory provisions (for example, statutory versus economic depreciation), on differences in the real costs of using debt rather than equity finance and also on the differing ease of tax evasion for different types of firms. Under expensing, all firms would save the same amount t_M in taxes, since they would be happy to report investment expenses in full. Yet, the size of subsidy needed to just offset in present value the taxes on the future return to the marginal investment will inevitably vary substantially across firms, due to variation across firms in their *effective* tax rates. The effective tax rates each firm faces would not be observable at the time that the statutory provisions are set. Therefore, the tax law will inevitably generate a misallocation of capital across firms.

State banks, in contrast, should have the ability to learn *something* about these effective tax rates when evaluating each loan application. State banks would then have the discretion to vary the required γ^* depending on their perception of the firm's effective tax rate. For example, effective tax rates are likely to be higher for large manufacturing firms, where auditing is easy. If so, then state loans should go more heavily to these firms. Conversely, if smaller firms pay little in taxes, then state banks would provide these firms little or no credit.[34]

Is a state bank preferable to allowing expensing of (some fraction of) new investment as a means of increasing capital investment? This depends on whether the potential gain under a state bank from being able to direct funds more heavily towards firms facing a higher effective tax rate is greater than the loss from the lower operating efficiency of the bank itself (due, for example, to overstaffing and weaker internal financial incentives). The potential advantage of a state bank is larger, the more that effective tax rates vary by firm. The higher are tax rates generally, the more room there is for such variation in effective tax rates by firm.

As tax rates increase, however, efficiency costs still rise with a state bank, since the bankruptcy costs c become larger, the costs of tax evasion become larger, and the misallocation of funds (due to the bank's lack of *full* knowledge of how effective tax rates vary by firm, or its lack of incentive to allocate funds based on this knowledge) becomes more costly. How then do these efficiency losses from use of a state bank compare with those arising from state ownership of the underlying firms? We have assumed that the government can induce managers of state-owned firms to choose the efficient level of K without use of debt finance, and the resulting costs c. Following the prior papers, we have assumed that state ownership of firms leads to some efficiency loss, αS_p, regardless of the tax rate t_M. If the loss with state-owned banks increases in t_M, then there can be three regimes: one at low values of t_M with no state ownership, a second at intermediate values of t_M with state-owned banks but no state-owned firms, and a third one at high values of t_M with a shift to state ownership of (some) nonfinancial firms.

The model therefore forecasts that following a drop in tax rates, countries will first privatize nonfinancial firms, but only following further cuts in tax rates will they fully privatize the banking sector. Given the recent sharp drop in tax rates in Germany, for example, it would be natural to expect to see its state-owned banks privatized shortly.[35]

6.4 Labor-Market Distortions and State Ownership

In the previous section, we argued that state-owned banks can be used to lessen the efficiency losses from corporate tax distortions, even while maintaining private ownership of nonbank firms. If so, then state ownership of nonbank firms is not needed to deal with corporate tax distortions. Also, any state-owned firms that do exist—for example, natural monopolies—would not have a systematically higher capital-labor ratio than equivalent private firms.[36]

While the role of state banks can therefore explain why state-owned firms are not systematically more capital-intensive than private firms, it cannot necessarily explain why they appear to be more labor-intensive. The corporate tax, however, is only one of many distortions affecting the allocation of resources under private ownership. The objective of this section is to describe a variety of other reasons why, from the government's perspective, private firms employ too few workers, and particularly too few low-skilled workers, on both efficiency and equity grounds. Cheap loans from a state-owned bank cannot induce firms to hire more low-skilled workers. Instead, state ownership of some firms can be used. If this is the explanation for state ownership, then these state-owned firms should be labor-intensive relative to private firms, should tend to attract low-skilled workers relative to private firms in the same industry, and should tend to lose money—for example, by paying wages above the marginal productivity of their workers. All of these forecasts seem consistent with the behavior of state firms.[37]

6.4.1   Redistribution through Changes in Relative Wage Rates

A recent paper by Naito (1999) argues implicitly that state ownership of firms may be an effective supplement to existing income taxes in order to redistribute from skilled to unskilled workers. The key consideration in his model is that the relative wage rates of different types of workers depend on their relative supplies. By reducing the supply of low-skilled workers to the private sector, through hiring more of them into the state sector, the government can raise their relative wage rate. Starting from an allocation satisfying production efficiency, a marginal change in this direction has no first-order efficiency costs. Yet, it results in a first-order change in relative wages. Accomplishing the same additional redistribution through the tax system will have clear efficiency costs.

If the public firm competes with private firms in the output market, yet has the same technology, then it will end up running a loss due to its deviating from the cost-minimizing input proportions chosen by private firms. The government is willing to absorb this loss because of the redistributional benefits. Note that these benefits go to all low-skilled workers, and not just to those hired by state-owned firms. This redistribution is accomplished most easily through government ownership of firms in which the marginal product of low-skilled workers drops least as their input share expands.

6.4.2   Minimum Wage

A similar argument can be made regarding the implications of the minimum wage. One way to rationalize the minimum wage is to view it as an alternative way for the government to reduce the supply of low-skilled workers to the private sector, in order to raise their wage rate. Rather than restricting supply directly, the minimum wage instead raises the price. The equilibrium, however, does not depend on whether quantity or price controls are used.

The costs and benefits of the restricted supply are not shared equally among the low-skilled, however. When the price of low-skilled workers is artificially raised through the minimum wage, some low-skilled get jobs at the minimum wage while others do not find employment. State-owned firms can then provide employment for some low-skilled workers, reducing the number who end up without jobs due to the minimum wage.[38] Presumably, the public firm also must pay the minimum wage. By hiring a larger fraction of low-skilled workers at the minimum wage than would a private firm, the public firm again will earn a lower rate of profit. On efficiency grounds, it should choose to hire further workers as long as their marginal productivity is above the value they place on their leisure, even if both are much below the minimum wage. While the firm will therefore have a low accounting profit rate, there can be important efficiency as well as distributional gains from hiring these low-skilled workers.

6.4.3   Redistribution Based on Income versus Wage Rate

Another potential consideration when a firm is publicly owned is that it may acquire information about the hourly wage rate of its workers, and not just their overall labor income. With the income tax alone, in contrast, the government can reliably learn only the total amount paid from a firm to each worker.[39]

With this extra information, the government can redistribute to these workers more cheaply than it could knowing just their overall labor income. For example, it can offer workers a contract providing them the same utility they receive in a job in a private firm, but in which they face undistorted incentives at the margin. As a result, redistribution towards the low-skilled will be cheaper than when done outside state-owned firms. The state-owned firms would then expand given this added benefit of public employment.

By this story, however, state-owned firms will plausibly be *more* skill-intensive than private firms. By observing an individual's wage rate, the government can avoid the efficiency costs of distorting their labor supply decisions. These efficiency costs are proportionately larger for more-skilled workers.

6.4.4 Distortions in Unemployment Insurance Programs

Unemployment insurance (UI) can serve an important efficiency enhancing function, providing insurance to workers against an unexpected fall in income as a result of a layoff, and also providing immediate liquidity.[40] The problem, as emphasized, for example, by Feldstein (1974), is that UI distorts both the incentives faced by firms when making hiring and layoff decisions and the incentives faced by unemployed individuals when deciding whether to accept a new job offer.

One important issue is whether the tax payments made by firms or workers to finance the program are experience rated. If tax rates adjust so that the firm in the end has to finance any unemployment benefits paid to its laid-off workers, then there is no net transfer to the firm and its workers together because of the program. The program simply allows the firm to precommit credibly to provide unemployment benefits to its former workers, making it easier to hire these workers initially.[41] Experience rating, however, requires that the government maintain complete records over time of the present value of benefits paid to past employees of the firm as well as the present value of the firm's past tax payments.[42] While some U.S. states come close to providing full experience rating in their UI programs, most programs elsewhere are not experience rated.

If the financing of the program is not experience rated, then there is a net transfer to the firm and its workers when a worker is laid off, and a net fall in this transfer when an unemployed individual is hired. Due to this price distortion, firms will lay off too many workers and hire too few workers, since they ignore the implications of their decisions for the net costs faced by the UI program. For example, if a worker's marginal product is w, the dollar equivalent loss in utility from forgone leisure is v, and the size of UI benefits is b, then a firm would, in equilibrium, gain by recalling a worker only when $w > v + b$. On efficiency grounds, however, the worker should be recalled whenever $w > v$.

In practice, due perhaps to distributional concerns, unemployment benefits tend to be a higher fraction of the normal wage for less-skilled workers. As a result, these distortions to hiring and firing decisions will be worse for less-skilled workers.

Under what conditions would there be a social gain from hiring unemployed workers in a state-owned firm, where the marginal productivity is m_p and the wage is w_p, rather than simply providing these workers UI benefits? Holding the utility of the worker constant, the worker would need to be paid $w_p = v + b$. However, having the worker employed rather than unemployed results in an efficiency gain of $m_p - v$. These efficiency gains are present even if $m_p < w_p$, so that the state-owned firm loses money on these workers. By optimizing over w_p, welfare could be improved further.

6.4.5   Unions

Whether unemployment resulting from union-negotiated increases in wage rates provides grounds for public employment is a trickier issue. On one level, the role of unions is closely analogous to the role described above for the minimum wage. One key difference is that union members tend to be relatively skilled, rather than low-skilled. Since unions represent the interests of only a part of the labor force, their actions can harm nonmembers (including less-skilled workers) by making it harder for them to obtain jobs.

The key difference between unions and the minimum wage, however, is that the government controls both the minimum wage and the amount of public employment, but it does not control the union-negotiated wage. By making it less costly for a union member to be out of work, the availability of extra public-sector jobs will induce the union to try to cut the supply of skilled workers further. When this induced increase in the union wage rate is taken into account, as well as any efficiency or equity gains from employing laid-off union members, the net welfare gain from the public sector jobs may or may not still look attractive.

6.5 Summary

Why have state-owned firms, and state-owned banks, existed in the past? Why were many of these firms privatized during the last decade or two? One possible answer is that state-owned firms were never in the public interest, but the realization of this became apparent to the general public only during the past two decades. Government officials can find it in their personal interests to control firms, as a source of economic rents. Until the last two decades, officials may not have faced enough pressure from voters to prevent this rent seeking.

The objective of this chapter is to provide an alternative and more benign explanation for the past state ownership, and one consistent as well with the more recent privatizations. The chapter builds on prior work by Gordon, Bai, and Li (1999) and Huizinga and Nielsen (2001). These papers argued that state ownership may be a way to avoid the efficiency losses from underinvestment caused by high corporate tax rates, at the expense of offsetting efficiency costs from public ownership per se (due, e.g., to weaker internal incentives).

The arguments in these previous papers cannot explain why state-owned banks are so common, since banks typically face relatively low effective tax rates. These papers also suggest that state-owned firms will be unusually capital-intensive, yet the stylized evidence is that they are unusually labor-intensive.

This chapter focuses first on the role of state banks. By providing cheap credit, these banks can induce firms to increase their capital stock, and in the process lessen the efficiency losses from the corporate income tax. While the banks may lose money from the cheap loans, this loss to the government can be more than offset by the resulting increase in corporate tax revenue on the profits from the new investments. While state banks may be less competitive than private banks, the gain from this improved allocation may be sufficient to offset any operating inefficiencies.

Given the presence of state banks, therefore, (nonbank) state firms need not be more capital-intensive than equivalent firms in the private sector. However, this does not explain why state-owned firms tend to be labor-intensive. Various possible explanations are examined. For one, by having state-owned firms hire unskilled workers, the government can drive up the equilibrium wage rate for the unskilled. Similarly, state-owned firms can beneficially hire workers who are unemployed due to the distortions created by the minimum wage, unemployment insurance programs, or unions. Finally, by observing each worker's wage rate as well as their overall labor income, a state-owned firm may be able to redistribute from skilled to unskilled more efficiently than can be done through the income tax system.

Notes

I would very much like to thank participants at the CESifo conference, "Public Finances and Public Policy in the New Millennium," University of Munich, January 12–13, 2001, Sijbren Cnossen, Ray Rees, and two referees for comments on an earlier draft. In addition, I would like to express my gratitude to Richard Musgrave, whose insightful teaching and writing have strongly influenced my own work as well as that of the field of public finance as a whole.

1. See, for example, Havrylyshyn and McGettigan (2000).

2. For example, Claessens, Djankov, and Pohl (1997) and Frydman et al. (1998) both document that concentrated outside ownership is a key factor explaining the productivity gains of privatized firms. Yet, voucher privatization is characterized, at least initially, by very diffuse outside ownership.

3. See, for example, Gordon, Bai, and Li (1999) and Huizinga and Nielsen (2001).

4. The compensation package of the manager is under the control of the government, and in principle can be designed to induce managers to focus on before-tax rather than after-tax profits.

5. For a summary of this evidence, see, for example, Lee (1998).

6. Papers by Ramamurti (1997), LaPorta and López-de-Silanes (1999), D'Souza and Megginson (1999), and Dewenter and Malatesta (2001) all document sharp declines in employment following privatization.

7. While a state-owned bank will lose money by making such cheap loans, from the government's perspective these losses will be offset by the resulting increase in corporate tax revenue.

8. A recent theoretical rationale for the soft-budget constraint is found in Dewatripont and Maskin (1995).

9. This was the key argument, for example, in Arrow (1951).

10. For further discussion, see Rees (1984).

11. While many empirical studies do find that state-owned firms operate less efficiently, this finding is by no means universal. See, for example, Pestieau and Tulkens (1993), who find that the degree of competition in the industry rather than the form of ownership may be the key factor affecting efficiency. Since state-owned firms often are in industries where there is little competition, on average they are less efficient.

12. Here, we generalize the past papers, where the output of public firms was assumed to equal $(1 - \alpha)F(K, L)$ for some value of α.

13. We implicitly assume here that the firm finances its capital with equity, and we ignore economic versus tax depreciation.

14. Note that p_K equals $r/(1 - \tau)$ in the market equilibrium and r at the efficient allocation.

15. Of course, one can also "explain" the association of high tax rates with public ownership by arguing that political parties in favor of big governments favor both high tax rates and public ownership. The argument proposed in the past papers eliminates the need for assuming a "taste" for public ownership, arguing that rational behavior in response to high tax rates is sufficient in itself to explain state ownership. In principle, data can be used to differentiate between the two hypotheses. The first argues that high tax rates of any sort should be associated with state ownership, while the latter argues that a high distortion to investment incentives (through a high corporate tax rate) leads to state ownership.

16. Similarly, any differences between personal and corporate tax rates can lead firms to shift between corporate and noncorporate status. Here, the key rate is not the effective personal tax rate on interest income embodied in market prices, but the personal tax rates of the shareholders of the smaller firms that can most easily change status. The same general issues arise, however.

17. Under certain assumptions, this weighted average tax rate will equal the implicit tax rate that reconciles the interest rates on taxable and tax-exempt bonds. In U.S. data, this implicit tax rate has been far below the statutory corporate tax rate.

18. The evidence in Gordon and Slemrod (2000), for example, shows that the amount of income shifting is large and very responsive to tax differentials. In contrast, Gordon and Lee (2001) find only very limited effects of taxes on corporate financial decisions.

19. For simplicity of notation, we ignore any personal taxes on equity income.

20. In the following discussion, we assume that these loans come from private banks. However, any private loans would be equivalent.

21. Many of these costs are borne by the lender, and then are passed along to the borrower through a higher interest rate.

22. Jensen and Meckling (1976), in contrast, describe reasons why a firm may use some debt finance, even ignoring tax incentives, in order to minimize agency costs.

23. In contrast, if the corporate tax rate could be set ignoring income-shifting pressures, then it would be set equal to t and these first-order conditions would imply $f_K = r$ and $c' = 0$, since a uniform tax avoids any portfolio distortions. Note, however, that the model ignores any effects of taxes on saving, by implicitly assuming that saving is inelastic.

24. If some costs were not fully deductible—for example, depreciation allowances were less generous than economic depreciation—then the bank could undo these distortions through charging a lower interest rate. But the government could also undo these distortions through shifting to economic depreciation for tax purposes.

25. We continue to assume, however, that the corporate tax is enforced.

26. The reduced rate of return earned by shareholders as a result of the extra investment represents an implicit tax on these inframarginal holdings of the firm's capital stock.

27. In fact, we will find that new loans from the state bank, by increasing the collateral available to private banks, induce some additional lending as well from these private banks.

28. Note that resulting changes in L or D have no first-order effect, due to the envelope condition.

29. This certainly occurs if $\mu = 1$. To see this, note that $c - \gamma c' < 0$ due to the convexity of the function c.

30. In this equilibrium, loans from private banks continue. Any equilibrium with loans from both state banks and private banks has to be described carefully, however, since the firm would clearly prefer a loan that it does not have to repay to one that it does need to repay. The approach above implicitly assumes that the state bank is a Stackelberg leader and chooses first how much to lend to the firm. Given the size of this loan, the firm then chooses how much to borrow in addition from private banks so as to satisfy equation (5). The key requirement in this equilibrium is that the amount of private loans not affect the amount of loans from the state bank.

31. Here, we calculate $\partial W^a / \partial \gamma^*$, recognizing that I is a function of γ^*, set the derivative equal to zero, and solve for $\partial W^a / \partial I$.

32. Auerbach and Kotlikoff (1987) document the size of the potential gains from this policy shift, arising from what amounts to a windfall tax on existing capital. Both the shift to expensing and the shift to lending from state banks are examples of time inconsistency in optimal tax structure, since in both cases the government takes past equity investments as given when determining current policies, yet past equity investments will be affected by investors' anticipations of future government policies.

33. Given distributional considerations as well as the distortions to debt decisions, the optimal policy as seen above is a bit more complicated, whether it is implemented through expensing or through state loans.

34. If private funds come from the world market and smaller firms face a positive effective tax rate, then some state loans would still be desired in order to lessen the degree of underinvestment in these firms. However, if funds are drawn from other domestic investments (e.g., in large manufacturing firms), then loans may not be attractive.

35. For a recent call for such a privatization, see Sinn (1999).

36. As noted earlier, under the optimal lending from state banks, the equilibrium capital stock for private firms may even be larger than that for state-owned firms, where the efficient allocation with $f_K = r$ would be chosen.

37. See Li (1997), for example, for detailed evidence on Chinese state-owned firms.

38. If all such workers were hired, the outcome would be the same as in Naito's framework.

39. If the government tried to elicit information from a firm on hours worked for each worker, the firm would lose nothing directly by reporting a high figure, while its workers would gain if the government then treats them as being lower skilled in its tax-transfer program. As a result, any information is not likely to be credible.

40. Individuals would have difficulty borrowing privately against (hoped for) future earnings, given their ability to declare bankruptcy before these future earnings materialize. See Bailey (1978) and Gruber (1997) for further discussion.

41. The better designed the program, the more attractive a worker will find the proposed compensation package, for any given ex ante cost to the firm.

42. True experience rating also requires that any net benefits a firm received from the program be a liability owed in the event of closure.

References

Arrow, K. 1951. *Social Choice and Individual Values*. New York: Wiley.

Auerbach, A., and L. Kotlikoff. 1987. *Dynamic Fiscal Policy*. Cambridge, UK: Cambridge University Press.

Bailey, M. 1978. "Some Aspects of Optimal Unemployment Insurance." *Journal of Public Economics* 10: 279–402.

Boycko, M., A. Shleifer, and R. W. Vishny. 1996. "A Theory of Privatization." *Economic Journal* 106: 309–319.

Bradford, D. F. 1989. "An Uncluttered Income Tax: The Next Reform Agenda?" In *A Supply-Side Agenda for Germany*, ed. G. Fels and G. M. von Furstenberg. New York: Springer.

Buchanan, J., and G. Tullock. 1962. *The Calculus of Consent*. Ann Arbor: University of Michigan Press.

Claessens, S., S. Djankov, and G. Pohl. 1997. "Ownership and Corporate Governance: Evidence from the Czech Republic." World Bank Policy Research Paper No. 1737.

Coase, R. 1988. *The Firm, the Market, and the Law*. Chicago: University of Chicago Press.

Dewatripont, M., and E. S. Maskin. 1995. "Credit and Efficiency in Centralized and Decentralized Economies." *Review of Economic Studies* 62: 541–555.

Dewenter, K., and P. H. Malatesta. 2001. "State-Owned and Privately-Owned Firms: An Empirical Analysis of Profitability, Leverage, and Labor Intensity." *American Economic Review* 91: 320–334.

D'Souza, J., and W. L. Megginson. 1999. "The Financial and Operating Performance of Privatized Firms during the 1990s." *Journal of Finance* 54: 1397–1438.

Feldstein, M. S. 1974. "Unemployment Compensation: Adverse Incentives and Distributional Anomalies." *National Tax Journal* 27: 231–244.

Frydman, R., C. W. Gray, M. Hessel, and A. Rapaczynski. 1998. "When Does Privatization Work? The Impact of Private Ownership on Corporate Governance in Transition Economies." C.V. Starr Center Working Paper No. 9832.

Gordon, R. H., C.-E. Bai, and D. Li. 1999. "Efficiency Losses from Tax Distortions vs. Government Control." *European Economic Review* 43: 1095–1103.

Gordon, R. H., and D. F. Bradford. 1980. "Taxation and the Stock Market Valuation of Capital Gains and Dividends: Theory and Empirical Results." *Journal of Public Economics* 14: 109–136.

Gordon, R. H., and Y. Lee. 2001. "Do Taxes Affect Corporate Debt Policy? Evidence from U.S. Corporate Tax Return Data." *Journal of Public Economics* 82: 195–224.

Gordon, R. H., and J. Slemrod. 2000. "Are 'Real' Responses to Taxes Simply Income Shifting between Corporate and Personal Tax Bases?" In *Does Atlas Shrug? The Economics of Taxing the Rich*, ed. J. Slemrod. New York: Russell Sage Foundation; Cambridge, MA, and London, UK: Harvard University Press.

Gruber, J. 1997. "The Consumption Smoothing Benefits of Unemployment Insurance." *American Economic Review* 87: 192–205.

Havrylyshyn, O., and D. McGettigan. 2000. "Privatization in Transition Countries." *Post-Soviet Affairs* 16: 257–286.

Huizinga, H., and S. B. Nielsen. 2001. "Privatization, Public Investment, and Capital Income Taxation." *Journal of Public Economics* 82: 399–414.

Jensen, M. C., and W. H. Meckling. 1976. "Theory of the Firm: Managerial Behavior, Agency Costs and Ownership Structure." *Journal of Financial Economics* 3: 305–360.

Kornai, J. 1979. *Economics of Shortage*. Stockholm: Institute for International Economic Studies.

Lange, O. 1938. *On the Economic Theory of Socialism*. Minneapolis: University of Minnesota Press.

LaPorta, R., and F. López-de-Silanes. 1999. "The Benefits of Privatization: Evidence from Mexico." *Quarterly Journal of Economics* 114: 1193–1242.

Lee, Y. 1998. "Essays on Chinese State-Owned Enterprise Reform." Ph.D. diss., University of Michigan.

Lerner, A. 1944. *The Economics of Control: Principles of Welfare Economics*. New York: Macmillan.

Li, W. 1997. "The Impact of Economic Reforms on the Performance of Chinese State Enterprises, 1980–1989." *Journal of Political Economy* 105: 1080–1106.

McLure, C. 1991. "Tax Policy for Economies in Transition from Socialism." *Tax Notes International* 27: 347–353.

Musgrave, R. 1959. *The Theory of Public Finance*. New York: McGraw-Hill.

Naito, H. 1999. "Reexamination of Uniform Commodity Taxes under a Non-Linear Income Tax System, and Its Implications for Production Efficiency." *Journal of Public Economics* 71: 165–188.

Pestieau, P., and H. Tulkens. 1993. "Assessing and Explaining the Performance of Public Enterprises." *Finanz Archiv* 50: 293–323.

Ramamurti, R. 1997. "Testing the Limits of Privatization: Argentine Railroads." *World Development* 25: 1973–1993.

Rees, R. 1984. *Public Enterprise Economics*. London: Weidenfeld and Nicholson.

Sinn, H.-W. 1999. *The German State Banks*. Cheltenham, UK: Edward Elgar.

Comments

Ray Rees

The starting point of Roger Gordon's chapter is the idea that corporation taxes distort the capital-labor ratio of privately owned companies, so that, even if state-owned enterprises are in some general sense inefficient, they may be more efficient than private firms. Whether or not this is true, I find it hard to believe that this can be advanced as an explanation for the actual existence of state ownership of firms in the past. An examination of the reasons for the creation of public enterprises, either ab initio or by the nationalization of privately owned enterprises, would in my view never suggest that among these was the correction of excessively low capital-labor ratios in private companies due to high corporation taxes.

It is therefore not surprising that some empirical predictions that would follow from the use of public ownership to correct for tax distortions of this kind do not seem to be confirmed by the evidence. State-owned firms should be more capital-intensive than privately owned firms in the same industry, and following privatization capital-labor ratios should fall. Instead of this, the usual criticism of state-owned enterprises is that they are excessively labor-intensive, and privatization is usually followed by large reductions in the labor force. All this is amply borne out by the experience with public enterprise and privatization in the United Kingdom in the 1950s to 1980s.

However, the chapter, though taking this kind of evidence as central to the discussion, does not interpret it as implying the irrelevance of corporation tax levels in explaining public ownership, but rather constructs an explanation based on the existence of state-owned banks. If state-owned banks make loans to private companies that do not have to be repaid, then this effectively removes at the margin the distortion due to corporation taxes, and so we no longer expect private enterprises to have lower capital-labor ratios than comparable nonbank public enterprises. It should be noted that the chapter advances this as an *explanation* of the fact that private firms are not less capital-intensive than public enterprises, rather than as a normative second-best proposition, that state-owned banks *should* be used in this way to undo the distortions created by the corporation tax. No evidence is, however, presented to confirm that state-owned banks have indeed functioned in this way. One problem is that in some countries with substantial state-owned sectors, such as the United Kingdom, there were no state-owned banks, and so the fact that private firms were not less capital-intensive cannot be explained in this way. In countries such as France, Germany, and Italy, where there are or were state banks, there is nothing to suggest that it was standard practice to advance nonrepayable loans to private firms, and indeed cases in which private firms defaulted on loans tended to be regarded as scandalous. It may be that the author has in mind an economy where this can be shown to be so, in which case the chapter should make this evidence explicit.

If the provision of nonrepayable loans by state banks is accepted as explaining why private firms are no less capital-intensive than comparable public firms, it still has to be explained why they are much more so, that is, why the "excessive" labor intensity of the latter? Here, the argument is that a number of distortions exist that lead private firms to underemploy labor, and publicly owned firms take on extra labor to undo these distortions. Such distortions are created by minimum wages and unemployment insurance programs, as well as possibly by unions. There is also the suggestion that state-owned enterprises were used to redistribute income to low-skilled workers by increasing demand for them and thus driving up their relative wage. Finally, they may be able to circumvent the problem underlying the Mirrlees approach to nonlinear income taxation, in that they can directly observe wage rates and so redistribute income more effectively than under such a tax system.

Again, it must be noted that these ideas are advanced as positive explanations of the evidence, rather than as normative propositions concerning how state-owned enterprises may be used to correct labor market distortions. Certainly, in the debates that took place, for example in the United Kingdom in the 1970s and 1980s, concerning the rate at which the labor force in declining sectors such as coal and steel should be run down, the point was made that the marginal social opportunity costs of labor in these sectors may well, for reasons such as labor market frictions, be well below the market wage rates, and this may have had some influence in slowing the rate of contraction. This does not, however, explain why in expanding sectors such as electricity and telecommunications, there was still excessive labor intensity, and privatization of these industries was accompanied by substantial labor-force reductions. In my view, the explanation for this excessive labor intensity is to be found in the nature of the control and decision structure of public enterprise, and the role played by unions within this, rather than in an attempt to correct for general labor market distortions. Indeed, the drive toward privatization is to be understood precisely as the attempt to achieve radical transformation of this control and decision structure, together with a change in enterprise objectives.

7   The Property Tax: Competing Views and a Hybrid Theory

John Douglas Wilson

7.1 Introduction

The incidence of the property tax remains a particularly controversial area in public economics. This chapter attempts to resolve some of the controversy by using a "hybrid model" containing important features of two competing views of the property tax. An earlier third view was that the burden of a locally imposed property tax on reproducible capital is shifted to the consumers of the goods produced from this capital, making it similar to a regressive excise tax. For example, a tax on housing capital is similar to an excise tax on housing services. But the development of general equilibrium models of tax incidence eventually led researchers to question this view. In a celebrated article, Micszkowski (1972) develops the "new view" of the property tax. The new view makes a critical distinction between a single city imposing a property tax on all of the mobile capital located within its borders versus all cities in the nation imposing property taxes. In the former case, the single city can be assumed to face a highly elastic supply of capital. Consequently, the burden of a higher property tax will be shifted to residents. However, the capital supply for the nation as a whole is far less elastic. In the benchmark case of a fixed capital stock, the entire system of local property taxes will lower the after-tax return on capital by "approximately" the average tax rate. Hence, Mieszkowski concludes that the property tax is largely a "profits tax," but with interjurisdictional differences in tax rates creating "excise tax effects."

Although Richard Musgrave had originally used the view of the property tax as an excise tax in empirical work (Musgrave et al. 1951), his work on tax incidence, with its emphasis on *relative* price changes and *real* income changes, was clearly important for the development of the new view. Mieszkowski and Zodrow (1989) note that the new view model is "based on the traditional national model of tax incidence developed by Richard Musgrave (1959) and Harberger (1962)." In fact, Mieszkowski studied public economics under Musgrave, and for his Ph.D. thesis he followed Musgrave's suggestion that "I work on a general equilibrium approach to tax incidence combining the uses and sources side of real income" (Mieszkowski 1999, x).

Mieszkowski's work appears to have influenced Musgrave's own thinking about the property tax. Musgrave (1974) devotes considerable attention to the "Harberger-Mieszkowski" model and incorporates the new view into empirical estimates of the incidence of the residential property tax. While these estimates show that the property tax remains regressive over the lower to middle end of the income scale, his final conclusion is that, with suitable reforms to provide low-income relief, "I would concur that the property tax on housing should be transferred from the regressive to the progressive column" (229).

The new view rests on general equilibrium exercises that employ Musgrave's (1959) concept of "differential tax incidence": When the property tax is imposed or increased, some other tax or subsidy is adjusted to maintain a balanced government budget. In a set of highly influential papers, however, Hamilton (1975, 1976) challenges the idea that the expenditure side of the budget can be ignored. Whereas Musgrave (1959) recognizes "balanced-budget incidence" as an alternative incidence exercise, where taxes and expenditures are increased by equal amounts, Hamilton goes further by effectively abandoning the study of exogenous changes in taxes and expenditures. He restricts his attention to the residential portion of the property tax, modeled as an excise tax on housing. Recognizing that it is a local tax in the United States, he observes that it can be viewed as an efficient "benefit tax," which households pay in order to receive local public goods. In an efficient equilibrium, each household's property tax payment equals the cost of providing it with public goods. Given this marginal-cost-pricing property, households are efficiently sorted across jurisdictions according to their incomes and preferences for public goods, and each jurisdiction's public good supply is efficiently tailored to the preferences of its residents.

Hamilton's "benefit view" of the property tax essentially extends Tiebout's (1956) theory of local public goods to take into account the widespread use of property taxation in the United States. Thus, the property tax is seen as having an important role in improving the allocation of goods and resources. This role is not present under the new view.

A critical assumption underlying the benefit view is that local governments utilize zoning policies to prevent the property tax from distorting housing choices. Since the property tax will normally reduce the demand for housing, "fiscal zoning" is needed to prevent households from demanding too little housing. Proponents of the new view appear to find this assumption particularly questionable. Thus, researchers have attempted to drop it, while still allowing public good levels to be endogenously determined. Zodrow and Mieszkowski (1986a) provide a "reformulated new view" with these properties. In their model, an exogenous fraction of expenditures are financed by a head tax on immobile households, with the remaining expenditures financed by taxing interjurisdictionally mobile capital. Zoning restrictions are not available to eliminate the distortions created by the latter tax. By reducing head tax payments and computing the resulting changes in equilibrium prices, they conclude that the profits tax effects of the property tax survive, along with excise tax effects resulting from interjurisdictional differences in the endogenously chosen tax rates. Mieszkowski (1999) concludes that "no reconciliation or hybrid theory is possible" (xv).

A single "hybrid model" cannot contain all of the important features of the new view and benefit view, since some of these features are incompatible. In particular, the assumption of perfect zoning, which underlies the benefit view, clearly eliminates the general equilibrium responses that generate the incidence effects for the new view. For this reason, I depart from the benefit view by eliminating zoning constraints. Thus, I will be asking whether the benefit view survives in some modified form if other important features of the benefit view are retained. The model contains both capital and labor mobility, since mobile labor is as critical to the benefit view as mobile capital is to the new view. I also follow Hamilton by considering a residential property tax.[1] On the other hand, the tax base is assumed to be fixed for the nation as a whole, since this assumption is critical to the new view's capitalization result.

Krelove (1993) has already examined a model with these properties, emphasizing inefficiencies in the choice of property tax rates by local governments. Although housing demands are not constrained by zoning rules in his model, he nevertheless finds that each household's tax payment equals the cost of providing it with the jurisdiction's public good. Hoyt (1991) and Wilson (1997) obtain the same result from slightly different models. Thus, the property tax appears to survive as a "distortionary benefit tax."

But how close are "appearances" to reality? If the property tax is really a benefit tax, then its use should lead to more efficient public good provision, since new residents compensate existing residents for the additional costs of public good provision. To investigate this issue, I depart from the traditional use of both differential tax incidence and balanced budget incidence and instead examine a switch in the tax systems used by local governments, while allowing the levels of expenditures to be endogenously determined by local government behavior. This exercise may be called "endogenous budget incidence." By making public good levels endogenous, I am inserting a major element of the new view into the hybrid model. Three tax systems are considered: the residential property tax; an actual benefit tax, consisting of a head tax on all residents; and a tax on a jurisdiction's land.[2]

Taken as a whole, the results suggest that the property tax retains elements of both the new view and the benefit view, as might be expected from a hybrid model. The first part of the chapter ignores excise tax effects by considering an economy with identical jurisdictions and households. Under land taxation, public goods are underprovided. Moving to a property tax induces jurisdictions to raise their public good supplies, but they remain below the first-best levels. Replacing the property tax with a system of head taxes raises the after-tax return on capital, as predicted by the new view, and induces governments to provide public goods efficiently. The latter part of the chapter extends the analysis to the case of heterogeneous households and reaches similar, though less clear-cut, conclusions. By emphasizing the welfare enhancing role of the property tax in a model that retains incidence features of the new view, this chapter provides one way of reconciling the new view with the benefit view.

The plan of this chapter is as follows. In the next section, I describe the model with homogeneous households, which is based on Krelove's model. Section 7.3 then derives the rules for public good provision and taxation under the alternative tax systems. These rules are then used in section 7.4 to investigate the effects of changes in tax systems. Section 7.5 considers the heterogeneous household case, and section 7.6 concludes.

7.2 The Model

Consider an economy with a large, but fixed, number of identical jurisdictions, each consisting of L units of land. A jurisdiction's land is combined with capital, K, to produce housing, H, via a constant-returns production function, $H(K, L)$. Capital is perfectly mobile across jurisdictions but fixed in supply for the entire system of jurisdictions. Under the traditional exercise of differential tax incidence, it follows that a property tax, levied as a uniform tax on every jurisdiction's capital and land, will be borne entirely by capital and land. In the present model, this tax may be viewed as an excise tax on housing, levied at the unit rate $t = q - p$, where q is the "consumer price" of housing and p is the "producer price." In equilibrium, profits equal zero in each jurisdiction's housing industry: $pH = rK + RL$, where r and R are the unit costs of capital and land, respectively. I also consider a land tax, T, in which case the after-tax return on land is $\rho = R - T$.

For now, let us assume that all households are identical. Each is endowed with k units of housing capital, one unit of land, and y units of a numeraire commodity, which can either be consumed as a private good or purchased by the government to produce a public good. Each household in a given jurisdiction receives the same amount of the public good, g, and $C(g, n)$ denotes the cost function, defined in units of the numeraire, where n is the jurisdiction's population level. The partial derivative, C_n, denotes "marginal congestion costs."

A household's utility function is denoted $u(x, h, g)$, where x is private good consumption and h is housing consumption. Utility maximization yields an indirect utility function, $v(q, g, b)$, where $b = y + rk + \rho$. Throughout the analysis, the factor prices used in the definition of income b should be viewed as the equilibrium returns on capital and land, which are equalized across jurisdictions (as discussed further in what follows). It does not matter where a household owns land, since the household receives the same equilibrium return everywhere.

Three conditions determine the equilibrium for a given jurisdiction. First, the free mobility of households across jurisdictions implies that the utility obtained in the jurisdiction must equal the utility available elsewhere. Using the indirect utility function and denoting this "outside utility" by u^*, we have

$$v(q,g,b) = u^*. \tag{1}$$

Each jurisdiction behaves competitively by treating u^* and r as fixed—that is, jurisdictions are "utility-takers" in the market for mobile households and "price-takers" in the capital market. Condition (1) can be solved for q:

$$q = q(g,b), \quad \frac{dq}{dg} = \frac{v_g}{hv_b}, \tag{2}$$

where u^* is suppressed. The derivative dq/dg is obtained by implicit differentiation of (1), using Roy's identity. Subscripts denote partial derivatives.

Next, the supply of housing must equal the demand. Given the jurisdiction's fixed supply of land, the housing supply is a well-defined function of the producer price, p, and the cost of capital, r: $H(p,r)$. To simplify matters, I assume that a household's demand for housing is independent of the public good, $h(q,b)$.[3] With n denoting the number of households in the jurisdiction, the equilibrium condition is

$$H(p,r) = nh(q,b). \tag{3}$$

This equation defines the population function, $n(p,q,r,b)$.

Finally, the government budget constraint must be satisfied:

$$C(g,n(\cdot)) = (q - p)H(p,r) + TL. \tag{4}$$

Turning to government behavior, the standard objective of land-value maximization is assumed. This objective is appropriate under the assumption that households are mobile across a large number of utility-taking jurisdictions. In this case, changes in a single jurisdiction's policies alter only the utilities of those households that own land within the jurisdiction. As a result, only these landowners care about policy choices; migration responses to policy changes will keep the utilities of nonlandowning residents unchanged at the levels they can receive elsewhere. As a result, the government should encounter support, and no significant opposition, in the pursuit of land-value-maximizing policies.

To state the maximization problem, observe that the requirement that profits equal zero in the housing industry defines the before-tax return on land R as a function of p and r, enabling us to write the after-tax return on land as $R(p,r) - T$. Solving (4) for T then gives the following maximization problem:

$$\max_{p,g} R(p,r)L - [C(g,n(\cdot)) - (q(g,b) - p)H(p,r)]. \tag{P1}$$

This setup assumes that both the property tax rate t and the land tax rate T can be chosen optimally. When only a land tax is available, there is no difference between the producer and consumer prices of housing, implying that $p = q(g,b)$. Thus, p is no longer a control variable and the problem becomes

$$\max_{g} R(q(g,b),r)L - C(g,n(\cdot)), \tag{P2}$$

where $q(g,b)$ replaces p and q as arguments in the function $n(\cdot)$, allowing us to redefine n as a function of g, b, and r. If there are no constraints on taxes, then any use of land taxes will be supplemented with a head tax, and the problem is

$$\max_{g,\tau} R(q(g,b-\tau),r)L - [C(g,n(\cdot)) - \tau n(\cdot)], \tag{P3}$$

where τ is the head tax and now $b - \tau$ replaces b as an argument in $n(\cdot)$.

With the equilibrium for each jurisdiction determined, given the values of u^* and r, these variables must now adjust to achieve an equilibrium for the nation as a whole. In particular, u^* and r adjust to equate the demand for households, summed across jurisdictions, to the fixed supply, and to equate demand with supply in the nation's capital market.

7.3   Tax and Expenditure Rules

To start the comparison of alternative tax systems, let us first examine the tax and expenditure rules under these systems. It is well-known that the use of head taxes leads to an efficient equilibrium, which satisfies the Samuelson rule for public good provision. This rule equates the sum of marginal rates of substitution between numeraire income and the public good to the marginal resource cost of the public good:

$$n\frac{v_g}{v_b} = C_g. \tag{5}$$

In addition, the head tax is set equal to marginal congestion costs: $\tau = C_n$. In other words, the head tax is an efficient "benefit tax" or "congestion tax." The land tax is then used to balance the government budget if scale economies cause marginal congestion costs to fall short of the average cost of public good provision, C/n.

Hoyt (1991), Krelove (1993), and Wilson (1997) all investigate the rules for taxes and the public good level when a distortionary property tax must be used instead of head taxes. Their surprising conclusion is that the property tax remains a congestion tax in the sense that a household's tax payment equals marginal congestion costs:

$$th = C_n. \tag{6}$$

This conclusion follows from the first-order condition for price p in problem P1.

This tax rule suggests that new residents are compensating the jurisdiction for marginal congestion costs, in which case such costs might be expected not to enter the rule for public good provision. However, this is not the case. The following proposition is taken from Wilson (1997).

Proposition 1: Assume that either a property tax or a land tax is available to finance the public good. In each case, the equilibrium public good level satisfies

$$n\frac{v_g}{v_b} = C_g + C_n\frac{dn}{dg}, \tag{7}$$

where dn/dg is the marginal population change induced by a rise in g financed with the available tax instrument. Rule (7) also remains valid when both taxes are present if either (i) the land tax is exogenously fixed or (ii) both taxes are chosen optimally. Under both (i) and (ii), the term dn/dg represents the marginal population change from a rise in g financed by a property tax.

Rule (7) tells us that the sum of the marginal rates of substitution between income and the public good equals a measure of the marginal cost of g that includes not only the usual resource cost C_g but also any additional "congestion costs" associated with a rise in g. In the case of property tax finance, increasing g produces an inflow of new households, because the accompanying rise in the price of housing q creates an excess supply of housing at the existing population level, requiring that this level rise to clear the housing market. Each of these new residents raises the cost of the public good by C_n at the margin, and the total additional congestion costs are therefore $C_n(dn/dg)$.

A critical aspect of this rule is that it applies to both the case of property tax finance and the case where only land taxation is available. But why are congestion costs fully included as a cost in the rule when the property tax is available, despite the congestion tax interpretation of the property tax suggested by tax rule (6)? The answer is that the housing market distortion created by the property tax offsets the congestion tax benefits at the margin. By raising the property tax rate to finance additional public good provision, the government further distorts housing decisions, and the deadweight loss from this distortion offsets the benefits from taxing new residents according to the congestion that they create. When only land is taxed, tax payments are unaffected by the migration response to a rise in g, that is, there is no equivalent to the congestion pricing rule given by (6). But there is also no deadweight loss in the housing market.

Despite the applicability of rule (7) to both property tax finance and land tax finance, the marginal impact of the public good on the population level n, denoted dn/dg in (7), does depend on which tax system is used. We now turn to the implications of this consideration for public good provision and welfare.

7.4   The Welfare Effects of the Property Tax

Suppose that local governments initially have access only to lump-sum taxation, in the form of a land tax, and consider how welfare is affected by allowing them access to a property tax. Following the benefit view of the property tax, let us not hold public good levels fixed, but rather allow them to be endogenously determined, along with tax rates, through the behavior of the independent local governments. I call this exercise "endogenous budget incidence," to distinguish it from balanced budget incidence and differential tax incidence. The next proposition shows what happens.

Proposition 2: Starting from an equilibrium in which only land taxes are available, suppose that the property tax is also made available to all jurisdictions. Then jurisdictions choose to increase their public good levels, and every household's utility rises.

Proof. The proof uses the rule for public good provision given by
(7). Hold g fixed and change tax systems. Then the only potential
change in rule (7) involves the marginal impact of g on a jurisdiction's population, dn/dg. Implicit differentiation of the condition
for housing market equilibrium (equation (3)) gives the following
formula:

$$\frac{dn}{dg} = \frac{1}{h}\frac{\partial H}{\partial p}\frac{dp}{dg} - \frac{n}{h}\frac{\partial h}{\partial q}\frac{dq}{dg}, \tag{8}$$

where, as already noted, $dq/dg = v_g/hv_b$. In the absence of property taxation, $dp/dg = dq/dg$ because $p = q$. But $dp/dg = 0$ when the
property tax is available, since g is chosen to maximize after-tax
land rents, $R - T$, implying that a marginal change in g financed by
the property tax has no impact on R and, therefore, on p. (R and r
determine p via the zero-profit condition, but the small jurisdiction
treats r as fixed.)

Thus, moving to a property tax eliminates the positive term
involving dp/dg in (8). But it has no impact on the remaining term.
In particular, there is no change in the consumer price required to
clear the housing market. Reducing the land tax lowers the cost of
housing production, thereby lowering p, but the introduction of
the property tax then keeps q unchanged. With tax payments being
held fixed, there is also no change in private income, b. With q and
b unchanged, the second term stays fixed. But the elimination of
the first term lowers dn/dg, causing the marginal cost of the public
good to fall from the viewpoint of a single jurisdiction. Local governments respond by raising their public good levels until rule (7) is
reestablished.

Finally, consider the welfare impact of this change in tax systems.
When property taxation is allowed in all jurisdictions and they all
raise g, there is no change in any single jurisdiction's population
level. Hence, the congestion cost term in (7) does not enter the welfare calculations of the benefits and costs of this rise in g. With the
marginal benefit of g, given by the left-hand side of (7), exceeding
the marginal resource cost, we may conclude that the increase in g
raises welfare. *QED*

This proposition suggests that at least a portion of the benefit view
survives in this hybrid model. Raising the property tax to finance
higher public good provision in a jurisdiction retards the entry of

new households into the jurisdiction. If only the land tax were available, then a higher land tax would raise gross land rents relative to the return on capital, causing more housing capital to be placed on each unit of land. This housing expansion would facilitate the movement of new individuals into the jurisdiction, adding to congestion costs. But when the property tax is used, there is no expansion in the housing stock, implying a smaller inflow of households and therefore lower additional congestion costs. Hence, public good levels rise from their depressed levels. In this sense, the property tax tends partially to control population flows, as a benefit tax should, leading to more efficient public good provision.

Consider now how much of the tax burden falls on land and capital. Holding g fixed, the assumption of fixed factor supplies clearly gives the "new view" incidence results. Capital and land share the burden of the property tax in proportion to their income shares in housing production. Note, in particular, that there can be no change in the ratio of gross factor prices, since the ratio of factor demands for the entire economy would differ from the ratio of exogenous factor supplies.

This reasoning tells us that a differential-tax-incidence exercise involving a shift from land taxation to property taxation will lower the tax burden on land and raise it on capital by identical amounts. However, the current exercise endogenizes expenditures, and we have seen that they rise when jurisdictions are allowed to use the property tax.[4] Thus, the rise in capital's burden exceeds the fall in land's burden.

As a final exercise, start by making both the property tax and the land tax available to all jurisdictions, and then allow them to use the efficient head tax. In this case, jurisdictions will obviously replace the property tax with the head tax, since the property tax distorts housing decisions from their individual viewpoints. Each household's head tax will be set equal to marginal congestion costs, and households will bear the head tax burden in their roles as residents of the jurisdictions levying the head tax, not as factor owners. Thus, the head tax becomes a fully efficient benefit tax, and public good levels increase to the point where the Samuelson rule holds.

The underprovision of public goods under the property tax relative to head taxation is similar to the underprovision results obtained in the tax competition literature; see Wilson (1999) for a review. What is different here is the demonstration that the property tax is actually preferable to a land tax. In standard tax competition models, such as Zodrow and Mieszkowski (1986b) or Wilson (1986), a tax on each jurisdiction's fixed factor would achieve a first-best allocation. In particular, each jurisdiction would view such a tax as a nondistortionary source of revenue and, therefore, follow first-best rules for public good provision. In contrast, the presence of household mobility in the current model implies that a tax on land is not first-best from a single jurisdiction's viewpoint, since it does not efficiently control the jurisdiction's population level. The property tax provides some limited form of control and is therefore better than the land tax.

To conclude, the hybrid model gives hybrid results: some benefit view in terms of the desirable effects of the property tax on public good supplies; but also some new view in terms of how the property tax affects factor rewards and how it falls short of an efficient benefit tax.

7.5 Heterogeneous Households

I now assume that there are different types of households, distinguished by preferences or incomes. These different types receive no benefit from occupying the same jurisdiction, and they incur the cost of not being able to receive their most desired tax-expenditure packages. Hence, I may limit consideration to equilibria in which each jurisdiction is occupied by one type of household. For simplicity, I assume two types, A and B, with type-B households paying higher property tax rates in equilibrium. An equilibrium need not exist, due to the well-known "musical suburbs problem" where the "poor" chase the "rich" in hopes of obtaining public goods that are subsidized by the high taxes paid by rich residents. Having investigated this problem elsewhere (Wilson 1998), I focus here on cases where an equilibrium does exist.

Land-value maximization is again assumed, but now the equilibrium utilities confronting each jurisdiction must adjust to leave them indifferent between the two equilibrium policies, one attracting type-A households and the other attracting type-B households. In other words, after-tax land rents are equalized across all jurisdictions. Otherwise, no jurisdiction would choose to attract the household that generates the lower land rents. Changing tax systems will generally alter the fraction of jurisdictions that must be occupied by each type of household to achieve this equality, causing the number of households in a given jurisdiction to change. For the subsequent analysis, I abstract from any scale effects of such changes by assuming a publicly provided private good (i.e., $C(g,n) = gn$). In this case, the congestion pricing rule for property taxation, $th = C_n$, implies that the government budget is balanced without the need for land taxation. In other words, allowing jurisdictions to impose a property tax means that this is the only tax that they will use (assuming no head tax), in which case $R = \rho$. Since the return on capital is also equalized across jurisdictions under property taxation, the zero-profit condition tells us that the producer price of housing is also equalized. Any differences in consumer prices are solely created by differences in property tax rates: $q^i = p^* + t^i$ for a jurisdiction with type-i households (a "type-i jurisdiction"), where p^* denotes the equilibrium producer price.

Suppose that jurisdictions are allowed to switch from their chosen property taxes to efficient head taxes, while holding fixed public good levels, for now. The elimination of property taxes can be expected to create an excess demand for housing at the existing producer price. As a result, p must rise, implying equal percentage increases in r and ρ to maintain zero profits. The new market-clearing producer price, p^{**}, will lie between $p^* + t^A$ and $p^* + t^B$. In line with Mieszkowski's (1972) reasoning, we might take p^{**} to be roughly an average across jurisdictions of the consumer prices under the property tax, with differences between these prices and p^{**} representing the excise tax effects of the property tax. By reversing the argument, we then see that capitalists and landowners everywhere bear the burden of the property tax in terms of the reduced nominal factor rewards associated with the decline in p from p^{**} to p^*, but the real values of these reductions depend on where the factor owners reside. Note, however, that the total fall in real factor income exceeds the tax revenue, because the differential property tax rates distort the allocation of housing across the different types of households, creating an "excess burden." Thus, the average tax rate may be a poor indicator of tax burdens, a point that Courant (1977) makes using a different model.[5]

Consider now the welfare effects of the move from property taxation to head taxation, taking into account the endogenous change in public good levels. With heterogeneous households, the changes in individual utilities will depend on the distribution of land and capital. Let us assume that all housing is owner-occupied under the initial property tax system, that is, there is no absentee ownership of the capital and land employed within any given jurisdiction. We move to the new equilibrium in steps. First, implement the tax change, while holding fixed housing and public good consumption for each type of household. Then there is no change in welfare, since we have merely altered the collection point of the tax, without changing the amount collected or behavior in the private sector. Moreover, raising r and p to their new equilibrium values also has no impact on welfare, since the higher incomes are fully offset by the higher price of housing (using our assumption of owner-occupied housing). If we now allow households to reoptimize their housing demands, revealed preference tells us that utilities will rise. Allowing public good supplies to change as well must further raise utilities. As previously discussed, the Samuelson rule is now applicable, and since it does not contain a congestion cost term, each jurisdiction increases its public good level to the efficient value.[6]

To conclude, the property tax fails to benefit anyone in the hybrid model, relative to a true benefit tax. This finding supports the new view.

Finally, how does the property tax compare to a land tax? The considerations discussed in the homogeneous case apply here also. In particular, moving from a land tax to a property tax tends to lower the marginal migration response, dn/dg, giving jurisdictions an incentive to raise g closer to its efficient level. But there are new considerations. Since after-tax land rents are equalized across jurisdictions under a land tax, differences in land taxes imply different gross rents and, consequently, different factor-price ratios in the two types of jurisdictions. It follows that land and capital are misallocated between the two types of jurisdictions. Moving from land taxation to property taxation removes this misallocation, raising the economy's total supply of housing. This additional benefit is not present in the homogeneous households case. However, the benefits of the higher housing supply need not be spread evenly between the two jurisdictions. In particular, it does not seem necessary that housing prices always fall in both jurisdictions, and this ambiguity complicates the analysis of how public good levels change. While the move to property taxation appears beneficial in the aggregate, additional assumptions may be needed to show that both types of households share in these benefits.

7.6 Conclusion

This chapter has constructed a hybrid model encompassing elements of both the new view and benefit view of the property tax. In an equilibrium with property taxation, each household's tax payment equals the cost of providing it with the public good, suggesting that the property tax is a benefit tax. Moreover, moving from land taxation to property taxation has been shown to raise public good levels from their inefficiently low levels, since the property tax does, to some extent, reduce the additional congestion associated with a rise in public good provision. But if the property tax is a benefit tax, it seems to be a most imperfect one at best. Capital and land throughout the entire economy bear the burden of the property tax, and moving to a true benefit tax (i.e., a head tax) raises all utilities, even in the case of heterogeneous households considered here.

It would be useful to explore other hybrid models of the property tax. I have stayed within the Tiebout tradition by working with a model (in section 7.5) where households sort themselves across jurisdictions according to incomes and preferences for public goods. But such sorting is far from perfect in practice, suggesting that future modeling efforts should attempt to capture the various reasons why different types of households might benefit from residing in the same jurisdiction. Schwab and Oates (1991) identify the existence of peer-group effects as one possible reason.[7] In the context of education, peer-group effects arise when the achievement of individual students in a class is positively related to the average ability (or achievement) of all students in the class. Desirable peer-group effects might result when the children of high-income households are mixed with the children of low-income households, since the former children tend to perform better in school. But while peer-group effects provide an efficiency justification for mixing households of different types, Schwab and Oates emphasize that taxes must generally differ across households to achieve this mixing as an equilibrium outcome. In particular, high-income households should pay lower taxes than low-income households in the same jurisdiction, to compensate the former for generating desirable peer-group effects. Under the property tax, however, high-income households tend to pay higher taxes, since they consume more housing. Schwab and Oates note "the troublesome issue of the existence of an equilibrium" when first-best taxes are not available.

These existence problems might be reduced or eliminated if we took a hybrid approach to modeling zoning restrictions on housing. The current model follows Mieszkowski's new view model by assuming the absence of zoning, whereas Hamilton's benefit view assumes a zoning policy that fully eliminates the distortionary effects of the property tax on housing consumption. The hybrid approach would attempt to capture the imperfect zoning that exists in practice. In a jurisdiction with heterogeneous households, it seems impractical to implement zoning arrangements that eliminate all inefficiencies in the housing market. A fundamental question is whether the property tax behaves more like a benefit tax or a profits tax under empirically reasonable zoning arrangements.

A more ambitious task would be to endogenize the imperfections in a jurisdiction's zoning policies. These imperfections can be viewed as an outcome of the existing political process. The assumption of perfect household mobility eliminates politics, even in the case of heterogeneous households, since households are able to "vote with their feet" (see Stiglitz 1983). But once mobility costs are recognized, the political process becomes an important consideration, and the design of a jurisdiction's zoning policies is typically a particularly contentious issue for a jurisdiction. Additional research is needed to learn whether the zoning arrangements that arise from a reasonable model of politics support the benefit view. Proponents of the benefit view might argue, however, that the theory is valid only in cases where individuals are highly mobile, leaving us to debate the validity of this assumption.

There are other worthwhile extensions of the analysis that retain the assumption of perfect mobility. I have assumed that capital is used only to produce housing. Alternatively, capital could be viewed as being divided between the production of housing and nonhousing consumption. In this case, a uniform property tax on all land and capital would seem even less like a benefit tax than the property tax in the current chapter, since part of the tax would fall on an interjurisdictionally traded good, nonhousing consumption. One approach would be to analyze a classified property tax, where "housing capital" and "industrial capital" are subject to separate tax rates. Wilson (1985) investigates the optimal classified property tax for a single jurisdiction, but without considering zoning restrictions.

To conclude, the current model suggests that Musgrave and Musgrave (1973) have largely got it right when they write in their textbook that "the part of the tax imposed on improvements is borne by the owners of capital in the nation at large" (415). I would add only that the property tax does seem to improve local decision making, but not as much as does a true benefit tax. This is a lesson from our excursion into endogenous-budget incidence. But there remain important theoretical and empirical avenues to explore in this area.

Notes

I am grateful to Panu Poutvaara, other participants at the CESifo conference, "Public Finances and Public Policy in the New Millennium," University of Munich, January 12–13, 2001, and the referees for helpful comments and suggestions.

1. White (1975) and Fischel (1975) extend Hamilton's argument to industrial and commercial capital.

2. In contrast, Krelove (1993) identifies Pareto improvements that could be obtained if a central government were able to alter the property tax and public good levels from their equilibrium values, without introducing alternative policy instruments.

3. This assumption holds when the utility function is weakly separable between g and private goods.

4. Recall from the introduction that Zodrow and Mieszkowski (1986a) also endogenize public expenditures for their reformulated new view. However, they depart from the current model and Hamilton's benefit view by assuming that labor is immobile and considering a tax on both residential and nonresidential capital.

5. Wilson (1984) provides another analysis of these excise tax effects, using a three-factor model with mobile capital and heterogeneous mobile workers.

6. For more general utility functions, where g is not separable from other goods, g might fall to satisfy the Samuelson rule, but the conclusion that welfare rises remains valid.

7. Another possibility is that different households supply different types of labor that are complementary with each other, in which case these households raise each other's productivity by living and working together. Brueckner (1994) describes such a model. Note, however, that the model assumes no commuting; households work where they reside.

References

Brueckner, J. K. 1994. "Tastes, Skills, and Local Public Goods." *Journal of Urban Economics* 35: 201–220.

Courant, P. 1977. "A General Equilibrium Model of Heterogeneous Local Property Taxes." *Journal of Public Economics* 8: 313–327.

Fischel, W. A. 1975. "Fiscal and Environmental Considerations in the Location of Firms in Suburban Communities." In *Fiscal Zoning and Land Use Controls*, ed. E. Mills and W. E. Oates. Lexington, MA: D. C. Heath.

Hamilton, B. W. 1975. "Zoning and Property Taxation in a System of Local Governments." *Urban Studies* 12: 205–211.

Hamilton, B. W. 1976. "Capitalization of Intrajurisdictional Differences in Local Tax Prices." *American Economic Review* 66: 743–753.

Harberger, A. C. 1962. "The Incidence of the Corporate Income Tax." *Journal of Political Economy* 70: 215–240.

Hoyt, W. H. 1991. "Competitive Jurisdictions, Congestion, and the Henry George Theorem: When Should Property Be Taxed Instead of Land?" *Regional Science and Urban Economics* 21: 351–370.

Krelove, R. 1993. "The Persistence and Inefficiency of Property Tax Finance of Local Public Expenditures." *Journal of Public Economics* 51: 415–435.

Mieszkowski, P. 1972. "The Property Tax: An Excise Tax or a Profits Tax?" *Journal of Public Economics* 1: 73–96.

Mieszkowski, P. 1999. *Taxes, Public Goods and Urban Economics: The Selected Essays of Peter Mieszkowski*. Northampton, MA: Edward Elgar.

Mieszkowski, P., and G. Zodrow. 1989. "Taxation in the Tiebout Model." *Journal of Economic Literature* 27: 1089–1146.

Musgrave, R. A. 1959. *The Theory of Public Finance*. New York: McGraw-Hill.

Musgrave, R. A. 1974. "Is a Property Tax on Housing Regressive?" *American Economic Review* 64: 222–229.

Musgrave, R. A., and P. B. Musgrave. 1973. *Public Finance in Theory and Practice*. New York: McGraw-Hill.

Musgrave, R. A., J. J. Carroll, L. D. Cook, and L. Frane. 1951. "Distribution of Tax Payments by Income Groups: A Case Study for 1948." *National Tax Journal* 4: 1–53.

Schwab, R. M., and W. E. Oates. 1991. "Community Composition and the Provision of Local Public Goods: A Normative Analysis." *Journal of Public Economics* 44: 217–237.

Stiglitz, J. E. 1983. "Public Goods in Open Economies with Heterogeneous Individuals." In *Locational Analysis of Public Facilities*, ed. J.-F. Thisse and H. G. Zoller. Amsterdam, Netherlands: North-Holland.

Tiebout, C. M. 1956. "A Pure Theory of Local Expenditures." *Journal of Political Economy* 64: 416–424.

White, M. J. 1975. "Firm Location in a Zoned Metropolitan Area." In *Fiscal Zoning and Land Use Controls*, ed. E. Mills and W. E. Oates. Lexington, MA: D. C. Heath.

Wilson, J. D. 1984. "The Excise Tax Effects of the Property Tax." *Journal of Public Economics* 24: 309–329.

Wilson, J. D. 1985. "Optimal Property Taxation in the Presence of Interregional Capital Mobility." *Journal of Urban Economics* 17: 73–89.

Wilson, J. D. 1986. "A Theory of Interregional Tax Competition." *Journal of Urban Economics* 19: 296–315.

Wilson, J. D. 1997. "Property Taxation, Congestion, and Local Public Goods." *Journal of Public Economics* 64: 202–217.

Wilson, J. D. 1998. "Imperfect Solutions to the Musical-Suburbs Problem." In *Topics in Public Economics*, ed. D. Pines, E. Sadka, and I. Zilcha. Cambridge, UK: Cambridge University Press.

Wilson, J. D. 1999. "Theories of Tax Competition." *National Tax Journal* 52: 269–304.

Zodrow, G. R., and P. Mieszkowski. 1986a. "The New View of the Property Tax: A Reformulation." *Regional Science and Urban Economics* 16: 309–327.

Zodrow, G. R., and P. Mieszkowski. 1986b. "Pigou, Tiebout, Property Taxation, and the Underprovision of Local Public Goods." *Journal of Urban Economics* 19: 356–370.

Comments

Panu Poutvaara

This chapter by John Wilson both summarizes existing views on property taxation and proposes a new framework to evaluate its efficiency effects and incidence. Wilson's framework encompasses features from both Mieszkowski's (1972) "new view" interpreting property tax as largely a profits tax and Hamilton's (1975, 1976) "benefit view" claiming that property tax is essentially a benefit tax paid for local public goods.

In Wilson's model, both capital and labor are mobile between jurisdictions. Capital is fixed at the national level, and households have exogenous income. Capital and land are combined to produce housing services, and there is no zoning. Jurisdictions use their tax revenue to provide local public goods with an endogenous expenditure level. Each jurisdiction maximizes land value, taking the utility level of mobile households and the interest rate on housing capital as given. Households are initially assumed to be identical.

Wilson compares public good provision and utility with head taxes, residential property taxes, land taxes, and their combinations. If there are no head taxes, public goods are underprovided due to congestion effects. Underprovision is worse with only land taxes than with a system of property taxes. The reason for this is that property taxes partially control population flows, whereas increasing land taxes creates congestion effects. Capital and land share the burden of property taxation proportionally to their income shares in housing production. Property taxes turn out to have features of both the new view and the benefit view.

The chapter also analyzes a model with two household types, one of which has a higher demand for the public good. It is assumed that an equilibrium in which different types live in different jurisdictions exists. With two household types, changes in tax structure imply changes in population levels in jurisdictions occupied by different household types, and therefore also changes in the number of jurisdictions occupied by each household type. As it is assumed that the public good is a publicly provided private good, congestion pricing with property taxes balances the budget. However, property taxes are still inferior to head taxes, as differential property tax rates distort the allocation of housing across different types of households. With heterogeneous households, land taxation leads to misallocation of land and capital between different household types. Although property taxes eliminate this distortion, it is uncertain whether everyone benefits from a change from land taxes to property taxes.

Wilson's contribution provides interesting and important new results. I would like to point out certain extensions and questions for further research. First of all, it is assumed that governments maximize land values and that all households are costlessly mobile. This corresponds to the Tiebout tradition, transforming local politics essentially into a market mechanism without any political tensions inside jurisdictions. Independently of their preferences as consumers, local populations owning the land are indifferent on policy pursued in their original home regions as long as this maximizes land values. This simplifying assumption has certainly permitted a large amount of interesting analysis. But to what extent do the results carry over under alternative assumptions on political process?

If the aim is to understand an economy in which only a minority of voters are perfectly mobile, it would be desirable to adopt another formulation of government decision making, allowing "political" motivations of local taxation and public good supply. By "political," I mean that not everyone agrees on what should be done, but there are conflicting interests. For example, the government could maximize the utility of immobile households owning the land. These immobile households might also demand housing services and public goods. One case to analyze might be such that immobile households are an identical group and mobile households another identical group, possibly with the same utility functions but with different endowments as they do not own land.

There are also avenues for further research without changing the assumptions on political process and costless mobility. In the chapter, it is assumed that capital is used only in housing. One alternative would be that a fixed capital stock is divided between housing and production facilities. Household income would be endogenous production combining capital and inelastically supplied labor. Another alternative would be to eliminate the assumption that there are constant marginal costs in public goods production with heterogeneous households. If the production function were more general, some distortion in housing demand might be desirable. Wilson's contribution provides a natural starting point for research aiming to learn more on these effects.

References

Hamilton, B. W. 1975. "Zoning and Property Taxation in a System of Local Governments." *Urban Studies* 12: 205–211.

Hamilton, B. W. 1976. "Capitalization of Intrajurisdictional Differences in Local Tax Prices." *American Economic Review* 66: 743–753.

Mieszkowski, P. 1972. "The Property Tax: An Excise Tax or a Profits Tax?" *Journal of Public Economics* 1: 73–96.

8 The Dutch Presumptive Capital Income Tax: Find or Failure?

Sijbren Cnossen and
Lans Bovenberg

8.1 Introduction

On January 1, 2001, the Netherlands introduced a new personal income tax act.[1] The most radical change concerns the introduction of a presumptive tax on personal capital income. Henceforth, the taxable return on personally held assets, such as deposits, stocks, bonds, and real estate (excluding owner-occupied housing), is set at a presumptive rate of 4 percent of the value of these assets net of liabilities, regardless of the actual returns. The amount thus computed is taxed at a rate of 30 percent. The presumptive capital income tax is therefore equivalent to a selective net wealth or assets tax levied at a rate of 1.2 percent. The presumptive capital income tax replaced the progressive tax on actual personal capital income— that is, interest, dividends, and rental income (capital gains on personally held assets were exempt)—as well as the old, broad-based net wealth tax.[2]

The presumptive capital income tax is unique in the industrialized world. In contrast to the Netherlands, other countries (including the United States and most member states of the European Union) impose a capital gains tax, separately or in conjunction with a personal income tax on other actual capital income. One drawback of a conventional realization-based capital gains tax is that the effective tax rate declines with the holding period of the asset. To counter the attendant lock-in effect, the scholarly literature has developed a retrospective capital gains tax which charges interest on the deferred tax at the time of realization. This literature has also drawn attention to the feasibility of a so-called mark-to-market tax, which taxes capital gains as they accrue.

This chapter evaluates the Dutch presumptive capital income tax as well as its principal alternatives. We first provide a brief overview of the Dutch tax reform, which takes a schedular approach to taxing personal income (section 8.2). Subsequently, we characterize the tax reform and review the major ways in which personal capital income, broadly defined, can be taxed (section 8.3). Against this background, the alternatives are explored in greater detail: the presumptive capital income tax (section 8.4), a conventional realization-based capital gains tax (section 8.5), a retrospective capital gains tax (section 8.6), and a mark-to-market tax (section 8.7). All alternatives appear to suffer from particular shortcomings, as summarized in section 8.8. In our view, the least unattractive option appears to be (i) a mark-to-market tax to capture the returns on easy-to-value liquid assets, such as financial products, and (ii) a capital gains tax with interest on the deferred tax to tax the returns on hard-to-value illiquid assets, such as real estate and small businesses.

8.2   Outline of the Tax Reform

Table 8.1 summarizes the main elements of the new Dutch income tax. Taxable personal income is assigned to one of three so-called *boxes* (we have added boxes 4 and 5 for purposes of analysis). Box 1 consists mainly of labor income items. These items include the labor income that a self-employed person (proprietor) earns in his or her business (labeled business profits for tax purposes) and the fictitious wage attributed to the manager-shareholder of a closely held corporation.[3]

Some capital income items are also included in box 1. The most important ones are the return on capital that proprietors employ in their own business and the income from owner-occupied housing (i.e., presumptive net rental income minus mortgage interest).[4] Also allocated to this box are interest, net rental income (i.e., net of operating expenses), and realized capital gains on assets put at the disposal of closely held corporations by dominant shareholders.[5] This anti-avoidance provision prevents these shareholders from shifting their taxable income out of box 1, which is subject to relatively high marginal tax rates, into box 3, which features a low proportional tax rate. The sum of labor and capital income assigned to box 1 is taxed at progressive rates ranging from 32.35 percent in the first bracket

Table 8.1
New income tax in the Netherlands, 2001

Boxes/tax rate(s)	Labor income	Capital income
Box 1 *(natural persons)* 32.35%, 37.6%, 42%, 52% General tax credit of €1,576. Earned income tax credit of up to €803. Other tax credits for children, single parents, and the elderly.	Wages, salaries. Labor income of self-employed.[a] Presumptive wage income of manager-shareholders of closely held corporations. Pensions, Social Security benefits. Other labor income.	Return on capital of self-employed.[a] Presumptive net rental income of owner-occupied housing minus mortgage interest. Interest, rental income, and capital gains on assets put at the disposal of closely held corporations by dominant shareholders.[b]
Box 2 *(dominant shareholders)* 25%[c]	Labor income of manager-shareholders of closely held corporations in excess of presumptive wage income.	Distributed profits and capital gains on shares in closely held corporations that form a dominant holding.
Box 3 *(personal wealth)*[d] 30%		Four percent presumptive return on the value of deposits, stocks, bonds, and immovable property.
Box 4 *(closely and publicly held corporations)*[e] 35%[f]	Labor income of manager-shareholders of closely held corporations in excess of presumptive wage income.	Profits.
Box 5 *(nontaxable entities)*[e] Exempt.		Capital income of pension funds.

[a] Labor and capital income of self-employed persons is taxed jointly as business profits subject to the personal income tax.
[b] A shareholder is deemed to be a dominant shareholder if he or she (and associated persons) holds at least 5 percent of the paid-up shares of a (closely held) corporation.
[c] The nominal tax rate is 25 percent, but due to cumulation with the corporation tax rate of 35 percent, the effective tax rate will be higher depending on the time at which profits are distributed. The effective tax rate on profits distributed out of current profits is 51.25 percent $(35\% + (100 - 35)25\%)$.
[d] Effective tax rates are lower due to a basic wealth exemption of €17,600 (€35,200 for couples).
[e] Boxes 4 and 5 are not mentioned in the income tax act.
[f] Profits up to €22,686 are taxed at 30 percent.

(largely earmarked for Social Security finance) to 52 percent in the top bracket. The tax thus computed is reduced by a number of tax credits that can be applied only to the income of this box.

Profit distributions to shareholders having a dominant holding in closely held corporations are taxed in box 2. Also included in this box are capital gains realized when a part or the whole of a dominant holding is sold. The nominal personal tax rate on these items of income is 25 percent, but the effective overall tax rate is higher, because the items have also been subject to the corporation tax of 35 percent in box 4. As table 8.1 indicates, the labor income of a manager-shareholder, if and to the extent this income exceeds his or her fictitious wage, is also taxed in box 4 (and box 2 if distributed or reflected in the capital gain realized on a dominant holding). Effective tax rates on capital gains assigned to box 2 (as well as boxes 1 and 4) vary, depending on the extent to which their realization can be deferred.

Box 3 includes (the returns on) individually held assets, such as deposits, stocks (including the shares of passive shareholders in closely held corporations), bonds, and real estate (except owner-occupied housing). The items in this box are subject to the presumptive capital income tax. The statutory rate is 30 percent on a *presumptive* return of 4 percent. The resulting nominal tax rate of 1.2 percent on the value of the taxable assets is thus proportional. Expressed as a percentage of the *actual* return, however, the tax liability differs between assets (depending on the actual return). The higher the actual return becomes, the lower is the tax expressed as a percentage of that return. In the case of shares, moreover, the presumptive tax comes on top of the corporation tax.

Table 8.1 includes a fourth box—not mentioned in the new income tax act, but relevant to the analysis in this chapter—in which the current profits of corporations, publicly and closely held, are subject to the corporation tax at a statutory rate of 35 percent. The tax reform does not affect this box; corporate entities are taxed under a separate act. The classical corporate tax system, under which distributed profits are taxed separately at the corporate level (under the corporation tax) and the shareholder level (under the income tax), is thus maintained. Nevertheless, the reform of the personal capital income tax importantly alters the economic effects of the classical system, as explained later.

A fifth box—also not mentioned in the new act—includes tax-exempt capital income. In particular, pension savings can accumulate without attracting capital income tax.

8.3 Alternative Ways of Taxing Capital Income

8.3.1 Characteristics of the New Income Tax

Under the presumptive tax, capital income is taxed on the basis of the expected (ex ante) investment return. This return represents the normal risk-free return to capital, that is, the return to waiting. In contrast, a capital gains tax, conventional or retrospective, and a mark-to-market tax include the actual (ex post) return of an asset in their bases. In addition to the risk-free return, an ex post tax includes in its base the return attributable to uncertainty, as well as the return originating in investor-specific abilities (which can also be viewed as remuneration for the application of human capital)—for example, the reward for information advantages.

Under the new Dutch income tax, capital income is sometimes taxed on an ex ante basis, sometimes on an ex post basis, and sometimes not at all. In addition, the rates at which (ex ante or ex post) capital income is taxed vary; sometimes the rates are proportional, but in other cases progressive rates apply. Specifically,

• The return on equity, including capital gains, invested in proprietorships and closely held corporations is taxed on an ex post basis—at progressive rates (in box 1) if earned by proprietorships, and at proportional rates (in boxes 2 and 4) if earned by closely held corporations. Capital gains are taxed on a realization basis without interest charged on the deferred tax.

• The return on equity (shares) invested in publicly held corporations is taxed twice: on an ex post basis at the corporate level and on an ex ante basis at the personal level. At both levels, proportional rates apply. Capital gains are taxed on a realization basis at the corporate level but on an accrual basis at the personal level.

• The return on individually held assets, such as deposits, debt claims, and real estate, is generally taxed on an ex ante basis at the personal level. This applies also to owner-occupied property—albeit that the presumptive return (i.e., the net rental value) is merely

0.8 percent (which is considerably lower than the presumptive return of 4 percent in box 3) and that the presumptive return is taxed at progressive rates (in box 1) instead of at a proportional rate (in box 3). Exceptionally, the return on debt capital and real estate put at the disposal of closely held corporations by dominant shareholders is taxed on an ex post basis at progressive rates (in box 1).

• The return on savings held in pension funds is not taxed. Depending on the difference between the tax rate at which pension contributions are deductible and the tax rate at which pension payouts are taxable, the return on pension savings is in fact subsidized through the tax system.[6]

8.3.2 What Are the Alternatives?

All types of capital income could be taxed uniformly: that is to say, only on an ex ante basis or only on an ex post basis—and in the latter case on a realization basis (with or without interest on the deferred tax) or a mark-to-market basis. Under each of these four alternatives, the capital income items in table 8.1 would have to be reallocated in the following manner:

• *Presumptive capital income tax.* All capital income would be taxed on an ex ante basis in the same manner as the assets in box 3. Accordingly, capital invested in proprietorships and owner-occupied housing (currently allocated to box 1) would have to be transferred to box 3. The same applies to capital invested in closely held corporations, whether directly (in box 2) or indirectly (in box 1). In principle, pension savings (box 5) could also be placed in box 3. The corporation tax (box 4) could be abolished. These changes would transform the presumptive capital income tax into a comprehensive net wealth tax and confine the base of the personal income tax to labor income (which would largely be taxed on a consumption tax basis on account of the deferred taxation of pension savings).

• *Capital gains tax.* All capital income, current as well as realized capital gains, would be taxed on an ex post basis in the same way as the income of assets assigned to box 2. This implies that the assets currently assigned to boxes 1 and 3 would be transferred to box 2. In principle, the exemption for capital income from pension savings would have to be abolished. The corporation tax could be maintained, but in taxing dividends and capital gains at the level of the individual shareholder, the corporation tax attributable to distributed profits should be credited against the personal income tax on the grossed-up dividends (imputation system), and a write up of basis of shares by retained profits net of corporation tax should be permitted when taxing capital gains.

• *Retrospective capital gains tax.* All capital income would be taxed in the same manner as under a conventional capital gains tax, but, in addition, interest would be charged on the deferred tax as if the gains had been taxed as they accrued.

• *Mark-to-market tax.* All capital income would be taxed on an ex post basis without regard to the realization rule. Specifically, capital gains would be taxed as they accrue (i.e., on the basis of the mark-to-market principle), including at the level of proprietorships and pension funds. The mark-to-market tax implies that the corporation tax could be abolished. Alternatively, the corporation tax could serve as a withholding tax at the corporate level, but creditable against the capital income and mark-to-market tax at the individual level.

The following sections evaluate these four alternatives on the basis of generally accepted criteria for a "good" income tax—namely, equity (ability to pay), neutrality, and enforcement. The ability-to-pay criterion requires a comprehensive definition of income, defined as the sum of consumption and the real accretion of wealth in some period (generally, the calendar year).[7] Neutrality implies that fundamental economic signals rather than tax considerations should guide the behavior of investors and entrepreneurs. This general principle is violated if the tax to be paid depends on the choice between lending or investing, the form in which a business is conducted, or its financing structure and dividend policy. Enforcement means that opportunities for arbitrage (strategic trading purely for tax advantages) are minimized.

8.4 Presumptive Capital Income Tax

8.4.1 Equity Considerations

Taxing capital income on a presumptive basis violates ability to pay measured in terms of income. First, under a presumptive capital income tax, the government exempts above-normal returns that originate in superior investment insight. These additional returns, which are attributable to the application of labor and other investor-specific production factors, escape tax. This is in contrast to above-normal returns due to superior entrepreneurial skills applied in businesses. These returns are taxed at the business level at the progressive personal income tax rates (of up to 52 percent) or at the corporation tax rate (of 35 percent).

Second, under a presumptive capital income tax, the government does not share in the good and bad luck of investors. This violates the ability-to-pay criterion and may also harm efficiency. Compared with the capital market, the government may be better equipped to pool investment risks—for example, because of its ability to share risks across generations through public debt policy (Atkinson and Stiglitz 1980). By stepping back as insurance agent under the presumptive tax, the government forgoes the insurance premium (i.e., the tax on the risk premium). If the government effectively pools risks, this latter tax is not a burden on the private sector; rather, it is the price that the private sector is willing to pay to the government for pooling macroeconomic risks.

8.4.2 Neutrality Considerations

The inconsistent treatment of various items of capital income affects economic choices, in particular business financing decisions and the form in which a business is conducted.

8.4.2.1 Debt versus Equity

The previous income tax regime encouraged publicly held corporations to finance their investments through profit retention rather than debt. This occurred because the corporation tax rate (35 percent plus the 0 percent tax rate on personal capital gains) was typically lower than the progressive rates (of up to 60 percent) of the personal income tax applying to interest income accruing to higher income groups (where shareholdings and debtholdings are concentrated). Accordingly, profit retention enabled shareholders to reduce the tax rate on the return of their investments from the relatively high personal income tax rate to the relatively low corporation tax rate.

The presumptive capital income tax reverses the privileged position of retained profits versus debt. The high personal income tax rate on actual nominal interest income is replaced by a low 30 percent rate on a presumptive return of only 4 percent. Furthermore, the presumptive tax of 1.2 percent on the value of debtholdings applies also to shareholdings. In fact, the old personal income tax on actual capital income, which taxed the return on debt but exempted capital gains (i.e., the return on equity), was replaced by a wealth tax (i.e., the presumptive capital income tax), which taxes not only debt but also equity. The tax discrimination against equity at the corporate level (the normal return on equity is, in contrast to interest, not deductible in ascertaining taxable profits) is therefore no longer mitigated by tax concessions for equity at the personal level (the old personal income tax exempted capital gains but taxed interest).

The quantitative analysis of Bovenberg and Ter Rele (1998) confirms that retained earnings became a less attractive source of finance than debt under the presumptive capital income tax. Applying the approach pioneered by King and Fullerton (1984), Bovenberg and Ter Rele compute the cost of capital for marginal investments under both the old and the new regimes. Their calculations assume an inflation rate of 2 percent and a real rate of interest that is exogenously fixed at 4 percent by international capital markets. Table 8.2 lists the costs of capital (under the old and the new regimes) for three types of investors: individual investors facing average marginal tax rates, individual investors paying the top marginal tax rate, and institutional investors paying no capital income taxes. Investors are assumed to arbitrage between debt (which yields a fixed before-tax rate of return of 4 percent in real terms) and equity, so that each investor earns the same after-tax yield on debt and equity. This net yield and the taxation of equity produce the required pre-tax real return on equity.

Table 8.2 shows that the tax reform leaves the cost of debt finance more or less unaffected. This cost rises slightly for proprietorships and owner-occupied housing, because the reduction of the top marginal income tax rates reduces the value of interest deductions. The required return on retained earnings increases substantially for shareholders subject to the personal income tax, and exceeds that on debt for all types of Dutch investors, including investors facing high marginal tax rates. The documented larger gap between the cost of retained earnings and debt finance encourages corporations that rely on Dutch investors for their equity capital to increase debt finance. The shareholdings of corporations that can also draw on nonresidents and tax-exempt institutions for their equity needs will shift away from Dutch individual investors.

Table 8.2
Real capital costs of marginal investments before/after the Dutch tax reform[a]

| Types of investors[b] | Equity[c] | Of which | | Debt |
		New shares	Retained profits	
Average marginal tax rates (1.2/3.0)[d]				
Corporations:				
Ordinary shareholders	2.9/5.9	6.1/6.1	2.6/5.9	3.0/3.0
Dominant shareholders	3.1/5.5	3.9/6.8	3.0/5.3	2.9/2.9
Proprietorships	2.2/4.5	—	—	2.2/2.5
Owner-occupied housing	2.3/3.8	—	—	2.0/2.4
High marginal tax rates (−0.3/2.8)[e]				
Corporations:				
Ordinary shareholders	1.6/5.9	6.1/6.1	1.1/5.9	3.0/3.0
Dominant shareholders	1.0/5.2	1.3/6.5	0.9/5.0	2.9/2.9
Proprietorships	0.6/5.0	—	—	1.4/1.8
Owner-occupied housing	1.2/3.8	—	—	1.2/1.8
Institutional investors (4/4)				
Corporations with ordinary shareholders	5.9/5.9	6.1/6.1	5.9/5.9	3.0/3.0

Source: Bovenberg and Ter Rele 1998.
[a] On the basis of a nominal interest rate of 6 percent and an inflation rate of 2 percent. Accordingly, without taxation, the real cost of capital would be 4 percent.
[b] Figures in parentheses show the after-tax real returns to savers before/after the tax reform.
[c] Equity-financed investments of corporations are assumed to consist of 10 percent newly issued shares and 90 percent retained profits.
[d] To compute the return after tax of equity-financed investments, 10 percent of the wealth of households is assumed to fall under the exemption (proposed at the time the calculations were made) of €10,000 (€20,000 for couples) of the presumptive capital income tax. The average marginal tax rate of the income tax in box 1 is 41 percent.
[e] The top marginal income tax rates are 60 percent before the reform and 52 percent (in box 1) after the reform. Personal wealth is assumed to exceed the exemption under the presumptive capital income tax.

The new tax system also raises the costs of equity finance in owner-occupied housing and proprietorships (see table 8.2), for two reasons. First of all, the abolition of the old system of personal wealth taxation, which included tax preferences for business equity and owner-occupied housing, differentially raises equity costs. Second, owner-occupied housing and the business equity of proprietors are taxed in box 1, but alternative financial investments are taxed in box 3. Hence, the costs of debt and equity are no longer treated symmetrically: The nominal interest costs of debt remain deductible at progressive rates in box 1, whereas the alternative investment of equity in the capital market is taxed at a proportional rate of only 30 percent on a presumptive return of only 4 percent. As is the case for corporate investments, the higher costs of equity finance will result in the substitution of debt for equity finance. Especially households subject to high marginal tax rates in box 1 face a substantial tax incentive to finance their own homes and businesses with debt and to invest their own equity in assets assigned to box 3.

8.4.2.2 Retained Profits versus New Shares

Under the old regime, financing through retained profits was more advantageous than financing through issuing new shares (see table 8.2). After all, the cost of profit retention (i.e., the net dividend that shareholders forgo) was lower than the cost of new equity. The presumptive capital income tax, in contrast, does not depend on the form in which the return on equity is enjoyed (dividend or capital gain). As a direct consequence, the decision to distribute profits is no longer being distorted, and issuing new shares is no longer less attractive (apart from transaction costs) than retaining profits.[8] This should shift equity capital from mature corporations (insiders), which generate retained profits, to new growing corporations (outsiders), which have to rely on the external capital market to attract equity. In this way, the new tax regime should promote a more efficient allocation of capital and facilitate the entry of new firms.

8.4.2.3 Business Form

The tax reform promotes the further demise of the closely held corporation set up to avoid the high personal income tax rates. Prior to 1997, this business form was greatly favored over the proprietorship, because current profits were taxed at the corporation tax rate of

35 percent, while (deferred) profit distributions and realized capital gains on dominant holdings attracted 20 percent tax, instead of the progressive income tax rates up to 60 percent levied on other income. Manager-shareholders, moreover, could transform their labor income into capital income without limit. In 1997, a fictitious wage was imputed to manager-shareholders and the tax rate on distributions and capital gains was raised to 25 percent. The new income tax further narrows the gap vis-à-vis the proprietorship form of doing business by lowering the top personal income tax rate to 52 percent and by introducing various anti-avoidance provisions.

8.4.3   Tax Arbitrage

Under the old regime, investors faced a tax incentive to borrow (and deduct the interest expense at high marginal tax rates) and to invest the funds in financial products that generated their returns mainly in the form of capital gains, which were not subject to the personal income tax. Under the new tax regime, in contrast, the tax incentive to borrow vanishes in box 3, because the presumptive capital income tax does not make a distinction between interest, dividends, and capital gains. However, by excluding owner-occupied housing, equity in closely held corporations and proprietorships, and pension wealth, the presumptive capital income tax features only a relatively small base. At the same time, the progressive tax rate structure is maintained in box 1, different proportional tax rates apply in boxes 2 and 4, the income tax on pension savings in box 5 can be deferred, and the return on debt remains exempt from the corporation tax. Thus, an incentive remains to relabel highly taxed income items into items subject to lower tax rates. This tax arbitrage erodes tax revenue, undermines the effective progressivity of the tax, and distorts the allocation of capital and risk.

8.5   Realization-Based Capital Gains Tax

Under the previous income tax regime in the Netherlands, a realization-based capital gains tax was levied on the sale of a dominant holding in a closely held company and on business assets. Capital gains were not taxed, however, when personally held assets, such as securities and real estate, were sold. In designing the tax reform, the Dutch Cabinet rejected a capital gains tax on these latter assets for the following reasons: Asset holders would defer the realization of capital gains (thus causing investors to lock in their investment), risk taking would be harmed, correcting capital gains for inflation would be difficult, and fairness required that tax be levied when liquid funds became available. These arguments are evaluated on the basis of the existing literature.[9]

The main objection to a capital gains tax based on the realization principle is that the effective tax rate declines with the holding period of the asset. In fact, the return on the capital gain attributable to the deferral goes untaxed. Accordingly, investors are encouraged to hold onto assets carrying accrued capital gains. This so-called lock-in effect interferes with the efficient functioning of the capital market and distorts ownership patterns. Lock-in can also destabilize the stock market because shares are sold when prices decline (to realize losses) and held onto when prices rise (to defer realization of the gains).[10] Beyond that, taxing capital gains on a realization basis invites tax arbitrage. Investments on which capital gains can be deferred can be financed by loans with interest expenses that can be deducted immediately. These tax-induced transactions, which permit investors to have their cake and eat it too, erode the tax base.

In rejecting a capital gains tax, the Dutch Cabinet argued that countries levying capital gains taxes are increasingly being confronted with the harmful effects of such taxes on risk-taking behavior. However, if capital losses are fully deductible, a capital gains tax should encourage rather than discourage risk taking. After all, loss taking (and the associated tax relief) can be accelerated, whereas profits (and the associated tax liability) can be deferred. Risky investments should thus become more attractive.[11] This subsidy to risk-taking behavior, however, erodes the tax base. To prevent this, the tax authorities might want to put limitations on the deduction of losses from other taxable income. Such limits on loss taking discourage risk-taking behavior. The government thus faces a trade-off between protecting the tax base and encouraging risk taking.

The Dutch Cabinet pointed also to the need for an inflation correction. This argument, however, applies not only to capital gains but also to other forms of capital income. If only capital gains were corrected for inflation, investors would be encouraged to buy assets yielding capital gains and to finance these purchases by loans (of which the inflation component of the nominal interest would be fully deductible).[12]

The realization rule is based on the notion that tax payments can be demanded only if liquid funds are available.[13] In modern financial markets, however, realization is a matter of portfolio management rather than income definition. Securities, especially if traded on the stock exchange, are as liquid as a deposit in a bank. In any case, other income items, such as the rental value of owner-occupied property, are also taxed in the Netherlands without liquid funds necessarily being available. The same holds true for ex ante taxes, such as the old net wealth tax and the new presumptive capital income tax.

8.6   Retrospective Capital Gains Taxation

The tax literature has developed various methods to eliminate the incentive to defer realization and hence the lock-in effect. Under the Auerbach (1991) method, when an asset is disposed of, the value at sale is deemed to have resulted from appreciation at the risk-free interest rate from the date of purchase. Tax is due on this deferred interest, with additional interest thereon to compensate for the value of deferral. Under the Auerbach method, the investor-specific risk premium escapes the tax.[14] Information requirements are minimal. Since the tax owed on the asset is independent of the purchase price, only the sale price and the length of the holding period have to be observed.

While the Auerbach method solves the efficiency (lock-in) issue, taxpaying capacity (in terms of income accretion) is not adequately measured because the investor-specific risk premium goes untaxed. The Bradford (1995) method, in contrast, does tax this risk premium. Bradford requires the taxpayer to set a gain reference date (GRD) and a gain tax rate (GTR) at the time of the investment. As under the Auerbach method, taxable income is computed at the time of realization by assuming that the capital asset has increased in value at the risk-free interest rate from the GRD. Furthermore, the purchase price is presumed to have increased in value at the risk-free rate until the GRD. Tax is charged on both presumed increases with interest on the deferred tax. In contrast to the Auerbach method, the Bradford method charges tax at the GTR on the investor-risk premium, which is presumed to have been capitalized at the GRD. Interest is also charged on this capital gain.[15] Obviously, the information requirements under the Bradford method are greater than those under the Auerbach method: In addition, values at the time of purchase have to be observed; also, the GRD and the GTR have to be set.

Retrospective capital gains taxation also brings problems in its train. While it does eliminate time-shifting tax planning, it creates an incentive for entity-shifting tax planning, whereby taxpayers shift income across assets. That incentive arises under a retrospective capital gains tax because effective tax rates on excess returns vary across assets.[16] Nevertheless, the general idea of maintaining the realization principle with interest on the deferred tax seems worthy of consideration if taxation at the time of accretion is problematic on account of valuation and cash-flow problems for particular assets, such as real estate and small businesses.

8.7 Mark-to-Market Tax

According to the S-H-S income concept, the annual accretion of wealth, measured in real terms, is the ideal base for taxing capital income.[17] Effective tax rates would coincide with statutory rates, and lock-in effects would be eliminated. The tax liability would be settled annually so that no large potential capital gains tax liabilities are carried forward that have to be paid at some future date. Tax avoidance is thus more difficult and less rewarding. As a direct consequence, administrative and compliance costs are lower.

In the United States, the desirability and feasibility of a capital accretion tax, or mark-to-market tax as the tax is called, are receiving increasing attention in the scholarly literature.[18] Most analysts agree, however, that political and administrative obstacles lie in the way of taxing illiquid assets, such as real estate (especially owner-occupied housing) and business assets, on a mark-to-market basis. The discussion therefore focuses on the distinction between these illiquid capital assets (which should continue to be subject to the prevailing capital gains tax) and the assets that should fall under the mark-to-market tax, on valuation issues, and on the relationship between the tax rate of the mark-to-market tax and the tax rate of the realization-based capital gains tax.

Agreement appears to be emerging that securities (such as stocks, bonds, derivatives, and debt claims) can be included in the base of the mark-to-market tax, while real estate and small businesses should be subject to a conventional capital gains tax. As regards the valuation of specified securities, the Financial Accounting Standards Board (FASB) in the United States believes that derivatives do not present insurmountable problems (Weisbach 2000). Indeed, corporations are already obliged to publish the market value of all their financial instruments. As regards tax rates, Weisbach points out that the average effective tax rate on capital gains should closely approximate the mark-to-market tax rate. This could be achieved by charging interest on realized capital gains tax under the assumption that the gains have accrued over the holding period in line with, say, the average price index for the hard-to-value asset, such as real estate.

Special attention should be given to the interaction of the mark-to-market tax and the corporation tax. In principle, the corporation tax would become redundant, because distributed and retained profits would already be taxed under the mark-to-market tax. The incentive to retain profits would be eliminated. If the corporation tax were retained and interest remained deductible in ascertaining taxable profits, equity would be discriminated against compared with debt. The corporation tax, however, could be reformed to function as a withholding tax for the mark-to-market tax—whereby the tax on the return on equity as well as debt would be levied at source.

8.8 Evaluation and Preferred Alternative

8.8.1 Comparative Analysis

The Dutch presumptive capital income tax does not include the investor-specific investment premium (which can be associated especially with wealthy investors) in the tax base. Also, the government does not share in the good and bad luck of investors. The presumptive capital income tax worsens the discrimination of equity vis-à-vis debt, because the tax on equity income at the corporate level is no longer offset by the exemption of capital gains at the personal level. Furthermore, the small tax base distorts economic choices, encourages tax arbitrage, and harms revenue. Last but not least, the presumptive capital income tax harms efforts to coordinate capital income taxes within the European Union. Whereas the Netherlands is resorting to ex ante taxes on a presumptive return, other member states are strengthening ex post taxes on capital income, including capital gains taxes and withholding taxes.

The major drawback of a conventional capital gains tax is that taxpayers are encouraged to defer the realization of capital gains and to accelerate the realization of capital losses. Complicated anti-avoidance provisions are often introduced to forestall this tax-driven behavior. Deferral and lock-in can be mitigated, but not eliminated, by deeming realization to occur at death and by charging interest on the deferred tax. This points in the direction of a mark-to-market tax. Generally, the problem with a mark-to-market tax is that it is difficult to apply to real estate (including owner-occupied housing) and small businesses due to serious valuation problems. For these assets, a capital gains tax regime (preferably with a rough-and-ready interest charge on deferred taxes) would have to be maintained.

The valuation problems are smallest under a capital gains tax, as long as no effort is made to charge interest on the deferred tax that correctly reflects the buildup of the gains over the holding period. In that case, the market generates the required information when the asset changes hands. For liquid financial products, financial markets provide the information required for a presumptive capital income tax (net wealth tax), a capital gains tax that attempts to charge interest as gains accrue, and a mark-to-market tax. Illiquid assets, however, have to be valued on a discretionary basis under these taxes. Interestingly, the Dutch presumptive capital income tax includes hard-to-value personal real estate in its base, including owner-occupied housing (albeit taxed in box 1 instead of box 3). This implies that the Dutch government believes that real estate, as well as liquid financial products, can be valued annually for tax purposes. Under the old net wealth tax, moreover, the equity capital of small businesses also had to be valued.

Under all alternatives, the position of the corporation tax is important. If the corporation tax were retained (after all, it also serves as a tax on the equity income of nonresidents), the double taxation of equity under the presumptive capital income tax could be eliminated by permitting the deduction of a normal return on equity capital at the corporate level. Under a tax on actual capital income, including capital gains, the double taxation of distributed profits could be eliminated through an imputation system or by exempting dividend income at the individual level (if the rate of the income tax equals the corporation tax rate). Permitting shareholders to write up bases of shares with retained profits net of corporation tax would prevent the double taxation of retained profits. Under a mark-to-market tax, differentiating the tax rate between equity and debt can prevent the double taxation of distributed profits.[19]

8.8.2 Preferred Choice

As the comparative evaluation clearly indicates, trade-offs have to be made between equity, efficiency, and feasibility in choosing between the various approaches to the taxation of capital income. On the basis of the arguments presented in this chapter, we conclude that if income is chosen as the best measure of taxpaying capacity, then the effective and neutral taxation of capital income can best be ensured through a combination of taxes at the business level and the individual level. At the business level, these taxes should include the corporation tax and a withholding tax on interest. At the individual level, a combination of the approaches discussed in this chapter would be our preferred choice: (i) a mark-to-market tax to tax the returns on financial products and (ii) a capital gains tax to tax the returns on real estate (with interest on the deferred tax to reduce lock-in).

We favor a single uniform tax rate on all capital income. This would minimize deadweight losses arising from the nonneutral taxation of capital income (Auerbach 1989). A flat rate (without a basic exemption), moreover, would reduce administrative and compliance costs, because capital income arising at the corporate level does not have to be attributed to individuals. If revenue needs dictate a higher tax rate on labor income, we favor the separation of actual (rather than presumptive) capital income (taxable at a moderate flat rate) from labor income (taxable at higher rates). This would result in a dual income tax, as found in Finland and Norway (Sørensen 1994; Cnossen 2000).

Notes

The authors are grateful to Len Burman, Richard Musgrave, and Deborah Schenk for helpful comments on a draft of this chapter. The chapter draws heavily on Cnossen and Bovenberg (2001).

1. See *Wet inkomstenbelasting 2001*, *State Gazette*, May 11, 2000, nos. 215 and 216. For the initial explanatory memorandum, see *Tweede Kamer*, 1998–1999, 26727, no. 2.

2. In contrast to the new presumptive capital income tax, the old net wealth tax also included in its base the value of owner-occupied property and the equity capital of proprietorships and closely held corporations.

3. The fictitious wage income of a manager-shareholder that is taxable in box 1 is generally deemed to be €40,454; exceptionally, however, the wage income can be higher or lower if commensurate with the manager's position. This anti-avoidance provision was introduced in 1997 to discourage manager-shareholders from relabeling their labor income as corporate profits. The provision has lost much of its significance following the reduction of the top income tax rate to 52 percent and the introduction of a relatively low effective tax rate in box 3, which should stimulate profit distributions.

4. Presumptive net rental income from owner-occupied housing (i.e., net of operating expenses) is deemed to be 0.8 percent of the value of the housing, which is well below market rental values. Since nominal interest on mortgages can be deducted in full, the income from owner-occupied housing is typically negative.

5. A shareholder is deemed to be a dominant shareholder for tax purposes if he or she (with or without associated persons) owns at least 5 percent of the paid-up shares of a (closely held) corporation.

6. The return on pension savings is taxed at the time the pension benefit is paid out. This tax is exactly equal to the advantage of tax deferral on the paid-in contributions if the rates at which benefits are taxed coincide with the rates at which the contributions are deductible. Under these circumstances, therefore, income from pension savings is in fact tax-exempt. However, since the rates at which pension benefits are taxed are generally lower than the rates at which contributions can be deducted, pension savings are typically subsidized through the tax system.

7. This is generally known as the S-H-S (Schanz-Haig-Simons) concept of income, after the authors who originally introduced the concept, that is, George Schanz, Robert M. Haig, and Henry C. Simons. See, especially, Simons (1938) and, for a modern interpretation, Goode (1975). Taking the criteria for a good income tax as our point of departure, we assume that ability to pay should be measured by income—largely a value judgment. We realize, however, that wealth and consumption can also be appropriate tax bases for assessing ability to pay.

8. Table 8.2 shows that new shares still suffer from a slight tax disadvantage compared with retained earnings. This is due to a separate low-rate tax on newly paid-in capital.

9. For one of the latest contributions to the voluminous literature on capital gains taxation, see Burman (1999). For the economic effects of a capital gains tax, see also Auerbach (1988) and Auten and Cordes (1991). For a compilation of the early literature on capital gains taxation, see Hoerner (1992).

10. The elasticities and time-series evidence presented in Burman and Randolph (1994) and Bogart and Gentry (1995) suggest that individuals are not very sensitive to capital gains taxation.

11. Even without the asymmetric realization of gains and losses, a capital gains tax could stimulate risk taking compared with the presumptive capital income tax (i.e., a wealth tax). This would be the case if the government, which shares the risks of investors under an ex post income tax, could pool risks better than the capital market.

12. Inflation corrections require complicated legislative provisions. At low inflation rates, therefore, most countries do not correct taxable capital income for inflation.

13. This rule also plays an important role in determining taxable profits. Indeed, the realization principle is closely associated with sound accounting principles.

14. Auerbach (1991) notes that his approach captures the capital gain attributable to the capitalized idea of the investor but fails to capture the initial income associated with the idea. He suggests that special rules would be necessary in "such special and easily identifiable cases."

15. In a recent paper, Auerbach and Bradford (2001) have further generalized their earlier work by showing the unique form that must be taken by a tax system based entirely on realization accounting to implement a uniform capital income tax or, equivalently, a uniform wealth tax. This system combines elements of an accrual-based capital income tax and a traditional cash-flow tax.

16. This issue is alluded to by Auerbach (1991). For a general treatment, see also Knoll (2001).

17. In the United States, this approach is already applied to specific derivatives, such as options, futures, forwards, and swaps.

18. For a pioneering article, see Shakow (1986), and for a general treatment, see Halperin (1997). The discussion in this section draws on Weisbach (2000), who favors a mixed mark-to-market/realization-based capital gains tax system. For an interesting view, see also Schenk (2000), who favors a presumptive capital income tax.

19. In considering these measures, one should bear in mind that double taxation does not interfere with investment and dividend payout decisions of mature firms if the corporation tax is confined to above-normal returns or if the tax on future profit distributions is capitalized in lower share values.

References

Atkinson, A. B., and J. E. Stiglitz. 1980. *Lectures on Public Economics*. New York: McGraw-Hill.

Auerbach, A. J. 1988. "Capital Gains Taxation in the United States: Realization, Revenue, and Rhetoric." *Brookings Papers on Economic Activity* 595–631.

Auerbach, A. J. 1989. "The Deadweight Loss from 'Non-Neutral' Capital Income Taxation." *Journal of Public Economics* 40: 1–36.

Auerbach, A. J. 1991. "Retrospective Capital Gains Taxation." *American Economic Review* 81: 167–178.

Auerbach, A. J., and D. F. Bradford. 2001. "Generalized Cash Flow Taxation." CESifo Working Paper No. 425, Munich, Germany.

Auten, G. E., and J. J. Cordes. 1991. "Policy Watch: Cutting Capital Gains Taxes." *Journal of Economic Perspectives* 5: 181–192.

Bogart, W. T., and W. M. Gentry. 1995. "Capital Gains Taxes and Realizations: Evidence from Interstate Comparisons." *Review of Economics and Statistics* 77: 267–282.

Bovenberg, A. L., and H. T. M. Ter Rele. 1998. *Reforming Dutch Capital Taxation: An Analysis of Incentives to Save and Invest*. CPB Research Memorandum 142. The Hague, Netherlands: Centraal Planbureau.

Bradford, D. F. 1995. "Fixing Realization Accounting: Symmetry, Consistency and Correctness in the Taxation of Financial Instruments." *New York University Tax Law Review* 50: 731–784.

Burman, L. E. 1999. *The Labyrinth of Capital Gains Tax Policy*. Washington, DC: Brookings Institution.

Burman, L. E., and W. C. Randolph. 1994. "Measuring Permanent Responses to Capital Gains Tax Changes in Panel Data." *American Economic Review* 84: 794–809.

Cnossen, S. 2000. "Taxing Capital Income in the Nordic Countries: A Model for the European Union?" In *Taxing Capital Income in the European Union: Issues and Options for Reform*, ed. S. Cnossen. Oxford, UK: Oxford University Press.

Cnossen, S., and L. Bovenberg. 2001. "Fundamental Tax Reform in the Netherlands." *International Tax and Public Finance* 7: 471–484.

Goode, R. 1975. *The Individual Income Tax*. Rev. ed. Washington, DC: Brookings Institution.

Halperin, D. 1997. "Saving the Income Tax: An Agenda for Research." *Tax Notes*, November 24, 967–977.

Hoerner, J. A. 1992. *The Capital Gains Controversy: A Tax Analysts Reader*. Arlington, VA: Tax Analysts.

King, M. A., and D. Fullerton. 1984. *The Taxation of Income from Capital*. Chicago: University of Chicago Press.

Knoll, M. S. 2001. "Tax Planning, Effective Marginal Tax Rates, and the Structure of the Income Tax." *New York University Tax Law Review* 54: 555–583.

Schenk, D. 2000. "Saving the Income Tax with a Wealth Tax." *New York University Tax Law Review* 53: 423–475.

Shakow, D. J. 1986. "Taxation without Realization: A Proposal for Accrual Taxation." *University of Pennsylvania Law Review* 135: 1111–1186.

Simons, H. C. 1938. *Personal Income Taxation: The Definition of Income as a Problem of Fiscal Policy*. Chicago: Chicago University Press.

Sørensen, P. B. 1994. "From the Global Income Tax to the Dual Income Tax: Recent Tax Reforms in the Nordic Countries." *International Tax and Public Finance* 1: 57–79.

Weisbach, D. A. 2000. "A Partial Mark-to-Market Tax System." *New York University Tax Law Review* 95: 95–135.

Comments

Alfons J. Weichenrieder

The recent Dutch tax reform described by Sijbren Cnossen and Lans Bovenberg seems to be a striking one indeed. Since January 2001, owners of certain assets have been taxed not according to the *actual* income derived from their assets but on the basis of an *imputed* income derived by applying an arbitrary rate of return to the actual (bank deposits, stocks, bonds) or estimated (real estate) value of assets. According to the authors, the main political motive for the reform was to tax capital income more widely and uniformly. The old income tax induced taxpayers to convert ordinary capital income into exempt capital gains. At the same time, a realization-based capital gains tax was eschewed because of its lock-in and deferral effects.

Taxation of capital gains and the correct value of capital depreciation have always been the Achilles heel of income taxation, and it is only fair to say that no simple and generally accepted solution has yet been found. Although not applied to all assets, the new Dutch approach to the problem looks like a quite drastic one that substitutes a wealth tax (the presumptive capital income tax) for the income tax on capital income and gains. It is a major merit of the chapter by Cnossen and Bovenberg that it explains to the non-Dutch community of public finance scholars the resulting changes and difficulties in a very clear and systematic way.

To evaluate the Dutch reform, I find it helpful first to identify the major implications of having an effective capital gains tax. In particular, such a tax should subject windfall profits (unanticipated gains) and anticipated capital gains to tax, and, in most real-world variants, would imply a discrimination against a corporation's retained earnings. This discrimination arises from the fact that retentions tend to make a firm more valuable and will lead either to an immediate tax on accrued capital gains or to a future tax on realizations once the shares are sold.

So how does the new wealth tax compare? If the aim is to tax capital gains, then at first sight it may not be at all clear why it is a good idea to pick a wealth tax. To take a simple example, consider a bond with a fixed return q in a world with a fixed interest (discount) rate r. Clearly, the value of this security would be q/r and it would be nothing but a replication of an income tax at rate x to introduce a wealth tax at a rate of $y = xr$. Now, to actually allow for capital gains, assume that for some reason the return of the bond increases from q to Q at time t_0. Assume the rise has not been anticipated before t_0. Then, given that the tax authorities correctly adjust the asset value from q/r to Q/r at time t_0, there is no difference between the wealth tax and the previous Dutch system which simply exempted capital gains. The jump in asset value at time t_0 is not taxed in either of the two approaches.

Of course, another possibility is the occurrence of anticipated capital gains. Assume the cash flow q of assets increases at a steady rate $g < r$. Then, the value of an asset at time t will equal $V_t = q_t/(r - g)$ and will increase at the rate g. The Schanz-Haig-Simons concept of income would comprise the current return q_t plus the capital gain and equal $I_t = gV_t - q_t = rq_t/(r - g)$. So, unlike in the case of unanticipated capital gains, in the case of anticipated capital gains the previous relationship $y = xr$ makes sure that the wealth tax and the ideal income tax are equivalent; this will also tend to be the case in settings that are more general than the above example.

As pointed out, capital gains may simply reflect profit retentions of a corporation. Indeed under the previous Dutch system, with a personal tax rate of up to 60 percent and a corporate tax rate of 35 percent, incentives to retain earnings and avoid the high personal taxes were paramount. It is in exactly this kind of system that a capital gains tax is helpful to foster financial neutrality as it punishes retentions. It is important to emphasize, though, that this was not a valid argument for the introduction of the wealth tax. In the Netherlands, the political consensus was to allow the effective tax on personal capital income to be lowered to the corporate tax rate or even below. So setting the maximum personal tax rate at 35 percent could have easily increased the financial neutrality without recourse to a capital gains tax or any substitute.

So, to sum up, of the three potential justifications for having a capital gains tax (taxing unanticipated windfall profits, taxing anticipated capital gains, and fostering financial neutrality), it is only the second one that is valid in the case of the Dutch wealth tax. The benefit that goes with the implied taxation of capital gains seems limited when compared with the several costs described in the chapter by Cnossen and Bovenberg.

Instead of levying a presumptive capital tax on securities, the authors propose to subject those assets to an accrual-based capital gains tax levied at a flat rate, which should be identical for all capital income. Given that the wealth tax requires a regular assessment of asset values, there should be no additional administrative cost, while on the benefit side windfall profits would then be included in the tax base. Thus, the proposal looks like a clear improvement. If the presumptive capital income tax is to work properly, then it requires adjustments of asset values on a regular basis. But if that is feasible, so is an accrual-based capital gains tax.

III

The Welfare State in an
Integrating World

9 The Crisis of Germany's Pension Insurance System and How It Can Be Resolved

Hans-Werner Sinn

9.1 Introduction

[I am concerned that] the feeling of human dignity, which I want even the poorest German to have, should be kept alive, that he should not simply be an object of charity without any rights, that he should have a peculium which belongs to him alone ... which makes it easier for him to open many doors which otherwise would be closed, and which, if he can take his contribution out again when he leaves, ensures him better treatment in the house to which he has been admitted.

—P. Stein, *Prince Bismarck's Speeches*

These are the words Bismarck used in his speech to the Reichstag on April 2, 1881, to justify his social legislation. It is significant that he used the word "peculium" for the public assistance he wanted the old and sick to receive. The peculium was the money Roman slaves were allowed to save up and could ultimately use to buy their freedom. Obviously, Bismarck saw the situation of the elderly as an underprivileged one, similar to that of the slaves in ancient Rome, and one from which it was necessary to liberate them.

Bismarck did succeed in liberating pensioners. People today are not stigmatized for being old and do not need to beg from their children to live a well-ordered life. However, a hundred years later, the pendulum has now swung in the opposite direction. The real problem today is the enormous burden facing contributors, not the stigma facing pensioners. The German pension system is strictly earnings related, with regard to both contributions and pensions. The combined rate of contributions by employers and employees to the pension insurance system in Germany is 20 percent of the gross wage. This burden will become even heavier in future, because there will be more and more pensioners and fewer and fewer people available to work. Even today, many people are finding the contributions burden oppressive, and there are grounds for believing that this burden is one of the reasons for the high wage costs in Germany and for the resulting unemployment.

This chapter discusses the impending problem of financing the German pension insurance system and the possibilities available for sensible reforms that can prevent the system from breaking down under the weight of excessive contributions and from endangering Germany's political system. It starts from research carried out by Munich's Center for Economic Studies (CES) for the Advisory Council to the Federal Ministry of Economics and Technology,[1] and it comments on the reform proposal the German government made in 2000 as a reaction to the council report.

9.2 The Implications of Demographic Developments for the Pension Insurance System

There were no special financing problems when Bismarck introduced the pension insurance system, because the number of old people affected was very small relative to the number of young people. Figure 9.1 compares the German age pyramid in Bismarck's time with that in 1995. It can be seen that the number of elderly at the top of the pyramid in Bismarck's time was extremely small relative to the number of young people lower down. If birth rates and death rates had been constant, the pyramid would have looked the same in 1995 as it did in 1875. However, this was not the case. The pyramid for 1995, which is shown on the right, belies its name. It should more correctly be called a pine tree, not a pyramid, as the younger age groups contain fewer people than the older ones.

It is quite obvious that the pine tree structure creates problems for a pension insurance system that operates with PAYGO financing. Fewer and fewer young people must finance more and more old people. It is also quite obvious that the greatest difficulties are yet to come. The problem will become severe when the heavy branches now at the lower levels of the pine tree move up to the pensionable levels. This is what is going to happen in the 2030s. By then, it will hardly be possible to keep the PAYGO process operating in its present form.

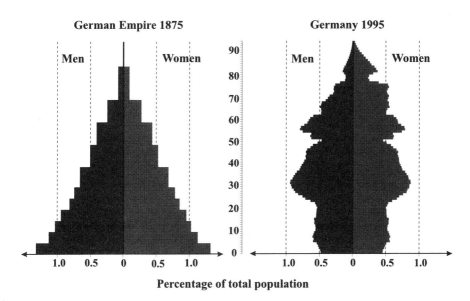

Figure 9.1
The German age pyramid in Bismarck's time (1875) and today (1995)
Sources: Statistisches Bundesamt, *Statistisches Jahrbuch*, table 3.11, Bevölkerung 1995
nach dem Alter, 62, 1997; Kaiserliches Statistisches Amt, *Statistisches Jahrbuch für das
Deutsche Reich*, Vol. 30, April, 7–9, table 4, Die Bevölkerung am 1 Dez 1875 nach
Geschlecht und 11 Altersklassen, 1878.

The pine tree has this shape because the growth rate of the German population has been falling continuously over time. Last century, this growth rate was about 1.1 percent, and it was the third
highest in Europe after Great Britain and Finland.[2] Today, the
growth rate is −0.1 percent in terms of the native German population and +0.6 percent when immigrants are included.[3]

The problem is that the Germans do not have as many children as
they used to. Ten Germans now only have, on average, seven children. The population growth rate in Germany is no longer third
from the top in Europe; in the OECD, it is now third from the bottom. Only Spain and Italy have even lower birth rates than Germany
has.

The declining number of children is not the only thing that creates
problems for the pension insurance system; increasing life expectancy does so, too. Medical advances are increasing the remaining
life expectancy of a 65-year-old German man or woman by around
1.5 months each year—that is, by an additional year every eight

years. The gap between the number of births and remaining life expectancy is widening all the time, and this will create more and more trouble for the pension insurance system because the number of people of pension age is rising continuously relative to those of working age.

Declining birth rates and increasing life expectancy are trends that are observable in other countries, too. Most OECD countries have problems similar to Germany. Nevertheless, the problem seems to be more severe in this country than anywhere else in the world. Unless the current trends change fundamentally, Germany will have the oldest population in the world by 2030.

9.3   Implications for the Development of the Contribution Rate

The demographic distortion has serious effects for the contribution rates of the pension insurance system. Currently, 100 Germans of working age (between 20 and 64 years) support 25 older people. In 2035, they will have to support between 50 and 55 older people, depending on which population forecast is used.[4] One does not need to set up a forecasting model to see that there will need to be either a very large increase in the contribution rate or a considerable reduction in pensions.

Up to 1992, Germany had a pension system in which pensions were linked to the growth of gross wages. Based on this, the range of possibilities open to politicians for 2035 is between doubling the contribution rates for the same pensions and halving the pensions with the same contribution rates. The politicians can choose some point within this range but they cannot perform miracles. If they are to succeed in preventing the contribution rate from increasing from 20 percent today to 40 percent in future, pensioners must make sacrifices.

The Bundestag has defined a comprehensive program of sacrifices with its previous pension reforms. In 1992, it replaced tying the pension to gross wages with tying it to net wages; it has done away with early retirement; it has abolished the pension for occupational invalidity (due to decline in earning capacity); and it has made it more difficult to get a general disability pension. In 1997, it decided that the so-called "standard pension"—that is, the pension of someone who has paid contributions based on average income for forty-five years—should fall from 70 percent to 64 percent of the net wage by 2030. However, this decision was quickly abolished by the new majority in the Bundestag, which instead imposed a moratorium on real pension adjustments to gain time for the implementation of more fundamental reforms. The reform implemented in 2001 has introduced a fiscal saving stimulus, which can be regarded as a first step toward a partially funded system,[5] as well as further implicit pension cuts resulting from redefining the net wage to which current pensions are tied. Net wages are now defined as gross wages minus taxes and contributions and minus recommended saving. The deduction of recommended saving reduces the base from which pensions are derived and therefore results in an effective pension cut without formally affecting the replacement rate, which is carefully watched by the public. For a while, it seemed that a PAYGO pension level of 64 percent, according to the new definition of net wages, was aimed at, which corresponded to about 61 percent according to the old definition; but then the proposal came under attack by various political groups that wanted to maintain a much more generous system. Ultimately, a level of 67 percent of net wages according to the new definition emerged, which corresponds to about 64 percent according to the old definition. This chapter discusses some of the alternatives for fundamental tax reform to shed some light on the general options available.

Figure 9.2 illustrates the results of the CES model for the case where the ultimate standard pension is 64 percent of net wages according to their old definition. Obviously, the contribution rate remains almost constant up to about 2020, increases rapidly after that, and by 2035 reaches its maximum value of between 28 and 31 percent.[6]

The two different figures refer to alternative population forecasts of the Federal Statistical Office and an Interministerial Working Group.[7] The lower forecast is based on the estimates of the Federal Statistical Office, which make the unrealistic, but cautious, assumption that life expectancy of west Germans will remain constant. The office also assumed that an additional eleven million foreigners will migrate to Germany up to 2030. The higher forecast assumes an increase in life expectancy of three years and lower immigration, of seven million people up to 2040.

Of course, the immigration figures assumed add a substantial degree of arbitrariness to the results. However, these are official assumptions which serve as useful benchmarks for the estimates. A

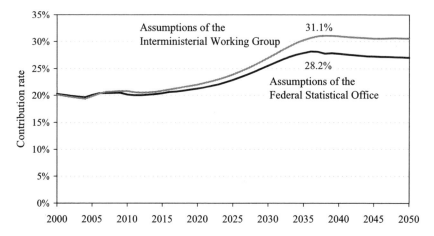

Figure 9.2
The development of the contribution rate with alternative population forecasts
Source: CES.
Note: The contribution rate is the sum of the employer's and the employee's contribution divided by gross wage income (net of the employer's contribution).

solution of the pension problem by immigration is theoretically conceivable, but not really a possibility. The immigration necessary by 2035 to keep the ratio of pensioners and persons of working age at today's level is more than 40 million people, or about 50 percent of Germany's current population.

The calculations are based on the essential characteristics of the German pension scheme, and they assume a constancy in the unemployment rate, the labor-force participation rate, the labor tax rate, the contribution rates for other social purposes, and the share of pensions covered by tax-financed contributions from the government budget. Sinn and Thum (1999) discuss the sensitivity of the results with regard to the assumptions, showing that official estimates that come up with lower contribution rates do so primarily by assuming increasing tax rates and higher sickness contributions which automatically reduce pension benefits. If these other components are taken into account, it turns out that the official estimates result in a significantly higher aggregate burden of contributions to the government sector than those presented here.

Contribution rates of the order of magnitude shown in figure 9.2 will not be affordable and would lead to a revolt by the young against the old. Undoubtedly, Germany is at the start of an initially insidious but increasingly alarming crisis of the statutory pension insurance system, one that could have serious consequences for the state itself if suitable countermeasures are not taken quickly. Fortunately, the German government seems to have understood this and is therefore considering a more substantial reform. However, whether the discussed cut in relative PAYGO pension rights by only 1–4 percentage points is enough is open to doubt. Section 9.6 discusses this in more detail.

9.4 Pay-As-You-Go versus Funding: Basic Remarks

Germany could have looked at the coming demographic distortion quite composedly if its pension insurance system had been a fully capital-funded system and not a contributory PAYGO one, because pensions could then have been financed by dispersing previous savings instead of by using the contributions of the working generation. With capital funding, the contributions to pension insurance are true savings which can be put onto the capital market and used to finance real investments. The stream of payments that the real investments produce can, if necessary, be used to pay back the loans to the savers, and thus the pensions can be paid without putting a burden on the contributors. The only problem then is to create the capital stock. It is great if you have one, but the accumulation process is arduous.

After the pension insurance system had been established by Bismarck, it proved possible to build up, in only ten years, a capital stock that could have financed pensions for seventeen years. Unfortunately, the World Wars and inflation thwarted the plan and destroyed the system's capital base. Today, the pension insurance system lives from hand to mouth. Its fund is only sufficient to cover it for eleven days.

Most Germans have no idea that the pension insurance system is a PAYGO one. They think that the money that they pay into the pension insurance system today is, in effect, savings that they will be able to use later. This belief is, of course, mistaken, as the contributions are all used up in financing today's pensioners. Nothing, but nothing, is being saved. The supposed savings are just an illusion.

The illusion is encouraged by the equivalence between contributions and pensions, which is the characteristic feature of the German pension system. The person who pays in twice as much as his neighbor gets a pension that is about twice as large. One's contributions give a right to future pension payments and, to the contributor, this seems like paying into a savings account. The Federal Constitutional Court has even included the earned right to pension payments among the legal rights of ownership under Article 14 of the German Constitution.

In a PAYGO system, each generation when young pays its pension contributions to the old generation and acquires the right to receive pensions when it is old. These pensions are paid for by the next young generation's contributions. The first generation pays nothing for its pensions; each of the following generations must make payments to its preceding generation to acquire the right to its own pensions. These rights are a hidden implicit government debt, which, like an explicit government debt, must be paid for by the next generation. This implicit government debt is created when the first generation comes into the pension insurance system, and it is turned over from generation to generation. Because the pensioners' rights are linked to wage developments, the size of the implicit government debt grows continuously over time, even when the population size is constant.

Today, the cash value of the rights already acquired—that is, the implicit government debt—is around DM 10 to 12 trillion. That is more than Germany's total fixed assets and a multiple of the explicit government debt, which comes to DM 2.3 trillion. When the euro was introduced, the German debt-to-GDP ratio was just above the Maastricht limit of 60 percent. If the implicit government debt of the pension insurance is added in, the total debt-to-GDP ratio becomes about 350 percent.[8]

The PAYGO system offers contributors only a very modest return on the contributions they have paid in. Those who only had a few years left to contribute when the system was introduced in 1957 could pocket the initial profit and get a very high return on their contributions, one that was much higher than returns in the capital market. But anyone who entered the scheme in 1957 or later made a worse deal than a capital market investment. Figure 9.3 shows the results of detailed calculations for this carried out at CES. The graph shows the real inflation-adjusted returns that the different age cohorts of sample male pensioners who entered the pension insurance system after 1957 have received, or will receive in future, based

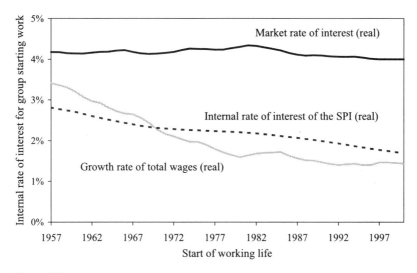

Figure 9.3
The internal return on the statutory pension insurance system (SPI)
Source: CES.
Note: The growth rates and interest rates are averages over periods of fifty years starting in the respective year shown on the abscissa. For the years after 2000, which gain importance in the right-hand part of the diagram, a constant annual real wage growth of 2 percent and a constant real rate of interest of 4 percent were assumed. These assumptions also underlie the calculations of section 9.6.

on current estimates. The cohort of the sample pensioners entered the pension insurance system at age 20. Some drew a normal age pension after forty-five years of contributing to the system, others drew an early general disability pension, and still others died before they had received any pension. Some of the age cohorts left widows and orphans who also drew pensions.

It can be seen that the real returns of the 20-year-olds who entered in 1957, and will normally become pensioners in 2002, are still almost 3 percent. Those who entered as 20-year-olds in 1990, however, can only expect a return on their contributions of 2 percent, and the young people who enter now can only count on a real return of about 1.5 percent. By contrast, savings invested in ten-year federal bonds and rolled over for fifty years would, as the top curve shows, have brought a real interest rate of about 4 percent.

It is not surprising that the returns on the PAYGO system are so low. Theoretically, they are explained by the real growth rate of total wages. Figure 9.3 shows that the theory comes pretty close to reality.

The growth rate of total wages has, in fact, fallen greatly in the last forty years. If, as a result of the demographic distortion, it falls further, the returns that the pension insurance system can offer will also fall.

At first sight, these data could be interpreted as a verdict on the German pension insurance system. In this interpretation, the system appears to be a completely inefficient way of arranging old-age provision; it should be abolished as quickly as possible and be replaced with a capital coverage system. Many observers have indeed interpreted the difference in returns in this way and see it as a reason to introduce a capital coverage system.

This appearance deceives. To call the difference in returns "inefficient" is to make a grossly mistaken economic interpretation. The truth is that the difference in returns is an essential feature of the intergenerational redistribution. The difference in returns is an integral part of the PAYGO system, from which one can no longer escape once this system has been set up. It is the mirror image of the initial profit that accrued to the first post-1957 pension cohort; it has already been distributed and cannot be taken back again. Each subsequent generation has acquired a claim against the next generation by paying its pension contributions, but these entitlements are never high enough to keep pace with a capital market investment. It is as if each generation is paying an implicit tax to service the implicit government debt that resulted from the gift made to the first generation. The pension insurance system is a zero-sum game being played by present and future generations in which the initial gain is mirrored by a loss of exactly the same amount for each subsequent generation when the present value of this amount is correctly calculated on an actuarial basis. In each period of time in an ongoing pension system, the present value of the implicit taxes to be paid by all future generations equals the present value of the then existing pension entitlements, that is, the implicit government debt.[9]

Naturally, changing over to capital funding is attractive, if by doing so the implicit tax hidden in the contributions can be avoided. But this is impossible because the pension entitlements already established cannot simply be swept under the table. An explicit tax would be needed to service these entitlements and, in present value terms, this would be just as high as the implicit tax that all successive generations would have to pay if the PAYGO system were to continue. Contrary to first appearances, it is not at all possible to exploit the returns advantage of the funded system in a way that results in a net advantage for society. The claim that the funded system is more efficient than the PAYGO system because it brings higher returns is completely false from an economic point of view, as the higher returns only show up if the tax required to service past entitlements is disregarded.[10]

9.5 Resolving the Crisis by Partial Capital Funding

All this does not mean that capital funding has no useful function. On the contrary, the statutory pension insurance system is in urgent need of help from capital funding, but it needs it for a different reason—not because it is inefficient. This reason is the demographic crisis that was described in section 9.2. The problem is not finding a system that promises more efficiency in the next 1,000 years; it is resolving the dangerous crisis that will affect the present 30- to 40-year-olds when they reach pension age.

If a generation is to enjoy retirement without having to keep on working, it must make provision for it, and there are, in principle, two ways of doing this. Either people can save and finance their keep by drawing on these savings, or they can have children so that these children will take care of them later. In harsh economic terms, people who want to have comfortable retirement must have previously accumulated either real capital or human capital. Those who do not do one or the other must starve—for nothing, you get nothing in return.

In the past decades, Germans have chosen not to accumulate as much human capital as was usual in the past. This is the reason for the crisis. If they, nevertheless, still want to live comfortably in their old age, their only option is to substitute real capital for the missing human capital. The additional real capital secures some of the present nominal pension entitlements, and it prevents the subsequent generation from having to carry an unjustified burden that is economically not affordable. The rule must be to cope with the pension burden, which would otherwise be crushing, by shouldering part of this burden now. This does not mean that changing over completely to a capital funding system would be necessary. Real capital need only be built up by the amount of the missing human capital. Full funding is not required if the goal is to keep the pension crisis under control.[11]

It is sometimes argued that the present employed generation cannot be expected to bear the burden of accumulating capital as well as the burden of their pension contributions. The transition to even partial capital accumulation, it is said, in itself implies an unfair double burden. This position fails to recognize that the employed generation must always bear a double burden since they must always maintain their own children as well as their parents. This was the case in the pre-industrial family, it is the case in today's world with government pension insurance, and it can never be otherwise. The pension problem has arisen because the current employed generation has preferred to get rid of one of these burdens by having fewer children than was usual in the past. It is in no way unfair to ask this generation to put the money they save from not bringing up so many children into the capital market and to secure their pensions in this way. The necessary ability to pay is certainly there and there is no unfair second burden.

Of course, a problem does arise here when it is considered that some families have enough children but other families have none. If those people who are already financing the older generation with their pension contributions and who are also maintaining a sufficient number of children are forced to save more, they will be faced with a third burden which can truly be called unfair. A partial dependence of the pension on the number of children could help solve this problem, but this is a matter of justice between families rather than between generations, which is not considered in this chapter.

9.6   Results of Simulation Calculations

It is now time to be more specific. This section reports on the results of simulation calculations to discover the quantitative effects of alternative suggestions for reforms aimed at resolving the pensions crisis. The comparison refers to (I) the present system, (II) a complete transfer to capital funding, (III) undermining the contribution mountain by setting up a fund within the statutory pension insurance system, (IV) partial funding with a fixed private saving rate, and (V) partial capital funding with a variable private saving rate. All calculations assume a time path of the sum of all pension components which, for the "standard pensioner," is 64 percent of net wages according to their old definition (gross wages minus taxes and other contributions to the government, but including recommended saving). It is important to note that the calculations take the time path of the sum of all pension components as given for all the alternatives, so that only the developments of the burdens differ. This assumption is typically not met by the reform proposals made in the political debate, but, without it, no meaningful comparison of the fundamental alternatives is possible. Pensions for widows, orphans, and the unemployable will, in any case, continue to be financed by way of PAYGO contributions. Capital funding will only be considered in relation to old-age pensions. The calculations are based on the assumptions mentioned above, including the relatively optimistic population estimates made by the Federal Statistical Office which abstract from the gradual increase in life expectancy. It is furthermore assumed that the real rate of interest remains constant over time and that wages grow at a constant real rate of 2 percent per annum.[12]

Figure 9.4 refers to the most radical reform conceivable: an immediate transfer to full capital funding of old-age pensions. All entitlements already established are respected and continue to be financed through PAYGO contributions. New entitlements, however, will be acquired entirely with capital accumulation from real saving. The lighter line in the graph gives the sum of the PAYGO contributions as a share of gross income and the saving contributions necessary to acquire entitlements the same as those with PAYGO financing. For comparison purposes, the development of the contribution rate in

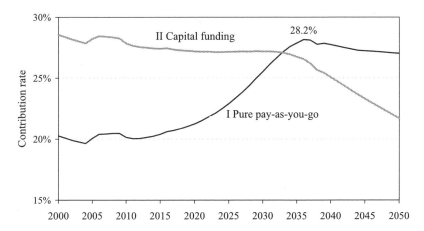

Figure 9.4
Contributions vs. full capital funding

the unreformed PAYGO system is shown again, by the darker line. It can be seen that the initial burden in the case of complete transfer to capital funding is very high because the transition generation must pay twice—once for old people's pensions which are based on entitlements already acquired and once for their own later pensions which are to be financed through savings. Only very gradually over the following decades does the PAYGO financing of the entitlements already built up become less important and the total burden fall. Complete transfer will only occur around 2070.

It can be seen that the transfer to full capital funding takes the system out of the frying pan into the fire, because it is a mirror image of the PAYGO path. The increase in charges to over 28 percent of gross wages, which, under the present circumstances, is to be expected in the 2030s, starts immediately and so does the pensions crisis. Because, as was argued earlier, the transfer to capital funding makes no comparable long-term increase in efficiency possible, one can confidently reject this scenario.

It would be ideal if there were a reform that would get rid of the impending crisis without a new burden turning up somewhere else, but this kind of reform could only occur in never-neverland. The best that can be achieved in the real world is an even distribution of the inevitable burden over time. Only in this way can a confidence crisis in the pension insurance system, which at the same time would be a crisis of the state itself, be averted.

One obvious way to even out the burden over time is for the pension insurance system itself to accumulate the capital that could be used in the crisis years to contribute to financing pensions. The pension contribution mountain would, so to speak, be undermined. Figure 9.5 shows this undermining. It can be seen that permanent stabilization would be possible if the contribution rate were to be raised immediately from the current 20 percent to 23.3 percent and kept at that level. In this way, the pension insurance system could accumulate a capital stock in the years up to about 2025 and this capital stock would then gradually be drawn down because the contribution rate would no longer be sufficient to finance pensions. In this version, capital would only be accumulated in a transition phase. In the long run, the pension insurance system's capital stock would once again be zero.

Regardless of how attractive the undermining solution may appear at first sight, it fails to take into account the covetousness

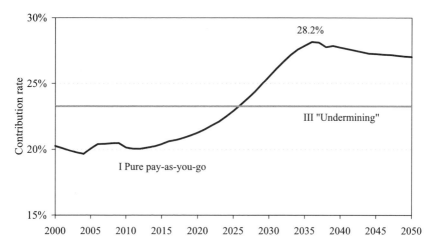

Figure 9.5
Pay-as-you-go vs. undermining

with which the politicians would look at a capital stock accumulated by the pension insurance system. It is hard to imagine a future federal minister, who wants to win the next election, resisting the pensioners' desire to use the capital stock prematurely. As a German proverb goes, dogs don't stockpile sausages.

Evening out the distribution must be brought about in another way, without the pension insurance system accumulating capital. One conceivable possibility is to oblige people to save a certain minimum fraction of their gross income so that part of the later pensions can be financed by dissolving the savings. The savings will have to be placed with private capital funds of the saver's choice, and the government will watch the average performance of these funds. It calculates the average funded pension entitlements accumulated by the single age cohorts and cuts the PAYGO pensions, and with them the contribution rates, accordingly. The funds are fully private and compete with one another, but their financial standing is strictly controlled by the regulatory authorities to reduce the investment risk involved. The saving is obligatory because many people with only low ordinary pension entitlements would not save voluntarily, knowing that by doing so they would only reduce their entitlement to receive social aid. As private saving creates a positive fiscal externality, voluntary decisions are insufficient. This is one of the many second-best examples where one type of intervention necessitates another one.

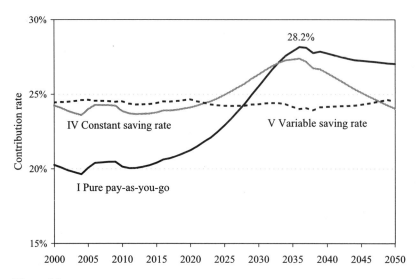

Figure 9.6
Two alternative saving models

Figure 9.6 demonstrates the implications of this proposal for the case of a saving rate of 4 percent of gross wages. It shows that the time path of the overall financial burden involved—the sum of PAYGO contributions and the saving rate—will remain in the neighborhood of 24 percent for a long time, but will rapidly increase after 2020 and eventually reach a peak level of 27 percent in 2035. Only in the following years will the overall burden be lower than it would have been with an ongoing PAYGO system that generates the same time path of pensions.

Obviously, a fixed saving rate is not able to smooth the time path of the financial burden involved with securing old-age pensions. Other alternatives with different values of the fixed saving rate were calculated, but the end result was always similar. In the neighborhood of the critical year, 2035, the remaining PAYGO contributions necessary to reach the desired pension level are still so high that the addition of a constant saving rate creates a problematic peak in the overall burden.

In 2000, the German government proposed a seemingly similar plan which foresees a gradual increase in the saving rate from 0 to 4 percent from 2008 onward. This plan, too, suffers from the problem described. It is a big step forward for the German debate to think about funded elements as such; however, the proposal will be unable to smooth the time path of the financial burden.

A problem with the German proposal is also that it defines the PAYGO pensions rather than the sum of these pensions and the funded pension elements. In the model analyzed here, about 50 percent of the old-age pensions will be funded in the very long run and, up to 2035, about a quarter of the old-age pensions will be funded. This means that the PAYGO component of the standard pension will have to decline to about 50 percent of net wages according to the old definition. By way of contrast, the government proposal sets the PAYGO component relative to the same base of at least 60 percent in 2030. This figure seems far too high if the goal is to maintain reasonable pension benefits and will lead to a significantly higher burden peak than that shown in figure 9.6.

Since the fixed saving rate policy does not work, it seems reasonable to try an alternative with variable saving rates. Path V in figure 9.6 shows a policy where the saving rate is initially 4 percent and is then adjusted over time so as to keep the sum of the PAYGO contributions and the saving rate roughly constant over the next fifty years, even in the critical fourth decade.

It can be seen that smoothing the time path of the burden is in fact possible, and that the burden is permanently lower in the crisis years after 2028 than with an ongoing PAYGO system. At the peak of the crisis in 2035, the contribution rate is more than 3 percentage points lower than the rate to be expected without a reform. Up to the peak of the crisis, a quarter of the old-age pensions can be financed from savings and, in the long run, half capital funding will be achieved, as in the case of a fixed saving rate of 4 percent. In the very long term—in the last quarter of this century—the burden will fall below that associated with the undermining solution. The transfer to partial capital funding is then complete.

In figure 9.7, it can be seen how the smoothing of the path of the burden comes about through varying its components. The top curve shows the sum of the PAYGO contributions and the compulsory saving rate, whose path is already known from figure 9.6. The curve below this shows the necessary PAYGO contributions. The curve begins with the present value of 20 percent, then rises only very slowly because more and more capital-funded pension components are available. At the peak of the demographic crisis, a contribution burden of only 23 percent will be reached, which is much lower

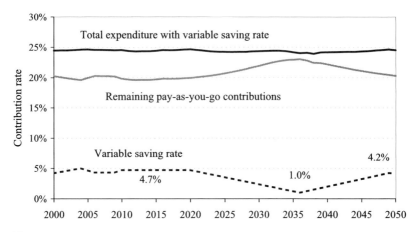

Figure 9.7
The path of the saving rate
Source: CES.

than the 28 percent that must be expected with the present system. The bottom curve shows the path of the compulsory saving rate which, together with the PAYGO contributions, makes up the total expenditures.

Up to about 2020, the compulsory saving rate is over 4 percent; it falls to only 1 percent up to 2036, when it again rises gradually. This variability in the compulsory saving rate is what determines the smoothing of the path of the total burden.[13]

In the next twenty years, the aggregate savings generated by this policy are between 3 and 4 percent of national income unless saving is crowded out that otherwise would have taken place. This is not too much and not too little. Some critics of capital funding maintain that the capital market cannot absorb more capital from savings, and others maintain that savings are irrelevant because national expenditure can only be financed from the national product of the current period. This is not the place to explain why these statements are misleading, if not completely wrong.[14] But one thing is certain. Germany's saving rate today of around 9 percent is well below the 15 percent that brought Germany prosperity and growth in the 1960s. It could only be to the economy's benefit if the saving rate were to rise by 3–4 percentage points as a result of capital funding of pension insurance. One would not reach the saving rate of the 1960s but one would be getting closer to it. An increase in saving produces an increase in national product, and that increase in national product will make future pension expenditure easier to afford than it otherwise would have been.

9.7   Concluding Remarks

It has been shown that the German pension insurance system is sliding into a demographic crisis and that partial capital funding on a private basis, but under government supervision, is a way to avoid disaster. Partial capital funding is the golden mean between the extremes of pure PAYGO financing and pure capital funding. It unites the strengths of both the systems and, last but not least, is the best insurance strategy with respect to the idiosyncratic risks involved with both alternatives.

Bismarck wanted to prevent the old and the sick from being "pushed aside" by the young. The reform presented in this chapter will prevent the pension insurance system from one day being pushed aside by the young and, with it, perhaps the state itself, too.

Appendix: Comments on Alternative Contributions Forecasts

The forecast shown in figure 9.2 is a conditional estimate in which the conditions are assumptions that need not be accepted. Other results follow from other assumptions. Figure 9.8 gives an overview of alternative forecasts that have been made recently in different places. It can be seen that the range of forecasts of the contribution rate for 2040 is about 25–31 percent. The third curve from the bottom shows the lower of the forecasts made at CES.

A look at the other forecasts shows how sensitive the calculations are to alternative assumptions. It is noteworthy how low the estimates of the contribution rates made by Prognos AG for the Federal Ministry of Labor and the Federal Association of Pension Insurance Institutions are.[15] A third of the difference between this and the CES forecast (1.25 percentage points) stems from the fact that Prognos AG assumes increases in the federal grant over and above that determined in 1997, and two-thirds (2.45 percentage points) from the fact that it assumes a large increase in other, differently based rates of taxes and charges on wage incomes. The higher the other charges, the lower the pension entitlements implied by the German pension formula and the lower the resulting contributions burden. Prognos

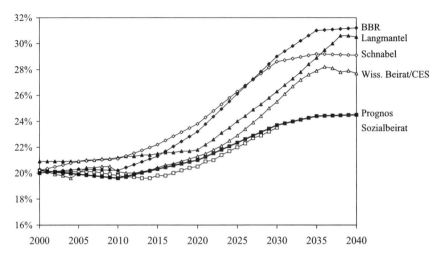

Figure 9.8
Alternative forecasts of the development of the contribution rate
Sources: Sozialbeirat (1998); Prognos (1998); Wissenschaftlicher Beirat beim Bundesministerium für Wirtschaft (1998); Schnabel (1998); Langmantel et al. (1997); Besendorfer, Borgmann, and Raffelhüschen (BBR) (1998).

implicitly assumes that the total burden on wage incomes from
income tax and charges for pension, health, unemployment, and
nursing insurance will be an alarming 70 percent, while the CES
forecast implicitly assumes a total burden of 66 percent. Here, the tax
needed to finance the increased federal grants, which Prognos really
must impute, is not even included. Reduced to a single denominator,
the pension burden indicated by Prognos is relatively low because
both the other burdens and the total burden on employees are
assumed to be relatively high. Looking at the Prognos calculations as
a whole, the arguments in favor of partial capital funding are considerably stronger than with the CES forecast. Since some politicians
have interpreted the Prognos forecast as giving an all-clear signal for
the pension problem, this indicates that the calculations published
by Prognos have been grossly misinterpreted.

The CES forecast is a status quo prediction. It assumes a constant
rate for charges for other purposes, because it wants to isolate the
effect of the demographic distortion on pension contributions. There
will be several more tax reforms and changes in the pattern of other
charges by the time the peak of the crisis arrives. In view of this
political uncertainty, it makes little sense to carry out the calcula-

tions on the basis of the current income tax progression scale. The pension reduction that will be produced through this mechanism as a result of adjustment of net wages is an artifact that will certainly not reflect the reality of the next four decades.

The CES forecast used in this chapter is the more cautious of its two alternative forecasts because it assumes a large immigration (11 million) and no further increase in life expectancy in west Germany. The east German life expectancy is assumed to increase until it reaches the west German level. If it is assumed, as the Interministerial Working Group assumes (see figure 9.2), that there will be a further increase in life expectancy of three years and lower immigration (7 million), then the CES forecast, too, largely coincides with the top three forecasts shown in figure 9.8.

Notes

The author wishes to thank Juli Irving-Lessmann, Marcel Thum, Jakob von Weizsäcker, and Frank Westermann for careful research assistance and the members of the Council of Advisers to the German Federal Ministry of Economics and Technology for stimulating discussions. The chapter has been developed from a lecture in German that was given to the annual assembly of the Bavarian Academy of Sciences and from calculations for the council. Useful comments of two anonymous referees are gratefully acknowledged.

1. Wissenschaftlicher Beirat beim Bundesministerium für Wirtschaft, 1998. See also Sinn (1997; 1998a, b).

2. See Mitchell (1981).

3. See Statistisches Bundesamt, *Statistisches Jahrbuch der BRD*, Wiesbaden, Germany, various issues.

4. See Statistisches Bundesamt (1994) and Interministerielle Arbeitsgruppe (1996).

5. Following 2008, those who are insured in the German Statutory Pension Scheme are expected to save an amount of up to 4 percent of their gross wages (to be phased in starting from 2002) in order to augment their retirement income. Provided that the money is invested in a special class of certified products, savings are subsidized at a rate that is at least equal to the marginal tax rate of the individual (which is at a maximum of 42 percent following 2005), with special allowances for low-wage earners and those who are raising children. Among a host of other regulations, legal restrictions require that the amount saved must be warranted on a nominal basis, that the funds cannot be drawn on before the individual reaches age 60, and that part of the accumulated funds must be annuitized no later than at age 85.

6. An outline of and commentary to alternative contribution forecasts are given in the appendix.

7. See note 4.

8. Of course, this is not a net debt if the taxpayers' obligation to service the debt is subtracted. The debt net of the present value of taxes necessary to service the debt is zero by definition for all states that do not go bankrupt, regardless of their pension and borrowing policies. The term "government debt" always refers to a gross debt concept.

9. For a formal proof of these statements, see Sinn (2000).

10. There are a couple of other arguments for an efficiency gain resulting from the transition to a funded system, including a reduction in the labor-leisure distortion or the ability to earn high-risk premiums in the world capital market. These arguments are not well-founded though, since the possible efficiency gains do not result from the funded system itself and can easily be achieved in an ongoing PAYGO system. For example, the introduction of individual accounts within a PAYGO system (e.g., as in Germany) will reduce the labor-leisure distortion to a minimum. This minimum cannot be reduced further by introducing a funded system, since the explicit tax this system requires in order to satisfy old pension entitlements will also result in a labor-leisure distortion. In fact, the labor-leisure distortion will be even more problematic since the transition concentrates the implicit tax burden that was formerly distributed over all generations on the transition generation without changing its present value. Similarly, the risk premiums could easily be earned by a society if the government borrowed funds in the capital market and invested them in international equities. See Sinn (2000) for proofs and extensive discussions of these issues as well as further references to the literature.

11. There are at least two straightforward ways of calculating the volume of partial funding necessary to compensate for the lack of children: (i) the replacement rate is constant, and funding is used to smooth the time path of the sum of contributions and required savings relative to wages; (ii) the replacement rate is constant, and funding is used to smooth the time path of the implicit wage tax rate. This chapter investigates possibility (i). For an investigation into possibility (ii), see Sinn and Werding (2000).

12. These assumptions are stylized status quo projections from the last two decades, reflecting partly a preference for simplicity and easy interpretability of the model and partly the belief that Germany is too small to affect the time paths of the world market rate of interest, the capital intensity of German industry, and technological progress. Even if many of the aging industrialized economies carried out similar reforms, it is not clear how strongly the world market rate of interest would be affected, given that the world is full of population-rich and underdeveloped economies which offer indefinite investment possibilities. Nevertheless, a general equilibrium formulation would, of course, have its merits. See Miles (1999) for pension forecasts in a general equilibrium framework.

13. Of course, in practice, executing the policy will be more difficult than in theory. If the population, growth, and interest forecasts assumed stay valid, policymakers could simply derive the required saving rate by deducting from the calculated value of four the increment of the contribution rate above 20 percent that follows by applying the pension formula to current wages. If the population forecasts and the expectations about growth and interest rates change, it will be necessary to recalculate the then-relevant starting value of the saving rate and proceed thenceforth again according to the rule described. The Council of Advisers to the Federal Ministry of Economics and Technology (Wissenschaftlicher Beirat beim Bundesministerium für Wirtschaft 1998) discussed the possibility of setting up a Pension Council that would regularly update the calculations along the lines suggested earlier.

14. The two problems relate to the Ricardian equivalence problem but seem to be mutually exclusive. If funding implies more aggregate savings, future national product will be higher and hence it will be easier to finance pensions, but there may be an absorption problem for the capital markets. (The moderate increase in saving rates cited in the text excludes this possibility.) If, on the other hand, Ricardian equivalence implies that funding does not imply more aggregate savings, future national product will not increase and the second fear will have some foundation. Clearly, however, the capital market could not be overcrowded with funds in this case. (There is a myriad of reasons why Ricardian equivalence may not hold or may not have this implication.) See Sinn (2000) and Wissenschaftlicher Beirat beim Bundesminsterium für Wirtschaft (1998) for a more thorough discussion of the alternatives.

15. Further details can be found in Sinn and Thum (1999) and Werding (1999).

References

Besendorfer, D., C. Borgmann, and B. Raffelhüschen. 1998. "Ein Plädoyer für intergenerative Ausgewogenheit: Rentenreformvorschläge auf dem Prüfstand." (The Case for Intergenerational Balance: An Examination of Pension Proposals.) Universität Freiburg Discussion Paper No. 65/98.

Interministerielle Arbeitsgruppe. 1996. "Bevölkerungsprognose." (Population Forecast.) Variante A. Bonn, Germany.

Kaiserliches Statistisches Amt. 1878. *Statistisches Jahrbuch für das Deutsche Reich.* Vol. 30. Berlin, Germany.

Langmantel, E., K. Vogler-Ludwig, A. Juchems, and W. Grunwald. 1997. *Entlastungspotential eines Teilkapitalstocks in der Rentenversicherung unter alternativen Bevölkerungsannahmen.* (Savings Potential of a Partial Capital Stock with Alternative Population Assumptions.) München, Germany: Ifo Institut.

Miles, D. 1999. "Modelling the Impact of Demographic Change upon the Economy." *Economic Journal* 109: 1–36.

Mitchell, B. R. 1981. *European Historical Statistics: 1750–1975.* Second revision. New York: Facts on File.

Prognos. 1998. *Auswirkungen veränderter ökonomischer und rechtlicher Rahmenbedingungen auf die gesetzliche Rentenversicherung in Deutschland.* (Consequences of Changes of the Economic and Legal Framework on the Statutory Pension System in Germany.) DRV-Schriften, Vol. 9. Frankfurt am Main, Germany: Verband Deutscher Rentenversicherungsträger.

Schnabel, R. 1998. "Rates of Return of the German Pay-As-You-Go Pension System." *Finanzarchiv N.F.* 55: 374–399.

Sinn, H.-W. 1997. "The Value of Children and Immigrants in a Pay-As-You-Go Pension System: A Proposal for a Partial Transition to a Funded System." National Bureau of Economic Research Working Paper No. 6229, Cambridge, MA.

Sinn, H.-W. 1998a. "The Pay-As-You-Go Pension System as a Fertility Insurance and Enforcement Device." Universität München CES Discussion Paper No. 154.

Sinn, H.-W. 1998b. "Comment on Axel Börsch Supan." In *Redesigning Social Security*, ed. H. Siebert. Tübingen, Germany: Mohr-Siebeck.

Sinn, H.-W. 2000. "Why a Funded System Is Useful and Why It Is Not Useful." *International Tax and Public Finance* 7: 389–410.

Sinn, H.-W., and M. Thum. 1999. "Gesetzliche Rentenversicherung: Prognosen im Vergleich." (Statutory Pension Insurance: A Comparison of Forecasts.) *Finanzarchiv* 56: 104–135.

Sinn, H.-W., and M. Werding. 2000. "Rentenniveausenkung und Teilkapitaldeckung: Ifo-Empfehlungen zur Konsolidierung des Umlageverfahrens." (Lowering Pension Benefits and Partial Funding: Ifo Recommendations for Consolidating the Pay-As-You-Go System.) *Ifo Schnelldienst* 53: 12–25.

Sozialbeirat. 1998. *Gutachten des Sozialbeirats zum Rentenversicherungsbericht 1998 und Stellungnahmen zu einigen weiteren Berichten zur Alterssicherung.* (Expertise of the Social Advisory Council on the Pension Insurance Report 1998 and Positions Regarding Other Reports on Old-Age Pensions.) Bonn, Germany: Bundesrat.

Statistisches Bundesamt. 1994. *Achte koordinierte Bevölkerungsvorausberechnung.* (Eighth Coordinated Population Forecast.) Variante 2. Wiesbaden, Germany.

Stein, P. Undated. *Fürst Bismarcks Reden.* (Prince Bismarck's Speeches.) Achter Band: Steuerreform und Socialpolitik 1880–1882. Leipzig, Germany: Reclam.

Werding, M. 1999. "Humankapitalbildung, Beschäftigung und Altersvorsorge." (Human Capital Formation, Employment and Retirement Provisions.) *Beiträge zur Arbeitsmarkt- und Berufsforschung* 224: 159–184.

Wissenschaftlicher Beirat beim Bundesministerium für Wirtschaft. 1998. *Grundlegende Reform der gesetzlichen Rentenversicherung.* (Fundamental Reform of the Statutory Pension Insurance.) Bonn, Germany: Bundesministerium für Wirtschaft.

Comments

Georges de Menil

Germany presents a paradigm of the implications of aging for pension systems in the European Union. Of all the countries in the region, it is the one that is facing the most dramatic change in demographic structure. According to some projections, the ratio in the population of people aged 65 and over to people aged 20–64 is expected to drop from four in 2000 to two in 2035. During that period, the population as a whole is expected to decline. Yet, Germany is also a country whose PAYGO system of old-age insurance still functions in exemplary fashion. Benefits are related to contributions through a system of points, which is broadly perceived to be credible and fair. Workers continue to have confidence that they will receive the pensions they have been promised. Evasion is limited. Germany faces the prospect of a dramatic demographic crisis, but has not yet crossed the threshold of an actual system crisis.[1] This makes the way that it chooses to deal with the demographic problems it faces particularly significant for others. If Germany succeeds, through fundamental reform, at avoiding a pension crisis, the approach it adopts could become a model for other countries. The fact that Germany was also the birthplace, and Bismarck the father, of modern social insurance adds to the significance of the German debate.

In his chapter, Hans-Werner Sinn provides an authoritative analysis of the problems facing Germany's Social Security system, describes the recently enacted "Riester" reforms, and proposes a further modification, which he argues would better address the underlying problem. The chapter presents a series of careful simulations, made with the CES Social Security model, of contributions and benefits through 2050, under alternative scenarios.

1   The End of the Ponzi Scheme

In general, PAYGO systems function well when population growth
ensures that the number of contributors rises more rapidly than the
number of beneficiaries. The day of reckoning arrives if the number
of contributors begins to decline while the number of beneficiaries,
and their aspirations, continue to rise. At that point, the only way
to maintain benefits is to raise taxes. Sinn presents simulations
which show that, in Germany, maintaining the current average replacement rate[2] requires that the average contribution rate rise from
its present level of 20 percent to at least 28 percent in 2035. This
sharp increase in the tax rate constitutes what Sinn calls the German
pension crisis.

The problem is a direct consequence of the nature of a PAYGO
system. If Germany did not have a PAYGO system of social insurance, its demographic slowdown would not generate a pension
crisis. Each generation would have provided in advance for its retirement, from the fruit of its own labor. It would not depend, for its
old-age income, on the size and the support of the next generation.

However, Sinn argues, societies such as Germany, with a mature
PAYGO system, are in a sense trapped in that system. The only fair
way to get out of it is to pay off the older generation, the one that has
already made its contributions and now expects to receive benefits.
This implies that the workers in the generation that decides to buy
out have to pay twice, once to support their parents and once to
accumulate for their own retirement. Sinn simulates the implications
for Germany of such a radical shift, and finds that this doubling-up
would advance the crisis from 2035 to 2000.[3]

2   Saving Now to Avoid Crisis Later

What a country faced with a problem like that of Germany can
reasonably do, Sinn argues, is to prefund its Social Security system
sufficiently to avoid the impending tax spike. This involves increasing contributions now and investing the resulting surpluses in capital market instruments, which can reasonably be expected, in the
German case, to bring a 4 percent real rate of return. Because this
return is higher than the expected rate of growth of pension liabilities (2 percent because of rising real wages, offset eventually by an
anticipated 0.5 percent per year decline of the population), prefund-

ing lowers the average contribution rate over time below the otherwise inevitable and dangerously high peak rate of 28 percent. In Sinn's simulations, if the contribution rate is raised to 24 percent immediately, it can then be kept at that level for the rest of time. Prefunding makes it possible to smooth the contribution rate at a level significantly below the peak level, which would otherwise come about in 2035.

However, Sinn forcefully rejects what, from an institutional point of view, would be the simplest approach to prefunding—namely, to have the state Social Security fund accumulate temporary (but perhaps quite large) surpluses. He argues, correctly in my view, that leaving such surpluses under the control of a state agency would invite their misuse for short-run political purposes. Sinn concludes that the only way to ensure that the accumulated funds are dedicated to providing retirement income is to have working people save them directly in individual accounts, of which they and their families are the sole beneficiaries. Contributions to the accounts must be mandatory in order to avoid the moral hazard created by the availability of state welfare support. As the retirement income from these accounts increases, payments from the state PAYGO system can be reduced and, with them, the taxes that support them.

Sinn thus arrives, by a process of elimination, at the proposal that is at the center of pension reform debates around the world—namely, the creation of a national system of mandatory individual retirement accounts, privately managed but regulated by the state.[4] He proceeds to analyze two proposals for Germany: (1) the Riester reform, in which individuals are encouraged to contribute a constant 4 percent of their wages, above and beyond their present Social Security payments, to these accounts,[5] and (2) a "variable saving rate" proposal, in which saving is slightly higher in the earlier years but is reduced later, in such a way as to keep the total of Social Security taxes plus mandatory saving below a critical threshold.

2.1 The Riester Reform

In principle, additional payments to individual accounts at a constant rate and offsetting reductions, in the retirement years, of PAYGO benefits can avoid what would otherwise be a demographic pension crisis. But Sinn demonstrates, in a revealing simulation, that the introduction of this variant of fundamental reform in Germany at the beginning of the century is not sufficient to ward off the crisis of 2035. With a constant saving rate in individual accounts of 4 percent from the outset, the combined total of mandatory saving and PAYGO taxes still rises to 27 percent in 2035. In a sense, the reform comes too late. Had it been introduced perhaps a decade earlier, the individual funds would have had more time to accumulate, and the retirement income they provided would have been sufficient to lower total mandatory contributions below the threshold of tolerance.

This stark result serves as a warning. The more the necessary adjustments are postponed, the less effective they will be.

2.2 The Variable Saving Rate Proposal

If a constant 4 percent rate of additional saving introduced in 2000 is insufficient to avoid a crisis thirty-five years later, the next logical step is to raise the saving rate more at the beginning, and then lower it later, when the PAYGO tax begins its sharp, still inevitable rise. It is funds contributed early that can contribute to the retirement needs of 2035. Increased saving in 2035 itself obviously provides no retirement relief in that year. In a further simulation, Sinn shows that by raising the saving rate to 4–5 percent before 2005 and reducing it as low as 1 percent in 2035, the sum of saving contributions and PAYGO contributions can be kept durably below 25 percent.[6]

Sinn argues that this variable saving rate variant succeeds at avoiding the pension crisis of 2035.

3   When Is a Contribution a Tax?

In the interests of describing Germany's dilemma in the simplest possible terms, Sinn implicitly treats mandatory savings contributions and PAYGO Social Security taxes as equivalently painful. His analysis focuses on reducing the sum of the two payments. This equivalence is not self-evident. It can be argued that mandatory saving incorporates little tax pain. It can also be argued that, even in demographically unfavorable circumstances, taxes paid to a fair PAYGO system are not all pain.

Let us look at mandatory saving first. If the system is carefully explained to its participants,[7] they will tend to perceive the contributions as similar to voluntary savings. Sophisticated individuals who are already placing substantial amounts of savings in financial markets may simply adjust their voluntary programs so as to offset the new mandatory saving. Though the mandatory payments may cause some inconvenience to these individuals, it is clearly less burdensome for them than redistributive taxes. Previously unsophisticated workers may, on the other hand, value the access to financial markets under prudent conditions that the system provides. For them, contributions to such a system may not be a burden at all. In general, mandatory savings should be compared not with free voluntary savings, but with what voluntary savings might be if the state had ways to stop gaming of the welfare system. (If they could be prohibited from planning indigence, low-income individuals might voluntarily save more.) All of these considerations suggest that the tax burden of mandatory savings may be moderate.[8]

Turn now to contributions to a PAYGO system of Social Security. If the system is one in which benefits are tied to contributions in a fair and transparent manner (as has been generally the case in Germany), those contributions are not equivalent to redistributive taxes either. They are part of a social contract in which individuals make certain payments and receive corresponding benefits. There is a difference. Individuals could expect to get larger benefits from those same payments if they placed them in the capital market. As Sinn (2000) explains lucidly, the spread between the real yield on prudent financial instruments and the implicit return of the PAYGO system is a very real tax, which provides intergenerational redistribution.

In short, neither mandatory savings nor PAYGO contributions (if fair) are the total equivalent of redistributive taxes. However, mandatory savings probably entail less of a tax burden than PAYGO contributions.

Two implications follow from the previous observations:

• A reform that replaces PAYGO contributions with mandatory savings is tantamount to a tax reduction. From the point of view of a worker in 2035, a mandatory saving contribution of 4 percent and a PAYGO contribution of 23 percent is significantly, not just marginally, better than a PAYGO contribution of 28 percent. Reforms with mandatory saving could do more to diffuse the 2035 crisis than Sinn's figure 9.6 at first suggests. This consideration strengthens the arguments for partial replacement of PAYGO with individual funding.

• The confidence that working people presently have in the PAYGO system is an important factor of social stability. A reform that undermines that confidence may tend to exacerbate and precipitate the tax revolt that the demographic crisis threatens. As presented by Sinn, both individual account reforms risk producing that result.

4 Breaking the Promise

As presented, both the constant rate reform and the variable rate variant break the link between contributions and benefits, which has been the firm foundation on which the German Social Security system has operated in the period since World War II. They transform what is now partially a contributory system into something much closer to pure intergenerational redistribution. They do so because they arbitrarily scale back the PAYGO benefits that today's workers will receive, in an ex post fashion. In 2035, when these individuals are retired, they will see their PAYGO benefits reduced, even though they continued, during much of the intervening period, to make full payment of PAYGO taxes at the old rates. They may be told that there is no reduction, because they are still receiving a target total of 64 percent of average wages as pensions at that time. Annuities from their individual account have simply replaced payments from the federal Social Security office. But if they had confidence at the outset in both individual accounts and the PAYGO system, they may expect to receive full payments from both. They will, in those circumstances, view the benefit reduction of 2035 as a violation of a promise.

Moreover, as soon as today's worker-contributors realize that the game has been changed and that their current contributions will no longer provide the same benefits they provided in the past, they may stop paying those contributions. The tax revolt may come sooner rather than later.

4.1 The Tax Burden of a Partial Shift to Funding Cannot Be Avoided

As Sinn makes abundantly clear, a partial shift to funding is a central requirement of any solution of the pending pension crisis. The change in demographic structure is such that the implicit rate of return of the PAYGO system has become, and is becoming, too low to provide for the retirement aspirations of the population. But, as Sinn has also explained, any shift to funding produces a tax burden. A promise has been made to the older generation, and if that promise is to be honored, someone has to pay twice.[9]

In the two reform scenarios analyzed by Sinn, that burden is paid entirely by today's workers. They are expected to continue to pay PAYGO benefits at current rates for some time, but to accept receiving reduced benefits when they retire.

One cannot avoid asking at this point why today's older generation should not bear part of the burden of the necessary partial shift to funding.[10]

4.2 Preserving the Point System by Scaling It Down in Advance

An alternative strategy, of which the Riester reform and the variable rate variant could be viewed as first steps, would be to begin cutting back entitlements now. We can infer from Sinn's simulations that if future entitlements were reduced by a seventh, they could be met by an exclusively PAYGO system in 2035 with a tax rate of 24 percent, which is significantly less than 28 percent. In order to preserve the credibility of the point system, the benefits to today's older generation would have to be reduced to a similar degree. Lower benefits today would mean that the Social Security budget could be balanced with lower contributions today, which would, in turn, justify paying today's workers lower benefits when they retire.

Scaling back PAYGO now would help make room for the additional saving, which is a necessary, central ingredient of any reform intended to compensate for the aging of the population. Because their PAYGO contributions would have been reduced, today's workers could better afford the new mandatory savings called for by "Riester-type" reforms.

Though it would be unreasonable abruptly to scale back the benefits of existing retirees or make them bear the full burden of the adjustment, it would not be unreasonable to make the retirees and today's older workers share in the burden, by beginning now to scale back those benefits progressively. This would allow for progressive reduction, also beginning now, in the PAYGO contribution rate. The planned, progressive scaling-up of mandatory saving (from 2 percent to 4 percent) would be justified if it were the counterpart of a similar progressive reduction of PAYGO benefits and contributions.

4.3 Political Feasibility

Beginning now to reduce PAYGO entitlements may be politically difficult. It would certainly require a lot of explanation. But once everyone realizes that PAYGO benefits will have to be cut back eventually, acting now may be the only way to preserve the credibility of the PAYGO system in the future. If the ultimate objective is a mixed funded and PAYGO system, as Sinn states clearly, preserving the credibility of the "first pillar" is an important consideration.

5 Conclusion

Germany, which faces the most dramatic population aging of any country in Europe, is grappling with a bold program of partial replacement of its PAYGO system with funded individual accounts. The model nature of the existing system and the magnitude of the impending demographic crisis give particular significance to the German debate.

The declared, central objective of the German reform process is the avoidance of sharp tax increases a generation from now. In this authoritative and informative chapter, Sinn, who is both an advocate and a critic of the process, argues that there are different ways of carrying out the program. He advocates a variable saving rate variant, which entails slightly higher encouraged savings in the early years than the program the government has enacted, and mandates that the saving rate will rise and fall in such a manner as to keep total Social Security contributions below a threshold of tolerance. In these comments, I have advocated that the German government, in addition to creating mandatory individual accounts or variable saving rate variants, should begin now to scale back existing PAYGO entitlements. I argue that reducing benefits now is the only way to protect the credibility of the PAYGO system in the future.

Notes

1. A system crisis can be described as a situation in which legally required contributions are not being paid and promised benefits are not being distributed. Hans-Werner Sinn warns that Germany may well find itself in such a situation in the future, but observes that the system still functioned well in the first years of the twenty-first century. By contrast, in many of the countries of Eastern Europe, preexisting Social Security systems collapsed after the fall of the Berlin Wall, even though the changes in demographic structure that those countries experienced were less dramatic than those

Germany faces. The problems there were a vicious circle of overly generous benefits, high tax rates (twice as high as in Germany), and rampant evasion. See, for example, de Menil and Sheshinski (2001b).

2. Ratio of the average pension to the average economy-wide wage at retirement.

3. He seems, in reaching this conclusion, to rule out a Chilean-style large-scale deficit financing of the transition with "recognition bonds," and to require that contributions be maintained at a level sufficient to avoid any increase in the Social Security deficit. Deficit financing would make it possible to spread the burden of the transition over many years. Deficit financing would require technical exemption from the constraints of the Stability Pact. It can be argued that such an exemption would not violate the spirit of the pact, because what it would permit is the replacement of an implicit debt (the unwritten liabilities of the Social Security system) with an explicit debt.

4. A partial move from PAYGO to funding can also be advocated in its own right, even in the absence of a demographic crisis. Under certain assumptions, funding will raise the national saving rate, and, in a world of uncertainty, a combination of the two systems permits the contributor to hedge the risks in each. See de Menil (2000) and de Menil and Sheshinski (2001a).

5. In some of its original reports, the Council of Advisers to the German Minister of Economics and Technology, Riester, recommended that contributions to these individual retirement accounts be mandatory. The mandatory feature was dropped in subsequent negotiations, and, in the law that was enacted in 2000 and implemented in 2001, the contributions are recommended but optional. The savings are subsidized if they are invested in a special class of certified products. They are expected to start at 2 percent of gross wages in 2002 and to rise to 4 percent of gross wages by 2008. As of the end of 2002, the sign-up rate was substantially below expectations. The analysis in this comment refers more particularly to the original recommendation of mandatory saving contributions.

6. It is possible that individuals who have acquired the habit of saving 4–5 percent will continue to save voluntarily in that neighborhood, after the mandatory rate is lowered. However, whatever they do that is voluntary cannot be considered a burden. It would, in fact, most likely be a welcome addition to total capital formation.

7. If they are, for instance, given passbooks, and can monitor and occasionally reallocate the investments in their account, they will be more likely to perceive their contributions as equivalent to voluntary savings.

8. Even if they cannot game the welfare system, myopic individuals may, left to their own devices, insufficiently provide for their old age. For these, mandatory savings are a burden that the benevolent state considers to be in their best interest. Others, who are indigent, may simply not have sufficient income to make those provisions. Those are the individuals for whom the welfare system is intended to provide support.

9. In Sinn (2000), the author makes a strong argument that there are no Pareto gains to a shift from PAYGO to funding. Sinn's insistence in this chapter that partial funding avoids a crisis can be interpreted as qualifying that argument. Certainly, there must be some Pareto gains to avoiding a crisis.

10. That they are the ones who decided not to have children is not a sufficient argument. They made that decision, and made their private saving decisions, at a time when today's PAYGO system was in full force. If PAYGO had not been in force,

they probably would indeed have provided with greater prudence for their own retirement.

References

De Menil, G. 2000. "A Comment on the Place of Funded Pensions in Transition Economies." *International Tax and Public Finance* 7: 431–444.

De Menil, G., and E. Sheshinski. 2001a. "The Optimal Balance of Intergenerational Transfers and Funded Pensions in the Presence of Risk." Manuscript, Delta, Paris.

De Menil, G., and E. Sheshinski. 2001b. "Romania's Pension System: From Crisis to Reform." In *Social Security Pension Reform in Europe*, ed. M. Feldstein and H. Siebert. National Bureau of Economic Research Conference Report. Chicago: University of Chicago Press.

Sinn, H.-W. 2000. "Why a Funded System Is Useful and Why It Is Not Useful." *International Tax and Public Finance* 7: 389–410.

10

Social Insurance Based on Individual Savings Accounts

Peter Birch Sørensen

10.1 Introduction

10.1.1 The Welfare State under Pressure

At the dawn of the new millennium, European Welfare States face financial pressure from several demographic, economic, and cultural trends. Population aging, earlier retirement, shorter working hours, stubbornly high unemployment, and increasingly mobile tax bases all combine to increase the demand for public spending relative to the potential for tax collection. Some critics, such as Lindbeck (1995), also argue that the Welfare State tends to undermine the social norms that have so far helped to secure its economic sustainability.

To avert the looming fiscal crisis, economists have made numerous proposals for reform of Welfare State programs. Much of the debate has focused on the arguments for and against switching from PAYGO to funded pension systems for the elderly (see, for example, Breyer (1989), Homburg (1990), Raffelhüschen (1993), Feldstein (1995, 1997), Kotlikoff (1996), Brunner (1996), Diamond (1998), Belan and Pestieau (1999), Hassler and Lindbeck (1999), Sinn (2000), Demmel and Keuschnigg (2000), and Hauenschild (2000) for contributions to this long-standing debate).

Although the issue of moving from unfunded to funded pensions is analytically distinct from the issue of moving from defined benefit to defined contribution pensions, most proposals for a transition to a funded pension system have assumed that such a reform would also involve a move from a system with defined benefits to a system with defined contributions paid into individual savings accounts. In this chapter, I consider the effects of financing part of the social insurance for people of *working age* via mandatory contributions to individual

Table 10.1
Social transfers in Denmark, 1999

	Percent of total transfers	Percent of GDP at factor prices
Transfers to individuals of working age		
Unemployment benefits	8.1	1.7
Social assistance	9.2	1.9
Sickness and maternity benefits	5.7	1.2
Child benefits	7.1	1.5
Parental leave benefits	0.8	0.2
Education leave benefits	0.8	0.2
Education benefits[a]	5.4	1.1
Disability benefits	13.1	2.7
Early retirement benefits	9.6	2.0
Transfers to individuals above retirement age		
Pensions to civil servants	6.4	1.3
General pensions	28.0	5.8
Transfers to all age groups		
Housing benefits	4.0	0.8
Other transfers	1.8	0.4
Total transfers	100.0	20.7

Source: Statistics Denmark, *Statistiske Efterretninger 2000* 17: table 8.
[a] Benefits to students above 18 years of age.

savings accounts rather than through general tax revenues. Various forms of such individual accounts have recently been proposed by Fölster (1994, 1997), Orszag and Snower (1997a, b), Feldstein and Altman (1998), and Orszag et al. (1999).

Table 10.1 suggests why it is relevant to ask whether part of the currently tax-financed social insurance for the working population ought to be based on individual savings accounts. The table records the level and structure of tax-financed social transfers in Denmark in 1999. Several of these transfers compensate for shortfalls of income due to circumstances such as education, childbirth, short-term sickness, short-term unemployment, and so forth that almost all people will experience sometime during their working career. To a large extent, these transfers and the associated taxes merely smooth the individual's disposable income over his active life, without redistributing lifetime income across individuals. In Sweden, where the structure of the Welfare State is very similar to Denmark's, a government report issued in 1994 estimated that roughly 25 percent of annual social transfers are essentially taxes which are transferred to the taxpayer himself within the same year, and that measured over the entire life cycle, only about 24 percent of total transfers serve to redistribute lifetime incomes (ESO 1994).

The problem is that even though a large part of the tax bill is actually transferred back to the taxpayer himself, the decoupling of taxes and social benefits creates large marginal tax wedges with all the associated disincentive effects. In continental Europe, where many social transfers are financed by Social Security contributions, the same disincentive effects tend to arise, since social benefits are rarely linked to Social Security taxes in an actuarially fair manner.

The problem may be said to stem from a failure to implement Richard Musgrave's famous separation of the Distribution Branch and the Allocation Branch of the public budget (Musgrave 1959, 1996). Social insurance that does not redistribute income should be seen as part of the Allocation Branch. There may be a role for government in securing provision of such insurance, to the extent that private insurance and capital markets are imperfect or altogether missing. However, if consumption smoothing over the individual's active life is the only aim, a linking of taxes and transfers through benefit taxation (as opposed to taxation based on ability to pay) seems appropriate to ensure efficiency, in accordance with the principles of the Allocation Branch developed by Wicksell (1896), Lindahl (1919), and Musgrave (1939). Social insurance based on individual accounts may be seen as an attempt to implement this idea.

Yet, just as a tax-financed PAYGO pension system with a flat pension does imply some redistribution of lifetime income (because the flat benefit makes up a larger fraction of the labor income of low-wage earners), the current tax-financed social insurance for the working-age population does involve some redistribution from rich to poor and from the lucky to the unlucky. Hence, the crucial questions are whether the introduction of individual accounts (IAs) could increase aggregate (utilitarian) welfare and whether all groups would share in the welfare gain, that is, whether IAs could generate a Pareto improvement by improving the government's equity-efficiency trade-off.

Addressing this issue, but focusing on social insurance for people of working age, this chapter may be seen as a parallel to previous papers that have discussed the possibility of a Pareto-improving reform of retirement pensions based on individual accounts. A potential for Pareto improvement exists if pension reform implies a reduction of labor market distortions (see, e.g., Belan and Pestieau 1999, 124–125, and Demmel and Keuschnigg 2000). If the existing system involves a distorting labor income tax financing a flat pension benefit that is unrelated to the pensioner's previous work effort, whereas the reformed system is based on individual accounts and actuarial fairness, the reform will clearly improve labor market efficiency. However, if workers are heterogeneous and the existing pension system implies some intragenerational redistribution from rich to poor, it is far from obvious that a switch to individual accounts can generate a Pareto improvement, as stressed by Brunner (1996). In a similar way, it is not obvious—and hence worthy of closer scrutiny—whether greater reliance on IA-based social insurance for people of working age could generate a Pareto improvement or an increase in the utilitarian sum of individual utilities.

The next two subsections offer a preliminary description and discussion of the design and likely effects of the system of IAs on which I will focus. In section 10.2, I then set up a simple formal model of an economy with IAs to analyze the conditions needed for the system to generate a welfare improvement. Section 10.3 discusses ways to offset the likely negative distribution effects of IAs and considers a specific Danish proposal of a system of social insurance partly based on IAs. Section 10.4 summarizes my findings and suggests some directions for future research on the effects of individual accounts.

10.1.2   A Design for Social Insurance Based on Individual Accounts

The system of IAs I have in mind is heavily inspired by Fölster (1994, 1997) and would work as follows.

For each taxpayer, an individual account is established. This IA system is a bookkeeping device which can be administered by the public sector or by private life insurance companies or other financial institutions. A part of each taxpayer's annual tax bill (or part or all of his current Social Security contributions) is replaced by a mandatory Social Security contribution which is credited to his IA. The contribution is calculated as a percentage of the taxpayer's income.

Whenever the taxpayer receives a benefit payment from one of the transfer programs included in the IA scheme, a corresponding amount is debited to his IA. A market rate of interest is added to or subtracted from the balance on the IA each year. At the time of the taxpayer's retirement from the labor market, the balance on his IA is converted into an annuity which is added to his ordinary public retirement pension. If the IA balance is negative at the time of retirement, the taxpayer simply receives the ordinary public pension during old age. To give every citizen a realistic chance of accumulating a surplus on his IA at the time of retirement, his benefit receipts from the social insurance system will no longer be debited to his IA if the negative balance on the account has reached a certain "debt ceiling." When the debt ceiling is exceeded, social insurance benefits are financed out of general tax revenues, with no consequences for the individual's IA balance. This means that even persons suffering from prolonged periods of income loss will have a possibility of obtaining an addition to their public pension if they are able to raise their earnings (and hence their contributions to their IA). The social insurance programs that could naturally be linked to the IAs would be those that serve, to a large degree, to smooth the individual's income over his working career, as further discussed in the next subsection. To be able to draw on these programs via his IA, a person would have to satisfy all of the eligibility criteria existing today, and the benefit rates would correspond to the current rates. For an individual who does not manage to accumulate a surplus on his IA, these rules will ensure that the IA system will work exactly like the present system of social insurance.

Like the existing tax-transfer system, this IA system provides two forms of social insurance:

• *Lifetime income insurance:* The debt ceiling on the IA combined with the minimum retirement pension ensures some redistribution by guaranteeing a minimum lifetime income. The debt ceiling implies that an unlucky individual who has to draw relatively large amounts from social insurance programs will have his benefits financed out of the general tax revenue contributed by all taxpayers, just like today, without any negative consequences for his minimum old-age pension.

• *Liquidity insurance:* The IA system allows the individual to collect social insurance benefits under eligibility rules identical to those existing at present, regardless of the size of the balance on his account. The IA therefore offers the same liquidity insurance as the current social insurance system, even though an individual who has not reached the debt ceiling on his account must accept a reduction of his supplementary retirement pension whenever he draws a social transfer via his IA.

The IAs would improve economic incentives in two important ways. First of all, marginal tax wedges would be reduced for all taxpayers who are able to accumulate just a single euro of surplus on their IAs at the time of retirement. Of course, the taxpayer will have to deposit an additional amount in his IA whenever he raises his income. However, this additional deposit will either enable him to draw more social insurance benefits without having his old-age pension reduced or, alternatively, entitle him to a larger old-age annuity. Because the contributions credited to the IA earn interest, they will entitle the contributor to increased social insurance benefits or increased retirement pensions that exactly match the contributions in expected present-value terms. As long as the taxpayer can expect to accumulate even the slightest surplus on his IA, every additional euro of contribution to his account will thus be repaid to him with interest added. Hence, the mandatory IA contributions do not have the character of a tax, since they are essentially money transferred by the taxpayer to himself, so marginal tax rates will tend to go down by the amount of tax replaced by the IA contributions. The qualification to this statement is that some taxpayers might be subject to credit rationing at the time when their mandatory contribution to the IA has to be paid. For these individuals, the contribution would work to some extent like an ordinary tax, since their subjective discount rate would tend to exceed the interest rate earned on their IA balance.

The second type of efficiency gain is that the IA system would reduce the problem of moral hazard associated with the existing social insurance system. When benefits are financed out of general tax revenue, the individual has no incentive to engage in behavior that minimizes the risk that he will have to draw on the social transfer system. By contrast, under the IA system, the individual who can look forward to a surplus on his IA does have such an incentive, since he will be entitled to a higher retirement pension to the extent that he takes up a smaller amount of social transfers.

10.1.3 Throwing the Baby Away with the Bath Water?

Since the IAs effectively turn part of existing transfers into government loans to taxpayers, one might ask whether the potential efficiency gains from IAs could not be reaped in a more straightforward manner by simply cutting the level of social insurance benefits. One might also argue that, if the introduction of IAs is really equivalent to a benefit cut, the IAs could never raise social welfare if the existing benefit levels have already been optimized with due attention to all distortionary effects of taxes and benefits. The analysis below shows that this line of reasoning is wrong because the existence of the lifetime income guarantee means that the IA system may be used to improve the incentives of high-income earners—whose taxes partly serve to finance transfers to themselves—without reducing the consumption possibilities of low-income earners. Hence, the IA system is *not* equivalent to a benefit cut, so even if the tax-transfer system has been optimized prior to the introduction of IAs, the IA system may increase social welfare by increasing the armory of fiscal instruments available to the government.

At the same time, it should be recognized that protection against income losses and redistribution of lifetime income are not the only purposes of the public transfer system. Some of the transfer programs listed in table 10.1 (e.g., parental leave and education leave) are also intended to induce behavior that is deemed socially desirable. If the social benefits from these activities are significant, the IA system may reduce social welfare to the extent that it discourages parental leave, education, and so forth by reducing the present value of the existing subsidies.

The decision on which transfer schemes to include in the IA system therefore requires careful consideration by policymakers. In the formal model presented later, the public transfers included in the IA scheme are interpreted mainly as unemployment benefits and early retirement benefits. The inclusion of unemployment benefits seems natural, since unemployment is not an "activity" that is seen as desirable in itself. Early retirement may sometimes offer a socially beneficial alternative to work for elderly workers who have been worn out by the high productivity requirements of modern labor markets. However, in most Western European countries, early retirement benefits are now granted to very broad segments of the labor force (including high-income groups) and not just to marginalized workers. With the prospect of a declining labor force due to population aging, the social costs of generous early retirement benefits are increasing. Against this background, it is now an explicit goal of many European governments to halt the strong trend towards earlier retirement that has been stimulated by the proliferation of early retirement benefits. Including such benefits in the IA system—perhaps combined with the preservation of special schemes for worn-out elderly workers—could be one way of limiting the existing subsidization of early withdrawal from the labor force.

In the specific policy proposal described in section 10.3.2, public income transfers to students in higher education are also included in the IA system. This proposal should be seen against the institutional background of the typical European country, where students in higher education pay no tuition fees (or only very modest fees) in public universities. Undoubtedly, the strong positive externalities associated with basic education justify extensive subsidization of this part of the education system (including high school). On equity grounds, there is also a case for means-tested benefits to college and university students from poor families. Beyond this, and considering the general waiving of tuition fees, the case for general income transfers to students in higher education seems less than obvious, especially since these students tend to be recruited mainly from the middle and upper classes. By including general education benefits in the IA system, the benefits would effectively be turned into a government loan. By offering such a loan, the government would acknowledge that students are often restricted in their ability to borrow against expected future labor income in the private capital market. At the same time, the transformation of an income transfer into a loan would eliminate the tendency of existing education benefits to redistribute lifetime income in favor of the middle and upper classes.

It should be stressed that this chapter does not advocate or validate that the current tax-financed system of social insurance be completely replaced by a system of individual accounts. The distributional consequences of a social insurance system entirely based on IAs would undoubtedly be unacceptable to most governments. The present analysis only suggests that a *combination* of tax-financed social insurance and individual accounts on a modest scale may be preferable to a fully tax-financed system.

With these preliminaries, let us turn to a formal analysis of the theoretical case for the IA system.

10.2   A Theoretical Framework for Analyzing Individual Accounts

10.2.1   The Setup: An Overlapping Generations Model with Endogenous Retirement Age

My analytical framework is an overlapping generations model in which individuals live for two periods.[1] During the first period of life, each individual wishes to work full time, but may be prevented from doing so by circumstances beyond his control, such as a negative labor market shock. In the second period, the individual chooses to work only a fraction e of the time and to be retired from the labor force during the remaining fraction $(1 - e)$ of the period. The choice of e may be interpreted as a choice of the time of retirement. Alternatively, e may be interpreted as "effort" invested in finding a job or simply as labor time, so that $1 - e$ is the amount of unemployment implied by the worker's (lack of) effort. Before the introduction of individual accounts, people are entitled to a tax-financed public transfer whenever they are out of work due to unemployment or (early) retirement. It is assumed that the preferred retirement age chosen in the second period of life is no lower than the age limit entitling people to (early) retirement benefits. In line with common practice in OECD countries, it is also assumed that public retirement benefits are not increased in an actuarially fair manner if a person decides to postpone retirement.

During each time period, the economy is populated by an equal number of young and old individuals. A certain fraction of the young are fully employed, but the remaining fraction of young workers are affected by adverse social contingencies keeping them out of work during an exogenous fraction $\bar{u}$ of the first period of their lives.

For simplicity, pre-tax factor prices are taken as constant, since endogenous factor price dynamics only complicate the analysis of the transition to individual accounts without adding anything of substance. The exogeneity of factor prices may be rationalized by assuming that the economy is small and open, producing and consuming a single good which is a perfect substitute for foreign goods, using a constant-returns technology, and facing perfect capital mobility. In such a setting, the exogenous world real interest rate ties down domestic capital intensity, which in turn pins down the domestic real wage.

Although highly simplified, this model has two features that are important for a relevant analysis of social insurance reform. First, the existence of taxes and transfers distorts private sector behavior (by distorting labor supply). Second, the model allows for involuntary as well as voluntary unemployment or nonemployment, recognizing that a person may be out of work either as a result of unfortunate circumstances beyond his control or as a result of a voluntary choice.

In the following subsections, I present the details of the model, starting with consumer behavior.

10.2.2 Consumer Behavior

For all consumers in the economy, lifetime utility $\hat{U}$ is given by a utility function of the form

$$\hat{U} = U(C_1) + \left(\frac{1}{1+\delta}\right)[U(C_2) - h(e)], \qquad U' > 0,\ U'' < 0,\ h' > 0,$$

$$h'' > 0,\ \delta > 0,\ 0 \le e \le 1, \tag{1}$$

where U is instantaneous utility from consumption, C_1 is first-period consumption, C_2 is second-period consumption, δ is the rate of time preference, e is the second-period employment rate, and $h(e)$ is the disutility from second-period work or effort. Since the working hours of employed workers are institutionally fixed, the disutility from first-period work is also exogenous and is therefore ignored in (1). Note that an increase in the value of e may be interpreted as a postponement of the consumer's date of retirement from the labor force.

Households are divided into those that are exposed to involuntary unemployment during their youth and those that are not. A consumer from the latter group, who has an employment rate of unity during the first period of his life, is subject to the budget constraints

$$C_1 = w(1 - t - s) - S, \tag{2}$$

$$C_2 = (1 + r)S + we(1 - t - s) + b(1 - e) + A, \tag{3}$$

$$A = (1 + r)sw + swe - \alpha b(1 - e),\ A \ge 0,\ 0 \le \alpha \le 1, \tag{4}$$

where w is the real wage rate before tax, t is the labor income tax rate, s is the mandatory rate of Social Security contribution to the consumer's individual account, S is financial saving (excluding the contribution to the IA), r is the real interest rate (determined in the world capital market), b is the flat rate of benefit received by people who are out of work (including retired people), and A is the balance on the consumer's individual account, which is paid out in the second period when he retires. From (4), we see that this balance consists of the contributions to the IA made during youth, uprated by the market interest rate, $(1+r)sw$, plus the contribution made in the second period, swe, minus that fraction α of the consumer's benefit receipts $b(1-e)$ that is financed by debiting his individual account. In the case of $\alpha = s = 0$, we have a conventional tax-financed system of social insurance without individual accounts. When $\alpha > 0$, part of the consumer's (early) retirement benefit is financed by withdrawals from his IA. Note that the IA may be a mere bookkeeping system kept by the public sector, or it may be a "genuine" savings account held in a private financial institution. In both cases, the behavioral effects of the system will be the same, as long as it is mandatory and consumers are allowed to draw benefits even if the balance on their account is negative.

The constraint $A \geq 0$ in (4) reflects the lifetime income insurance built into the IA system: If the balance on the IA is negative at the time of retirement, the account is set at zero and the consumer still receives his (retirement) benefit at the rate b. Realistically, some workers with relatively low earnings and/or relatively long spells of unemployment will end up with a negative balance on their IA.[2] To capture this phenomenon in the model, I assume that those workers who are exposed to involuntary unemployment during their youth would end up with a negative value of A for all admissible values of $e \leq 1$. Using a superscript l to refer to this group of low-income workers, assuming that they are out of work during an exogenous fraction $\bar{u}$ of the first period of their working career, and recalling that their negative IA balance will be set at zero at the time of retirement, we may then write the budget constraints for the two periods of their life as

$$C_1^l = w(1-t-s)(1-\bar{u}) + b\bar{u} - S^l, \tag{5}$$

$$C_2^l = (1+r)S^l + we^l(1-t-s) + b(1-e^l). \tag{6}$$

Consumers are assumed to be able to (re)optimize after their labor
market status during youth has been revealed. A worker who is fully
employed during youth maximizes lifetime utility, (1), with respect
to C_1, C_2, and e, subject to (2) through (4). Assuming that the constraint $A \geq 0$ is satisfied, the first-order conditions for such a worker
are

$$U'(C_1) = \left(\frac{1+r}{1+\delta}\right) U'(C_2), \tag{7}$$

$$U'(C_2)[w(1-t) - b(1-\alpha)] = h'(e). \tag{8}$$

Equation (7) is the familiar Keynes-Ramsey rule equating the marginal rate of substitution between present and future consumption to
the marginal rate of transformation allowed by the international
capital market. Equation (8) states that the marginal utility gain from
an additional unit of work during the second period (the left-hand
side) must be equated to the marginal disutility of work (the right-
hand side). Consolidating (2) through (4) into a single lifetime budget constraint on the assumption that $A \geq 0$, the reader may easily
verify that the Social Security tax rate s drops out.[3] Hence, the Social
Security contribution does not affect the behavior of workers who
are fully employed during their youth, so "effort," e, is influenced
only by the remaining policy instruments, that is, $e = e(b, \alpha, t)$. By
comparative static analysis of (7) and (8), using (2) through (4), one
can show that

$$e_b \equiv \frac{\partial e}{\partial b} < 0, \; e_\alpha \equiv \frac{\partial e}{\partial \alpha} > 0, \; e_\alpha = -b e_b \text{ for } \alpha_o = 0, \tag{9}$$

where α_o denotes the initial value of α. Thus, a higher rate of Social
Security benefit will stimulate earlier retirement, whereas a higher
degree of self-financing of benefits via the IA system (an increase in
α) will lead to postponed retirement. Equation (9) also indicates that
the labor supply effect of introducing IAs is equivalent to the effect
of a benefit cut for workers with nonnegative IA balances. The labor
supply effect of a higher labor income tax rate (e_t) cannot be signed,
due to offsetting income and substitution effects.

The optimal levels of C_1 and C_2 will also depend on b, α, and t (but
not on s), so the indirect utility function of a worker who is fully
employed during his youth may be written as $V = V(b, \alpha, t)$, and the
Envelope Theorem may be used to demonstrate that

$$V_b \equiv \frac{\partial V}{\partial b} = (1 - e)\frac{U'(C_2)}{1 + \delta} > 0, \tag{10}$$

$$V_\alpha \equiv \frac{\partial V}{\partial \alpha} = -b(1 - e)\frac{U'(C_2)}{1 + \delta} = -bV_b < 0, \tag{11}$$

$$V_t \equiv \frac{\partial V}{\partial t} = -[w(1 + r) + we]\frac{U'(C_2)}{1 + \delta} < 0. \tag{12}$$

For the group of low-income workers, lifetime utility, (1), must be maximized subject to (5) and (6). The latter two equations imply that consumption and effort will be affected by the policy instruments b, s, and t, but not (directly) by α.[4] The first-order conditions for low-income workers still include the Keynes-Ramsey rule (7), but (8) is replaced by

$$U'(C_2^l)[w(1 - t - s) - b] = h'(e^l). \tag{13}$$

From (5), (6), and (13), one finds that

$$e_b^l < 0, \ e_s^l = e_t^l. \tag{14}$$

Denoting a low-income worker's indirect utility function by $V^l = V^l(b, s, t)$, one can also show from his first-order conditions that

$$V_s^l = V_t^l < 0. \tag{15}$$

Thus, a rise in the Social Security tax rate has the same effect on the behavior and welfare of low-income workers as a rise in the ordinary labor income tax rate, as is immediately apparent from (5) and (6).

These results will be useful for the analysis of the welfare effects of introducing individual accounts.

10.2.3 The Government Budget Constraint and the Transition to Individual Accounts

We will now consider the behavior of government. For the moment, I assume that the IA system is administered by the public sector, so the mandatory Social Security contributions accrue to the government and the IA balances paid out to retirees form part of government expenditure (in section 10.2.5, I deal with a privatized IA system). To ensure that the welfare gains for the current young and future generations are not achieved at the expense of the current old generation, I assume that, during the first period following the fiscal reform, the rules of the new system apply only to new entrants to the labor market (the current young), whereas a transition scheme ensures that the current old are effectively treated according to the old fiscal rules until the end of their lives.

In the analysis below, variables with a subscript "o" refer to the situation prevailing before the fiscal reform, while variables without such a subscript refer to the post-reform situation. Prior to the reform, the government balances its budget in accordance with the government budget constraint

$$b[p^l\bar{u} + p^l(1 - e_o^l) + (1 - p^l)(1 - e_o)]$$

$$= t_o[p^l w(1 - \bar{u}) + (1 - p^l)w] + t_o[p^l we_o^l + (1 - p^l)we_o], \quad (16)$$

where p^l is the exogenous fraction of young workers who are exposed to involuntary unemployment or other social contingencies. The left-hand side of (16) measures current expenditure on social benefits to the young plus (early) retirement benefits to the old. The first term on the right-hand side is the labor income tax collected from the current young, and the second term on the right-hand side is the labor income tax paid by the current old. For simplicity, I abstract from taxes on income from capital. Note that since the IA reform does not involve any change in b, the pre-reform and post-reform values of this variable coincide.

In the first period following the introduction of the IA system, the government adopts "grandfathering" rules ensuring that the current old continue to be treated in accordance with the old fiscal rules during the transition period. The new Social Security tax s and the post-reform level of the labor income tax t therefore apply only to young workers in the first time period following the reform. To be able to keep s and t constant through all post-reform time periods, I assume that the government finances the transition to the new fiscal system by issuing (or retiring) an appropriate amount D of government debt. Hence, the government budget constraint for the first period following the reform becomes

$$b[p^l\bar{u} + p^l(1 - e_o^l) + (1 - p^l)(1 - e_o)]$$

$$= \overbrace{(t + s)[p^l w(1 - \bar{u}) + (1 - p^l)w]}^{\text{taxes on young workers}} + \underbrace{t_o[p^l we_o^l + (1 - p^l)we_o]}_{\text{taxes on old workers}} + D.$$

$$(17)$$

When the single transition period is over, the new fiscal rules apply to all workers, and the government budget constraint for all the subsequent periods is

$$b[p^l\bar{u} + p^l(1 - e^l) + (1 - p^l)(1 - e)] + (1 - p^l)A + rD$$

$$= (t + s)[p^l w(1 - \bar{u}) + (1 - p^l)w + p^l we^l + (1 - p^l)we], \tag{18}$$

where the second term on the left-hand side of (18) is public expenditure on the supplementary pensions based on positive IA balances, and the third term on the left-hand side is the cost of servicing the public debt incurred to finance the transition to the IA system. Using (4), (16), and (17), we may rewrite the post-reform government budget constraint (18) as

$$b[p^l\bar{u} + p^l(1 - e^l) + (1 - \alpha)(1 - p^l)(1 - e)]$$

$$- p^l w(t + s)[(1 + r)(1 - \bar{u}) + e^l] - (1 - p^l)tw(1 + r + e)$$

$$+ rt_o w[p^l(1 - \bar{u}) + 1 - p^l] = 0. \tag{19}$$

To provide a full account of the budgetary implications of the IA reform, we must supplement the government budget constraint (19) by a rule for the determination of the Social Security tax rate s. For concreteness, I assume that the level of s is just sufficient to ensure that the high-income workers who are fully employed during their youth end up with a nonnegative IA balance. Setting $A = 0$ in (4), this requires

$$s = \frac{\alpha b(1 - e)}{w(1 + r) + we} \Rightarrow \frac{ds}{d\alpha} = \rho \equiv \frac{b(1 - e)}{w(1 + r) + we} \quad \text{for } \alpha_o = 0, \tag{20}$$

where the variable ρ is a fully employed worker's ratio of lifetime benefit income to his lifetime labor income.

Having described the behavior of the private and the public sectors, we are now ready to analyze the welfare implications of introducing individual accounts.

10.2.4 The Welfare Effects of Introducing Individual Accounts

The transition scheme described in the previous subsection ensures that the welfare of the current old is unaffected by the IA reform and that all workers of a given category (low-income or high-income) entering the labor market after the time of the reform will attain the

same level of welfare. Hence, the IA reform will be welfare improving (in an aggregate sense) if it raises the total welfare $\hat{V}$ of individuals born after the time of the reform, given by

$$\hat{V} = p^l V^l + (1 - p^l) V. \tag{21}$$

This specification of social welfare may be interpreted as the ex ante
expected utility of a consumer whose labor market status has not yet
been revealed, or as the utilitarian sum of individual ex post utility
levels (with population normalized at unity).

I wish to analyze whether the introduction of mandatory individual accounts on a small scale could raise $\hat{V}$, starting from an initial
situation with purely tax-financed social insurance. Formally, this
can be done by analyzing the welfare effect of a marginal increase in
the policy parameter α (the fraction of social benefits financed via the
IAs), starting from an initial value $\alpha_o = 0$ and accounting for the facts
that the increase in α will be associated with a rise in the social
security tax s and a fall in the ordinary labor income tax t. From (21),
we thus get

$$\frac{d\hat{V}}{d\alpha} = p^l \left[\left(\frac{ds}{d\alpha} \right) V_s^l + \left(\frac{dt}{d\alpha} \right) V_t^l \right] + (1 - p^l) \left[V_\alpha + \left(\frac{dt}{d\alpha} \right) V_t \right]. \tag{22}$$

Using (20), we have

$$\frac{dt}{d\alpha} = \frac{ds}{d\alpha} \frac{dt}{ds} = \rho \frac{dt}{ds}. \tag{23}$$

From (11), (12), and (20), it follows that $V_\alpha = \rho V_t$, and from (15), we
know that $V_s^l = V_t^l$. Inserting these relationships along with (23) into
(22), we get

$$\frac{d\hat{V}}{d\alpha} = \rho \left(1 + \frac{dt}{ds} \right) [p^l V_t^l + (1 - p^l) V_t]. \tag{24}$$

Since V_t^l and V_t are both negative, (24) shows that the introduction
of individual accounts will be welfare improving if and only if
$dt/ds < -1$, that is, if and only if the new Social Security tax paves
the way for a more-than-compensating fall in the labor income tax
rate.

In the government budget constraint, (19), we may treat α as a
function of s, noting from (20) that $d\alpha/ds = 1/\rho$. Moreover, since s
and t have identical effects on the behavior of low-income workers,

we have $e_s^l = e_t^l$, as stated in (14). Using these results and the definition of ρ given in (20), and assuming $\alpha_o = s_o = 0$, we find from (19) that

$$\frac{dt}{ds} = -\left[\frac{R_t + (1 - p^l)(b + tw)(\rho^{-1}e_\alpha - e_t)}{R_t}\right],\tag{25}$$

where $R_t \equiv w\{(1 + r)[p^l(1 - \bar{u}) + 1 - p^l] + p^l e^l + (1 - p^l)e + (b + tw) \cdot [p^l e_t^l + (1 - p^l)e_t]\}$. R_t is the effect of a rise in the labor income tax rate on net public revenue. Inserting (25) into (24), we obtain

$$\frac{d\hat{V}}{d\alpha} = (1 - p^l)(b + tw)\left(\frac{\rho e_t - e_\alpha}{R_t}\right)[p^l V_t^l + (1 - p^l)V_t] > 0 \text{ for } e_t \leq 0.\tag{26}$$

From (8), we know that $e_\alpha > 0$, and the absence of Laffer curve effects implies $R_t > 0$. Hence, we see from (26) that $e_t \leq 0$ is a *sufficient* (but *not* a necessary) condition for the IA reform to be welfare improving. In other words, as long as a fall in the labor income tax rate does not *reduce* the labor supply of high-income workers—that is, as long as the income effect does not dominate the substitution effect—we can be sure that the fall in the labor income tax rate will be greater than the new Social Security contributions to the IAs, thereby paving a way for a welfare improvement.

The intuition for this result may be explained as follows: Since a high-income worker receives social benefits (e.g., early retirement benefits) in the second stage of his life, part of the taxes he pays are really transferred to himself. Yet, this part of his tax bill and the associated social benefits distort his labor supply, since there is no actuarial link between taxes and benefits. The introduction of IAs establishes such a link, which improves incentives and increases net public revenue via an increase in the labor supply of high-income workers. At the same time, the IA system protects the consumption possibilities of low-income workers via the lifetime income guarantee. In this way, the IA system effectively enables the government to implement a selective efficiency improving cut in taxes and benefits for high-income workers without hurting the low-income workers. Indeed, the latter group will share in the overall welfare gain, because low-income workers also benefit from the labor income tax cut, so the IA reform will generate a genuine Pareto improvement.

Notice that this conclusion does not rely on an assumption that the tax-transfer system has been optimized before the introduction of IAs. It is a general result that is valid even if such optimization has

taken place. The possibility of a welfare gain stems from the fact that
the IA system is a new fiscal instrument which provides the government with better opportunities to tailor the fiscal system to the different needs of different taxpayers.

10.2.5 The Equivalence of a Privatized and a Publicly Administered IA System

I have so far assumed that the IA system would be administered by
the public sector. I shall now demonstrate that the same effects could
be achieved by mandatory contributions to savings accounts held by
private financial institutions. In section 10.2.2, we noted that the
microeconomic behavioral effects of publicly administered and private IAs will be identical, assuming that the IA balances earn the
going market rate of interest in both cases. It remains to be shown
that the general equilibrium effects on labor taxation and on private
capital formation will also be the same, even though a privatized IA
system will have a different impact on the government budget from
that of a public IA system.

Under a privatized IA system, the mandatory Social Security contributions will be paid into private IA accounts and hence will not be
recorded as part of public sector revenue. Moreover, in periods of
unemployment or nonemployment, a part of the worker's benefit
income will be financed by withdrawals from his IA account, until
the account is emptied. For concreteness, we can imagine that all
benefits from the first day of unemployment are paid out by the
public sector—which checks that the eligibility requirements are
met—and that the private financial institution transfers funds from
the worker's IA account to the public sector as long as the IA balance
is positive. Hence, the *publicly financed* unemployment benefits paid
out to young workers will only amount to $p^l[b\bar{u} - sw(1 - \bar{u})]$. In the
transition period following the reform, old workers will still be
treated according to the old rules, so the government budget constraint for the first time period after the reform becomes

$$b[p^l(1 - e_o^l) + (1 - p^l)(1 - e_o)] + p^l[b\bar{u} - sw(1 - \bar{u})]$$

$$= t[p^lw(1 - \bar{u}) + (1 - p^l)w] + t_o[p^lwe_o^l + (1 - p^l)we_o] + \tilde{D}, \quad (27)$$

assuming that the government issues an amount of debt $\tilde{D}$ during
the transition to be able to maintain a constant post-reform value t of
the labor income tax rate. When the single transition period has

expired, the new rules apply to all workers, and part of the (early) retirement benefits to old workers will be financed by withdrawals from the private IA accounts. The post-reform government budget constraint therefore becomes

$$
\overbrace{p^l[b\bar{u} - sw(1 - \bar{u}) + b(1 - e^l) - swe^l]}^{\substack{\text{tax-financed transfers to}\\ \text{low-income workers}}} + \overbrace{(1 - p^l)b(1 - \alpha)(1 - e)}^{\substack{\text{tax-financed transfers to}\\ \text{high-income workers}}} + r\tilde{D}
$$

$$
= t[p^l w(1 - \bar{u}) + (1 - p^l)w + p^l we^l + (1 - p^l)we]. \tag{28}
$$

By substituting (16) and (27) into (28), the reader may easily verify that one ends up with a post-reform government budget constraint identical to (19). This means that the magnitude of dt/ds will be the same under a privatized IA system as under a publicly administered IA system, provided the rule (20) for the setting of the mandatory Social Security contribution is the same in the two cases. Hence, the welfare effects of the IA reform will also be identical in the two scenarios.

Consider next the effects on private capital formation. The level of public debt needed to finance the transition to a privately adminis-tered IA system is found from (16) and (27):

$$
\tilde{D} = (t_o - t)[p^l w(1 - \bar{u}) + (1 - p^l)w] - sp^l w(1 - \bar{u}). \tag{29}
$$

For comparison, we may solve (16) and (17) for the level of debt needed to finance a public IA system:

$$
D = (t_o - t)[p^l w(1 - \bar{u}) + (1 - p^l)w] - s[p^l w(1 - \bar{u}) + (1 - p^l)w]. \tag{30}
$$

We see that the stock of public debt under a privatized system will be higher by the amount $sw(1 - p^l)$. However, this additional public debt is exactly offset by the aggregate reserves built up in private IA accounts by the fully employed young workers during the transition period.[5] Hence, the funds left to finance private capital formation will be exactly the same under a privatized IA system as under a publicly administered IA system: The reserves accumulated in pri-vate accounts under the former system simply serve to absorb the additional public debt under this system.

10.2.6 Modifications and Extensions

The model analyzed above captures the lifetime income insurance effect of social insurance, but not the liquidity insurance effect, since no agents are subject to credit constraints. But as demonstrated in Sørensen (2001b), the model may easily be extended to allow for the possibility that low-income workers are liquidity-constrained during their youth, due to an inability to borrow against expected future labor income. In that case, the introduction of individual accounts will offer an additional source of welfare improvement by strengthening the capacity of the fiscal system to shift consumption possibilities towards those periods of an individual's working career when he is liquidity-constrained. The point is that, since the IA system allows taxpayers to collect benefits at the normal rate when they are involuntarily out of work, the system allows a cut in the present value of tax-financed benefits without significantly reducing consumption possibilities in that stage of life where the marginal utility of consumption is the highest. By thus reducing the utility cost of a cut in the present value of benefits, the introduction of IAs means that social welfare can be improved by a marginal cut in public spending and taxation, even if the level of taxation and spending has been optimized prior to the IA reform (see Sørensen 2001b).

On the other hand, the model above paints an optimistic picture of the effects of IAs by assuming that all workers collect some amount of tax-financed social insurance benefits (for example, early retirement benefits) during their career. Suppose, instead, that there is a significant group of "low-risk" workers collecting no public benefits at all. This group would clearly not contribute to the (partial) self-financing of benefits implied by the IA system, but they would still gain from the cuts in the ordinary labor income tax made possible by the introduction of IAs. Ceteris paribus, the resulting fiscal redistribution towards the low-risk workers (who are likely to earn relatively high incomes) will make it more difficult to achieve a Pareto improvement via the introduction of individual accounts, as shown by Sørensen (2001a). The next section will discuss how such undesirable distributional effects of IAs could be minimized.

10.3   Individual Accounts and Income Distribution

10.3.1   *Introducing Equity Concerns in the Design of Individual Accounts*

The analysis in section 10.2 assumed that the fall in a worker's net benefit income under an IA system would be proportional to his initial benefit income, and that the labor tax cut made possible by the IAs would be granted in proportion to each worker's labor income. Even if the IA system might yield a Pareto improvement, these design features would imply that the distribution of disposable incomes would tend to be twisted in favor of individuals with high wages and a low dependence on benefits.

However, using alternative designs, it would be possible to moderate these distributional effects of IAs. First of all, since the introduction of IAs is likely to redistribute income away from low-income earners, it would be natural to concentrate the labor tax cuts in the lower end of the income scale, reducing average tax rates more for low-wage earners than for high-wage earners. Second, in addition to the lifetime income insurance implied by the "debt ceiling" on each IA, policymakers could design the IA system such that benefits drawn during spells of long-term unemployment, long-term illness, and so forth would not be debited to the person's IA. This could be done by requiring that once the number of days of unemployment or illness exceeds a certain maximum, the benefits received will no longer be debited to the IA. Since almost all people experience some short-term illness and a lot of people also go through one or several spells of short-term unemployment over their working career, such rules would be a way of concentrating the IA system on those social transfers that are granted to the great majority of workers, in line with the rationale for IAs.

Finally, since students in higher education tend to be recruited mainly from the middle and upper classes, the inclusion of education benefits in the IA system would also tend to work as an equalizing mechanism offsetting the regressive incidence of the system.

I turn now to a specific proposal for an IA design exploiting these ideas.

10.3.2 A Specific Proposal for a System of Individual Accounts

In 1995, a Danish group of business leaders and academics—the so-called Alternative Welfare Commission—proposed the introduction of an IA system in response to a government report on the future of the Danish Welfare State. According to the proposal, part of the Danish income tax would be replaced by a mandatory Social Security contribution, levied on labor income and to be credited to the taxpayer's IA. The following social transfers would be debited to the IAs:

1. Unemployment benefits and social assistance benefits related to unemployment, but only for periods of unemployment below three months, and only for taxpayers having experienced no more than six months of unemployment over the last ten years.

2. Sickness benefits for the first twenty days of illness during the last ten-year period.

3. Child benefits (to the first two children).

4. Benefits paid during maternity leave (for the first two children) and parental leave.

5. Education benefits to students above the age of 18.

6. Benefits paid during education and sabbatical leave.

7. Early retirement benefits for able individuals below 62 years of age. Only individuals with a surplus on their IA would be entitled to draw early retirement benefits before the age of 62, unless declared disabled.

For purposes of lifetime income insurance, it was also proposed that benefits should no longer be debited to the IA if the negative balance on the account were to exceed a "debt ceiling." The proposed debt ceiling was 150,000 kroner for people below 40 years of age, 100,000 kroner for people between 40 and 50, and 50,000 kroner for individuals above 50 (1995 price level). This sliding scale was meant to ensure that individuals at different stages of their working career would still have some chance of accumulating a surplus on their IA, thus preserving the positive incentive effects of the system. However, as an equalizing device, the debt ceiling would not apply to negative IA balances arising from the take-up of education benefits.

The Alternative Welfare Commission estimated that its proposal would allow a 5 percentage point cut in the proportional Danish labor income tax. The introduction of an IA system on a rather moderate initial scale was intended to avoid significant effects on income distribution and to allow for experimentation and the building of administrative capacity. The commission recognized that some socially beneficial activities (such as those promoted by the various leave schemes) would tend to be discouraged by its IA proposal and that policymakers might have different preferences regarding the transfer schemes to be included in the IA system. But the commission pointed out that adverse demographic developments would force the government to give higher priority to the stimulation of labor supply and labor-force participation and that this might justify lower subsidies to activities keeping people out of the labor force.

Langhoff-Roos (2000) has recently undertaken a microsimulation study of the distributional effects of the IA system proposed by the Alternative Welfare Commission. Using Danish microdata on the frequency of unemployment, sickness, education activity, childbirth, participation in leave schemes, and early retirement, Langhoff-Roos constructed typical working careers (covering the age interval from 18 to 66) for two cohorts of 1,000 males and 1,000 females, each divided into five categories of education levels. On this basis, she was able to offer a rough estimate of the distributional effects of the proposed IA system, assuming that the system would involve a 5 percentage point cut in the proportional Danish payroll tax and a 5 percent Social Security tax rate, and *disregarding any behavioral changes induced by the IA system*. If the IA system is politically credible, the appropriate market interest rate on IA balances is the risk-free rate, which could be proxied by the interest rate on short-term government bonds. To simplify the analysis, Langhoff-Roos assumed a "golden rule" scenario in which the real interest rate on the IA balances equals the growth rate of real wages.

The distributional effects for the male cohort simulated by Langhoff-Roos are summarized in table 10.2. We see that two-thirds of the male group would end up with a positive IA balance at the time of retirement. For all education levels, the average magnitude of the positive IA balance would correspond to roughly one year's pre-tax salary. Not surprisingly, the two higher education levels would have a higher frequency of positive balances, but the debiting of education benefits to the IAs would limit the redistribution implied by the system. Comparing the last two columns in table 10.2, we see that income distribution under the IA system would be only slightly more uneven than under the existing tax-transfer system. According to Langhoff-Roos (2000), the distributional effects of the IA system would be rather similar for females, although only about half of the women would manage to accumulate an IA surplus because they tend to have lower wages and to rely more on the transfer system than men.

Since the positive IA balances involve the payout of additional pensions compared with the present system, the combination of a 5

Table 10.2
Simulated effects of the Danish proposal of a "citizen account" (males)

Education level	Individuals with positive balance at retirement (% of total)	Average account balance for individuals with positive balance (% of average annual pre-tax income)	Lifetime income before tax (% of average)	Disposable lifetime income	
				Current tax-transfer system (% of average)	Citizen account system (% of average)
Unskilled	65	98.3	87	92	91
Skilled	65	102.7	96	98	97
Short college education	52	99.0	93	96	96
Medium-length college education	74	99.1	122	113	115
Long college education	82	94.3	147	129	133
Average	67	101.3	100	100	100

Source: Langhoff-Roos 2000.
Note: The details of the proposed citizen account system are given in the text.

percentage point payroll tax cut and a 5 percent Social Security tax would imply an estimated government budget deficit of 0.89 percent of the aggregate wage bill, assuming no behavioral changes. However, accounting for changes in behavior, one would expect a deficit of such limited magnitude to be eliminated by a reduced take-up of benefits and by an increase in the tax base, since the effective marginal labor income tax rate would fall by 5 percentage points for all individuals with an IA surplus.[6]

Moreover, the slightly regressive effect of the IA system recorded in table 10.2 could be modified by introducing more progressivity into the remaining part of the income tax. Indeed, as a supplement to the IA system, the Alternative Welfare Commission proposed to increase the existing nondistortionary Danish property tax on pure land values for the purpose of financing an Earned Income Tax Credit which would weigh more heavily in the budgets of low-income workers.

Thus it would seem that a carefully designed IA system could avoid significant redistribution from poor to rich. However, redistribution in this dimension is not the only purpose of the tax-transfer system, and it seems inevitable that the IA system will involve some redistribution from the unlucky (with more frequent spells of income shortfalls) to the lucky within each income group. In deciding whether or not to introduce individual accounts, policymakers would have to weigh this unfortunate distribution effect against the efficiency gains offered by the system.

10.4 Summary and Conclusions

In the modern European Welfare State, a substantial part of the tax bill is transferred back to the taxpayer himself in the form of social transfers received during his working career. Hence, the tax-transfer system tends to generate "excessive" distortions in the sense of creating tax wedges that do not help to redistribute lifetime income. This provides a potential rationale for financing part of social insurance for people of working age via individual accounts based on mandatory saving. In the system of IAs discussed in this chapter, a worker drawing higher Social Security benefits would ceteris paribus receive a lower supplementary retirement pension from his IA. At the same time, the IA system would involve a lifetime income guarantee, ensuring a minimum tax-financed public pension for low-income workers with a deficit on their IAs at the time of retirement.

To analyze the incentive and welfare effects of such a fiscal reform, I set up a simple overlapping generations model with endogenous retirement decisions where some workers were exposed to involuntary unemployment or nonemployment due to social contingencies or negative labor market shocks. These low-income workers were assumed to end up with negative IA balances at the time of retirement, but would then be protected by the minimum lifetime income guarantee. The remaining group of high-income workers would accumulate nonnegative IA balances and would thus be affected by the incentive effects of the IA system. Within this framework, I found that the introduction of IAs to finance a (modest) fraction of unemployment benefits and early retirement benefits would generate a Pareto improvement under very mild conditions, even if the pre-existing tax-transfer system had been optimized. The introduction of IAs would generate a welfare gain by establishing an efficiency-enhancing actuarial link between taxes and benefits for high-income workers, without reducing the consumption possibilities of the low-income workers who are protected by the lifetime income guarantee. This result would hold whether the IA system were administered by the public sector or whether the mandatory individual accounts were held at private financial institutions.

I then described a specific Danish proposal for an IA system and reviewed an estimate of the effects of this system on the Danish distribution of income. On this basis, I concluded that the potentially regressive distributional effects could be minimized by carefully designing the IA system with a view to equity concerns, but at the same time it would be hard to prevent some amount of redistribution from "unlucky" to "lucky" individuals.

The analysis in this chapter is preliminary in nature, adding to a still very limited literature on individual accounts for the working population. More research is obviously needed before robust policy conclusions on the merits and demerits of IAs can be drawn. On the theoretical side, there is scope for a more careful modeling of the labor market effects of IAs—for example, by allowing more explicitly for uncertainty and by endogenizing educational choice. It would also be desirable to disaggregate the transfer system to be able to allow for the specific functions of the various public transfer schemes. On the empirical side, there is scope for a more detailed analysis of the distributional effects of IAs using microdata. Ultimately, one would like to build a microsimulation model accounting for the heterogeneity of the working population and incorporating behavioral responses based on empirically estimated elasticities.

Notes

Without implicating them in any remaining shortcomings or controversial policy views, I wish to thank Henry Aaron, Sijbren Cnossen, Assar Lindbeck, Pierre Pestieau, and an anonymous referee for critical comments on an earlier version of this chapter.

1. The model presented here is a simplified version of the model developed in Sørensen (2001b). In contrast to the present model, that model allows for the possibility that low-income workers may be subject to liquidity constraints during periods of unemployment. The role of liquidity constraints is discussed in section 10.2.6.

2. In Sørensen (2001b), I also consider a scenario where the Social Security tax rate s is sufficiently high to ensure that all workers end up with a nonnegative IA balance.

3. The lifetime budget constraint of a worker with a nonnegative IA balance is

$$C_1 + \frac{C_2}{1+r} = w(1-t) + \frac{we(1-t) + b(1-e)(1-\alpha)}{1+r}.$$

4. As we see in section 10.2.3, there is a link between the magnitude of α and the magnitude of s, so a change in α will have an *indirect* effect on V via its impact on s.

5. Recall that the low-income workers exposed to unemployment do not build up any reserves during their youth, since their IA accounts are emptied to finance part of their unemployment benefits. Hence, the aggregate reserve building amounts only to the mandatory IA contributions paid by the fully employed young workers, $sw(1-p^l)$.

6. In a competitive labor market, the response of the aggregate labor income tax base wL to a reduction in the labor income tax rate t would be given by the formula

$$\frac{d(wL)}{wL} = \left(\frac{dt}{1-t}\right)(1-\varepsilon^d)\left(\frac{\varepsilon^s}{\varepsilon^s + \varepsilon^d}\right),$$

where ε^d is the numerical wage elasticity of aggregate labor demand and ε^s is the net wage elasticity of labor supply. For, say, $\varepsilon^d = 2$, $\varepsilon^s = 0.2$, and an initial tax rate of $t = 0.5$, a 5 percentage point drop in the tax rate would generate an increase in the labor income tax base of 0.9 percent. In practice, the marginal tax rate for workers with negative IAs would not drop, but at the same time there would be a lower take-up of benefits tending to improve the budget from the spending side.

References

Alternative Committee on Welfare. 1995. (Den Alternative Velfærdskommission.) *Fra Forsørgerkultur til Udviklingskultur.* (From Dependency Culture to Development Culture.) Report published by the weekly magazine Mondag Morgen, Copenhagen, Denmark.

Belan, P., and P. Pestieau. 1999. "Privatizing Social Security: A Critical Assessment." *Geneva Papers on Risk and Insurance* 24: 114–130.

Breyer, F. 1989. "On the Intergenerational Pareto Efficiency of Pay-As-You-Go Financed Pension Schemes." *Journal of Institutional and Theoretical Economics* 145: 643–658.

Brunner, J. K. 1996. "Transition from a Pay-As-You-Go to a Fully Funded Pension System: The Case of Differing Individuals and Intragenerational Fairness." *Journal of Public Economics* 60: 131–146.

Demmel, R., and C. Keuschnigg. 2000. "Funded Pensions and Unemployment." *Finanzarchiv* 57: 22–38.

Diamond, P. 1998. "The Economics of Social Reform." National Bureau of Economic Research Working Paper No. 6719, Cambridge, MA.

ESO. 1994. (Expertgruppen för Studier i Offentlig Ekonomi.) Ds 1994: 135, *Skatter och Socialförsikringar över Livscykeln: En Simuleringsmodell.* (Taxes and Social Insurance Over the Life Cycle: A Simulation Model.) Stockholm: Ministry of Finance.

Feldstein, M. 1995. "Would Privatizing Social Security Raise Economic Welfare?" National Bureau of Economic Research Working Paper No. 5281, Cambridge, MA.

Feldstein, M. 1997. "Transition to a Fully Funded Pension System: Five Economic Issues." National Bureau of Economic Research Working Paper No. 6149, Cambridge, MA.

Feldstein, M., and D. Altman. 1998. "Unemployment Insurance Savings Accounts." National Bureau of Economic Research Working Paper No. 6860, Cambridge, MA.

Fölster, S. 1994. "Socialförsikring genom Medborgarkonto: Vilka Är Argumenterne?" (Social Insurance Through a Citizen Account: What Are the Issues?) *Ekonomisk Debatt* 22: 387–397.

Fölster, S. 1997. "Social Insurance Based on Personal Savings Accounts: A Possible Reform for Overburdened Welfare States?" *European Economy*, no. 4: 81–100.

Hassler, J., and A. Lindbeck. 1999. "Can and Should a Pay-As-You-Go Pension System Mimic a Funded System?" Mimeo., Institute for International Economic Studies, Stockholm University, Sweden.

Hauenschild, N. 2000. "Pareto-Improving Transition from Pay-As-You-Go to Fully Funded Social Security under Uncertain Incomes." *Finanzarchiv* 57: 39–62.

Homburg, S. 1990. "The Efficiency of Unfunded Pension Schemes." *Journal of Institutional and Theoretical Economics* 146: 640–647.

Kotlikoff, L. 1996. "Simulating the Privatization of Social Security in General Equilibrium." National Bureau of Economic Research Working Paper No. 5776, Cambridge, MA.

Langhoff-Roos, L. 2000. *Social Insurance Based on Personal Savings Accounts.* Master's thesis, Institute of Economics, University of Copenhagen, Denmark.

Lindahl, E. 1919. "Die Gerechtigkeit der Besteuerung: Positive Lösung." Reprinted as "Just Taxation: A Positive Solution." In *Classics in the Theory of Public Finance*, ed. R. Musgrave and A. Peacock. London and New York: Macmillan, 1994.

Lindbeck, A. 1995. "Hazardous Welfare State Dynamics." *American Economic Review* 85: 9–15.

Musgrave, R. 1939. "The Voluntary Exchange Theory of Public Economy." *Quarterly Journal of Economics* 53: 217–237.

Musgrave, R. 1959. *The Theory of Public Finance*. New York: McGraw-Hill.

Musgrave, R. 1996. "Combining and Separating Fiscal Choices: Wicksell's Model at Its Centennial." *Public Economics Review* 1: 1–34.

Orszag, J., P. Orszag, D. Snower, and J. Stiglitz. 1999. "The Impact of Individual Accounts: Piecemeal versus Comprehensive Approaches." Paper presented at the Annual Bank Conference on Development Economics, World Bank, Washington, DC.

Orszag, J., and D. Snower. 1997a. "Expanding the Welfare System: A Proposal for Reform." *European Economy*, no. 4: 101–118.

Orszag, J., and D. Snower. 1997b. "From Unemployment Benefits to Unemployment Support Accounts." Mimeo., Birkbeck College, London, UK.

Raffelhüschen, B. 1993. "Funding Social Security through Pareto-Optimal Conversion Policies." *Journal of Economics* 7(suppl.): 105–131.

Sinn, H.-W. 2000. "Why a Funded Pension Is Useful and Why It Is Not Useful." *International Tax and Public Finance* 7: 389–410.

Sørensen, P. B. 2001a. "Social Insurance Based on Individual Savings Accounts." Paper presented at the conference on Public Finances and Public Policy in the New Millennium, University of Munich, Germany.

Sørensen, P. B. 2001b. "Social Insurance for the Working Population: Is There a Role for Individual Accounts?" Paper presented at the 57th conference of the International Institute of Public Finance, Linz, Austria.

Wicksell, K. 1896. "Ein Neues Princip der Gerechten Besteuerung." Reprinted as "A New Principle of Just Taxation." In *Classics in the Theory of Public Finance*, ed. R. Musgrave and A. Peacock. London and New York: Macmillan.

11 Social Insurance and Redistribution

Robin Boadway,
Manuel Leite-Monteiro,
Maurice Marchand, and
Pierre Pestieau

11.1 Introduction

One of the most compelling and lasting methodological insights of Richard Musgrave's 1959 classic *The Theory of Public Finance* was the conceptual separation between the Allocative and Distributive Branches of government. It represented an operationalization of the First and Second Theorems of Welfare Economics. In ideal circumstances, the Allocative Branch should be concerned with taking the economy to the society's utility possibilities frontier by exploiting all gains from trade, while the Redistributive Branch alone need be concerned with choosing the ethically preferred point. From a policy perspective, the ability to separate efficiency and equity considerations is of enormous importance. To the extent that the Allocative Branch can go about its business of ensuring that resources are allocated efficiently, willingness to pay can be used as the benchmark for public project evaluation and interpersonal welfare comparisons can be set aside. Much influential normative public economics has revolved around investigating the circumstances under which this separation applies and the consequences of its not applying.

Two types of reasons have been stressed in the literature as to why efficiency and equity might not be separable. The first devolves from the theory of second-best formalized by Lipsey and Lancaster (1956).[1] This literature focused initially on the agnostic implications of exogenously given second-best distortions for the use of market prices as signals of efficiency. Subsequently, with the advent of the optimal commodity tax literature, the existence of second-best distortions was found to make it necessary to incorporate equity weights into shadow pricing rules for public projects.[2] However, the mere existence of commodity tax distortions did not vitiate the

Musgravian separation of branches. Indeed, arguably the most important result of Diamond and Mirrlees's (1971) seminal contribution to optimal commodity tax analysis was their so-called Production Efficiency Theorem. According to this theorem, if commodity taxes were set optimally and all pure profits were taxed away, public sector shadow prices would be producer prices, at least for private commodities. This essentially revitalized the Musgravian separation result after the onslaught of the theory of second-best. Unfortunately, the Production Efficiency Theorem only applied with respect to private commodities, and only then if taxes were in fact set optimally. In the case of public goods, the Samuelson rule had to be modified not only to include the effect of (perhaps optimal) linear tax distortions, but also to incorporate equity considerations.[3]

The second reason why equity and efficiency considerations might not be separable is, in a sense, more profound. It is because of an imperfectly informed government. The classic work of Mirrlees (1971) implied that if the government cannot observe private attributes of households, the Second Theorem of Welfare Economics would be violated, and economic outcomes would be restricted to the second-best utility possibilities frontier. Effectively, this theory supplied a fully endogenous explanation for why lump-sum redistributive taxation was not optimal: Second-best tax distortions were useful as a way of eliciting information, albeit in a costly way.[4] Even here, however, it is conceivable that efficiency considerations alone might be used to determine public sector allocation rules. Indeed, the Production Efficiency Theorem survives: With optimal nonlinear income taxes in place, public sector shadow prices for private commodities are still producer prices. With public goods, matters are slightly more complicated. Unlike with linear taxes, the Samuelson rule for public goods applies with optimal nonlinear taxes as long as leisure is separable from public and private goods (Boadway and Keen 1993).

While the above literature is concerned with public spending on goods and services, this chapter focuses on another prominent sort of spending—that on social insurance. Why do we have social insurance and not private insurance for such things as healthcare and disability? In a perfect Musgravian world, one might expect that private insurance based on market efficiency principles would suffice. Yet, in most countries, social insurance takes a much larger share of GDP than private insurance, and in fact often preceded private insurance.

Traditionally, there are three types of reasons for public intervention in the field of insurance: transaction costs, market failures, and redistribution. In the healthcare sector, private insurance exhibits higher transaction costs than social insurance. This is partly because of high administrative costs.[5] Market failures, the second reason, arise primarily from asymmetric information, such as that between insurers and insurees (adverse selection and moral hazard) and that between healthcare providers and healthcare consumers. In keeping with the Musgravian tradition, our interest is in the third reason, that is, the role of social insurance as a redistributive device.

In a full-information world of first-best, there is little reason for redistribution using social insurance. The distributive and allocative functions of the government can be separated, so one would expect income taxation to achieve all the desired redistribution, and social insurance to operate according to the market rule of actuarial fairness. However, in a second-best world of distortionary taxation, we will show that social insurance can be a powerful device for redistribution, complementing the tax-transfer system.

It has been established in the literature that if risks are negatively related to income so that the poor face higher risks on average, then we have an obvious redistributive argument for social insurance. As shown by Rochet (1989) and Cremer and Pestieau (1996), social insurance combined with a standard distortionary income tax can redistribute more effectively. The reason is that redistributing through social insurance does not involve the same distortion, and this is even more so when social insurance is less administratively costly than private insurance.[6]

This result has been developed in a setting where the risk probability is given and any loss can be compensated for without restriction. In other words, ex ante and ex post moral hazards were assumed away. When either one is taken into account, it appears that the case for social insurance is not as strong, and that, unlike in the earlier analyses, full coverage is no longer necessarily socially desirable. The purpose of this chapter is to study those two types of moral hazard in an economy in which a linear income tax and a social insurance can be used jointly along with a private insurance that is actuarially fair, possibly up to some loading factor.[7]

The chapter is organized as follows. Section 11.2 presents the basic model and assumptions. Sections 11.3 and 11.4 consider two benchmark cases. In the first, there is perfect information and the government can make lump-sum redistributive transfers. In this case, Musgravian separation applies: Despite moral hazard, actuarially fair insurance can be provided by the private sector, and all redistributive objectives can be accomplished by the tax-transfer system. In the second benchmark, there is no moral hazard, but the public sector is restricted to distortionary taxation—linear progressive income taxation for simplicity. In this case, full social insurance is provided, crowding out private insurance. Section 11.5 then considers ex post moral hazard along with linear progressive taxation, and section 11.6 ex ante moral hazard. In each case, there is generally a redistributive role for public intervention in private insurance markets, though the direction of intervention is ambiguous. Section 11.7 extends the ex post moral hazard case to a setting in which there are extra administrative costs associated with private insurance provision. Finally, section 11.8 offers some concluding remarks.

11.2   Model and Assumptions

The economy consists of three types of decision makers—households, insurance firms, and the government. Households face an idiosyncratic risk of accident, but might be able to take actions that affect the size of the loss in the event of an accident—ex post moral hazard—or that affect the probability of the accident occurring—ex ante moral hazard. These actions cannot be directly controlled by the government. Households differ both in productivity and in accident risk. Insurance companies can observe household risk, and they provide insurance competitively and—except in the case described in section 11.7, where administrative costs are introduced—actuarially fairly.[8] The government's objective is to redistribute income among households, but because it cannot observe productivities, it is restricted to using distortionary policy instruments (except as described in section 11.3). Decision making can be thought of as occurring sequentially. The government chooses its policies first, followed by the insurance firms and then households. In each case, the outcomes of subsequent stages are fully anticipated, so that equilibria of interest will be subgame perfect.

To be more specific, we use as an example the case of health insurance, though the analysis would apply more generally to other types of personal risks faced by households. We consider two states of the world, denoted by 0 for good health and 1 for ill health. There are n types of individuals indexed by $i = 1, \ldots, n$, each characterized by a wage rate and a risk characteristic. The wage rate for a type i person is exogenously given by w_i. In the absence of ex ante moral hazard, his or her exogenous probability of illness is π_i. All households with a given wage have the same probability of illness, which simplifies the analysis considerably. The proportion of households of type i is given by f_i, where $\sum f_i = 1$. With ex ante moral hazard, type i households can affect the probability of illness according to the function $\pi_i(x)$, where x is preventive spending which takes place before the state of health is revealed to the household. The function $\pi_i(x)$ is decreasing in x with $\pi_i(\infty) > 0$.

In the good state, health status is exogenously given as h^0. In the bad state, health status is $h^1 = \bar{h} + m(z)$, where z is curative expenditure on health improvement, $m'(z) > 0$, and $m''(z) < 0$. Expenditures z that are chosen by the household in the case of ex post moral hazard are undertaken after the state of health is revealed to the household. In this case, we assume that $h^1 = \bar{h} + m(z) < h^0$ for all values of z (i.e., $m(\infty) < h^0 - \bar{h}$), so treatment cannot bring health status if ill to a level as high as health status if not ill (we depart from this assumption in section 11.4). Notice that the parameters h^0 and $\bar{h}$, as well as the function $m(z)$, are the same for all types of households. Only the probabilities of good health differ.

Households have identical state-independent utility functions:

$$u(c_i^j, h_i^j, \ell_i^j), \tag{1}$$

where c_i^j is consumption and ℓ_i^j is labor supply of a type i household in state $j(= 0, 1)$. In some cases, we shall assume that utility takes the quasi-linear form $u[c_i^j + h_i^j - g(\ell_i^j)]$, where $g(\ell_i^j)$ is increasing and strictly convex. In this case, labor supply depends only on the after-tax wage rate and z on its out-of-pocket price: There are no income or cross-price effects. In particular, labor supply is then state-independent. With a more general utility function, labor could be higher in the bad state if the individual has to compensate for private healthcare spending or lower if ill health increases the disutility of labor.[9] Naturally, households maximize expected utility, weighted by the probabilities π_i for state 1 (ill health) and $1 - \pi_i$ for state 0 (good health). Households take government policies and private insurance premiums as given. They choose x before the state of health is determined, and c, ℓ, and z after the state is determined.

Insurance firms are perfectly competitive. They offer insurance policies $\{p_i, P_i\}$ to households of type i, where p_i is the proportion of curative health expenditures z_i that are covered (reimbursed) and P_i is the total premium. Insurance companies anticipate the effect of their insurance policies on curative expenditures z_i in the case of ex post moral hazard and on preventive expenditures x_i in the case of ex ante moral hazard. Initially, we ignore administrative costs, in which case competition entails that premiums are given by

$$P_i = \pi_i(x_i)p_i z_i \qquad i = 1, \dots, n. \tag{2}$$

In a later section, we let there be a loading factor equal to $k \geq 0$. Then premiums for type i households are $P_i = (1 + k)\pi_i(x_i)p_i z_i$.

The government has two sorts of policy instruments—tax-transfer policies and social insurance. Except in the following section, where the government can impose lump-sum taxes and transfers on households according to their types, tax-transfer policy consists of a linear progressive income tax with marginal tax rate t and a lump-sum poll subsidy a per household. Social insurance covers a proportion s of curative expenditures z_i, financed out of general tax revenues. Throughout the chapter, we impose the condition $0 \leq s \leq 1$. Notice that the same rate of social insurance applies to all households. However, in the full-information case considered in the next section, the government is able to offer a separate social insurance rate s_i to each household type. Denote total insurance coverage by $\sigma_i = p_i + s$ (or $p_i + s_i$ in the full-information case).

As mentioned, there are three main stages of decision making in this economy, representing the sequence in which the decisions occur:

Stage 1: The government chooses its policies $\{t, a, s\}$. It cannot observe individual types or individual demands for goods, leisure, or insurance, but it can observe incomes. It knows preferences and the distribution of individuals by type i. The government anticipates the effect of its policies both on the insurance market and subsequently on households.

Stage 2: The competitive insurance industry sells private insurance to households. Market equilibrium (competition for customers, with zero profits) determines p_i and P_i. The insurance industry is assumed to be able to observe household risk types, so there is no adverse selection problem. Thus, insurance firms are better informed than the government since they can observe π_i. In this stage, $\{t, a, s\}$ are taken as given and household behavior is correctly anticipated.

Stage 3: Households select $\{x_i, c_i^1, \ell_i^1, z_i, c_i^0, \ell_i^0\}$. Preventive expenditures x_i are chosen before the state of health is revealed. All other variables are state-specific since they are chosen after the state is revealed (z_i is chosen only in the bad state). Households take $\{t, a, s, p_i, P_i\}$ as given from the previous two stages.

The equilibrium is assumed to be subgame perfect, so we proceed to solve it by backward induction. The method of solution can best be illustrated by considering as a benchmark the full-information case.

11.3   The Full-Information Benchmark

In this benchmark, the government can observe individual types i, so all policies can be type-specific. The government gives a lump-sum transfer of a_i to households of type i, as well as an individualized social insurance coverage rate of s_i.[10] Total coverage is then $\sigma_i = s_i + p_i$. We begin by analyzing household choice and proceed backwards to earlier stages.

11.3.1   Stage 3: Household Choice

Households of type i face the following budget constraints in the bad and good states:

$$c_i^1 = w_i \ell_i^1 + a_i - x_i - (1 - \sigma_i) z_i^1 - P_i, \tag{3}$$

$$c_i^0 = w_i \ell_i^0 + a_i - x_i - P_i, \tag{4}$$

where the household can choose ℓ and z after the state has been revealed. Given that no z will be chosen in the good state, the problem for household i is

$$\max_{x_i, \ell_i^j, z_i} \{ \pi_i(x_i) u[w_i \ell_i^1 + a_i - x_i - (1 - \sigma_i) z_i^1 - P_i, \bar{h} + m(z_i), \ell_i^1]$$

$$+ [1 - \pi_i(x_i)] u(w_i \ell_i^0 + a_i - x_i - P_i, h^0, \ell_i^0) \}. \tag{5}$$

The first-order conditions are (using self-evident notation for partial derivatives)

$$\ell_i^j: w_i u_{cj}^i + u_{\ell j}^i = 0 \text{ for } j = 0, 1, \tag{6}$$

$$z_i: -(1 - \sigma_i)u_{c1}^i + m'(z_i)u_{h1}^i = 0, \tag{7}$$

$$x_i: \pi_i'(x_i)[u^i(1) - u^i(0)] - \pi_i(x_i)u_{c0}^i - [1 - \pi_i(x_i)]u_{c1}^i = 0, \tag{8}$$

where $u^i(j)$ is the utility level achieved in state $j = 0, 1$. The solution to this problem yields $\ell_i^0(a_i - P_i)$, $\ell_i^1(a_i - P_i, s_i + p_i)$, $z_i(a_i - P_i, s_i + p_i)$, $x_i(a_i - P_i, s_i + p_i)$, and the indirect utility function $v_i(a_i - P_i, s_i + p_i)$. Applying the Envelope Theorem gives

$$v_a^i = -v_P^i = \pi_i u_{c1}^i + (1 - \pi_i)u_{c0}^i = E[u_c^i], \tag{9}$$

$$v_s^i = v_p^i = \pi_i z_i u_{c1}^i. \tag{10}$$

11.3.2 Stage 2: Insurance Market Equilibrium

Insurance firms are perfectly competitive and compete in insurance policies. Firms take as given the policies offered by other firms and the level of utility that households can achieve by those policies. Each firm then offers households of type i a combination $\{p_i, P_i\}$ to maximize profits, given the utility level achieved elsewhere and anticipating household behavior in stage 3. Thus, the problem of a representative insurance firm with respect to each type i can be written as

$$\max_{P_i, p_i}\{P_i - \pi_i[x_i(a_i - P_i, s_i + p_i)]p_i z_i(a_i - P_i, s_i + p_i)\}$$

$$\text{s.t.} \quad v_i(a_i - P_i, s_i + p_i) \geq \bar{v}^i, \tag{11}$$

where $\bar{v}^i$ is given by the industry as a whole. In market equilibrium, all firms behave identically and profits are driven to zero by free entry. In effect, the industry-wide utility level $\bar{v}^i$ is competed up until profits equal zero. Thus, equilibrium in the insurance industry can be characterized as the solution to the following problem using the zero-profit condition, which is dual to the individual firm's problem:

$$\max_{P_i, p_i}\{v_i(a_i - P_i, s_i + p_i)\}$$

$$\text{s.t.} \quad P_i = \pi_i[x_i(a_i - P_i, s_i + p_i)]p_i z_i(a_i - P_i, s_i + p_i). \tag{12}$$

The Lagrangean expression is

$$\mathcal{L} = v_i(a_i - P_i, s_i + p_i) + \lambda_i\{P_i - \pi_i[x_i(a_i - P_i, s_i + p_i)]p_i z_i(a_i - P_i, s_i + p_i)\}.$$
(13)

The first-order conditions for this problem are

$$P_i: v_p^i + \lambda_i(1 - \pi_i p_i z_p^i - p_i z_i \pi_i' x_p^i) = 0,$$
(14)

$$p_i: v_p^i - \lambda_i(\pi_i z_i + \pi_i p_i z_p^i + p_i z_i \pi_i' x_p^i) = 0,$$
(15)

where v_p^i and v_p^i are given by (9) and (10) in anticipation of stage 3. The solution to this problem gives $P_i(a_i, s_i)$ and $p_i(a_i, s_i)$, and the value function is defined as $V_i(a_i, s_i)$. Note that because of the moral hazard problem, $p_i < 1$, since $p_i = 1$ leads to z_i being indefinitely high. Also, as long as $s_i < 1$, $p_i > 0$ generally. Indeed, at $p_i = 0$, $d\mathcal{L}/dp_i = \pi_i z_i (u_{c1}^i - E[u_c^i])$ and it is plausible to assume that $u_{c1}^i > u_{c0}^i$ since one can expect that $c_i^1 < c_i^0$. It is noteworthy that if $s_i < 1$, inequality $p_i > 0$ always holds with a quasi-linear specification of the utility function, $u[c + h - g(\ell)]$. Again applying the Envelope Theorem to this problem, we obtain

$$V_a^i = v_a^i - \lambda_i[\pi_i p_i z_a^i + p_i z_i \pi_i' x_a^i] = \lambda_i,$$
(16)

$$V_s^i = v_s^i - \lambda_i[\pi_i p_i z_s^i + p_i z_i \pi_i' x_s^i] = \lambda_i \pi_i z_i,$$
(17)

where we have used (9), (10), and the first-order conditions for P_i and p_i.

11.3.3 Stage 1: Government Policy

The government chooses lump-sum taxes a_i and public insurance s_i to maximize the sum of utilities subject to its budget constraint, anticipating the outcomes of the subsequent two stages. Thus, its objective function is $\sum f_i V_i(a_i, s_i)$ and its budget constraint is

$$\sum f_i\{a_i + s_i \pi_i[x_i(a_i - P_i(a_i, s_i), s_i + p_i(a_i, s_i))]$$
$$\times z_i[a_i - P_i(a_i, s_i), s_i + p_i(a_i, s_i)]\} = 0.$$
(18)

The Lagrangean expression is

$$\mathcal{L} = \sum_{i=1}^{n} f_i V_i(a_i, s_i) - \gamma \sum_{i=1}^{n} f_i\{a_i + s_i \pi_i[x_i(a_i - P_i(a_i, s_i), s_i + p_i(a_i, s_i))]$$
$$\times z_i[a_i - P_i(a_i, s_i), s_i + p_i(a_i, s_i)]\}.$$
(19)

The first-order conditions are, using the envelope results (16) and (17) from stage 2,

$$a_i: \lambda_i - \gamma \left[1 + s_i \pi_i \frac{dz_i}{da_i} + s_i z_i \pi_i' \frac{dx_i}{da_i} \right] = 0, \tag{20}$$

$$s_i: \lambda_i \pi_i z_i - \gamma \left[\pi_i z_i + s_i \pi_i \frac{dz_i}{ds_i} + s_i z_i \pi_i' \frac{dx_i}{ds_i} \right] = 0. \tag{21}$$

Note that the total effects of a_i and s_i on z_i and x_i take into account the effect that government policies will have on private insurance coverage and premiums. Combining these two conditions, we obtain

$$\gamma s_i \left[\pi_i \left(\frac{dz_i}{ds_i} - \pi_i z_i \frac{dz_i}{da_i} \right) + \pi_i' z_i \left(\frac{dx_i}{ds_i} - \pi_i z_i \frac{dx_i}{da_i} \right) \right] = 0. \tag{22}$$

Therefore, $s_i = 0$: *There is no role for public insurance in the full-information benchmark.*[11] That also means that there would be no role for social insurance s that would not discriminate among households of different types.[12] Blomqvist and Horn (1984) reach the same conclusion in a framework similar to ours where there is, however, no moral hazard.[13] Also, from the first-order condition on a_i, $s_i = 0$ implies $\lambda_i = \gamma$ for all households. Therefore, from the first-order conditions on P_i from stage 2, and using (9), we obtain

$$E[u_c^i] = \gamma[1 + \pi_i p_i z_a^i + p_i z_i \pi_i' x_a^i]. \tag{23}$$

Thus, the government does not equalize expected utilities in the full-information case because of the moral hazard problem.

We turn now to the case where the government is imperfectly informed and is restricted to pursuing its redistributive objectives using a linear progressive tax.

11.4   The Case without Moral Hazard

It is useful also to consider the case where there is no moral hazard of either type. Assume for simplicity that, unlike the previous case, there is only one value of curative expenditures $\hat{z}$ and that it fully restores health status in the ill-health state. That is, $\hat{z}$ is such that $h^1 = \bar{h} + m(\hat{z}) = h^0$. Assume also that π_i is exogenously fixed for all i. There is a private insurance market that offers households coverage p_i and charges a premium P_i adjusted to their illness probability, so that $P_i = \pi_i p_i \hat{z}$.

Suppose first that there is public insurance that covers a proportion s of expenditures $\hat{z}$, and that households can purchase private insurance freely. We omit explicit consideration of the insurance industry here because the absence of moral hazard makes the solution of the stage 2 problem straightforward. It is clear that a competitive insurance industry would replicate the extent of coverage most preferred by each type of household. With a linear income tax, we can now write the expected utility of each household of type i as

$$U^i = \pi_i u[(1-t)w_i\ell_i^1 + a - \pi_i p_i\hat{z} - (1-s-p_i)\hat{z}, h^1, \ell_i^1]$$
$$+ (1-\pi_i)u[(1-t)w_i\ell_i^0 + a - \pi_i p_i\hat{z}, h^0, \ell_i^0]. \tag{24}$$

Focusing first on the choice of p_i, we obtain, by differentiating U^i,

$$\frac{\partial U^i}{\partial p_i} = \pi_i\hat{z}(u_{c1}^i - E[u_c^i]). \tag{25}$$

As long as there is less than full insurance, we have $u_{c1}^i > E[u_c^i]$. This implies that $\partial U^i/\partial p_i > 0$ for any value of $p_i < 1-s$. Therefore, as is well-known, in the absence of moral hazard, it is optimal for all households to choose full insurance coverage, $p_i = 1-s$ for any s. In addition to their private insurance coverage, households choose their labor supplies conditional on the two health states, $\ell_i^j(t,a,s)$ for $j = 0,1$. If there is full insurance, consumption and labor supply are identical in the two states of health. However, to keep the analysis as general as possible, we continue to distinguish the two states of health.

Let us now look at the optimal behavior of the public sector. It will implement a linear progressive tax for redistributive reasons. The question is whether it will also want to intervene in insurance markets. If it does, we know that whatever the value of s, households choose their private insurance coverage so that their health expenditures are fully reimbursed ($p_i = 1-s$).

Given the tax parameters t and a and social insurance coverage s, the government revenue constraint is simply

$$\sum f_i\{\pi_i tw_i\ell_i^1(t,a,s) + (1-\pi_i)tw_i\ell_i^0(t,a,s) - \pi_i s\hat{z} - a\} = 0. \tag{26}$$

The Lagrangean expression for the government's problem can then be written as

$$\mathcal{L} = \sum f_i \{ \pi_i u[w_i(1-t)\ell_i^1(\cdot) + a - \pi_i p_i(\cdot)\hat{z} - (1-s-p_i(\cdot))\hat{z}, h^1, \ell_i^1(\cdot)]$$
$$+ (1-\pi_i)u[w_i(1-t)\ell_i^0(\cdot) + a - \pi_i p_i(\cdot)\hat{z}, h^0, \ell_i^0(\cdot)]$$
$$+ \gamma[\pi_i tw_i \ell_i^1(\cdot) + (1-\pi_i)tw_i\ell_i^0(\cdot) - a - \pi_i s\hat{z}]\}, \tag{27}$$

where γ is the Lagrange multiplier associated with the revenue constraint and $(\cdot) = (t, a, s)$.

Using the Envelope Theorem, the first-order conditions can be written as

$$\frac{\partial \mathcal{L}}{\partial s} = \sum f_i \left\{ \pi_i \hat{z} u_{c1}^i + \gamma \pi_i tw_i \frac{\partial \ell_i^1}{\partial s} \right\} - \gamma \bar{\pi}\hat{z} = 0, \tag{28}$$

$$\frac{\partial \mathcal{L}}{\partial a} = \sum f_i \left\{ E[u_c^i] + \gamma \left(tw_i E\left[\frac{\partial \ell_i}{\partial a}\right] - 1 \right) \right\} = 0, \tag{29}$$

$$\frac{\partial \mathcal{L}}{\partial t} = \sum f_i \left\{ -E[w_i \ell_i u_c^i] + \gamma \left(tw_i E\left[\frac{\partial \ell_i}{\partial t}\right] + w_i E[\ell_i] \right) \right\} = 0, \tag{30}$$

where $\bar{\pi} = \sum f_i \pi_i$. We can rewrite (29) as follows:

$$\bar{b} \equiv \sum f_i E[b_i] \equiv \sum f_i[\pi_i b_i^1 + (1-\pi_i)b_i^0] = 1, \tag{31}$$

where

$$b_i^j = \frac{u_{cj}^i}{\gamma} + tw_i \frac{\partial \ell_i^j}{\partial a} \quad \text{for } j = 0, 1 \tag{32}$$

is the so-called net marginal social utility of income of type i households in state of health j. Note that in the case of complete insurance, $b_i^1 = b_i^0$ (since health status, consumption, and labor supply are identical in the two states) and $\bar{b}^1 = \bar{b} = 1$, with $\bar{b}^1 \equiv \sum f_i b_i^1$. Using these definitions and subtracting (29) multiplied by $\bar{\pi}\hat{z}$ from (28) yields[14]

$$\frac{\partial \mathcal{L}}{\partial s} \frac{1}{\gamma \hat{z}} = \text{cov}[b_i^1, \pi_i]. \tag{33}$$

Whether it is optimal to have some public coverage of health expenditures therefore depends upon the sign of $\text{cov}[b_i^1, \pi_i]$. Suppose that π_i and w_i are negatively correlated. Then π_i and b_i^1 are positively correlated, and as a consequence it is desirable to push s up to its ceiling value, namely unity.[15] When $s = 1$, there is no need for private insurance. This result, which is the polar opposite of the full-information case, is that obtained by Rochet (1989) and Cremer and Pestieau (1996).

Even though this is not our main concern, we can also derive the optimal tax formula from (29) and (30):

$$t = \frac{-\text{cov}[E[b_i], E[w_i\ell_i]]}{\sum f_i w_i E[\partial \tilde{\ell}_i / \partial \omega_i]}, \tag{34}$$

where $\omega_i = w_i(1 - t)$ and $\partial \tilde{\ell}_i^j / \partial \omega_i$ is the compensated derivative of labor supply of a type i household in state j. This expression is standard, with the numerator being the equity term and the denominator the efficiency term. Note that since health expenditures are fully reimbursed, (34) could be simplified by dropping the expected value operator.

The weakness of the preceding analysis is that it implicitly assumes that both social and private insurance have no influence on the size of the loss, z, to be compensated, nor on the probability, π, of loss. We now turn to these two possibilities. Thus, the amount of the loss that can be recouped depends on each agent's behavior, and the probability of the loss is also the responsibility of each agent. With these two additions, we will see that full insurance is no longer desirable. It is useful to treat the two sorts of moral hazard separately.

11.5 Ex Post Moral Hazard

Here, we assume that the π_is are given (and either negatively or positively correlated with wages, w_i), but that individuals can influence their health status following an illness. By investing in curative expenditures z_i, they can reach a health status $h^1 = \bar{h} + m(z_i) < h^0$. A proportion of expenditure on health improvement is covered by social insurance (s) and another by private insurance (p_i). As before, we solve for the subgame-perfect equilibrium by backward induction.

11.5.1 Stage 3: Household Choice

Households of type i take as given government policies a, t, and s and private insurance policy parameters p_i and P_i. The budget constraints in the two states of health are now

$$c_i^1 = (1 - t)w_i\ell_i^1 + a - (1 - \sigma_i)z_i - P_i, \tag{35}$$

$$c_i^0 = (1 - t)w_i\ell_i^0 + a - P_i. \tag{36}$$

The problem for a type i household is

$$\max_{\ell_i^j, z_i}\{\pi_i u[(1-t)w_i\ell_i^1 + a - (1-\sigma_i)z_i - P_i, \bar{h} + m(z_i), \ell_i^1]$$

$$+ (1-\pi_i)u[(1-t)w_i\ell_i^0 + a - P_i, h^0, \ell_i^0]\}. \tag{37}$$

The first-order conditions are

$$\ell_i^j: (1-t)w_i u_{cj}^i + u_{\ell j}^i = 0 \text{ for } j = 0,1, \tag{38}$$

$$z_i: -(1-\sigma_i)u_{c1}^i + m'(z_i)u_{h1}^i = 0. \tag{39}$$

The solution to this problem yields $\ell_i^0(t, a - P_i), \ell_i^1(t, a - P_i, s + p_i)$, $z_i(t, a - P_i, s + p_i)$, and the indirect utility function $v_i(t, a - P_i, s + p_i)$. Applying the Envelope Theorem gives

$$v_t^i = -E[w_i\ell_i u_c^i], \tag{40}$$

$$v_a^i = -v_P^i = E[u_c^i], \tag{41}$$

$$v_s^i = v_p^i = \pi_i z_i u_{c1}^i. \tag{42}$$

11.5.2   Stage 2: Insurance Market Equilibrium

As before, insurance industry equilibrium can be characterized as the outcome from choosing private coverage p_i and premiums P_i to maximize household expected utility by type, subject to a type-specific zero profit (or actuarial fairness) condition, and anticipating the consequences for stage 3. The insurance equilibrium for a type i household is the solution to the maximization of the following Lagrangean:

$$\mathcal{L} = v_i(t, a - P_i, s + p_i) + \lambda_i[P_i - \pi_i p_i z_i(t, a - P_i, s + p_i)]. \tag{43}$$

The first-order conditions for this problem are

$$P_i: v_P^i + \lambda_i[1 - \pi_i p_i z_P^i] = 0, \tag{44}$$

$$p_i: v_p^i - \lambda_i[\pi_i z_i + \pi_i p_i z_p^i] = 0, \tag{45}$$

where $v_P^i = -E[u_c^i]$ and $v_p^i = \pi_i z_i u_{c1}^i$ from (41) and (42). The solution to this problem gives $P_i(t, a, s)$ and $p_i(t, a, s)$. As already mentioned in section 11.3, it is plausible that $p_i > 0$ as long as $s < 1$. The maximum value function for this problem is defined as $V_i(t, a, s)$. By the Envelope Theorem, we obtain its properties:

$$V_t^i = -E[w_i \ell_i u_c^i] - \lambda_i \pi_i p_i z_t^i, \tag{46}$$

$$V_a^i = \lambda_i, \tag{47}$$

$$V_s^i = \lambda_i \pi_i z_i, \tag{48}$$

where we have used the first-order conditions on P_i and p_i as well as (40), (41), and (42).

11.5.3 Stage 1: Government Policy

The government chooses the linear tax parameters, t and a, and the level of social insurance, s, to maximize the sum of utilities subject to its budget constraint, anticipating the outcomes of the subsequent stages. The Lagrangean expression is

$$\mathcal{L} = \sum f_i V_i(t, a, s) + \gamma \sum \{ t w_i [\pi_i \ell_i^1(t, a - P_i(\cdot), s + p_i(\cdot)) $$
$$+ (1 - \pi_i) \ell_i^0(t, a - P_i(\cdot))] - a - s \pi_i z_i(t, a - P_i(\cdot), s + p_i(\cdot)) \}, \tag{49}$$

where $P_i(t, a, s)$ and $p_i(t, a, s)$ are determined in stage 2.

The first-order conditions are

$$t: \quad \sum f_i V_t^i + \gamma \sum f_i \left\{ w_i E[\ell_i] + t w_i E\left[\frac{d\ell_i}{dt}\right] - s \pi_i \frac{dz_i}{dt} \right\} = 0, \tag{50}$$

$$a: \quad \sum f_i V_a^i + \gamma \sum f_i \left\{ -1 + t w_i E\left[\frac{d\ell_i}{da}\right] - s \pi_i \frac{dz_i}{da} \right\} = 0, \tag{51}$$

$$s: \quad \sum f_i V_s^i + \gamma \sum f_i \left\{ -\pi_i z_i + t w_i E\left[\frac{d\ell_i}{ds}\right] - s \pi_i \frac{dz_i}{ds} \right\} = 0. \tag{52}$$

Using (46), (47), and (48), these can be rewritten as

$$\sum f_i \left\{ \frac{E[w_i \ell_i u_c^i] + \lambda_i \pi_i p_i z_t^i}{\gamma} - w_i E[\ell_i] - t w_i E\left[\frac{d\ell_i}{dt}\right] + s \pi_i \frac{dz_i}{dt} \right\} = 0, \tag{53}$$

$$\sum f_i \left\{ \frac{\lambda_i}{\gamma} - 1 + t w_i E\left[\frac{d\ell_i}{da}\right] - s \pi_i \frac{dz_i}{da} \right\} = 0, \tag{54}$$

$$\sum f_i \left\{ \frac{\lambda_i}{\gamma} \pi_i z_i - \pi_i z_i + t w_i E\left[\frac{d\ell_i}{ds}\right] - s \pi_i \frac{dz_i}{ds} \right\} = 0. \tag{55}$$

From (54), we obtain

$$\sum f_i E[b_i] = \bar{b} = 1, \tag{56}$$

where $b_i^j = \lambda_i/\gamma + tw_i[d\ell_i^j/da] - s\pi_i[dz_i/da]$ is the net marginal social utility of income for a type i person in state of health j. Next, combining (53) and (55), we obtain

$$E[b_i\pi_i z_i] - \bar{b}E[\pi_i z_i] - s\sum f_i\pi_i\left[\frac{dz_i}{ds} - \pi_i z_i\frac{dz_i}{da}\right]$$

$$+ t\sum f_i w_i E\left[\frac{d\ell_i}{ds} - \pi_i z_i\frac{d\ell_i}{da}\right] = 0 \tag{57}$$

or

$$s = \frac{\text{cov}[E[b_i], \pi_i z_i]}{\sum f_i\pi_i \, d\tilde{z}_i/ds} + \frac{t\sum f_i w_i E[d\tilde{\ell}_i/ds]}{\sum f_i\pi_i \, d\tilde{z}_i/ds}, \tag{58}$$

where $d\tilde{z}_i/ds = dz_i/ds - \pi_i z_i \, dz_i/da$ is a compensated total demand derivative, and similarly for $d\tilde{\ell}_i/ds$. These are total demand derivatives since, for example, dz_i/ds is the total derivative of z_i with respect to s, meaning that z_i is a function not only of s but also of P_i and p_i, which are in turn functions of s. Indeed, an increase in s causes p_i and P_i to fall, which is accounted for in these total derivatives.

Equation (58) consists of two terms. The first term is analogous to the standard expression for the optimal marginal tax rate as in (34) earlier. The denominator is the efficiency term and gives the compensated effect of an increase in s (financed by a state-invariant lump-sum tax) on curative expenditures. We expect this term to be positive, though it is not necessarily so. The larger it is, the smaller is the value of s. The numerator—the covariance between the expected marginal social utility of income, $E[b_i]$, and $\pi_i z_i$—is the equity term. If, as in Rochet (1989), the covariance between $E[b_i]$ and π_i is positive, we still have to verify if taking $\pi_i z_i$ instead of π_i changes the sign. If we assume that π_i and w_i are "sufficiently" negatively correlated and that z_i does not increase much with w_i, then the covariance term is positive.

The second term in (58) is related to a second-best effect. Changes in s induce indirect changes in the deadweight loss due to the distortion imposed by the marginal tax rate t. If ℓ increases with s, an increase in s will indirectly increase tax revenues. Since the social value of an additional unit of tax revenues is greater than one, this would enhance the case for social insurance.[16]

In general, it is difficult to say whether (58) yields s greater or less than zero,[17] despite the fact that in the absence of moral hazard, we earlier obtained $s = 1$. More precise results can be obtained only by using specific functional forms. Consider, for example, the quasi-linear case introduced earlier, $u[c_i^j + h_i^j - g(\ell_i^j)]$. In this case, labor supply is independent of s. Moreover, z_i depends only on $\sigma_i = s + p_i$. More precisely, $dz_i/d\sigma_i = -1/m''(z_i) > 0$. Thus, (58) reduces to

$$s = \frac{\text{cov}[E[b_i], \pi_i z_i]}{\sum f_i \pi_i \, d\tilde{z}_i/ds} = \frac{\text{cov}[E[b_i], \pi_i z_i]}{-\sum f_i \pi_i (1 + \partial p_i/\partial s - \pi_i z_i \partial p_i/\partial a)/m''(z_i)}. \tag{59}$$

In the appendix, we show that for this quasi-linear utility function, $\partial p_i/\partial s - \pi_i z_i \partial p_i/\partial a > -1$, so that the denominator of (59) is positive. Then, assuming that the correlation between π_i and w_i is negative enough for the covariance term to be positive, the optimal value of s will be positive. However, unlike in Rochet (1989), $s < 1$ because of moral hazard. This can be seen from (52). As s approaches 1, z_i goes to ∞, so that $\partial \mathcal{L}/\partial s$ becomes negative.

11.6 Ex Ante Moral Hazard

Ex ante moral hazard involves preventive expenditures that can affect the probability of illness. For simplicity, we assume that, as in section 11.4, curative expenditures are fixed at the level $\hat{z}$, and thus the good health status h^0 is also attained in the ill-health state. We can thus exclude the health status variable from the utility function. We proceed as usual by backward induction, looking first at the household's choices, then at private insurance market equilibrium, and finally at the government's optimization.

11.6.1 Stage 3: Household Choice

Given government policies a, t, and s and private insurance policies p_i and P_i, each type i household solves the following problem:

$$\max_{x_i, \ell_i^j} \{\pi_i(x_i) u[(1-t)w_i\ell_i^1 + a - x_i - (1 - \sigma_i)\hat{z} - P_i, \ell_i^1]$$

$$+ [1 - \pi_i(x_i)] u[(1-t)w_i\ell_i^0 + a - x_i - P_i, \ell_i^0]\}. \tag{60}$$

The first-order conditions are assumed to be interior and are given by

$$\ell_i^j: (1-t)w_i u_{cj}^i + u_{\ell j}^i = 0 \text{ for } j = 0, 1, \tag{61}$$

$$x_i: \pi_i'(x_i)[u^i(1) - u^i(0)] - E[u_c^i] = 0, \tag{62}$$

where $u^i(j)$ is the utility level achieved in state $j = 0, 1$. This yields supply functions $\ell_i^0(t, a - P_i)$ and $\ell_i^1(t, a - P_i, s + p_i)$, $x_i(t, a - P_i, s + p_i)$, and the indirect utility function $v_i(t, a - P_i, s + p_i)$. Applying the Envelope Theorem gives Roy's identities:

$$v_t^i = -E[w_i \ell_i u_c^i], \tag{63}$$

$$v_a^i = -v_P^i = E[u_c^i], \tag{64}$$

$$v_s^i = v_p^i = \pi_i(x_i)\hat{z}u_{c1}^i. \tag{65}$$

11.6.2 Stage 2: Insurance Market Equilibrium

In equilibrium, insurance policies offered by the private sector to type i households maximize

$$\mathscr{L} = v_i(t, a - P_i, s + p_i) + \lambda_i\{P_i - \pi_i[x_i(t, a - P_i, s + p_i)]p_i\hat{z}\}. \tag{66}$$

The first-order conditions for this problem are

$$P_i: v_P^i + \lambda_i[1 - p_i\hat{z}\pi_i'(x_i)x_P^i] = 0, \tag{67}$$

$$p_i: v_p^i - \lambda_i[\pi_i(x_i)\hat{z} + p_i\hat{z}\pi_i'(x_i)x_p^i] = 0, \tag{68}$$

where $v_P^i = -E[u_c^i]$ and $v_p^i = \pi_i(x_i)\hat{z}u_{c1}^i$ from (64) and (65). The solution to this problem gives $P_i(t, a, s)$ and $p_i(t, a, s)$, where, as before, it is plausible that $p_i > 0$ as long as $s < 1$. The maximum value function is $V_i(t, a, s)$. By the Envelope Theorem and using (63), (64), and (65), we obtain its properties:

$$V_t^i = -E[w_i \ell_i u_c^i] - \lambda_i p_i\hat{z}\pi_i'(x_i)x_t^i, \tag{69}$$

$$V_a^i = \lambda_i, \tag{70}$$

$$V_s^i = \lambda_i\pi_i(x_i)\hat{z}. \tag{71}$$

11.6.3 Stage 1: Government Policy

As usual, the government chooses $\{t, a, s\}$ to maximize a utilitarian social welfare function subject to its budget constraint and the reaction functions of the private sector. The Lagrangean expression is

$$\mathscr{L} = \sum f_i V_i(t, a, s) + \gamma \sum f_i\{tw_i[\pi_i(x_i(\cdot))\ell_i^1(\cdot) + (1 - \pi_i(\cdot))\ell_i^0(\cdot)]$$
$$- a - s\pi_i(x_i(\cdot))\hat{z}\}, \tag{72}$$

where $(\cdot) = (t, a - P_i(t,a,s), s + p_i(t,a,s))$, in which $P_i(t,a,s)$ and $p_i(t,a,s)$ are determined in stage 2. Proceeding exactly as before, rearrangement of the first-order conditions yields the analog of (58):

$$s = \frac{\text{cov}[E[b_i], \pi_i(x_i)\hat{z}]}{\sum f_i \hat{z}\pi_i'(x_i)\, d\tilde{x}_i/ds} + \frac{t\sum f_i w_i E[d\tilde{\ell}_i/ds]}{\sum f_i \hat{z}\pi_i'(x_i)\, d\tilde{x}_i/ds},\qquad(73)$$

where $b_i^j = \lambda_i/\gamma + tw_i[d\ell_i^j/da] - s\hat{z}\pi_i'[dx_i/da]$. Note that all indirect effects on the government budget of changing a are accounted for, including those through induced changes in the probability π_i.

The interpretation of the terms in this expression is identical to that for (58) in the ex post moral hazard case. The denominator—the efficiency term involving the effect of social insurance on preventive expenditures—is expected to be positive, since $\pi_i' < 0$ and we expect that a compensated increase in s will reduce preventive expenditures. The equity effect, reflected in the covariance term, is positive provided that x_i is normal, given that $\pi_i(x_i)$ decreases as w_i increases and that π_i is not positively correlated with w_i. The second term reflects the indirect, or second-best, effect. Its sign depends upon how labor supplies are affected by changes in the social insurance rate s.

In general, it is difficult to sign s from (73), especially given the fact that the derivatives of ℓ_i and x_i are total ones.[18] It is instructive again to consider as a special case that of quasi-linear preferences, which are here given simply by $u[c_i^j - g(\ell_i^j)]$ since health status is the same in both states. In this case, (73) reduces to

$$s = \frac{\text{cov}[E[b_i], \pi_i(x_i)\hat{z}]}{\sum f_i \hat{z}\pi_i'(x_i)\, d\tilde{x}_i/ds}.\qquad(74)$$

It can be shown by a comparative static analysis of household and insurance industry behavior that a sufficient condition for $s > 0$ is that private insurance is a normal good.

11.7   Administrative Costs

As mentioned, it has been documented that there are administrative costs of operating a competitive insurance industry that may be avoided by a single-payer government system. Administrative costs effectively increase the cost of private insurance relative to a public scheme. There are two consequences of this. First, and most obviously, the attractiveness of social insurance is enhanced relative to private insurance, despite the informational disadvantages the public sector might face. Second, from the fact that the cost of private insurance is not actuarially fair, it is no longer the case that all households will necessarily purchase private insurance. To illustrate this, we employ the case of ex post moral hazard. The model is the same as in section 11.5 except for the administrative costs associated with private insurance. In particular, we assume that there is a loading factor equal to a proportion $k \geq 0$ of insurance premiums.[19] The no-profit condition then becomes $P_i = (1 + k)\pi_i p_i z_i$.

The same three stages of decision making apply. Household behavior in stage 3 is essentially the same as before, with Roy's identities from (40), (41), and (42) applying. In stage 2, the insurance market equilibrium for type i households solves

$$\max_{P_i, p_i}\{v_i(t, a - P_i, s + p_i)\}$$

$$\text{s.t.} \quad P_i = (1 + k)\pi_i p_i z_i(t, a - P_i, s + p_i). \tag{75}$$

We can no longer be sure that there will be an interior solution for p_i, even if $s = 0$. That is, a nonnegative constraint on coverage, $p_i \geq 0$, may be binding. Given that, the first-order conditions for this problem are

$$P_i: v_p^i + \lambda_i[1 - (1 + k)\pi_i p_i z_p^i] = 0, \tag{76}$$

$$p_i: v_p^i - \lambda_i(1 + k)[\pi_i z_i + \pi_i p_i z_p^i] \leq 0, \tag{77}$$

where the inequality holds if the constraint $p_i \geq 0$ is binding. We might expect that higher-wage groups will demand greater coverage. In fact, a comparative static analysis on these first-order conditions reveals that, in general, it is not clear on which income groups the inequality constraint is binding. That is, $\partial p_i / \partial w_i \lessgtr 0$. It turns out that, as in the appendix, a sufficient condition for $\partial p_i / \partial w_i > 0$ is the familiar one that private insurance is a normal good. In any case, the solution to this problem gives $P_i(t, a, s)$ and $p_i(t, a, s)$, along with the value function $V_i(t, a, s)$. By the Envelope Theorem, we obtain, in the usual way,

$$V_t^i = -E[w_i \ell_i u_c^i] - \lambda_i(1 + k)\pi_i p_i z_t^i, \tag{78}$$

$$V_a^i = \lambda_i, \tag{79}$$

$$V_s^i \le (1+k)\lambda_i \pi_i z_i, \tag{80}$$

where the inequality holds when $p_i \ge 0$ is binding.

Let I_0 be the set of household types i such that the constraint $p_i \ge 0$ is binding, that is, the set that purchases no private insurance. Then government optimization yields a set of conditions analogous to (53), (54), and (55). Solving them for s, we obtain

$$s = \left\{ \sum f_i \pi_i \, d\tilde{z}_i / ds \right\}^{-1} \left\{ \operatorname{cov}[E[b_i], \pi_i z_i] + t \sum f_i w_i E\left[\frac{d\tilde{\ell}_i}{ds} \right] \right.$$

$$\left. + k \sum_{i \notin I_0} f_i \pi_i z_i \lambda_i / \gamma + \sum_{i \in I_0} f_i \pi_i z_i (u_{c1}^i - E[u_c^i]) / \gamma \right\}. \tag{81}$$

The denominator on the right-hand side of (81) and the first two terms in the numerator are the same as before. They capture respectively the efficiency, the equity, and the second-best indirect effects. As before, they have ambiguous signs except in special cases. We expect the denominator and the equity term to be positive, but in general these terms are all ambiguous. The second-best term, reflecting the indirect effect of changes in s on the deadweight loss of taxation, will disappear if the utility function is quasi-linear in consumption and health status. The last two terms of the numerator are related to the inefficiency of private insurance; they vanish if $k = 0$. The term involving k reflects the efficiency cost of having individuals purchase expensive private insurance. The term involving those households that are quantity-constrained ($i \in I_0$) reflects the benefits of providing social insurance to those households for which private insurance coverage is too expensive. Overall, since the last two terms are both positive, the existence of administrative costs of private insurance tends to enhance the case for public insurance coverage s, which is not surprising.

11.8   Conclusion

The starting point of this chapter was the finding of Rochet (1989) that with distortionary income taxation, social insurance is desirable as a redistributive device. The gist of his argument was the distortionary feature of income taxation. With a nondistortionary redistributive tax, there would be no need for social insurance as long as it is not cheaper than market-provided insurance. One of our purposes was to see how robust this finding was when introducing moral hazard.

We distinguished between ex ante and ex post moral hazard and showed that the case for public intervention in insurance markets remains. However, while in Rochet's analysis optimal social insurance is complete and crowds out private insurance, in the presence of moral hazard it is no longer the case. Public and private insurance will generally exist side by side. Moreover, it is no longer necessarily the case that optimal social insurance rates be positive. That is even true in the case where there is a negative correlation between productivity and the expected value of spending incurred to correct for the loss. We also introduced the idea that social insurance could be less costly than private insurance. This clearly strengthens the case for social insurance and increases the chances that it should be positive.

A number of extensions to the current analysis could be contemplated. First, it might be interesting to see whether or not an optimal nonlinear tax would dampen the case for social insurance. Evidence from related literature suggests that even when nonlinear taxes are set optimally, the case for second-best policy instruments typically remains intact. Second, for the case of ex ante moral hazard, we could consider the possibility of subsidizing preventive spending. Third, the viewpoint adopted here was purely normative. It would be interesting to adopt a political economy approach, with social insurance being determined by voting.[20] Finally, instead of treating both types of moral hazard separately, it would be useful to combine them in a single model, although that will certainly increase the complexity without resolving the ambiguity.

Appendix

In this appendix, we assume that the utility function is quasi-linear and derive the comparative statics for p_i under ex post moral hazard. These will then be used to show the necessary conditions to have a positive value for s.

If the utility function is $u[c_i^j + h_i^j - g(l_i^j)]$, the first-order conditions for the household's problem simplify to

$$(1 - t)w_i - g'(l_i^j) = 0, \tag{82}$$

$$-(1 - \sigma_i) + m'(z_i) = 0, \tag{83}$$

and solve as $l_i^1 = l_i^0 = l[(1-t)w]$ and $z_i = z(\sigma_i)$. Thus, labor supply depends only on net-of-tax wages and is state-independent, and curative expenditures only depend on the coverage rate. Using these results, the stage 2 first-order condition on p_i can then be written as

$$\Delta \equiv u_{c1}^i z_i + E[u_c^i](z_i + p_i z_p) = 0. \tag{84}$$

Differentiation of this expression yields

$$\Delta_{p_i}\, dp_i + \Delta_{w_i}\, dw_i + \Delta_{\pi_i}\, d\pi_i + \Delta_a\, da + \Delta_t\, dt + \Delta_s\, ds = 0, \tag{85}$$

with

$$\Delta_a = u_{c1c1}^i z_i - E[u_{cc}^i](z_i + p_i z_p^i), \tag{86}$$

$$\Delta_t = -w_i l_i \Delta_a, \tag{87}$$

$$\Delta_s = \pi_i p_i z_p^i \Delta_a + z_i u_{c1c1}^i [z_i - \pi_i(z_i + p_i z_p^i)] + E[u_c^i](z_p^i + p_i z_{pp}^i) - u_{c1}^i z_i p_i, \tag{88}$$

$$\Delta_{w_i} = (1-t)l\Delta_a, \tag{89}$$

$$\Delta_{\pi_i} = -p_i z_i \Delta_a - (u_{c1}^i - u_{c0}^i)c(z_i + p_i z_p^i), \tag{90}$$

$$\Delta_{p_i} = \Delta_s - \pi_i z_i \Delta_a - E[u_c^i]z_p^i < 0 \text{ (by the SOC).} \tag{91}$$

In general, the effects of the exogenous variables on the sign of p_i are ambiguous. However, if we assume that private insurance is a normal good (i.e., $\partial p_i/\partial a > 0$), $\Delta_a > 0$ and thus we have

$$\frac{\partial p_i}{\partial a} > 0, \frac{\partial p_i}{\partial t} < 0, \frac{\partial p_i}{\partial s} > -1, \frac{\partial p_i}{\partial w_i} > 0, \text{ and } \frac{\partial p_i}{\partial \pi_i} > 0 \text{ (by the SOC).} \tag{92}$$

Note that even though an increase in s may raise or lower p_i, total coverage σ_i ($=s+p_i$) increases: There is less than complete crowding out of private insurance. As well, using the previous comparative static effects,

$$1 + \frac{\partial p_i}{\partial s} - \pi_i z_i \frac{\partial p_i}{\partial a} = \frac{1}{-\Delta_{p_i}}\{Eu_c^i z_p^i\}, \tag{93}$$

which is positive. Therefore, the compensated effect of a change of s in z_i ($d\tilde z_i/ds$) is also positive. Thus, the denominator in expression (59) is positive, guaranteeing that, with a positive covariance term, social insurance coverage is never negative.

Notes

We are grateful for comments by Gabrielle Demange, Dominique Demougin, Louis Eeckhoudt, and two referees. This chapter presents research results of the Belgian Program on Interuniversity Poles of Attraction initiated by the Belgian State, Prime Minister's Office, Science Policy Programming. The scientific responsibility is assumed by the authors.

1. The idea of the theory of second-best has been around for a long time. Elements of it may be found, for example, in the work on public sector pricing by Boiteux (1956), in the taxation literature by Hotelling (1932) and Harberger (1964), and in the trade literature by Meade (1955). For a survey of the theory of second-best and its relation to public economics, see Boadway (1997).

2. The most complete summary of this can be found in Drèze and Stern (1987).

3. The modified Samuelson rule reflecting linear tax distortions was obtained by Atkinson and Stern (1974). The further modification to incorporate equity considerations may be seen in Atkinson and Stiglitz (1980).

4. Guesnerie (1995) provides the most comprehensive account of the relationship between asymmetric information and distortionary taxation.

5. These costs are linked to the small scale of private insurance firms and to their advertisement costs. On this, see Diamond (1992) and Mitchell (1998). The point goes back to Arrow (1963).

6. See also Petretto (1999).

7. The paper by Blomqvist and Horn (1984) bears some similarities to this chapter even though it is not concerned with moral hazard. These authors also examine the case of public insurance when actuarially fair private insurance is available and individuals differ in both labor productivity and illness probability. No labor is supplied when ill, and public insurance consists of a uniform lump-sum benefit to the ill.

8. That is, there is no adverse selection. Our assumptions are generally designed to ensure that private insurance firms can provide insurance efficiently, thereby eliminating insurance market failure as a reason for government intervention.

9. A natural extension of this modeling would be to have the labor supply falling to zero in the bad state of health.

10. An extension here and elsewhere in the chapter could involve imposing a subsidy on preventive expenditures as well.

11. Social insurance is not needed but cannot be excluded. Indeed, what matters in the present setting is total coverage σ_i, which can result from any combination of s_i and p_i. Any imposition of s_i would be offset by a reduction in p_i. Of course, lump-sum subsidy a_i must be adjusted according to each combination.

12. The result that $s_i = 0$ runs counter to a standard result in the insurance literature that there will be market failure under ex ante moral hazard, though not necessarily under ex post. See, for example, Pauly (1974) and Marshall (1976). See also Gaynor, Haas-Wilson, and Vogt (2000), who show that imperfect competition does not alleviate the moral hazard problem.

13. See proposition 2 in their paper.

14. Given that $s + p_i = 1, \ell_i = \ell_i(t, a, 1)$, and $\partial \ell_i / \partial s = 0$.

15. It is worth noting that even with identical w_i, social insurance is desirable as the only way from "good" to "bad" risks.

16. By the same token, an expression for the optimal tax rate t would include an interaction effect of the tax rate on curative expenditures. This would be analogous to the results of Arnott and Stiglitz (1986), who argue that an indirect way for government policy to address the moral hazard problem would be to tax commodities that are complementary with the moral hazard activity.

17. A negative s could be interpreted as a tax on curative spending, which is an imperfect way of taxing private insurance premiums.

18. It is, however, possible to show that the solution will generally be an interior one. It is impossible that $s = 1$ as this would induce x_i to go to ∞. On the other hand, it is possible that $s = 0$, though this would be by chance only.

19. We are assuming that $k > 0$. Positive loading factors in private health insurance are well-documented in the literature. See, for instance, Phelps (1992, chap. 10). In some sectors, private insurance might be less costly than social insurance. The results should then be modified accordingly.

20. In that respect, see Hindriks and De Donder (2000).

References

Arnott, R., and J. E. Stiglitz. 1986. "Moral Hazard and Optimal Commodity Taxation." *Journal of Public Economics* 29: 1–24.

Arrow, K. J. 1963. "Uncertainty and the Welfare Economics of Medical Care." *American Economic Review* 53: 942–973.

Atkinson, A. B., and N. H. Stern. 1974. "Pigou, Taxation and Public Goods." *Review of Economic Studies* 41: 119–128.

Atkinson, A. B., and J. E. Stiglitz. 1980. *Lectures on Public Economics*. New York: McGraw-Hill.

Blomqvist, A., and H. Horn. 1984. "Public Health Insurance and Optimal Income Taxation." *Journal of Public Economics* 24: 352–371.

Boadway, R. 1997. "The Role of Second-Best Theory in Public Economics." In *Trade, Technology and Economics: Essays in Honour of Richard G. Lipsey*, ed. B. C. Eaton and R. G. Harris. Cheltenham, UK: Edward Elgar.

Boadway, R., and M. Keen. 1993. "Public Goods, Self-Selection and Optimal Income Taxation." *International Economic Review* 34: 463–478.

Boiteux, M. 1956. "Sur la Gestion des Monopoles Publics Astreints à l'Equilibre Budgétaire." *Econometrica* 24: 22–40.

Cremer, H., and P. Pestieau. 1996. "Redistributive Taxation and Social Insurance." *International Tax and Public Finance* 3: 281–295.

Diamond, P. A. 1992. "Organizing the Health Insurance Market." *Econometrica* 60: 1233–1254.

Diamond, P. A., and J. A. Mirrlees. 1971. "Optimal Taxation and Public Production: Part I and Part II." *American Economic Review* 61: 8–27 and 261–278.

Drèze, J., and N. Stern. 1987. "Theory of Cost-Benefit Analysis." In *Handbook of Public Economics*, vol. 2, ed. A. Auerbach and M. Feldstein. Amsterdam: North-Holland.

Gaynor, M., D. Haas-Wilson, and W. B. Vogt. 2000. "Are Invisible Hands Good Hands? Moral Hazard, Competition and the Second-Best in Health Care Markets." *Journal of Political Economy* 108: 992–1005.

Guesnerie, R. 1995. *A Contribution to the Pure Theory of Taxation*. Cambridge, UK: Cambridge University Press.

Harberger, A. C. 1964. "Taxation, Resource Allocation, and Welfare." In *The Role of Direct and Indirect Taxes in the Federal Revenue System*, ed. J. Due. Princeton: Princeton University Press.

Hindriks, J., and P. De Donder. 2000. "The Politics of Redistributive Social Insurance." Mimeo., Queen Mary and Westfield College, London.

Hotelling, H. 1932. "Edgeworth's Taxation Paradox and the Nature of Demand and Supply Functions." *Journal of Political Economy* 40: 577–616.

Lipsey, R. G., and K. Lancaster. 1956. "The General Theory of Second Best." *Review of Economic Studies* 24: 11–32.

Marshall, J. M. 1976. "Moral Hazard." *American Economic Review* 66: 880–890.

Meade, J. E. 1955. *Trade and Welfare: Mathematical Supplement*. Oxford, UK: Oxford University Press.

Mirrlees, J. A. 1971. "An Exploration in the Theory of Optimum Income Taxation." *Review of Economic Studies* 38: 175–208.

Mitchell, O. 1998. "Administrative Costs in Public and Private Retirement Systems." In *Privatizing Social Security*, ed. M. Feldstein. Chicago: University of Chicago Press.

Musgrave, R. A. 1959. *The Theory of Public Finance*. New York: McGraw-Hill.

Pauly, M. V. 1974. "Overinsurance and Public Provision of Insurance: The Roles of Moral Hazard and Adverse Selection." *Quarterly Journal of Economics* 88: 44–62.

Petretto, A. 1999. "Optimal Social Health Insurance with Supplementary Private Insurance." *Journal of Health Economics* 18: 727–745.

Phelps, C. E. 1992. *Health Economics*. New York: Harper Collins.

Rochet, J.-C. 1989. "Incentives, Redistribution and Social Insurance." *Geneva Papers on Risk and Insurance* 16: 143–165.

Comments

Dominique Demougin

1 Introduction

The chapter by Robin Boadway, Manuel Leite-Monteiro, Maurice Marchand, and Pierre Pestieau builds upon a result from Rochet (1989) and Cremer and Pestieau (1996) where it is shown that under some circumstances, the social insurance system may become an efficient tool to redistribute income. The gist of the argument runs as follows: Suppose that the government is hindered in efficiently redistributing income via a tax-transfer scheme because lump-sum taxes are not feasible, and also assume that labor productivity is the private information of individuals. On the other hand, suppose that health expenditures are correlated to labor productivity. Then we can already conclude, from the optimal mechanism design literature, that a government could improve the efficiency of its redistribution scheme by including the additional information from healthcare.

Following that logic, Rochet (1989) and Cremer and Pestieau (1996) show that a social insurance scheme can be interpreted as part of a redistribution mechanism. In their contribution, Boadway et al. introduce moral hazard problems into the above setup. Not surprisingly, the additional frictions are shown to reduce the usefulness of employing the social system for redistributive purposes. In doing so, the chapter provides an interesting justification, based on efficiency, for the use of a dual system in healthcare, where part of the health expenditures are publicly funded while the rest must be privately financed via a competitive insurance sector.

The next section of this comment uses a simplified version of Boadway et al.'s model to provide a simple heuristic of the main results, while the final section offers some concluding remarks.

2 A Heuristic Interpretation

For parsimony, suppose that there are only two types of agents, differentiated solely by their labor productivity. Under laissez-faire,
the more productive agents will attain a higher level of income
and utility. Thus, under standard assumptions, a benevolent plan-
ner maximizing the sum of utilities would want to redistribute
income from the high to the low productivity agents. Furthermore,
assume that due to asymmetric information, distortionary taxation
is required. Initially, only considering redistribution through a tax-
transfer scheme, it is well known from the work of Mirrlees (1971)
that full equalization is not welfare maximizing. At the second-best
optimum, though high productivity agents maintain a higher utility
than low productivity individuals, redistribution is not further
increased due to the additional distortion it would create in the labor
market.

For simplicity's sake, let us consider the case where only low productivity agents require health expenditures (obviously, the same
argument applies if we assume that high productivity agents also
require healthcare but face a smaller probability of health hazard). In
keeping with the notation of the chapter, let us define the following:

a = transfers to agent independent of type;

P_l = premium paid for private insurance by low productivity agents;

π_l = probability that a low productivity agent becomes ill;

z = health expenditures required in the case when an agent becomes
ill;

α = proportion of high productivity agents;

s = share of health expenditures financed out of taxes.

Private health insurance companies are assumed to be able to
observe the distribution of health expenditure of each of its customers (i.e., insurance companies are assumed to face no adverse
selection problems). If, in addition, there is no moral hazard, full
insurance becomes optimal. Thus, in that case, depending on public
coverage,

$$P_l = \pi_l(1 - s)z \text{ for } 0 \leq s \leq 1. \tag{1}$$

In the budget constraint of a low productivity agent, consider the
term $a - P_l = \Delta$. Suppose the state were to reduce the transfer term a,

but, simultaneously, to increase the share of publicly financed health expenditures s, thereby inducing a reduction of the health premium P_l in such a way that Δ remains constant. Altogether, unless something else were to change in the system, low productivity agents would be just as well off as before.

Consider now the per capita budget constraint of the state, where the right-hand side gives the average tax revenue and the left-hand side the average expenditure:

$$T = a + (1 - \alpha)\pi_l sz. \tag{2}$$

Note that since lump-sum taxation is not feasible, tax revenue is assumed to be generated by distortionary taxes. Keeping Δ constant and substituting yields

$$T = \Delta + \pi_l z(1 - \alpha s). \tag{3}$$

Thus, the larger s, the lower the tax requirement to provide a given Δ for low productivity agents. The reason is obvious: Whereas using the tax-transfer scheme the government is forced—due to lack of information—to subsidize both types of agents, it will only subsidize the unproductive agents if it covers health expenditures.

Of course, reducing T lowers the distortion on the labor market, thereby increasing welfare. There should be a second indirect effect. Indeed, because marginal distortions of subsidizing the poor have been reduced, one should expect an improvement of the income distribution between low and high productivity agents. This again would have a positive effect on overall welfare.

The preceding argument suggests that in the absence of moral hazard, the government should set $s^* = 1$, implying a fully publicly funded healthcare system.[1] A similar argument applies with many types of agents. Suppose, as before, that productivity is negatively correlated to expected health expenditures. If the government fully funds the health system, it is as if it were paying the premium of members of society. Since low productivity agents would have to pay a higher premium in the case of a privately funded health system, it becomes equivalent to subsidizing the poor more heavily than the rich, thereby improving redistribution within society.

In their contribution, Boadway et al. introduce into the above framework the possibility of ex ante and ex post moral hazards. Ex ante moral hazard stands for the possibility of agents investing in preventive medicine, thereby reducing expected health expenditures.

Ex post moral hazard models the idea that, in the case of a health problem, different levels of curative expenditures are possible. In either case, covering health expenditures distorts private incentives, thereby creating two sorts of problems. First, full insurance becomes suboptimal. Thus, even in the case of fully publicly funded healthcare, the presence of moral hazard requires setting $s < 1$ due to the adverse incentive effect. This creates a three-way trade-off between aligning individual incentives in healthcare, efficiency in the labor market, and redistribution of income.

Second, in the more general case where there are many types of agents facing different likelihoods of health problems, optimal insurance coverage in the second-best solution should differ across the various risk groups. However, it does not appear realistic to assume that a publicly funded healthcare system can provide different coverage across individuals, both for informational reasons and, perhaps more importantly, due to political pressure. A natural way out would be for the state to cover some of the health expenditures, thereby improving the income distribution, while simultaneously allowing part of health coverage to be organized by private insurance companies that are better equipped to offer incentive schemes.

3   A Few Critical Remarks

By assuming a linear tax system, Boadway et al. unnecessarily restrict their analysis. It creates the impression that the result is an artifact of the state not using all the available information about productivity that is hidden in the agents' incomes. However, the result is more general, since the heuristic argument in the foregoing section would remain valid, even if income taxes had been set at the second-best level.

Furthermore, though it is correct that governments should use health expenditures, it is not clear that they should use them by providing health coverage. In that respect, the example of the foregoing section is quite telling. Since productive agents do not face a health risk, observing health-related expenditures fully signals the agent's type. A priori, there is no reason why the state should not choose even to "overinsure" the agent in order to improve its redistribution objective. More specifically, it would be useful to ask the question in terms of the optimal redistribution scheme while allowing the state to use all the information available through health expenditures.

Finally, correlation between the agent's type and health expenditures is presumed to be given exogenously. Of course, there is no particular reason why less productive individuals should be genetically more prone to illness than others. Stated differently, the correlation between health expenditures and type is endogenous. Changing incentives within the system will also affect the resulting correlation. Though I do not think it would change any of the results significantly, it might provide an interesting extension.

Note

1. Implicitly, I have assumed that $s = 1$ is compatible with the other parameters of the system. Specifically, I have implicitly assumed that $T^* - \alpha \pi_l z \geq 0$. Otherwise, fully funded state health insurance will not occur, simply because it would induce more redistribution than desired by the government.

References

Cremer, H., and P. Pestieau. 1996. "Redistributive Taxation and Social Insurance." *International Tax and Public Finance* 3: 281–295.

Mirrlees, J. A. 1971. "An Exploration in the Theory of Optimum Income Taxation." *Review of Economic Studies* 38: 175–208.

Rochet, J.-C. 1989. "Incentives, Redistribution and Social Insurance." *Geneva Papers on Risk and Insurance* 16: 143–165.

12

Insurance and the Utilization of Medical Services among the Self-Employed

Craig William Perry and
Harvey S. Rosen

12.1 Introduction

About 44.2 million Americans, over 16 percent of the population, lack any kind of medical insurance. This phenomenon is central to policy debates about healthcare. As former President Clinton observed, "This is a problem that America cannot let go." Self-employed people have received particular attention in this context because of their lower-than-average insurance rates—only 68 percent of those under 63 years of age had any coverage in 1996, according to our tabulations from the Medical Expenditure Panel Survey (MEPS).

The principal public policy response to the situation of the self-employed has been to subsidize their purchases of health insurance through the personal income tax. Currently, self-employed workers are allowed to deduct 60 percent of their health insurance premiums, which is up from 45 percent in 1998. According to recent legislation, this figure is scheduled to increase to 70 percent in 2002 and 100 percent in 2003 and thereafter.[1] Rules Committee Chairman David Dreir hailed the bill's passage by saying: "The American people are concerned that they can't gain access to quality health care ... Accessibility is our key. We're moving toward it" (Murray and McGinley 1999). According to news reports, insurance companies have been lobbying the Congress to accelerate this schedule,[2] a proposal supported by Elizabeth Dole during her brief run for the Republican presidential nomination.

Congressman Dreir's statement is useful because it spells out clearly the putative reasoning behind the policy of subsidizing insurance purchases for the self-employed—lack of insurance translates into lack of utilization of healthcare.[3] It is, in fact, well documented that the self-employed are less likely to be insured than wage earners, even after taking into account their differing demographic characteristics (Holtz-Eakin, Penrod, and Rosen 1996; Hamilton 2000). However, it is not obvious that, for this group of people, lack of insurance does indeed translate into lack of utilization of healthcare services. Healthcare, after all, can be financed from sources other than insurance. In fact, we know of no research that examines whether the self-employed utilize health services less than their wage-earning counterparts. This chapter investigates the links between health insurance and utilization among the self-employed. The centerpiece of the study is a statistical analysis of the differences in utilization rates for various medical services between the self-employed and wage earners.

Section 12.2 provides a brief review of previous literature. Section 12.3 outlines the empirical strategy and describes our data set, the 1996 wave of the MEPS. The MEPS has rich information on individuals' utilization of a variety of medical services, including a set of important diagnostic tests. Section 12.4 discusses econometric issues and presents the results. The main finding is that even though the self-employed are less likely to have insurance than wage earners, the gap in the utilization of healthcare services is generally fairly small. Indeed, for some important services, there is no substantial gap at all. In section 12.5, we turn to the closely related question of whether the medical expenditures incurred by the self-employed substantially reduce their capacity to purchase other commodities, and find no evidence to support this concern. Further, in section 12.6, we find that, to the extent that we are able to measure, the children of the self-employed are no less likely to have access to medical services than the children of wage earners. Hence, concerns that the self-employed need insurance subsidies in order to increase their utilization of medical services, to maintain their standard of living, or to help their children obtain healthcare may be misplaced. Section 12.7 provides a summary and suggestions for future research.

12.2   Previous Literature

The determinants of healthcare utilization have been the subject of several studies. Kass, Weinick, and Monheit (1999) used the MEPS data to examine differences in utilization rates by race. A noteworthy aspect of their study is that they moved beyond the conventional approach of considering only doctor visits or hospital admissions. Instead, they studied a wide variety of health services, including diagnostic tests such as breast examinations, which many medical practitioners view as being important for maintaining good health. Their analysis, however, was confined to comparisons of means by race. They did no multivariate analysis to take into account other variables that might affect utilization rates. Gilleskie (1998) studied utilization decisions in the context of worker absentee decisions, but only considered doctor visits. Currie and Gruber's (1995) careful examination of the effect of changes in Medicaid eligibility on medical care utilization looked only at doctor visits and hospitalizations and focused on the low-income part of the population. In the RAND Health Insurance Experiment, individuals were randomly assigned to health insurance plans with different copayments and deductibles (Newhouse 1993). The results suggested that the greater the cost sharing, the smaller the individual's health expenditures. Similarly, Hurd and McGarry (1997) found that, among the elderly, those who have the most insurance use the most healthcare services. None of these studies considered issues relating to self-employment.

In short, the papers in the existing empirical literature either look at a restrictive set of utilization measures or ignore the multivariate nature of the problem of explaining differential utilization rates across groups. What is more important given the public policy debate on subsidizing health insurance for the self-employed, none of them studies the links among insurance, utilization, and self-employment.[4]

Our focus has been on the literature analyzing the *positive* question of how insurance relates to utilization rather than the *normative* question of whether the government should subsidize insurance purchases in order to increase utilization. The issue is particularly cogent in the United States, where, in general, the government provides insurance only to certain low-income individuals (through Medicaid) and to the elderly (through Medicare). The normative literature has noted that adverse selection can lead to underprovision of health insurance in such a (primarily) private market. In this context, a tax subsidy to encourage purchases of health insurance can enhance efficiency. On the other hand, authors such as Feldstein (1995) have argued that adverse selection is not of major practical importance in the U.S. context and that the tax subsidy leads to overprovision of health insurance. Determining the optimal government intervention in a private health insurance market is a complicated issue beyond the scope of this chapter. We merely note that the answer to the normative question must ultimately depend, inter alia, on the positive question of how utilization of healthcare, and ultimately health status itself, are linked to insurance coverage.

12.3 Data

12.3.1 Description

Our basic goal is to see whether the differences between the self-employed and wage earners in their insurance rates are associated with differences in their utilization of various medical services. We require information on individuals' utilization of various medical services and insurance coverage, along with a set of exogenous characteristics that might be expected to influence utilization and insurance decisions. We draw upon the household component of the 1996 Medical Expenditure Panel Survey. The panel consists of approximately 22,000 respondents, who comprise 9,500 families. The respondents were asked a series of questions relating to their demographic characteristics, insurance coverage, employment status, and medical care use. We exclude from the sample those with missing information on education and insurance status as well as individuals who were not employed. Further, we exclude any persons younger than 18 and older than 62.[5] Those under 18 are unlikely to have developed a strong attachment to the labor market, and the decisions of those over 62 are complicated by impending retirement. Further, about 95 percent of individuals over 65 are covered by Medicare. All of these exclusions left a group of 9,552 individuals, of whom 1,158 (12 percent) were self-employed. This corresponds fairly closely to other estimates of the self-employment rate in 1996 (U.S. Bureau of the Census 1998, 412).

As noted in section 12.2, most previous studies of access have relied on a very limited set of utilization measures. An important strength of the MEPS is that in addition to insurance status, it contains information on a large variety of medical services, including not only conventional items, such as doctor visits and hospital stays, but also visits to other kinds of practitioners, such as dentists and chiropractors. As well, it provides data on the utilization of some important diagnostic procedures, such as breast examinations and blood pressure tests. Somewhat arbitrarily, we divide the procedures into two groups. The first group—site-based services—consists of doctor visits, hospital admissions, hospital stays, chiropractor visits, optometrist visits, and alternative care. The second group— screening and preventative care services—consists of breast exams, physical exams, dentist checkups, flu shots, mammograms, prostate exams, prescription medicine purchases, blood pressure tests, and cholesterol tests.[6]

Of course, utilization rates do not necessarily measure adequately the quality of services received. Two people who both visit the doctor during the year are not automatically receiving the same healthcare. For example, during a given visit, a physician might spend more time with an insured patient than with an uninsured patient, or order more diagnostic tests for the former than for the latter. In section 12.5, we examine this conjecture using data on expenditures per doctor visit. Another possible problem with studying utilization measures is that we ultimately care about the "output" health status rather than the health services' "inputs" per se. This is a legitimate concern, and we have examined health outcomes in Perry and Rosen (2001). However, access to healthcare is of independent interest, if for no other reason than it clearly drives the public policy debate. Recall Congressman Dreir's statement quoted above: "Accessibility is our key."

12.3.2   A Preliminary Look at the Data

Table 12.1 focuses on insurance coverage and rates of healthcare utilization by employment status. For each variable, column (1) shows the mean for the entire sample, column (2) the mean for the self-employed, and column (3) the mean for wage earners. The last column displays the t-statistics associated with the hypothesis that the means of the relevant variables are equal.

The first row of the table shows rates of insurance for each group. It is based on a dichotomous variable in the MEPS file that takes a value of one if the individual has health insurance coverage and zero otherwise. Specifically, the variable equals one if the individual is covered under Medicare, Medicaid, CHAMPUS/CHAMPVA,[7] other public hospital/physician, or private hospital/physician insurance. (An individual who receives spousal coverage is construed as being

Table 12.1
Summary statistics: insurance and utilization rates of healthcare services

	(1) Entire sample	(2) Self- employed	(3) Wage earners	(4) Test statistic of difference in means between columns (2) and (3)
Insurance	0.794 (0.405)	0.681 (0.470)	0.809 (0.393)	−10.2
Doctor visits	0.623 (0.485)	0.585 (0.493)	0.628 (0.482)	−2.79
Hospital admissions	0.0534 (0.225)	0.0423 (0.201)	0.0549 (0.228)	−1.79
Hospital stays	0.0537 (0.225)	0.0440 (0.205)	0.0550 (0.228)	−1.56
Chiropractor visits	0.0380 (0.191)	0.0604 (0.238)	0.0349 (0.184)	4.27
Optometrist visits	0.0420 (0.200)	0.0458 (0.209)	0.0412 (0.199)	0.725
Alternative care	0.0652 (0.247)	0.100 (0.300)	0.0604 (0.238)	5.15
Blood pressure exam	0.713 (0.452)	0.662 (0.473)	0.720 (0.449)	−4.08
Cholesterol exam	0.363 (0.481)	0.355 (0.479)	0.364 (0.481)	−0.623
Breast exam	0.290 (0.454)	0.208 (0.406)	0.301 (0.459)	−6.57
Physical exam	0.404 (0.491)	0.358 (0.480)	0.410 (0.492)	−3.35
Dentist checkup	0.432 (0.495)	0.440 (0.497)	0.430 (0.495)	0.643
Flu shot	0.166 (0.372)	0.142 (0.349)	0.169 (0.375)	−2.33
Mammogram	0.107 (0.309)	0.0959 (0.295)	0.109 (0.311)	−1.30
Prostate exam	0.104 (0.305)	0.135 (0.342)	0.0994 (0.299)	3.70
Prescription medicine purchase	0.599 (0.490)	0.560 (0.490)	0.604 (0.489)	−2.88

Notes: Each entry in columns (1), (2), and (3) shows the proportion of the relevant group that utilized each healthcare service within the last year. Figures in parentheses are standard errors. The first row shows the proportion of individuals who were covered by health insurance. Means for breast exams, prostate exams, and mammograms are taken only over the appropriate gender group. Column (4) shows t-tests on the differences in the means in columns (2) and (3).

covered for purposes of defining this variable.) The results in the first row of the table indicate that the self-employed are substantially less likely than wage earners to have any health insurance. Only 68 percent of the self-employed in our sample have insurance compared with 81 percent of the wage earners. From column (4), this difference is significant at all conventional levels, a finding consistent with tabulations from other data sets.[8]

A key question is whether the relative lack of insurance on the part of the self-employed is associated with a commensurate lack of utilization of health services. The results in table 12.1 are quite interesting in this respect. For some services (hospital admissions, hospital stays, cholesterol exams, dental checkups, mammograms, optometrist visits), there are no statistically significant differences in utilization rates. Second, for other services, there are statistically significant differences, but the self-employed have *higher* utilization rates (alternative care, prostate exams, chiropractor visits). In the cases where the utilization rates are statistically significantly lower for the self-employed, the question is whether or not the differences are large. "Large," of course, is in the eyes of the beholder. It strikes us that at least some of the differences are not substantial. For example, the probability of visiting a doctor is only 4.3 percentage points (or 7 percent) less. On the other hand, the probability of receiving a breast exam is 9.3 percentage points (or 31 percent) less.

In short, the tabulations in table 12.1 suggest that despite their relatively low insurance rates, the self-employed are not necessarily less likely than their wage-earning counterparts to utilize a variety of healthcare services. Further, where the self-employed are statistically less likely to use services, the percentage differences are often not very large.[9] That said, we should not make too much of the specific results in table 12.1, because a variety of factors might influence utilization of healthcare services, and some of these could be correlated with self-employment status. Hence, while the results are suggestive, we now turn to a multivariate approach.

12.4 Multivariate Analysis of Utilization Rates

The preliminary calculations in table 12.1 suggest that self-employed individuals' low propensity to have medical insurance does not necessarily translate into less utilization of medical services. But such univariate comparisons ignore the fact that variables other than employment status may affect utilization rates. An appropriate empirical model should allow the probability that an individual utilizes a given medical service to depend on his or her relevant personal characteristics as well as on self-employment status. We use the conventional probit model, which posits that the probability that individual i utilizes some service is given by

$$\text{Prob}(Util_i > 0) = F(\beta X_i + \delta SE_i), \tag{1}$$

where X_i is a vector of observable demographic characteristics, SE_i is a dichotomous variable equal to one if the individual is self-employed and zero otherwise, and $F(\cdot)$ is the cumulative normal distribution.

An important issue is what variables to include in the vector of demographic characteristics, X_i. The MEPS contains fairly extensive demographic information. We attempted to select only those characteristics that were very likely to be exogenous to insurance and healthcare utilization decisions. Age is included because it affects the likelihood of needing health services—health problems tend to increase with age (Lakdawalla and Philipson 1998). Also, certain procedures, such as mammograms and prostate exams, become highly recommended only after certain ages are reached. We also include the square of age because previous research suggests that a quadratic function may be appropriate.[10] Education can be expected to influence both individuals' physical condition and their capacity to pay for care (Taubman and Rosen 1982); hence, we include a set of dichotomous variables for educational attainment. On the basis of previous analyses, we also include a set of race/ethnicity dichotomous variables (Kass, Weinick, and Monheit 1999), a set of indicator variables for the region of the country in which the person lives (Skinner and Wennberg 1998; Cutler and Sheiner 1999),[11] a dichotomous variable for the individual's sex,[12] a dichotomous variable for marital status, and a continuous variable for family size—number of adults plus dependents (Taubman and Rosen 1982).[13]

Our specification omits certain variables that have appeared as covariates in several previous studies of healthcare utilization. For example, Stabile (2001) and Ross and Mirowsky (2000) included on the right-hand side of their utilization equations indicator variables for the individual's insurance status, self-assessed health, and the presence of any chronic health conditions. Ross and Mirowsky included income as well. Such variables might very well be endogenous, however. With respect to insurance, for example, Gruber (2000, 46) notes: "Insurance coverage itself may be a function of health status, leading to endogeneity bias in estimates of the effects of insurance on health and on the utilization of medical care." In the same way, there is a substantial literature documenting the links between income and health status, but the direction of causality is not known. (See, e.g., Deaton and Paxson 1999 and Ettner 1996.) To the extent that individuals' incomes are low because they are in poor health (and utilizing healthcare services intensively), income is an endogenous variable and should be excluded from the reduced form.[14] Using income in the context of comparisons between wage earners and the self-employed is particularly problematic. Self-employment income may be measured incorrectly because individuals fail to take into account, among other things, the opportunity cost of the capital they have invested in their enterprises (Hamilton 2000).

We try to include only exogenous variables on the right-hand side of (1). While this makes it difficult to attach a structural interpretation to the results, it does increase the likelihood of obtaining consistent parameter estimates.[15]

As noted earlier, we control for a number of demographic variables.[16] A relevant question in this context is whether there is unobservable heterogeneity with respect to the utilization of healthcare services. Do the self-employed and wage earners differ systematically in their underlying demands in a way that cannot be captured by our covariates? In particular, might there be unobservable variables that drive both the demand for healthcare services and the propensity to become self-employed? Suppose, for example, that self-employment requires a lot of energy and vigor. Healthy people (who tend not to demand many medical services) will therefore tend to enter self-employment, ceteris paribus. The self-employed, then, utilize fewer health services simply because they are healthier than wage earners. Put another way, if there is some underlying relationship between health and employment status, it may muddy the interpretation of our results.

Previous research suggests that this is probably not much of a problem. Holtz-Eakin, Penrod, and Rosen (1996) employed both the Survey of Income and Program Participation (SIPP) and the Panel Study of Income Dynamics (PSID) data to examine transitions from wage earning to self-employment. Both data sets indicate that in a given year, those wage earners who become self-employed in the future are not statistically different in their health status or health-care utilization from the ones who remain wage earners.[17] This result is confirmed by Perry and Rosen (2001), who analyze transitions from wage earning to self-employment and vice versa in the MEPS data. While these findings cannot definitively exclude the possibility of unobservable heterogeneity, they certainly provide no evidence that people who select into self-employment are systematically different with respect to health-related attributes.[18]

12.4.1 Basic Results

Following the same tack as our discussion of the unadjusted differences between self-employed and wage-earning individuals surrounding table 12.1, our first multivariate analysis uses an equation analogous to (1) to examine the probability of being insured; we then turn to the various utilization measures.

12.4.1.1 Insurance Coverage
The results are presented in column (1) of table 12.2. The figures are the marginal effects of each of the variables on the probability of having insurance coverage. Importantly, the coefficient on the self-employed variable is both negative and statistically significant. To put the coefficient of -0.203 in perspective, note that 80.9 percent of the wage earners have insurance. Hence, the self-employed are 25.1 percent less likely to be insured even after controlling for other variables such as education and race.

12.4.1.2 Utilization
With the results on insurance coverage in hand, we now turn to the analysis of the various utilization measures. Column (2) of table 12.2 reports the results for the probability of a doctor visit in 1996. The coefficient on the self-employment variable is negative (-0.0585) and significant ($t = -3.58$). Given that the probability of a wage earner visiting the doctor is 0.63, this implies that the self-employed are about 9.3 percent less likely to visit the doctor than wage earners. As before, we face the problem of determining whether this figure is "large." While nontrivial, it is considerably less than one might expect given the differential in insurance probabilities, especially in light of Hurd and McGarry's (1997, 131) observation that, in gen-

eral, "the empirical literature does demonstrate a strong correlation between insurance coverage and service use."

As stressed above, we are interested in a variety of medical services, not just doctor visits, so we next reestimate the model for each of a series of utilization measures. These results are displayed in columns (3) through (7) of table 12.2. Taken in conjunction with the insurance results in column (1), the coefficients on the self-employment variables in columns (3) through (7) suggest several related conclusions. First, for some services, such as hospital admissions, hospital stays, and optometrist visits, the differences in utilization probabilities between wage earners and the self-employed are not statistically significant at conventional levels. The absence of any differences for optometrist visits comes as no surprise because they are generally not covered by insurance, but this is not the case for hospital admissions and hospital stays. Second, for two categories—visits to chiropractors and alternative care—the self-employed have higher utilization rates. We conjecture that relative price effects are at work here. To the extent that services in these categories are not covered by insurance for a particular individual, they are expensive relative to other medical services that are covered. In effect, the prices of chiropractors and alternative care relative to conventional medical services are lower for those without insurance. Because the self-employed are less likely to be insured, their demand is higher than that of their wage-earning counterparts. Tastes may play a role here as well. The benefits from alternative medicine—acupuncture, massage, biofeedback training, hypnosis, and so forth—are far less well documented than those from conventional therapies. Schumpeterian tradition views the self-employed as being less risk averse and more adventuresome than wage earners; hence, they may find such treatments more attractive.

Table 12.3 presents the probit results for screening and preventative care utilization. In general, the self-employed are less likely to utilize such services than are wage earners. For three services (mammograms, prostate exams, and flu shots), the percentage differences are quite large; the others are modest in magnitude in light of the insurance differential.

An important message from tables 12.2 and 12.3 is that the utilization differentials vary across services. A natural question is whether the services with particularly large differentials are in some

Table 12.2
Probit estimates for insurance coverage and for site-based services utilization

	(1) Insurance status	(2) Doctor visits	(3) Hospital admissions	(4) Hospital stays	(5) Chiropractor visits	(6) Optometrist visits	(7) Alternative care
Self-employed	-0.203 (0.0160) [-25.1%]	-0.0585 (0.0163) [-9.32%]	-0.0115 (0.00618) [-20.9%]	-0.0106 (0.00626) [-19.2%]	0.0172 (0.00649) [48.7%]	0.000133 (0.00593) [3.23%]	0.0322 (0.00805) [53.3%]
Age	0.00532 (0.00249)	-0.00842 (0.00323)	-0.00268 (0.00136)	-0.00278 (0.00136)	0.00148 (0.00118)	-0.00211 (0.00118)	0.00557 (0.00242)
Age squared	-0.0000205 (0.0000316)	0.000155 (0.0000409)	0.0000375 (0.0000173)	0.0000388 (0.0000171)	-0.0000198 (0.0000144)	0.0000318 (0.0000143)	-0.0000556 (0.0000177)
GED[a]	0.0872 (0.0129)	0.146 (0.0225)	0.0157 (0.0133)	0.0157 (0.0134)	-0.0118 (0.00902)	0.0421 (0.0203)	0.0300 (0.0183)
High school diploma	0.203 (0.0111)	0.129 (0.0154)	-0.00772 (0.00668)	-0.00750 (0.00671)	0.0161 (0.00644)	0.0330 (0.00787)	0.0185 (0.00808)
BA	0.197 (0.00687)	0.187 (0.0156)	-0.0114 (0.00723)	-0.0114 (0.00727)	0.0196 (0.00949)	0.0503 (0.0141)	0.0538 (0.0136)
MA	0.178 (0.00579)	0.206 (0.0188)	-0.00975 (0.00963)	-0.00980 (0.00967)	0.0282 (0.0141)	0.0738 (0.0219)	0.0726 (0.0199)
Ph.D.	0.171 (0.00581)	0.204 (0.0312)	0.0175 (0.0222)	0.0246 (0.0234)	-0.00599 (0.0158)	0.0735 (0.0363)	0.0376 (0.0283)
Other degree	0.157 (0.00722)	0.129 (0.0109)	-0.00417 (0.00933)	-0.00300 (0.00948)	0.0221 (0.00122)	0.0608 (0.0191)	0.0421 (0.0161)
Family size	-0.0123 (0.00271)	-0.0338 (0.00355)	0.00278 (0.00145)	0.00275 (0.00146)	-0.00542 (0.00138)	-0.00408 (0.00138)	-0.00866 (0.00176)
American Indian	-0.000836 (0.0336)	0.0556 (0.0431)	0.00806 (0.0201)	0.00808 (0.0202)	-0.0101 (0.0131)	-0.0166 (0.0126)	-0.00916 (0.0206)

Aleut, Eskimo	−0.0566 (0.185)	0.237 (0.122)	0.266 (0.200)	0.265 (0.200)	—	—	0.118 (0.166)
Asian	−0.0645 (0.0289)	−0.0683 (0.0322)	−0.0208 (0.0101)	−0.0210 (0.0101)	−0.0133 (0.00766)	−0.0179 (0.00752)	0.00963 (0.0136)
Black	−0.0298 (0.0131)	−0.0397 (0.0161)	−0.00806 (0.0201)	−0.00801 (0.00625)	−0.0187 (0.00426)	−0.0117 (0.00523)	−0.0192 (0.00579)
Other	−0.204 (0.200)	−0.198 (0.202)	0.0366 (0.0833)	0.0378 (0.0843)	—	0.112 (0.143)	—
Northeast	0.0320 (0.0116)	0.0416 (0.0155)	0.00868 (0.00753)	0.00850 (0.00756)	−0.00828 (0.00464)	−0.0141 (0.00455)	−0.0323 (0.00434)
Midwest	0.0515 (0.0108)	0.0315 (0.0151)	0.00248 (0.00690)	0.00242 (0.00693)	0.00980 (0.00539)	−0.0129 (0.00447)	−0.0284 (0.00446)
South	−0.00371 (0.0108)	0.0256 (0.0139)	0.00934 (0.00633)	0.0103 (0.00693)	−0.0173 (0.0426)	−0.0224 (0.00439)	−0.0432 (0.00474)
Male	−0.0371 (0.00808)	−0.213 (0.00987)	−0.0375 (0.00460)	−0.0379 (0.00462)	−0.0117 (0.00356)	−0.0162 (0.00390)	−0.0387 (0.00452)
Married	0.135 (0.0103)	0.0963 (0.0122)	0.0167 (0.00504)	0.0167 (0.00506)	0.0107 (0.00394)	0.00309 (0.00431)	−0.0109 (0.00452)
Log likelihood	−4,179	−5,841	−1,932	−1,940	−1,465	−1,600	−2,013
Observations	9,552	9,552	9,552	9,552	9,536	9,546	9,500

Notes: The coefficients give the marginal effects of the associated right-hand-side variable on the probability of being covered by insurance (column (1)) and on the probabilities of utilizing various services (columns (2) through (7)). The standard errors appear in parentheses. The figures in square brackets in the "self-employed" row give the implied percentage differences in the probabilities between self-employed and wage earners. Empty cells have no observations in them.

[a] General educational development (high school equivalency examination).

Table 12.3
Probit estimates for utilization of screening and preventative care services

	(1) Breast exam	(2) Physical exam	(3) Dentist checkup	(4) Flu shot	(5) Mammo-gram	(6) Prostate exam	(7) Prescription medicine purchase	(8) Blood pressure test	(9) Cholesterol test
Self-employed	-0.0800 (0.0265) [-26.6%]	-0.0649 (0.0153) [-15.8%]	-0.0159 (0.0166) [-3.70%]	-0.0518 (0.0101) [-30.7%]	-0.0694 (0.0345) [-63.6%]	-0.0541 (0.0140) [-54.4%]	-0.0598 (0.0164) [-9.90%]	-0.0825 (0.0155) [-11.5%]	-0.0648 (0.0155) [-17.8%]
Age	-0.00596 (0.00466)	-0.0113 (0.00323)	-0.000880 (0.0033)	-0.00126 (0.00249)	0.143 (0.0305)	0.00495 (0.00427)	-0.0122 (0.00326)	-0.00579 (0.00291)	0.00496 (0.00346)
Age squared	0.0000849 (0.0000591)	0.000198 (0.0000403)	0.0000257 (0.00004)	0.0000823 (0.0000309)	-0.00126 (0.000306)	0.0000764 (0.0000513)	0.000204 (0.0000411)	0.000124 (0.0000377)	0.0000843 (0.0000432)
GED[a]	0.0519 (0.0383)	0.0453 (0.0290)	0.109 (0.031)	0.0689 (0.0267)	0.00849 (0.0702)	0.127 (0.0426)	0.111 (0.0252)	0.0845 (0.0197)	0.0630 (0.0308)
High school diploma	0.105 (0.0240)	0.0373 (0.0163)	0.212 (0.017)	0.0530 (0.0131)	0.0754 (0.0376)	0.0797 (0.0195)	0.0713 (0.0158)	0.0778 (0.0137)	0.0719 (0.0170)
BA	0.206 (0.0229)	0.0833 (0.0198)	0.347 (0.018)	0.0905 (0.0182)	0.144 (0.0438)	0.134 (0.0272)	0.127 (0.0175)	0.129 (0.0132)	0.131 (0.0209)
MA	0.257 (0.0231)	0.0994 (0.0266)	0.413 (0.020)	0.124 (0.0260)	0.167 (0.0488)	0.134 (0.0374)	0.141 (0.0227)	0.147 (0.0153)	0.164 (0.0278)
Ph.D.	0.198 (0.0524)	0.169 (0.0464)	0.329 (0.037)	0.207 (0.0457)	0.347 (0.0707)	0.130 (0.0604)	0.149 (0.0384)	0.125 (0.0280)	0.188 (0.0486)
Other degree	0.182 (0.0258)	0.0846 (0.0245)	0.277 (0.023)	0.0987 (0.0229)	0.194 (0.0485)	0.159 (0.0371)	0.101 (0.0218)	0.123 (0.0155)	0.104 (0.0257)
Family size	-0.0391 (0.00549)	-0.00522 (0.00357)	-0.0230 (0.004)	-0.0137 (0.00294)	-0.0311 (0.00913)	-0.000731 (0.00434)	-0.0303 (0.00362)	-0.0226 (0.00311)	-0.00611 (0.00381)

American Indian	-0.0606 (0.0648)	0.0126 (0.0460)	-0.0573 (0.046)	-0.0106 (0.0336)	-0.139 (0.0965)	0.0572 (0.0564)	-0.0423 (0.0442)	-0.00438 (0.0397)	0.0784 (0.0496)
Aleut, Eskimo	0.179 (0.154)	0.314 (0.166)	-0.0809 (0.194)	-0.00964 (0.127)	—	—	0.0680 (0.201)	0.0570 (0.168)	0.447 (0.157)
Asian	-0.0334 (0.0478)	0.0171 (0.0312)	-0.0496 (0.031)	0.0322 (0.0247)	-0.0568 (0.0686)	-0.0615 (0.0291)	-0.119 (0.0322)	-0.0538 (0.0297)	0.0518 (0.0324)
Black	0.0886 (0.0206)	0.143 (0.0163)	-0.123 (0.016)	-0.0254 (0.0116)	0.0756 (0.0344)	0.0526 (0.0216)	-0.0555 (0.0163)	-0.00649 (0.0146)	0.101 (0.0173)
Other	-0.0404 (0.287)	0.138 (0.172)	0.101 (0.195)	—	—	—	-0.425 (0.174)	0.152 (0.0918)	0.333 (0.160)
Northeast	0.00891 (0.0236)	0.139 (0.0164)	0.0323 (0.016)	-0.0218 (0.0114)	0.107 (0.0358)	0.0846 (0.0209)	0.0191 (0.0159)	0.0534 (0.0132)	0.108 (0.0172)
Midwest	-0.0267 (0.0225)	0.0219 (0.0156)	0.0428 (0.016)	-0.00481 (0.0112)	0.0322 (0.0344)	-0.00220 (0.0179)	0.0549 (0.0151)	0.0519 (0.0128)	0.00487 (0.0160)
South	-0.0259 (0.0207)	0.0451 (0.0142)	-0.0469 (0.014)	-0.00810 (0.0104)	0.0214 (0.0321)	0.00854 (0.0165)	0.0370 (0.0140)	0.0403 (0.0120)	0.0634 (0.0148)
Male	—	-0.119 (0.0102)	-0.122 (0.010)	-0.0466 (0.00774)	—	—	-0.210 (0.0100)	-0.166 (0.00901)	-0.0735 (0.0106)
Married	0.114 (0.0169)	0.0665 (0.0119)	0.0585 (0.012)	0.0183 (0.00901)	0.0926 (0.0259)	0.0730 (0.0144)	0.104 (0.0123)	0.0714 (0.0112)	0.0462 (0.0125)
Log likelihood	-2,719	-6,171	-6,041	-4,005	-1,333	-2,067	-5,996	-4,956	-5,527
Observations	4,352	9,552	9,552	9,283	2,060	5,009	8,110	9,263	8,976

Notes: The coefficients give the marginal effects of the associated right-hand-side variable on the probabilities of utilizing various screening services. The standard errors appear in parentheses. The figures in square brackets in the "self-employed" row give the implied percentage differences in the probabilities between self-employed and wage earners. Empty cells have no observations in them.

[a]General educational development (high school equivalency examination).

sense "important." Should there be public policy concern over the fact that the self-employed are substantially less likely than wage earners to consume these particular services? The three services with the largest differentials in percentage terms are mammograms, prostate exams, and flu shots. The relative infrequency of mammograms and prostate exams seems a serious issue. It may be, however, that the figures in table 12.3 overstate the differential for these two tests. They are generally recommended only for people over the age of 40. When we reestimated the relevant probit equations including only individuals over 40, we found that, within this age group, self-employed women are 14 percent less likely to have mammograms than their wage-earning counterparts, and self-employed men are 17 percent less likely to have prostate exams than their wage-earning counterparts. These figures are substantially smaller than those in table 12.3. In any case, to the extent that there are substantial differentials in the utilization of certain tests, it is not clear that the solution is a special deduction for health insurance in the tax code. Targeted policies such as price subsidies might be more appropriate.

12.4.2   Alternative Specifications

We subjected our model to a variety of tests to see whether our substantive results were sensitive to changes in specification.

12.4.2.1   Males versus Females

The canonical specification in tables 12.2 and 12.3 imposes the constraint that men and women differ in their insurance coverage and utilization rates only by an intercept. However, medical conditions and risk aversion differ by sex, so the process governing the relationships among insurance, utilization, and employment status may be different as well. We therefore reestimated the basic specification separately by sex. The results, available upon request, suggest that, in general, there are no substantial differences by sex in the magnitudes of the self-employment effects on the utilization of the various services.

12.4.2.2   Hours of Work

It is well documented that the compensation packages of part-time workers are less likely than those of full-time workers to include benefits such as medical insurance (Campling 1987; Committee on

Ways and Means 1998, 1107). At the same time, hours of work might be correlated with self-employment status. In fact, the correlation in our data is 0.106. Hence, our estimates of the effects of self-employment on insurance coverage and utilization rates might be biased because of the failure to take into account differences in hours worked. We therefore augmented our basic specifications from tables 12.2 and 12.3 with a set of dichotomous variables for hours worked per week.[19] Of course, hours of work might itself be endogenous—people who use healthcare intensively may be ill and work fewer hours, ceteris paribus. This is why we chose not to include hours of work in our canonical model.

In results available upon request, we found that the inclusion of hours of work has barely any impact on the self-employment effect. The most substantial changes occurred in the estimates for breast exams and cholesterol tests. Interestingly, in those cases, the coefficients on the self-employment variable become less negative once indicators for hours of work are included on the right-hand side. The changes are of the order of 2 percentage points. Thus, the inclusion of hours of work in the model reduces the differences in utilization rates associated with self-employment.

12.4.2.3 Organizational Form

So far, we have assumed that the self-employed are a homogeneous group with respect to the institutional environments in which they function. However, self-employed individuals operate in different organizational forms—sole proprietorships, partnerships, and corporations—and the probability of being insured could vary with organizational form. In particular, those who are incorporated might be more likely to have insurance, for two reasons. First, their expenditures for health insurance are fully deductible; for members of partnerships and sole proprietors, they are not. Second, to the extent that corporate enterprises have more employees, the owners can purchase insurance at advantageous group rates.[20] Under these assumptions, we can use the MEPS data on organizational form to examine further whether differences in insurance coverage drive differences in utilization. Specifically, to the extent that insurance is an important factor, one would expect incorporated self-employed individuals to utilize more medical services than their unincorporated counterparts, ceteris paribus.

To investigate this possibility, we augment our basic specification with a set of interactions between organizational form and self-employment status:

$$\text{Prob}(Util_i > 0) = F(\beta X_i + \delta SE_i + \gamma SE_i INCORP_i + \lambda SE_i PROP_i), \quad (2)$$

where $INCORP_i$ is a dichotomous variable equal to one if an individual is incorporated, $PROP_i$ equals one if the individual is organized as a sole proprietor, and the other variables are as defined previously. This augmented specification allows for differential effects by organizational form—δ is the effect if the self-employed individual is in a partnership, $\delta + \gamma$ if incorporated, and $\delta + \lambda$ if a sole proprietor (all relative to being a wage earner).

Table 12.4 reports the estimates of the key parameters of (2)—δ, γ, and λ. The first row shows the results for the probability of having insurance. According to the point estimate in column (1), a self-employed individual in a partnership is 25 percentage points less likely to have insurance coverage than a wage earner. From columns (1) and (2), an incorporated individual is only 15 percentage points ($= -0.25 + 0.10$) less likely to have insurance, and from columns (1) and (3), a sole proprietor is 24.2 percentage points ($= -0.25 + 0.008$) less likely, essentially the same figure as for a partner. Column (4) is the p-value of a chi-square test of the hypothesis that the effect of self-employment is zero; it is rejected at all conventional levels. Column (5) provides the p-value of the test of the hypothesis that the total effect for incorporated individuals is zero, and column (6) presents the result for sole proprietors. In both cases, one can easily reject the hypothesis that the effects are zero. The key result is that the data are consistent with our conjecture above: Relative to their counterparts in partnerships and sole proprietorships, incorporated individuals are more likely to have insurance (although still less likely than wage earners).

Is this differential in insurance coverage associated with differential utilization of medical services for incorporated individuals? As we move down column (2) of table 12.4, the answer is generally no. Except for blood pressure tests and flu shots, the interaction terms are statistically insignificant. Further, according to the figures in column (5), for about half the procedures, the incorporated self-employed have about the same utilization rates as wage earners, despite the fact that their coverage rates are 15 percentage points less.

An implicit assumption behind this discussion is that operating as a corporation is primarily an indicator for insurance status. It could reasonably be argued, however, that it is mainly an indicator for income—self-employed individuals who have gotten to the stage where it is worthwhile to incorporate have higher incomes than partners and sole proprietors, ceteris paribus. Note that we would expect income and insurance to work in the same direction as far as their effects on utilization of medical services are concerned—both would tend to have a positive effect. While this clouds the meaning of statistically significant interaction terms in column (2), it does not substantially affect our interpretation of insignificant effects—a zero is entirely consistent with no insurance effect.

12.4.2.4 Intensity of Utilization: Doctor Visits

In general, the MEPS tells us only whether or not an individual utilized a given kind of healthcare, not how intensively. This accounts for our focus on the probabilities of using various medical services. However, information on the number of times that the individual went to the doctor is available. We take advantage of these data to estimate how the self-employed differ from wage earners with respect to the number of doctor visits. The idea is to see if our story on differences in the use of medical services changes when we allow the intensity of utilization to vary across individuals.

We employed the same explanatory variables as in our basic model, equation (1). A complication is introduced by the fact that a substantial number of observations are at zero hours. We therefore use a tobit estimator. The coefficient on the self-employment variable is -0.69 with a standard error of 0.25—the self-employed pay fewer visits to their doctors, ceteris paribus.[21] To assess the quantitative significance of the coefficient, we began by computing the expected number of visits assuming SE is equal to zero and setting all the other variables at their means. We then repeated the exercise assuming SE is one. This exercise suggested that the impact of being self-employed is 0.03 fewer visits, or 1.09 percent.[22] Thus, taking advantage of the extra information on intensity of utilization of doctor visits reinforces the results from table 12.2 on the dichotomous choice—the differential between the self-employed and wage earners with respect to doctor visits is not very large, particularly in light of the differential in insurance coverage.

Table 12.4
Differential self-employment effects by organizational form

	(1) Self-employed (δ)	(2) Incorporated × SE (γ)	(3) Proprietorship × SE (λ)	(4) Test of $\delta = \gamma = \lambda = 0$	(5) Test of $\delta + \gamma = 0$	(6) Test of $\delta + \lambda = 0$
Insurance coverage	-0.255 (0.0450)	0.101 (0.0220)	0.00815 (0.250)	0.000	0.0018	0.000
Doctor visits	-0.0853 (0.0459)	0.0201 (0.0508)	0.0324 (0.0461)	0.0032	0.0277	0.0094
Hospital admissions	-0.0235 (0.0157)	-0.0101 (0.0231)	0.0306 (0.0333)	0.0623	0.0155	0.774
Hospital stays	-0.0167 (0.0164)	-0.0175 (0.0188)	0.0197 (0.0280)	0.0840	0.0152	0.873
Prescription medicine purchase	-0.0562 (0.0472)	-0.0220 (0.0540)	0.00397 (0.0490)	0.0027	0.0074	0.0089
Chiropractor visits	0.0325 (0.0194)	-0.0150 (0.00898)	-0.008 (0.0104)	0.0081	0.413	0.0051
Optometrist visits	0.014 (0.018)	-0.012 (0.013)	-0.0123 (0.012)	0.842	0.962	0.977
Cholesterol test	-0.0881 (0.0439)	0.0762 (0.0567)	0.00617 (0.0509)	0.0001	0.559	0.000
Breast exam	-0.142 (0.0775)	0.118 (0.0761)	0.0468 (0.0742)	0.0076	0.891	0.0029
Blood pressure test	-0.170 (0.0452)	0.108 (0.0329)	0.0646 (0.0354)	0.000	0.251	0.000
Physical exam	-0.0866 (0.0428)	0.0503 (0.0541)	0.0152 (0.0492)	0.0004	0.168	0.0002

	(1)	(2)	(3)	(4)	(5)	(6)
Alternative care	0.00989 (0.0197)	0.0142 (0.0243)	0.0264 (0.0250)	0.000	0.0374	0.000
Dentist checkup	−0.00883 (0.0436)	0.0202 (0.0520)	0.00940 (0.0473)	0.420	0.794	0.112
Flu shot	−0.106 (0.0237)	0.122 (0.0606)	0.0851 (0.0522)	0.000	0.150	0.0001
Mammogram	−0.147 (0.0940)	0.144 (0.112)	0.0703 (0.105)	0.131	0.956	0.0592
Prostate exam	−0.0809 (0.0381)	0.0373 (0.0600)	0.0403 (0.0581)	0.0041	0.0063	0.0006

Notes: These are the results for the self-employment variables when we augment our canonical model with interaction terms to control for differences in organizational form. (See equation 2.) Column (1) gives the effects if the individual is in a partnership, column (2) if incorporated, and column (3) if a sole proprietor. In each cell, the figure is the marginal effect on the probability of the relevant left-hand-side variable, and the number in parentheses is the standard error. Columns (4) through (6) give the p-values of the associated tests.

12.5   Healthcare Expenditures

So far, our focus has been on differential utilization rates. This reflects the dominant question in the public policy debate: "Are the relatively low rates of insurance among the self-employed associated with less access to healthcare?" The MEPS data also contain information about expenditures on healthcare, both out-of-pocket and total. Analysis of these data can cast further light on the question of whether a public policy response is required to the relatively low rates of health insurance among the self-employed.

To begin, we note that the debate over healthcare sometimes loses sight of the key function of insurance—to spread consumption over different states of the world. Hence, even if the self-employed have access to healthcare, we cannot necessarily be sanguine about their relative lack of insurance. We need to know if paying for healthcare causes serious reductions in their standard of living.

The MEPS data contain information about family out-of-pocket expenditures on healthcare (including expenses on insurance and medical services). To examine whether the self-employed's lack of insurance forces large reductions in their living standards, we began by analyzing how these expenditures vary with employment status. Specifically, we estimated a model in which individual out-of-pocket expenditures depend upon the same variables as the basic utilization equations of table 12.2. Because a substantial number of individuals have zero out-of-pocket healthcare expenditures (21.7 percent), we again use the tobit statistical model.

The coefficient on the self-employment variable is 141 with a standard error of 28.3. This result confirms what intuition might suggest—the self-employed have more out-of-pocket healthcare costs than wage earners, ceteris paribus. However, from a quantitative standpoint, the difference is not very large—using the same computational method as in section 12.4.1, the expected difference in out-of-pocket expenditures is only $84.42. A similar exercise indicates that total expenditures on healthcare are smaller for the self-employed (by $228), again as one might expect.

In this context, it is perhaps more informative to ask how out-of-pocket expenditures *relative to income* depend on employment status. We therefore reestimated the model with expenditures as a fraction of income on the left-hand side, again using a tobit model.[23] The coefficient on the self-employment variable is both positive (0.00748) and significant (s.e. $= 0.00194$), indicating a higher fraction of out-of-pocket costs for the self-employed. However, again proceeding as in section 12.4.1, our results imply that, on average, the self-employed devote only 0.4 percent more of their incomes to out-of-pocket medical expenditures than wage earners do.

Because the purpose of insurance is to smooth consumption, if a substantial number of the self-employed experience major health expenditures relative to their incomes, we might be concerned even if, on average, the ratios of out-of-pocket expenditures to income are about the same. It is therefore useful to know more about the distribution of the ratio of out-of-pocket costs to income than its mean. Hence, we computed the ratio at various percentiles. Within the sample of wage earners, the ratio of out-of-pocket costs to income at the seventy-fifth percentile is 0.0137; for the self-employed, it is 0.0160. At the ninetieth percentile, the figures are 0.0347 and 0.0479 for wage earners and the self-employed, respectively. The distributions of the level of out-of-pocket expenditures are qualitatively similar. At the seventy-fifth percentile, expenditures are $454 and $335 for the self-employed and wage earners, respectively. At the ninety-fifth percentile, the comparable figures are $1,877 and $1,226. It is hard to imagine that such differences are sufficient to merit public policy concern.

Another problem in the interpretation of our results on utilization is that they do not take into account possible differences in the quality of services. For example, we showed in table 12.2 that the self-employed were only about 9 percent less likely to visit the doctor than wage earners. But what if the quality of their visits was lower because they lacked insurance? In the absence of insurance, perhaps the self-employed visit less-experienced physicians who charge lower fees. Or perhaps a given physician demands a lower fee from an uninsured self-employed patient, but then spends less time with him or her.

The MEPS provides no direct way to investigate this issue. However, as a very rough measure for quality, we can compare total expenditures (i.e., out-of-pocket plus insurance) per doctor visit for wage earners and the self-employed. Given that a "doctor visit" is far from a homogeneous commodity,[24] it is not clear how much one can learn from such an exercise. Without making too much of it, therefore, we merely note that, conditional on making at least one visit to the doctor, mean expenditures per visit are $625.04 for wage earners and \$450.69 for the self-employed, a difference that is not statistically significant at conventional levels ($t = 1.160$). In this context, recall from table 12.3 that, for a variety of diagnostic tests, there are not substantial differences in utilization rates between wage earners and the self-employed. To the extent that such tests themselves can be viewed as indicators of the quality of healthcare, the table 12.3 findings are consistent with insubstantial differences in quality between the two groups.

12.6 Children's Issues

In recent years, much of the debate over health insurance has focused on the needs of children. In the fall of 2000, for example, the *New York Times* noted that "Health care for children has become a major issue in the presidential campaign" (Pear 2000, A1). Even if health services utilization is not a problem for the self-employed, one still might make a case for insurance subsidies if this promoted access to healthcare for their children. The MEPS data contain a set of questions relating to preventative care for children as well as information on their doctor and hospital visits.[25] In this section, we examine how children's medical services utilization depends on their parents' employment status.

Because the relevant question is the impact on the child's utilization of the parents' self-employment status, we create a dichotomous variable, *PARENTSE*, which is equal to one if both parents are self-employed or only one parent works and he or she is self-employed, and equal to zero otherwise. Following the same strategy as before, we begin by asking how the probability of the child's having health insurance varies with *PARENTSE*, ceteris paribus. We estimate a probit model in which the probability of insurance coverage depends upon the child's age, race, sex, and region as well as *PARENTSE*. The coefficient on the self-employment variable is 0.040 with a standard error of 0.0322—children of the self-employed are about as likely to have insurance coverage as wage earners' children. In light of the insurance gap between self-employed and wage-earning adults (see table 12.2), this result is striking. It suggests that parents place a premium on having their children insured. There is certainly anecdotal evidence to this effect. In the fall of 2000, the *New York Times* interviewed a father who continued to purchase health insurance for his children even after a very substantial increase in the premium.

The father observed: "These are my kids we're talking about here. You never know what might happen ... I wouldn't dream of them being without insurance" (Verhovek 2000, A1).

In short, whatever problems the self-employed have in getting insurance for themselves do not seem to stand in the way of their obtaining insurance for their children. With this information in hand, the rest of the analysis is somewhat anticlimactic. We found that, ceteris paribus, the children of the self-employed are about as likely to visit the doctor or be admitted to hospital as the children of wage earners, are more likely to receive hepatitis vaccinations, and are about as likely to be vaccinated for measles/mumps/rubella.[26] In short, analysis of this admittedly limited set of children's utilization measures suggests that a child-based justification for an insurance subsidy for the self-employed is implausible.

12.7   Conclusion

Using data from the 1996 Medical Expenditure Panel Survey, we have analyzed differences between the self-employed and wage earners with respect to insurance coverage and utilization of a variety of healthcare services. Our results suggest that for the self-employed, the link between insurance and utilization of healthcare services is weaker than some have suggested. For a number of medical care services, the self-employed had the same utilization rates as wage earners, despite the fact that they were substantially less likely to be insured. In most cases where the self-employed did utilize services less, the differences were not major. These findings were robust to a number of reasonable changes in the specification of our statistical model, and are particularly striking against the backdrop of a literature that, in general, finds strong correlations between insurance coverage and utilization of healthcare services (Hurd and McGarry 1997, 131).

The self-employed thus appear to be able to finance access to healthcare from sources other than insurance. Perhaps the source is their own wealth, or perhaps they have better access to borrowing than wage earners.[27] In any case, to the extent that the goal of public policy is to increase the utilization of healthcare services among the self-employed, providing them with health insurance subsidies may not be an efficacious measure. That said, there are reasons other than increasing utilization that might lead one to favor a subsidy.

For example, to the extent that other parties are incurring the costs of treating the self-employed, there may be an efficiency rationale for inducing them to buy insurance (Coate 1995). Another possible justification for a subsidy is horizontal equity—health insurance purchases of wage earners and the self-employed should be treated in the same way (although to the extent that differences in the taxation of health insurance are capitalized into the returns to self-employment, this rationale is less compelling).

Of course, as Fuchs (1998), Gruber (2000), and others have observed, despite the focus of the public policy debate on insurance coverage and utilization rates, what we ultimately care about is health outcomes. The extent to which medical care has a positive effect on health is not clear. According to some studies, access to healthcare accounts for only a relatively small part of health, and more important determinants are genetics, environment, and health behaviors (Institute for the Future 2000, 23). Consistent with this notion, Meara (1998) shows that access to healthcare is less important than maternal behaviors when it comes to explaining low birth weights, and Skinner, Fisher, and Wennberg (2001) document that at a given point in time, variation in healthcare intensity appears not to improve survival probabilities among the elderly. An important question for future research is whether the large differences in their propensities to be insured lead to substantial differences in health status between wage earners and the self-employed.[28]

Notes

We are grateful to Brookes Billman, Sijbren Cnossen, Gebhard Flaig, Jonathan Gruber, Douglas Holtz-Eakin, Helen Levy, James Poterba, Amy K. Taylor, Diane Whitmore, and participants of seminars at Princeton and Columbia for useful suggestions, to Karen Neukirchen for help in preparing the manuscript, and to Princeton's Center for Economic Policy Studies and the National Science Foundation for financial support. We thank the participants at the CESifo conference, "Public Finances and Public Policy in the New Millennium," University of Munich, January 12–13, 2001, and two referees for their comments.

1. See Internal Revenue Service Code section 162(1).

2. See *Wall Street Journal*, October 7, 1999, p. A2.

3. Conventional economic analysis suggests other reasons why a subsidy might be worth considering—for example, horizontal equity. Nevertheless, utilization per se appears to be the primary issue in much of the policy debate, and is our focus here. Other possible rationales for a subsidy are discussed below.

4. In contrast, there is a substantial literature on how the implicit subsidy for health insurance in the tax code affects insurance coverage for the self-employed. See, for example, Gruber and Poterba (1994) and Marquis and Long (1995).

5. We lose twenty-eight observations because of missing data on education, 3,612 because of missing data on employment, four because of missing insurance data, and 10,034 from the exclusion of those over 62 years old.

6. For several of these procedures (e.g., breast exam, cholesterol test, prostate exam), the MEPS provides the history of utilization. That is, we know whether the individual had the procedure within the past year, within the past two years, within the past five years, more than five years ago, or never had it. Since we only have insurance data from the past year, we focus exclusively on utilization within the past year.

7. CHAMPUS is a health benefits program designed to provide medical coverage for the dependents of active-duty military servicemen and servicewomen. CHAMPVA is intended for dependents and survivors of severely disabled veterans.

8. See, for example, Holtz-Eakin, Penrod, and Rosen's (1996) tabulations from the Survey of Income and Program Participation (SIPP) data or Health Insurance Association of America (2000).

9. We also did two-way comparisons of utilization rates by employment status and insurance status. For most services, the average utilization rates are less for the self-employed than for wage earners, even when they have the same insurance status. This is consistent with the message of table 12.1, that insurance cannot entirely "explain" the differences between wage earners and the self-employed. However, this finding must be viewed with caution, because it is based on stratification by an endogenous variable (insurance status).

10. We also entered age as a set of dichotomous variables instead of as a quadratic, and this change had no impact on our substantive results.

11. The regional classifications correspond to those used by the Census Bureau.

12. See Hagan, Simpson, and Gillis (1987) and Barber and Odean (2000) on differences in risk preferences by sex.

13. However, one can imagine that marital status and family size may be endogenous to medical services utilization. We therefore estimated our models without these two variables. Doing so had no impact upon the basic results.

14. Nevertheless, as an experiment, we estimated our canonical model including income on the right-hand side. We found that while income was positively related to insurance coverage and utilization, our substantive results did not change. Specifically, the self-employment effect on insurance coverage was still about the same magnitude and statistically significant (-0.220 with a standard error of 0.017). The self-employment differential on doctor visits was even smaller than in table 12.2 (-0.0195 with a standard error of 0.00686), and for most of the other services, the self-employment differentials were about the same as in tables 12.2 and 12.3 (for example, the prostate exam differential was -0.0558 (s.e. $= 0.0143$) and the cholesterol test differential was -0.0743 (s.e. $= 0.0158$)). In the same spirit, we also augmented the equation with dichotomous variables for the industry in which the individual worked. This, too, left our substantive results unchanged.

15. Despite the likely endogeneity of insurance status, for the sake of completeness, we estimated the basic equation including the insurance dichotomous variable and its interaction with the self-employment indicator on the right-hand side. As expected, for most healthcare services, the coefficient on the insurance variable is positive and significant. Importantly, the results with respect to the impact of self-employment are very similar to those reported in what follows.

16. In our sample, on average the self-employed are more likely to be white, male, and married with a spouse present. Further, the self-employed tend to be older (5.2 years) on average than wage earners. These findings on demographic differences between self-employed and wage-earning individuals generally echo those of previous research; see, for example, Fairlie and Meyer (1999). Summary statistics are available upon request to the authors.

17. In the SIPP data, the health measures were combined days in bed during the last four months and a self-reported health status variable. The utilization measures were combined nights in a hospital in the last four (and twelve) months and the combined number of doctor visits in the last four (and twelve) months. In the PSID, the health measures were hours of work lost due to illness and a self-reported health variable. The utilization measure was number of nights in a hospital during the year. These results are cited in Holtz-Eakin, Penrod, and Rosen (1996); more detailed documentation is reported in Holtz-Eakin, Penrod, and Rosen (1994).

18. These considerations suggest that to obtain a consistent estimate of the impact of insurance on utilization, one could use instrumental variables, with self-employment status as an instrument for insurance. Such a strategy would not enable one to obtain a direct estimate of the impact of self-employment on utilization.

19. There are three indicator variables. The first is equal to one if the individual works between 20 and 35 hours per week; the second is one for between 35 and 45 hours of work; and the third for more than 45 hours. The omitted category is less than 20 hours per week.

20. See Thomasson (2000) on the advantages of group coverage.

21. The full set of tobit results is available upon request.

22. The expectations were computed according to the standard formula $E(Y) = F(\beta X/\sigma)\beta X + \sigma f(\beta X/\sigma)$, where σ is the standard error associated with the tobit index, $F(\cdot)$ is the cumulative normal distribution, and $f(\cdot)$ is the standard normal distribution (Maddala 1983, 159).

23. For families with implausibly low incomes, the ratio of expenditures to income may be very high, possibly skewing the results. Hence, for this exercise, we exclude observations for which income is less than $5,000. This reduced the sample size by 601.

24. See Eichner, McClellan, and Wise (1999) for a careful analysis of sources of differences in healthcare expenditures among employer-provided health plans.

25. The preventative care information is for children aged 7 or under, and the doctor visit information is for children aged 17 or under.

26. Detailed results are available upon request.

27. Recent press reports indicate that self-employed individuals are particularly likely to take advantage of "buyers' clubs" for healthcare services, which offer below-market

prices on doctor visits, medical tests, and so on (Freudenheim 2000, A1). However, there are no data on the importance of this phenomenon.

28. For some results along these lines, see Perry and Rosen (2001).

References

Barber, B. M., and T. Odean. 2000. "Boys Will Be Boys: Gender, Overconfidence, and Common Stock Investment." Working paper, University of California, Davis.

Campling, R. F. 1987. "Employee Benefits and the Part-Time Worker." Working paper, School of Industrial Relations, Queen's at Kingston, Ontario, Canada.

Coate, S. 1995. "Altruism, the Samaritan's Dilemma, and Government Transfer Policy." *American Economic Review* 85: 46–57.

Committee on Ways and Means, U.S. House of Representatives. 1998. *1998 Green Book.* Washington, DC: U.S. Government Printing Office.

Currie, J., and J. Gruber. 1995. "Health Insurance Eligibility, Utilization of Medical Care, and Child Health." National Bureau of Economic Research Working Paper No. 5052, Cambridge, MA.

Cutler, D., and L. Sheiner. 1999. "The Geography of Medicare." *American Economic Review* 89: 228–233.

Deaton, A., and C. Paxson. 1999. "Mortality, Education, Income and Inequality among American Cohorts." Working paper, Research Program in Development Studies, Princeton University.

Eichner, M., M. McClellan, and D. A. Wise. 1999. "The Sources of Cost Difference in Health Insurance Plans: A Decomposition Analysis." National Bureau of Economic Research Working Paper No. 7443, Cambridge, MA.

Ettner, S. L. 1996. "New Evidence on the Relationship between Income and Health." *Journal of Health Economics* 15: 67–85.

Fairlie, R. W., and B. D. Meyer. 1999. "Trends in Self-Employment among White and Black Men: 1910–1990." National Bureau of Economic Research Working Paper No. 7182, Cambridge, MA.

Feldstein, M. 1995. "The Economics of Health Care: What Have We Learned? What Have I Learned?" Working paper, National Bureau of Economic Research, Cambridge, MA.

Freudenheim, M. 2000. "'Buyers' Clubs for Medical Services Crop Up." *New York Times*, August 25, p. A1.

Fuchs, V. 1998. "Health, Government, and Irving Fisher." National Bureau of Economic Research Working Paper No. 6710, Cambridge, MA.

Gilleskie, D. 1998. "A Dynamic Stochastic Model of Medical Care Use and Work Absence." *Econometrica* 66: 1–46.

Gruber, J. 2000. "Medicaid." National Bureau of Economic Research Working Paper No. 7829, Cambridge, MA.

Gruber, J., and J. M. Poterba. 1994. "Tax Incentives and the Decision to Purchase Health Insurance: Evidence from the Self-Employed." *Quarterly Journal of Economics* 104: 701–733.

Hagan, J., J. Simpson, and A. R. Gillis. 1987. "Class in the Household: A Power Control Theory of Gender and Delinquency." *American Journal of Sociology* 92: 788–816.

Hamilton, B. H. 2000. "Does Entrepreneurship Pay? An Empirical Analysis of the Returns to Self-Employment." *Journal of Political Economy* 3: 604–631.

Health Insurance Association of America. 2000. *Source Book of Health Insurance Data, 1999–2000.* Washington, DC: Health Insurance Association of America.

Holtz-Eakin, D., J. Penrod, and H. S. Rosen. 1994. "Health Insurance and the Supply of the Entrepreneurs." National Bureau of Economic Research Working Paper No. 4880, Cambridge, MA.

Holtz-Eakin, D., J. Penrod, and H. S. Rosen. 1996. "Health Insurance and the Supply of the Entrepreneurs." *Journal of Public Economics* 62: 209–235.

Hurd, M. D., and K. McGarry. 1997. "Medical Insurance and the Use of Health Care Services by the Elderly." *Journal of Health Economics* 16: 129–154.

Institute for the Future. 2000. *Health and Health Care 2010: The Forecast, the Challenge.* San Francisco: Jossey-Bass Publishers.

Kass, B. L., R. M. Weinick, and A. C. Monheit. 1999. *Racial and Ethnic Differences in Health, 1996.* Washington, DC: Agency for Health Care Policy and Research.

Lakdawalla, D., and T. Philipson. 1998. "The Rise in Old Age Longevity and the Market for Long-Term Care." National Bureau of Economic Research Working Paper No. 6547, Cambridge, MA.

Maddala, G. S. 1983. *Limited-Dependent and Qualitative Variables in Econometrics.* New York: Oxford University Press.

Marquis, M., and S. Long. 1995. "Worker Demand for Health Insurance in Non-Group Market." *Journal of Health Economics* 14: 47–63.

Meara, E. 1998. "Why Is Health Related to Socioeconomic Status?" Working paper, Harvard University.

Murray, S., and L. McGinley. 1999. "House Approves Insurance-Access Bill." *Wall Street Journal*, October 7, p. A2.

Newhouse, J. 1993. *Free for All? Lessons from the RAND Health Insurance Experiment.* Santa Monica, CA: RAND.

Pear, R. 2000. "40 States Forfeit Health Care Funds for Poor Children." *New York Times*, September 24, p. A1.

Perry, C. W., and H. S. Rosen. 2001. "The Self-Employed Are Less Likely to Have Health Insurance than Wage-Earners. So What?" National Bureau of Economic Research Working Paper No. 8316, Cambridge, MA.

Ross, C. E., and J. Mirowsky. 2000. "Does Medical Insurance Contribute to Socioeconomic Differentials in Health?" *Milbank Quarterly* 78: 291–321.

Skinner, J., E. S. Fisher, and J. E. Wennberg. 2001. "The Efficiency of Medicare." National Bureau of Economic Research Working Paper No. 8395, Cambridge, MA.

Skinner, J., and J. Wennberg. 1998. "How Much Is Enough? Efficiency and Medicare Spending in the Last Six Months of Life." National Bureau of Economic Research Working Paper No. 6513, Cambridge, MA.

Stabile, M. 2001. "Private Insurance Subsidies and Public Health Care Markets: Evidence from Canada." *Canadian Journal of Economics* 34: 921–942.

Taubman, P., and S. Rosen. 1982. "Healthiness, Education, and Marital Status." National Bureau of Economic Research Working Paper No. 611, Cambridge, MA.

Thomasson, M. A. 2000. "The Importance of Group Coverage: How Tax Policy Shaped U.S. Health Insurance." National Bureau of Economic Research Working Paper No. 7543, Cambridge, MA.

U.S. Bureau of the Census. 1998. *Statistical Abstract of the United States: 1998*, 118th ed. Washington, DC: U.S. Bureau of the Census.

Verhovek, S. H. 2000. "Frustration Grows with Cost of Health Insurance." *New York Times*, September 18, p. A1.

Comments

Gebhard Flaig

Craig Perry and Harvey Rosen's chapter starts with the observation that self-employed people have a significantly lower health insurance rate than wage earners and asks whether this difference in insurance coverage is associated with a comparable difference in the utilization rates of medical services. This is, in many respects, an interesting and important problem, which is tackled in the chapter by a series of econometric estimations. The study is carried out very professionally and presents some novel results.

In my comment, I will be mainly concerned with some specification and estimation issues. It is a difficult task to model the interactions between the decisions analyzed in the chapter. So we should look for the most efficient and reliable methods to extract useful information from the data. Before I can trust in all of the presented results and the conclusions drawn from them, I would like to see some extensions and amendments to the empirical specification in order to get a feeling of whether the results are really robust with respect to the underlying assumptions.

The first point concerns some more technical problems. The study takes the standard assumption that the disturbance term in the utility function is normally distributed. This allows use of the well-known probit model to estimate the model parameters. But we should be aware that this is not an innocuous assumption. Suppose we have two distinct groups that differ in an unmeasured characteristic—for example, health status. Within each group, the error term may be normally distributed, but for the entire sample we have a mixture of two distributions with unknown effects on the properties of the estimated coefficients. Other departures from normality emerge when the unmeasured characteristics have a

distribution with fat tails or a high degree of skewness. It would be
useful to conduct some specification tests, based on generalized
residuals (see, e.g., Pagan and Vella 1989). A violation of the normality assumption is not harmless, since it implies inconsistent
parameter estimates. The use of a heteroskedastic consistent variance-
covariance matrix is not a sufficient remedy.

A further possibility is that the variance of the disturbance terms
is different for wage earners and the self-employed. This implies that
the parameter vector differs between the two groups by a proportional factor. Imposing equality, as is done in the chapter, may be too
restrictive and can distort the empirical results. If the employment
status is exogenous with respect to the decision on using a medical
service, the simple solution is to estimate a separate probit model for
each group.

If the employment status is correlated with the disturbance variable in the utility function for using a medical service, a switching
regression model with endogenous switching is appropriate (see
Maddala 1983, sec. 8.3).

The utility functions for being self-employed and for the utilization of a medical service can be specified as follows:

$$U_{SE} = \beta_0 x_0 + \varepsilon_0 \quad \text{(utility of being self-employed);} \tag{1}$$

$$U_{MS} = \beta_1 x_1 + \varepsilon_1 \text{ if } U_{SE} > 0 \quad \text{(utility of medical service} \atop \text{for self-employed);} \tag{2}$$

$$U_{MS} = \beta_2 x_1 + \varepsilon_2 \text{ if } U_{SE} \le 0 \quad \text{(utility of medical service} \atop \text{for wage earner).} \tag{3}$$

In these equations, x_0 and x_1 are vectors of observed determinants of
the utility functions and the ε variables denote unobserved random
shocks.

In the chapter, a reduced form is estimated where the potentially
endogenous variable, insurance coverage, is left out as an explanatory variable. The parameter on the self-employment dummy measures both the direct effect of employment status on the utilization of
medical services and the indirect effect via insurance coverage. In a
more structural setting, we are interested in decomposing the total
effect into the causal effects of employment status and of health
insurance on the utilization rate. We can accomplish this task using a

bivariate probit model of the following form:

$$U_{IC} = \beta_1 x_1 + \delta_1 SE + \varepsilon_1 \quad \text{(utility of insurance)};\tag{4}$$

$$U_{MS} = \beta_2 x_2 + \delta_2 SE + \gamma IC + \varepsilon_2 \quad \text{(utility of medical service)};\tag{5}$$

$$\text{Prob}(IC = 1, MS = 1) = \Phi_2(\beta_1 x_1 + \delta_1 SE, \beta_2 x_2 + \delta_2 SE + \gamma IC, \rho),\tag{6}$$

where IC is a dummy variable that takes the value of one if the individual chooses to be insured and zero otherwise, the dummy variable MS is one if a medical service is used and zero otherwise, and ρ is the correlation coefficient between ε_1 and ε_2.

If ε_1 and ε_2 are correlated, there may exist an unobserved variable that has an effect on the decisions concerning both insurance coverage and usage of medical services. If, in addition, the employment dummy SE is correlated with ε_1 (being self-employed depends on health status, which is measured by ε_1), we will get inconsistently estimated parameters. The remedy to this problem is to estimate a trivariate probit model in which employment status, insurance coverage, and utilization of medical services are specified as endogenous choice variables:

$$U_{SE} = \beta_0 x_0 - \varepsilon_0 \quad \text{(utility of self-employment)};\tag{7}$$

$$U_{IC} = \beta_1 x_1 - \delta_1 SE - \varepsilon_1 \quad \text{(utility of insurance)};\tag{8}$$

$$U_{MS} = \beta_2 x_2 + \delta_2 SE + \gamma IC + \varepsilon_2 \quad \text{(utility of medical service)}.\tag{9}$$

This model can be extended by simultaneously modeling more than one medical service. In this case, computing the likelihood function involves the evaluation of high-dimensional integrals. The progress in simulation-based estimation methods makes this approach more and more feasible. A simpler but somewhat restrictive model relies on a one-factor structure of the residuals, which requires the numerical quadrature of only a univariate integral (see Heckman 1981).

A possible drawback of the Perry-Rosen study is that it uses only cross-sectional information for estimating the empirical models. Generally, it is a profitable approach to exploit the panel structure of a data set. Panel data allow us to control in an efficient way for unobserved heterogeneity—for example, concerning chronic illness—and to study the persistence of big shocks to health status and the implied effects on doctor visits and healthcare expenditures.

With panel data, not only have we a snapshot for one year but also we can analyze the permanent effects of health insurance coverage on the time path of the utilization of medical services. Even if the utilization rate within a year is not very different between insured and uninsured individuals, over time there may emerge great gaps between the two groups. For instance, chronically ill individuals who are not insured may suffer a great loss in wealth.

The advantages of using panel data come not without costs. Since the decisions over time are not independent, due to unobserved heterogeneity, one has to specify multinomial probit models which require the evaluation of high-dimensional integrals. As already mentioned, the advances in simulation-based estimation methods have reduced the problems considerably.

An interesting aspect of the chapter is the analysis of the utilization intensity of medical services. The dependent variable here is the number of doctor visits. The estimation is carried out using a tobit model in order to account for the nonnegativity of the dependent variable. While being a useful tool for many applications, the tobit model may be somewhat restrictive in the present context. A more suitable approach may be found within the class of count data models (see Winkelmann 2000). An especially interesting specification is given by a "hurdle" model. The model contains two equations, the first being a participation equation, which determines whether an individual is active in the sense of using at least one medical service, and the second being the frequency equation, which determines the number of doctor visits, conditional on being active. In this way, we can account for unobserved heterogeneity with regard to the health condition of the individuals in the sample.

The study presents important and interesting results concerning the relationship between health insurance coverage and the utilization of medical services. It is an important first step into an underresearched field. But more can be done.

Analyzing cross-sectional data with reduced form models may not be the most efficient way to extract as much useful information as possible from the data. A more structural approach combined with the use of panel data will probably deliver many new insights. I would like to encourage the authors to extend their future work on this subject in some of the proposed directions.

References

Heckman, J. 1981. "Structural Models for Discrete Panel Data." In *Structural Analysis of Discrete Data with Econometric Applications*, ed. C. Manski and D. McFadden. Cambridge: MIT Press.

Maddala, G. S. 1983. *Limited-Dependent and Qualitative Variables in Econometrics*. Cambridge, UK: Cambridge University Press.

Pagan, A., and F. Vella. 1989. "Diagnostic Tests for Models Based on Individual Data: A Survey." *Journal of Applied Econometrics* 4: 529–559.

Winkelmann, R. 2000. *Econometric Analysis of Count Data*. Heidelberg, Germany and New York: Springer-Verlag.

IV   Fiscal Federalism

13

Sharing the International Tax Base in a Changing World

Richard M. Bird and
Jack M. Mintz

One might describe the current international tax system as the second worst imaginable—the worst system being whatever would replace the current system.

—R. L. Doernberg, "Electronic Commerce: Changing Income Tax Treaty Principles a Bit?"

All laws stand on the twin pillars of territoriality and enforceability, and tax laws cannot exist outside this framework. Yet, when one enters the world of cyberspace, these twin pillars become loose at their foundation. How does one mark territory in a seamless, digital world? How does one map nations and taxing jurisdictions in a world that is not based on geography?

—Ajay Thakkar, qtd. in Dressel and Goulder, "IFA Asia Regional Conference Focuses on E-Commerce and International Taxation"

13.1 Introduction

It is not easy to achieve a consensus on international tax issues. The conceptual, institutional, and administrative problems besetting international taxation are formidable, and we have no simple solutions to them. Our more modest aim in this chapter is simply, first, to explore the extent to which a game-theoretic framework may, despite its limitations, help us to understand better some critical aspects of international tax coordination and, second, to set out some aspects of the institutional setting within which these problems are dealt with that may, over time, help point the way towards a workable solution.

This topic seems particularly relevant to a symposium in honor of Richard Musgrave, since the coordination of tax systems in different jurisdictions is an issue in which he has long been interested and to which he has contributed substantially.[1] It is also one with respect to which much of his work has been done in collaboration with Peggy

Musgrave,[2] who is herself, of course, one of the world's leading authorities on tax coordination issues.[3]

The two epigraphs, taken from a recent issue of an international tax journal, neatly set out the parameters of the problem we consider in this chapter. The present system of international taxation is in many ways in a terrible state. Nations whose economic relations with each other require acknowledgment of intersecting fiscal claims have the choice of recognizing and accommodating competing tax claims or going it alone and letting others worry about any resulting problems. Over a century of negotiation and refinement, the fiscal interests of residence and source states have become precariously balanced in what may perhaps be called the "OECD consensus." Over time, less through the systemic or normative application of international tax principles than by the incremental evolution of rules deemed to be both roughly fair and roughly feasible, a regime that acknowledges and accommodates competing claims developed, for the most part with substantial international agreement as to both the underlying objectives and the means to achieve them.

Essentially, source countries have claimed primary jurisdiction over profits generated by economic activities where there was a physical presence or at least some credible basis for asserting a "permanent establishment." Residence countries, on the other hand, have asserted primary claim to taxing portfolio remittances. They have also often, in effect, smoothed out the differential source rates imposed on direct investors by subjecting remitted profits to residence tax with crediting for source tax. The balance that has been thus achieved, however, is both logically suspect in some respects and often difficult to enforce and interpret. Moreover, the future looks even more obscure and uncertain in the face of globalization and new developments in financial innovation and electronic commerce. The bilateral tax treaties through which the present system is largely implemented, for example, inevitably rely on characterizations of income, which are not only inherently arbitrary but are also becoming increasingly obscure. Similarly, the concept of permanent establishment that is central to the present consensus is becoming increasingly tenuous, as illustrated by recent discussions on taxing profits from computer servers (Cockfield 2000). The question of whether national governments with different interests can cooperate sufficiently to rescue the international tax system is thus becoming ever more prominent.

At least some of the gloom that many seem to feel with respect to the international tax system may perhaps be attributed to the implicit perception that the international tax game is essentially noncooperative in nature since there are few binding agreements amongst participants, except for the bilateral tax treaties already mentioned. Strategic decisions tend to result in "beggar-thy-neighbor" practices so that governments fail to achieve a consensus since there is a strong incentive to defect rather than cooperate (the so-called Nash equilibrium). Many papers have been written using this noncooperative framework to analyze international tax problems, such as Hamada (1966), Mintz and Tulkens (1986), and Gordon (1992), and indeed, as Tulkens (chapter 14) notes in another context, it is sensible to examine such noncooperative fiscal equilibria closely since they constitute, as it were, the "fallback" position if all else fails.

Despite the obvious difficulties of reaching consensus, however, the fact is that countries have over the years managed to achieve a surprising degree of agreement on a multilateral framework in many areas of finance and trade (Keohane and Nye 2001) as well as with respect to the provision of many international public goods (Sandler 2002). In the tax field, for example, the OECD model has often been used as the basis for bilateral tax treaties. Similarly, considerable agreement has been reached among major countries with respect to a multilateral transfer-pricing regime. Most recently, an OECD initiative has both identified so-called harmful tax competition practices and called for the elimination of special preference regimes for financial service entities.[4] Further, the European Union has also developed its own list of harmful practices, and some European countries have already begun to comply with the rules (Osterweil 2000).

Such multilateral agreements are more consistent with a cooperative game-theoretic framework. Yet, the multilateral approach to international tax coordination remains fairly limited so far. Countries have generally preferred to approach international tax issues either unilaterally or, at most, bilaterally, which results in only a limited degree of coordination. Interestingly, considerably more sweeping multilateral agreements have been reached in other policy areas such as trade (NAFTA and the WTO) and military cooperation (NATO).[5] As the lengthy and thus far inconclusive EU discussion of direct taxes suggests, there are good reasons why tax policy has seldom been coordinated through explicit multilateral treaty negotiations.[6] Given the problems now arising at the international level, however, some increase in multilateral coordination in tax matters seems to be required—at least if the taxation of international income flows is to be sustained.[7] Our principal aim in this chapter is simply to outline some of the problems involved in adopting such a multilateral approach.

There is, of course, already a fair amount of literature on cooperative methods for international tax coordination with respect to such issues as tax harmonization (Keen 1987), transfer pricing (Bond and Gresnik 1996), minimum tax rates (Kanbur and Keen 1993; Huizinga and Nielsen 2000), the exchange of information (Bacchetta and Espinosa 2000; Tanzi and Zee 1999), and allocation methods for profits (Mintz 1999). But this literature seldom attempts to take into account either the motivations that countries have to cooperate or how these motivations ultimately impact the methods used to achieve cooperation.[8] In particular, the literature does not deal with the "rights" that countries may attempt to assert in defining their tax regimes even in a cooperative setting, a point suggested by Musgrave and Musgrave (1972).[9] One of our aims in this chapter is to consider some of the implications of the rights or entitlements that countries might wish to assert in determining their tax policy for the prospects of multilateral cooperation on fiscal matters.

More generally, we attempt three tasks in this chapter, although only in a modest way. First, we examine the basic framework of cooperative game theory to see how international tax issues might be resolved in such a setting. The key point to cooperative game theory is to understand not just the strategic decisions made by participants in the game but also the rules of the game. Since the current institutional setting for international taxation contains substantial elements of several different seemingly alternative models, it is by no means clear exactly what the game is. Second, we consider in more detail various rules of the tax coordination game that seem critical for developing an agreement. In particular, we consider the role of what Musgrave and Musgrave (1972) call "inter-nation equity" and relate it to the broader concerns of "fair shares" that have motivated much of the development of the system that is now in place and that seem likely to govern whatever emerges in the future. Third—and going well beyond the game-theoretic framework which, suggestive as we think it is, neither explains the process to date nor offers a clear guide for the future—we offer some thoughts on how the ongoing process of developing a "new" international tax system for the "new" world economy might best proceed.

13.2   The Formal International Tax Game

To begin, let us list some of the basic elements of a formal game. There are *players* who choose *actions* using *strategies* to maximize their *payoffs*. Games can be one-shot, with player actions taken simultaneously or sequentially (one player may move first). Alternatively, games can be repeated in finite time or indefinitely (the latter is a "supergame"). Players may have *complete information* about payoffs and actions or *incomplete information* whereby some players may know more than others about the elements of the game (such as a firm knowing its true costs while another firm only knows the distribution of other firm costs).

The above elements apply to both a cooperative and a noncooperative game. The distinction between these two types of games is that a noncooperative game involves no binding commitments. Players choose strategies that maximize their payoffs that are best responses to strategic decisions made by other players. The choices made may not achieve what is "first-best" in the sense that if the players could collude and divide up the proceeds, they could do better than in a noncooperative setting.[10]

In a noncooperative game, actions taken by the private sector include decisions on consumption, saving, and work effort for consumers and on investment, hiring, and output for firms. Governments take fiscal actions—choosing the level and mix of public goods and services and taxes. Governments are usually assumed to be first movers, anticipating the reactions of the private sector to fiscal decisions.[11] If tax rates are the strategic variable, they are chosen so that there is sufficient revenue to finance public goods—that is, to satisfy the government's budget constraint. Governments may be interested in maximizing the welfare of citizens (defined over private and public goods as in Mintz and Tulkens 1986), tax revenues (Kanbur and Keen 1993), political rents (Persson, Roland, and Tabellini 1997), or some combination of these objectives (Edwards and Keen 1996). Typically, it is assumed that governments use Nash strategies, choosing the best response, given the best responses of other governments. Alternatively, if one government is a "leader," it might move first, anticipating the reactions of other governments whose actions follow the leader (the equilibrium has been referred to as a subgame-perfect equilibrium). Games can be either one-shot or repeated, although many models tend to concentrate on finite time horizons.

Such noncooperative models suggest that governments will generally choose suboptimal tax rates—that is, rates that are either too high or too low relative to a coordinated solution, depending upon the nature of "fiscal externalities" present (see Gordon 1983; Mintz and Tulkens 1986). Fiscal externalities are the effect that one government's decision has on the welfare of other governments. In some cases, fiscal externalities are positive, implying tax rates will be set too low. For example, if there is "tax base flight," a government, by raising taxes on a mobile base, will lose the base to another jurisdiction that thus benefits from the larger tax base. Or, the fiscal externality may be negative, as in the case of "tax exportation." Tax rates will then be chosen too high when a government can impose taxes on nonresidents who benefit little from public goods and services provided in the taxing jurisdiction.[12]

In contrast to a noncooperative game, a cooperative game allows players to communicate or negotiate a binding agreement for dividing up the joint payoffs.[13] Such communication increases the payoffs to all players compared with the payoffs achieved under the noncooperative game. The following features characterize a cooperative game:

• *Pareto optimality:* The joint payoff should be taken from a set of payoffs that achieves the highest level of payoff for the coalition of all players in the game. Pareto-optimal payoffs are those in which no other player can be made better off without making some player worse off.

• *Coalition stability:* Some players may participate in a coalition to the exclusion of other players if this is in their interest. The *core* of a cooperative game is comprised of outcomes that are coalitionally stable in the sense that any other outcome can be blocked by a subset of the participants.

• *Individual rationality:* The players need to agree to a binding agreement that would make themselves as well off as in a situation where there is no agreement. The game must be "individually rational," meaning that each player does better than the payoff achieved without cooperation.

• *Side payments:* Cooperation may or may not be achieved through negotiation of side payments. Side payments (transferable utilities) expand the possible outcomes for cooperation (the core of a game). Without side payments, cooperation is more difficult to achieve.

We next review the issues that arise with a tax coordination problem in a cooperative game setting. Specifically, we consider the problems that arise in identifying players, determining payoffs, and negotiating "fair" agreements of a game.

13.2.1 The Players

The game of tax coordination involves at least two types of players: the private sector (consumers and/or firms) and governments. But who are the players in a cooperative game? Is it only governments and not the private sector? Even if only governments are included as part of a coalition, what criteria determine which governments participate?

In most models, the private sector is not considered to be part of the coalition in a cooperative agreement. This raises the question of coalition stability, since the private sector could try to block potential cooperative agreements among governments. In formal models, the willingness of the private sector to block cooperative agreements depends on the nature of payoffs assumed for government decisions. If governments are benevolent and act in the interests of their residents, then implicitly the private sector is included in the coalition. Agreements reaching Pareto-optimal allocations will at the same time improve the welfare of citizens. However, if governments pursue other objectives, such as maximization of total tax revenue or political rents, the interests of the public and private sectors will not coincide. Moreover, in any political model with private-sector participants having different objectives (such as capitalists versus workers), a coalition-stable agreement needs to take into account the various interests of private participants.[14]

Even with a more limited coalition of governments, there are significant issues in determining which governments would be included in an agreement. To be part of an agreement, a government would need to have the *right* to tax a particular base. For example, under the income tax, governments may tax businesses operating in their jurisdiction. But what rules determine when a business is operating in the jurisdiction? Among industrialized countries, there is a long history of establishing legal rules for taxation of source income that is now the basis for the OECD model tax treaty. These rules include definitions of *residence, permanent establishment*, and *carrying on business*.

Under current practice, individuals are treated as residents of a country if they have a "sufficient connection" to it, which might be determined on the basis of factors such as physical presence, the availability of a fixed abode, permanent resident status, or economic conditions, with the rules in different countries differing in details. A corporation (or other legal person) is deemed to be resident if it is formed or incorporated in the jurisdiction or if its central management and control are exercised in the jurisdiction, again with different countries taking different approaches. A permanent establishment is generally defined as a fixed place of business in which business is wholly or partly carried on. This concept clearly includes a place of management, branch, office, factory, workshop, quarry, mine, or oil or gas well. However, it generally does not include a place of storage, advertising, or the collection of information. The carrying on of business is defined as the production, creation, manufacturing, or improvement of a product or service, the solicitation of orders or offers through an agent, and the disposition of real property. The profits from a permanent establishment would be subject to income tax. On the other hand, income derived without a permanent establishment (such as using an agent to carry on business) may only be subject to withholding tax.

Several "gray" areas have arisen with respect to determining which player should be part of a cooperative game of international tax coordination:

• For example, the test of "central management and control" used in some countries to determine the residence of a corporation is being increasingly challenged owing to such developments as the international consolidation of businesses and the use of international boards of directors who may reside in different countries and meet via videoconferencing.

• With globalization of business activities, employees increasingly travel abroad for short periods of time to carry out business. In response, some countries have broadened the notion of permanent establishment to tax profits even if there are only agents working on behalf of a company. At the extreme, if an employee of a company simply rents a hotel room, a jurisdiction might claim the right to tax income earned at source, contrary to the OECD model treaty. Exporting countries, needless to say, have not welcomed such moves.[15]

• Most recently, the development of electronic commerce has raised additional questions about who the players are. Are Internet Service Providers (ISPs) or Web sites "permanent establishments" and therefore subject to taxation? Even if they are determined to be permanent establishments, ISPs and Web sites are difficult to tax in practice since they may easily move to tax-free jurisdictions. Indeed, one entrepreneur has already provided as a potential base for such activities a ship anchored in international waters which is not subject to any national taxing jurisdiction.

It is thus by no means always clear which jurisdictions are the relevant players in the international tax game. While this problem is especially obvious with respect to the right to tax profits under an income tax, even under a VAT there are increasing difficulties determining the players of the game since the VAT depends on determining both the source of supply and the place of consumption. In particular, the taxation of services in a jurisdiction depends on determining the place of supply. If services (or digitized goods) are provided through a Web site, which jurisdiction has the right to tax such services?

13.2.2   Payoffs

Once the players are identified, the next problem is to determine the payoff. Is it the welfare of citizens? Which citizens? Are governments interested in maximizing tax revenues? Are politicians mainly concerned with their rents derived from political power? Since games are played over a time horizon, what discount rate would competing players use?

There are no simple answers to such questions. However, the success of any cooperative agreement depends upon how governments react to each other and on whether they perceive improvements in their positions, which in turn clearly depends upon the payoffs that are important to them.[16] If governments are benevolent—that is, concerned about the welfare of their citizens—they will be concerned about efficiency and distributive issues within their jurisdictions. If they are really benevolent, they may care about the welfare of the world as a whole. If, on the other hand, governments are "Leviathan" (Edwards and Keen 1996), they may only care about tax revenues or the size of the budget. In this case, governments will seek to protect their revenues rather than being concerned about efficiency of markets and the distributive impacts of their policies.

Most models assume that governments have the same payoff functions. But suppose cooperating governments have different payoffs—say, one is benevolent and the other is Leviathan and interested only in maximizing tax revenues. The cooperative game should lead to the joint maximization of payoffs, but the relevant payoff in this case would be tax revenues for one government and national welfare for the other. Maximizing such a mixed joint payoff is not at all the same as maximizing the welfare of residents in both countries—presumably the goal of interest to those who wish to promote globally efficient markets.

Indeed, perhaps the most important difference between a noncooperative and a cooperative game relates to whether countries pursue *global* or *national* objectives.[17] In a noncooperative game, for instance, even a benevolent government is presumably concerned only about national efficiency—maximization of the welfare of its own citizens (who are usually assumed in the literature to be identical, to abstract from the internal distributive concerns that often dominate, in practice, in shaping policy). On the other hand, the players in a cooperative game may ultimately pursue global efficiency in the interest of achieving higher payoffs for their own citizens than would be possible without cooperation.

Peggy Musgrave (1969) discusses a good example of the difference between these two objectives with respect to capital income taxation. Under the national efficiency objective, capital allocation is not distorted if the capital exporter's tax system does not affect the allocation of capital between foreign and home jurisdictions. This implies that foreign taxes should be *deducted* from income so that the return on foreign investments, net of foreign taxes, is equal to the return on capital in the home country.[18] On the other hand, under global efficiency, capital location should not be influenced by either the home or the host country tax system. To achieve this aim, the home country should *credit* the host country's tax against its own taxes so that the total tax burden in both countries would be the same—even if a refund has to be paid when the foreign tax is in excess of home-country tax liability. Of course, no government, however benevolent, goes this far.[19]

Whether governments pursue global or national objectives has also been raised in the trade literature. A general view is that governments should eliminate trade barriers even unilaterally in the interest of national welfare. However, in the case of taxation, unlike trade, there is a conflict between national and global objectives, since taxes are levied on both traded and nontraded activities. Nonetheless, as Slemrod (1995) points out, governments might in their national interests still pursue global objectives, such as worldwide capital market efficiency, to achieve cooperation from other governments. Of course, even if governments did pursue global objectives in order to secure international tax coordination, they would presumably only agree to policies that would make them better off compared with the payoffs achieved in a noncooperative game (individual rationality). Even in a cooperative game, national objectives are never abandoned.

Such a game, however, may be one in which players are concerned not just about their level of welfare but also about the welfare of other players in the game. The presence of altruism or envy, for instance, implies that players are concerned about not just the level but also the distribution of income (or taxes) among countries. For example, if payoffs are jointly maximized, the core of a game might result in both countries being made better off, but the richer country might obtain a greater proportional increase in its payoff than the poorer country. This outcome may not be acceptable if the relative position of countries matters to one or both countries. If countries are concerned with *inter-nation equity*, and not just their own level of welfare, the payoff objective is obviously different.

It is interesting to note that some of the key "principles" often cited with respect to international taxation, such as capital export neutrality (CEN) and capital import neutrality (CIN), simply do not arise in the framework discussed to this point. The argument in favor of CEN, although essentially based on achieving world economic efficiency, has also been put forward as an essential component of interpersonal equity with a global progressive income tax (Musgrave and Musgrave 1972). Countries can achieve the highest level of global welfare if the tax burdens on home and foreign investments by a multinational are the same, so that capital is unimpeded in flowing between jurisdictions. This aim can be achieved, for example, if countries abandon source-base corporate taxes and only impose income taxes on residents (or, alternatively, full credit is given to the investor to offset any source-base tax in the foreign jurisdiction). Mintz and Tulkens (1996) and Dickescheid (1999) show that the CEN principle will achieve a form of Pareto efficiency in the sense of eliminating fiscal externalities amongst governments when choosing tax rates. However, CEN will not achieve a globally efficient capital market if investors, worldwide, bear different taxes, resulting in different costs of capital for businesses.

The argument for CIN, which is more controversial, is strictly efficiency-based. Taxes borne by corporations should be the same no matter who owns them. In this case, if only source-base taxes are used, the tax burden on investments within a jurisdiction is the same regardless of ownership of the firm. Clearly, both CEN and CIN cannot hold simultaneously unless source-base and residence-base tax rates are the same in all jurisdictions. Although CEN, and perhaps even CIN, might be invoked to achieve global efficiency, neither of these principles deals with the critical question of the distribution of revenue across countries.

13.2.3 Negotiations and Fairness

As the extensive development of bilateral tax treaties over the years demonstrates, countries are often willing to be parties to binding agreements. Countries do not generally rely on the tacit collusion that might be a possible outcome of a supergame. Instead, they generally agree to binding terms of a tax treaty. Bilateral treaties have achieved certain important aims—the avoidance of double taxation, agreements on withholding tax rates, exchange of information, and acceptance of certain rules such as nondiscrimination towards foreign investment. A key feature in such treaties is usually formal *reciprocity* or "equal treatment."[20] Moreover, to a considerable extent, treaties, though independent legal documents, exhibit tacit collusion in the sense that many of their provisions are usually modeled closely on the OECD model tax convention.

To understand the basis of an agreement, one must understand what factors influence negotiations. Formal economic models of negotiation (Nash 1950; Rubinstein 1982) suggest that participants will maximize the weighted product of gains in individual payoffs resulting from the agreement.[21] The weights are determined from the bargaining strengths of the participants. If players are equally strong and are identical, then each of the participants would get half of the gains from cooperation. In many situations, this would, of course, be viewed a "fair" allocation.

However, countries are not identical. Nor do they have equal strengths. Those countries with greater power would get a greater share of the gains from cooperation. Even if the participants have equal weights, the country with a higher level of welfare in the absence of cooperation would have a higher level of welfare after the agreement, as predicted by the Nash bargaining model.

Although such bargaining models provide some useful results in predicting outcomes, it is difficult to apply these models to the specific problems faced by countries trying to reach a cooperative arrangement on taxes.[22] First, payoffs are often not easy to measure, in part because the objectives may not be the same for all participants. Second, the cooperative arrangements usually deal with only a limited set of instruments (such as withholding taxes), and other considerations may be equally if not more important, with the result that a narrow cooperative arrangement may result in a loss, not a gain, in welfare, making such an agreement impossible to negotiate. Third, since the gains received by participants ultimately depend upon their bargaining power, gains are unlikely to be equally shared—and this outcome may run against the notion of "fairness" held by some participants. As noted earlier, the relative position of each participant may in some instances turn out to be as important as the actual gain achieved.

How the tax base is shared is clearly important to each participant. This critical aspect of cooperative game theory suggests that securing a satisfactory outcome will both be difficult and require a pragmatic approach to international tax coordination. We take this up further in the following sections.

13.3 The Rules of the Real Game

In the preceding discussion, some elements of the present international tax game have already been mentioned. We now turn to consider in more detail some of the rules of this game, with particular attention to how the principles that appear to have been followed in international tax policy up to now suggest that international tax cooperation might develop in the future.

Perhaps the most fundamental rule of international taxation is that there are really no explicit rules of international taxation (Bird and Wilkie 2000). Instead, there are simply domestic tax rules applied to cross-border flows that may, or may not, take into account the fact that such flows may be subject to taxation in more than one jurisdiction. If income (in some sense) arises (somehow defined) within a jurisdiction, that jurisdiction is likely to tax it. From this perspective, tax treaties can be seen as international agreements on how to allocate income among those jurisdictions with which the taxpayer arguably has a sufficiently strong connection for them to assert their right to tax. The overt purpose of such arrangements is generally to limit "double taxation," to mitigate tax avoidance, and to provide greater certainty for investors. In an important sense, however, the fundamental significance of treaties is that the countries involved admit that other countries are in some sense *entitled* to impose tax.

International tax rules, whether applied through domestic law or bilateral treaty, are thus in essence an attempt to work out a division of economic income between two political jurisdictions. Such rules are inherently pragmatic, and purpose-driven. Normative rationalizations of particular sets of operational rules—such so-called principles of international taxation as the residence principle or capital export neutrality—may come along later and may become widely accepted as the language in which issues are discussed. But it is important to understand not only that the pragmatic rules applied precede the principles, but also that the results of applying such rules have to be broadly acceptable to all (or at least to all major) participants. If they are not, the rules will be changed.[23]

The aim of the existing international tax system is essentially to allocate the worldwide tax base among jurisdictions based on the economic connection of the activity to jurisdictions. The fundamental question is "How can countries assert an inherently territorially based claim to income that arises in whole or in part outside their territorial jurisdiction?" Regardless of what form it takes— domestic foreign tax credit systems or contractual arrangements in tax treaties—international tax allocation attempts to establish a correspondence (historically on a transactional basis) between economic and financial income. The distortionary effects that may arise from the interaction of differing direct capital income tax systems can realistically be ameliorated only by either eliminating the differentiation—giving up tax sovereignty—or intelligent mutual coordination and case-by-case accommodation of competing national tax claims. Given the apparently strong attachment of national governments to their direct tax systems—as evidenced by the prolonged EU discussion of this issue—solutions requiring harmonization to succeed appear to have a low probability of success in dealing with these problems. In the circumstances, as mentioned above, a more pragmatic (though perhaps less "principled") approach seems the only feasible way to deal with international tax conflicts, consistent with a game-theoretic approach for understanding the motivations for cooperative arrangements.

13.3.1   The Crisis in International Taxation

Globalization in the fiscal context means increased interaction of national economies, in a setting in which fewer intrinsic characteristics of economic activity associate it with (or locate it in) any particular political jurisdiction ("dematerialization," as King 1996 calls it). The problem is how to establish a meaningful correspondence between measurable economic income associated with a tax jurisdiction and the financial income that in practice is subject to that jurisdiction's tax rules, on a basis that compels respect for that claim by other jurisdictions that have an interest in the activity, its outcome, or the actors engaged in the activity. The growing dichotomy between economic reality and the assumptions underlying the existing international tax system needs to be bridged.

The objective of international tax rules is to achieve some degree of measurable and administrable correspondence between economic and financial/tax income. As Sasseville (2000) and others have noted, this aim lies at the root of the concept of permanent establishment. When factor inputs were more clearly associated with specific jurisdictions, traditional accounting concepts of financial income or profit generally approximated some meaningful measure of economic income. Increasingly, however, important factor inputs that contribute to the earning of income do not need to be closely tied to any specific jurisdiction. Neither political divisions nor the formal characteristics of corporate organization and commercial

activity any longer serve necessarily to indicate the location of economic activity, or of the "owner" of the income stream, or the
"source" of economic income.

In these circumstances, any feasible solution to the problem of
assessing and dividing the international tax base in the changing
context of today's world will inevitably be somewhat artificial. But it
need not be as artificial as in the present system, rooted as it is in
simpler times in which, as Bird and Wilkie (2000, 93–94) put it,
"there was, on the whole, a much closer correspondence between
financial flows and economic activities, when a bond was a bond, a
dividend a dividend, and a foreign investment was physical—a hole
in the ground or a building on top of it." Times have changed sufficiently that the rules also need to be changed to secure results that
will be accepted as "fair." As noted earlier, what is really at issue in
sharing the international tax base is the difficult and controversial
concept of "fairness" in an international context. "Fair shares" for all
relevant claimants to the tax pie appear to be an essential element of
any acceptable (and hence sustainable) international tax system.

Of course, if two countries have such different concepts of what is
fair that the claims of one seem to the other to be beyond the realm
of plausible fairness, agreement is unlikely to be reached. On the
other hand, as a recent survey of the growing literature on such
"self-serving biases" suggests, "there are many problems that people
are unable to solve in the abstract, but are able to solve when
placed in a real-world context" (Babcock and Loewenstein 1997,
122). That is, what principle cannot resolve, practice sometimes can,
particularly if practice is carried out within an appropriate institutional setting.

Since the first League of Nations efforts in the 1920s (Picciotto
1992), the international tax community has developed a set of rules
and principles that have served moderately well in devising and
implementing a regime that can both identify taxable international
flows and collect taxes. The existing rules—and the principles
derived from them—were designed to divide income between jurisdictions in a fashion that both roughly proxied economic reality and
could be implemented in practice.

Economists such as Frenkel, Razin, and Sadka (1991) often favor
the pure residence principle because of the undesirable allocative
effects (from a worldwide perspective) of the source principle if
effective tax rates differ between countries. Many legal scholars also

favor the residence principle as a logical component of achieving horizontal equity among domestic taxpayers.[24] Administrators and those more concerned with what *can* be done than with what *should* be done, on the other hand, often tend to favor the source principle for pragmatic reasons, owing to the considerable practical difficulties of extending the residence principle beyond national borders without hard-to-secure cooperation from foreign tax authorities.[25] In practice, how this balance has been struck over time has reflected the outcome of the ongoing and sometimes overt conflict between countries that lies at the root of international tax policy.

The central problem of the international tax game is common to both source- and residence-based tax systems. Both approaches allocate tax base and revenues on the assumption that there are identifiable and measurable economic activities by identifiable actors that may be assessed to tax in accordance with flows attributable to a particular jurisdiction. These "principles" are thus simply ways of dividing up the pie in accordance with (1) some notion of what is going on where and (2) a concept of who has what right to share in the fruits of international economic activity. The first of these points is, as we have noted, becoming increasingly difficult to determine in practice in this changing world. Our major concern here, however, is to bring out some of the implications of the second point with respect to how the first point might potentially be resolved in practice.

Countries that play in the international tax game assert their jurisdiction over international capital income by associating some financial flow of which they are aware with some economic activity that can reasonably be asserted to fall within their political jurisdiction. As Schanz noted over a century ago (Vogel 1988), and as Portner (2000) recently reemphasized, the critical question is thus one of establishing a measure of "economic allegiance" for dividing the international tax base that will be generally accepted as fair and feasible. What matters in the end is not the extent to which any particular solution accords with some presumed normative principle but rather how well it works and how likely it is to prove acceptable to most major players in the international tax game.

In practice, the key aspect to this game is the division of tax base between nations rather than the division of returns between state(s) and investor. These two questions are related, since the battle for tax share may result in heavier (or conceivably lighter) taxation in total, but this issue, although obviously important, is secondary in this discussion.[26] Since nation states are the players in this game, this question will generally be approached from a national rather than a world perspective.[27] The question is simply whether countries achieve their best interests by competing or by cooperating. If the former, what are the conditions required to achieve favorable outcomes? If the latter, what sort of cooperation is required (and what must be given up to achieve it)?

Unfortunately, there do not appear to be principles that are both acceptable and feasible with respect to how to divide up such a complex and changing target as the international tax base in the multiplayer international tax game—even if the players and payoffs are more clearly defined than our earlier discussion suggests (Brams and Taylor 1996). Neither the source nor residence concept, for example, provides very useful guidance on how to assign economic income to a particular territorial jurisdiction, and, as McLure (2000) notes, the meaningfulness of the key concept of permanent establishment as a guide to determining economic allegiance—who the players are—is also very much in question these days.

13.3.2 Approaches to Solutions

One way to attempt to solve the problems that arise from the broader span of economic enterprise than of political jurisdiction is to take a holistic approach—to adopt some grand design, either to restructure the form of taxation (by moving to cash-flow taxes or consumption taxes, for example) or to turn over the problem to some higher, and presumably wiser, authority.

Some, for instance, have suggested that one way to resolve many of the problems arising for taxation as a result of recent global financial changes is by revamping company taxation—for example, by adopting a dual income tax system (Cnossen 1996) or some form of cash-flow or consumption tax (King 1996). To some, the income tax problem seems so complicated, the negotiations required to get anywhere sensible likely to be so long and difficult, and the results likely to prove so unsatisfactory that they will be unstable, that the only answer seems to be to abandon income taxes and move to consumption taxes. This solution has the great advantage of eliminating the problems arising from the tax treatment of interest and especially the problems arising from interest deductibility. As Musgrave (2000b) discusses in detail, consumption (cash-flow) taxes in their various forms simplify the problem both by eliminating timing problems and by defining financial flows as the relevant economic activity to be taxed. On the other hand, they solve the international problem only if they are simultaneously adopted everywhere, and the reality appears to be that it seems unlikely that this approach will soon be adopted in major countries (Munnell 1992; Cnossen and Bird 1990).

Another holistic approach, favored by, for example, Tanzi (1995, 1999), is to formalize and multilateralize international tax information exchanges through what used to be called "a GATT for taxes" or what may perhaps now be called a WTTO (World Tax and Trade Organization). The need for increased supranational authority to resolve many of the problems bedeviling international taxation is clear in the writings of such prominent academic commentators as Avi-Yonath (2000a), for example. In the absence of an international tax police—that is, an overriding sovereign jurisdiction—however, it seems unlikely that this approach will prove to be much more productive than the current unsatisfactory experience with information exchange (Tanzi and Zee 1999). No country's tax administration seems likely to give high priority to enforcing another country's taxes.

Yet another holistic approach—that generally favored to date in the EU context—is some form of imposed harmonization or uniformity. At one level, this approach again requires either international tax policing or the cession of national sovereignty.[28] Imposed harmonization seems to be neither workable nor desirable. At another level, short of the achievement of a "one-world" government, in any case such harmonization seems unlikely to be achieved soon, if ever, in the world as a whole, even if the European Union someday achieves this goal.

On the whole, such holistic approaches to international problems seem overly ambitious, even utopian. They are also perhaps unnecessary. The mere existence of "borderless" transactions does not mean that the only solution is for everyone to do the same thing. Of course, because the actions of one impinge on others, we are more likely to come close to maximizing joint welfare if each acts taking into account the actions of others to some extent—in other words, if a cooperative game is played.

International laws may not be needed to reap gains from trade and investment flows, but a certain degree of international comity *is* necessary. An alternative way to approximate to this end may be, so to speak, to "muddle through"—to search for incremental changes in existing fiscal institutions that may be (1) acceptable, (2) workable, and (3) an improvement—to establish a viable cooperative game in the international tax context, rules to which key players will agree are needed (Shelton 1997). The critical questions are not so much what the rules are as who sets the rules, how they are implemented, and why they are accepted.[29]

Accretionary and voluntary harmonization from below, we suggest, largely accounts for the limited amount of progress that has been made to date in the EU directives with respect to parent-subsidiary relations and mergers and takeovers and the transfer-pricing convention (Bird and Wilkie 2000). This approach is obviously partial and conceptually unsatisfactory in some respects. But it is also not only happening but workable. The main problems encountered in the EU context relate to the treatment of interest (Huizinga 1994) and the existence of tax-exempt providers of capital such as pension funds (Alworth 1998). So long as some capital suppliers are tax-exempt and some flows of capital income are privileged, tax arbitrage will persist, and neither in administrative nor in allocative terms can a fully satisfactory solution be reached. It may thus still be a long way from "here to there" (Brean 1992). Nonetheless, some progress has been made and more probably can continue to be made in what seems to be the right direction, so long as the right questions are posed to the right players in the right forum.

If flows between countries are roughly equal, and their treatment in the different countries is roughly similar, for instance, the results of the prevailing rules (the "OECD consensus") may continue to be (roughly) allocatively acceptable to some players. More generally, however, as noted earlier, the problem in the real world is not how to achieve the tax collector's nirvana of no arbitrage, but rather how to coordinate the limits of disagreement between countries.

In a sense, so long as there is a rough correspondence between economic and financial realities, it may not matter too much how one determines the territorial tax base—whether on the basis of the characteristics of transactions, or entities, or whatever. But when there is no longer such a correspondence, as seems increasingly to be the case, such mainstays of the OECD consensus as permanent establishment and nondiscrimination (formal reciprocity) are unlikely to suffice. Such concepts essentially emerged over time as rough guidelines as to how to carve up the tax base, given economic reality. To the extent that reality has changed, new guidelines are needed. The basic question is not whether change is needed. It clearly is. The question is rather whether it is reasonable to expect the needed new guidelines to be derived from voluntary cooperation. In the world as a whole, this task seems certain to be much more difficult than within the European Union.

This may be viewed as a question of whether a Coasian solution to fiscal externalities can be reached. As is well-known, the answer to this question depends upon both the level of transaction costs relative to the level of externalities and the distribution of both sorts of costs among the players in the game, as well as on how often the game is played (Cornes and Sandler 1996). We do not know enough about these costs to tell whether it is plausible to expect such a solution, or whether countries may instead voluntarily decide that the most efficient way to resolve the problem may be by ceding some authority to a central authority, as may perhaps ensue in the European Union— or even, though we are skeptical, in the perhaps future WTTO.

What we do know is that countries respond to common economic influences, that the response of each affects others, and that the overall outcome of such actions is likely to be better if they are carried out with mutual critical awareness both of the underlying influences and of the policy responses of others.[30] From this perspective, the problem is not so much one of designing an appropriate system of international tax rules as it is to ensure that the process by which such rules are established is known to all and as open and as well informed as possible. In other words, the key to reaching a viable solution to the inherently intractable problems facing the international fiscal community is, through repeated discussions and interactions, to reach at least rough agreement on the key "principles" to be applied in dividing the international tax pie. The argument for pragmatic modesty rather than utopian idealism in approaching this question is essentially that the fundamental problems in taxing capital income in the global economy seem unlikely ever to be resolved except by the application of arbitrary solutions, and that the only way we know to make such solutions tolerable— "fair," if one will—is by ensuring that those who are affected agree to them.[31]

Two general approaches to reaching a cooperative agreement with respect to international taxation may be considered. One is to reach a formal international agreement as to international tax principles and practices. This approach has, to some extent, been followed in the past, from the early days of the League of Nations to the development of the postwar OECD consensus and the current OECD process with respect to harmful tax competition, the taxation of electronic commerce, and so on. More ambitious recent proposals for formal international tax cooperation—Intertax (Surr 1966) as it were—are in this tradition. As Tanzi (1995, 140) puts it, "There is no world institution with the responsibility to establish desirable rules for taxation and with enough clout to induce countries to follow those rules. Perhaps the time has come to establish one." We think, on the contrary, that this time is not yet here. Instead, we suggest that what needs more thought right now is the nature of the institutions within which a set of rules can be developed—rules that, even though (like the elements of the OECD consensus) they may not be legally enforceable, will be largely followed in practice.

An alternative approach to resolving these problems—which may, to a large extent, explain the relative success of the first approach in the past—might be described as "Big Boys" rule (Bird 1994). That is, the major players in effect develop rules that suit their interests and then persuade (or bully) others into agreeing to play by these rules. U.S. hegemony in the postwar era clearly underlay the development of the OECD consensus, abetted in no small degree by the relative congruence of U.S. national interests over most of the latter half of the twentieth century with the achievement of worldwide efficiency in capital markets. The question now, however, is whether a three-bloc world (United States, European Union, and Eastern Asia) will have the same incentives to reach a consensus that will be both relatively efficient and "fair" enough to be sustainable not only for these players but ultimately for other affected countries as well.

13.3.3 "Fair Shares" or Feasible Shares?

Whatever institutional framework is developed or employed, in the end agreement will depend upon the key players getting what they consider to be their "fair share." The critical issue in international taxation thus concerns not efficiency but concepts of justice, although of course how such concepts are implemented may definitely affect the size of the pie to be divided. As we mentioned earlier, from the perspective of worldwide efficiency, what is usually called for is capital export neutrality, which can best be implemented by full and immediate crediting of source-country taxes by residence countries. What is not as well-known as it should be, perhaps, is that no country actually grants such credits, nor is any country likely to do so, since in effect it would be giving the keys to the national treasury to source countries.[32] What seem needed to make progress in the international tax area are not further attempts to develop "envy-free" incentive mechanisms to induce countries to act in what none of them believes is in their own interests, but rather more careful and explicit discussion of pragmatic sharing principles—that is, rationales for dividing the tax base that are both workable (feasible, acceptable) and still accord with a logical (or principled) rationale. Although differences in perceived fairness may not, in the end, be reconcilable through bargaining on shares of surplus, a number of relevant ideas may be found in the literature.

Perhaps the most obvious idea, if not always the easiest to implement, is the *benefit principle*. To the extent that countries provide public services that are cost-reducing (and hence presumably profit-enhancing), those who benefit should obviously be charged for such services. When, as is commonly the case, an array of such services exist that cannot be—or are not—charged for specifically, there is an obvious case in both equity and efficiency terms for imposing a generalized "benefit" tax on those who benefit from public-sector activity but would not otherwise pay for the benefits they receive.

Although arguments along these lines have been used to support corporate profits taxes (Mintz 1999; Musgrave 2000a), an alternative and more appropriate form of business taxation from this perspective would appear to be total factor costs. In fact, as Bird and Mintz (2000) demonstrate, the most appropriate fiscal instrument to implement this principle is an income-based origin principle tax on value added.

What McLure (2000, 6:4) has recently referred to as the "somewhat squishy" concept of the *entitlement principle* derives from Locke (Musgrave 1983).[33] As Musgrave (2000a) has recently spelled out in detail, both source and residence countries can be argued to be "entitled" to a share of the revenues generated by cross-border investments.

In the case of source countries, the entitlement argument is essentially that, since, to at least some extent, the profits generated within their borders arise from the presence of such cooperating factors as natural resources or a skilled labor force, it seems only reasonable for the country that possesses or provides such factors to claim a "fair share" of the profits. At the same time, residence countries may feel "entitled" to exercise a similar claim for their fair share of the global income generated by the activities of their residents. The question, of course, is how to reconcile these conflicting entitlements.

Arguments as to which country—source or residence—"contributes more to the production of income" (Vogel 1988, 86) are likely to be singularly futile with respect to multinational enterprises where, as one of us has said earlier, "the allocation of profits is ... inherently and unavoidably arbitrary since such businesses are ... inevitably 'unitary' in character" (Bird 1986, 334).

While we hesitate to call it a principle, another obvious approach to dividing the tax base is to apply what Oldman (1966) called the *traffic principle* of charging what the traffic will bear—in effect, a discriminatory pricing (or surplus absorbing) approach. This approach is sometimes referred to in the international tax literature as the "soak-up" principle and is most commonly illustrated by the suggestion that source countries should impose taxes at least equal to those levied by residence countries that provide foreign tax credits, in order to ensure that any revenue that goes to the treasury goes to their treasury rather than that of the residence country.

As Musgrave (2000a) notes, such measures may make perfect sense in a noncooperative environment—so long as one can get away with them. It is clear, however, that this approach must be excluded in a cooperative framework, except perhaps to the extent that—as indeed in the OECD consensus—it is pragmatically recognized that since source countries (where they can be clearly identified) get the first "kick at the can" (Brean, Bird, and Krauss 1991), they are more likely to be able to impose effective taxes than are residence countries.

While considered utopian by most tax practitioners, there is also an obvious role, at least in theory, for some version of a *redistribution principle* (Musgrave and Musgrave 1972). There are poor nations, just as there are poor people. Recently, measures have been taken, for example, to relieve certain poor nations of some of the unpleasant economic consequences of being highly indebted. Similarly, in the past, many OECD countries have explicitly permitted poor countries wider latitude in terms of international tax arrangements through such measures as "tax sparing."

More generally, there has long been some recognition in the international tax world—compare for instance the OECD and UN model conventions (Vann 1991)—that it may not be appropriate to apply the same rules to all countries. Some Latin American countries, for example, long asserted the primacy of territorial (source) rights in part on redistributive grounds.[34] Although this subject would appear to repay more careful exploration in the cooperative environment we are discussing—for example, it is clearly, in part, dislike of the "rich" designing rules to be imposed largely on the "poor" that lies behind some of the adverse reaction to the OECD's harmful practices agenda (Langer 2000)—we shall not consider it further here.

A principle that definitely requires further exploration in the cooperative framework, however, is the *reciprocity principle*. Reciprocity in the sense of "you scratch my back, I'll scratch yours" is well established as a principle in international trade and tax negotiations. As a strategy, it leads to cooperative behavior as noted in the game theory literature discussed earlier. As Sasseville (2000, 5:3) says, in reality tax authorities are less concerned about conceptual principles than they are about "enforcing and collecting taxes with a minimal disruption of economic activities, *having regard to what other countries can do to their own taxpayers*" (emphasis added).

Unfortunately, the prevalent convention under the OECD consensus is to interpret such "reciprocity" solely in terms of nominal rates, especially of withholding taxes, even though, as was demonstrated decades ago (P. Musgrave 1967; Sato and Bird 1975), what is really called for in terms of efficiency is so-called effective reciprocity in terms of combined corporate and withholding rates. Interestingly, reciprocity and redistribution may to some extent be combined by, for example, applying different reciprocity standards to poorer countries (e.g., with respect to tax sparing).

A final, and in the end perhaps the most important, guide to dividing the international tax base is what might be called, again at the risk of stretching the word, the *feasibility principle*. In the words of McLure (2000, 6:5), "Whether source-based taxation is administratively feasible trumps conceptual arguments." Much the same may be said with respect to all of the other concepts that are so often raised in international tax literature. Sasseville (2000, 5:11), for example, argues convincingly that "the success of the permanent establishment concept can be explained by the advantages it offers in making sure that tax can actually be collected with a reasonable compliance burden."

Similarly, many of the arguments that have been made in favor of increased explicit recognition of the need for agreed formulary methods to share international tax bases rest, in the end, on pragmatic grounds of feasibility. The formulary approach cuts through the obfuscation of conflicting principles by going directly to the pragmatic resolution of who gets what in a mutually agreed fashion. Of course, it may not always be judicious in a complex multilayered bargaining process to "cut to the chase" in this fashion. But doing so certainly focuses the discussion more sharply on the key issue of who gets what.

Two common criticisms of formulary approaches are that (1) they result in intractable "tax-grabbing" conflicts between jurisdictions to the detriment of both international comity and allocative efficiency and (2) they are terribly difficult and arbitrary in implementation. The first criticism assumes unilateral action and is hence irrelevant in the present context. The second is simply wrong: It is no more difficult (or easier) to implement an agreed formulary approach than any other internationally agreed approach (Mintz 1999).

The need for a "formula split" was recognized over a century ago in a pioneering paper by Schanz in 1892, where a 75:25 split between source and residence countries was suggested (Vogel 1988). The complex and lengthy process that took place over many decades under the auspices of the League of Nations and the OECD was essentially an attempt to find conceptual hooks upon which to hang what the participants recognized to be an acceptably fair split along these lines. Interestingly, a proposal not that far removed from that of Schanz was recently made with respect to e-commerce by Doernberg (1998). Good ideas, it appears, are hard to keep down, although they often seem to be equally hard to implement!

One should not despair, however, since, as the history of the ideas that developed into the OECD consensus shows, the key principles and concepts underlying that consensus largely originated as an attempt to develop a pragmatic and workable approach to allocating the international tax base in a manner that could be considered "fair" by all participants. The key point recognized by Schanz and other early writers on this subject was that what is most important is to establish a plausible and enforceable "economic connection" (nexus) for would-be taxing jurisdictions—that is, something they could really do and that others would respect. The League of Nations work in the 1920s, for example, was explicitly a search for a workable way to define "economic allegiance." As we have noted earlier, the problem currently facing the international tax community is that the compromises worked out over the last fifty years seem unlikely to hold much longer, so that it is necessary to rethink these issues again, with the same objective in mind.

13.4 How to Get There from Here

We are hardly the first to recognize that a certain degree of international cooperation is essential to any feasible resolution of current and future international tax problems. An important question, however, is when and how it might make sense to delegate some decision authority to an international body. As we noted earlier, such delegation does occur to some extent—for example, as the various working groups (Technical Assistance Groups, or TAGs) of the OECD countries attempt to work out the details of how to tax e-commerce. But as with the existing model tax conventions, no state is necessarily bound by any rules that emerge from such discussions even if they assented to their formulation; though presumably by so doing they have deliberately raised the costs of any subsequent dissent. As with Elster's (1984) famous example of Ulysses and the sirens, countries may consciously ask others to, as it were, "bind them to the mast" of internationally agreed principle so that they are less easily tempted to stray into the paths of short-run political or fiscal advantage.

As Zajac (1996) notes, decisions are always made in particular institutional frameworks, and all institutions develop well-defined notions—conventions or norms—that "frame" particular decisions in terms of who and what are formally considered "equal" in some relevant sense. The international tax system is no different, although the problem of how to develop what may be called the necessary degree of "trust" to think of it as a cooperative game is exceptionally complex. As the recent reviews by Ostrom (2000) and Slemrod (chapter 2) on the emergence of norms and trust amongst groups and within nations demonstrate, this subject is an extremely complex one about which we have still much to learn. Since we obviously know even less about the even more complex subject of how to establish trust amongst countries which are themselves made up of many divergent groups and interests, the argument that follows is obviously largely speculative and based more on suggestive inferences than on any well-developed analysis.

An encouraging lesson that some have drawn from experience with the resolution of some international trade disputes, for example, is that it appears that those who are actually involved in such processes on an ongoing basis sometimes seem to resolve issues on bases other than narrow national interests, apparently responding to conventions and norms that have emerged in practice to foster cooperation rather than open conflict (Woodside 1995). On the other hand, it is quite discouraging to see how often such resolutions by "expert tribunals" have not been accepted by those in power who are not themselves engaged in the process but respond, it seems, solely to national (or sectional) interests. As an example, witness the current U.S. discussion with respect to the WTO decision on foreign sales corporations (FSCs).[35] While there are many ways of interpreting this experience, we suggest that to some extent it reflects both the primacy of politics over expertise—which some may, of course, consider to be a good thing—and the perceived primacy of "fairness" over efficiency.

Efficiency is certainly important, but, as we have stressed earlier, it is not the only relevant outcome. Fairness also matters. Indeed, experience suggests strongly that perceived fairness is generally a more critical element than efficiency in international policymaking. Real-world arguments are less about efficiency than about what is perceived to be fair. Perceptions of fairness impinge on attitudes and affect behavior in the international tax game. Economists have, for the most part, carefully constructed their professional discourse to avoid explicitly discussing this issue except in the most sterile fashion in which, for example, allocations are both efficient and equitable simultaneously (Varian 1975). As Zajak (1996, 99) notes, however, compared with the concerns motivating players in the real world, "envy-free theory seems sterile, abstract, and unworldly." In the risky, dynamic, and imperfectly informed real world, there are few, if any, Pareto-improving moves available and, even if there are such moves, there are virtually always losers as well as arguments among the winners about how to divide the surplus.

Moreover, simply setting out the abstract properties of a desirable fair-division scheme does not get us very far. Rather, as Brams and

Taylor (1996) develop at length, we need to go further and provide a feasible algorithm or solution procedure that will achieve the desired goal if we want to contribute to the debate in the real world. One way this can be done in many cases, they show, is in effect to redefine the game by placing it in a broader class of games. It is always easier to resolve a problem of fair division if more than one thing is being divided and balances can be struck simultaneously in several different areas. As we mentioned earlier, for example, federations have to some extent resolved some problems of tax competition and harmonization by "sweetening the pot" for perceived losers through intergovernmental fiscal transfers. Unfortunately, such solutions are not often open with respect to international taxation.[36]

The task is thus how to reconcile differing interests and perceptions in a way that participants will find acceptable and practicable in an arena in which side payments are generally infeasible. If the world is truly evolving into a "global" society, then, like any domestic society, it will have to find ways to develop and implement conventions or even laws that institutionalize the division of the world's goods with a modicum of fairness. We are a long way from this ideal yet (Sandler 1997), but even if countries are not yet much concerned with ensuring either interpersonal equity across national borders or interjurisdictional equity in accordance with any abstract principles of distributive justice, they are very much concerned with dividing the international tax base. Perhaps, as Brams and Taylor (1996) say, the most we can strive for at present is to introduce a more explicit awareness of the need for cooperative behavior or, to put it another way, some more farsighted behavior into the game.

Actually, as we mentioned at the beginning of this chapter, the international tax game has to a surprising extent already demonstrated such behavior, in large part because of the extent to which it has met the criteria set out by Sandler (1997) for solving "global challenges" as we discuss shortly. Assuming that each nation acts independently—for example, through the unilateral approach of the foreign tax credit and so on—at one level, the problem may be interpreted as how to induce them to do so constructively in the interest of all. Much of the economic literature on international taxation may be construed along these lines as attempting to exhort the virtues of world efficiency as a goal of tax policy. This approach has not been notably successful except when, as was arguably the case in the postwar era, it coincided with the perceived interests of both important public and private sector players in a "lead" country (the United States).

If this approach fails, as we think it is likely to do in the world as it is, the next step is to try to build a "club" or a stable coalition of cooperating states. To do so is always tricky in the international arena—as the European Union has so often shown with respect to direct taxes—since it invariably requires delegating some degree of sovereignty for at least a limited sphere of action.[37] More success is likely to be achieved, Sandler (1997) suggests, the more closely the following principles are adhered to:

• *Keep it simple.* "Complex interactions among states may best be fostered with the help of very simple structures that respect the nation-state as crucial player" (Sandler 1997, 143). In the international tax context, this suggests that building on the OECD-led approach may indeed be a better way to go than any more ambitious attempt to erect a new "global" tax body. Critics such as Langer (2000) may attack the lack of representativeness of the OECD, and important countries such as India and China may well balk at following rules that they had no explicit role in making. Nonetheless, this approach seems more likely to succeed in working out a revised "sharing" system than setting up yet another ineffective worldwide body.[38] But will any such solution prove widely acceptable?

• *Keep the numbers of those involved in the negotiations small* and their interests as homogeneous as possible. Again, the OECD—or perhaps even the G7 or some smaller forum that recognizes more explicitly the emerging major "blocs" of the world economy (NAFTA, European Union, Eastern Asia)—would appear to offer the most appropriate venue. As in the current OECD process, where appropriate, nonmembers (such as Singapore) can and should be involved in the core discussion process through, for example, membership of the relevant TAG. The critical question, of course, is whether and to what extent solutions devised by the few will be accepted as "fair" by countries not themselves involved in the negotiations. Applied at the level of countries, the "democratic deficit" stressed by Keohane and Nye (2001) suggests that unless countries are explicitly involved in reaching a particular solution, they are unlikely to be willing to accept that solution. Recognizing this problem, the OECD, the United Nations, and others concerned with international taxation are currently considering whether and to what extent a new "Global Tax Forum" can or should be created as a forum to carry on such discussions. Inevitably, however, the broader the representation, the more diverse the interests, and the more difficult to reach a clear solution.

• *Use expert studies to reduce uncertainty.* The first two "principles" mentioned do not offer much hope since the way to reach a solution—through a simple, focused negotiation within a relatively small and homogeneous group—seems incompatible with wide acceptance of the fairness of any such solution by a heterogeneous world. In contrast, this third approach, which has a long and honorable tradition in international taxation starting with the League of Nations and more recently exercised with the OECD, has some promise, essentially by gradually building up "common knowledge" about the problems and possible solutions.[39] As noted earlier, it would seem advisable to build on and strengthen the work of the OECD in this respect, perhaps extending its ambit still more into nonmember countries than has already been done, rather than turning to more inclusive bodies such as the IMF or the WTO as some have suggested. The earlier parallel discussions in the OECD and the United Nations with respect to the model tax convention, with substantial overlap between the participants in the two groups, might be one way to proceed, although it should again be recognized that neither of these groups would likely have made much progress had the United States not taken a lead role in both forums.

• *Set sights low enough to achieve success.* One can always improve later, but only if the process gets started. To become sustainable, any process needs to produce success in the sense of yielding outcomes that are broadly acceptable to all or most participants. Of course, what different people perceive to be fair depends upon both history and procedures.

• *Look for a leader.* There is no question that the United States led the way in forming the postwar consensus on international taxation. There is less certainty that it will equally lead the way into the future. Bird (1987) suggested some years ago that there might be a role for smaller developed countries to lead the way, but the relative lack of success of this approach in the "Cairns group" approach to international agricultural trade casts doubt on this scenario. Unless the United States, the European Union, or some equally powerful and persuasive leader takes charge, the process of developing acceptable principles seems likely to be long and may well be ultimately unsuccessful. The point is not that what the leader proposes must, should, or will be accepted. It is rather that only with some key player pushing for a solution is anything likely to get done.[40] This appears to be perhaps the major problem in developing a sustainable solution to the cooperative international tax game right now.

Simple principles such as the above may not be all that easy to reconcile either with the more formal game-theoretic framework with which we began or with the considerably more complex and fuzzy realities of international political economy. Nonetheless, we suggest that at this stage of the evolution of the international tax system, what is most needed is not a grandiose scheme that will resolve all our problems, present and future, but rather some small, doable steps that may, if sustained, lead us over time into developing the new world tax order that seems necessary to match the changing nature of the international economy.[41]

From this perspective, continued development and discussion in the OECD and other forums of the principles and methods of sharing the tax base seems the right way to go—although in the absence of a leading player with clear ideas and sufficient influence, it is by no means clear where this process will lead. No one has a monopoly on the "right" answer for the international tax system, in part because the answer that is right can only be reached by a process of discussion and experience that is both sufficiently focused to reach a conclusion and sufficiently inclusive to ensure that those affected feel they have been treated fairly. The balance of these factors is delicate, and the outcome can be reached only over time as the world gradually moves to a new (relative) consensus about how best to divide up the international tax base. What those interested in maintaining the degree of international tax comity needed to facilitate world trade and investment need to do, we think, is to pay much more attention to the difficult institutional questions involved in establishing a setting within which countries can play the game of sharing the international tax base in this changing world.

Notes

We are grateful for useful comments from an anonymous reviewer, Sijbren Cnossen, Thomas Moutos, Peggy Musgrave, Victor Thuronyi, Henry Tulkens, and other participants in the CESifo conference, "Public Finances and Public Policy in the New Millennium," University of Munich, January 12–13, 2001.

1. A classic text in the field of international taxation is R. Musgrave (1969); see also Musgrave (1960) for an earlier formulation.

2. See, notably, Musgrave and Musgrave (1972), recently reprinted in Musgrave (2000).

3. See, for example, two of her recent contributions: Musgrave (2000a, b).

4. The OECD (1998) report has been strongly supported by some (e.g., Avi-Yonath 2000b; Weiner 2000) and equally strongly criticized by others (Langer 2000; Penalosa 2000). For a recent review of the "harmful tax competition" debate, see Sieker (2001). Makhlouf (2001) is the most recent OECD report on this subject.

5. See Sandler (2002) for further discussion.

6. See Thuronyi (2001) for a useful discussion of the likelihood of a multilateral EU treaty and Sørensen (2001) for an analysis of regional tax coordination. As Goulder (2001) notes, the OECD has moved faster in this area than the European Union in some ways because, unlike the European Union, in which any member state can block action, the OECD operates as a "consensus" organization, which can act even though some members disagree—as, for example, Belgium, Switzerland, Portugal, and Luxembourg do with respect to "harmful tax practices."

7. We focus in this chapter on the taxation of capital income and especially corporate taxation since that is clearly the critical area. As Bird and McLure (1990) noted, if international capital income taxation cannot be sustained, the long-run viability of the income tax in general is called into question. Moreover, as Musgrave (2000b) argues, only if *all* countries shift to consumption taxation will the problems plaguing the present system of international taxation diminish.

8. Some recent papers (Fuest 1995; Fuest and Huber 1999) consider whether tax coordination will work when only some tax instruments are coordinated.

9. A recent exception is Cappelen (1999).

10. One must not be misled by terminology: A "noncooperative" game could be—like a competitive market—more welfare-enhancing than is a cooperative (cartel-like) game.

11. We do not discuss the important question of how conflicting domestic interests in different countries may influence government policy. Several commentators on an earlier draft suggested that the existing system can best be explained by the dominance of producer interests and domestic special-interest politics which enables these groups to block effective international tax cooperation. We do not dispute that such an interest group political model may indeed have considerable explanatory power. Nonetheless, in the present chapter we adopt a more systemic and institutional approach to international taxation. As Barkdull and Harris (2001) note in a recent analysis of foreign policy, these (and other) approaches are best viewed not so much as competing models of reality as different facets of the complex reality, all of which may be needed to grasp the whole picture.

12. See Wilson (1999) and Sørensen (2001) for more extensive consideration of the tax competition literature.

13. It is not necessary to have a binding agreement to achieve cooperation. In a supergame with noncooperative behavior (Telser 1988), a strategy of "tit-for-tat" could lead to cooperative behavior among governments if each believes that cheating would cause consequences that are more negative than continuing cooperation. However, cooperation is not the only possible outcome in a supergame.

14. As mentioned in note 11 earlier, these issues may be particularly important with respect to international taxation but this aspect is not further discussed here.

15. Similar problems arise with shipping and airlines. In extreme cases, a single stop by a ship at a port has led to the imposition of profits taxes. Special arrangements have evolved over the years to handle such cases, including visiting rock stars and other entertainers. Presumably, with time, similar arrangements may be evolved to handle problems such as those mentioned in the text.

16. As discussed later, the extent of "common knowledge" (Chwe 2001) among different governments is also important.

17. Graetz (2001) argues that U.S. policy should be based on national interests, not on global interests such as capital export or import neutrality. However, in our view, the essential nature of a cooperative agreement is that it achieves something other than that achievable by national interests alone. In a cooperative game, countries will only participate in the game if they can achieve a higher payoff than the "national interest" payoff achieved in a noncooperative game.

18. In practice, some governments have credited foreign corporate income taxes even on a unilateral basis, rather than restricting foreign taxes to be deducted from income. Several models have looked at whether a capital-exporting country should credit foreign taxes from its own national perspective. Gordon (1992), for example, suggests that a large country, operating as a first mover, might credit foreign taxes to encourage smaller capital-importing countries to assess withholding taxes on income. The withholding taxes paid by the residents of the home country in the foreign jurisdiction would limit the scope for tax evasion.

19. In reality, governments as a rule restrict the crediting of foreign taxes to the amount of home tax liability on the income earned in foreign jurisdictions. Some recent literature (e.g., Devereux and Hubbard 2000) shows that the conventional views discussed in the text are not always optimal from a national standpoint. On the whole, however, as Thomas Moutos notes in his comment on this chapter, "it is hard to imagine that the tax authorities of any country decide their tax regime by keeping track of the ever-changing rules for optimal taxation advocated by the academic literature."

20. As Musgrave (1967) and Sato and Bird (1975) demonstrated, formal or nominal reciprocity is allocatively distorting when countries have different systems of corporate and personal taxation.

21. More generally, the Nash bargaining solution can be viewed as an approximation of other bargaining solutions, including the sequential game proposed by Rubinstein (1982).

22. For perhaps the best attempt to date, see Sørensen (2001).

23. This is not to deny that there may not be a potentially important role to be played by a clear normative vision of what a "good" international tax system should look like.

Such a vision may both motivate players in seeking solutions and guide them in deciding which solutions they will accept (e.g., by creating "common knowledge" (Chwe 2001)). Nonetheless, we argue in this chapter that what matters more than the internal logic of a system or its conformity to some vision is its acceptability and workability. Visions determine outcomes only to the extent they mold minds to think in the same way and hence to accept a particular system.

24. See Kingson (1981) for a classic statement; also P. Musgrave (1969). For a contrary position, see Vogel (1990).

25. As Sørensen (2001) argues, agreement on minimum source taxation may provide a more feasible approach than universal effective residence taxation (which in turn, he suggests, seems more attainable than a world—or regional—coordinating body).

26. Of course, to the extent that multinational firms are influential "players," their main concern is more likely to be the level of taxes than the jurisdictions to which they pay them, so the comment in the text reflects the "government" perspective adopted in this chapter, as discussed in note 11 earlier.

27. To the extent that a "world" perspective is adopted by any country, as noted earlier, it is in any case generally done in its own national interest.

28. This approach perverts the meaning of harmonization from the achievement of common goals to the imposition of uniform rules, which again denies the reality of national differences and member-state sovereignty: See Dosser (1966) and Bird (1989) for further discussion.

29. See, for example, the strenuous objections of Langer (2000) to the OECD's harmful tax competition proposals on the grounds that the rules are being made by a self-selected and hypocritical group of countries and are being thrust upon other countries with different and—he assumes—equally legitimate interests.

30. Another way to put this is that a certain degree of "common knowledge" (Chwe 2001) is needed to facilitate understanding of each other's likely reactions and hence the attainment of agreement.

31. This problem is much more complex in the international setting than in the context of a federal state, in which there is not only a clear overarching authority but also alternative channels through which conflicts may be resolved, so that what a player loses in one field may be regained in another. From one perspective, this may be viewed as another argument for a WTTO, in which, for example, trade and tax issues may be considered together and hence more scope opened for such "issue bargaining." In the absence of a formal hierarchical structure (a constitution, a central government), however, we think the mere creation of such a body would not help much in devising credible side payments in the international setting. Indeed, as we suggest in section 13.4, introducing too many issues (and players) may well make it even more difficult to reach sustainable solutions.

32. What is equally interesting, and perhaps more surprising, is that no country appears to implement as its primary approach what P. Musgrave (1969) has demonstrated is the way to maximize national (rather than world) efficiency—namely, subjecting foreign-source income to full current taxation while allowing foreign taxes to be deducted. The absence of this appears to reflect (1) the importance of the "exporter" interest in reciprocal treatment, (2) the usual "mercantilist" preferences expressed in public policy—in this case, fostering foreign investment—and (3) more optimistically

in the present context, perhaps the perceived desirability of conforming to prevalent international conventions in tax treatment.

33. The entitlement argument was labeled "national rental" in Musgrave and Musgrave (1972). This terminology is also used in Musgrave (2000a).

34. Of course, this advocacy was undoubtedly linked to the fact that such countries (e.g., Argentina) had territorial systems themselves. Most major Latin American countries have now moved to a "worldwide" system in principle.

35. See Culbertson and Drummond (2000) for discussion of the general reluctance of the United States to submit to international decisions.

36. See the discussion in note 31 earlier. Of course, the statement in the text is overly strong since treaties are often made in a broader "trading" context. For example, the withholding rate on dividends in the Canada-U.S. treaty is generally considered to have been set at the level it is in part in exchange for U.S. acceptance of Canada's not granting dividend tax credits to U.S. investors.

37. For a recent discussion of the relevance of the "club model" of international organizations, see Keohane and Nye (2001), who emphasize what they call the "democratic deficit" of such organizations—that is, the extent to which they are dominated by experts and hence insufficiently "politicized" in the sense of lacking effective political links to their constituencies.

38. We thus do not agree with Avi-Yonath (2000a), who favors moving the harmful tax competition debate "upstairs" to the WTO both because it is a more inclusive body and because of its enforcement capacity. In part for the reason mentioned in the last note (the democratic deficit of the WTO), we instead agree with Green (1998), who notes that tax sovereignty is too key for most players—not least the United States—for them to give it up in any substantial degree to any international body in the foreseeable future.

39. As Chwe (2001, 111) says, "When we face each other, when we are both awake, that fact is common knowledge, and successful coordination, although not guaranteed ... is at least possible. When you are facing away, successful coordination is not possible, even when both of us get the message."

40. This might be because the "leader" provides, as it were, an "umbrella" under which others can shelter (Sandler 2002), as the United States arguably did in the development of the postwar consensus on international taxation. Or it might be because its position provides an anchor or a "focal point" (Chwe 2001) around which discussion can coalesce.

41. For earlier attempts to sketch such a "new tax order," see Bird (1988) and Bird and Mintz (1994).

References

Alworth, J. S. 1998. "Taxation and Integrated Financial Markets: The Challenges of Derivatives and Other Financial Innovations." *International Tax and Public Finance* 5: 507–534.

Avi-Yonath, R. 2000a. "Globalization, Tax Competition, and the Fiscal Crisis of the Welfare State." *Harvard Law Review* 113: 1575–1603.

Avi-Yonath, R. 2000b. "Tax, Trade, and Harmful Tax Competition: Reflections on the FSC Controversy." *Tax Notes International* 21: 2840–2845.

Babcock, L., and G. Loewenstein. 1997. "Explaining Bargaining Impasse: The Role of Self-Serving Biases." *Journal of Economic Perspectives* 11: 109–126.

Bacchetta, P., and M. Espinosa. 2000. "Exchange of Information Clauses in International Tax Treaties." *International Tax and Public Finance* 7: 275–294.

Barkdull, J., and P. G. Harris. 2001. "Ecology and Foreign Policy: Theoretical Lessons from the Literature." Lingnan University Working Paper No. 112, Hong Kong.

Bird, R. M. 1986. "The Interjurisdictional Allocation of Income." *Australian Tax Forum* 3: 333–354.

Bird, R. M. 1987. *The Taxation of International Investment Flows*. Wellington, New Zealand: Institute of Policy Studies.

Bird, R. M. 1988. "Shaping a New International Tax Order." *Bulletin for International Fiscal Documentation* 42: 292–299.

Bird, R. M. 1989. "Tax Harmonization in Federations and Common Markets." In *Public Finance and Performance of Enterprises*, ed. M. Neumann and K. W. Roskamp. Paris: International Institute of Public Finance.

Bird, R. M. 1994. "A View from the North." *Tax Law Review* 44: 745–757.

Bird, R. M., and C. E. McLure Jr. 1990. "The Personal Income Tax in an Interdependent World." In *The Personal Income Tax: Phoenix from the Ashes?* ed. S. Cnossen and R. M. Bird. Amsterdam: North-Holland.

Bird, R. M., and J. M. Mintz. 1994. "Future Developments in Tax Policy." *Federal Law Review* 22: 402–413.

Bird, R. M., and J. M. Mintz. 2000. "Tax Assignment in Canada: A Modest Proposal." In *The State of the Federation, 2000–01: Towards a New Mission Statement for Canadian Fiscal Federalism*, ed. H. Lazar. Montreal: McGill-Queen's University Press.

Bird, R. M., and J. S. Wilkie. 2000. "Source- vs. Residence-Based Taxation in the European Union: The Wrong Question?" In *Taxing Capital Income in the European Union: Issues and Options for Reform*, ed. S. Cnossen. Oxford, UK: Oxford University Press.

Bond, E., and T. Gresnik. 1996. "Regulation of Multinational Firms with Two Active Governments: A Common Agency Approach." *Journal of Public Economics* 59: 33–53.

Brams, S. J., and A. D. Taylor. 1996. *Fair Division*. Cambridge, UK: Cambridge University Press.

Brean, D. J. S. 1992. "Here or There? The Source and Residence Principles of International Taxation." In *Taxation to 2000 and Beyond*, ed. R. M. Bird and J. M. Mintz. Toronto: Canadian Tax Foundation.

Brean, D. J. S., R. M. Bird, and M. Krauss. 1991. *Taxation of International Portfolio Investment*. Ottawa: Center for Trade Policy and Law and the Institute for Research on Public Policy.

Cappelen, A. W. 1999. "National and International Distributive Justice in Bilateral Tax Treaties." *Finanzarchiv* 56: 424–442.

Chwe, M. S.-Y. 2001. *Rational Ritual: Culture, Coordination, and Common Knowledge*. Princeton: Princeton University Press.

Cnossen, S. 1996. "Company Taxes in the European Union: Criteria and Options for Reform." *Fiscal Studies* 17(4): 67–97.

Cnossen, S., and R. M. Bird, eds. 1990. *The Personal Income Tax: Phoenix from the Ashes?* Amsterdam: North-Holland.

Cockfield, A. J. 2000. "Should We Really Tax Profits from Computer Servers? A Case Study in E-Commerce Taxation." *Tax Notes International* 21: 2407–2415.

Cornes, R., and T. Sandler. 1996. *The Theory of Externalities, Public Goods, and Club Goods*. Cambridge, UK: Cambridge University Press.

Culbertson, R. E., and A. S. Drummond. 2000. "Is the Country that Developed the Advance Pricing Agreement Finally Ready to Take Arbitration Seriously?" In *2000 World Tax Conference Report*. Toronto: Canadian Tax Foundation.

Devereux, M. P., and R. G. Hubbard. 2000. "Taxing Multinationals." National Bureau of Economic Research Working Paper No. 7920, Cambridge, MA.

Dickescheid, T. 1999. "Tax Competition with Multinational Firms." *Finanzarchiv* 56: 500–517.

Doernberg, R. L. 1998. "Electronic Commerce and International Tax Sharing." *Tax Notes International* 16: 1013–1022.

Doernberg, R. L. 2000. "Electronic Commerce: Changing Income Tax Treaty Principles a Bit?" *Tax Notes International* 21: 2417–2430.

Dosser, D. 1966. "Economic Analysis of Tax Harmonization." In *Fiscal Harmonization in Common Markets*, ed. C. S. Shoup. (Two volumes.) New York: Columbia University Press.

Dressel, A., and R. Goulder. 2000. "IFA Asia Regional Conference Focuses on E-Commerce and International Taxation." *Tax Notes International* 21: 2331–2335.

Edwards, J., and M. Keen. 1996. "Tax Competition and Leviathan." *European Economic Review* 40: 113–134.

Elster, J. 1984. *Ulysses and the Sirens*. Rev. ed. Cambridge, UK: Cambridge University Press.

Frenkel, J. A., A. Razin, and E. Sadka. 1991. *International Taxation in an Integrated World*. Cambridge: MIT Press.

Fuest, C. 1995. "Interjurisdictional Competition and Public Expenditure: Is Tax Co-ordination Counterproductive?" *Finanzarchiv* 52: 478–496.

Fuest, C., and B. Huber. 1999. "Can Tax Coordination Work?" *Finanzarchiv* 56: 443–458.

Gordon, R. H. 1983. "An Optimal Taxation Approach to Fiscal Federalism." *Quarterly Journal of Economics* 98: 567–586.

Gordon, R. H. 1992. "Can Capital Income Taxes Survive in Open Economies?" *Journal of Finance* 47: 1159–1180.

Goulder, R. 2001. "Worldwide Tax Review." *Tax Notes International* 7: 873–874.

Graetz, M. J. 2001. "Taxing International Income: Inadequate Principles, Outdated Concepts and Unsatisfactory Policies." *Brooklyn Journal of Law* 26: 1357–1448.

Green, R. M. 1998. "Antilegalistic Approaches to Resolving Disputes between Governments: A Comparison of the International Tax and Trade Regimes." *Yale Journal of International Law* 23: 79–139.

Hamada, K. 1966. "Strategic Aspects of Taxation of Foreign Investment Income." *Quarterly Journal of Economics* 80: 361–375.

Huizinga, H. 1994. "International Interest Withholding Taxation: Prospects for a Common European Policy." *International Tax and Public Finance* 1: 277–291.

Huizinga, H., and S. B. Nielsen. 2000. "The Taxation of Interest in Europe: A Minimum Withholding Tax?" In *Taxing Capital Income in the European Union: Issues and Options for Reform*, ed. S. Cnossen. Oxford, UK: Oxford University Press.

Kanbur, R., and M. Keen. 1993. "Jeux sans Frontières: Tax Competition and Tax Coordination when Countries Differ in Size." *American Economic Review* 83: 877–892.

Keen, M. 1987. "Welfare Effects of Commodity Tax Harmonization." *Journal of Public Economics* 33: 107–114.

Keohane, R., and J. S. Nye Jr. 2001. "Between Centralization and Fragmentation: The Club Model of Multilateral Cooperation and Problems of Democratic Legitimacy." Kennedy School of Government (Harvard University) KSG Working Paper No. 01-004.

King, M. 1996. "Tax Systems in the 21st Century." Paper presented to International Fiscal Association, Geneva, Switzerland.

Kingson, C. 1981. "The Coherence of International Taxation." *Columbia Law Review* 81: 1151–1289.

Langer, M. J. 2000. "Harmful Tax Competition: Who Are the Real Tax Havens?" *Tax Notes International* 21: 2831–2839.

McLure, C. E., Jr. 2000. "Source-Based Taxation and Alternatives to the Concept of Permanent Establishment." In *2000 World Tax Conference Report*. Toronto: Canadian Tax Foundation.

Makhlouf, G. 2001. "Statement on the OECD's Harmful Tax Practices Initiative." *Tax Notes International* 7: 875–891.

Mintz, J. M. 1999. "Globalization of the Corporate Income Tax: The Role of Allocation." *Finanzarchiv* 56: 389–422.

Mintz, J. M., and H. Tulkens. 1986. "Commodity Tax Competition between Member States of a Federation: Equilibrium and Efficiency." *Journal of Public Economics* 29: 133–172.

Mintz, J. M., and H. Tulkens. 1996. "Optimality Properties of Alternative Systems of Taxation of Foreign Capital Income." *Journal of Public Economics* 60: 373–399.

Munnell, A. H. 1992. "Taxation of Capital Income in a Global Economy: An Overview." *New England Economic Review* (September–October): 33–52.

Musgrave, P. B. 1967. "Harmonization of Direct Business Taxes: A Case Study." In *Fiscal Harmonization in Common Markets*, Volume 2, ed. C. S. Shoup. New York: Columbia University Press.

Musgrave, P. B. 1969. *United States Taxation of Foreign Investment Income*. Cambridge: Harvard Law School International Tax Program.

Musgrave, P. B. 2000a. "Interjurisdictional Equity in Company Taxation: Principles and Applications to the European Union." In *Taxing Capital Income in the European Union: Issues and Options for Reform*, ed. S. Cnossen. Oxford, UK: Oxford University Press.

Musgrave, P. B. 2000b. "Consumption Tax Proposals in an International Setting." *Tax Law Review* 54: 77–100.

Musgrave, R. A. 1960. "Criteria for Foreign Tax Credit." In *Taxation and Operations Abroad*. Princeton: Tax Institute of America.

Musgrave, R. A. 1969. *Fiscal Systems*. New Haven: Yale University Press.

Musgrave, R. A. 1983. "Who Should Tax, Where, and What?" In *Tax Assignment in Federal Countries*, ed. C. E. McLure Jr. Canberra, Australia: Centre for Research on Federal Financial Relations, Australian National University.

Musgrave, R. A. 2000. *Public Finance in a Democratic Society, Volume III: The Foundations of Taxation and Expenditure*. Cheltenham, UK: Edward Elgar.

Musgrave, R. A., and P. B. Musgrave. 1972. "Inter-Nation Equity." In *Modern Fiscal Issues*, ed. R. M. Bird and J. G. Head. Toronto: University of Toronto Press.

Nash, J. 1950. "The Bargaining Problem." *Econometrica* 18: 155–162.

OECD. 1998. *Harmful Tax Competition*. Paris: Organization for Economic Cooperation and Development.

Oldman, O. 1966. "Tax Policy of Less Developed Countries with Respect to Foreign Income and Income of Foreigners." In *Taxation of Foreign Income*. Princeton: Tax Institute of America.

Osterweil, E. 2000. "The OECD Report on Harmful Tax Competition and the EU Code of Conduct." In *2000 World Tax Conference Report*. Toronto: Canadian Tax Foundation.

Ostrom, E. 2000. "Collective Action and the Evolution of Social Norms." *Journal of Economic Perspectives* 14(3): 137–158.

Penalosa, J. L. de J. 2000. "Harmful Tax Competition Measures: A Critique." In *2000 World Tax Conference Report*. Toronto: Canadian Tax Foundation.

Persson, T., G. Roland, and G. Tabellini. 1997. "Comparative Politics and Public Finance." Centre for Economic Policy Research mimeo, London.

Picciotto, S. 1992. *International Business Taxation*. London: Weidenfeld & Nicolson.

Portner, R. 2000. "Permanent Establishment: Rethinking Definitions, Effects, and Requirements." In *2000 World Tax Conference Report*. Toronto: Canadian Tax Foundation.

Rubinstein, A. 1982. "Perfect Equilibrium in a Bargaining Model." *Econometrica* 50: 97–109.

Sandler, T. 1997. *Global Challenges*. Cambridge, UK: Cambridge University Press.

Sandler, T. 2002. "On Financing Global and International Public Goods." In *International Public Goods: Developing Global Incentives*, ed. M. Ferroni and A. Mody. Dordrecht, Netherlands: Kluwer.

Sasseville, J. 2000. "The Future of the Treaty Rules for Taxing Business Profits." In *2000 World Tax Conference Report*. Toronto: Canadian Tax Foundation.

Sato, M., and R. M. Bird. 1975. "International Aspects of the Taxation of Corporations and Shareholders." *International Monetary Fund Staff Papers* 22: 384–455.

Shelton, J. 1997. "Emerging Issues in Taxing Business in a Global Economy." *Tax Notes International* 14: 221–223.

Sieker, S. 2001. "Offshore Financial Centers and 'Harmful Tax Competition': The Year 2000 in Review." *Tax Notes International* 22: 557–573.

Slemrod, J. B. 1995. "Free Trade Taxation and Protectionist Taxation." *International Tax and Public Finance* 2: 471–489.

Sørensen, P. B. 2001. "International Tax Coordination: Regionalism or Globalism." CESifo Working Paper No. 483, Munich, Germany.

Surr, J. V. 1966. "Intertax: Intergovernmental Cooperation in Taxation." *Harvard International Law Journal* 7: 179–237.

Tanzi, V. 1995. *Taxation in an Integrating World*. Washington, DC: Brookings Institution.

Tanzi, V. 1999. "Is There a Need for a World Tax Organization?" In *The Economics of Globalization*, ed. A. Razin and E. Sadka. New York: Cambridge University Press.

Tanzi, V., and H. H. Zee. 1999. "Taxation in a Borderless World: The Role of Information Exchange." In *International Studies in Taxation: Law and Economics*, ed. G. Lindecrona, S.-O. Olin, and B. Wiman. London: Kluwer Law International.

Telser, L. G. 1988. *Theories of Competition*. Amsterdam: North-Holland.

Thuronyi, V. 2001. "International Tax Cooperation and a Multilateral Treaty." *Brooklyn Journal of International Law* 26: 1641–1682.

Vann, R. 1991. "A Model Tax Treaty for the Asian-Pacific Region?" *Bulletin for International Fiscal Documentation* 45: 99–131.

Varian, H. R. 1975. "Distributive Justice, Welfare Economics and the Theory of Justice." *Journal of Philosophy and Public Affairs* 4: 223–247.

Vogel, K. 1988. "The Search for Compatible Tax Systems." In *Tax Policy in the Twenty-First Century*, ed. H. Stein. New York: John Wiley & Sons.

Vogel, K. 1990. "World-Wide vs. Source Taxation of Income: A Review and Re-Evaluation of Arguments." In *Influence of Tax Differentials on International Competitiveness*. Deventer, Netherlands: Kluwer.

Weiner, J. M. 2000. "The OECD's Forum on Harmful Tax Practices and the New Spirit of International Cooperation." In *2000 World Tax Conference Report*. Toronto: Canadian Tax Foundation.

Wilson, J. D. 1999. "Theories of Tax Competition." *National Tax Journal* 52: 269–304.

Woodside, K. B. 1995. "Institutions for the Settlement of Trade Disputes: The Case of the Canada–United States Free Trade Agreement." In *Institutional Design*, ed. D. L. Wiemer. Boston: Kluwer Academic Publishers.

Zajac, E. E. 1996. *Political Economy of Fairness*. Cambridge: MIT Press.

Comments

Thomas Moutos

The chapter by Richard Bird and Jack Mintz is an interesting, wide-ranging, and judicious presentation of the problems bedeviling the international tax system. These problems arise from the difficulties in allocating the worldwide tax base among jurisdictions when there are conflicting claims about what constitutes a country's tax base. These problems have been recently exacerbated by the combination of a seamless world economy and the continuing absence of coordination among national tax systems. The authors, instead of using a stylized model in order to present an "efficient solution" to the international tax problem, have sensibly chosen to adopt a pragmatic approach to come down in favor of some simple guidelines that could be used to effect the much-needed improvements in the international tax system. The discussion is informed by the framework of cooperative game theory, with enough attention being paid to identify the rules of the international tax game, the relevant players, and the expected payoffs.

Bird and Mintz focus their attention not on whether some combination of the residence or the source principle of international taxation should be preferred on grounds of different efficiency criteria, but —rightly so— on what general principles should guide the procedure leading to an agreement that the interested parties will consider as "fair." In support of their approach, they rely on two observations. First, they note that there is no country in the world that grants a full foreign tax credit system (which is required if worldwide efficiency is to be achieved in conjunction with the residence principle). Second, they note that there is also no country that implements the national efficiency criterion (the Musgrave-Feldstein-Hartman (MFH) principle) since firms are *not* allowed to deduct foreign taxes in order to determine the home tax base. Based on the second observation, the authors conclude that tax policies are not decided with an eye to national (never mind world) efficiency considerations.

However, in the real world, policymakers may have in mind a more sophisticated principle for national welfare maximization than the MFH one. For example, the MFH principle may not be the relevant one if we take a modern view of multinational firm decision making in which, unlike portfolio investment, foreign direct investment (FDI) is determined by strategic choices. In this view, key decisions about the location of a plant (as opposed to marginal additions to existing investment) are determined by comparing the after-tax profits in different locations. Devereux and Hubbard (2000) show that, in this case, the MFH principle is not optimal from a national viewpoint. Nevertheless, it is hard to imagine that the tax authorities of any country decide their tax regime by keeping track of the ever-changing rules for optimal taxation advocated by the academic literature. In this sense, the emphasis by the authors on issues of (inter-country) fairness rather than efficiency appears justified on pragmatic grounds. Yet, on the same grounds, it seems likely that domestic special-interest politics have played and will continue to play a more important role in determining the content of international tax agreements than international equity considerations.

The literature on the political economy of trade policy leaves one in no doubt that special-interest politics are major determinants of trade policy. It would thus be surprising if special-interest politics were not also important determinants of international taxation issues. Yet, although the authors admit to the importance of this issue, they have not attempted to examine how political economy considerations may dilute the importance of "perceived fairness" in international policymaking. Indeed, there is enough evidence that private interests have been as important as national interests or efficiency considerations in shaping the rules of international taxation. For example, the coexistence of tax havens and the application of the residence principle to some incomes has allowed many wealthy individuals to avoid paying taxes in their own countries by establishing tax addresses in tax havens. It is important to note that for a country to qualify as a tax haven, it must have, in addition to low or zero tax rates, developed a significant treaty framework with important countries so that the incomes channeled to the tax-haven country are not heavily taxed at the source. Political economy considerations appear a more sensible explanation for the development of these treaties than concerns for an equitable sharing of the international tax base. Thus, although the residence principle is, in general, considered to be superior to the source principle on both allocation and equity grounds, its interaction with the existing institutional framework creates some shortcomings.

One of the most interesting points made by Bird and Mintz relates to broadening the bargaining agenda. Yet, although they accept, in principle, that it is always easier to resolve a bargaining problem if more than one thing is the objective of negotiations (since in this case it becomes possible to accept "losses" in some areas which are balanced by "gains" in others), they dismiss the relevance of this to international taxation. However, there is ample evidence from intra-EU negotiations that countries have been induced to accept a package of deals—some of which they would not be willing to accept in isolation (see Moravcsik 1998). A particularly suitable issue with which international taxation could be paired is international trade. The close connection between trade policy and taxation issues is amply demonstrated by yet another dispute between the European Union and the United States. In 1997, the European Union brought a complaint to the World Trade Organization (WTO), accusing the United States of violating the rules prohibiting WTO members from subsidizing exports. The European Union maintained that the United States provides export tax subsidies through the exemption of part of export profits from U.S. taxation by giving firms the ability to allocate export profits to foreign-source income. This is typically done by routing export sales through tax-avoiding devices such as foreign sales corporations (FSCs) located in offshore locations. Although a fraction of the profits made by the FSCs is subject to U.S. taxation, two-thirds of them are forever exempt, thereby providing to U.S. exporters the equivalent of a 1 percent ad valorem subsidy (see Desai and Hines 2000). What the above example demonstrates is that Tanzi's (1995) suggestion—to create an international institution equivalent to the WTO or the International Monetary Fund (IMF) which would be responsible for overseeing developments in tax systems—should be modified in favor of an institution whose function would be to provide surveillance over both tax and trade policies. Having said that, the recent WTO ruling on this issue in favor of the European Union, and the unwillingness of the United States to accept the ruling and modify its policy, provides evidence in support of Bird and Mintz's claim that the creation of a "formal hierarchical structure" will not much mitigate the need for a workable compromise between the interested parties.

The authors' pragmatic approach makes them pessimistic about
the possibility of shaping the international tax system according to
some principle of worldwide efficiency. They conclude by listing
some principles, suggested by Sandler (1997), that they think may
prove helpful in the redesign (or creation) of the international tax
system. However, one of them (i.e., *keep the numbers of those involved
in the negotiations small*) is hardly compatible with notions of fairness
(especially if the notion includes not only fairness in terms of outcomes but also fairness in terms of procedures). Moreover, in addition to the lack of legitimacy (in the eyes of nonparticipating
countries), this particular guideline is not likely to lead to a consensus even if it is restricted to the G7 or even a smaller forum. The
previous OECD consensus was a result of a congruence of interests
between the hegemonic country (the United States) and the major
European countries—all of which had a national interest in the
application of the residence principle, given that their net foreign
asset position was positive. The mutation of the United States from a
net creditor to a net debtor has disrupted this congruence of interests
between the major players. When this is coupled with the relative
decline in the hegemonic position of the United States (vis-à-vis the
European Union and Japan), one is left with the impression that
even the guidelines adopted by the authors suffer from the lack of
those attributes that the authors themselves have described as being
essential to any workable compromise on the reform of the international tax system. Of course, this observation can only make one
agree even more with the authors that "it is not easy to achieve a
consensus on international tax issues."

References

Desai, M. A., and J. R. Hines Jr. 2000. "The Uneasy Marriage of Export Incentives and
the Income Tax." National Bureau of Economic Research Working Paper No. 8009,
Cambridge, MA.

Devereux, M. P., and R. G. Hubbard. 2000. "Taxing Multinationals." National Bureau
of Economic Research Working Paper No. 7920, Cambridge, MA.

Moravcsik, A. 1998. *The Choice for Europe: Social Purpose and Political Power from Mes-
sina to Maastricht*. Ithaca: Cornell University Press.

Sandler, T. 1997. *Global Challenges*. Cambridge, MA: Cambridge University Press.

Tanzi, V. 1995. *Taxation in an Integrating World*. Washington, DC: Brookings
Institution.

14

On Cooperation in Musgravian Models of Externalities within a Federation

Henry Tulkens

14.1 Introduction

In my home country, Belgium, cooperation between federated entities has become of vital importance—vital in the very first sense of
the word. While the Belgian state is by now 170 years old, the Belgian federation is in fact very young: only ten years old, even a little
less. And the federalization process being a decentralizing (some
people say centrifugal) one, the issue sometimes arises: Why is it a
state, after all?

This is my motivation for the topic I chose for this chapter. I
realize that asking such a question in Germany, where just the
reverse did occur ten years ago with the reunification, may seem
inappropriate.

But this celebratory volume invites thinking of a general nature.
By writing the first treatise entitled *The Theory of Public Finance*,
Richard Musgrave brought the general language of economic theory
into public finance and thereby pioneered a new way to cover the
field. Following that example, I have endeavored to cover my subject
matter in as general a way as I can.

Starting from some description of the interactions that occur within the components of a federation and from a characterization of the
efficient amount of such interactions (section 14.2), I move to the
pretty classical issue of how to achieve that efficiency in a federal
framework, under alternative institutional settings (section 14.3).
Leaving aside efficiency, I consider noncooperative equilibria and
evaluate their interest in a federal context (section 14.4). While considering further steps of decentralization, I cannot escape the issue of
a federation's dismantling and ask the question, "What can public

finance theory tell us about that extreme case?" (section 14.5). I conclude in a Musgravian spirit (section 14.6).

14.2 Describing Interactions and Optimality in the Presence of Externalities

Interactions between jurisdictions may be represented in many different ways. For the present chapter, I find it justified to make use of one such representation actually due to Richard Musgrave (published as Musgrave 1969). It was not designed for the study of federalism, but instead for a discussion on the nature of public goods, and a lively exchange took place on that basis between Richard and Paul Samuelson at the IEA-CNRS conference in Biarritz, France, in 1966 for which the paper had been prepared. I do not plan to reopen that discussion here,[1] but I do plan to exploit two diagrams presented by Musgrave in the paper.

There are two economic agents, A and B, who are not identified explicitly in the paper as individuals or as political parties or as regions in a federation, but later in this chapter I shall adopt this last interpretation.

Each agent's preferences are described by a preference function $U_A(\cdot)$ and $U_B(\cdot)$, respectively, whose arguments are (a) some standard private good X—thus, X_A and X_B for A and B, respectively—and (b) another good, denoted Y, which generates an externality on the other agent. The purpose of Musgrave's Biarritz paper was, to a large extent, to describe and characterize several alternative forms of the externality conveyed by Y, and to compare these forms with the concept of public good in the strict Samuelsonian sense. I select here two of these forms.[2] One is called by the author the case of "nonsubstitute externalities" and is expressed as follows in terms of the arguments of the preference functions of A and B:

$$U_A(X_A, Y_A, Y_B) \text{ and } U_B(X_B, Y_B, Y_A).$$

The other case is called the one of "mixed benefit goods," expressed as

$$U_A(X_A, Y_A, Y_A + Y_B) \text{ and } U_B(X_B, Y_B, Y_A + Y_B).$$

In the first case, good Y produced by A is like a public good for B, since he consumes the same amount of it as A. If there were several

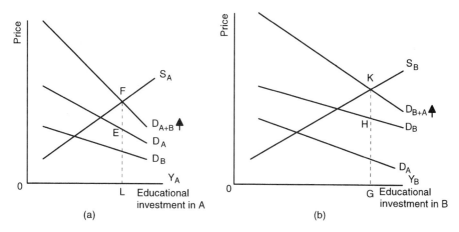

Figure 14.1
Nonsubstitute externalities

agents, $C, D, \ldots$, with Y_A entering their utility function just as is the case for B, Y_A would be a standard Samuelsonian public good. A similar argument can be made for Y_B, mutatis mutandis, which is also a (different) public good.

In the second case, Y_A and Y_B are in fact the same physical commodity, provided by both A and B and whose sum has the virtue of being a Samuelsonian public good.[3]

With the help of two sets of diagrams, Musgrave determines the optimality conditions for the supply of the externality-generating good, Y, as appears in figures 14.1 and 14.2. Thus, we have that at an optimum in the first figure, agent A produces and consumes OL of Y_A and agent B produces and consumes OG of Y_B. In the case of the second figure, the efficient total production of Y is OE, with OH produced by A and HE produced by B. (Musgrave is not too clear on what the respective supply curves are in this case, but this is unimportant in capturing the essence of the argument.)

While much of the discussion between Musgrave and Samuelson[4] bears in fact on the proper definition of what a public good is, I am referring to it here because the analytics I just recalled include a feature not much stressed in the literature on public goods—namely, that the good Y is produced by both A and B. That is, Musgrave is writing a model with *many producers* of the public good (or of the externalities). All of the literature until then, and most of it after, has

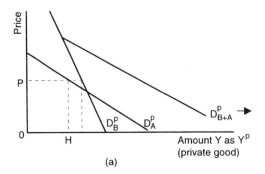

(a)

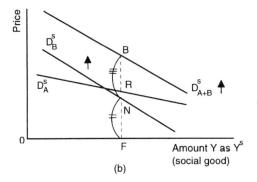

(b)

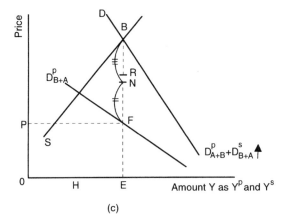

(c)

Figure 14.2
Mixed benefit goods

always dealt with economies with one producer only, or a single aggregate production function for the public good.

Where lies the interest in dealing with two (or more) producers of the public good instead of just one? Well, precisely where issues relating to cooperation are at stake.

Indeed, in that context, it is not only the (aggregate) amount of the public good that matters (for the determination of which preferences must be revealed in some appropriately cooperative way) but also the share taken by each producer in that production and, as a consequence, the amount of resources devoted to that by each unit. In addition, in an interpretation of A and B as regions with both consumers and producers, the possibility arises of transfers between regions that ought to be taken into account as they, of course, can play a role in the likelihood of cooperation.

14.3   How to Achieve Efficiency?

While efficient solutions were thus well-defined for each of the two cases, Musgrave (1969) was not very explicit on the question of how these efficient solutions could be obtained. Just a "combination of a market mechanism and a tax-subsidy scheme" was called for by the author, but hardly elaborated upon.

An answer was to be offered to that kind of question in the late 1960s and in the 1970s by means of "resource allocation processes"[5] for public goods, formulated in terms of differential equations. In short, these were essentially mathematical algorithms allowing one to compute,[6] in a tâtonnement-like succession of steps, an efficient solution.

But these processes were rather poor from an institutional point of view. And institutions are of paramount importance[7] if one is to understand *how* an efficient, or equilibrium, state of the economy can emerge.

A richer interpretation of the model can therefore be offered if we consider it in the institutional framework of a federation. In this context, the issue at stake becomes the one of achieving efficiency for the federation, the members of which are A and B.

Several new and interesting problems arise when this view is adopted, and these are best revealed by thinking in the terms offered recently by Inman and Rubinfeld (1997a) on federalism. These authors distinguish between three forms of federalism:[8]

1. planned federalism;[9]
2. cooperative federalism;
3. majority-rule federalism.

By the very definition of federalism, all of these institutional forms share the common feature that a decentralized structure of government prevails for handling local issues. The way in which the three forms differ is in how the issues of common interest that require federal policies—for example, handling of interregional externalities, supplying national or international public goods, and making tax choices on geographically mobile bases—are resolved. Specifically, the above three-way distinction by the authors corresponds to procedures of:

• technocratic planning conducted at the federal level, under institutional form (1);

• unanimous agreement between representatives of each of the lower-tier governments, under institutional form (2);

• majority vote of elected representatives of the lower-tier governments, under institutional form (3).

This taxonomy of alternative forms of federal coordination can readily be applied to the Musgravian models of interactions presented above (thinking, if relevant, in terms of more than just the two entities A and B; both the models and the diagrams perfectly allow for that). It can, of course, be similarly applied to most other forms of interaction between federated entities.

What does it teach us about the outcome of cooperation in a federation? If planning is understood in the old sovietic mode, its authoritarian character is contradictory to the idea of cooperation; it is thus of no interest to us. If, instead, planning is viewed in the sense of the resource allocation processes referred to earlier, it is essentially an information device. In particular, it identifies and computes the economic surplus that is generated along the path of efficiency gains. It can also compute various ways of sharing that surplus among the parties involved: fair ways, strategically stable ways, incentive-compatible ways,[10] and so forth. Planning in this democratic and "enlightened" sense should apparently solve completely the problem of achieving efficiency.

However, is such information sufficient for collective decisions to occur? Negotiations between the parties involved always follow their gathering of information. This is where the second Inman and Rubinfeld institutional form of federalism—cooperative federalism, in their terms—comes in. The focus is on the negotiation process itself, seen as Coasian bargaining. The authors' evaluation of it is a skeptical one, due to a number of difficulties: "inability of the parties to agree on how the surplus ... should be divided," poor estimates of each other's threat point, concealment of information, complications of strategic interplay when the number of jurisdictions is large. "The overall record has not been impressive," they conclude, adding: "Our reading of the historical and contemporary evidence does not provide much support for the claim that lower-tier governments can solve their important collective action problems on their own through unanimous Coasian agreements" (Inman and Rubinfeld 1997a, 50).

Should this disappointing evaluation make us abandon the idea of cooperative federalism? I do not think so, because we probably do not know enough yet, in economics and public finance, about what fundamentally determines cooperation. Even between individuals, the source of cooperation is poorly understood, as witnessed in a synthesis proposed recently by Ostrom (2000). Yet, there are remarkable advances reported in that paper; they should provide inspiration for improvement in our understanding of cooperation between jurisdictions.

That leaves us with the third institutional form: majority-rule federalism. I shall not attempt to collect here the pros and cons of it; Inman and Rubinfeld (1997a) analyze them in much detail and with subtlety. Let me simply record, on the one hand, that the equilibria yielded by majority voting at the federal level may not be efficient; and, on the other hand, that even when these equilibria are efficient, the majority vote always implies, by nature, a minority whose frustration may not be negligible.

Thus, each one of the three institutional forms of federalism has its limitations, and none of them can pretend to guarantee full efficiency.

14.4   Noncooperative Equilibria as "Fallback Positions" in Federal Affairs

Having noticed that cooperation has limitations, one is naturally led to ask, "What is the outcome if cooperation does *not* take place?" The

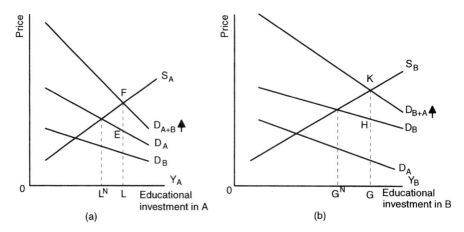

Figure 14.3
Noncooperative equilibrium between A and B for the case of "nonsubstitute externalities"

federal framework suggests as an answer that each entity will then seek to implement, on the issues of common interest, the policies that are best for itself, given the policies chosen by the other entities in the federation.

This situation is nothing else than a noncooperative equilibrium between the entities in the sense of Nash (1951). It can be illustrated by means of the Musgravian diagrams of 1969. In the case of the figure 14.1 diagrams, for instance,[11] under no cooperation, region A chooses[12] OL^N and region B OG^N (see figure 14.3).

This well-defined outcome, which, of course, generalizes to any number of regions, was not pointed out in Musgrave's paper because his interest was only in characterizing efficiency in the presence of externalities in general. But in the federal setting that I want to deal with presently, this particular situation is of considerable relevance and interest for several reasons.

First, it makes clear that a conceptual alternative to cooperation within the federation can be conceived of—and that this alternative is not necessarily chaos, or dismantling of the country, or disappearance of the public sector, or some other catastrophic event—as hinted by some in political debates.[13] Instead, noncooperative fiscal equilibria are to be seen as reasonable "fallback positions" that will prevail in case cooperation cannot be achieved.

Notice that there is no reason to believe that a Nash equilibrium will involve the parties making aggressive threats against each other:

The concept indeed rests on maximizing their own regional benefit rather than maximizing harm to others.

Second, it follows from this first argument that noncooperative equilibria are worth studying for their own sake, so as to enable one to formulate relevant policy statements. In the literature of the last fifteen to twenty years, much research and attention have been devoted to Nash equilibria between jurisdictions.[14]

A common trait of these works has been to emphasize the inefficiency feature of these equilibria; and, on that basis, many authors have just dismissed the subject. But others have gone a few steps farther, for instance, in attempting to answer all sorts of questions on the economic magnitudes involved: "Is public spending at such equilibria larger or smaller than at federally efficient levels?"; "Are the taxes too high or too low?" As a result, directions of tax "reforms" are being identified, in the search for improvements on these equilibria.

A major example of noncooperative arrangements in federations is the phenomenon of tax competition. Within the European Union,[15] this phenomenon plagues the correct levy of taxes on saving and on capital income, as everybody knows. The conceptual apparatus I am recalling here suggests that we are now at a noncooperative equilibrium of some sort in this matter.

But I note from statements accompanying the reforms currently under preparation that a distinction is being made between "harmful" and "not harmful" fiscal competition. This amounts to recognizing that not all fiscal competition equilibria are bad ones. Those that are not bad may not necessarily be efficient; but their degree of inefficiency may be small or innocuous.

This is why I would claim that better and more detailed knowledge of these equilibria and measurement of their distance from efficiency is desirable, for each category of taxes as much as for expenditures with spillovers. That the early Musgrave diagrams were in fact offering a first step in that very direction is a comforting fact to engage us further in that task.

14.5   Searching for the Roots of Federalism

Let us now pursue the reasoning sketched out at the beginning of section 14.4, with the following further question: "If no cooperation is taking place and just a Nash equilibrium prevails between the members of the federation, what distinguishes this outcome from a confederation or even from a set of separate states?"[16] In fact, the Musgrave diagrams, interpreted above in a federally decentralized context, apply equally well to two separate and independent states that interact with one another through the externalities generated by commodity Y.

Entertaining this kind of question should bring us into the area of constitutional law, for which I have no particular competence. Let me therefore remain within the domains of public finance, with its unmistakable support from economic theory.

Notice that in all my themes thus far on federalism, economics provides rich conceptual supports: externalities and public goods to describe interactions between entities;[17] efficiency and equity to specify objectives for cooperation; noncooperative equilibria to illustrate decentralization; bargaining and voting models to formalize decision processes within the federation; and so forth. Most of these concepts have been developed during the last half-century. In short, one can say that public finance has thereby contributed a lot to a better understanding of the logic of federations and to deriving from them improved levels of welfare.

Do public finance and economic theory provide similar conceptual tools to handle my question on decentralization beyond federalism? To make my point sufficiently precise, let me remind us from constitutional law that, according to standard legal categories,[18] a federation is a nation (or a state) whose existence results from a *constitution* adopted by its population as a result of some voting procedure. A confederation, on the contrary, is neither a nation nor a state; it owes its existence not to a constitution but to a *contract*—a treaty—unanimously signed by representatives of its member states and ratified by their respective domestic institutions.

Thus, decentralization beyond federalism amounts essentially to an abandonment of the constitutional link—while in the opposite direction, the creation of a federation, say in the European Union, implies writing and adopting a constitution.

For understanding what determines these steps—from constitution to contract, or from contract to constitution—I see in our discipline no tool presently available that is well accepted and of sufficient generality.

There is, however, an important contribution in that direction. Section 2.3 of Inman and Rubinfeld's (1997b) extended survey on the political theory of federalism (companion to Inman and Rubinfeld

1997a) formulates a model of constitutional choice based on benefits and costs of alternative institutional specifications of the federation as to (1) assignment of policy responsibility across levels of government and (2) degree of representation of local interests within the central government. While the details of the model do account for essential components of the problem, the authors recognize that their formulation does not lend itself, as yet, to conclusions of a general nature. The proposed approach, though, is promising.

14.6   Conclusion

In the Musgravian world, we can also find a hint towards answering the difficult question of the existence of a nation in spite of possible extreme decentralization. In his reply (Musgrave 1997) to Inman and Rubinfeld (1997a), one finds a sentence that points in the following terms to the heart of the issue: "Ultimately, finding the appropriate jurisdiction [has mainly to do] with the question, very much with us today, of how *closely-knit* a nation the member jurisdictions of the federation wish to form" (67, italics added).

It is not clear how the prevailing concepts of utility functions, private and public goods, equilibria, and optima can accommodate the idea of a "closely-knit nation." We probably need to discover or construct new conceptual tools to master it. If someone could succeed in this task, public finance would bring about still another valuable contribution to the understanding and welfare of our nations.

Notes

I express grateful thanks to my colleague Hughes Dumont for valuable discussions on some aspects of the themes developed here, to Magali Verdonck for a careful reading, and to an insightful referee for his suggestions.

1. Let me only suggest having a look at the record of it, which takes twelve pages of small text in the proceedings book!

2. I skip the many other cases expounded in the paper, as my purpose here is not to discuss the taxonomy of externalities and public goods.

3. In my joint work with Parkash Chander, dealing with international environmental problems, I have made extensive use of this formulation, using the term "environmental externalities" (Chander and Tulkens 1995, 1997). The first of these references was built on a variant found in Mäler (1989). The model is still in use today in further applications to climate change issues (see, e.g., Germain et al. forthcoming). Another instance of use of a model in that same spirit is the one referred to in footnote 2 of Ostrom (2000), a paper to which I refer again in what follows.

4. With Sen spicing up the debate, as he was the discussant of Musgrave's paper in Biarritz.

5. In the terminology of Arrow and Hurwicz (1977). These were often called planning models (after Malinvaud 1970–1971) or tâtonnement models (Drèze and de la Vallée Poussin 1971). They find their origin in the Lange-Lerner theory of socialism.

6. An exercise effectively achieved for a real-life international environmental externality (sulfur dioxide emissions) in Kaitala, Mäler, and Tulkens (1995) and further pursued in Germain, Toint, and Tulkens (1995).

7. As I argued in Tulkens (1978, section 4).

8. Which they call "principles" of federalism.

9. The authors call this "economic" federalism. (Apologies to the authors for substituting my own words again.)

10. This takes unexpected forms in the case of sharing the surplus generated by a public input in a federal setting, as was discovered in Cattoir and Tulkens (2000).

11. To handle the second case mentioned earlier, more should be specified concerning the supply curves.

12. Strictly speaking, this is correct only under an assumption of separability in the preference functions of both A and B between the demands for Y_A and Y_B.

13. This attitude is often observed in young federations, and typically in Belgium, where at each step taken in the devolution process, litanies of fearful statements on the future of the country are recited even by otherwise competent intellectuals.

14. Bergstrom, Blume, and Varian (1986) provide an early and rich analysis of Nash equilibria in a model of voluntary provision of public goods. However, the actors involved in their model are individuals rather than jurisdictions. They are thus led to consider issues less directly relevant to federalism.

15. Which is not—yet—a federation, of course, but has many traits of one.

16. This is pretty much a European question. Indeed, it is a characteristic of the U.S. economic literature on fiscal federalism that, while authors pay much attention to how spending and taxing powers are devolved to higher or lower tiers of government, and seek optimal or equilibrium degrees of decentralization, they hardly ever consider the question of the extreme degree of decentralization—that is, the breaking up of a federal state into separate states. A major exception is, of course, Inman and Rubinfeld (1997b), to which I return later.

17. And I would add the one of "reaction functions" if I had gone into more detail on noncooperative equilibria.

18. As reported, for example, in Schmitt (1994).

References

Arrow, K., and L. Hurwicz, eds. 1977. *Studies in Resource Allocation Processes*. Cambridge, UK: Cambridge University Press.

Bergstrom, T., L. Blume, and H. Varian. 1986. "On the Private Provision of Public Goods." *Journal of Public Economics* 29: 25–49.

Cattoir, P., and H. Tulkens. 2000. "Federalism, Cooperation and Voluntary Transfers." Paper presented at the ISPE Conference on Public Finance and Redistribution held at CORE in honor of Maurice Marchand, Louvain-la-Neuve, Belgium.

Chander, P., and H. Tulkens. 1995. "A Core-Theoretic Solution for the Design of Cooperative Agreements on Transfrontier Pollution." *International Tax and Public Finance* 2: 279–294.

Chander, P., and H. Tulkens. 1997. "The Core of an Economy with Multilateral Environmental Externalities." *International Journal of Game Theory* 26: 379–401.

Drèze, J., and D. de la Vallée Poussin. 1971. "A Tâtonnement Process for Public Goods." *Review of Economic Studies* 38: 133–150.

Germain, M., P. Toint, and H. Tulkens. 1995. "International Negotiations on Acid Rains in Northern Europe: A Discrete Time Iterative Process." In *Economic Policy for the Environment and Natural Resources*, ed. A. Xepapadeas. London: Edward Elgar.

Germain, M., P. Toint, H. Tulkens, and A. de Zeeuw. Forthcoming. "Transfers to Sustain Cooperation in International Stock Pollutant Control." Université Catholique de Louvain (Louvain-la-Neuve, Belgium), Center for Operations Research and Econometrics (CORE) Discussion Paper No. 9832; *Journal of Economic Dynamics and Control*.

Inman, R. P., and D. L. Rubinfeld. 1997a. "Rethinking Federalism." *Journal of Economic Perspectives* 11(4): 43–64.

Inman, R. P., and D. L. Rubinfeld. 1997b. "The Political Economy of Federalism." In *Perspectives on Public Choice: a Handbook*, ed. D. C. Mueller. Cambridge, UK: Cambridge University Press.

Kaitala, V., K. G. Mäler, and H. Tulkens. 1995. "The Acid Rain Game as a Resource Allocation Process, with Application to Negotiations between Finland, Russia and Estonia." *Scandinavian Journal of Economics* 97: 325–343.

Mäler, K. G. 1989. "The Acid Rain Game." In *Valuation Methods and Policy Making in Environmental Economics*, ed. H. Folmer and E. Van Ierland. Amsterdam: Elsevier.

Malinvaud, E. 1970–1971. "Procedures for the Determination of a Program of Collective Consumption." *European Economic Review* 2: 187–217.

Musgrave, R. 1959. *The Theory of Public Finance*. New York: McGraw-Hill.

Musgrave, R. 1969. "Provision for Social Goods." In *Public Economics*, ed. J. Margolis and H. Guitton. Proceedings of the IEA-CNRS conference held at Biarritz, France, 1966. London: Macmillan and New York: St. Martin's Press.

Musgrave, R. 1997. "Devolution, Grants and Fiscal Competition." *Journal of Economic Perspectives* 11(4): 65–72.

Nash, J.-F. 1951. "Non Cooperative Games." *Annals of Mathematics* 54: 289–295.

Ostrom, E. 2000. "Collective Action and the Evolution of Social Norms." *Journal of Economic Perspectives* 14(3): 137–158.

Schmitt, N. 1994. "Confédération et Fédération." In *Dictionnaire International du Fédéralisme*, ed. D. de Rougemont and F. Saint-Ouen. Brussels, Belgium: Bruylant.

Tulkens, H. 1978. "Dynamic Processes for Public Goods: An Institution-Oriented Survey." *Journal of Public Economics* 9: 163–201.

Comments

Clemens Fuest

Henry Tulkens's chapter starts out with one of Richard Musgrave's contributions to the theory of externalities and discusses the application to the theory of fiscal federalism. The notion of externalities plays a crucial role in the literature on interjurisdictional competition. Externalities may take the form of technological spillovers, where citizens in one jurisdiction benefit from public goods provision in other jurisdictions or suffer from border-crossing pollution, for instance. They may also take the form of fiscal externalities, which imply that the tax policy of one jurisdiction affects the welfare of citizens in other jurisdictions. A theory of federalism based on either type of externality leads to the result that cooperation or policy coordination among (benevolent) governments is necessary to reach efficient outcomes.

However, while the theory claims that policy cooperation is welfare enhancing, real-world governments often seem to find it difficult to cooperate. One prominent example is the field of tax policy. In the European Union, for instance, various attempts have been made to bring about corporate tax coordination but very little progress has been made so far. One possible explanation for this reluctance to coordinate tax policy is that countries are different. If countries differ in size or population, the gains from cooperation may be distributed unevenly across countries and some countries may even be made worse off. The problem with this explanation is that, under such circumstances, Pareto-improving policy cooperation may still be reached through side payments. If this does not happen, the question arises of whether noncooperative solutions are really as bad as the traditional theory of federalism and interjurisdictional competition based on externalities suggests. Tulkens puts it this way: "I would claim that better and more detailed knowledge of these [noncooperative] equilibria and measurement of their distance from efficiency is desirable." In fact, a theory of federalism should be able to show that there are noncooperative equilibria that are more efficient than cooperative ones. If this is not possible, the theory implies that a centralized or unitary state would be a more efficient institutional structure.

In the literature, several arguments in favor of noncooperative solutions or decentralized policymaking have been developed. In the traditional theory of fiscal federalism (Oates 1972), the main argument in favor of decentralization is based on the idea that local governments have better information about local preferences than central governments. This argument is certainly important, but it is also incomplete because it does not tell us why the central government could not set up a local agency that collects the information and passes it on to the central government. Of course, the answer to this second question is that the central government may well do so but faces the problem that the local agency may have incentives not to pass on the information. This problem is the focus of a more recent, growing literature that analyzes fiscal federalism from the perspective of principal-agent theory (see, e.g., the literature cited in Qian and Weingast 1997).

A second argument in favor of decentralization can be found in Kehoe (1989). He shows that cooperation among governments may not be desirable if there are time-consistency problems. For instance, capital taxes may be too high because, once an investment has been made, governments have incentives to raise taxes above the level announced ex ante. Since investors anticipate this, investment projects that generate a surplus for the economy as a whole may not be realized. In this case, decentralization may serve as a commitment device if the mobility of capital across borders reduces the level of capital tax rates.

Probably the most important argument in favor of decentralization, though, claims that it helps to improve the efficiency of the political process. A very simple and provocative model of the political process that has been used to show this is the well-known Leviathan model of government (Brennan and Buchanan 1980). It assumes that governments, rather than being benevolent, extract as much revenue from the private sector as they can and waste a large part of it. From this point of view, decentralization has the advantage of limiting the taxing power of government. Of course, the Leviathan model is a caricature of modern democratic governments.

However, it has inspired a literature on interjurisdictional competition that uses more realistic models of government. This literature does not always confirm the result that decentralization improves the efficiency of the political process[1] but it shows that it may happen under plausible conditions.[2] The policy conclusion emerging from these contributions seems to be that the optimal degree of decentralization balances the marginal cost of further centralization—a reduced efficiency of the political process—against the marginal benefit, which is the internalization of (fiscal and other) externalities.

In my understanding, this balanced view is very much in line with Richard Musgrave's approach to public policy problems. Interestingly, Richard Musgrave is sometimes seen as emphasizing the issue of externalities, which call for government intervention, while neglecting problems of the political process. The preface to the first edition of *Public Finance in Theory and Practice* reveals that he is well aware of both problems: "The existence of externalities ... pose[s] issues which require political processes for their resolution. A public sector is needed to make society work and the problem is how to do this in a framework of individual freedom and justice" (Musgrave and Musgrave 1973, xviii).

Notes

1. See, for example, Musgrave and Musgrave (1973, 523) on the protection of minorities.

2. See, for example, Fuest (2000) and the literature cited there.

References

Brennan, G., and J. Buchanan. 1980. *The Power to Tax: Analytical Foundations for a Fiscal Constitution.* Cambridge, UK: Cambridge University Press.

Fuest, C. 2000. "The Political Economy of Tax Coordination as a Bargaining Game between Bureaucrats and Politicians." *Public Choice* 103: 357–382.

Kehoe, P. J. 1989. "Policy Cooperation among Benevolent Governments May Be Undesirable." *Review of Economic Studies* 56: 289–296.

Musgrave, R., and P. Musgrave. 1973. *Public Finance in Theory and Practice.* Auckland, New Zealand: McGraw-Hill.

Oates, W. E. 1972. *Fiscal Federalism.* New York: Harcourt Brace.

Qian, Y., and R. B. Weingast. 1997. "Federalism as a Commitment to Preserving Market Incentives." *Journal of Economic Perspectives* 11: 83–92.

15

Fiscal Federalism and Risk Sharing in Germany: The Role of Size Differences

Kai A. Konrad and
Helmut Seitz

15.1 Introduction

The literature on fiscal federalism has extensively discussed federal transfer systems. As Richard Musgrave points out in the introduction to his seminal paper on "Approaches to a Fiscal Theory of Political Federalism" in 1961, there are many possible reasons why the central government in a federation may interfere with state finances. The complexity of actual transfer arrangements reflects the multiplicity of reasons for such transfers.[1] Musgrave (1961) distinguishes several objectives. First, the central government may try to influence the amount or type of public services, or the terms on which public services are provided at the state level. Second, the federal government may try to make a citizen's situation in terms of public services more independent of the state to which the citizen belongs. All these objectives may be at work in the German case, where not only are state and federal revenues redistributed according to a complex scheme, but also the provision of public services by states and by the federal government is highly integrated. In November 1999, the German Supreme Court demanded a major reform of this system.

A central aspect that provides legitimation for a system of unconditional transfers between states in a federation[2] is idiosyncratic regional risk and the potential for intergovernmental risk sharing. We will concentrate on this aspect here. The potential for risk sharing in federations is a hotly debated issue. Of course, like any risk-sharing device, risk sharing between regions involves some problems of moral hazard.[3] Mutual insurance among states against random variations in the provision of public services would be provided by ex post equalization of actual outlays or performance. As

Musgrave (1961) points out when discussing equalization of actual outlays or performance, fiscal equalization systems that force regions with above-average per capita tax revenues to pay transfers to regions with below-average fiscal capacity generate strong disincentives for tax-revenue-generating policies in both fiscally weak and fiscally strong regions.

A large number of recent contributions have addressed the fundamental trade-offs between risk sharing, redistribution between regions that differ with respect to their expected wealth, and incentives.[4] This chapter revisits the fundamental trade-off between risk sharing and incentives for local governments. Much of the literature has focused on federal transfers as a risk-sharing device to smooth private consumption (see, e.g., Fatás 1998 and Forni and Reichlin 1999 for two views and brief surveys on the empirical literature). We concentrate on risk sharing of government revenues, and leave private-sector risks aside. This choice is made for two reasons. First, we can expect that global private capital markets can take care of risks in the private sector much better than any smoothing via countercyclical taxation and the insurance effect of tax transfers within a federation, because it encompasses a larger set of risky assets that involve idiosyncratic risks.[5] This argument is stronger the smaller the federation under consideration, and hence particularly relevant for a federation such as Germany that represents only a small share in global economic activity. Second, it is known that government revenue is more volatile than aggregate income itself. Hence, governments' revenue risks are of particular relevance.

The central aspect we address is asymmetry in regions' population sizes. All existing federations are composed of regions of asymmetric population size. Differences in size within Germany are almost as dramatic as in the European Union.[6] For instance, the largest state in 1999—North Rhine-Westphalia—had 18 million inhabitants, which is 27.1 times the size of the population of Bremen—the smallest state in terms of population size—which had a population of 0.66 million. The second-largest state—Bavaria—had 12.1 million inhabitants, which is 11.4 times the size of the second-smallest state—Saarland— which had a population of 1.07 million. Suppose two states form a federation, one state (A) about ten times the size of the other state (B). Neglecting the issue of moral hazard, the best mutual insurance outcome would be obtained if both states collect their risky tax revenue, sum their tax revenues, and divide this total between them (not necessarily evenly). However, moral hazard incentives on the side of states would typically make this maximum mutual insurance suboptimal. With revenue sharing, each state's incentive to enforce the (uniform federal) tax laws and to spend money on tax auditing is diminished. In this chapter, we consider linear mutual insurance schemes. We characterize the optimal linear mutual insurance scheme.[7] We show that the per capita share of a region's tax revenue that should enter the insurance scheme is higher the larger the relative size of this region. Further, even though the optimal insurance scheme has larger contributions by larger regions, which increases their moral hazard incentives, it holds that, for optimal contribution shares, the larger region chooses higher per capita tax revenue than the smaller region.

In what follows, we first briefly survey the empirical literature on risk sharing in federations, consider whether there is scope for risk sharing within a federation such as Germany (which could possibly justify some of the federal transfer mechanism that exists under the current law), and survey the incentive properties of the current system of federal transfers in section 15.2. Then we establish the main results regarding the impact of relative size on the optimal mutual insurance contract within a federation in section 15.3 and draw conclusions for the optimal design of the federal transfer system.[8] Section 15.4 summarizes the findings and concludes.

15.2 Empirical Evidence

To assess the importance of size effects in the trade-off between risk sharing and the disincentive effects of mutual insurance arrangements in a federal system of taxes and transfers as in Germany, we consider two types of evidence. We consider the scope for risk diversification in federations and we consider how size affects the incentive effects of a proportional redistribution mechanism.

Whether region-specific (idiosyncratic) economic performance risk in federations is of major importance and whether federal tax-transfer systems can provide a quantitatively important amount of insurance is a debated issue. The empirical literature mainly concentrates on the effect of federal taxation on consumption risk in the European Union, the United States, and Canada, and, for assessing the scope for interstate insurance in Germany, we may follow the general insights from this literature.

Fatás (1998), for instance, examines GDP growth rates across U.S. states from 1969 to 1990. He calculates standard deviations ranging from 10.36 (North Dakota) to as low as 1.64 (Pennsylvania), with an average of 2.17. Standard deviations relative to the aggregate are between 6.53 (North Dakota) and 0.96 (Pennsylvania), with an average of 1.36. Finally, correlations of growth rates with the average growth rate (of all states in the federation, excluding the particular state under consideration) range between 0.13 (Wyoming) and 0.93 (Ohio), with an average of 0.72. Fatás (1998) also compares these values with those for the EU countries. There, for the pre-EMU (European Monetary Union) period from 1979 to 1996, the standard deviation of growth rates had an average of 1.71, the average of standard deviations relative to the aggregate was 1.41, and the average correlation was 0.56. Fatás then considers the consumption smoothing that was generated by federal taxation. Consumption smoothing via federal tax and transfer systems can be attributed to two effects: interregional smoothing (sharing idiosyncratic variations of state tax bases) and intertemporal smoothing (sharing fluctuations of the aggregate tax base over time). Only the first effect is the "insurance effect" of federal tax-transfer systems. The second effect is the "substitution effect." Fatás argues that the insurance effect contributes most to explaining consumption smoothing if there is no variation in growth rates in the aggregate over time but much variation in growth rates across regions within each period. Similarly, consumption smoothing can mainly be attributed to intertemporal smoothing, and not to an insurance effect, if growth rates across regions within periods are highly correlated and if there is considerable variation in the aggregate growth rate over time. The insurance effect contributes little to consumption smoothing if the growth rates fluctuate much over time and are highly correlated across states, and the insurance part of consumption smoothing is large if there is little intertemporal variation in growth but large variation across states. For the United States, Fatás concludes that federal taxation smooths consumption, but that two-thirds of this effect should be attributed to intertemporal tax smoothing and only about a third to an insurance effect.

In the light of these results, the respective data on west Germany in table 15.1 draw a gloomy picture about the possible benefits of interregional insurance. The average standard deviation in Germany

Table 15.1
Volatility and correlation of real GDP growth rates, 1971–1999, of states in west Germany (excluding Berlin-West)

State	σ_i	$\sigma_i/\bar{\sigma}_i$	Corr
North Rhine-Westphalia	1.922	0.995	0.951
Bavaria	1.884	0.977	0.953
Baden-Wuerttemberg	2.331	1.263	0.934
Lower-Saxony	1.901	0.880	0.890
Hesse	2.377	1.264	0.882
Rhineland-Palatinate	2.009	1.053	0.929
Schleswig-Holstein	1.932	0.993	0.625
Saarland	1.976	1.033	0.772
Hamburg	1.922	0.886	0.714
Bremen	1.905	0.740	0.780
Weighted average	2.073	1.073	0.933

Source: Calculated from *Volkswirtschaftliche Gesamtrechnung der Länder*, 2000. Statistisches Landesamt Baden-Württemberg, Arbeitsgemeinschaft Volkswirtschaftliche Gesamtrechnung der Länder, Stuttgart, Germany.
Notes:
σ_i denotes the standard deviation of real GDP growth rate in state i.
$\bar{\sigma}_i$ denotes the standard deviation of real GDP growth rate in west Germany (excluding state i).
Corr denotes the correlation coefficient between the real GDP growth rate in state i and real GDP growth rate in west Germany (excluding state i).

is in the same range as those in the United States and in Europe, but the correlation of states' growth has been much larger in Germany than in the United States or across EU countries. Fatás's (1998) verdict on the role of insurance in consumption smoothing would therefore apply even more strongly for Germany: The share of the "insurance effect" for consumption smoothing in Germany would be very small.

Forni and Reichlin (1999) review the results that point to insurance effects being of little importance. They argue that autocorrelation of regional growth can change these results: Regions can take care of high-frequency changes in growth performance by intertemporal smoothing, particularly borrowing and lending, and this is true for both the private and public sectors. Hence, the main purpose of insurance via federal taxation is to insure against long-lasting shocks—that is, states would like to insure their citizens against long-lasting changes in economic performance, relative to other states.[9]

Indeed, in Germany, there is some evidence that such long-term
changes in regional prosperity do exist. For instance, as reported in
Färber (1998, 112), Bavaria had a much steeper growth path than all
other states in Germany. In 1950, per capita GDP in Bavaria was
about 87 percent of average per capita GDP in Germany, and this
ratio increased to about 108 percent in 1997. Similarly, Hesse moved
from 99 percent in 1950 to 124 percent in 1997, whereas relative per
capita income in North Rhine-Westphalia dropped from 120 percent
in 1950 to 94 percent in 1997. Hamburg shows a U-shaped pattern,
starting from 186 percent of average GDP per capita in 1950, dropping to 162 percent in 1990, and rising again to 176 percent in
1997. Figure 15.1 depicts these changes for all west German states.[10]
For the tax revenue, changes can be expected to be even more
pronounced, as the progressivity of many taxes leads to a more-

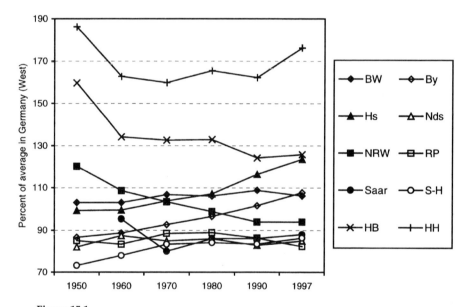

Figure 15.1
Regional long-term economic performance risks in Germany
Key:

BW	Baden-Wuerttemberg	By	Bavaria
Hs	Hesse	Nds	Lower-Saxony
NRW	North Rhine-Westphalia	RP	Rhineland-Palatinate
Saar	Saarland	S-H	Schleswig-Holstein
HB	Bremen	HH	Hamburg

Source: Färber 1998.

than-proportional reaction of tax revenue to changes in the tax base. Because government revenue is strongly procyclical with GDP growth, any random shock on GDP growth is magnified with respect to growth rates, and, hence, the variation of government revenue may be larger than the variation in GDP.

This suggests that there is some long-run variation in tax bases across German states, leaving some scope for an insurance motive in the federal tax-transfer system. Of course, we should note that there are some caveats. The long-term changes in performance are only partially the outcome of exogenous developments. First, the federal system, in which considerable interaction between states occurred both in terms of tax revenue sharing and in terms of public service provision, may have had an impact on regional growth and development. It is likely that the interaction had an equalizing effect, so that the variation in figure 15.1 may understate the exogenous risks.

Second, regional growth and development depend on factors such as regional investment and other regional policy. Regional investment along relevant dimensions (infrastructure, human capital) may have been higher in the states that outperformed other states, or these states may simply have had better government. However, there are also some seemingly exogenous developments that can be seen as "natural" explanations for the most notable changes that occurred in Bavaria, Hesse, North Rhine-Westphalia, Hamburg, and Bremen. For instance, North Rhine-Westphalia, Hamburg, and Bremen were "rich" in the 1950s, because the former state had a lot of mining and iron and steel industries and the latter two had a lot of shipbuilding industry. The global crisis in recent decades in these industries had not been anticipated in the 1950s by most economists. Similarly, the tremendous importance of fashion, media, communication, air transport, and the financial sector in the 1990s, which contributed to the economic prosperity increase in Bavaria and Hesse, was also not anticipated by many economists in the 1950s.

A second issue that has to be addressed is whether size differences between the German states really matter. Table 15.2 presents several measures. The first column simply presents state population, which indicates rather dramatic differences in population size across states. The next presents the population share of the various states. With a per capita uniform transfer mechanism, this relative size is a measure of how much returns to a state in terms of transfers if the state

Table 15.2
Population shares, implicit tax rates from redistribution, and marginal tax rates of the German fiscal equalization system

State i	n_i	$n_i/\sum n_j$	ITR_{100}	ITR_{90}	MTR
North Rhine-Westphalia	18.000	0.219	0.781	0.703	0.712
Bavaria	12.155	0.148	0.852	0.767	0.745
Baden-Wuerttemberg	10.476	0.128	0.872	0.785	0.755
Lower Saxony	7.899	0.096	0.904	0.814	0.851
Hesse	6.052	0.074	0.926	0.833	0.798
Saxony	4.460	0.054	0.946	0.851	0.898
Rhineland-Palatinate	4.031	0.049	0.951	0.856	0.872
Saxony-Anhalt	2.649	0.032	0.968	0.871	0.909
Schleswig-Holstein	2.777	0.034	0.966	0.869	0.878
Thuringia	2.449	0.030	0.970	0.873	0.910
Brandenburg	2.601	0.032	0.968	0.871	0.910
Mecklenburg West Pomerania	1.789	0.022	0.978	0.880	0.914
Saarland	1.072	0.013	0.987	0.888	0.919
Berlin	3.387	0.041	0.959	0.863	0.898
Hamburg	1.705	0.021	0.979	0.881	0.914
Bremen	0.663	0.008	0.992	0.893	0.916

Notes:
n_i denotes population in millions in state i in 1999. (Source: *Statistical Yearbook of the Federal Republic of Germany*, 1999. Statistisches Bundesamt, Weisbaden, Germany.)
$n_i/\sum n_j$ denotes population in state i as a share of aggregate population.
$\text{ITR}_{100} = 1 - n_i/\sum n_j$ is the implicit tax rate that results from a federal redistribution system if all state tax revenues are summed and shared evenly on a per capita basis between all states. ITR_{100} corresponds to $\gamma = 1$ in section 15.3.
$\text{ITR}_{90} = 0.9(1 - n_i/\sum n_j)$ is the respective implicit tax rate that results from a federal redistribution system if 90 percent of all state tax revenues are summed and shared evenly on a per capita basis. ITR_{90} corresponds to $\gamma = 0.9$ in section 15.3.
MTR is the marginal tax rate on state tax revenue in Germany (the net outflow share from an increase in income tax revenue in state i of DM 1 million) as reported in Baretti et al. (2000, 106) on the basis of actual data in Germany for 1996.

raises its tax base by one additional deutschemark, if this deutschemark fully enters into the transfer system. The third column reports the implicit tax rate, ITR_{100}, if all tax revenues are taken into account in the fiscal equalization system. For comparison, the penultimate column reports the implicit tax rate if only 90 percent of state tax revenues enter the fiscal equalization system, ITR_{90}. The final column, MTR, reports the implicit marginal tax rates for the actual federal tax-transfer mechanism that operated in Germany, based on 1996 data reported in Baretti et al. (2000). Simple eyeballing reveals that there is a close relationship between ITR_{90} and MTR. This is not an accident. The German federal tax-transfer system is rather complex, and consists of a number of steps involving both interstate equalization of tax revenues and further equalizing transfers from the federal government to the states.[11] However, an important element is that a major share of VATs and federal transfers is used to equalize more broadly defined tax revenues per capita (including revenues from income taxation and some others, but not all state revenues), and we can expect that this effect contributes to making ITR_{90} and MTR rather similar.

Table 15.2 shows that size differences generate substantially different marginal incentives for generating tax revenue for the different German states. States in Germany audit and enforce the tax laws. Most of these tax laws are uniform throughout the federation. However, states have some discretion as to how strictly they enforce tax laws and how much they spend on monitoring and auditing, and the implicit tax rates may influence these decisions.[12]

Now we turn to the theoretical aspects of size differences in a mutual insurance scheme between states in a federation.

15.3 Optimal Insurance

Transfer schemes in federations are typically symmetric, in the sense that all states in the federation participate with the same share in their government revenues in the tax-transfer scheme. In this section, we highlight that this is suboptimal. The optimal tax-transfer mechanism should account for relative size. We consider the role of population size for the optimal mutual insurance contract in a simple framework.

Consider a federation that consists of two states, A and B. The states are inhabited by n_A and n_B identical individuals, respectively, with $N = n_A + n_B$ being the total number of individuals. There is no information asymmetry between individuals and the state government so that the governments behave in the best interest of their citizens.[13] Simplifying as much as possible, the utility of a citizen in region i is described by

$$u_i = \theta E g_i - \beta S(g_i) - \varphi(e_i), \tag{1}$$

where g_i is the per capita amount of a publicly provided good in region i, Eg_i is the expected amount of provision, $S(g_i)$ is the variance of this per capita amount, and β is the relative weight of variance in units of expected amount. The factor θ measures the marginal utility of a unit of expected public provision of goods in units of private income, and we assume $\theta > 1$. The term $\varphi(e_i)$ measures the cost of taxation and will be explained in detail later.

The per capita amounts of a publicly provided good are determined as follows. The two governments' tax collections per capita are e_A and e_B. In addition to these amounts, they receive random per capita revenues ε_A and ε_B. These random variables have mean zero and variance σ^2. They are perfectly correlated between citizens of the same state. They may or may not be correlated across the two states, and the covariance is $\text{cov}(\varepsilon_A, \varepsilon_B) \equiv \rho^2$. We can think of ε_i as consisting of a state-specific shock and a federation-wide shock—for example, in terms of random variation of the statutory tax base or of random factors that determine the tax collection cost. Each state government learns the value of its own state-specific shock after its collection efforts are already chosen.[14] Once e_i and ε_i are determined, each country can observe its own e_i, but only the sum of e_i and ε_i becomes observable for the other country.

Consider now the term $\varphi(e_i)$. This term measures the individuals' cost of governmental revenue collection activity in units of private income. For instance, this cost is the tax burden itself that reduces private consumption, but also the excess burden that is caused by distortionary taxes, and the cost of monitoring and enforcing the tax laws. In line with standard results on the cost of taxation, this cost is assumed to be strictly convex, that is, $\varphi' > 0$ and $\varphi'' > 0$. We also assume convex marginal cost, $\varphi''' \geq 0$. This assumption is mainly for analytical convenience. It is a well-known assumption from standard moral hazard models (see Laffont and Tirole 1993).

Note that all regions are symmetric with respect to preferences of individuals, tax collection cost per capita, and so forth. We disregard, for instance, the issue of wealth per capita differences in different regions that have been the focus of recent interest in the literature. The only asymmetry we consider is that states differ in population size.

There is a redistribution mechanism of tax revenues between the states that provides mutual insurance. We denote by $1 - \gamma_i$ the share of revenue that remains with the state and by γ_i the share of region i's tax revenue that enters the mutual insurance mechanism. Then we obtain

$$g_i = (1 - \gamma_i)(e_i + \varepsilon_i) + \sum_{k=A,B} \gamma_k n_k (e_k + \varepsilon_k) \frac{1}{N}.$$ (2)

Hence, we assume that the payments that enter the redistribution mechanism are distributed evenly over the total population. This is the case, for instance, if the state contributions go to a central government in the federation that redistributes it among the states on a per capita basis, or if the same procedure is implemented by way of an agreement among the states. We are interested in the optimal linear redistribution mechanism here, and, hence, the problem will be to determine the optimal γ_A and γ_B. We will compare our results then with the redistribution mechanism that is at work in Germany.

Note that uniform $\gamma_i = \gamma = 1$ and $\gamma_i = \gamma = 0.9$ applied to population sizes in Germany generate the implicit tax rates ITR_{100} and ITR_{90} in table 15.2. Recall that the actual redistribution mechanism in Germany yields a marginal tax burden on state tax revenue that is very closely approximated by a *constant* γ of 0.9, the same for all states and independent of population size.[15]

It is also important to note that, with two states, the two variables γ_A and γ_B span the whole set of linear mutual insurance contracts that are budget balanced, except for a possible revenue-independent transfer from one state to the other. However, given that the payoff functions as in (1) are linear in expected government expenditure, the revenue-independent transfer is irrelevant for characterizing the optimal insurance contract, and there is no loss of generality if we set this transfer equal to zero.[16]

The per capita risks in state A become

$$S(g_A) = \left(1 - \gamma_A + \gamma_A \frac{n_A}{N}\right)^2 \sigma^2 + \left(\gamma_B \frac{n_B}{N}\right)^2 \sigma^2$$

$$+ 2\left(1 - \gamma_A + \gamma_A \frac{n_A}{N}\right)\left(\gamma_B \frac{n_B}{N}\right)\rho^2,$$ (3)

and $S(g_B)$ is obtained from (3) by replacing all subscripts A by B and vice versa.

It is important to note, however, that the point here is more general and also applies if the federal government uses the contributions in a welfarist way among the states—for instance, for the provision of a global public good that is nonrival among all citizens, the amount of which is a function of total contributions

$\sum_{k=A,B} \gamma_k n_k(e_k + \varepsilon_k)$, or for per capita contributions of publicly provided private goods.

We can now consider the problem of constitutional design
and seek the linear sharing rules (γ_A, γ_B) that maximize the sum of
utilities

$$U = n_A u_A + n_B u_B \tag{4}$$

in the two states, taking into account that redistributions cannot be
made contingent on states' choices of e_i, as these choices cannot be
observed due to the random shocks that add to states' actual tax
collection efforts.

We disregard several important issues here. First, we disregard a
participation constraint for each state. This is not a major shortcoming. Given the quasi-linear payoff functions, an ex ante participation
constraint can always be met by appropriate outcome-independent
transfer payments that are determined at the constitutional stage
and compensate the (large) states that lose from participating in the
optimal mechanism. Second, we do not allow for endogenous formation of states. As small states have an advantage here, there would
be a tendency for states to split up into smaller units. In existing
federations, typically there are major hurdles that make such structural changes difficult. Third, we disregard the most important
questions of the optimal size and structure of federations.[17]

The problem of finding the optimal sharing rules (γ_A, γ_B) resembles
a standard insurance problem with proportional insurance with
moral hazard, as in Shavell (1979). However, there are two important differences that make this problem different from a standard
optimal insurance problem. First, we consider mutual insurance
among a small number of agents. There is no risk-neutral agent here,
and also aggregate risk does not vanish. Second, and more importantly, the agents here differ in size in a nontrivial way: The problem
is different from mutual insurance between two agents that differ in
their wealth and in their wealth risks, because our "agents" consist
of sets of individuals and these sets differ in the number of their elements. A large region represents large aggregate income risk but
also consists of a large number of people among whom risks can be
shared. The number of people matters particularly if this region
shares in the risks from another region.[18]

For any given values γ_A and γ_B, regions maximize the utility of
their respective citizens by a choice of e_i, anticipating the other

region's equilibrium choice and taking this choice as given. Straightforward calculations yield first-order conditions for choices of e_i as

$$1 - \gamma_i + \frac{n_i}{N}\gamma_i = \frac{\varphi'(e_i)}{\theta} \text{ for } i = A, B. \tag{5}$$

Efficient tax collection would require $\varphi'(e_i) = \theta$. The first-order conditions reveal that states choose inefficiently low tax collection if they participate in the revenue-sharing mechanism. A state chooses a higher tax revenue e_i if the share γ_i of revenue that goes into the redistribution mechanism is small and if the relative size of the state compared with the total population in the federation is large. In particular, if contribution shares γ_i are uniform across states, in expectation large states generate more revenue per capita than small states do, and we would expect that there is net redistribution from large to small states.

Here, we are interested in the normative question of *optimal* contribution shares. From (5) and maximization of (4), we obtain a system of equations that characterizes the second-best optimal sharing rules.

$$\begin{bmatrix} 2\beta\sigma^2 + \dfrac{\theta^2 n_B}{N\varphi''(e_A)} & -2\beta\rho^2 \\[2ex] -2\beta\rho^2 & 2\beta\sigma^2 + \dfrac{\theta^2 n_A}{N\varphi''(e_B)} \end{bmatrix} \begin{pmatrix} \gamma_A^* \\ \gamma_B^* \end{pmatrix} = \begin{pmatrix} 2\beta(\sigma^2 - \rho^2) \\ 2\beta(\sigma^2 - \rho^2) \end{pmatrix}. \tag{6}$$

Asterisks denote variables at their optimum values. Cramer's rule yields the optimal share,

$$\gamma_A^* = \frac{2\beta(\sigma^2 - \rho^2)\left[\left(2\beta\sigma^2 + \dfrac{\theta^2 n_A}{N\varphi''(e_B)}\right) + 2\beta\rho^2\right]}{\left(2\beta\sigma^2 + \dfrac{\theta^2 n_B}{N\varphi''(e_A)}\right)\left(2\beta\sigma^2 + \dfrac{\theta^2 n_A}{N\varphi''(e_B)}\right) - (2\beta\rho^2)^2}, \tag{7}$$

and γ_B^* is obtained from (7) by replacing all subscripts A by B and vice versa. Note that this condition (7) explicitly determines the optimal shares only if φ'' is constant, as otherwise this is an implicit function because the choices of effort depend on the respective shares γ_i^*.

Condition (7) reveals that the share of tax revenue that should be redistributed for risk-sharing purposes is generally higher if state risks are more idiosyncratic. For instance, if $\rho = \sigma$, the state risks are perfectly correlated and risk sharing is useless. Accordingly, from (7), $\gamma_A^* = \gamma_B^* = 0$ in this case. This reproduces as a by-product the result in Bucovetsky (1997), according to which federal tax-transfer mechanisms are less attractive as an insurance device if regional shocks are more strongly positively correlated. In turn, if $\rho = 0$, the condition (7) simplifies to

$$\gamma_i^* = \frac{2\beta\sigma^2}{2\beta\sigma^2 + \dfrac{N - n_i}{N}\dfrac{\theta^2}{\varphi''(e_i)}}. \tag{8}$$

For this condition, it can be shown that the optimal share of tax revenue that should take part in the redistribution mechanism increases in β.

The main question we address in this chapter is the impact of asymmetry in population size. The following proposition holds.

Proposition 1: $\gamma_A^* > \gamma_B^*$ if $n_A > n_B$.

Proof. The denominators of γ_A^* and γ_B^* are identical. Hence,

$$\gamma_A^* > \gamma_B^* \text{ if } \frac{n_A}{\varphi''(e_B)} > \frac{n_B}{\varphi''(e_A)}. \tag{9}$$

If $\varphi''(e_i)$ is constant, this implies that $\gamma_A^* > \gamma_B^*$ if $n_A > n_B$ for any $\rho < \sigma$, that is, if the regions' risks are imperfectly correlated. However, the result holds more generally also if $\varphi''' > 0$. This can be shown by contradiction. Suppose $\gamma_A^* < \gamma_B^*$ and $n_A > n_B$; hence, $\gamma_A^* n_B < \gamma_B^* n_A$, or, equivalently,

$$1 - \gamma_A^* \frac{n_B}{N} > 1 - \gamma_B^* \frac{n_A}{N}. \tag{10}$$

By the first-order conditions (5), it follows from inequality (10) that $\varphi'(e_A) > \varphi'(e_B)$, and, by $\varphi'' > 0$, we have $e_A > e_B$. If $\varphi''' \geq 0$, this implies $\varphi''(e_A) \geq \varphi''(e_B)$ and hence, by $n_A > n_B$, this implies $\varphi''(e_A)n_A > \varphi''(e_B)n_B$, or $n_A/(\varphi''(e_B)) > n_B/(\varphi''(e_A))$. This in turn implies $\gamma_A^* > \gamma_B^*$ by (9). Hence, we end up with a contradiction. *QED*

Proposition 1 has a simple intuition. In order to find the optimal γ_i values that enter the risk-sharing mechanism, we have to consider the trade-off between incentives and risk sharing. Suppose, for example, $n_A = 99$ and $n_B = 1$. If state A contributes to the redistribution mechanism, it receives back 0.99 units per unit of tax revenue, whereas B gets back only 0.01 units per unit of tax revenue. The share that is returned to the state is proportional to relative population size. Hence, for equal contribution shares, the tax collection incentives are more strongly distorted in smaller regions. At the same time, a similarly strong asymmetry as regards risk sharing does not hold. More precisely, at $\gamma_A = \gamma_B < 1$, we can change the γ_i values in a way that keeps constant the sum of disutilities from risk. It turns out that, at $\gamma_A = \gamma_B$, the sum $n_A \beta S(g_A) + n_B \beta S(g_B)$ stays constant if γ_A is increased by one marginal unit if γ_B is reduced by precisely the same marginal unit. Hence, we have a comparative static experiment that keeps the amount of total risk cost constant and can ask how this affects the other components of overall utility. By $d\gamma_A > 0$, region A will further reduce tax collection effort by $de_A / d\alpha_A = -\theta n_B / N \varphi''$, whereas region B will increase its tax collection effort. However, for given $\gamma_A = \gamma_B$, the tax collection effort is more distorted in the region that has fewer inhabitants, by (5). Hence, if the share of tax revenue that goes into the redistribution mechanism from the smaller region is reduced, the reduction in distortion is larger than the induced increase in distortion in the larger region in which the share of tax revenue that enters the redistribution mechanism increases.

From proposition 1, we obtain a simple rule for the design of intergovernmental transfer mechanisms on a constitutional stage. If the transfer system is motivated by risk-sharing incentives, smaller regions should keep a larger share in their tax revenues than larger regions. This result is in strong contrast to the existing system of intergovernmental transfers. For instance, in Germany, states are treated symmetrically and the federal redistribution mechanism does not account for state size as is suggested by proposition 1. Note that we do not argue for a transfer mechanism that would add to the existing system. The existing redistribution is considerable, and may or may not be too high, depending on regions' risk preferences, on the amount of diversifiable risk, and on the size of distortions from moral hazard that are generated by given contribution rates. The point made in proposition 1 is that, whatever the levels of optimal risk sharing, the optimal contribution levels are not identical for small and large regions.

The optimal mutual insurance mechanism with asymmetric population sizes has another interesting property that is stated as follows:

Proposition 2: If the optimal mutual insurance mechanism is implemented, it holds that the larger state has the larger expected tax revenue: $e_A^* > e_B^*$ if $n_A > n_B$.

Proof. The proof is by contradiction. Let $n_A > n_B$. Suppose $e_A^* < e_B^*$. This implies $\varphi'(e_A) < \varphi'(e_B)$, or, using (5), $\theta(1 - \gamma_A^*(n_B/N)) < \theta(1 - \gamma_B^*(n_A/N))$. Simplifying yields $\gamma_A^* n_B > \gamma_B^* n_A$. Inserting for γ_A^* and γ_B^* and simplifying yields

$$2\beta n_B(\sigma^2 + \rho^2) + \frac{\theta^2 n_A n_B}{N} \frac{1}{\varphi''(e_B^*)} > 2\beta n_A(\sigma^2 + \rho^2) + \frac{\theta^2 n_A n_B}{N} \frac{1}{\varphi''(e_A^*)}. \quad (11)$$

By $n_A > n_B$, this implies $\varphi''(e_B^*) < \varphi''(e_A^*)$, and, by $\varphi''' \geq 0$, we find $e_A^* > e_B^*$, which establishes a contradiction. QED

Recall that, for identical shares γ_A and γ_B, the government in the state with the larger population size has a stronger incentive to collect revenue, because the share of an additional unit of revenue that is collected by this government that will be spent on this region's population is larger than the respective share of an additional unit of revenue for the smaller region. The property of the optimal mechanism that is characterized in proposition 1 counteracts this incentive: The smaller state optimally contributes a smaller share to the redistribution mechanism than the larger state, and this reduces the moral hazard incentives of the small state and increases the moral hazard incentives of the large state, compared with equal shares that average the optimal shares. However, this process stops in an interior optimum, given the trade-off between incentives and risk sharing, and stops short of where the two states' incentives would be equal. Hence, the optimal difference in shares is too small to overcome the effect that a smaller region receives back a smaller share of its contributions to the federal redistribution mechanism.

We briefly discuss an assumption that led to this result. The linear specification of utility and mean-variance utility is mainly for analytical convenience and because our empirical analysis is also within a mean-variance framework. With expected utility, however, income effects matter. For instance, the two regions' choices of effort are not separable as in (5), and this adds some complexity to the model. It should be straightforward, however, that the quintessential property, according to which a smaller region's tax-collecting incentives are lower than those of a large region, should yield qualitatively similar results to the ones derived here.

We carried out the analysis here for the case with two regions; the same design question emerges for federations with more than two states. In general, and in particular if the correlation between states is not uniform, this problem is more complex, and the optimal mechanism will sometimes involve making one state's transfer payment a function of one other state's (or a group of other states') observed total tax revenue. Analyzing these more complex mechanism design questions is left to future research. However, we expect that the basic result in this chapter is robust: With a uniform transfer mechanism, regions face a moral hazard incentive that increases if their share in the aggregate federal revenue becomes smaller, and the federal transfer mechanism should therefore account for size in order to counterbalance this effect.

15.4 Conclusions

In this chapter, we have considered the role of the German federal tax-transfer scheme as a device for revenue risk sharing between states in Germany. We briefly reviewed the empirical literature and the data on whether there is a role for risk sharing among German states. Piecemeal evidence suggests that there are a limited number of state-specific long-lasting shocks in Germany that could generate some demand for risk sharing between state governments. We also saw that one of the properties of fiscal federalism in Germany is that states differ considerably in size, and that size matters for the states' incentives to raise revenues in a homogeneous and proportional federal tax-transfer system. We then considered mutual insurance between states in a federation from a theoretical perspective, asking whether size differences matter. We found that they do. For the optimal incentive system, a proportional contribution from states to the tax-transfer mechanism is suboptimal. A small state should contribute a smaller share of its per capita share of tax revenues than a large state, in order to compensate for the fact that a given share of contributions to the tax-transfer mechanism has stronger disincentive effects for a smaller state than for a larger state. However, the adjustment of contribution shares should not go so far that the marginal disincentive effects for large and small states are the same: In the optimum, the disincentive effect for a small state should indeed be stronger than that for a large state.

For the optimal design of a federal tax-transfer mechanism, there are many aspects that must be taken into account, and some of these may reinforce, weaken, or even overcompensate the effect derived here. However, given everything else constant, our analysis provides an efficiency reason for why small states should keep a larger share of their own per capita revenues than large states so as to balance optimally the benefits of risk sharing and the harmful disincentive effects.

Notes

We thank Helmut Bester, participants of the Microeconomic Theory Workshop at the Free University of Berlin, participants of the CESifo conference, "Public Finances and Public Policy in the New Millennium," University of Munich, January 12–13, 2001, participants of the Public Economics Seminar at CORE, and three referees for many valuable comments. The usual caveat applies.

1. Sometimes this is a scheme in which regions redistribute some share in their government budgets among themselves. Sometimes the redistribution occurs via regional contributions to a federal layer of government, or via the way the federal government allocates revenues that stem from all regions for purposes that benefit some regions more than others, or both. Transfer systems become even less transparent through matching grants provisions and other joint funding of regional expenditure. Also, there seems to be a tendency for the complexities of these transfer mechanisms to grow over time. Hence, it may be not an accident that the German system is particularly complex, as it has been in place now for fifty years. Another example is the EU budget, particularly the complication that is introduced by the special provisions for the United Kingdom and the way these have developed from one reform to the next (see, e.g., Messal and Klein 1993).

2. As has been discussed in the literature on fiscal federalism, conditional transfers or matching grants play a major role in internalizing interregional spillovers. See, for example, Oates (1972).

3. There may also be issues of adverse selection, and several papers—for example, those by Cremer and Pestieau (1997), Bordignon, Manasse, and Tabellini (2001), and Cornes and Silva (2000)—consider this aspect.

4. See, for instance, contributions by Bucovetsky (1997, 1998), Lee (1998), Alesina and Perotti (1998), Persson and Tabellini (1996a, b), and Lockwood (1999).

5. For instance, Asdrubali, Sørensen, and Yosha (1996) estimate that in the United States in the period from 1964 to 1990, private capital markets and credit markets accounted for 39 percent and 23 percent of total consumption smoothing, respectively, compared with a contribution of 13 percent by the federal fiscal transfer system.

6. In the European Union, the largest country (Germany) has about two hundred times the population size of the smallest country (Luxembourg), and the second-

largest country (France) has more than sixteen times the population size of the second-smallest country (Ireland).

7. Existing federations are more likely to be a political economy outcome than the outcome of a welfare-maximization calculus. However, the efficient allocation is of some interest as a benchmark case. One may then ask why actual political outcomes deviate from this efficient outcome.

8. Our aim is not to draw conclusions about whether existing federal transfer mechanisms redistribute too much or too little. Instead, we derive an optimality property by which regions' contribution shares should be differentiated according to relative size.

9. Such insurance need not be desirable in a world with perfectly mobile citizens, because it reduces migration and prevents individuals from making use of productivity differences. However, mobility is rather imperfect. If we assume that the migration cost for the old generation is prohibitive, but the young can migrate, the exodus of the young may actually aggravate economic shocks. Migration cannot be expected to work as an instantaneous buffer. Adjustment to permanent changes in productivity takes time, leaving a considerable role for insurance against long-lasting shocks.

10. The former Berlin (West) is not included in the empirical stocktaking because Berlin (West) and Berlin (East) merged in 1990 to form the state Berlin and therefore consistent time-series data on Berlin are not available.

11. Another major element of interregional redistribution in Germany is social insurance. As we are considering government budgets, and social insurance is organized independently and is not part of the government budget in Germany, we disregard redistribution within social insurance.

12. Whether such disincentives exist or not is hotly debated in German politics, and essentially this is an empirical question. Some results supporting the existence of disincentive effects are presented in Baretti, Huber, and Lichtblau (2000). Given the importance of the question, and the problems of measuring these effects, this issue is likely to trigger more empirical work in the future.

13. This assumption is for simplicity here, as we concentrate on a simple point which would also emerge if we chose a political economy approach.

14. Accordingly, we consider a simple moral hazard problem. A different time structure in which a region learns about ε_i before it chooses its effort e_i would be interesting as well and leads to some mechanism design issues.

15. As discussed previously, the assumption that states enforce federal tax laws approximates the German system, and tax law enforcement is more centralized in many federations. However, the principal result that requires taking size differences into consideration is of more general validity and may also be applied to issues such as public goods spillovers or fiscal externalities.

16. Note also that, due to possible nonzero correlation in outcomes, the optimal incentive contract that determines the transfer that a region receives would be a function not only of the region's own revenues in absolute terms, but also of how the region performed compared with the revenue that is obtained in the other region. In order to make use of this type of yardstick competition, a residual claimant would be needed who receives any budget surplus or deficit. However, if the redistribution mechanism has to be budget balanced, any linear redistribution mechanism can be characterized simply by some γ_A and γ_B.

17. This problem has many dimensions. For instance, there could be an optimal degree of centralization in enforcement of the tax laws. Further, idiosyncratic risk is needed to make federations optimal from a risk-sharing point of view, and population size, risk preferences, and the size and correlation of state risks would be important determinants for these design questions.

18. As is known from the Arrow-Lind theorem, or portfolio theory, it makes a difference whether the agent, A, who shares in the risks of another agent, B, is a big single investor or consists of many small investors.

References

Alesina, A., and R. Perotti. 1998. "Economic Risk and Political Risk in Fiscal Unions." *Economic Journal* 108: 989–1008.

Asdrubali, P., B. E. Sørensen, and O. Yosha. 1996. "Channels of Interstate Risk Sharing: United States 1963–1990." *Quarterly Journal of Economics* 111: 1081–1110.

Baretti, C., R. Fenge, B. Huber, W. Leibfritz, and M. Steinherr. 2000. *Chancen und Grenzen des föderalen Wettbewerbs*. Ifo-Beiträge zur Wirtschaftsforschung, Band 1. Munich, Germany: ifo Institut.

Baretti, C., B. Huber, and K. Lichtblau. 2000. "A Tax on Tax Revenue, the Incentive Effects of Equalizing Transfers: Evidence from Germany." CESifo Working Paper No. 333, Munich, Germany.

Bordignon, M., P. Manasse, and G. Tabellini. 2001. "Optimal Regional Redistribution under Asymmetric Information." *American Economic Review* 91: 709–723.

Bucovetsky, S. 1997. "Insurance and Incentive Effects of Transfers among Regions: Equity and Efficiency." *International Tax and Public Finance* 4: 463–483.

Bucovetsky, S. 1998. "Federalism, Equalization and Risk Aversion." *Journal of Public Economics* 67: 301–328.

Cornes, R. C., and E. C. D. Silva. 2000. "Local Public Goods, Risk Sharing, and Private Information in Federal Systems." *Journal of Urban Economics* 47: 39–60.

Cremer, H., and P. Pestieau. 1997. "Income Redistribution in an Economic Union: The Trade Off between Inter- and Intra-National Redistribution." *International Tax and Public Finance* 4: 325–335.

Färber, G. 1998. "Finanzverfassung." In *50 Jahre Herrenchiemseeer Verfassungskonvent-Zur Struktur des deutschen Föderalismus*, ed. Bundesrat. Bonn, Germany: Deutscher Bundesrat.

Fatás, A. 1998. "Does EMU Need a Fiscal Federation?" *Economic Policy* 26: 163–203.

Forni, M., and L. Reichlin. 1999. "Risk and Potential Insurance in Europe." *European Economic Review* 43: 1237–1256.

Laffont, J.-J., and J. Tirole. 1993. *A Theory of Incentives in Procurement and Regulation*. Cambridge: MIT Press.

Lee, K. 1998. "Uncertain Income and Redistribution in a Federal System." *Journal of Public Economics* 69: 413–433.

Lockwood, B. 1999. "Inter-Regional Insurance." *Journal of Public Economics* 72: 1–37.

Messal, R., and A. Klein. 1993. "Finanzlasten und Eigenmittelstruktur der Europäischen Gemeinschaft." *Wirtschaftsdienst* 93 / VIII: 375–383.

Musgrave, R. 1961. "Approaches to a Fiscal Theory of Political Federalism." In *Public Finances: Needs, Sources and Utilization*, National Bureau of Economic Research. Princeton: Princeton University Press. Reprinted in *The Economics of Fiscal Federalism and Local Finance*, ed. W. Oates. Brookfield, VT: Harcourt Brace Jovanovich Inc., 1972.

Oates, W. 1972. *Fiscal Federalism*. New York: Harcourt Brace.

Persson, T., and G. Tabellini. 1996a. "Federal Fiscal Constitutions: Risk Sharing and Moral Hazard." *Econometrica* 64: 623–646.

Persson, T., and G. Tabellini. 1996b. "Federal Fiscal Constitutions: Risk Sharing and Redistribution." *Journal of Political Economy* 104: 979–1009.

Shavell, S. 1979. "On Moral Hazard and Insurance." *Quarterly Journal of Economics* 93: 541–562.

Comments

Marko Köthenbürger

How should regional population asymmetries be reflected in federal risk sharing? Kai Konrad and Helmut Seitz approach this interesting and policy-relevant question in two steps. First, they provide empirical results on the trade-off between risk sharing and incentives with some emphasis on the German interregional transfer system. Second, the authors give a characterization of the optimal contribution rates to a risk-sharing mechanism in the presence of moral hazard.

Why are tax revenues more volatile than private incomes? The authors argue that this effect may be traced back to the existence of a progressive tax system. Any idiosyncratic variation of regional tax bases leads to an even larger variation in tax revenue under a progressive income tax scheme, thereby creating demand for an interregional transfer scheme conditioned on tax revenue as a risk-sharing device. In Germany, the income tax system is progressive, confirming scope for risk sharing. It would be interesting to have more information about how the German transfer system actually meets the demand for interregional insurance and what impact population size has. For instance, in Germany, almost all major tax revenues are shared vertically (between different levels of government) as well as horizontally (between governments at the same level). Tax revenues are pooled and distributed to the states according to formulae related to the regional tax base, suggesting that the tax progression effect might already be spread over all states.

To take an extreme example, consider two regions that participate in a tax-sharing scheme. Regional tax revenues are pooled and allocated relative to the regional tax base. Let the tax base decrease by €1 in one region and increase by €1 in the other region. Given a progressive tax system, the shock translates into a change in regional tax revenues of €1.5. In this simple example, tax sharing insures both regions against the tax progression effect. Note, the tax-sharing system still implies a change in tax revenues allocated to each region independent of the progressive tax system. This change in tax revenues is only due to the tax base shock.

Furthermore, incentives might already be adversely affected by revenue pooling to such an extent that a reduction in the total amount of risk shared among German states is justified on efficiency grounds. If this turns out to be true, implementing the optimal degree of risk spreading might imply a diminished role of fiscal equalization for risk sharing. A detailed analysis of the interaction between revenue sharing and fiscal equalization in Germany would shed more light on the risk-sharing and incentive properties of both transfer systems.

The data presented on the volatility and correlation of GDP growth rates suggest that there is only a limited scope for risk sharing in Germany. However, long-term differences in GDP growth rates across states exist and, according to the authors, they might be a rationale for mutual insurance. Some more empirical analysis could provide a more thorough underpinning for the last conclusion. Since interstate GDP growth rate differences are the result of exogenous shocks and endogenous reactions of the transfer system, one could calculate the size of potentially insurable risk beyond what is already insured by the existing system (Forni and Reichlin 1999). This estimate would offer a useful characterization of the amount of risk sharing in Germany (see Buettner 2002 for a related analysis). Furthermore, one should note that long-term interregional differences in economic performance may be compatible with optimal risk sharing (see Konrad and Seitz's proposition 2).

In the theoretical part of the chapter, the optimal contribution rate to a risk-sharing mechanism is characterized. Regions are risk-averse and, thus, in the presence of idiosyncratic shocks, risk sharing is welfare enhancing. To create an economic trade-off, regions are allowed to decide on their tax collection effort. The authors show that larger regions should contribute a larger fraction of per capita tax revenues to the transfer scheme. At this point, it would be useful to extend the analysis by introducing some explicit modeling of the political economy. Voting could, for instance, take place at the federal as well as the regional level. In this case, each region should also operate a transfer system for risk sharing among municipalities within the region (as is the case in Germany).

This extension has two advantages. First, it enables a comparison of the results with those derived in Persson and Tabellini (1996a, b). Second, it allows Konrad and Seitz to model some political features of the German fiscal federalism relevant for the authors' advocated reform of the transfer system.

Some skepticism concerning the political feasibility of the policy implications seems to be justified. German states with a high population are net contributors under the equalization system, reducing the prospects that the normative results prevail in a political equilibrium. Indeed, some net contributors appealed to the German supreme court for a reduction in the burden imposed by the existing system.

References

Buettner, T. 2002. "Fiscal Federalism and Interstate Risk Sharing: Empirical Evidence from Germany." *Economics Letters* 74: 195–202.

Forni, M., and L. Reichlin. 1999. "Risk and Potential Insurance in Europe." *European Economic Review* 43: 1237–1256.

Persson, T., and G. Tabellini. 1996a. "Federal Fiscal Constitutions: Risk Sharing and Moral Hazard." *Econometrica* 64: 623–646.

Persson, T., and G. Tabellini. 1996b. "Federal Fiscal Constitutions: Risk Sharing and Redistribution." *Journal of Political Economy* 104: 979–1009.

16

Delayed Integration of Mobile Labor: A Principle for Coordinating Taxation, Social Security, and Social Assistance

Wolfram F. Richter

16.1 Introduction

In a world in which constrained labor mobility is the sole impediment to allocational efficiency, integrating labor markets is clearly efficiency enhancing. However, there are losers and winners of market integration. Losers are among those factors whose marginal product comes under competitive pressure. In this chapter, the focus is exclusively on the factor of labor, which divides into a mobile and an immobile part. The differentiation is exogenous and nonlabor factors of production are assumed away.

From an ex ante point of view, labor migration is driven by regional productivity shocks. Such shocks may be favorable or adverse. As a result, market integration affects mobile and immobile labor differently. Whereas market integration helps to insure mobile labor against regional shocks, immobile labor suffers from increased income volatility. The latter may evoke a demand for market-provided insurance. Market insurance, however, suffers from adverse selection. Governments may therefore see reason to intervene with taxation and social insurance. The reason to intervene is strengthened if mobility is skill-driven. In this case, skill and volatility of income will be negatively correlated. This makes nonskilled immobile labor the natural target of distributive policy.

In this chapter, three critical assumptions are made. First, distributive policy is pursued at the regional level; second, there is no fiscal equalization across regions; and third, discriminatory policies and institutional restrictions on labor mobility are not admissible. This specific set of assumptions is characteristic of the state of integration achieved by the European Union. The union does not really assign the power to redistribute income to the regions. Rather, distributive competence is with the member states. Still, the Treaty of the European Community prohibits any discriminatory policy directed by the member states against migrant labor. Such an institutional setting is more characteristic of an interregional context than of an international one. That is the reason why the following theoretical analysis does not refer to countries and nations but to regions and jurisdictions.

If distributive policy is pursued by autonomous jurisdictions, there is a need to assign mobile individuals to these jurisdictions in an unambiguous way. There are competing rules of assignment, however, and their comparative advantages are the subject of this chapter.

The literature tends to restrict consideration to two extreme rules of assignment, the Home Country Principle and the Employment Principle. The latter means that individuals are assigned to the competent jurisdiction in the region of employment. The Home Country Principle requires, instead, assignment of individuals to the competent jurisdiction in the region from which they originate. This may be, though need not be, the region in which an individual was born. A less rigid application of the Home Country Principle would allow individuals to opt for a specific jurisdiction once at the beginning of their working life (Sinn 1994, 100). Alternatively, one can consider assigning individuals to the country of citizenship. This possibility is, however, not considered in this chapter, the reason being that the Treaty of the European Community explicitly rules out any discrimination on the grounds of nationality.[1]

The Principles of Employment and Home Country have their direct counterparts in capital income taxation. To see this, interpret labor income as the return to human capital. It is then obvious that the Employment Principle amounts to taxing capital at source. It may be less obvious that the Home Country Principle amounts to taxing capital in the country of residence. Note, however, that (labor's) home country shares two specific features with the country of (capital's) residence. In both cases, reference is made to the region in which wealth has been accumulated and which cannot be substituted ex post by taxpayers seeking to avoid local taxation.

It is common practice to assign mobile labor according to the Employment Principle. The OECD Model Tax Convention is based on the Employment Principle, just as is the coordination of Social Security among the member states of the European Union.[2] The disadvantages of source taxes are well documented in the literature. If nonharmonized, they induce production inefficiency and they harm immobile factors of production. Source taxes on mobile factors are shifted backward. In fact, mobile factors can be taxed on a benefit basis only (Musgrave 1999, 170). There is, however, an additional problem if labor is taxed at source. The Employment Principle is inherently discriminatory. It is not easily extended to cover non-working individuals. This may not be considered a pressing political problem for Europe. It may still become an impediment for the further political integration. The right of free movement ranks high among the agreed values of the European Union. According to the Treaty of Maastricht, every citizen of the union has the right to reside wherever (s)he wishes to. This ruling contrasts with the legal practice, which ties the freedom to move to employment. In particular, welfare recipients lose their claim to support if they choose to migrate. This hardly complies with the notion of a European citizenship and it might not be wise to leave it to the courts to close the gap between European visions and common practice.

The tension between the restricted granting of social assistance and the declared right of free movement of all citizens could easily be resolved by requiring the home country to export social assistance. Countries are, however, reluctant to adopt this straightforward solution. One can only speculate about the reasons. An obvious one will be monitoring. Social assistance is designed as support to people in need. Such need has to be monitored. Countries are reluctant to delegate monitoring functions to foreign administrations. Although social assistance is not the primary focus of the present chapter, it will be given due consideration when weighing competing rules of assignment.

The Home Country Principle has been proposed as a rule for assigning working individuals to jurisdictions. The justification has been an allocational one. In contrast to the Employment Principle, the Home Country Principle sustains production efficiency. Some authors plead for the Home Country Principle not only with a view to production efficiency. For Sinn (1994), it safeguards the Welfare State. In Sinn's conception, the Welfare State provides insurance against income risk and uncertain life careers. It works best if it is not left to the individual's discretion whether and when to opt out of the system. The freedom to opt out would only result in adverse selection. At most, individuals should be allowed to choose between competing redistributive systems ex ante when young and ignorant about career prospects. The Home Country Principle allows the realization of such a conception.

However, the underlying view of redistribution can be criticized, as it relies on coercion. The implicit assumption is that people have to be forced if they are to bear a fair share of the cost of distributive policy. The competing conception suggests that distributive policy needs to be approved by the population. Such approval is best ensured if there is a strong feeling of solidarity between the winners and losers of redistribution. Such a feeling of solidarity must, however, grow. It grows in neighborhoods and fellowships. The Home Country Principle ignores this, as it is oriented toward the past. The Employment Principle is more integrative. It is responsive to changes in neighborhoods.

The Home Country Principle can also be criticized for the weak incentives it gives jurisdictions to respond to citizens' preferences. After individuals have been assigned to a particular jurisdiction, they cannot threaten to exit. That makes them exploitable. The Home Country Principle imposes little discipline on Leviathan governments. The Employment Principle is more supportive of efficiency enhancing competition among jurisdictions.

If neither the Home Country nor the Employment Principle is a fully convincing rule of assignment, a mix of the two might promise better results. And, in fact, one particular mix has recently been suggested by the Advisory Board to the Federal Ministry of Finance in Germany (Wissenschaftlicher Beirat 2001) as a rule for assigning citizens of the European Union. The idea is to leave migrants— working and nonworking individuals alike—assigned to their home country for a coordinated period of transition and to reassign them to the country of immigration thereafter. Hence, jurisdictional reassignment follows migration only with delay. The council calls this assignment rule "Delayed Integration."[3] It is integrative insofar as migrants are eventually assigned to the country to which they move. Integration is delayed, as reassignment becomes effective only after a period of transition. For the sake of illustration, the council assumes a transition period of five years.

It is not that the idea of Delayed Integration is totally novel. In fact, there are rules in foreign tax codes that catch the very spirit of Delayed Integration. An example is the foreign tax code of Germany (Weichenrieder 2000). When a German taxpayer emigrates and moves to a low-income-tax jurisdiction, (s)he continues to be subjected to German taxation on that part of her/his income that originates in Germany. There are other rules that resemble Delayed Integration but are dissimilar to it in an important respect. An example is the granting of social assistance within Germany or Switzerland. By citing Feld (2000), Weichenrieder reports that Swiss cantons provide welfare support to immigrants from other cantons as if they were residents and that the home canton reimburses the canton of residence for its full expenses during the first two years after migration and for half its expenses during the following six years. A similar rule applies to migration within Germany (Wissenschaftlicher Beirat 2001). The obligation to refund costs for an initial time period is reminiscent of Delayed Integration. However, the rule differs with respect to the incentives given to migrants. It is as if a residence principle were in place. Migrants are entitled to the welfare support granted at the place where they choose to reside. This differs from Delayed Integration. During the period of transition, this principle entitles immigrants only to the welfare support granted in their home jurisdiction.

Weichenrieder takes a critical view of Delayed Integration. He argues that it weakens tax competition. Regions' incentive to undercut other regions' tax rates is undermined. The promise of low tax rates after a period of transition lacks credibility. There is always the risk that jurisdictions resort to policy surprises.

The present chapter tries to work out the merits of Delayed Integration. This is done in a model that ignores strategic aspects of tax competition. The model, an adaptation of Wildasin (2000), is introduced in section 16.2. Section 16.3 analyzes the equilibrium that migration brings about in a world of laissez-faire. In the remaining sections, it is assumed that regional governments pursue autonomous policies of redistribution. That raises the question of which rule of assignment between individuals and jurisdictions should apply. Section 16.4 looks at the Employment Principle, section 16.5 at the Home Country Principle, and section 16.6 at the Principle of Delayed Integration. Section 16.7 summarizes and draws conclusions.

16.2 A Simple Model of Skilled Labor Mobility

The model is largely a simplified version of Wildasin (2000). The focus is on a representative jurisdiction endowed with $\bar{L}$ immobile and $\bar{H}$ mobile native workers. The division into immobile and mobile workers is exogenous. In contrast to Wildasin (2000), we regard mobility to be an innate ability. It is out of personal control. Without loss of generality, one may therefore normalize the immobile workforce to be one, $\bar{L} = 1$. Wildasin (2000) assumes, instead, that mobility is the result of skill acquisition, which is endogenously determined by human capital investment.

Production is assumed to require labor only. The output of the jurisdiction under consideration is a function $\Theta F(H)$ of the number H of mobile workers employed. $\bar{H} < H$ stands for immigration and $\bar{H} > H$ for emigration. We assume positive but decreasing marginal productivity, $F' > 0 > F''$. The factor Θ reflects a stochastic regional shock. This means that its value may well deviate from Θ^*, which holds outside the jurisdiction. In contrast, technology is the same throughout the economy $(F = F^*)$. In what follows, an asterisk refers to parameters of foreign jurisdictions. They are exogenous, reflecting the fact that our region is small compared with the rest of the economy.

Linear homogeneity implies that the full product, ΘF, is distributed as income to the workforce employed in the jurisdiction. Income per capita is $\Theta F/(1 + H)$. A key assumption for the following analysis requires

$$\Theta F' > \frac{\Theta F}{1 + H}. \tag{1}$$

Hence, the marginal product of mobile labor exceeds the average product of the locally employed workforce. Inequality (1) is far from being self-evident. Major results derived in this chapter turn into their opposite if (1) holds with a reversed inequality sign. Still, it is suggestive to interpret (1) as a condition of *skill-driven mobility*. Note that (1) is equivalent to $r = \Theta F' > \Theta[F - HF'] = w$, which says that the return to mobile labor exceeds the return to immobile labor. This is plausible only if mobile labor can be equated with skilled labor.

16.3   Laissez-Faire

When jurisdictions refrain from intervening in labor markets, the wage income of mobile labor, r, is determined by the foreign rate of return, $r^* = \Theta^* F'^*$.[4] This has some immediate though important implications. First, the resulting allocation of mobile labor is production-efficient: $\Theta F' = r = r^* = \Theta^* F'^*$. Second, mobile labor is perfectly insured against the income risk of regional shocks. The variable r does not vary with Θ but only with Θ^*. As the given jurisdiction is small and as there are many small jurisdictions, it is reasonable to assume that Θ^* is nonstochastic and independent of Θ.

Regional shocks are completely absorbed by variations in employment. Let $H^{LF} = H^{LF}(\Theta)$ solve $\Theta F'(H^{LF}) = r = $ constant and let it denote mobile labor employed in a regime of laissez-faire. Employment is positively correlated with regional shocks, $dH^{LF}/d\Theta = -F'/\Theta F'' > 0$. This makes the return to immobile labor, $w = \Theta[F - H^{LF}F']$, more volatile. Without adjustment in H^{LF}, we have

$$\frac{\partial w}{\partial \Theta} = F - H^{LF}F', \tag{2}$$

which falls short of

$$F = \frac{\partial w}{\partial \Theta} + \frac{\partial w}{\partial H}\frac{dH^{LF}}{d\Theta} = \frac{dw}{d\Theta}. \tag{3}$$

The effects that the integration of labor markets have for immobile labor are therefore ambiguous. The exposure of immobile labor to regional shocks increases. It is not clear whether such increased risk is compensated for by an increase in the expected return.[5] It depends not least on risk preferences. The results derived by Wildasin (2000, proposition 1) are less ambiguous and more positive. Since mobility is not fate in Wildasin's setting but the result of investment decisions taken ex ante, expected utilities are equalized in equilibrium across skill levels. As a consequence, labor market integration raises the equilibrium return to all kinds of labor and eliminates all income risk. Hence, there is little reason for government intervention. Welfare is maximized by laissez-faire. This is not necessarily the case in the present framework, in which characteristics of mobility and skill are exogenous.

16.4   The Employment Principle

If governments wish to redistribute labor income in a world of free labor mobility, the rule assigning individuals to jurisdictions becomes focal. In this section, it is assumed that workers pay taxes to and receive public transfers from the jurisdiction in which they are employed. This is the Employment Principle. It is the principle recommended in Article 15 of the OECD Model Convention for the taxation of labor income. It is also the principle governing Social Security in the European Union as laid down in Regulation (EEC) No. 1408/71. In what follows, we do not explicitly differentiate between taxation and Social Security. We simply assume that an individual has to pay taxes T to the jurisdiction to which (s)he is assigned and that (s)he receives some transfer S from the same jurisdiction. A crucial assumption is that such taxes and transfers do not discriminate between mobile and immobile workers. For the sake of further simplification, we assume linear taxation at the rate $t \in [0, 1]$. Hence, tax revenue is $T^E = t\Theta F(H^E)$. The index E indicates that taxation is in accord with the Employment Principle. If the government budget is to be balanced, we must have $S^E = t\Theta F(H^E)/(1 + H^E)$. Note that nondiscrimination means that each worker pays the same wage tax rate t and that (s)he receives the same transfer S^E.

Net wage income of mobile labor is $\rho^E \equiv (1 - t)\Theta F' + S^E$, which, by wage arbitrage, equals the net wage income paid abroad, $(1 - t^*)\Theta^* F'^* + S^*$. The Employment Principle is known to threaten production efficiency. See, among others, Frenkel, Razin, and Sadka (1991, section 2.1). In the present model, production inefficiency ($\Theta F' \neq \Theta^* F'^*$) follows from wage arbitrage if transfers are harmonized ($S^E = S^{E*}$) but tax rates are not ($t \neq t^*$).

Given the Employment Principle, the level of employment, $H^E = H^E(\Theta, t)$, of a small jurisdiction follows from solving $\rho^E =$ constant. Let H_Θ^E, H_t^E, S_H^E, and so forth denote partial derivatives. Implicit differentiation gives us

$$H_\Theta^E = -\frac{(1 - t)F' + tF/(1 + H^E)}{(1 - t)\Theta F'' + S_H^E}, \tag{4}$$

$$H_t^E = \frac{F' - F/(1 + H^E)}{(1 - t)F'' + S_H^E/\Theta}. \tag{5}$$

In what follows, it is assumed that employment is positively correlated with regional shocks:

$$H_\Theta^E > 0 \Leftrightarrow (1 - t)\Theta F'' + S_H^E < 0. \tag{6}$$

The first term in the sum of (6) is clearly negative. The second term may be nonnegative, however, because transfer payments may react positively to immigration. This is just the case when mobility is skill-driven in the sense of (1):

$$S_H^E = \frac{t\Theta}{1 + H}\left[F' - \frac{F}{1 + H}\right] \geq 0, \tag{7}$$

where equality holds if $t = 0$. If (6) and (1) hold jointly, taxation drives mobile labor out of the country ($H_t^E < 0$).

The only income on which local policy has an impact is the income of immobile labor, $\omega^E = \omega^E(t, \Theta) \equiv (1 - t)\Theta[F - H^E F'] + S^E$. The income of mobile labor ρ^E is fixed by wage arbitrage. However, redistributive policy in favor of immobile labor fails to be effective if the Employment Principle applies. This follows from the well-known result that taxing perfectly mobile production factors at source is harmful for the immobile factors. The burden of taxation is shifted backwards and local production decisions are distorted.

Proposition 1: Given the Employment Principle, $t = 0$ maximizes the net income of immobile labor, $\omega^E(t, \Theta)$.

The proof is skipped as the result is considered to be known. The proof follows from demonstrating $\partial \omega^E / \partial t = 0$ at $t = 0$, and $\partial^2 \omega^E / \partial t^2 = \Theta[F' - F/(1 + H^E)]^2 / F'' \leq 0$ at $t = 0$.

Although the income of immobile labor is maximized by setting $t = 0$, it is interesting to study the effects of some positive choice of t. Of major interest is the effect that $t > 0$ has on the volatility of immobile labor income. One might be inclined to conjecture that reducing ω^E is just the price one has to pay for smaller volatility with respect to regional shocks. However, the contrary is true. To see this, we compare $\partial \omega^E / \partial \Theta$ with $dw/d\Theta = F$ at $H = H^E$ and at small values of $t > 0$. $t = 0$ is excluded as any difference vanishes in absence of taxation. If $\omega^E_\Theta > F$, this is interpreted as a volatility-increasing effect of taxation.

Proposition 2: If the Employment Principle applies, if (1) holds, and if $t > 0$ is sufficiently small, then the volatility of immobile labor income exceeds the laissez-faire level of volatility at $H = H^E$.

The proof is straightforward. It relies on showing

$$F(H^E) = \left.\frac{dw}{d\Theta}\right|_{H=H^E} < \frac{\partial \omega^E}{\partial \Theta}$$

$$= \left[(1-t) + \frac{t}{1+H^E}\right]F - (1-t)H^E F' + [-(1-t)\Theta H^E F'' + S^E_H]H^E_\Theta$$

$$\Leftrightarrow 0 < -\frac{S^E_H}{(1-t)\Theta F'' + S^E_H}. \tag{8}$$

The latter inequality follows from (6) and (7).

Condition (8) helps us to understand proposition 2. If mobile labor did not respond to shocks ($H_\Theta^E = 0$), then taxation would be volatility reducing. For $H_\Theta^E = 0$, we obtain $\omega_\Theta^E < F$. However, by (6), employment is positively correlated with regional shocks. This reverses the volatility-reducing effect.

From the perspective of immobile labor, the Employment Principle has unfavorable effects only. When assessing such a result, one should note, however, that the present analysis disregards nonlabor income. This is clearly restrictive. One could assume, instead, that immobile nonlabor factors of production exist. In this case, much would depend on whether the returns to such nonlabor factors are included in the tax base and on how tax proceeds are distributed. Immobile labor can well benefit from the taxation of mobile factors if the tax burden and the efficiency loss are shifted to the immobile nonlabor factors of production.

16.5 The Home Country Principle

Taxing labor in the country of employment is not the only option. Taxing labor in the home country is a prominent alternative. Much of the literature, however, focuses on capital income taxation. In this context, taxation in the country of employment amounts to taxation at source, whereas taxation in the home country amounts to taxation in the country of residence. See, among others, Frenkel, Razin, and Sadka (1991). A more or less implicit assumption is that households do not change their place of residence. At most, they commute and supply labor abroad. However, this is not the relevant case in practice. In the European Union, fewer than 400,000 people work in a country that is not their country of residence. In the terminology of Regulation (EEC) No. 1408/71, they are frontier workers. More people migrate, which means that they change their place of residence along with the place of work. In this context, it is better not to speak of the residence principle but to speak of the Home Country Principle instead.

Home country taxation is theoretically appealing as it preserves *production efficiency*. This is easily demonstrated. Home country taxation implies that neither tax rates nor transfer payments change when labor is supplied abroad. By wage arbitrage, we obtain $(1 - t)\Theta F' + S^{HC} = \rho^{HC} = (1 - t)\Theta^* F'^* + S^{HC}$, or $\Theta F' = \Theta^* F'^*$. As a result, employment is not affected by taxation and it equals the level of employment in a regime of laissez-faire, $H^{HC} = H^{HC}(\Theta) = H^{LF}(\Theta)$.

H^{HC} is implicitly defined by $\Theta F' = \text{constant}$. Hence, $H_\Theta^{HC} = H_\Theta^{LF} = -F'/\Theta F'' > 0$.

In a regime of home country taxation, revenue amounts to $T^{HC} = t\Theta F + t(\bar{H} - H^{HC})\Theta^* F'^*$. This covers both the case of emigration, $\bar{H} > H^{HC}$, and the case of immigration, $\bar{H} < H^{HC}$. With a balanced budget, transfer payments are

$$S^{HC} = S^{HC}(t, \Theta, H^{HC}) = \frac{t[\Theta F + (\bar{H} - H^{HC})\Theta^* F'^*]}{1 + \bar{H}}. \tag{9}$$

Again, the focus is on net wage income of immobile labor, $\omega^{HC} = \omega^{HC}(t, \Theta) = (1 - t)\Theta[F - H^{HC}F'] + S^{HC}$. As H^{HC} is constant in t and as $\Theta F' = \Theta^* F'^*$, we obtain

$$\frac{\partial \omega^{HC}}{\partial t} = -\Theta[F - H^{HC}F'] + \frac{\Theta F + (\bar{H} - H^{HC})\Theta^* F'^*}{1 + \bar{H}}$$

$$= \frac{\bar{H}\Theta}{1 + \bar{H}}[F'(1 + H^{HC}) - F] > 0 \Leftrightarrow (1). \tag{10}$$

Proposition 3: Assuming home country taxation, net wage income of immobile labor increases in t if and only if mobility is skill driven in the sense of (1).

The benefits accruing to immobile labor do not result from efficiency gains. Their only source is intrajurisdictional redistribution. The losers are mobile workers. To see this more clearly, compute the income accruing to natives. This income turns out to be constant in t:

$$\omega^{HC} + \bar{H}\rho^{HC} = (1 - t)\Theta[F - H^{HC}F' + \bar{H}F'] + (1 + \bar{H})S^{HC}$$

$$= \Theta[F + (\bar{H} - H^{HC})F'] = w + \bar{H}r. \tag{11}$$

Much in contrast to what has been shown for the Employment Principle, home country taxation helps to decrease the volatility of immobile labor income. The decreasing effect is stronger, the larger $t > 0$. This follows from noting that

$$\frac{\partial \omega^{HC}}{\partial \Theta} = \frac{d}{d\Theta}\left\{\left[(1 - t) + \frac{t}{1 + \bar{H}}\right]\Theta F + \left[t\frac{\bar{H} - H^{HC}}{1 + \bar{H}} - (1 - t)H^{HC}\right]\Theta^* F'^*\right\}$$

$$= \left[(1 - t) + \frac{t}{1 + \bar{H}}\right]\left[F + \frac{F'^2}{F''}\right] < F = \frac{dw}{d\Theta}, \tag{12}$$

making use of $\Theta F' = \Theta^* F'^*$.

Proposition 4: Assuming home country taxation, the volatility of immobile labor income decreases in $t > 0$.

The Home Country Principle thus has a volatility-decreasing effect. It provides insurance against regional shocks. However, note that regional income rather than income accruing to natives is insured. Whereas the income accruing to natives depends on $\bar{H}$, regional income depends on H^{HC}. It amounts to

$$\omega^{HC} + H^{HC}\rho^{HC} = (1-t)\Theta F + (1 + H^{HC})S^{HC} > \Theta F = w + H^{LF}r$$

$$\Leftrightarrow (\bar{H} - H)[(1 + H^{HC})F' - F] > 0. \tag{13}$$

Given (1), this means that the Home Country Principle implies income redistribution from jurisdictions of immigration, $H > \bar{H}$, to jurisdictions of emigration, $\bar{H} > H$. Hence, the Home Country Principle insures regional income against regional shocks. Summarizing, we obtain the following proposition.

Proposition 5: Home country taxation has no effect on the level of aggregate income accruing to natives. Given (1), it damps, however, the volatility of regional income.

It may look as if the Home Country Principle has a clear advantage compared with the Employment Principle. The latter impedes production efficiency and works against the interests of immobile factors, as shown above. The Home Country Principle does not share these deficiencies. Still, it has its shortcomings which can, however, only be addressed by stepping out of the model. For instance, the Home Country Principle is known to impede consumption efficiency if combined with income taxation. The marginal rates of substituting leisure for consumption fail to be equalized across jurisdictions. See, among others, Frenkel, Razin, and Sadka (1991). Furthermore, the Home Country Principle is at variance with the political objective of integrating immigrants. Integration suggests treating immigrants like inhabitants. The Home Country Principle makes this impossible. Individuals stay assigned to their home country even if they decide to leave it forever. This has very much the flavor of slavery in the name of states. Although individuals are free to migrate, the home country continues to claim its share of all the returns earned, wherever earned. This is against the interests of immigration countries, especially if various benefits are made available to immigrants.

Above all, it weakens competition among jurisdictions, even when such competition can be considered to be desirable and efficiency enhancing.

16.6   Delayed Integration

If both the Employment and the Home Country Principles have their deficiencies, it is inviting to look for a compromise. Such a compromise may provide that migrants are reassigned for purposes of taxation and Social Security to the country of immigration only after an agreed period of transition has elapsed since migration. Just for the sake of illustration, let us assume a transition period of five years. The ruling would then be that migrants are treated according to the Home Country Principle for the first five years and thereafter according to the Employment Principle. Let us call this practice "Delayed Integration." Conflicts between tax authorities are ruled out if all adhere to the same span of delay. This kind of coordination is assumed throughout in what follows. The difference from current European practice is not so much the institution of some delay. In fact, workers posted abroad temporarily remain assigned to their home jurisdiction under current law.[6] Hence, the novel element of Delayed Integration is the use of the length of delay as an explicit policy instrument. Furthermore, part of the proposal is the suggestion that Delayed Integration should be applied to all citizens alike and that there should be no differentiation between (1) recipients of welfare payments and (2) individuals who are employed or treated as if they were employed like family members and students.

This section takes a closer look at the properties of Delayed Integration. Some basic results are derived within the given static model. As Delayed Integration is an inherently dynamic concept, it has to be adapted to the static framework. The adaptation is straightforward, however. It requires labor income earned abroad to be taxed at the rate $\delta t + (1 - \delta)t^*$. The value $\delta = \delta^* \in (0,1)$ measures the coordinated rate of delay. Hence, Delayed Integration can be interpreted as a convex combination of the Home Country Principle and the Employment Principle. This property helps to explain the following results. With δ approaching zero (one), Delayed Integration turns into employment (home country) taxation. The concept of Delayed Integration is equally applied to transfer payments. This means that $\delta S + (1 - \delta)S^*$ is paid to those working abroad, whereas inhabitants of the home jurisdiction receive S and pay taxes at the rate t. By wage arbitrage of emigrants, we have

$$(1 - t)\Theta F' + S = [\delta(1 - t) + (1 - \delta)(1 - t^*)]\Theta^* F'^* + \delta S + (1 - \delta)S^*. \quad (14)$$

Obviously, the Home Country Principle is recovered for $\delta = 1$ and the Employment Principle is obtained for $\delta = 0$. For what follows, much depends on whether wage arbitrage is bilateral or unilateral. Wage arbitrage is said to be *bilateral* if both (14) and its counterpart,

$$(1 - t^*)\Theta^* F'^* + S^* = [\delta(1 - t^*) + (1 - \delta)(1 - t)]\Theta F' + \delta S^* + (1 - \delta)S,$$
$$(14^*)$$

hold jointly. Wage arbitrage is called *unilateral* if only one of (14) and (14*) holds with equality and the other with inequality. Unilateral wage arbitrage results if emigration from one jurisdiction excludes emigration from the other. Such a pattern of migration is sustained in equilibrium if we have equality in either (14) or (14*) and if the left-hand side exceeds the right-hand side otherwise. Let us call this a corner equilibrium. It is informative, however, also to analyze interior equilibria characterized by bilateral wage arbitrage. We do one after the other and start with the latter.

16.6.1   Bilateral Wage Arbitrage

Consider Delayed Integration with $\delta \in (0, 1)$. Bilateral wage arbitrage is feasible only if fiscal policies are sufficiently harmonized. This does not necessarily require the equalization of policy instruments, $t = t^*$ and $S = S^*$. However, differences in tax rates $(t \neq t^*)$ are compatible with bilateral wage arbitrage only if the marginal products of mobile labor as well as net tax payments are equalized among jurisdictions. The former is the requirement for production efficiency. The latter means

$$t\Theta F' - S = t^* \Theta^* F'^* - S^*, \quad (15)$$

which is best interpreted as *harmonization of distributive policy*. Hence, whenever there are good reasons not to harmonize distributive policy across jurisdictions, bilateral wage arbitrage will not be viable. This is different from the regimes in which either the Employment or the Home Country Principle applies, and it may be considered a disadvantage of Delayed Integration.

Proposition 6:   Assume Delayed Integration with $\delta \in (0,1)$, bilateral wage arbitrage, and $t \neq t^*$. The implications are (1) production efficiency and (2) harmonization of distributive policy.

For a proof, solve (14*) for S^* and eliminate S^* from (14). After canceling various expressions, we end up with $\delta(t - t^*)\Theta^* F'^* = \delta(t - t^*)\Theta F'$, which implies production efficiency. Inserting $\Theta F' = \Theta^* F'^*$ into (14) and dividing through by $1 - \delta$ gives us (15).

From now on, assume $\Theta F' = \Theta^* F'^*$. Denote by H^{DI} mobile labor employed. Then $H^{DI} = H^{DI}(\Theta) = H^{LF}(\Theta)$ and $H_\Theta^{DI} = -F'/\Theta F'' > 0$. Tax revenue is

$$T^{DI} = t\Theta F + t\delta(\bar{H} - H^{DI})\Theta^* F'^*. \tag{16}$$

The first term on the right-hand side is tax revenue collected from home income. The second term is tax revenue collected from income earned abroad. If there is immigration, the second term is negative. It is then tax revenue accruing to foreign jurisdictions. By budget balance, we obtain

$$S^{DI} = S^{DI}(t, \Theta, H^{DI}) = t\frac{\Theta F + \delta(\bar{H} - H^{DI})\Theta^* F'^*}{1 + H^{DI} + \delta(\bar{H} - H^{DI})}. \tag{17}$$

Our focus is again on net wage income of immobile labor,

$$\omega^{DI} = \omega^{DI}(t, \Theta) = (1 - t)\Theta[F - H^{DI}F'] + S^{DI}. \tag{18}$$

As H^{DI} is constant in t and as $\Theta F' = \Theta^* F'^*$, we obtain

$$\frac{\partial \omega^{DI}}{\partial t} = -\Theta[F - H^{DI}F'] + \frac{\Theta F + \delta(\bar{H} - H^{DI})\Theta^* F'^*}{1 + H^{DI} + \delta(\bar{H} - H^{DI})}$$

$$= \frac{[H^{DI} + \delta(\bar{H} - H^{DI})]\Theta}{1 + H^{DI} + \delta(\bar{H} - H^{DI})}[F'(1 + H^{DI}) - F], \tag{19}$$

which is a straightforward generalization of (10).

Proposition 7:   Assuming Delayed Integration and production efficiency, net wage income of immobile labor increases in t if and only if mobility is skill-driven in the sense of (1).

For proposition 7 to hold, nothing has to be said about the exact degree of delay. δ only needs to be positive. The degree of delay is more critical for the effect that Delayed Integration and production

efficiency have on the volatility of immobile labor income. As we
show next, the volatility is reduced only if $\delta \in (0,1]$ is sufficiently
large. This follows from verifying

$$F = \frac{dw}{d\Theta} > \frac{\partial \omega^{DI}}{\partial \Theta} = \left[(1-t) + \frac{t}{1+H+\delta(\bar{H}-H)}\right] F$$

$$- (1-t)HF' - [(1-t)\Theta HF'' - S_H^{DI}]\frac{\partial H^{DI}}{\partial \Theta} \tag{20}$$

$$\Leftrightarrow [H + \delta(\bar{H}-H)]F > -\frac{(1-\delta)F'}{F''}\frac{(1+H)F'-F}{1+H+\delta(\bar{H}-H)}. \tag{21}$$

The derivation of the equivalence is straightforward. Use is made of
$\Theta F' = \Theta^* F'^*$, $t > 0$, and $H^{DI} = H^{LF} = H$.

Let us have a closer look at (21). Obviously, it does not depend on
the value of $t > 0$ whether the volatility of immobile labor income is
reduced or not. The tax rate, t, enters (21) neither directly nor indirectly via H. More critical is the choice of δ and the question of
whether mobility is skill-driven or not. If mobility is skill-driven in
the sense of (1) and if δ is fixed below one, the right-hand side of (21)
is positive, just as the left-hand side is. Under such circumstances,
unconditional statements about the effect on volatility are not feasible. This would be different if mobility were restricted to unskilled
labor, a constellation that is ruled out by (1). The impact that the
kind of labor mobility has on (21) disappears for $\delta = 1$. In this case,
the right-hand side vanishes and the volatility of immobile labor income is unambiguously reduced, as already stated by proposition 4.
We need not set $\delta = 1$, however, if (21) is to hold true. It suffices that
δ is chosen sufficiently close to one that the right-hand side becomes
small relative to the left-hand side. Note that H does not depend on
$\delta > 0$.

Proposition 8: Assuming production efficiency, Delayed Integration has a reducing effect on the volatility of immobile labor income
for all $t > 0$ if δ is chosen sufficiently close to one.

It is not surprising that proposition 8 only holds for large values of
δ. The smaller δ is, the smaller the difference between Delayed Integration and the Employment Principle. Proposition 2, however,
taught us that the volatility-reducing effect may well be reversed if
the Employment Principle applies.

It has to be stressed that propositions 7 and 8 rely on production efficiency, which, according to proposition 6, is guaranteed only if Delayed Integration with $\delta \in (0,1)$ sustains bilateral wage arbitrage. If Delayed Integration sustains unilateral wage arbitrage only, the implications become less clear-cut.

16.6.2 Unilateral Wage Arbitrage

If wage arbitrage is unilateral, either (14) or (14*) holds with equality. Equality of (14) captures the case in which workers emigrate from the home jurisdiction. Vice versa, equality of (14*) stands for a situation in which workers emigrate from the foreign jurisdiction. The two cases have to be analyzed separately. Since the analysis becomes a bit messy, we focus on a single question—whether the net income of immobile labor can be increased via taxation. The question has to be seen in connection with proposition 1. This proposition states that the net income of immobile labor cannot be increased by taxation if the Employment Principle holds. This result applies equally to jurisdictions of emigration and immigration. One may easily conjecture that things are different if Delayed Integration is adopted. In fact, we are going to show that the prospects for redistributing income towards immobile labor are better if Delayed Integration applies. More detailed statements have to differentiate between jurisdictions of emigration and those of immigration. We start by looking at jurisdictions of emigration.

Respecting budget balance, a jurisdiction of emigration pays transfers in the amount of

$$S^e = t \frac{\Theta F + \delta(\bar{H} - H^e)\Theta^* F'^*}{1 + H^e + \delta(\bar{H} - H^e)}. \tag{22}$$

The index e indicates emigration, $\bar{H} > H^e$. The variable H^e denotes equilibrium employment in the home jurisdiction. Its level is determined by (14) or $(1-t)\Theta F' + (1-\delta)S^e + \delta t\Theta^* F'^* = $ constant. Implicit differentiation gives us

$$\left.\frac{\partial H^e}{\partial t}\right|_{t=0} = \frac{\Theta F' - \delta\Theta^* F'^* - (1-\delta)S_t^e}{\Theta F''}. \tag{23}$$

Net income of immobile labor is $\omega^e = (1-t)\Theta[F - H^e F'] + S^e$. It is straightforward to derive

$$\frac{\partial \omega^e}{\partial t}\bigg|_{t=0} = \frac{\delta \bar{H}}{1 + H^e + \delta(\bar{H} - H^e)}[(1 + H^e)\Theta^* F'^* - \Theta F]. \tag{24}$$

We can see that two things must come together if ω_t^e is to be positive at $t = 0$. First, integration must be delayed ($\delta > 0$). Second, the marginal product that mobile labor can earn abroad must exceed the average product earned at home:

$$\Theta^* F'^* > \frac{\Theta F}{1 + H}. \tag{1*}$$

At first sight, (1*) looks very much like (1). In fact, (1*) equals (1) if production efficiency holds. However, unlike (1), (1*) cannot be interpreted as skill-driven mobility. Inequality (1*) is obtained, for instance, if the foreign jurisdiction experiences a strongly positive shock.

Proposition 9: If (1*) holds and if integration is delayed ($\delta > 0$), then the net income of immobile labor residing in the jurisdiction of emigration is increased by marginal taxation.

Let us compare this result with the case in which the home jurisdiction is characterized by inflowing labor. With the index i denoting immigration, transfer payments amount to

$$S^i = t\frac{\Theta F + \delta(\bar{H} - H^i)\Theta F'}{1 + H^i + \delta(\bar{H} - H^i)}. \tag{25}$$

This is obtained from dividing up tax revenues

$$T^i = t\Theta[F - H^i F'] + t\Theta\bar{H}F' + (1 - \delta)t(H^i - \bar{H})\Theta F'$$

$$= t\Theta F + t\delta(\bar{H} - H^i)\Theta F' \tag{26}$$

among $1 + \bar{H} + (1 - \delta)(H^i - \bar{H})$ equal shares. H_t^i is obtained by implicit differentiation of (14*) or $(1 - \delta)[(1 - t)\Theta F' + S^i] + \delta(1 - t^*)\Theta F' = $ constant. Net income of immobile labor is $\omega^i = (1 - t)\Theta[F - H^i F'] + S^i$. It responds to marginal taxation according to

$$\frac{\partial \omega^i}{\partial t}\bigg|_{t=0} = \delta\Theta\frac{(1 + H^i)F' - F}{1 + H^i + \delta(\bar{H} - H^i)}\left[\bar{H} - \frac{(1 - \delta)t^*}{1 - \delta t^*}H^i\right]. \tag{27}$$

For $t^* = 0$, (27) looks very much like (24). Hence, skill-driven mobility and Delayed Integration with $\delta > 0$ jointly ensure positivity of (27). The sign of (27) is more ambiguous if $t^* > 0$. The reason is that the tax elasticity of home employment increases in the foreign tax rate. More precisely, the absolute value of $H_t^i|_{t=0}$ increases in t^* when $\delta > 0$. On the other hand, positivity of (27) can be ensured even for $t^* > 0$ if δ is sufficiently close to one.

Proposition 10:   If mobility is skill-driven in the sense of (1) and if integration is delayed $(\delta > 0)$, then the net income of immobile labor residing in the jurisdiction of immigration is increased by marginal taxation either if $t^* = 0$ or if $t^* > 0$ and δ is sufficiently large.

16.7   Conclusions

The major conclusion to be drawn from the preceding analysis is that every rule of assignment has its specific shortcomings. There is no rule that can be said to outmatch the competing ones, both on allocational and distributional grounds. The rules that have been discussed in detail are the Employment Principle, the Home Country Principle, and the Principle of Delayed Integration. It remains to summarize their major characteristics. In doing so, we focus on the following objectives: (1) allocational efficiency, (2) compatibility with a policy of integration, (3) applicability to social assistance, (4) the power to redistribute in favor of immobile nonskilled labor, and (5) the power to insure immobile labor income against regional shocks.

Allocational efficiency relates to production and to consumption. Only production efficiency has been the explicit subject of the preceding analysis. This can be justified in view of the Production Efficiency Theorem of Diamond and Mirrlees (1971) giving priority to production efficiency in cases where policy has to choose.[7] Still, a broader view of efficiency should not leave consumption unconsidered.

We have seen that the only rule of assignment that sustains production efficiency is the Home Country Principle. Delayed Integration with positive delay sustains production efficiency only if wage arbitrage is bilateral, a situation requiring harmonization of distributive policy. The specific appeal of assigning individuals to their country of employment rests on the consumption efficiency that the assignment brings about. Delayed Integration with unilateral wage arbitrage tends to violate both efficiency conditions. The mere fact that Delayed Integration violates two efficiency conditions, whereas the Employment Principle violates only one, does not allow us to make strong inferences. After all, it is not the number of distortions that counts but the total efficiency loss. Still, given the framework adopted in this chapter, one may well conjecture that efficiency losses are minimized by the Home Country Principle and that they tend to decrease in the length of delay that is applied under Delayed Integration.

The model employed in this chapter assumes that the public sector performs efficiently. Hence, competition among jurisdictions has no efficiency-enhancing function as it would have in a Tiebout-like setting. This obviously biases the results against the Employment Principle and against the choice of some small value of δ under Delayed Integration. This has to be kept in mind when drawing policy conclusions.

The criterion to which we turn next is compatibility with a policy of integration. We have mentioned that it is not fully clear why we should pursue such an objective. Two tentative reasons have been suggested. One refers to the efficiency of administration. Incentives to monitor are stronger if monitoring is the responsibility of institutions that collect tax payments and that fund transfer payments. The other reason refers to distributive policy. Distributive policy is most effective if it is grounded in ethical values approved by those bearing the burden of redistribution. This is widely acknowledged (Pauly 1973) and implies that distributive policy should aim at exploiting the feeling of solidarity. Solidarity, however, develops best in neighborhoods and similar structures. All this provides strong arguments for integrative rules of assignment such as the Employment Principle. As a corollary, it indicates limits of the Home Country Principle. A shortcoming of the Employment Principle is its restricted coverage. It is not easily extended to social assistance. Social assistance, however, deserves special consideration.

It would not be prudent policy to put the burden of social assistance on the jurisdiction of immigration. It would only bring the Welfare State under competitive pressure. Jurisdictions would have strong incentives to cut welfare payments in order to deter the immigration of entitled persons. The widely practiced solution to the problem rests on discrimination. The rule is that welfare recipients are withdrawn support if they choose to migrate. It is not totally clear whether such practice complies with the spirit of the European Treaty in the post-Maastricht era. After all, one must admit that territorially restricted social assistance severely curtails the freedom to move. This freedom, however, ranks high among the agreed values of the European Union. It is therefore doubtful that territorially restricted social assistance is a politically and legally viable long-run solution for the European Union.

The solution that appears appealing at first sight puts the burden of social assistance unilaterally on the home jurisdiction. Extraterritorial welfare support would then have to be funded exclusively by the home jurisdiction and monitoring would be delegated to the jurisdiction of residence. Such a solution is not really convincing, however. This is not only for the reasons raised before against the Home Country Principle. Particular problems would appear if one were to combine the Home Country Principle for welfare recipients with the Employment Principle for the working population. The two groups are not easily separated in practice. According to a ruling of the European Court of Justice, ten to twelve hours of work per week suffice for a person to be qualified as working. The point is that the working status has far-reaching implications. Under the current law, it implies unrestricted assignment to the jurisdiction of employment. This assignment is not even revised in practice if the worker loses his or her job and becomes eligible for social assistance. Hence, the separation between working individuals and welfare recipients is difficult to enforce in practice. For the same reason, any hybrid regime of assignment rules fails to be a convincing solution.

It is the specific appeal of Delayed Integration that it is equally applicable to employed individuals and to welfare recipients and that it allows one to balance the legitimate interests of both the jurisdiction of immigration and the jurisdiction of emigration. There is only the problem that Delayed Integration requires delegated administration for a period of transition. But that should be manageable if it is handled on a mutual basis and if the period of transition is not excessive.

The final criterion we have chosen to discuss refers to the welfare of immobile labor. It is not totally clear whether this criterion deserves special notice. For one, immobile labor constitutes only one segment of the workforce, and for another, one must be aware that any policy designed to alleviate the fate of immobile labor may produce severe distortions. Mobility generates efficiency gains so that any policy targeted at immobility tends to be costly in terms of efficiency.

In the preceding analysis, such efficiency costs are ruled out by assuming an exogenous division in mobile and immobile labor.

Given this arguable assumption, there is good reason to target distributive policy to immobile labor. For one, it makes sense to assume immobile labor to be nonskilled and, hence, the deserved object of welfare support. For another, the effectiveness of redistribution decreases with the degree of mobility. If the Employment Principle applies, the welfare of mobile labor is out of the control of regional policy. It is then natural to ask what effect competing rules of assignment have on the welfare of immobile labor.

The results derived in this chapter suggest that immobile labor benefits most from the Home Country Principle. If Delayed Integration applies, a long period of transition is beneficial. The reason is fairly obvious. It does not pay for immobile labor to tax mobile labor at source (proposition 1). It even makes the variance of immobile labor income increase if there are regional shocks (proposition 2). Insurance against regional shocks is provided only if Delayed Integration is applied and if the period of transition is sufficiently long (proposition 8). An extended period of transition is also preferable if immobile labor is to be the clear winner of distributive policy (proposition 10).

In summary, we can say that Delayed Integration deserves to be considered an appealing compromise between the extreme Principles of Home Country and Employment. The preceding analysis does not lend itself to a forceful plea. Clearly, we would like to see results that prove optimality of Delayed Integration in some relevant sense. This chapter does not provide this kind of results. However, some attractive features of Delayed Integration could be identified. Hence, it is a rule of assignment that policy should seriously consider as an optional basis for coordinating the policies of autonomous jurisdictions committed to free movement of all their citizens.

Notes

I wish to thank my discussant Søren Bo Nielsen for many helpful comments and a thorough reading of an earlier draft. Thanks are equally due to the referees.

1. One may argue that the prohibition of the Nationality Principle extends to the Home Country Principle and that the Home Country Principle is therefore not a viable policy option for the European Union. On the other hand, the Home Country Principle has some attractive features which deserve to be analyzed theoretically.

2. See Regulation (EEC) No. 1408/71.

3. Sakslin (1997) has made a proposal that comes close to Delayed Integration. However, the proposal refers to residence-based benefits only. Michel, Pestieau, and Vidal (1998) study the effect that some delayed granting of citizenship has on distributive policy. In contrast to the model of the present chapter, they assume low-skilled labor to be mobile.

4. F'^* is a short form for $F'(H^*)$. One referee does not like the use of r for denoting the wage income of mobile labor. On the other hand, there is a straightforward analogy between mobile labor and mobile capital, which makes this notation particularly suggestive.

5. The gains from labor market integration are not our theme. Still, one would like to know how the expected return to immobile labor in the closed economy, $E\Theta[F(\bar{H}) - \bar{H}F'(\bar{H})]$, compares with the expected return in the open economy, $E\Theta[F(H^{LF}) - H^{LF}F'(H^{LF})]$. E denotes expectation. The question is easily answered if production is Cobb-Douglas ($F = H^{1-\alpha}$), if regional shocks are completely absorbed by unbiased variations of employment ($\bar{H} = EH^{LF}(\Theta)$), and if the return to mobile labor, $r = \Theta F'$, is nonstochastic. It is then straightforward to show that

$$H^{LF}(\Theta) = \bar{H}(E\Theta^{1/\alpha})^{-1}\Theta^{1/\alpha}$$

and that

$$E\Theta[F(\bar{H}) - \bar{H}F'(\bar{H})] < E\Theta[F(H^{LF}) - H^{LF}F'(H^{LF})] \Leftrightarrow E\Theta < (E\Theta^{1/\alpha})^\alpha,$$

which holds true by Jensen's inequality. The expected return to immobile labor then increases as a result of market integration.

6. For the purpose of Social Security, the rule is that the duration of the posting does not exceed twelve months (see Article 14, Regulation (EEC) No. 1408/71 and Watson 1980, 127). For the purpose of taxation, the duration may not exceed six months (Article 15, OECD Model Convention).

7. Søren Bo Nielsen rightly pointed out that the Production Efficiency Theorem is only applicable in absence of pure profits. Hence, reference to this theorem is questionable in the present model, which assumes limits to the taxation of immobile factor incomes.

References

Diamond, P. A., and J. A. Mirrlees. 1971. "Optimal Taxation and Public Production." *American Economic Review* 111: 8–27, 261–278.

Feld, L. 2000. *Steuerwettbewerb und seine Auswirkungen auf Allokation und Distribution: Eine empirische Analyse für die Schweiz.* (Tax Competition and its Effects on Allocation and Distribution: an Empirical Analysis for Switzerland.) Tübingen, Germany: Mohr.

Frenkel, J. A., A. Razin, and E. Sadka. 1991. *International Taxation in an Integrated World.* Cambridge: MIT Press.

Michel, P., P. Pestieau, and J.-P. Vidal. 1998. "Labor Migration and Redistribution with Alternative Assimilation Policies: The Small Economy Case." *Regional Science and Urban Economics* 28: 363–377.

Musgrave, R. A. 1999. "Fiscal Federalism." In *Public Finance and Public Choice: Two Contrasting Visions of the State*, ed. J. M. Buchanan and R. A. Musgrave. Cambridge: MIT Press.

Pauly, M. V. 1973. "Income Redistribution as a Local Public Good." *Journal of Public Economics* 2: 35–58.

Sakslin, M. 1997. "Can the Principles of the Nordic Conventions on Social Protection Contribute to the Modernization and Simplification of Regulation (EEC) No. 1408/71?" In *25 Years of Regulation (EEC) No. 1408/71 on Social Security for Migrant Workers*. Report from the European Conference on Social Security, Sweden, 1996. Stockholm, Sweden: Swedish National Social Insurance Board.

Sinn, H.-W. 1994. "How Much Europe? Subsidiarity, Centralization and Fiscal Competition." *Scottish Journal of Political Economy* 41: 85–107.

Watson, P. 1980. *Social Security Law of the European Communities*. London: Mansell Publishing.

Weichenrieder, A. 2000. "A Simple Rule for Taxing the Mobile Rich." University of Munich, Discussion Paper.

Wildasin, D. E. 2000. "Labor-Market Integration, Investment in Risky Human Capital, and Fiscal Competition." *American Economic Review* 90: 73–95.

Wissenschaftlicher Beirat beim Bundesministerium der Finanzen. 2001. "Freizügigkeit und soziale Sicherung in Europa." (Freedom of Movement and Social Security in Europe.) *Schriftenreihe des BMF*, Heft 69. Bonn, Germany: Stollfuß Verlag.

Comments

Søren Bo Nielsen

Wolfram Richter has written a nice and timely chapter on an issue that, unfortunately, has been somewhat neglected by public finance theorists and practitioners in Europe—namely, the proper treatment of mobile labor in terms of taxation rights and transfer obligations. The point of departure of the chapter is a concern about the consequences of increased mobility of especially high-skilled labor for the welfare of less-skilled and immobile labor, as well as for allocational efficiency. With interregional as well as international mobility of at least certain groups of labor expected to rise within Europe, it is important to find the most appropriate way of taxing labor and of handing out transfers.

Richter takes an analytical approach to these questions. In a simple model of a small country with a large rest of the world, in which mobile high-skilled labor combines with immobile low-skilled labor in production, he investigates in turn the characteristics of treating mobile labor in accordance with the Employment Principle, the Home Country Principle, and the Principle of Delayed Integration. Delayed Integration is inherently dynamic, but Richter illustrates it in his static model as a weighted average of the Employment Principle and the Home Country Principle, identified by the weights δ $(1 - \delta)$ on the Home Country Principle (the Employment Principle).

Comparing the two polar principles within his model, Richter notes that the Home Country Principle has the lead in terms of enabling production efficiency as well as being able to raise and provide insurance of income accruing to low-skilled immobile labor. The Employment Principle is not compatible with production efficiency and is counterproductive in regard to securing immobile labor income. On the other hand, the Home Country Principle scores less well in respect of compatibility with a policy of integration and practical provision of social assistance. Delayed Integration in some circumstances preserves the preferable features of the Home Country Principle. It can be interpreted as a principle for revenue and obligation sharing between two countries—one from which the mobile worker originates and the other where he or she currently resides and works.

The taxation of mobile workers has probably been discussed more in Germany than in any other EU country, and with good reason— Germany has experienced pronounced internal labor mobility since its unification and also has the second largest share in the European Union of immigrants from Eastern Europe. The Principle of Delayed Integration was proposed by the Scientific Council of the German Ministry of Finance; whether Delayed Integration is superior for tackling future labor mobility in Europe is not yet clear to me, but there is still time to contemplate the most appropriate principle before labor mobility takes off.

In selecting such a principle, one might wish to take into account that only part of tax revenue goes to finance transfers (to people of working age), while other parts instead finance the provision of private goods and pensions. With such alternative uses of public funds, the choice between the Employment Principle and the Home Country Principle and thus of design of Delayed Integration will be affected. If tax revenue instead of transfers goes to finance goods that (for simplicity, here) are perfect substitutes to ordinary private goods and that accrue to individuals on the basis of residence, the migration equilibrium is characterized by (with Richter's notation)

Employment Principle: $(1 - t)\Theta F' + G = (1 - t^*)\Theta^* F'^* + G^*$;   (1)

Home Country Principle: $(1 - t)\Theta F' + G = (1 - t)\Theta^* F'^* + G^*$.   (2)

Here, G and G^* denote the levels of goods provision in the small country and abroad. In general, G and G^* will differ, as will t and t^*. Therefore there is no reason to expect production efficiency under either regime, and there is probably no reason for the Home Country Principle to lead to a superior allocation of production compared with the Employment Principle. The reason is that the benefit side of the public sector shows up as goods provision (in schools, hospitals, etc.) that will be dependent on the worker's residence and not on his or her home country. Moving to another country thus means receiving these goods from a new supplier, whereas the transfers will still be received from the home country under the Home Country Principle. Contrary to the situation where tax revenue finances transfers, there is thus no presumption for Delayed Integration with a long delay (thus approaching the Home Country Principle) when taxes finance goods provision.

As an aside, not only workers but also pensioners are mobile. With the current tradition in Europe of allowing deductions for pension contributions and taxing pension benefits, the choice of how to tax pensions (public as well as occupational) is not about the Employment Principle versus the Home Country Principle, but rather between the source and residence principles. The concept of Delayed Integration will be harder to fit in for pensioners.

When contemplating taxation and individual mobility, it is also worth noting that labor migration implies moving both workplace and residence. Border-crossing commuters only move one of the two—they take up a job abroad while staying at home or they move abroad while keeping their former job at home. Interestingly, it can be seen that the Home Country Principle will work towards production efficiency in the situation where individuals are willing to work abroad but wish to live at home, regardless of whether tax revenue is used to finance transfers or provision of goods. Conversely, if they are willing to live abroad but not to give up their job, there will be no mechanism working towards production efficiency.

For Europe as a whole, border-crossing commuters may not be that important. But in the Øresund region between Denmark and Sweden, they are. During the last decade, thousands of Danes have settled down in southern Sweden while continuing to work in Denmark. Initially, they were able to enjoy a combination of minimal Social Security contributions (and thus high pre-tax wages) in Denmark and low personal income taxes in Sweden. A tax agreement between the two countries in 1997 endowed Denmark with the right to tax labor income of border-crossing commuters at source, implying that the Swedish municipalities in which the Danes live receive no personal income tax from them. Understandably, Sweden is now demanding yet another change in the tax treatment of these commuters, showing that the tax treatment of "Grenzgänger" is a complicated affair, just like taxation of mobile workers.

Returning to the Principle of Delayed Integration: For it to work, it should be able to handle rather complicated patterns of mobility. Consider this example. A person, born in Germany, at some point

decides to move to Belgium. After three years in Belgium, he spends
another three in the Netherlands, after which he settles down in the
United Kingdom with the intention of working there for a longer
time period. Unfortunately, he loses his job after only one year and
begins a two-year spell of unemployment. Now, with Delayed Integration and a five-year delay, which country should finance his
unemployment benefit? One possible answer is Belgium in the first
year and the Netherlands in the second, but these countries might
conceivably claim that the person did not stay in these countries long
enough for them to have the obligation to pay out future transfers.
Instead, they might refer to Germany, which, on its side, might claim
that the person left Germany more than five years before, so that it
no longer bears any responsibility.

Authors and Commentators

Henry J. Aaron, Brookings Institution

Alan J. Auerbach, University of California, Berkeley and NBER

Richard M. Bird, University of Toronto

Robin Boadway, Queen's University

Lans Bovenberg, Tilburg University and CEPR

David F. Bradford, Princeton University and NYU School of Law

Michael Burda, Humboldt University, Berlin

Sijbren Cnossen, Erasmus University Rotterdam and Maastricht University

Georges de Menil, Ecole des Hautes Etudes en Sciences Sociales, Paris

Dominique Demougin, University of Magdeburg

Jeremy Edwards, University of Cambridge and CESifo

Gebhard Flaig, CESifo

Clemens Fuest, University of Munich

Roger H. Gordon, University of California at San Diego

James R. Hines Jr., University of Michigan and NBER

Kai A. Konrad, Free University of Berlin and Wissenschaftszentrum Berlin für Sozialforschung

Marko Köthenbürger, University of Munich

Manuel Leite-Monteiro, Catholic University of Portugal

Assar Lindbeck, Stockholm University

Maurice Marchand, Catholic University of Louvain

Jack M. Mintz, University of Toronto

Thomas Moutos, Athens University of Economics and Business and CESifo

Richard A. Musgrave, University of California at Santa Cruz

Søren Bo Nielsen, Copenhagen Business School

Craig William Perry, King Street Capital Management

Pierre Pestieau, University of Liège, Catholic University of Louvain, and DELTA

Panu Poutvaara, Center for Economic and Business Research (CEBR), Copenhagen

Ray Rees, University of Munich

Wolfram F. Richter, University of Dortmund

Harvey S. Rosen, Princeton University

Agnar Sandmo, Norwegian School of Economics and Business Administration

Helmut Seitz, Europa-University Viadrina, Frankfurt (Oder)

Hans-Werner Sinn, University of Munich and CESifo

Joel Slemrod, University of Michigan

Peter Birch Sørensen, University of Copenhagen, EPRU, and CESifo

Henry Tulkens, Catholic University of Louvain

Alfons J. Weichenrieder, Goethe University Frankfurt and CESifo

John Douglas Wilson, Michigan State University

Index